FOOD & BEVERAGE OPERATIONS AND SUPERVISION/CAREER DEVELOPMENT

THE INTERNATIONAL CULINARY SCHOOLS℠
at The Art Institutes

John Wiley & Sons, Inc.

This custom textbook includes content from the following books:

Presenting Service: The Ultimate Guide for the Foodservice Professional, Second Edition by Lendal H. Kotschevar, PhD, FMP and Valentino Luciani, CHE (ISBN: 978-0-471-47578-1)

The Restaurant: From Concept to Operation, Fourth Edition by John R. Walker and Donald E. Lundberg (ISBN: 978-0-471-45028-3)

Supervision in the Hospitality Industry: Applied Human Resources, Fifth Edition by Jack E. Miller, John R. Walker, and Karen Eich Drummond (ISBN: 978-0-471-65748-4)

So You Want to Be a Chef? Your Guide to Culinary Careers by Lisa M. Brefere, CEC, AAC, Karen Eich Drummond, EdD, FMP, RD, and Brad Barnes, CMC, CCA, AAC (ISBN: 978-0-471-64691-4)

Library of Congress Cataloging-in-Publication Data:

ISBN: 978-0-470-17917-8

Printed in the United States of America

10 9 8 7 6 5

CONTENTS

PART 2 MANAGEMENT AND SUPERVISION/CAREER DEVELOPMENT

PREFACE

We are pleased to present this first edition of The International Culinary Schools at The Art Institutes' *Food & Beverage Operations and Supervision/Career Development*. This unique combination of materials reflects a philosophy of culinary education carried out at The International Culinary Schools at The Art Institutes' programs across the country. We are committed to collaborative, learner-centered instruction that encourages students to combine effective business leadership skills with excellent culinary fundamentals. This new book brings the management skills that we believe are absolutely essential to a contemporary chef into a single text for our students. These are the skills that distinguish our program and that will allow our graduates to reach their full potential as leading culinarians.

As a group of professional chefs and educators, we undertook this project with a strong sense of purpose and focus. One of the hallmarks of our program is its integration of classical culinary technique with core employability skills such as communication, time management, problem solving, teamwork, diversity appreciation, leadership and social responsibility. We wanted to provide a text which would support the development of these skills in a context specific to the world of the professional chef—and that would be relevant to our students from their first jobs as line cooks through their development to executive positions. We present the project with grateful appreciation to the many chefs, industry leaders, educators and students who contributed to its content. May their work and generosity of spirit be repaid by the contributions of a new generation of culinary leaders.

Michael Nenes, MBA, CEC, CCE
Assistant Vice President, Culinary Arts, The International Culinary Schools at
The Art Institutes

Matthew Bennett, M.Ed. CEC, CCE, CWPC, CFBE
The International Culinary Schools at The Art Institutes, Colorado

Gary Eaton, MA
The International Culinary Schools at The Art Institutes, Houston

Sarah Gorham, MS, CEC
The International Culinary Schools at The Art Institutes, Atlanta

Walter Leible, CMC
The International Culinary Schools at The Art Institutes, Phoenix

Robynne Maii, MA
The International Culinary Schools at The Art Institutes, New York

PART 1

FOOD AND BEVERAGE OPERATIONS MANAGEMENT

THE PROFESSIONAL SERVER*

Outline

---

* Authored by Lendal H. Kotschevar and Valentino Luciani.

Learning Objectives

After reading this chapter, you should be able to:

- Outline the skills and behaviors common to professional servers.
- Explain how hiring qualified employees helps an operation deliver excellent customer service.
- Describe laws that affect employees and employers.

INTRODUCTION

This chapter looks at the process of finding work as a server, and then at the factors that make a server professional in the eyes of guests, colleagues, and employers. These factors include a professional, neat appearance; a positive and helpful demeanor; courtesy and tact; a high level of knowledge of food and service; and the ability to suggest menu items and stay organized throughout the workday. This chapter provides an overview of these topics. In addition, it covers some of the basics of tips and unions, as well as the laws that affect servers.

FINDING WORK

Finding a good server position is not always easy. There might be many job openings, but it might be a challenge to find one that is a good match with your talents and availability. Word of mouth is one good way to find a position. This gives the server first-hand information from someone who knows the operation. Other sources of job openings include help-wanted advertisements, union headquarters, employment agencies, and just walking into operations.

The Interview

Remember when going to an interview to present yourself as a desirable employee. Do not brag but present yourself in a positive manner. Precisely explain your qualifications. Remember that body language tells the interviewer a lot. Display your confidence. Show the interviewer the same professional behavior you will use on the job. Dress and grooming should be neat, simple, and appropriate to the operation.

As a manager, hold interviews only when you are seriously considering an individual for a position. Interviews are designed to gather information about skills, personality, and job knowledge. Often a review of the application leads to interview questions. A broad amount of information is obtained by asking open-ended questions, such as, "You have worked at several places during the last year. Why did you leave each one of them?" This can lead to further questions that might give some revealing information about the applicant. A server may go through a preliminary interview with the manager or supervisor of the operation. The supervisor who is to immediately oversee the work of the server should be the final interviewer.

Interviewing

As a manager in the competitive foodservice industry, you will have the greatest success only if you actively strive to hire and retain the most qualified, talented, and motivated employees. The process begins with screening the most qualified and appropriate job applicants, identifying outstanding job candidates through effective interviewing, and selecting employees who are likely to remain and develop within your operation.

Most interviews will be divided into four parts: (1) preparation; (2) the interview; (3) ending the interview; and (4) evaluation. The key to conducting effective employee interviews is to plan your part of the interview in advance. By preparing interview questions and structuring the interview's direction before the meeting, you are much more assured of getting valuable information about the candidate than by simply winging it.

Most operations will find it helpful to establish job description specifications, which are written definitions of the requirements of the job and the person that should be hired to fill these requirements. It takes a person who knows the job and what it entails to write these. The job specification lists knowledge, skills and abilities, work experience, and education and training. Write specifications based on the information needed to perform job duties; the ability to perform a task, or behave in a certain way; and any specific skills, if applicable.

Another item that should be done before interviewing is to set up questions to use to get the information needed to judge the candidates' suitability for the job. These should cover the areas of: (1) education; (2) motivation; (3) ability to work with others; and (4) relevant personal characteristics. See Figure 1.1 for some examples of questions that might be asked in these four areas.

Open-ended questions require more than a yes or no answer, and they encourage candidates to talk about themselves and their experiences. By asking open-ended

Education

1. Who was your favorite teacher? Why did you like her or him?
2. What courses did you take? In which did you excel?
3. In what extracurricular activities did you participate?

Motivation

1. I see you have had previous experience as a server at _____. What were your job responsibilities? Did you enjoy doing them?
2. What are your professional goals? What do you want to be doing one year from now? Five years from now?
3. What do you expect from supervisors? From co-workers? From buspersons or others who work for you?
4. What did you like about your contacts with the kitchen crew? What did you not like?

Ability to Work with Others

1. What advantages do you see in working with others?
2. Describe some unpleasant experiences you have had with co-workers and how you handled them.
3. If you were given an inexperienced person to work with and train, what would you do to help this person learn, while at the same time doing the required work?

Relevant Personal Characteristics

1. When you are a guest in a restaurant, what type of service do you expect?
2. If you saw a co-worker stealing, what would you do?

FIGURE 1.1 Some open questions to ask in interviewing.

questions the interviewer gets a chance to get much more desirable information about the candidate that might be helpful in estimating the candidate's suitability for the position. Listen carefully to the candidate's answers. In fact, you should spend most of your time in the actual interview listening to the candidate.

There are other things one needs to do in planning for the interview. The room in which the interview occurs should be private, orderly, and unintimidating. Arrange to sit next to the applicant. Do not have anything such as a desk or table between you and the candidate, in order to help put the candidate at ease. Have materials ready to give the applicant. Notify others who will be interviewing the person. Make arrangements so you will not be interrupted during the interview. Have a note pad handy to use in taking notes.

One must remember in conducting the interview that the interviewer is also under scrutiny, and that the applicant is often making an evaluation of whether he or she wants to work there. The interviewer should greet the applicant warmly and be pleasant during the entire interview. Body language, such as facing the person who is talking and maintaining eye contact, also should be positive. Listen actively by nodding, maintaining eye contact, asking questions, and at times repeating what the candidate is saying. The only way you are going to find out what you want to know is to listen and hear it from the candidate. Of course, there are other factors to note, such as dress, the way the candidate conducts himself, and so forth, but the main source is through what the candidate says. Short comments, such as "Yes, that's good" or "I see," also indicate active listening. Don't expect spontaneous answers. Let the candidate think out answers before giving them.

One should not mislead candidates or make false promises. State frankly what is good and what is bad about the position. It is much better to be honest with the candidate about the hard parts of the job.

Before ending the interview, give the candidate a tour of the facility, explaining things that are of interest about the job. Introduce the candidate to others in the operation. Be sure to ask the applicant if there is anything more that he or she desires to know before ending the interview.

In ending the interview, thank the candidate, and indicate what will be done to inform her or him of the decision. If a date and time is given, be sure to observe it. Go with candidates to the exit and wish them well. Even if the interview went poorly, still be positive and courteous. The fact that the candidate would take the time and trouble to come for an interview is worthy of polite, considerate treatment.

After the interview, quickly review your notes, adding anything that you might have wanted to jot down but did not have the time. Summarize your judgment as to the candidate's suitability for the position. Before making any decision, be sure to weigh all the facts. Today, with the shortage of labor, one is apt to make hasty decisions; avoid this. Interviewing and hiring good employees is crucial to a successful operation.

The Legal Side of Hiring

There are legal restrictions to observe in the screening, interviewing, and hiring of employees, and violators will find they face severe penalties for not observing them.

Federal Insurance Contributions Act (FICA) (1937)	Source of federal payroll tax law, especially regarding Social Security
Fair Labor Standards Act (1938)	Establishes requirements for minimum wages, work time, overtime pay, equal pay, and child labor
Equal Pay Act (1963)	Requires employers to provide employees of both sexes equal pay for equal work
Civil Rights Act (1964)	Forbids discrimination in employment on the basis of race, color, religion, or national origin; sex and pregnancy are covered in the employment section
Age Discrimination in Employment Act (1967)	Prohibits discrimination against job applicants and employees over age 40
Equal Employment Opportunity Act (1972)	Prohibits discrimination based on race, color, religion, sex, or national origin (amended Civil Rights Act of 1964)
Vietnam Era Veterans Readjustment Act (1974)	Protects Vietnam veterans from any job-related discrimination
Immigration Reform and Control Act (IRCA) (1986)	Forbids employers from knowingly hiring anyone not legally authorized to work in the United States
Americans with Disabilities Act (1990)	Prohibits discrimination against qualified individuals in employment; requires employers to make reasonable adjustments in facilities and practices to permit participation of disabled persons

FIGURE 1.2 Federal laws affecting recruiting and hiring.

Only the federal laws in this area are reviewed below, but managers and supervisors should also know and observe all state or local requirements.

The laws and their limitation affecting recruiting and hiring appear in Figure 1.2. At no time should one mention or ask the candidate to give information on any of the following:

- Race, religion, age, or gender
- Ethnic background
- Country of origin
- Former or maiden name or parents' name
- Marital status or information about spouse
- Children, child-care arrangements, pregnancy, or future plans to become pregnant
- Credit rating or other financial information, or ownership of cars or other property
- Health
- Membership in an organization
- Voter preference
- Weight, height, or any questions relating to appearance
- Languages spoken, unless the ability to speak other languages is required of the position
- Prior arrests (convictions are legal)

The key is to ask only job-related questions. Questions such as, "Can you work nights and weekends?" and "Are you available to work overtime when needed?" are appropriate. Careful planning enables the interviewer to ask questions that are both legal and effective.

LOOKING PROFESSIONAL

Servers who wear crisp, clean uniforms and are properly groomed will make a positive first impression on guests, their employers, and colleagues. This typically translates into higher tips, better shifts and table sections, and enhanced opportunities for recognition and advancement.

Uniforms

Styles of uniforms vary greatly from operation to operation. Many bars, family-style restaurants, and casual-theme operations feature servers in khaki pants, shorts, T-shirts, cotton button-downs, or polo shirts. Servers in upscale fine-dining restaurants often wear ties and black aprons over formal clothing. Institutional food service uniforms typically resemble traditional uniforms rather than casual street clothes. No matter

FIGURE 1.3 A well-dressed, well-groomed server makes a positive impression to guests. Courtesy Corbis Digital Stock.

what an operation's server uniform, several things are consistent. For instance, the uniform should be clean, wrinkle-free, and well-fitting. Shoes should be comfortable and sturdy enough to withstand hours of standing, walking, and direct contact with slippery surfaces.

If servers carry pens, order pads, corkscrews, or matches, the items should be kept in pockets below the waist to prevent them from dropping. Never put a pen or pencil in your mouth or behind an ear. Extra uniforms should be on hand for emergencies. Jewelry should be limited to post earrings, rings, and watches, since anything dangling could end up on or near guests' food.

Although personal hygiene may be a sensitive subject, it is vital to food safety and proper server presentation. Unclean servers can disturb guests, and even spread illness or other contamination. Servers should bathe and wash hair frequently. Clean clothes should be worn. It is preferable to have workers change into clean clothes at the workplace. If unable to do this, workers should come from home directly to work. Servers are on their feet almost all their shift, so comfortable shoes should be worn—no platform, high-heeled, or open-toe shoes. Wear hair restraints. These are often required by health authorities. Nets, caps, or hats may be used. If hair is longer than collar length, it should be tied back or pinned up.

Basic hand care includes keeping nails short and clean. Wearing garish nail polish or artificial nails should not be permitted. Plastic gloves or using tongs should be required in handling food. All sores, cuts, or infections should be neatly covered by bandages or bandaids.

There are some sanitation do-nots in handling eating utensils:

1.   Do not touch the inside of cups, glasses, silverware, or dishes where food or liquid or lips will touch.

2.   Do not handle clean utensils without washing hands after clearing tables.

3.   Do not leave trays used for serving with soil on them.

4.   Do not use soiled napkins, serviettes, or other linens.

DEMEANOR AND ATTITUDE OF SUCCESSFUL SERVERS

A pleasant demeanor and positive attitude have as much or more to do with success in serving as knowing how to do the work. In fact, a survey of managers to find out the cause of servers' failure on the job indicated that only 10 percent were discharged because they did not know how to do the job. The other 90 percent were discharged largely because of personal traits or negative attitudes.

Delivering What Customers Expect: Operation Knowledge

To serve guests well and answer their questions intelligently, servers must be informed about the company for which they work and the products offered. Employees should know the following:

- Days and hours of operation
- History and background of the company
- Theme and concept of the decor
- Names of managers, management assistants, and supervisors
- Places of interest in the local area

Maintaining a Positive Attitude

One of the most important personality traits a good server must possess is a positive attitude toward work, colleagues, and serving the public. Good servers believe they can deliver and try not to dwell on failures, but correct their mistakes and learn from them.

Having a positive attitude toward work allows the server to make progress in learning and to develop increased proficiency. Setting small goals and achieving them builds confidence. After this, more difficult goals appear within reach. It is important to be prepared to take advantage of opportunities when they appear.

Making an earnest effort to be friendly with guests and to please them brings with it both financial and professional rewards. Servers should try to develop challenges for themselves, such as trying to win over difficult guests. Figure 1.4 contains a list of the fundamentals of professional service.

Servers should never talk about personal problems or inappropriate topics with guests or within guests' hearing. They should never complain in the dining room about the lack or paucity of a tip. In fact, it is not the server who should be the focus of attention at all, but the guest. Although this separation is certainly a challenge, support

Adhering to these standards ensures professionalism in manner and service.

- Be sure your personal style matches the style (formal, casual) of the operation.
- Don't initiate a superfluous conversation unless at the request of the guest.
- Humor can be positive and pleasing to the guest when properly applied.
- Timing is of crucial essence. For instance, if a guest orders a glass of wine served with the entree, and it comes even five minutes after, it can annoy the guest.
- Little things mean a lot. Everything that can be done to make a guest's experience more enjoyable, comfortable, and easy will always be appreciated.
- In a family restaurant, provide activities for children, such as crayons or puzzles, so parents can enjoy their meal.
- Always present the check face down, so that only the host(ess) can see the total.
- When saying goodbye, if the guest should extend the hand, the server should offer a firm handshake.
- Maintain proper eye contact, which is a sign of attentiveness and sincerity, at all times.
- Place dishes on the table gently.
- Guests should never be hurried, and should never be given the impression that they are being rushed so that others can be accommodated.
- In handling china and glassware, never touch the top or inside of a glass, or the surface or edges of a plate.
- To be a team player is a must. Help other servers whenever possible.

FIGURE 1.4 Professional service fundamentals.

from colleagues and good cooperation can go far in keeping servers focused on their guests and giving great service.

Courtesy

In life, courtesy means being polite, gracious, and considerate toward others. In food service, it means putting the guest's needs before one's own. Respect for others and a willingness to help are key. Courtesy should be automatic and natural. It is displayed through words and actions. Being courteous does not mean being servile or fawning. Good servers are professionally courteous, showing a serious regard for their work.

Even difficult guests, when treated courteously, will return the favor. The few who don't are rare, and servers should try to meet their needs and not take their mistreatment personally.

Tact

Tact is the art of saying and doing the right thing, using the right words at the right time. It is also an intuitive sense of what to do or say in order to maintain good relations and avoid offending guests. Behaving tactfully might be remembering and using guests' names, using diplomacy in adverse circumstances, or asking a guest to take a phone call when it is necessary to tell her that her credit card has been rejected. Being tactful means handling sensitive situations so that everyone involved is left with their dignity intact.

Sincerity and Honesty

Sincerity and honesty are shown by behaving naturally, and not in a forced or phony way, toward guests. A forced smile and "canned" lines ("Have a nice day") are obvious clues to insincerity. Being pleasant while serving is really all that is needed.

Being frank and telling the truth are important. Servers who make mistakes should simply admit the mistake and correct it as quickly as possible. Guests will appreciate the forthrightness and the effort. Excellent service will be easy to perform if servers follow the tips in Figure 1.5. And listed in Figure 1.6 are some helpful phrases that servers can use.

Camaraderie

Camaraderie is the ability to get along with people. When team relationships falter, guests suffer. No matter how you serve guests in the foodservice industry, your ability to work with others to serve them well will help you move ahead professionally.

LEARNING SKILLS

Professional servers must learn continually throughout their jobs or careers. Learning and training in service skills is accomplished in several ways: through DVDs and videotapes, study courses, computer programs, CD-ROM programs, simulations, online courses, training sessions, and other servers. No matter what the method, both

Providing excellent service is a good way to establish loyal customers.

- Do not correct guests if they mispronounce item names.
- Anticipation is a fundamental component of service. Guests should not have to ask for refills on coffee, water, and so on.
- Even the most helpful service, given with improper timing, can be perceived as poor service.
- Only talk about yourself when asked. Guests are the celebrity at the meal.
- Never allow your emotions to get the best of you. The service you give must remain consistent and professional, especially when dealing with difficult guests.
- If a napkin or piece of flatware falls on the floor, replace it immediately with a fresh one.
- Before clearing something, ask if the guest is finished.
- Describe items in an appetizing manner, such as, "Our special, Southern Fried Chicken, comes from an old southern recipe using special herbs and spices; it is crisp outside and moist and tender inside."
- Too much zeal in serving can bother guests. This usually discourages tips. Service that brings in tips is pleasant, effective, and unobtrusive.
- Do not stand nearby when a guest is paying the bill. Most guests want privacy when figuring out a tip or counting out money. They may wish to discuss the tip without the server being present.

FIGURE 1.5 Excellent service on the job.

the trainer and server are responsible for seeing that learning takes place and is put into practice on the job.

PRODUCT KNOWLEDGE

Just as a doctor knows the human body and the mechanic knows cars, servers must know about the products they serve. If a guest asks about a menu item, the server should provide all possible answers. Servers should study their menu to know how items are prepared and what they contain, and know all specials before a shift begins. This increases a server's opportunities for suggestive selling and increasing check averages and tips.

Pleasant, courteous phrases are always appropriate when dealing with customers.

- Good evening (morning, afternoon), and welcome to _____.
- My name is _____, and I'll be your server this evening (morning, afternoon). If there is anything that I can get for you, please let me know.
- May I take your order now, or would you prefer a little extra time to go over the menu?
- Do you have any questions about our menu?
- May I suggest a wine to complement your entree (or coffee with your dessert)?
- How is everything? Is the _____ done to your order?
- Thank you. It's been a pleasure serving you. We look forward to your return.
- I hope to see you again soon, Mr. _____ or Ms. _____.

FIGURE 1.6 Helpful phrases.

In addition to basic knowledge about the operation, servers must know a good deal about the menu. In the meeting of servers before the meal, servers should taste unusual dishes on the menu and know ingredients and methods of preparation of menu items. Know the following:

- What items are on the menu
- Signature items
- Promotional items
- Specials
- Estimated runout time
- Items of interest: For example, oysters flown in from the west that morning

SUGGESTIVE SELLING

Suggestive selling involves the extremely important role your servers have in suggesting items to guests, selling individual menu items, and increasing check averages and tips. Suggestive selling involves offering all of your guests the full range of products and services available in your operation. The more guests know about what menu items are available, how they are prepared, and why your operation is pleased to offer them, the more likely they are to enjoy every aspect of their meal. Suggesting menu items benefits your servers in increased tips, guests in increased enjoyment, and the operation in increased profits.

A knowledge of menu terminology is also essential. The best servers not only know what menu terms mean but also the explanation of the terminology. Knowing menu items can be a matter of pride and accomplishment in the profession of serving.

Inexperienced servers may not know many menu terms. The way to learn is to take a menu and ask the chef or manager to explain what is unfamiliar. Usually, in the line-up session before the meal, servers are told what menu items are.

ORGANIZATION

Organizing one's own work and time is essential. A disorganized server will have trouble with timing, such as knowing when to take an order, pick up items, or present the check. Disorganization breeds a frantic pace, tension and nervousness, and frequent attempts to catch up. Good servers have a rhythm.

Good organization will also help you anticipate guests' needs. Good observation is one of the most important factors in organization and timing.

TIPS

The meaning of tips—**T**o **I**nsure **P**rompt **S**ervice—is important to remember. Many servers take tips for granted, and make little or no effort to do additional work to earn one. This may be the fault of guests who tip 15 to 20 percent of the bill regardless of the quality of the service, so that servers know that extra effort is really not needed. However, with guests becoming more service and value minded, more discrimination is being shown in giving tips. Servers are expected to give good service, and in return, can expect a fair tip.

Some servers far outdistance others in earning tips. This comes through actions and words. They always welcome guests and thank them, and give the extra effort needed to please guests. Figure 1.7 outlines the basics every server should know in order to please guests.

Tips are considered part of a server's salary, and must be reported as such to the Internal Revenue Service. An employer is required to report 8 percent tips for each server in an establishment. This is calculated by dividing the total sales check amount by the number of guests served.

Be sure to remember these service tasks when attending to guests' needs.

- Serve items from the guest's left side.
- Remove items from the guest's right side.
- Serve and remove beverages from the guest's right side.
- Serve main food items at the six o'clock position.
- Handle fine glassware by the stem.
- Keep water glasses two-thirds full.
- After filling a tray or bus pan with soiled and leftover food, cover it with a napkin.
- Serve all bar beverages with a napkin or coaster.

FIGURE 1.7 **Basics of good service.**

UNIONS

Working in a unionized operation means that servers are represented to management by union representatives. In a unionized operation, the employer company typically signs a contract with union representatives covering job classifications, job duties, scheduling, pay, grievance procedures, vacation time, length of work week, break times, sick leave, termination, and so on. Unions charge their members dues to sustain their operation.

It is advisable for an operation's manager to have job descriptions and job specifications written before signing a labor contract if he or she does not want to forfeit that function to the union.

Union contracts often require that employees performing unsatisfactorily be warned orally and in writing a specified number of times before termination. This also happens to be a very wise management policy, since it protects managers in the case of wrongful termination lawsuit. Warnings should state a specific cause and incident description, and a description of how performance is expected to improve. Employees must be given a chance to correct their actions within a certain time period.

Managers should make every effort to settle employee matters internally. However, if a worker has a grievance which is not satisfied, he or she can contact the union and have it take up the matter with the company management. If the union believes the company has violated a contract term, it contacts the company to settle the matter amicably. If the matter is not settled, the union may appeal to a grievance committee to hear the case and make a decision. A union contract usually contains an agreement by both the union and management that the committee's decision will be binding on both parties. If not, the employee or the company could appeal to a court for a decision. Grievance committees are limited to hearing cases that arise within a specified area.

LAWS AFFECTING SERVERS

A number of laws relating to hiring and work affect both employers and servers. The most important of these follow.

Privacy Act

The Privacy Act of 1974 forbids employers from asking non-job-related questions that might discriminate against a group of qualified job applicants. The act applies not only to interviewing potential employees but also to discussing matters with current employees.

Fair Labor Standards Act

The Fair Labor Standards Act of 1938 protects workers between ages 40 and 70 from discharge because of age. This act also covers teenage workers, working hours, and union activities.

Family and Medical Leave Act

The Family and Medical Leave Act (FMLA) of 1993 requires employers with 50 or more employees to offer up to twelve weeks of unpaid leave in any twelve-month period for any of the following reasons:

- Birth, adoption, or foster care of a child
- Care for a child, dependent, spouse, or parent with a serious health condition
- Care for the employee's own serious health condition

The act includes some other provisions for both employer and employee that guide their relations dealing with family and medical leaves.

Civil Rights Act

Discrimination against job applicants and employees is prohibited in Title VII of the Civil Rights Act of 1964 and 1991. The act is administered and enforced by the Equal Employment Opportunity Commission (EEOC). It is unlawful to "fail or refuse to hire or discharge any individual or otherwise discriminate against any individual" on the basis of race, color, religion, sex, or national origin. The reason for not hiring an applicant must be job-related. For instance, in New York City a group of restaurants refused to hire women as captains and servers, saying that males only would be accepted by their guests. The EEOC ruled against them. In some cases, foodservice operations must train applicants to become suited to the work.

The Civil Rights Act further covers wrongful discharge on the basis of age, disability, and participation in collective bargaining or union activities. The penalty to the employer may be reemployment of the fired employee, court costs, attorney's fees, and in some claims penalties for committing an act against public policy or outrageous employer conduct.

The act now also covers sexual harassment on the job, which is defined as "unwelcome sexual advances, requests for sexual favors, and other verbal or physical conduct of a sexual nature . . . when:

1. Submission to such conduct is made either explicitly or implicitly a term or condition of a person's employment; or,

2. Submission to or rejection of such conduct . . . is used as the basis of employment decisions, affecting such person; or,

3. Such conduct has the purpose or effect of unreasonably interfering with a person's work performance or creating an intimidating, hostile, or offensive working environment."

A majority of cases on sexual harassment have favored the plaintiff and imposed substantial penalties on offenders. Judgments against defendant employers can be substantial.

Beverage Alcohol

Sale of alcohol is regulated by state and local laws. They generally cover licensing, permits, and how liquor may be sold. Some states called control states handle the sale and distribution, while others permit retail beverage establishments to purchase from prescribed dealers. They also typically address how to handle disruptive patrons. It is wise to call in the police to help handle a difficult guest.

FIGURE 1.8 Knowledge of the menu by the server allows for suggestive selling, which will also likely increase check averages and tips. Courtesy PhotoDisc, Inc.

Dram shop laws hold anyone serving alcohol liable if an intoxicated patron injures or kills a third person; hence, the equivalent term *third-party liability*. Courts may grant large damages against establishments and servers for violating dram shop laws. Insurance companies faced with paying such penalties have raised insurance fees to cover these costs.

To reduce such liability, many jurisdictions require that those serving alcohol be trained in serving it responsibly. Responsible service includes never serving alcohol to three types of people: intoxicated patrons, minors, and known or habitual alcoholics. Detecting a minor can be difficult. An operation should have specific steps in place for verifying identification. Documents without pictures or dates should not be accepted. If in doubt, examine the documents carefully. At times, minors accompany older persons who buy them beverage alcohol. Some operations or laws may prohibit minors from entering the premises of an operation selling beverage alcohol.

Detecting intoxicated people and alcoholics also is difficult. Servers must be trained to observe and interpret guests' behavior, and monitor guests' drinking. If an intoxicated guest tries to drive away, a server or manager should call the guest a cab, or, if all else fails, call the police.

Immigration Reform and Control Act

The Immigration Reform and Control Act (IRCA) of 1986 makes it illegal to hire aliens not authorized to work in this country. Employers must verify citizenship at the time of hiring. If asked before hiring (during the interview), nonhired applicants can claim discrimination. There is a grandfather clause that says that aliens hired before November 7, 1986, can be kept on the job. In addition to these, some aliens may be given a permit to work in this country. Every new employer must complete a Form 1–9 upon hiring and put it into the employee's file; its purpose is to verify that the new employee has submitted satisfactory proof of identity and work authorization, if the latter is required.

Americans with Disabilities Act

The Americans with Disabilities Act prohibits discrimination against people with differing levels of ability, requires reasonable accommodation for employees with disabilities, and requires public places and services to accommodate guests with disabilities. This means that not only is it good business to accommodate all guests, regardless of ability, but it is also the law.

CHAPTER SUMMARY

Looking professional is key to a server giving a good first impression. When looking for work, word of mouth can be a reliable source, as are newspaper advertisements, employment agencies, and walking into operations. The art of applying and interviewing for work is very important in finding desirable positions.

Demeanor and a positive attitude are crucial. Servers must be sincere, honest, and courteous. Good teamwork helps give better service. It is important for servers to know menu terms and how items are prepared.

Some servers are able to make more tips than others. Much of their success comes from knowing how to please guests. Tips are considered salary and must be reported as such to the IRS.

Unions sometimes represent employees in dealing with management.

Certain laws have an influence on how servers get work and how they perform it. The Privacy Act protects candidates and employees from inappropriate inquiries. The Fair Labor Standards Act protects servers from the ages of 40 to 70 from discharge because of age and has sections governing the work of teenagers. The Family and Medical Leave Act requires employers with 50 or more employees to offer up to twelve weeks of unpaid leave in any twelve-month period for reasons related to family and personal health.

The Civil Rights Act bars discrimination against employees because of race, color, religion, sex, or national origin. The Equal Employment Opportunity Commission (EEOC) enforces the act, which also covers cases involving sexual harassment on the job.

State and local dram shop laws create third-party liability on people serving beverage alcohol. The laws hold servers responsible to third parties injured or killed by intoxicated patrons, and encourage servers to be trained in monitoring alcohol service to guests.

The Immigration Reform and Control Act holds employers responsible for verifying the legal working status of employees. With a few exceptions, illegal aliens are prohibited from working in the United States.

RELATED INTERNET SITES

Tips on how to be a professional server

www.soyouwanna.com/site/syws/waiter/waiter3.html

KEY TERMS

Civil Rights Act	Equal Employment Opportunity Commission (EEOC)	Immigration Reform and Control Act
contol states		job description specifications
	Fair Labor Standards Act	Privacy Act of 1974
dram shop laws	Family and Medical Leave Act	unionized operation

CHAPTER REVIEW

1. What is a grievance committee, and of what use can it be to a server?

2. Is the question, "Do you have any disabilities?" appropriate to ask in a job interview?

3. What should servers do to maximize tips?

4. What constitutes sexual harassment?

5. What is third-party liability?

6. Describe a typical server's uniform for a casual operation.

7. How does being tactful help a server when a guest's credit card has been denied?

8. What do job specifications contain?

9. Describe some ways to show you are listening actively during an interview.

10. Is it appropriate to ask a female candidate if she is planning to have a baby anytime soon?

Case Studies

ESTABLISHING JOB DESCRIPTIONS

You are the manager of a family restaurant and want to establish job descriptions for the various jobs on the staff. In the service area you will need descriptions for the head waiter, servers, cashier, and hostess. Write these job descriptions for the service staff.

UNWANTED SUITOR

Christine works nights at Charlie's restaurant while going to college during the day. In three years of attending the university in the day time she has earned her B.S. degree. She is continuing to work at Charlie's while earning her master's degree. Things are proceeding well until a young man, whose first name is Bob, is hired as an evening server. He is a bit older than normal college age and is attending the same college as Christine while working on a business degree. He is attracted to Christine, who at first accepts his attentions. They have several dates together, but it turns out that Bob is more interested in her than she is in him. Christine tries to cut him off, but he is persistent and begins to annoy Christine so much she feels she can no longer work at Charlie's. However, she really doesn't want to leave. She has made the job fit her needs so well that she could never duplicate it elsewhere nor find a job that pays as well as her current job does. What should she do? How does she get rid of Bob? How would you as a manager help to resolve this situation.

SERVICE MISE EN PLACE*

Outline

Learning Objectives

After reading this chapter, you should be able to:

- Oversee the maintenance of well-stocked and organized service stations.

- Explain the importance of mise en place for servers.

---

* Authored by Lendal H. Kotschevar and Valentino Luciani.

INTRODUCTION

Many preparation steps must be completed before guests arrive to eat in a dining area. Not only must the place be clean and in good order, but equipment, food, beverages, dishes, and a host of other things must be ready for use. Without such prework, service becomes chaotic and disorganized. Not only are guests dissatisfied, but servers are frustrated and tired. Preparing well for the busy period of service that follows can pay off in making the work much more efficient, easier, satisfying, and financially rewarding.

The prework that takes place both in the kitchen and guest areas before service begins is often called mise en place, which means in French, "put into place." It means getting everything ready for serving guests, but it also means keeping things in good order as one works. In food production it means the same thing—have everything ready, and work to continuously keep things in order. Another commonly used term is *side work*.

Have a place for everything, clean up as you work, and think ahead. In both the service and production areas, good mise en place often denotes an effective worker—and a much happier one. Good mise en place makes work fun; the lack of it makes it a drudgery. Most importantly, good mise en place makes for satisfied guests.

Mise en place work is usually divided into three parts:

1.   Getting ready
2.   Sidework during service
3.   Ending the meal

The first part consists of all work done before guests arrive, such as setting up the station, preparing ahead to meet guest needs, and arranging for service in an orderly fashion.

One group of guests may leave a table full of soiled dishes and linens, dirty ash trays, crumbs, and other things that need attention in order for a fresh, neat, correctly set table to be ready for the next group of guests. This is the second part, the first being greeting guests and seating them correctly. The last part is the work required in the departure of guests, closing the station and leaving it in good shape for the next guests. No one part is more important than the other. Each must be done correctly to achieve totally satisfactory mise en place.

Mise en place work differs for different serving situations. For breakfast, the table setting is different: perhaps a superfine sugar is put into sugar bowls rather than regular, table sugar. The condiments required might be minimal compared to those set out for lunch.

As an example of how a different situation can influence the mise en place, the type needed for counter service differs from that of a regular meal, and the mise en place needed for a buffet dinner is quite different from that of a banquet. In general, banquet service will not require clearing and resetting the table because there is just one setting. If another banquet, party, or meal is to follow one banquet, the mise en place is different and the work to prepare starts all over. In quick-service restaurants, employees and managers must be diligent in their efforts to keep guest areas clean, since guest turnover is quite fast.

GETTING READY

First Impressions

Upon arriving at a food service establishment, guests see the outside and the surrounding grounds first. This must be inviting and give a favorable impression of what is to follow. Grimod de la Reynière, editor of the first gourmet magazine, said, "The soup to a meal should be like a porch to a house or the overture of an opera; it should be an inviting prelude to what is to follow." The same could be said of the entrance and grounds of an operation, no matter whether it is a drive-in, restaurant, or a boat waiting at a dock to take an evening party sailing in the bay while serving dinner.

The grounds should be clean and in good order. There should be good lighting and good security. Signs should be well lighted and visible from some distance so guests can be prepared to stop. Landscaping should be attractive, well groomed, and appear fresh. Walkways should be uncluttered and in good condition, and guests should not have to walk too far to enter. If valet parking is available, it should be prompt and courteous. Valet employees should be neatly groomed and uniformed, and should assist guests exiting their vehicles.

Lighting Good outdoor lighting is essential. Employees and customers need to see well in parking lots, on walks leading to the establishment's front and back doors, in stairways, near entrances, and in vestibules. These areas should be lit well enough to read a newspaper. Wire cages should protect exterior lights. A backup power supply is desirable.

Lighting serves as a deterrent to crime. Criminals do not usually want to be seen or identified, so they avoid a well-lit establishment in favor of one that has dimmer lighting. Lighting in hallways, storage rooms, and basements should also be bright enough so that anyone hiding in them can be clearly seen. Lighting should be sufficient such that no shadows are cast.

FIGURE 2.1 The exterior of an establishment is the first impression for guests. The exterior should always be kept clean and inviting. Courtesy Corbis Digital Stock.

When patrons enter a foodservice operation, they will form an overall first impression. Lighting is a key element in that impression, along with color, sound, and décor. Quick-service facilities and employee cafeterias strive for a feeling of brightness and movement because they are busy places where people do not linger. Such a feeling helps contribute to higher guest turnover. In fine-dining restaurants, conversely, people come to dine slowly and relax. These operations need less light and should be quieter and slower-paced.

The effective use of indirect lighting can add depth to a dining room. Shadowing helps give a pattern and breaks up the lighting. The light, however, should not be so dark as to make it difficult for people to see as they dine or move about. Sufficient lighting should be provided at tables so guests can easily read menus. In addition, because of the danger of accidents, candles or burning lamps for table light or decoration must be properly protected and used with care. All table lighting should function properly.

In the kitchen, there should be enough light so there are no shadows on work places. Heatproof lighting is desirable in cooking areas. Fluorescent lighting provides the most uniform and lowest energy cost.

Lighting fixtures throughout the foodservice establishment should be cleanable. Light bulbs should be replaced on a regular schedule, while they are still giving adequate light. Lights are designed to burn efficiently for a specific number of hours. Studies have shown that changing all lights at this run-out time saves money over waiting to replace lights singly as they burn out.

General Security Decor is an important part of making a good first impression. Many operations decorate entrances with pictures, plants, or art. The decor should not interfere with safe passage through the establishment. In full-service restaurants, the host stand should be neat, uncluttered, and out of guests' and employees' walkways. First impressions on entering the dining room should be pleasing and should give guests a welcome feeling of cleanliness and order. If the first impression is negative, it could linger on through the entire meal, and might affect an otherwise perfect experience.

Almost all operations will have a telephone available where guests can make calls. The area should be neat and clean, and phone books should be available. Check frequently to see that these books are in order and do not have missing pages. Also, make sure telephone areas are well lit.

All doors and windows should be clean and bright. The vestibule or hall should be well lit and attractive. If there is a coatroom or area for accommodating guests' outerwear or other items, it should be near the entrance. A sign should indicate that guests are responsible for the items left, but employees should be observant of any breach of security. Signs are no guarantee that the facility will not be held liable for theft or vandalism.

Foodservice operations are, unfortunately, not immune from criminal activity, regardless of how elite the establishment is. Pickpockets love busy places, and automobile vandalism or theft is a possibility. When a criminal activity is suspected, management should call the police and then investigate, detaining anyone suspected of committing the crime until the police arrive. Remove the disturbance to the manager's office and try to maintain a calm atmosphere in the establishment. Your establishment's attorney should provide employees with guidelines on dealing with suspected criminal activity.

The Dining Area

All guest areas should be neat, orderly, and inviting. Dirt or spills will spoil an otherwise perfect impression and negatively color a guest's feelings about your establishment.

A dirty spot on the entryway carpet may spoil the cordial welcome the facility is trying so hard to create. That's why it's important for all employees to see that the areas for which they are responsible contribute to an overall favorable impression.

The decor of the dining area should be fitting to the ambiance and clientele of the operation. Simplicity at times can be better than too much lavish decor. In full-service operations, what guests should see is a neat, orderly grouping of tables, set with the proper flatware, decor, and glassware. (Some authorities recommend that glassware be turned upside down, while others object to this practice, saying that inverted glassware indicates the table is not ready for guests.) Candles and table decorations should blend in with or complement the decor.

Quick-service operations should have only clean, neat tables and booths. There should be a convenient place for depositing waste and trays.

Whatever the case, the arrangement of tables should be neat, not too close together, and clean. Chairs should be squarely set slightly under the table.

Before a meal begins, make an inspection to see that the dining area is ready for guests, and make any necessary corrections. Ask yourself, "Would I want to eat here?" Your servers might also ask themselves this same question. Figure 2.2 is a checklist used in one operation to see if a dining room is in order.

Environmental Control The lighting, air conditioning, heating, and ventilation should be comfortable. Check for drafts. Be careful to eliminate any unpleasant cooking odors in the dining area.

Managers should know the basics of mechanical adjustments so they can help maintain a comfortable environment and correct problems. A manager should always be notified of heat and humidity problems.

Humidity can cause guest and employee discomfort. When the air is too moist, it does not evaporate well from the body, and this causes body heat to build up. The air in a dining room should have around 50 percent relative humidity. To check whether the dining area is too humid, just fill a glass with ice and water and set it down on a dish. If beads of moisture quickly build up on the surface, the room is too humid. Treat air to remove excess moisture as well as cool it down.

Servers should check to see that tables near cool air outlets are not blasted with cold air. Nobody wants to sit in a cold draft. Direct sunlight coming through a window quickly builds up heat. Proper window coverings can control the sun's rays. A desirable temperature in the dining area is around 70°F (21.1°C). If the temperature is hot and dry outside, the temperature can be somewhat higher and guests will still feel comfortable. Dry air helps people feel cool even though the temperature may be higher than 70°F.

Answering yes to each item indicates excellent mise en place.

DINING ROOM CHECKLIST

Inspected by _____

Time and Date _____

Area _____

Temperature _____ Humidity _____ Air Quality _____

Yes	No		Yes	No	
❑	❑	All lights turned on?	❑	❑	Traystands stored in proper locations?
❑	❑	Fixtures clean?			
❑	❑	Windows clean?	❑	❑	Silencer on properly?
❑	❑	Draperies properly arranged?	❑	❑	Table linen clean and pressed?
❑	❑	Furniture and decorative items clean and dusted?	❑	❑	Table cloth arranged properly?
❑	❑	Stations inspected?	❑	❑	Napkins properly folded and placed?
❑	❑	Tables level?			
❑	❑	Tables arranged properly?	❑	❑	Table lamps clean and in good working order?
❑	❑	Aisle space adequate?	❑	❑	Flower vases clean and filled with fresh flowers?
❑	❑	Chairs in good condition?*			
❑	❑	Clean?	❑	❑	Flowers nicely arranged?
❑	❑	Chairs arranged properly at the tables?	❑	❑	Covers set properly for meal or occasion?
❑	❑	Carpeting clean?	❑	❑	Dishes clean?**
❑	❑	Floors clean?	❑	❑	Flatware clean?
❑	❑	Floors polished?	❑	❑	Glassware clean?

*Check legs for splinters; check seat covers for rips and stains.

**Check each setting for proper flatware and placement; check also for proper placement of dishes, etc.

FIGURE 2.2 Sample dining room checklist.

Those in charge of dining areas should understand that guests themselves give off heat and moisture from their bodies and from the air they are exhaling. It is said that every adult gives off as much heat as a 100-watt light bulb. Thus, in a well-lighted dining room filled with guests and servers, heat can build up considerably and must be monitored to ensure everyone's comfort.

FIGURE 2.3 Servers should have access to dishes, flatware, glasses, and linen to reset tables quickly between guests.

Station Mise en Place Dishes, flatware, glassware, and linens are usually kept in a pantry or storeroom, and servers may have to retrieve these items before each meal. A steward is usually in charge of these items in large, formal operations. In some operations, these items might be located in the service station or on the service table near the dining area. This helps to speed service. Normally, servers get their own supplies for their stations, but buspersons may help them. Often, the server sets up the original stock and then, during the busy time of service, buspersons maintain supply levels and bring items to the station sidestand, or to the tables themselves.

Besides dishes and linens, salt and pepper shakers, condiments like mustard, ketchup, steak sauce, oil and vinegar in cruets, filled sugar bowls, and other items must be there, if their need is expected. All bottle necks on condiments, sugar bowls, salt and pepper shakers, and other items should be clean. Special attention should be paid to necks, mouths, and caps of bottles. Figure 2.5 on page 36 lists a suggested inventory of items for a sidestand.

Clean dishes can be brought to the sidestands on trays. The bottom of the tray should be lined with a clean cloth so dishes do not slide as they are carried. Be careful not to stack items too high, they may tip over and cause an accident or at least cause a server to lose time, and breakage can be costly. Cups and glasses can be brought to a service station in the racks they were washed in or on a tray. They should be placed inverted on the trays or in the racks.

Dishes, glassware, and other items that show cracks or chipping should be discarded, as should bent or otherwise damaged flatware.

Dishware, flatware, and glassware should be clean and sparkling. However, just because something looks clean and sparkling does not mean it is sanitary. Bacteria can be present without being seen. That is why these items are given a last minute or two of sanitizing while in the washing machines. In sink washing, the final rinse is extremely hot and usually includes a sanitizing agent. Wiping ware dry is not recommended. Health authorities frown on it because it can pass contamination from one utensil to another.

High temperatures and dishwashers using sanitizing compounds aids in providing a high volume of guest-safe dishware. The following steps are recommended:

1. Check cleanliness of dish machines and see sanitizing equipment are operating correctly and are filled with an adequate supply of sanitizing medium. Wash and rinse tanks should start with fresh, clear, hot water.

2. Scrape, flush, or soak items before washing. Pre-soak with dried or cooked food on items.

3. Use racks constructed so all item surfaces are exposed for cleaning. Correctly load machines. Do not overload. Washing and sanitizing efficiency is increased. Second pass throughs are avoided.

4. Check temperatures frequently.

5. Check items as racks are unloaded. Run items needing it through again. Proper equipment and proper work methods insure one-pass dish washing.

6. Air dry everything; do not use towels.

7. Keep machines in good repair.

Hard water can cause spotting on items, and over time, a mineral buildup can occur. This spotting and mineral buildup can be avoided by using the proper detergents and other washing compounds, usually a compound associated with phosphoric acid. If spotting cannot be avoided, wiping might be necessary to remove the spots. Mineral buildup is not as easily taken care of. Soft abrasive material is needed to remove the built-up soil, and it can be very time consuming. For these reasons, preventing the buildup in the first place is the best practice. Detergent companies often can be of help in solving these problems.

FIGURE 2.4 Servers should keep their workstations clean and organized, the better to respond to guests' needs.

Sterling silver flatware and other items should be well polished. If the operation has a silver polisher, these items will come from the dishwashing section in satisfactory condition. If not, servers themselves may have to polish or touch up some pieces. Soiled flatware should be separated at the service station. Some operations allow flatware to be kept in the containers in which they are washed with the handles up. This is sanitary, but may not be very presentable.

In some types of service, additional equipment will be brought to the table. For French service, a *guéridon* with all the necessary items will be brought tableside so the *chef de rang* may prepare the items. Service carts or wagons (*voitures*) may be brought to the table to display items for guest selection, or a carving station or other mobile equipment may be brought to the table. They should be so clean they shine, and metal parts should be polished. Glass or plastic covers should be clear. All equipment—tray stands, high chairs, and other equipment that may be needed from time to time—should be clean, neat, and in good working order.

Servers must often operate hot and cold food and liquid holding equipment. Follow these procedures to ensure the equipment is functioning properly:

1.   Hot food should be kept at temperatures above 140°F or higher. Holding equipment includes steam tables, double boilers, bain maries, heated cabinets, and chafing dishes.

2. *Never* use hot-holding equipment to cook or warm items—use only to keep foods hot.

3. Measure equipment temperatures every two hours and enter temperatures on a log.

Cold and raw foods and cold liquids must also be kept at proper temperatures to avoid contamination and retain textures and flavor. Servers should do the following:

1. Hold cold foods and liquids at about 40°F or lower.

2. Hold ready-to-eat cold foods in pans, plates, or other suitable containers, never directly on ice. Be sure ice surrounding food drains away as it melts. Sanitize drip pans after a day's use.

3. Measure temperatures every two hours and log them.

Before the station is ready, all food items needed by servers, such as butter, cream, coffee, ice, water, condiments, and garnishes should be on hand and properly stored. Usually such storage is close to the station and other servers may use it so the servicing of this area in mise en place is a joint responsibility. Buspersons might do this.

Frequently servers operate the coffee equipment. Before service starts, there should be a check to see that coffee and other items needed are on hand. Usually a 12-cup filter unit will be used. Coffee should always be fresh and prepared properly. Once a batch is made, remove the grounds immediately. If the grounds are allowed to stand over the brew, bitter compounds can drip down from them and reduce brew quality. Coffee should be held no longer than 45 minutes.

Table Mise en Place The first thing a server in a full-service restaurant should check before placing linens on tables is the tables themselves. Are they sturdy and not wobbly? Is gum deposited under the edges? Are they clean? Are they level? Are chairs clean and the seats free of crumbs? Is the area around the table clean and in good repair? If not, any undesirable condition should be corrected before the table is set.

Some operations cover their tables with a silencer and tablecloth. A silencer is a felt pad that quites the noise of the table service and absorbs spills. The server brings the silencer and tablecloth to the table and places them on a tray stand or another table. If items are on the table, these are removed and placed on a tray stand, cart, or service station counter. The silencer is then placed on the table first; it might just fit the shape of the tabletop or it might hang down not more than eight inches over the side. To lay the silencer, pick it up at the centerfold at both ends and, with arms extended, lay it so

All quantities are recommendations. The items and quantities in individual operations will vary.

FLATWARE

Dinner forks	30	Soup spoons	24
Dessert/Salad forks	30	Cocktail forks (dinner only)	12
Dinner knives	30	Grapefruit spoons (breakfast only)	12
Teaspoons	30	Fish knives (lunch and dinner only)	12

(Other flatware according to menu needs)

DISHWARE

Dinner plates	25	Salad plates	25
Bread plates	25	Cups and saucers	25
Soup bowls	15	Bouillon or soup cups	15

(Platters and other dishware according to menu needs)

GLASSWARE

Water glasses or goblets	30	White wine glasses	15
Red wine glasses	15		

(Other glassware as needed)

CONDIMENTS

Ketchup bottles	4	Dijon mustard	2
Worcestershire sauce	2	A-1 sauce	2
Tabasco sauce	2	Soy sauce (If needed)	2

(Chutney, oil and vinegar, grated cheese, etc. as needed)

REFRIGERATOR

Milk, regular	4	Milk 2%	4
Cream or substitutes, indiv.	36	Butter pats (144/box)	1 box

(Lemon, etc. as needed)

LINENS

Napkin, folded	30	Naperones (if used)	5
Tablecloths	5	Hand towels	5
Serviettes	5		

MISCELLANEOUS

Sugar substitute packets, salt substitutes, ice with tongs, syrups, jellies, jams, water pitchers, water, ash trays, pencils or pens, menus, peppermills, plate warmers, coffee makers, coffee packets, coffee maker cleaners, various trays, check trays, finger bowls, crumbers, tote boxes or buspans, etc., as needed.

FIGURE 2.5 Example of a standard inventory for a station of 20 to 25 covers.

the centerfold is in the center of the table and the silencer covers half the table on the side opposite you. Unfold the other half and place it so the table side on your side is covered. Sometimes the silencer may be given a quarterfold rather than a halffold. The procedure in this case is much the same as with the centerfold in the center, but the two top folds must be lifted up with the fingers and placed so as to cover the half of the table opposite the server. Now the underfolds must be carefully pulled from under and moved to the table edge where the server stands.

The method for laying the cloth on the silencer is similar to that used for laying the silencer. Smooth the silencer out before laying the cloth. The tablecloth should hang down at least eight, but no more than ten inches over the table sides, with hangover equal on all sides. Some may wish to have the hangover so the tablecloth edge almost touches the chair seat. Smooth the tablecloth out and step back and check to see that the cloth is centered. If not, adjust the cloth. Examine all table coverings for holes, cigarette burns, and stains and replace them if necessary. A naperone, also called a laycloth, may be laid on the table in a similar manner to that used to lay the silencer and tablecloth.

The placement of napkins can vary. Some operations place them in a stemmed wine glass, although some health inspectors have raised concern because lint particles can remain in the stemware. Others place them folded in the center on the service plate, if used, or on the tablecloth between knives and spoons and forks, if no service plate is used. Place plainly folded napkins, either paper or cloth, with one corner facing the guest, so when the guest picks up the napkin, it can easily be unfolded with one hand. Often in fine-dining establishments servers pick up the napkin and either hand it to the guest or place it across the guest's lap. Napkin folding has reached a high art of skill and many operations have intricately folded napkins that add to the table decor.

If the table is to be set with place mats or have no covering at all, wash the table top with a mild detergent in warm water and wipe dry. The tabletop should shine and have no sticky or soiled areas. Next, place the place mats squarely about two inches from the table edge. If these are the type that are reused, see that they are clean and free from grime or stickiness.

Items that are to go at the table center, such as flowers, candles, and salt and pepper shakers should now be placed on the table, as well as ashtrays, matches, table tents, and any other items. Then, proceed to set the table with the necessary covers. It is accepted practice to place flatware in the following manner: forks on the left, and knives (with blades facing inside) and spoons on the right. A dessert spoon or fork may be placed in the cover center above the napkin. Normally, flatware is set in place with the first piece to be used on the outer edge, and then as the meal and need for items proceed, the guest uses items from the outer edge inward.

FIGURE 2.6 It is important to have all tables set properly before the dining operation is open to guests.

The bottom ends of knives and forks should be placed at least one inch away from the edge of the table. When placing silverware on the tables, use a plate lined with a napkin to hold the ware. In casual dining, servers may use a cocktail tray, a plate, or simply a clean service towel as an underliner; servers should avoid walking around the dining room holding flatware with bare hands. Touching flatware by any part other than the handles should be absolutely avoided.

If the table setup requires it, the bread and butter plate is placed next to, but slightly above, the salad or appetizer fork. A butter knife is placed across the plate horizontally. Some operations prefer placing the butter knife vertically, so the tip of the knife points in the same direction as the dinner knife. In this case, the blades of both knives should face left.

The water glass is placed near the tip of the dinner knife. The wine glass (if required) is placed to the right of the water glass. If the operation offers two different shaped wine glasses (one for white wine, and one for red wine) the smaller of the two (usually the white wine glass) is placed slightly above the water glass, and the taller glass is placed slightly above and between the two. This might seem unimportant at first, but it will make a difference when serving wine, as it is difficult to pour any liquid into a glass when a taller glass is in the way.

If additional glasses are used, such as those for sherry, champagne, and brandy, they should be set toward the center of the table, so that they will not cramp the space available between guests. This should be kept in mind when setting a table for four or more.

Whether in casual or fine-dining operations, symmetry is a must. An effective method to ensure symmetry in flatware placement is to draw an imaginary line between the tip of the dinner knife and the dinner fork on the opposite side of the table. If the line is straight, the setup is symmetrical. This can be applied to any table shape and size, with the only exception being a round table where an odd number of covers are placed.

Centerpieces and condiments should not be placed in a manner inconvenient to guests; for example, flower vases should not keep guests from seeing others sitting on the opposite side of the table. Additional items that might be requested during the meal should be placed conveniently to the right side of the guest.

In some operations, such as a cafe, the table setup is simpler. Often there is no linen on the table and paper napkins may be used. A sugar bowl, salt and pepper shakers, ashtray, and matches (if there is a smoking section), and perhaps a bud vase or table decoration and some condiments are placed in the center. If the table is set against the wall, these items are placed on the edge of the table near the wall. Paper napkins may be in a container. Sometimes the table is set after the orders are placed, the server then bringing the correct items such as paper placemats, or flatware settings wrapped in paper napkins.

Often in coffee shops, cafes, or other busy operations, coffee cups might be on the table for breakfast. The flatware is usually limited to a knife, fork, and teaspoon. Other flatware will be brought as needed, such as a steak knife, soup spoon, iced tea spoon, or dessert spoon or fork. Tables are often not covered with linen for breakfast or lunch—placemats might be used—while linen might or might not be used for dinner.

In most quick-service and self-service operations, the table is bare and guests bring to the table the items they need. However, this may vary; some may still set tables with a limited amount of items.

Figure 2.7 contains a list of some basic mise en place instructions that will assist in any service style setup. Figure 2.8 is a reminder list of common side work.

Guest Checks

Order or guest check systems vary from operation to operation. Some restaurants still issue servers a supply of guest checks. With computerized POS (point-of-sale) systems, which are used by many restaurants today, this usually is unnecessary. Instead, checks, properly coded as to server, station, and table, are given to the server at the time guests are brought to the table, or are produced once order information is entered into the computer.

Where paper checks are used, servers are usually given a set quantity of numbered checks. Servers sign for them and are responsible for seeing that guest checks are properly used and that they get to cashiers with payment. In some operations, checks are issued

1. Be on shift and station on time.
2. Be sure to punch in on the time clock when you arrive.
3. Be prepared regarding personal appearance and uniform.
4. Check your station for adequate supplies of glassware, garnishes, straws, napkins, picks, etc.
5. See that all equipment is clean and ready to use.
6. Sign in for and receive change money.
7. Check station to make sure all areas are in proper condition (tables/chairs clean, arranged properly, floor clear, ashtrays on table, etc.)
8. If you are relieving another server, check with her/him for any instructions as to guests that might be in the station, pending orders.
9. The service area at the bar is to be kept clean at all times, free of litter, soiled towels, dirty ashtrays, and so on. All garnishes and supplies must be stored in an orderly fashion. Wipe the bar service area frequently to keep it clean. Keep garnish containers clean and filled with fresh items. It is advisable that different servers on each shift be made responsible for specific service area tasks; thus, one server can be made responsible for garnishes, another for picks, napkins, and so on.
10. Be sure you have a bottle and can opener at your station.
11. Be sure the ice bin area is kept clean. Use the scoop whenever filling glasses with ice. Every station should keep about a dozen glasses iced up.
12. Drink tower areas and sinks for drawing fresh water should be kept clean. Do not wash ashtrays under drink towers. This may create serious drainage problems.
13. Always use a large service tray in giving service. Prepare and stack no more than six trays. Arrange service items on trays on one side of cocktail tray. Each tray should contain:
    - ashtrays (if the restaurant has a smoking section)
    - tip trays
    - matchbooks
    - pens
    - bar towel
    - cocktail napkins
14. Check ashtrays frequently if the establishment has a smoking section. Remove as necessary, replacing with clean ones. Use the capping method by placing the clean ashtray on top of the dirty one; remove from table and place the dirty ashtray on side tray. Then put clean ashtray back on table.
15. The floor around your station must be kept free of litter (straws, napkins, empty sugar packets, etc.)
16. Unoccupied chairs should be pushed close to the tables to allow free movement between tables. This will also help to keep the station organized.
17. At the end of the shift and at closing, all tables and chairs should be returned to their proper places as per station chart. They should all be wiped clean with a bar towel.
18. At the end of a shift, all ashtrays should be washed and returned to their storage area in the station.
19. S-O-S (stay on station). Be ready to offer more service. Take that second order. Pick up soiled napkins, discarded stirrers, and so on. Put chairs back in place.
20. Circulate; don't congregate.
21. Utilize the round trip. Don't return to the station empty handed. Clear tables before going to the bar. With light loads from the bar, bring station supply replenishments.

FIGURE 2.7 A partial list of mise en place instructions.

A. Condiments
   1. Fill partially full containers with other partially filled ones. Fill to half-inch from the top.
   2. If containers are to be refilled, wash and dry first and then refill.
   3. With a damp cloth, wipe tops of containers; clean caps and replace.
   4. Store perishable condiments in neat rows in the refrigerator.
   5. Day servers will empty and refill relishes.

B. Sugars, salts, and peppers
   1. Fill and wipe salt and pepper shakers; make sure holes are clear.
   2. Refill sugar trays. Be sure old packets are not allowed to rest on the bottom under the row of packets on the tray.
   3. Wipe holders.
   4. On Monday nights all containers and trays should be emptied and washed. Refill only after being sure the containers are dry.

C. Butter and cream
   1. Don't use broken or partially melted butter patties. Place unusable patties in a dish to be taken to kitchen for use in cooking.
   2. Keep butter containers iced and free from melted water.
   3. Return emptied butter containers to pantry for washing and refilling.
   4. Keep coolers clean at all times; wipe out as needed. On Sundays, empty and wash, refilling with butter and cream.
   5. Fill creamers to about half-inch from the top. Do not refill creamers; use only clean ones.
   6. At end of shift, empty filled creamers into cream containers and send the emptied creamers to the dishwashing area.
   7. Keep at least two containers of cream and two filled butter containers in the cooler; more may be needed at busy times. Pick these up at the pantry.

D. Dining room buffet and water cooler
   1. Have placemats, napkins, salt packets, sugar packets, and takeout containers on hand.
   2. Have clean water pitchers on hand.
   3. Stock all these items on the shelves under the buffet.
   4. Stock tip trays and ashtrays on top of buffet. Keep the remainder of this area free for use during service.
   5. Stock glasses under water cooler.
   6. Remove daily the tray under spigot and wash drain area. Once a week use drain cleaning solution. Wipe down entire cooler daily.

E. Coffee urn area
   1. Clean iced tea dispenser and tray daily.
   2. Empty ice cubes for closing work; return lemon slices to kitchen pantry.
   3. Stock ramekins, iced tea glasses and spoons, teapots, children's cups, cups, and saucers on undershelves of coffee urn stand.
   4. Stock coffee, tea bags, instant tea bags, and coffee filters on undershelf of urn stand.
   5. Wipe entire area down daily.
   6. Clean coffee urn thoroughly at the end of each emptying. On closing, leave urn filled with water that has had a fourth cup of soda added. Mix well after adding. Rinse urn thoroughly in the morning after emptying and before using. On Saturdays add one bag of cleaning solution instead of soda and mix well. (Store this cleaning solution in box on bottom shelf.)
   7. Send bar trays through dishwasher once a week.

FIGURE 2.8 Side work reminder.

F. Bread warmer, boards, and knives
1. Wipe bread boards and bread knives with damp cloth after each use.
2. On closing, empty all trays of bread supplies and take to bake shop. Clean drawers. Be sure they are free of crumbs.
3. Wipe entire outside of warmer daily.
4. Have a good supply of napkins.
5. Clean bread baskets once a week.

G. Salad dressings
1. On closing, empty dressing jars into their storage containers and place the storage containers back into the refrigerator.
2. Stack the empty containers on a tray with ladles in between and take to dishwashing section.
3. Wipe racks with a damp cloth daily. Empty and clean refrigerator once a week.
4. Store condiments on tabletop. Clean tops and store perishable ones in refrigerator on closing.
5. Store French and Italian dressings on shelf under shrimp cocktail containers.

FIGURE 2.8 (Continued).

to servers at the time guests are seated. These checks are kept at the cashier stand. Servers sign for the checks given to them at the start of the shift, usually next to the check number on a form commonly called the traffic sheet.

Employee Theft Employees may be able to steal money by manipulating guest checks. Managers should watch for a slower flow of checks, or missing checks from those given out to servers, fake checks among legitimate ones, or checks that are regularly turned in late by an employee.

Other ways of stealing follow:

- Destroying checks, not ringing up the sale and keeping the money.
- *Bunching checks* by ringing up only one of several checks with identical amounts, collecting all the money, and keeping all the money except that for the rung-up check.
- Giving guests incorrect change.
- Raising prices on checks or charging for items not served.
- Stealing guest checks from the establishment's supply, and using these and never turning in the check and pocketing the money. False checks may also be brought in.
- Taking payment money left on another server's table.

One way to help protect against theft is to have the server present the check, receive cash or a credit card, and take this to a cashier. The cashier rings up the sale and gives the server any overpayment, which is returned along with the rung-up check to the guest. The guest signs the credit card receipt, giving it back to the server so the establishment has something to offer for its payment. The payer usually puts the tip amount on this signed receipt. If it's a cash deal, the guest paying the bill picks up the money returned, usually leaving the tip money on the tray for the server while keeping the rest.

An inspection should be made to see if all checks given to a server are returned either as used or unused checks. Some operations require servers to pay a certain amount for missing checks. POS systems as previously described alert management to problems. If guests are given checks to be taken to cashiers, servers are not considered responsible for missing checks. Cashiers are.

Some servers are not alone in finding creative ways to defraud restaurants. Some guests wait until there's a crowd at the cashier's station and then skip out on the check. It is the obligation for any employee to see that this does not happen.

Guest Fraud Other forms of fraud involve lying about the bill. Diners may purposely fail to report when their bar bill is not carried over to their food order. They may erase or alter entries on checks. Careful register use, stapling of all related checks, and keeping control of the checks as long as possible can help avoid check trouble. Customers may sometimes claim they were given insufficient change. To avoid this, servers should leave the change on a plate and name the change amount as the money is set down. Cashiers should leave the payment on the cash register and then pay the guest the correct change, naming the amount given as payment is made.

Getting Servers Ready

Scheduling In full-service restaurants, specific mise en place planning must be done by the host, hostess, maitre d', or other head of service. This includes forecasting server staffing needs. This is typically done by estimating the total number of covers, and then dividing this total by the number of covers one server can take care of during the meal period. Thus, if an operation estimates 120 guests for lunch, and the number of covers a server is expected to serve is 40, the number of servers scheduled is determined: 120 ÷ 40 = 3. The forecast may be made for a week, and daily work assignments should be made so servers know when they are to be at work (see Figure 6.5). Servers should be informed of their schedules well in advance so they can plan their other priorities.

It is important to plan the number of servers needed and the station assignments on a practical and realistic basis. Each operation's staffing needs differ based on the size and type of the establishment. Only the number of servers needed should be scheduled, and no more. If more customers come than were expected, or a server misses work, a well-organized staff of servers can smooth over the unexpected and still have happy, satisfied guests. It is important in such cases that the service staff be well trained to ensure that things run smoothly.

Wisely, some operations maintain a list of *extra board* service employees, which are not included in the payroll on a steady basis but are called in case of emergency. Larger operations use an on-call system.

The person in charge of service will assign stations. Station assignments let the servers know which stations they will be working, so they can move ahead and complete the necessary mise en place. Often a chart is posted showing station locations and the name of the server(s) responsible for them. As the customer flow fluctuates, stations may be restructured or reassigned. This allows for servers to cover stations while others take a break or end their shifts.

The Preshift Meeting Operations often have a short meeting of servers or all employees—sometimes called lineup, or preshift meeting—just before the meal period begins. Tables should be set, all other arrangements should be completed, and only last-minute things should be done. The meeting is usually conducted by the manager, host or hostess, or a supervisor. Often a quick inspection of grooming and dress occurs, but this is informal.

This preshift meeting is to go over the menu and any details of service that need to be brought to the attention of the service staff—whether any menu items are not available that day, the soups or fish of the day, and so on. Perhaps some important guests have made reservations or a special group is coming in which should be brought to the attention of servers in the station where they will be seated. Any special menu items should be covered with a description of how they are prepared and served. The correct items to use with various dishes and the manner of the service of the items, along with price and preparation time, should be included.

Each server should copy this information down since it may not appear on the menu and all information will have to be given verbally. Specials are usually items management wishes to promote, but others on the menu may be highlighted. Planned runout times may be given and suggested substitutes indicated. A bulletin board in the kitchen can give some of this information. A visit may be made to the kitchen where the chef may briefly add any details he or she wishes the server group to hear.

Sometimes the meeting covers complaints or compliments received. These can be helpful in indicating trouble spots and also indicating what guests like about the service or food. Since the time that follows can be stressful, the meeting should end on a positive note so servers are motivated to deliver great service.

CLEARING AND RESETTING TABLES

When a full-service dining room is full and other guests are waiting to be seated, tables cannot remain vacant long without angering customers. Clearing and setting tablecloths properly is important in maintaining a good image for the establishment. Thus, servers, buspersons, hosts/hostesses, and managers must work together to ensure that tables are cleared and reset in a swift, appealing manner.

Changing the linen is actually more difficult than the original set-up. One recommended method is as follows: Come to the table with a clean, folded cloth. Avoid holding it under the arm. Remove all items from the table to a tray, cart, or service station. Place the folded cloth on top of the soiled one. Next, pull the soiled cloth toward you so the hem of the soiled cloth is even with the far edge of the table. Unfold the fresh cloth by holding the center crease and the top hem between the index and middle finger. Then gently flip over the bottom section. Now hold the top edges of both cloths between the thumb and the index finger. By pulling on the opposite direction, you will pull the soiled cloth out while the fresh cloth remains in place. Step back to make sure the new cloth is centered and make adjustments as necessary. This method allows you to change cloths without exposing the naked table surface to patrons.

Another popular technique is to first place tableware items on the far side of the table. Then, with the forefingers of either hand, hold the two corners of both the soiled and the new cloth, pull up toward the center of the table, slightly raising both cloths' edges, and lower your fingers so as to fold the new cloth in half under the soiled one. Holding the corners of both cloths, fold them over again in the opposite direction. This should leave you with the soiled cloth folded in half under the clean one. Pull out the soiled cloth in one swift motion from the other side of the table. The tableware items are then returned to the center of the table.

Some other methods are faster and more suitable for a large-volume operation, but they involve uncovering the table. A common method is to fold back one edge of the soiled cloth and move the tableware items to that corner. The soiled cloth should be folded together to seal in the crumbs so they do not fall onto chairs or the floor. Place the clean cloth on the table, using the unfolding technique described earlier. Move the tableware items back to the center of the table and straighten the new cloth. With this

FIGURE 2.9 In preparation for new guests, tables should be reset quickly and properly soon after guests leave.

and all methods, if the table is against the wall, pull it a few inches away from the wall for easier clearing.

When a bare table is used, wipe it clean with a cloth dipped in warm water with detergent, wring completely dry.

Reset the table with the proper dishes, flatware, and glassware, and any items that had temporarily been removed. Place napkins accordingly. Once the table is reset, it is ready for the next guests.

ENDING THE MEAL

Mise en place is also required to prepare for guest departure. The bill should be totaled and ready to deliver. Some facilities deliver the bill by placing it face down on a small tray in front of the person paying, or in the middle of the table if the payer is not known.

If the payment is by credit card, provide a pen for writing down the required information. A rapid return with the change or the credit card and credit charge slip should be made. Any personal items that servers have taken care of during the meal, such as crutches, should be quickly brought. Help may be needed to put on coats. A sincere thanks from the server is appreciated. As the guests leave the dining area, the host, hostess, maitre d', or other individual at the entrance thanks them and invites them to return. In very informal situations, such as a quick-service operation, this may not occur. In those establishments, payment is made when the guest gets the food, and there is little formality needed on departure. Nevertheless, when guests are leaving, a warm thank-you makes all the difference.

The departure of guests should be given as much attention and care as the arrival. Cashiers, coatroom attendants, managers, doorpersons, valet parkers, and others should be friendly and helpful.

As a shift winds down, servers should complete their sidework. All soiled dishes should be taken to the dishwashing area and clean stock should be replenished. Soiled linen should be taken to its designated receptacle. Salt and pepper shakers should be filled, cleaned, and checked to see that holes are not plugged. Sugar bowls should be filled and cleaned. All other condiment containers should be filled and cleaned according to the operation's standards. Periodically, all salt and pepper shakers, sugar bowls, and other equipment should be emptied, washed thoroughly, dried, and then refilled. Check the sidestand to see that it is clean and the inventory is up to par. Old coffee should be emptied out and the containers cleaned. It might be necessary on a regular basis to put into the coffee machine a compound that frees it of lime buildup.

Health regulations in communities differ and must be followed. Perishable condiments should be placed in a refrigerator. Iced or refrigerated butter may be returned to refrigeration. Items not in sealed containers that have been put onto guest tables should never be reused for service. However, items such as jams or jellies in sealed containers are reusable. Be sure to know the expiration date for all perishable products and discard any items that have not been kept sanitary and at a safe temperature.

The closing work differs according to the operation and the meal. In most operations, closing includes setting up the dining and service areas for opening the next day. Each operation should establish complete checklists that outline what must be done at the end of each meal period to prepare for the next. For maximum efficiency, tasks may be assigned to individuals based on service area or shift length, for example.

The inspection checklist in Figure 2.10 can be used at closing, as well as before guest arrival. Servers should leave their stations clean, stocked, and prepared for the next shift. The next server will appreciate help on getting a good start. Likewise, each server profits from the servers who previously worked the station.

QUICK-SERVICE MISE EN PLACE

Attention to detail is as important in quick-service operations as it is in full-service restaurants. The primary servers are the counter employees and employees out on the floor cleaning and stocking amenities. When taking the order, the server should

Inspected by _____

Time and Date _____

Yes   No

❑   ❑   Lights off except designated ones?*

❑   ❑   Air conditioning turned off?

❑   ❑   Proper doors, windows, etc. locked?

❑   ❑   Alarm set properly?

❑   ❑   Tables cleared properly?

❑   ❑   Chairs inverted on tabletops?

❑   ❑   Perishable food supplies cared for?

❑   ❑   Cups, glasses, etc., inverted on trays?

❑   ❑   Sidestand top cleared except for allowed items?

❑   ❑   Heating and other equipment turned off?

❑   ❑   Soiled linen taken to soiled linen receptacle?

❑   ❑   Traystands properly stored?

❑   ❑   Proper amount of flatware, dishware, and glassware on sidestand
         for breakfast?

*Leave lights on for the inspection; turn off just before leaving.

FIGURE 2.10 Sample closing checklist.

repeat the order so the guest can hear and verify it before it is totaled up on the preset register. Payment is usually taken before the food is served.

When the order is assembled and put on a tray or in a bag, the guest typically takes it to a table or a service area for eating utensils, napkins, and condiments. In some operations, guests bus their own tables and dump their own trash. In others, employees perform this task.

In operations with drive-through pickup windows, the employee is responsible for helping guests select items, taking and placing orders, expediting, and giving a courteous, positive impression to guests.

To give such service requires precise and considerable mise en place. At peak service times, long lines challenge servers to work quickly and accurately. Without good mise en place, quick service is doomed. For service staff, this means that plenty of bags, wrappers or containers, condiments, coffee stirrers, cream and sugar, napkins, and straws must be on hand. Cash drawers should never be allowed to get low. Only the very last-minute details of assembly should be left. Because of the speed and efficiency expected by guests, mise en place is crucial.

THE CASH BANK

In some operations, cocktail and other servers carry their own money or cash bank. This allows quick payment of a check and reduces the amount of work required of the staff. Procedures for some servers may have to make cash transactions from a cash fund. If used, one of the first steps of coming on shift is to obtain a cash bank to use in making change when collecting bills. The server should be sure to verify the correctness of the sum given.

Servers may carry the bank, but often the bank may be kept at a cash register in a drawer that only that server can operate. The register must be turned on and the server must enter his or her server number, perhaps a password or drawer number. The check for payment will be inserted into the machine, allowing it to read information on it, such as check number, table number, server number, items on the check with their price, and check total. The amount of payment is entered; the proper sum is put into the register and the drawer is closed, which closes the transaction. The check is filed in a special spot or may be kept by the server for closing out the cash bank at the end of the shift.

Sometimes cash is not given by the guest, but some other type of payment is used. A common way of paying in clubs and hotels is to charge to one's account. In clubs, no identification is usually needed. If one is needed, the club member usually makes identification by offering a club membership card. In hotels, the person charging the bill may show for identification a key or key card or some card issued at the time of registration. If there is any doubt as to identification, a call can be made to a front desk or other agency to verify a name, room number, and other pertinent information.

Credit card use is common. Servers must know what credit cards are honored by the operation. Some operations subscribe to some system of credit card verification that indicates whether the card should be honored. The server should use this system; if the card is verified, the server makes out the charge slip. The card with the slip is brought to the card owner who signs the slip, puts in the amount of tip, and receives a slip copy along with the credit card and a sincere thanks. On closing out the servers bank, these slips are offered instead of cash. Some operations ask the server to fill in a sheet indicating individual credit card charges and totals. A sheet reporting complimentaries, discounts, or other such transactions may also be required in the closing report.

At times, corrections must be made on ring-ups. An overring may be corrected by processing a void system set up by the operation. Similarly, a coupon or complimentary system sometimes requires that the check be adjusted to reflect the discount. Often, a ticket, card, coupon, or other item is offered by the guest to verify the right to the lower payment, and this is filed with the checks. If there is an overring, the server may have to write this on the check and also fill in the transaction on an overring sheet.

When no cash register is used, and the server carries the bank, discount and complimentary records are usually written up by the server on a record sheet. Servers must have an adequate mathematical and writing background to complete such reporting.

At the end of the shift, the register will give a total printout of transactions made by each server during the shift. The operation may also wish to have a form filled out recording the check number and check amount, with total sales given at the bottom. Servers must accompany such a form with the proper amount of money. When servers keep tips in the register, any overage in the register after the amount due on sales is set aside and belongs to the server. The server presents the original cash bank, the sale money, and other records to the appropriate authority for a signed release, and is freed of all further responsibility unless some discrepancy is found in the report or funds turned in.

CHAPTER SUMMARY

Mise en place—preparing ahead for the service period—is essential if excellent service is to occur. Time is saved and serving is organized. Prepreparation of needs should be planned and accomplished to cover all phases of a guest's visit, from the time of arrival to departure.

Grounds must be neat and clean. Good security and safety are important. Entrances, hallways, phone booths, coatrooms, and other areas guests encounter upon arriving require attention. Sanitation standards also are a must for todays service personnel.

Mise en place work needed to care for guests can be divided into three parts: (1) Getting ready. (2) Between-guests work. (3) Ending the meal. The first covers all preparations needed for the arrival of guests until they arrive at the dining area, and the work that has to be done before a meal starts, such as getting all items and condiments ready, getting checks, having a lineup meeting, and so on. The second part covers the activities that take place when one group of guests leave and the table must be readied for another. It requires fast work if the dining area is busy and guests are waiting for tables. The last part consists of the preparations that must be made for guest departure and the work that must be done to see that the dining area is ready for the next meal.

RELATED INTERNET SITES

M*ise en Place while cooking*

www.hertzmann.com/articles/2003/mise/

KEY TERMS

cash bank	Grimod de la Reynière	traffic sheet
mise en place	silencer	

CHAPTER REVIEW

1. View several different kinds of facilities and look over the grounds, the entrance, and the way into the dining area. What do you find good and bad? What would you do differently?

2. What are some of the requirements of valet parkers?

3. How can a busperson assist the server in mise en place duties?

4. You are a server and have just arrived at the station assigned to you. What tasks should you perform, and in what order should you perform them?

5. What is a preshift meeting? What is its purpose?

6. How do some computers help stop security problems?

7. What is the proper way to clear a table of items before resetting it?

8. When guests are preparing to leave, what mise en place must be done to see that their departure is facilitated and they receive adequate attention to make them feel they were welcome?

9. Why shouldn't you wipe-dry wet dishes and glasses?

10. What system would you want management to have for the control of guest payment of checks?

Case Study

GOOD MISE EN PLACE IS MISSING

George is a new server in a section that during meal times is a busy place. This is his first service job since graduating from a school where service is taught as a part of the curriculum. The first day, he comes to work a bit early and is assigned a section of tables. He notes other servers around him are busy in their stations. He, however, studies the menu and goes to the kitchen to introduce himself to the cooks. He returns as the place opens up for the dinner hour. A few customers arrive and these tables are quickly waited upon by the other wait staff. George waits on his customers also, but he notices he's a bit busier than the others. The other servers seem to need to move around less than he does to serve the same number of guests. As the place gets busier and busier he feels a lot of pressure to keep up. He has to rush. He becomes frustrated and panics. Coworkers and the hostess have to step in and help him.

After the busy period is over and things are moving slowly, a woman coworker says, "You seem to know your stuff when it comes to waiting tables, but you sure don't know how to get ready to wait on them. Next time, you need to get ready. You didn't have your station prepared. If you had, you would have been able to serve a lot better and easier. We old timers know we've got to really get ready to make it through our busy hour. Next time I'd advise you to pack your station with things you'll need so that you can save steps when the rush period is on." George thanks her and says that the night has taught him a lesson. "I was told in class how important it is to do all your mise en place before and during the meal to provide good service. I guess I just forgot. Thanks for reminding me."

Plan a setup for George's station. Describe what he needs to do to get ready for the next time he serves.

SERVICE AREAS AND EQUIPMENT*

Outline

---

* Authored by Lendal H. Kotschevar and Valentino Luciani.

Learning Objectives

After reading this chapter, you should be able to:

- List and describe the equipment typically found in the dining area of an operation, as well as items used in table service.
- Describe the traditional hierarchy of a service staff.

INTRODUCTION

Servers use many kinds of service equipment and should know what these items are called and how they are used. Each cover, or a guest's place at the table, must have the proper equipment set in the proper way. Different service styles require different equipment.

Menus are a means of communication between guests and servers, and servers should know the items that are on them. Servers also work with two distinct staffs: the kitchen staff and the dining staff. They need to know the organization of each so they can work with them.

DINING AREA EQUIPMENT

Personal Items

Servers should always carry an order pad or order checks, with a pen or pencil. Very formal service requires a serviette or service napkin. Matches or a lighter can be carried to light candles.

Service Stations

The service station, or wait station, assists the service staff in performing their duties. Depending on the type of the operation, a service station may be small with only a minimal amount of dishes and flatware, or it can take up a large portion of the floor space and have many types of equipment.

What is stored in a service station depends on your type of operation. Some items found in service stations include flatware, dinnerware, table condiments, various paper goods, hot and cold prepared foods, glasses, cups, linens, trays, and tray stands.

All service stations perform one or more basic functions:

1.   They store basic goods so the server does not have to make numerous trips to the main storage area for each customer's request.

2.   They hold items for cleaning the dining room.

3.   They act as command and communication centers where orders can be placed with the kitchen and management and the kitchen can communicate information to servers.

4.   They serve as a production center.

5.   In some instances, they serve as host/hostess stations.

6.   They act as a link between the servers and kitchen staff.

In a banquet operation, the service station might be as simple as a table along a wall with extra silverware, napkins, bread and butter, and water and coffee pitchers. In a large chain quick-service operation, it might take up 50 percent of the floor space, including the area between the counter where the customers order, and the pass-through area where the kitchen places prepared food before it is brought to the customer.

Storage Center   The service station, as a storage area, varies greatly from one operation to another. At the most basic level, the setup is simple and the costs are minimal. However, larger operations have service areas that are more complex. They sometimes contain temperature storage units that hold both hot and cold prepared foods. The most common cold storage machines are ice bins, soda dispensers, and milk machines. They are found in most operations. Cold storage might also include dessert cases, or small reach-in refrigerators that hold premade salads, garnishes, or side dishes. Hot or warm storage are usually soup wells and bread warmers. In both hot and cold storage, the item is completed earlier in the kitchen, and the servers may have to plate or bowl the item before serving the customers.

As the costs of building restaurants increase, operators try to decrease the amount of space that does not directly have contact with the customer. Because of this, floor space in service stations is decreasing. To accommodate this change, restaurants are using vertical space—the space from the ceiling to the floor—to expand the usable space in service stations. It is important that managers are sure that proper sanitation and safety procedures are followed.

Cleaning Area The service station is sometimes used for storing cleaning items for the dining area. In some operations, the service station includes a place for dirty dishes/glasses, used linen, and garbage cans. Most also have sanitizing solutions to clean a table after it has been bussed. These solutions are used to clean a table after each use so it may be used, or *turned*, again.

Service stations or an attached area usually include the items needed for major cleaning after meal periods, at the end of the shift, or at closing. These include vacuums, polish, and cleaners.

It is management's job to establish strict, high sanitation rules for its operation and also see that employees have read and understand them. Management should see to it that all employees go through training programs on sanitation procedures. Many localities require that employees take an approved course, and are certified after successful completion as sanitarians qualified to supervise the kitchen and/or dining areas.

The established rules should apply to all areas of the operation, but special rules may apply to specific areas to fit special needs. The rules applying to kitchen and dining areas should be the same, except the rules may have to also cover sanitation for guests in non-kitchen areas. As an example, most states require that soups and other liquid or semiliquid foods be heated to a sufficiently high temperature in the kitchen as to guarantee the destruction of all microbiological agents (as opposed to being heated in a steam table). This is only one of many state and local sanitation regulations that must be followed.

It is important for safety reasons to keep used eating utensils, dishes, glasses, and used linens away from food and clean items. Some states require a hand washing sink to be available in the kitchen and service areas and that this sink be used only for that purpose.

Command Center In many foodservice operations, the service stations act as a command and communication center. POS (point of sale) systems allow servers to place orders to the kitchen in an orderly and traceable way. The POS system not only records and informs the kitchen of the customers order, but prompts needed information such as appropriate temperature and side dishes, tracks open checks, counts customers, totals check sales, and monitors amount of sales. The service station is also where management and the kitchen communicate important information to the service staff. There might be a board that lists the soups of the day, specials, or what the kitchen might be out of. Management can use it to inform the service staff of schedules, section assignments, or special circumstances. In most operations, the service station allows the staff to communicate with each other.

Production Center It is incorrect to assume that all production in a foodservice operation takes place in the kitchen. Many operations now require their service staff to be involved in some aspect of production. It might be as simple as making coffee and tea, or as complicated as preparing an entree-type salad. Beverages are most commonly filled in a service station. Almost all operations require the service staff to make coffee. Iced tea and lemonade are other simple beverages often produced by the service staff. Operations that offer malts and shakes usually require the servers to prepare them. With the growth of premium coffee and specialty drinks, the skills level and training required of the staff has increased. In operations that are food oriented but offer beverage alcohol, the servers might perform bartending duties. The necessary equipment must be located in the service station.

The production of food in a service area is usually limited to cold foods that are prepared beforehand, but do not hold well in their final state. These include ice cream, desserts with whipped cream, and salads. All the needed ingredients are prepared earlier by the kitchen staff or the server and are assembled as ordered to ensure the highest-quality product for the customer.

Host or Hostess Station

All operations have an area where the customers first have contact with an employee. Most often this is a host/hostess station area. Most stations have a few basic items; phone, reservation book, menus, and a floor diagram (including open tables, server areas, and smoking/nonsmoking sections). Some have POS systems that allow them to function like a cashier. Depending on the operation, it might combine some functions of a service station.

Kitchen or Service Area The kitchen or service area is in direct contact with the kitchen. Usually a manager or an expediter is in charge of the area. The main function this person is to act as a communication link between the servers and kitchen staff (with the assistance of or instead of a POS system). If servers need to communicate with the kitchen, they tell the expediter, who relays the information to the kitchen. The

FIGURE 3.1 The host/hostess station is often the first interior area where guests have first contact with the staff.

expediter is also used if the kitchen needs to talk to a server about clarifying an order. Most operations that use an expediter require the service and kitchen staff to communicate through the expediter. They also help servers with tray orders and assist in any production the server might have to perform.

Furniture

Tables Tables for seated service are used in most operations. In others, counters with stools are used. Stand-up areas may only have high counters at which people stand while eating. Tables are usually sized to accommodate different-sized groups, but may be put together for larger groups. Some square tables have hinged leaves that can be lifted up and locked into place to make a larger table, square or round. Table arrangements are dictated by serving needs and the dining area shape. Whatever the arrangement, it should be symmetrical and neat. Many tables are equipped with levelers; servers should know how to use these.

It is important that tables be far enough apart as to permit easy passage of people going by. Also, guests like tables to be far enough apart as to not allow a low conversation to be heard at an adjoining table. Aisle space between tables will be less wide than aisle space for guests walking through to get to other areas of the room.

Chairs Chair sizes and shapes will vary, but all should be very sturdy. Usually, the chairs do not have arms. Chairs should be large enough so guests can sit comfortably. Chairs on rollers are easy to move, but may be dangerous because they can easily slip out from under a guest as they are about to sit or stand up. Many chairs are equipped with glides so they move easily over a surface. Servers should check these to see that they are secure. Also, they should check to see that the chairs are clean. Some high chairs may be needed for small children, while booster seats for larger children might be needed. Chairs should be checked to note rough edges or legs that can snag on guests' clothing.

Other Furniture A guéridon is a small cart often carrying a réchaud, a small heater on which one cooks or reheats foods and liquids. The cooking items needed are on the cooking top or on a shelf under. The dishes on which to serve the food are usually kept on a shelf under the food-preparing top. Carts called voitures are used to move hors d'oeuvres, appetizers, salads, fruits, desserts, beverages, wines, or liqueurs around the dining area. Offerings should be neatly arranged. Some voitures may be refrigerated, while others may be heated and hold roasts and other items for carving and serving. A bus cart is used by servers or buspersons to hold used wares until they are transported to the warewashing area. Most operations do not allow the cart to be brought into the dining area when guests are present. Usually it is placed in an inconspicuous place and used wares are brought to it.

Tables are usually covered first with a silencer—a felt pad that quiets the noises of dishes and utensils and absorbs spills—and then with a tablecloth. Cotton, linen, and ramie are the most commonly used fabrics for tablecloths. Tablecloths should fit the table and hang down only about eight inches. They should be plain and smoothly pressed. The proper placement of silencers and tablecloths is described in Chapter 2.

Fine-dining operations may use naperones to cover the tablecloth. These are square, and do not cover the entire table.

Napkins, about 18 to 20 inches square, are often used in fine-dining establishments for dinner. Smaller ones may be used for lunch or breakfast. In more casual dining, paper napkins may be used. Small cocktail or hors d'oeuvre paper napkins may be used at receptions, cocktail parties, or teas.

A serviette or hand napkin is usually made of cloth and hangs over the arm of the server to protect his hands when serving hot items and as a general serving towel. Serviettes should be used in all kinds of service situations. Placemats are individual covers, about 18 inches to 24 inches long and about 12 inches wide. They are made of various materials, and can be decorated with advertising or information the operation wants a guest to read, or games for children. Some placemats have the menu printed on them.

TABLE SERVICE EQUIPMENT

Dishes

Dishware costs money and servers should give it good care. A dinner plate can cost $12 or more. Some operations prominently display the cost of individual dish items in the dishwashing area. A server who drops a tray of dishes costs the operation—or themselves—a lot of money. Sliding dishes and glassware from a tray onto a dishwasher table should never be allowed. Keeping flatware (forks, knives, spoons, etc.) separate from dishes is a must; some operations have a special sink or container where flatware can be dropped to soak before washing. Glassware should be given special care and kept separate from dishes.

Soiled ware may be loaded into dish baskets or tote boxes and taken to or from the kitchen. Servers who come to an area carrying a very heavy basket with no place to set it down can cause breakage or accidents. Know there is a landing space before you carry. Areas where soiled items are brought should have sufficient space so crowding and cross-traffic are avoided.

Most operations use a heavy reinforced china (porcelain) for dishware. Some may use lighter china, but this is often too fragile and expensive for ordinary use. It cannot stand the heavy wear and handling. Others may use ceramics or plastic, and some use paper. Whatever is used should be sanitary and clean. All china should be sparkling clean and sanitized when placed before guests. Glassware or china that is chipped, cracked, or has lost some of its glaze should not be used.

A description of some of the most used dishes follows.

Platter	Platters are long, oval dishes used to hold several portions of food; some smaller ones may be used instead of plates. Sizzling platters are almost always made of metal and are heated to a very high heat so the food sizzles on them as they are taken to the guests. Often an underliner is used. Guests should be warned not to touch them when the platter is set down.
Service/show plate	In fine-dining operations, a plate larger than the dinner plate sits on the table at the cover when the guest is seated. Hors d'oeuvres, soups, and other first-course foods in their serving dishes are placed on this plate. In many cases, management instructs servers to immediately remove the plate after the cocktail is served. Once removed, show plates are not used again. Show plates are usually 11 to 12 inches in diameter. They can be expensive and should be handled carefully. After their use, they should be wiped gently with a service napkin wet with vinegar and never brought to the dishwasher.
Dinner plate	This is used for dinners and even lunch to hold the main part of the meal. It can also be used as a service plate for other purposes, and is usually 10 to 11 inches in diameter. In many establishments, oval shapes are used instead of the traditional round plate.
Salad plate	A 7- to 8-inch-diameter plate used to hold salads, soups in bowls, desserts, and other foods.
Bread plate	Often called a bread and butter plate, it is usually 4 to 5 inches in diameter. Used for breads, rolls, toast, butter, jellies, jams, and so forth. Can be used as an underliner with a doily over it.
Demitasse	A round container with handle holding four to six ounces of hot beverage; a saucer is placed below the cup. Primarily used to serve espresso and specialty coffees.
Finger bowl	A cuplike container holding lukewarm water, usually with a slice of lemon or a rose petal floating in it. Used for lightly rinsing or washing the fingers. It is placed on an underliner with a doily on it. It may also be called a *monkey dish*.
Cocotte	Small casserole for cooking and serving entree preparations. It often has a cover over it.
Cloche	A bell-shaped cover used with a serving dish; the cover holds in the heat. Can be made of glass, plastic, or metal.
Snail dish	Metal or ceramic stoneware with six deep indentations for holding snails cooked out of their shells. A shallower one with six indentations is used for snails in the shell.
Sauce boat	For serving gravies, au jus, and other liquids.

Glassware

All glassware should be sparkling clean and sanitized. Often an all-purpose wine glass is used in place of various wine glasses. However, interest in the beverage selections can be increased by using a variety of specialized glassware.

Service Utensils and Flatware

All foodservice operations have special utensils that are only used by service staff. They can be as simple as plastic tongs for portioning salads, or as formal as sterling silver serving sets. The most common utensils are ice scoops, tongs, ladles, stirrers, and spatulas. The utensils your servers need will depend on your operation. In any operation, the utensils must be in good shape, clean, and sanitized.

A list of commonly used utensils follows.

Dinner fork	Used for main entrees and other foods eaten from a dinner plate. Can also be used as a general utility fork.
Salad fork	For salads, appetizers, some desserts, or fruits.
Fish fork	Used for fish and sometimes seafood dishes.
Cocktail fork	Used for seafood and other cocktails.
Lobster fork	For lobster when served in the shell.
Dessert fork	For pies, cakes, pastries, and other solid desserts.
Oyster fork	For eating clams, oysters, and other bivalves.
Fondue fork	A long fork used to pick up bread cubes and dip them into a cheese fondue; a shorter fork holds meat in hot oil for a meat fondue.
Teaspoon	Used for eating vegetables, fruit sauces, puddings, fruits, etc., and other foods that are difficult to eat with a fork.
Tablespoon	Larger than a teaspoon, used for soups or cereals.
Soup spoon	Used mainly for soups.
Coffee spoon	For beverages, some cocktails, and ice cream.
Espresso spoon	For liquids served in a demitasse cup.
Sundae or iced tea spoon	For ice cream sundaes, ice sodas, tall iced beverages, or similar beverages served in deep glassware.
Sauce spoon	A wide, shallow spoon used for sauces and lifting foods out of casseroles.
Snail tongs	For holding snails in the shell so the snail fork can extract them.
Lobster tongs	Used for holding lobsters in the shell.
Pastry tongs	For picking up and serving pastries.
Cake or pie server	For serving cakes, pies, pastries, tortes, and similar desserts.

FIGURE 3.2 Behind the bar, glassware should also be clean, organized, and easily accessible.

Other Items

Some other items commonly used by servers are pepper mills, water pitchers, coffee servers, teapots, bottle openers, oil and vinegar cruets, mustard holders, bread baskets, cheese graters, service trays, tray stands, check holders, and guest caddies.

MENUS

Menus are important to service because they inform the guest what your operation offers. Most operations have menus in readable form. This may be a traditional individual menu, a sign listing specials, or a board above the counter. Some operations require servers to recite what the menu offers. This limits the menu size, but adds a certain atmosphere.

It is usual to print menus on hard paper called *bristol* or cover stock, but they can be on a sign board as used in a cafeteria or a drive-in. In informal restaurants, a placemat may hold the menu. Some operations have the menu on their order tickets.

Meal plans and menus differ. A meal plan lists the type of food served at each course of the meal, while the menu lists the exact items served. Figure 3.3 shows this difference.

MEAL PLAN	⚜ MENU ⚜
Appetizer	Melon au Kirsch
Soup	Lobster Bisque
Entree	Baked Ham, Champagne Sauce
Side dishes	Sweet Potato, Roll, Harvard Beets
Salad	Pear and Grape with Honey French Dressing
Dessert	Hazelnut Cream

FIGURE 3.3 A meal plan and its menu.

Menus may be designed for specific meals or occasions. Thus, we can have a breakfast, lunch, afternoon, dinner, or evening menu, a room service menu, or a banquet menu. Some may even be designed for the person, such as a children's menu, an early bird menu, or a vegetarian menu for guests with special dietary needs. Some menus are not intended to be used for ordering by guests, but only to inform cooks of preparation needs.

Menus are sometimes named by their nature. An a la carte menu prices all menu items individually. A table d' hôte menu is one that prices foods together in a group, often as a nearly complete meal. A du jour menu (*du jour* means of the day) lists foods available only that day, and often there is little choice in selection—many times, only one du jour meal is offered. A cycle menu is one that runs for a period of time with foods changing daily. Then the cycle is repeated. A California menu is one that lists snacks, breakfasts, lunches, and dinners all on one menu. A general menu is the main menu of a hospital from which special diets are planned. Thus, from the general menu the dietitian selects food that a specific patient might have.

It is customary to list foods on a menu in the order in which they are usually eaten. Others may even have a separate menu for appetizers or desserts. Although less usual, menus may list different food groups by courses.

Menu items often carry some designator indicating how they are prepared. Thus, the menu may list a grilled cheese sandwich, which means it is browned on both sides on a griddle. It is not toasted. However, the word *grilled* used with a steak usually means the steak is broiled over or under direct heat. A menu listing Prime Rib of Beef

BROILED STEAKS, LARGE SIRLOINS		CHICKEN	
Rare	20–24 minutes	Broiled or sautéed	20–45 minutes
Medium	28 minutes		
Well done	28–32 minutes	FISH AND SEAFOOD	
		Filets	6–10 minutes
LAMB CHOPS		Steaks	6–16 minutes
Medium	12–25 minutes	Whole	13–20 minutes
Well done	14–30 minutes	Baked oysters	12–16 minutes
		Steamed clams	20 minutes
PORK CHOPS		Boiled lobster	20 minutes
Well done	15–30 minutes	Broiled lobster, split	15–20 minutes
		Broiled tails, split	8–10 minutes
BARBECUED RIBS			
Well done	45 minutes		

FIGURE 3.4 Some common preparation times (cooking times only).

is not saying the meat is of prime grade, but that the cut comes from the area known as the *prime* area of beef. *Roasting* means baking in dry heat, while braising means cooking in a small amount of liquid. *Boiled* means cooking in a lot of liquid. *Florentine* means the item comes prepared in some way with spinach. Servers should know what terms of this type mean. If they do not know a menu term they should look it up or ask the chef or manager, so when guests ask they are prepared to give an accurate answer.

Servers likewise have to know the time it will take to prepare orders so they can inform guests on approximate waiting times and also plan their service time schedule for that particular table. Figure 3.4 gives some preparation times, but these are averages, and may vary from the preparation time of a particular item on a menu based on the facility in which one is serving.

The times in Figure 3.4 can vary according to cooking method. As servers gain experience, they begin to almost intuitively know about the time needed for menu items. However, if this experience is lacking, it is best to check.

Beverages, when offered on menus, are listed in various ways. Banquet or fine-dining menus often list the wine to the right of the menu items with which it is served. Or the beverages served with the meal may be listed on the bottom of the menu:

Oysters Rockefeller
Boston Bean Potage, Croutons
Crab Mousse, Bercy Sauce
Grilled Loin Lamb Chops, Mint Sauce
Orange Glazed Carrots
Baked Stuffed Potato
Oriental Salad with Shiitake Mushrooms
Baked Stuffed Apple

Cocktails
Moet and Chandon Champagne
Cousino Masul Reservas Cabernet Sauvignon—1988
Chateau d' Y' chem Sauternes—1988
Liqueurs

Some operations may have a separate menu listing all beverage alcohol, usually aperitifs, cocktails, spirit drinks, brandies and liqueurs, after-dinner drinks, beers, and nonalcohol drinks. The wine list usually separates domestic wines from foreign ones and in the order of listing in each is usually aperitif wines, dry white wines, dry red wines, sweet dessert wines, fortified wines, sparkling wines, and alcohol-free ones. Wines are often numbered and coded on the menu, and guests can then order by the number. The server also lists on the check the wine by its number or code.

SERVICE STAFF

Two staffs are used to work in food preparation and serving: the production or kitchen staff, and the service staff. Servers are in frequent contact with the production staff where the type of staffing impacts what servers do in ordering and picking up orders. A thorough knowledge of kitchen staffing can help servers move more smoothly in the kitchen.

Kitchen Staff

Many food services operate with only one cook on a shift, along with a helper or two, and a dishwasher, and even the dishwasher can be missing. The cook usually directs the other kitchen workers, but frequently receives direction from an owner, manager, or assistant manager. If there is more than one cook, one is usually designated as head cook or chef, and this person is in charge, working under the direction of a manager. Kitchen staffs can grow to a considerable size with departments such as baking, salad, vegetable preparation, and cooking. Each department usually has a head that directs the work in that department; in many, the overseer of the kitchen may be a kitchen manager or chef. In some health facilities this may be a dietitian; dietary aids may assist the dietitian and also work closely with cooks in food preparation and in the dishing of foods and beverages to see that the foods meet the nutritional needs of the guests.

In the typical French organization there is often a continental kitchen. An executive chef is in charge, and is the overall manager of all food preparation and functions associated with it. A steward works with the chef in ordering, storage, and perhaps in menu planning. The steward is also in charge of much of the dining equipment, nappery, and other dining room equipment.

In food production, the *sous chef* (second to the main chef) runs the kitchen for the executive chef, who usually has an office some place away from the kitchen. The continental kitchen is divided into various departments headed by *chefs de parti*, such as the *garde manger* (cold foods and pantry), *patisserie* (bake shop), *legumier* (cooked vegetable and garnishes), *potager* (soups and stews), and *entremetier* (sauced and roasted dishes). Under these chefs de parti will be assistants and helpers. The great chef Auguste Escoffier introduced this continental type of kitchen organization. He wanted to keep his kitchen quiet, and so instead of having a number of servers calling orders to various units, servers brought their orders to an *aboyeur* (announcer) who, after receiving an order from a server, called it out in a clear, loud voice so the cooks who had to prepare the items could hear.

Some kitchens use checkers to make sure orders are correct, to price orders, and to give them to the aboyeur to call out. It is the duty of the checker to check the food and beverages leaving the kitchen against the order to see that everything is correct, even the garnishes. In this manner, servers take from the kitchen only the correct order, nothing else. Some checkers act as cashiers, receiving money for the orders and giving back the proper change.

In addition other helpers, sanitarians, and employees will be on the staff. Servers do not come into contact with many of these employees. There are frequent opportunities for conflict when working under stress, and friendly, cordial relationships among employees can do much to smooth over times when the work is highly demanding. Servers and kitchen staff work under the pressure of getting orders out promptly and in the standard required. A large number of orders may come in so fast that they pile up, and the kitchen staff may be under high pressure to get the food out in time and in proper quality. This is no time to make special demands. In some cases, servers may share tips with cooks; this often creates a high degree of cooperation between cooks and servers.

Traditional Service Staff

Service staffs vary considerably. All servers are usually responsible to someone who heads the operation or a representative of management. Management hires, sets up schedules and stations, sets up service standards and training, and directs other service work. In larger organizations, some of these duties may be delegated.

Some operations such as drive-ins or quick-service operations have little or no staff organization. Orders are taken at a counter or window, and the food is brought there to give to guests.

Seated service operations are more complex. Usually a manager or some representative of management is in charge, with one or several servers working on a shift. If the service staff is large, a hostess or host may be in charge.

The most complex staff is modeled after that used in Europe, which grew out of the staffs used by Escoffier and Ritz. It is labor intensive and expensive, but elegant and lavish. The manager of serving is usually called *maitre d' hotel*, but may be called host or head waiter. Often this person is in charge of assigning stations and may even hire the serving staff. Under this leadership may be *captains* who are in charge of a group of servers, often called *chefs de rang*, who may also be called front servers. Each chef de rang is assigned a station numbering up to 25 seats. A *commis*, also called assistant waiter or back server, assists the chef de rang. Buspersons in this organization are often called *commis debarasseur*.

In some French server staffing the chef de service acts as the maitre d', and may have an assistant called the *chef d' étage* who directs serving in the dining areas. An individual called the *maitre d' hotel de care* supervises a dining room section, somewhat as captains do.

Other persons who may be included in the serving staff are the food and beverage manager, who is in charge of all food production and service. Banquet managers head up banquet catering staffs and are usually under the food and beverage manager. The wine steward, or *sommelier*, is responsible for wines and other beverage alcohols and their service. Some units use bartenders who only fill orders for servers, but usually do not serve the public.

FIGURE 3.5 A service busperson assists servers and clears the table once guests have left. Courtesy Corbis Digital Stock.

In almost any type of service buspersons are used to bring trays of orders to a station, take away soiled items, and assist servers.

In a healthcare facility, a dietitian is usually in charge of service, but nurses who are not accountable to this person often deliver the food after it is sent from the kitchen. Servers may serve in visitor's or doctor's dining rooms.

CHAPTER SUMMARY

Servers work with a lot of equipment, and to serve properly they must know what this equipment is and how it is to be used. In some operations the amount of knowledge required is much less than in others. A server working in a restaurant serving French food will use a wide variety of equipment, while one working in a drive-in will use a very different variety of equipment.

Each server needs certain personal items such as an order pad, pencil or pen, and other equipment needed to take orders and complete the serving of them.

Servers serve guests seated at tables or booths. These should be clean and neatly set. Service stations hold much equipment needed by servers. Servers should see they are properly stocked and are kept clean and orderly. In some food services mobile equipment may be used, and this also should be neat and clean, and not left where it can interfere with the work of serving. Other equipment will be used according to the serving needs and type of operation.

Tablecloths, napkins, naperones, placemats, and other napery may be required, and servers need to know how to use these so that tables appear neat and well maintained.

Some servers have to handle a wide assortment of dishes, glassware, and eating utensils. The use of glassware or dishes with certain eating utensils is prescribed for certain foods or beverages, and servers must know the proper ones to use. Different dishes, glassware, or eating utensils require specific placement at covers. Without a thorough knowledge of all the factors that go with the proper use of these items, good service cannot occur.

Menus are used to communicate to guests the items available and how they are prepared, along with the price. Servers need to know what the items are and how they are prepared so they can completely inform guests about menu offerings. Servers may have to explain menu items and also indicate preparation times. Servers have to be sales people as well as do the work of serving.

The highest of sanitation standards must be kept by servers who inter a with guests. The sever, area, server stations, tabletop, items on the table, and menu should be immaculate when guests arrive. Dishes and other tableware should be handled so that no place where food might rest is touched by the server.

Servers need to know to whom they report and the role other employees on staff play in accomplishing food production and service. They need to know the kitchen organizations so they know how to place orders and pick them up. They also need to know this organization so they can work with the food preparation staffs.

RELATED INTERNET SITES

Virtual Trade Show
This site links burgers and sellers of food and beverage industry products.

www.nightclub.com/virtual_new

KEY TERMS

a la carte menu	du jour menu	maitre d' hotel
	expediter	*réchaud*
California menu	general menu	table d' hôte menu
cycle menu	*guéridon*	voiture

CHAPTER REVIEW

1. What is a service station? What is its use? What does it normally hold?

2. Match the terms on the left with their definition on the right.

    _____ (1) Guéridon   a. Small casserole
    _____ (2) Naperone   b. Used with a dish having small indentations in it
    _____ (3) Snail tongs   c. Covers tablecloth
    _____ (4) Demitasse   d. Holds about 4 ounces of espresso
    _____ (5) Cocotte   e. Used to hold food and equipment for tableside preparation

3. Match the terms on the left with their definition on the right.

    _____ (1) Aboyeur   a. Assistant waiter
    _____ (2) Maitre d' hotel   b. Front waiter
    _____ (3) Commis debarasseur   c. In charge of a group of waiters
    _____ (4) Commis   d. Busperson
    _____ (5) Chef d' étage   e. In charge of wine service
    _____ (6) Sommelier   f. Assistant to chef de service
    _____ (7) Chef de rang   g. Calls out food orders

4. What is a cycle menu?

5. In what order are items usually presented on menus?

6. What kind of menus are not meant to be used by guests for ordering?

7. What is cover stock?

8. Explain the difference between a *guéridon* and a *voiture*.

9. What is the difference between an *a la carte* and a *table d' hôte* menu?

10. What advantages and disadvantages do you see in servers sharing tips with the cooks?

Case Study

SERVER STATIONS

You are assisting an architect who is planning a kitchen, and the architect asks you to design the service stations. Design the service station she should use as an individual server station. Also design one that can act to supply the needs of three or four servers.

SERVING THE MEAL*

Outline

---

* Authored by Lendal H. Kotschevar and Valentino Luciani.

Learning Objectives

After reading this chapter, you should be able to:

- Oversee proper setting of tables, proper meal service, and clearing.
- Describe receiving correct payment from customers based on accurate guest checks.

INTRODUCTION

Every profession has its rules and procedures for accomplishing required tasks; table service is no exception. Up to this point, many general service rules and procedures have been given. This chapter focuses on the tasks of serving guests. First, we will cover some of the more general rules and techniques of handling trays and other service equipment. Next, rules and procedures for casual dining are covered, followed by special rules and procedures for formal dining.

STEPS IN SERVING

Serving food and beverages involves a sequence of five steps: (1) greeting and seating guests, (2) taking the order, (3) serving, (4) clearing, and (5) presenting the check and saying goodbye. The tasks of each step vary according to different meals and type of operation. Thus, breakfast is served differently from dinner; a drive-in serves differently from a cafeteria; and counter service differs from table service. Service requirements also depend on whether guests want a leisurely or a quick meal. At breakfast, guests are usually in a hurry and things are done so that guests can be on their way. Lunches can be hurried or leisurely, and it is crucial for servers to take their cues from guests. At dinner, the pace is likely to be more leisurely. Banquet service, buffet service, and other specialized services have special requirements.

GREETING AND SEATING THE GUESTS

The first employee that a customer comes in contact with represents the first opportunity to make your customer's experience a positive one. All employees, the owner, manager, host, and server, should know how to properly welcome a guest to the operation. How a customer is welcomed is dictated by the type of service your customer expects. Guests are typically greeted by a host or hostess or even the owner, but in other casual dining situations the greeter might be the server. The greeter should see that the greeting includes the most convivial elements: a pleasant attitude, a warm smile, eye contact, and a brief but welcoming phrase. If the guest has a reservation, it should be honored by immediate seating. However, this is not always possible and the guests might have to wait a few minutes. The procedure for handling this is discussed in Chapter 6 under reservations.

Hosts and hostesses must be well trained in the operation's procedures for seating people. With regular clientele, their desires for a table may be known. Some like to be seated where they are seen. Others do not. Many restaurants have smoking and nonsmoking sections, and guest preference should always be followed in this instance.

Hosts and hostesses should be alert and accommodating to guests' seating preferences. It is customary for hosts or servers to pull out the guest's chair so guests can seat themselves. Also be aware of special needs, such as those for people with disabilities and families with children.

The First Approach

The server's first contact with guests is crucial. At this point, guests make a summary of what to expect in service, and this often sets the size of the tip. The greeting, the seating, and the first approach to guests at the table should create a positive impression on the part of the guests and establish their estimate of the server's competence and ability to serve. The more pleasant one can make these first few minutes, the more likely it is that the server will have an easier and more pleasant time of serving, and that guests will enjoy their experience.

A friendly attitude is essential when dealing with guests, but the attitude should not be too familiar; some dignity should be observed. Do not indulge in unnecessary conversation or encourage familiarity.

The server or the captain (leader of a group of servers), if there is one, should help guests with their coats or other items. In some operations, the server is not expected to seat guests, but in some fine-dining establishments, the captain and server might do this.

Servers should make sure that their stations are ready to receive guests. Items such as candles, flowers, table tents, and place settings should be in place. The candle may or may not be lit, according to the operation. Some operations feel that unlit candles and upside-down glassware on the table indicates the table is not ready for guests, so it has glassware right side up when guests arrive. Flatware may or may not be on the table;

in some operations, it might be placed only after orders are taken so the server knows what is required. In other operations, only a basic setting of flatware—knife, fork, and spoon—is set and the other items are added as needed. Unless an all-purpose wine glass is used, the proper wine glasses and other required glassware will be set after the wine order is taken. In full-service establishments, salt and pepper shakers may or may not be on the table. Condiments are not placed on the table until guests order. However, coffee shops and other more casual dining units often have salt and pepper shakers and condiments on the table when guests are seated.

Servers should be watchful of guests coming to their station. Let guests know you have seen them. Take a step forward to greet them and say the appropriate, "Good morning," "Good afternoon," or "Good evening" with a smile. If you know guests' names, use them. Take them to their table if the host or hostess does not do so, and ask if the table is suitable. At times this cannot be done because the server is busy with others. However, enough time should be taken to let the new guests know the server knows they are there. A short, "I'm sorry, we're so busy. I'll be with you in a minute," can help to give the server a chance to finish what is being done and come back to the guests.

The Introduction

In some operations, when everyone is seated, the server introduces himself or herself by name, saying something like, "My name is ____. I will be your server this evening." Some operations do not like servers giving their names and only have the server greet the guest. If there are complementary snacks, they should be brought immediately, and water should be poured. It is also appropriate at this time to pre-bus or remove extra place settings from a table. If a table is set for six, but there are only four customers, the server should ask if additional guests are expected. If no other guests will be joining the party, remove the two extra settings. This gives the customers more room on the table, and saves the operation money.

Presenting Menus

Menus are frequently handed out right away, but some operations prefer to wait until the premeal beverage order is taken. If a premeal beverage menu is given out, the regular menu is then given out later. The person handing out menus depends on the operation. In most operations, the manager, or host, gives them out after the guests have been seated. Menus might already be placed at each cover. Or the server gives them out after

FIGURE 4.1 Servers can add a special touch to their service by explaining the menu to guests.

the server's introduction or after the beverage order has been taken. The server should hand out menus to each guest's left, unless space does not permit this.

It is traditional to hand guests their menus, either opened or unopened. It is discourteous to drop menus on the table so guests have to pick them up and open them. An operation might or might not specify that menus be given first to women. The server also might hand out a wine list, or a sommelier will do this separately.

After the menus have been given out, the server should describe all food and beverage specials along with their prices. Servers should have tasted all specials so they describe them honestly and appetizingly. The server should also mention items on the menu that are especially good or unique, or that management wants to push. A remark such as, "The chef is particularly proud of this dish. He is planning on using the recipe for the next culinary contest," might arouse interest in an item. A description of the basic methods of preparation of some dishes also arouses interest.

Servers should be familiar with all menu items, their ingredients, and the methods used to prepare them. It is embarrassing, and bad for business, to not be able to answer guests' questions about the menu. Guests also may wish to receive information about the nutritional qualities of some dishes. However, servers should not give out information unless they are positive they know the correct answer. If a customer needs to know if the specific ingredients in a recipe for medical or dietary reasons, the server should ask the kitchen and give the customer the correct answer.

GENERAL RULES AND PROCEDURES FOR SERVING

P roper serving is a craft that, when done correctly, flows so smoothly it appears simple to the untrained eye, yet when the novice attempts to do the tasks required, they become a challenge to one's knowledge and serving skills. What seems so simple when observed becomes extremely difficult when it has to be done. Just organizing the task alone so the service proceeds in a logical manner becomes a trial. However, with sincere application in learning the basics of service and by acquiring some dexterity in handling trays, china, glassware, and flatware, the novice server can become quite proficient in serving patrons, and in a short time can handle quite competently a fairly good-sized station.

Servers cannot be considered professionals until they become well acquainted with handling all service equipment confidently. Although the restaurant industry is in constant evolution, the following discussion covers some of the recommended serving procedures and rules that apply to most forms of service. Proficiency in these procedures along with some others can go far in making a professional of the novice.

Some servers like to develop their own methods; some of these methods may be acceptable, but often they are not. The rules and procedures cited here have been tested over time and have been found to give the most satisfactory service.

As indicated throughout the various chapters in this book, there are many personal requirements of a server. The most basic one is the ability to quickly get food and drinks from order, to the kitchen, and these back the guests. This is a demanding task.

It is essential that servers observe what is right and are not allowed to develop the wrong habits from the beginning. We are all creatures of habit and once we adopt certain methods and become accustomed to them, it is found that one learns to work smoothly, easily, efficiently, and quickly, giving a desirable level of service.

All dining operations should establish a flow pattern that servers should follow when moving in the dining area and kitchen. Breaking the flow can cause accidents because a fellow worker may not expect someone to act in a varying manner. Management should plan the flow pattern to follow, and train the service staff to follow it.

Serving Water and Ice

One of the first things done is to give guests a glass of water with ice. When pouring at the table, the pitcher should be positioned two to three inches away from the glass rim. If it is too close there is a risk of touching and chipping the glass; if it is too far, even the most skillful server runs the risk of spilling. The glass should not be filled to the rim; two-thirds to three-fourths full is sufficient. Patrons dislike to handle a glass that is completely full. The busperson or server should be alert during the meal to see that water glasses are kept filled. Some operations provide a pitcher or carafe of water so guests may fill their own glasses.

Dining area supervisors should see that employees know that spills require *immediate* attention. If the spill is in a busy area, an employee should remain there and direct traffic around the spill. The employee should warn nearby customers and fellow employees of the spill. While clean-up is in progress, the employee should post a sign, such as "Caution—Wet Floor." The sign must be left in place until the area is safe. If the spill is liquid and cannot be cleaned up for a time, an approved absorbent compound may be used to contain the liquid. If water or chemicals are used in the clean-up process, the employee should avoid wetting any more area than necessary.

Carrying Trays

Carrying a tray is one of the first tasks a server should learn. Trays come in various shapes and sizes, but the most common are the 27-inch to 30-inch oval tray, used for large loads, and the 15-inch cocktail tray, used primarily to serve beverages. Trays are customarily carried by the left hand raised slightly above the left shoulder. For sanitary reasons, the edge of the tray should be at least four inches away from the head or neck. Servers' hair must not in any way come in contact with items.

Almost all lifting in foodservice establishments involves carrying, especially for servers who must carry trays or plates. Servers and buspersons need to plan a route so they will not bump into other employees and guests.

When servers and buspersons plan their route, they should check the condition of the floor along the route, and look closely for any hazards, such as pieces of furniture or equipment out of place, spills, sharp corners, narrow passageways, and stairs.

Employees should use their whole hand to grip the load, not just their fingers. They need to keep the load close to their body and centered. Other carrying procedures include the following:

- Keep the ears, shoulders, and hips going in the same direction.
- Keep elbows against sides, for additional balance and so nothing is bumped.
- Keep stomach muscles firm and the lower back tucked in. The load should be carried by the legs and hips, not the back.

- To turn, move the whole body as a unit instead of twisting at the waist. Face the load when lifting it and setting it down. This might feel somewhat robotic, but the back will benefit.

It is not recommended to carry trays on the tips of the fingers. Using the palm of the hand gives more firm support and better control. (An exception might be when one is carrying a tray through a crowded area; raising the tray on the fingertips may help raise the tray high enough to get through.) The cocktail tray can be carried securely between the thumb and index finger, with added help from the other fingers, giving better control. This is especially true when carrying such a tray with glasses filled for a party of six or more. It is also recommended when carrying tall, fragile stemware or large items such as coffee pots.

Items on a smooth surface of a tray can slide; trays should be covered with cork, plastic, or a rubber mat to prevent this. A wet napkin spread over the surface of a smooth tray can also help reduce sliding. All trays should be kept clean for use.

Trays should not be placed on a table being cleared. Instead, the tray should be placed on a tray jack (also called a tray stand) near the table being cleared. (A bus cart can replace the tray on the tray stand.) Trays should never be placed on a table at which guests are seated. They can be placed on a table, primarily in a large banquet or buffet operation, once guests have gone.

FIGURE 4.2 Trays should be carried on the palm of the hand to keep them stable and reduce the risk of dropping the food. Courtesy PhotoDisc, Inc.

Some servers, especially in setting tables, like to carry stemware without trays by inserting the glasses by their stems through the fingers. While this is efficient and speeds table setting, for reasons of safety the use of a tray is recommended.

Perfect balance is the secret to carrying trays safely. Balance must be absolute to allow freedom of action and maneuverability when opening a door with the other hand, making turns, or just carrying the tray. Good balance can be obtained by distributing the weight of the items equally throughout the surface. The heaviest items should be placed in the tray's center with the lighter ones on the outside. When a tray is properly loaded by placing the palm of the hand exactly in the bottom center, there is no tilting from any side and the tray rests securely, with the fingers able to control any slight variation.

In some operations, tray jacks are permanently set up, ready to receive the loaded tray. In other establishments, the server brings the jack to the table with the free hand, opens it next to the table, and places the tray on it. If the tray is quite heavy, servers should place the jack prior to bringing out the tray. Sometimes another employee may come ahead of the server carrying the heavily loaded tray, open the jack, and help the employee place the tray on the stand. Once the tray is in place, service occurs with one or two dishes being removed from the tray at one time. When the tray is emptied, it is removed.

When resting a heavy tray on a tray jack, bend the knees slightly and put the tray down cautiously while holding it with both hands. Many times it is better to ask a fellow server to help place the tray on the jack.

Loading trays require attention, not only to achieve balance, but to get a maximum, but safe, load. This takes experience, and servers should note how more experienced servers load their trays. Food covers are used for many items. This allows another plate of similar size to be placed on top of the first plate. The cover also helps keep foods hot. It is possible using covers and stacking in this manner to get eight dishes on one tray. (In banquets, as many as sixteen entrees may be put on one tray.) Being able to stack in this manner gives good balance while at the same time helping the server to get more entrees to guests, saving travel time. It's also important to carefully load beverages so that the server can bring all the beverages to the guests in one trip, without spilling.

Servers should take care not to place hot and cold items on top of one another or even allow them to touch. Pots holding hot liquids should not be filled so full that the hot liquid easily spills from the spouts when the tray is carried. Most experienced servers also do not put cups on saucers or dishes of varying sizes or shapes on top of one another. Such items fail to nest and can slide easily. When carrying filled containers that will be set on another saucer, dish, or tray, place the filled container on the tray and not the item on which it will sit. In this way, any spills occur on the tray and not on the item on which the container will sit.

Handling China and Glassware

Sometimes a server is seen carrying a tall stack of dishes with one hand underneath while holding the stack firmly against the chest with the other hand. This is both risky and unsanitary. Keep the fingers off the rim of the dish. If carried as a stack, put both hands underneath and hold the stack away from the body. A serviette or service towel may be wrapped around the stack to help hold it in place. Do not try to carry too high a stack.

Handle tumblers from their bases and stemware from the stems. Handle dishes with the hand under and with the thumb along the rim of the plate. Watch to see that soiled, chipped, or cracked china or glassware is never used. Fruit juice and cocktail glasses, cereal dishes, soup bowls, dessert dishes, and pots should be set on underliners when placed on the table. Set iced beverages on an underliner or coaster. In some operations, a doily is set on the underliner before placing the item down.

If an item is hot while setting it before a guest, the server should use a fold-over-twice serviette or napkin between the thumb and index finger to protect the fingers. The server should also notify the guest that the item is very hot. If the guest does not hear the warning, the server should repeat the warning until the guest has acknowledged it.

Handling Flatware

Handling flatware properly is as important as handling china and glassware. Never touch the part of flatware that will go into a guest's mouth; hold only its handle. All flatware should be wiped thoroughly before setting it on the table, not only during mise en place but also at other times. If flatware is extremely spotted, management should be notified so it can check dishwashing procedures. In particular, the blades of knives need to be wiped more than once; the spots from hard water and films left by cleaning agents and dishwashing machines are visible on the blades more than any other place. A cloth or towel wet with a bit of vinegar and water is good for cleaning; the scent of vinegar quickly disappears but the acid of the vinegar removes the alkaline agents that spot the object. Do not put bent, tarnished, or soiled flatware at a cover. Placing flatware properly on the table is an essential of good service.

When resetting tables, some servers prefer to use a cocktail tray loaded with flatware organized so like ware is together. Others prefer to use flatware caddies loaded by kind in separate compartments. Whenever carrying flatware around the dining room, at least a plate with a napkin on it should be used. In handling spoons, forks, and knives, the fingers should touch only the lower part of the handle and never the business end.

TAKING THE ORDER

After the premeal beverages have been served and there are no reorders, the server should ask if the guests have made their selections. It is not unusual for some to have not even looked at the menu; the server should suggest appetizers and offer to return a little later. An alert server will note when the guests have seemingly made their choices, or when they may need assistance in making selections. The server should be there promptly to take care of guests' needs. Readiness to order is often indicated when a guest closes the menu and sets it down.

Guests may have difficulty in finding items or in reading the menu. Servers should note this and give assistance. Sometimes the guest cannot read well. The server may, in this instance, read the menu to the guest, explaining each item. Some may wish to know how items are prepared. Guests often want to know about a food's type, quality, grade, or preparation. For example, "Are the strawberries on the shortcake fresh or frozen?" "Are the oysters bluepoints or pacifics?" "Is the beef Choice or Prime?" "Are your pies

FIGURE 4.3 When guests are ready to order, the server should be prompt and friendly, and ready to make suggestions when questions are asked. Courtesy PhotoDisc, Inc.

baked here?" The time it takes to prepare might be important to some guests, and servers should be prepared to answer on any time questions. Servers must be prepared to answer a host of questions.

Some guests know immediately what they want; others may be undecided because they are not familiar with the service, are not hungry, have limited funds, or do not understand the menu. Servers can be a big help with these guests.

In most cases, the server takes the order, but in the more formal situations a captain might. Orders are often written on a guest check. These are usually serially numbered; servers are given a certain number of such checks, which they must sign for, before a shift. Some operations hold servers responsible for checks that disappear. There may be a standard charge levied against a server if a check is missing, which can occur with someone walking out without paying. Unused checks at shift's end are returned and credited to the server. However, where the POS system is used, as it is in many operations, servers are no longer held responsible.

When taking the order, the server should ask whether the guests want separate checks or one check. The server should stand at the left of the guest ordering. For small groups, the server may stand in one place where each guest can be seen and heard. Do not hover over guests. Be sure to get complete information, such as the kind of vegetable, the doneness of the meat, and so on. If an item takes long to prepare, tell the guest. It is desirable that servers also try to learn who is to pay the check so that presenting the check is clear.

Servers use systems on their order pads to help them remember who ordered what. The most common method is to establish the cover directly pointing toward a set point in the dining room as cover 1 or A, and to number the others clockwise. This standard system of guest order location is often called the pivot system. Cover No. 1 starts with the guest always sitting with his or her back to the kitchen. When the server returns with the orders, the server knows that this cover gets the New York steak cooked medium rare with a baked potato, house salad, and green beans. Cover No. 2 gets the chicken fricassee, mashed potatoes, peas, and tomato salad. No one is sitting at cover No. 3, but cover No. 4 gets the seafood salad and toast. Beverage and dessert orders will follow; the server will code these properly so service is easy and fast. All servers should follow the same system. In this way other servers can step in and work the table without asking a lot of questions.

Today much order taking is computerized. Servers send orders through the computer in the dining room to cooks in specific kitchen stations. It is possible for servers using this device to code in cover locations so that the server knows which guest ordered what when the orders are brought to the table. Usually the time the order is placed, the time it is ready, and the time it is picked up are recorded so management has a check on how long the flow of order taking to service takes and where to spot responsibility for delays. The computer system will also print sales tickets. Handheld computer systems are increasing in popularity, but, they still require an operational system, like a pivot system, for taking orders.

In any guest-check system, servers should write out orders in a legible and organized manner. If second and third copies are made, the server should press hard so each copy is readable. Good copies and legibility can help management in making check-duplicate reconciliation or any other control system used. For clearer writing, a booklet or menu under the pad or check can be used. When writing on a plain pad, it is recommended that a line be drawn after each course. This indicates to cooks when items are desired in the meal. (There might be a request where the guest asks for the salad to be served before the soup, or the salad to be served with the entrees, etc.)

Abbreviations are necessary to save time. (See Figure 4.4.) However, they should be standardized. Every server should know and use the abbreviations used in the operation. Following are some common abbreviations:

Extra rare (blue)	b	XR	Very well done	b	VWD
Rare	b	R	Chicken sautéed	bCh saut	
Medium rare	b	MR	Chicken fried	b	Ch f
Medium	b	M	Steak	b	St
Medium well	b MW		Roast Beef	b	Rst B
Well done	b WD		Prime Rib	b	PR
Baked	bBKD		Sour cream	b	SC
Creamed	b	CR		b	

It is helpful to underline extreme degrees of doneness, such as extra rare and very well done. This reinforces the fact that the guest wants the item that way. The server should also note any special requests. At the beginning of the shift, abbreviations for specials will be given by management to both servers and kitchen staff. Abbreviations help speed up order taking. If they later cause confusion and errors, then their purpose is lost and it would be far better not to use them.

Always repeat the order after the guest gives it. This prevents errors and misunderstandings. Be sure to get all the information needed, such as type of salad dressing, doneness of meat, and any special requests. Sometimes a guest may just give the entree order, close the menu, and hand it to the order taker. It is then necessary for the order taker to find out what the guest desires for the rest of the meal, such as an appetizer, the kind of soup or salad desired, beverage, and perhaps even the dessert, although dessert orders are usually taken after everyone has finished with the entree.

Using standard abbreviations saves time when taking orders.

GUEST CHECK

TABLE NO.	NO. PERSONS	CHECK NO. 339540	SERVER NO.
St, MR			
PR, R			
2 bkd pot, sc on side			
2 cr spin			
TAX			

FIGURE 4.4 Guest check with abbreviations.

Suggestive Selling

Servers do more than take orders, serve, and clear dishes. They are important sales people, and a great part of the sales function is suggestive selling. More than a sales tool, suggestive selling helps guests make up their minds so they are pleased with what they have selected. It is an essential part of excellent service.

Every encounter with a guest is different. You will have to ask questions and watch for cues to find out what guests like and dislike, how much time they have, and how much they want to spend. Remember that guests can neither see nor taste menu items before ordering them. They depend on servers to help them make the right decision.

Appropriate attitude, dress, and confidence will encourage guests to take your suggestions. Let guests know that you're there to please them, and that they can trust you. It is important not to oversell; don't be pushy. This brings resentment and distrust. But don't be afraid to suggest; the bigger the check, the bigger the tip.

When taking orders, servers should use open-ended rather than closed-ended questions. Open-ended questions allow further discussion of the subject, while closed-ended questions stop it. By asking an open-ended question, the server has a chance to discover something a guest might like. An open-ended question might be, "What would you like for dessert?" Even if the answer is "Nothing. I don't eat dessert," the server has a chance to make a sale by suggesting other options, such as a low-calorie fresh fruit plate or a cordial or other nondessert item. A closed-ended question might be, "Do you want an order of sautéed fresh mushrooms to go with your steak?" In this instance, the only response is yes or no.

Here are some tips for effective suggestive selling:

- Suggest beverages and appetizers to start a meal.
- Suggest premium liquors when guests order generic drinks.
- Suggest fresh fruit if the guest hesitates on the desserts.
- Suggest side orders with entrees.
- Suggest definite menu items; don't ask, "Will there be anything else?"
- Know the menu and suggest low-calorie items when appropriate.
- If the order will take some time to prepare, suggest an appetizer.
- If the guest orders an a la carte item and it is also on the dinner menu, suggest the complete dinner.
- Use appetizing words, such as *steaming, sweet, spicy, juicy, fresh, savory,* and *refreshing.*
- Sometimes certain items are also sold for takeout, such as pies and cakes, salad dressings, and some prepared foods. If a guest particularly likes an item, an alert server recommends that the guest purchase the item to take home (for a bigger check).
- Suggest desserts, desserts to split, and after-dinner drinks.

Placing and Picking Up Orders

When orders are sent by computer to the kitchen, servers do not have to go there to see that the right cooks get their orders. Servers are given a key, code number, or authorizing card to enter the computer system. After entering, the server usually has an identifying number or code. The table number, number of guests, and the check

number is usually entered after this is done. The time may be automatically recorded. The guest check is now inserted into the computer and the orders are entered. Often there is a preset keyboard or touch screen with almost all items on the menu listed. All the server has to do is touch one of these keys to order items. In some cases, the machine may ask for further information such as doneness of meat, or flavor of ice cream, and the server must then add this information. When all orders are placed, the server punches a key to print out the guest check.

With manual systems, servers must still place their orders in the kitchen. In some fine dining operations, the order in the kitchen is first checked by a checker, who then places the order. In formal dining, an aboyeur, or expediter, may take the order and place it with the proper sections. In some kitchens, servers call out their orders to the proper preparation personnel, but many avoid this because it can cause confusion and noise in the kitchen when several or more servers are calling out their orders. Quieter methods are often used. In the spindle method, servers put the order on a spindle for cooks to remove. In some operations, orders are placed on a rotating wheel, which keeps them in order as placed. The cooks then rotate the wheel to arrive at orders in sequence. In larger kitchens, servers must rewrite parts of the order so these separate parts can be placed in the proper section for preparation. Thus, a cold plate order might be separately written and go to the cold food section, the roast beef order rewritten to go to the steam table section, and a broiled steak order rewritten for the broiler section.

Various methods are used to notify servers that orders are ready. It is possible to have pagers send a signal to a specific server. Lights can be set in a dining area, and when this light is on, the server knows the kitchen is signaling that the order is ready. One novel way is to have a large clock that can light up an assigned number of a server.

Before taking an order from the kitchen, the server should check to see that everything ordered is there and is correct. (In some cases, a checker does this.) The server should take something out that does not appear right. Dished-up food should be neatly placed; garnishes should be right and attractive. Food spills on dish rims should be wiped away. Do this with a serviette, or towel, in the kitchen and not in front of guests. Servers should use a serviette or napkin to pick up hot dishes.

Servers should not pick up a course of a meal and bring it into the dining area until the previous course has been finished and cleared. However, in some faster-service operations, it is acceptable to clear one course while serving the next.

Servers need to organize their orders on pickup so everything is on hand when service at the table begins. One must be sure in the kitchen to pick up the correct items. Different menu items can look very similar, and if in doubt servers should ask the cook which meal they ordered. In some cases, cold foods should be brought to the service station before the hot ones, to be ready for service. When the hot items are brought from the kitchen, the cold and hot items are then served together. Pickup may require getting order items from various kitchen sections. For example, hot entrees may be waiting on a counter under a heat lamp, hot rolls may be waiting in a roll or bread warmer, and garnishes and salads may be in a refrigerator. Pick up hot foods last. Good organization simplifies the service task at the table. When the pick-up is complete, a last-minute check should be made to see that the food is the correct temperature, and has an overall pleasing appearance and superior quality. Some operations use expediters who do the picking up, and they act as the link between service and the kitchen.

SERVING THE GUESTS

Serving the order is the total of all efforts of everyone involved in the operation. Much thought and labor go into the production of the items servers put before guests; none of this should be lost during service. As noted in Chapter 2, everything must be ready and in its place. All mise en place must be done before bringing food to guests. All supplementary serviceware must be at the server station.

Where specific food items are placed depends on the table setting used. First courses, soup, and appetizers of single servings are placed directly in front of the guest. In placing the entree, see that the main food item is in front of the guest. Appetizers to be shared are placed in the center of the table with appetizer plates placed before guests. Entrees are also placed directly in front of guests. Other items, such as bread and salads, are placed to the right or left of the guest. Side salads are placed to the left, while breads are placed to the right.

In more formal meals, the placement of certain items are more or less prescribed. Beverage glassware should be on the right. This text indicates these, but there is so much variation today, that one might say that there is no consistent standard. Follow the standards of the operation, and try to make things convenient for guests. Managers in setting standards should see they provide the type of service guests want and that servers are able to meet.

Servers, whenever possible, should use the left hand to place and remove dishes when serving at the guest's left, and the right hand when working at the guest's right. This allows the server to have free arm movement and avoid colliding with guests' arms. Never reach in front of guests, or reach across one guest to serve another. Present dishes from which guests serve themselves on the guest's left, holding the dish so the guest can conveniently help himself of herself. Set serving flatware on the right side of the dish with handles turned toward the guest so it is easy to pick up the item for self-service. In most operations, salt and pepper shakers, sugar bowls, and condiments are placed in the center of the table. In booths and on tables set against a wall, these items are placed on the wall side. Bread trays and baskets are placed in the table's center. Cups and saucers go to the right of the guest, with the cup handle to the right.

Normally, entrees are served with the main item placed on the lower part of the plate closest to the guest, called the six o'clock position on the plate. The garnish and whatever side items are on the plate should be neatly arranged to make an attractive presentation.

Breakfast Service

Breakfast service must usually be fast. Fruits and juices should be served chilled. Milk is required with cereals and some operations also offer a finer sugar than regular, called berry sugar. Toast should be freshly made, and buttered or not, as the guest indicates. Hot breads should be hot and fresh. Hot cakes and waffles should be served as soon as possible; they lose quality rapidly as they cool. Eggs cooked to order must be correct, and served immediately. Hot beverages should be very hot.

Many operations today offer buffet breakfasts. This helps guests move quickly through the meal and allows them to take what they wish. Some guests may not wish as much food as is offered on a buffet, so most operations find that in addition to the buffet breakfast, they still must offer a menu and allow guests to select what they want.

Lunch Service

A lunch may consist of only one dish, such as a soup or salad, and a beverage. In a luncheon with courses, each course is placed directly in front of the guest. Vegetable dishes are placed above the entree to the right. Salad is placed on the left, with bread to the left of the salad. If a chilled beverage is served, place it to the right and a bit below the water glass. The handles of cups on the saucer should be turned to the right at the three o'clock position. At formal luncheons, servers *crumb* the table between courses. (Crumbing is removing crumbs and other items from the table surface.)

Formal Dinner Service

The first course in a full-course meal is placed directly in front of the guest. If a cocktail fork or other utensil is needed, place it on the right side of the plate or to the right of the plate. If flatware is already in place for the rest of the meal, this appetizer utensil is placed to the right of these. If guests are to serve themselves from a dish, place appetizer plates in front of the guest to the left. Sometimes a salad is served as a first course instead of an appetizer. The placement is the same and, if served from a dish, service again is from the left.

In some cases a finger bowl may be served after the first course, especially after finger foods such as cracked crab. The water in the bowl should be warm and have a lemon slice floating in it. A new napkin should be offered.

Soup is typically served as a second course. The soup bowl is placed on a serving plate, and put directly in front of the guest. The soup spoon should be to the right. Offer crackers. Crumb between courses as needed.

Entrees are placed directly in front of the guest. A vegetable dish, if used, is placed above and to the right. Side salads are placed to the left of the forks. The butter plate is to the right above the knife. Sometimes guests serve themselves from a platter. Put an empty, warm dinner plate directly in front of the guest with the platter and serving utensils above this.

At the more formal dinners, the salad is served after the entree and is set directly in front of the guest after the entree has been removed. Sometimes a salad bowl is offered; if so, the salad plate goes directly in front of the guest with service from the left.

In some operations, a fresh fruit sorbet is automatically offered before the entree. It is usually served in a tulip champagne glass over a doily and underliner with a teaspoon. A flower petal or lemon wheel can be used to decorate the glass.

Often dessert utensils are not placed with the original table setting but are brought in with the dessert. The dessert is set directly in front of the guest. If the dessert is triangular in shape, such as a piece of pie, place the point toward the guest. Sometimes there may be some doubt as to whether a guest would like a spoon, fork, or some other utensil. In this case, place both at the guest's place and let the guest decide.

Booth Service

Booth service is often difficult because of the need to serve guests at the far end of the table. Service to guests seated there should come first to avoid having the server reach across dishes served to those closer to the server. Serving those at the far end of the table usually requires the server to lean over and reach to get the items in their proper place. To serve those on the right, place the left hip against the table and with the left hand, reach out and set the items down. For the guests on the left, place the right hip against the table and reach out with the right hand. In serving a small booth or a dish used by all, it is acceptable for the server to stand flat against the booth and reach over.

FIGURE 4.6 Boothlike service requires the server to lean over guests furthest from the wall. Courtesy PhotoDisc, Inc.

Because booths often have less space than tables, it may be necessary to clear items as soon as possible.

CLEARING TABLES

In some operations clearing is not done until all guests have finished the course. In other operations it is acceptable to clear as each guest finishes. Some guests do not like to have dirty dishes in front of them and may ask for their removal. In such a case, the request is followed in spite of house rules. Servers should watch to see if guests wish their dishes to be cleared. Some signal this by setting their eating utensils down on the plate. If in doubt, the server should ask the guest if he or she has finished.

Clearing is done to the right using the right hand. Left-handed servers can make an exception to this rule if they don't feel comfortable handling certain items, such as heavy entree plates.

If beverages are not finished, leave them at the table unless the guests want them to be removed. Offer after-dinner drinks. Leave hot tea and coffee on the table for the dessert course. Water glasses remain on the table as long as the guest remains; keep them filled. Cracker wrappers and other miscellaneous items should also be cleared.

Crumb a table, with or without a tablecloth. If a crumber (or crumb brush) is not available, the blade of a dinner knife or a napkin folded into a roll shape will do the job. Do not sweep loose food particles onto the floor; use a plate or small tray covered with a napkin. The objective of crumbing is to get the table neat and clean and ready for dessert; coffee, and after-dinner drink service.

PRESENTING THE CHECK AND SAYING GOODBYE

When guests have finished and are ready to go, they resent having to wait for the check. The server, as well as the host or hostess, should be watching for signals from the guests that they are ready to leave, such as reaching for coats, purses, or packages. The last thing a server wants is a guest shouting, "Please bring the check!" Don't let guests rise and start to leave without the check, forcing you to rush over with the check. Difficulty getting the check can cause ill feelings, which might make guests decide not to come back or leave a paltry tip.

Present the check after the last clearing has occurred. It is an act of courtesy to ask, before presenting the check, if anything more is desired—even if the guest is seemingly in a hurry—so no oversight occurs.

The accurately totaled check may be presented in two ways. It may be brought to the table and placed face down on the table. This signals that the guest is to pay the cashier. It is appropriate to say something like, "Thank you. I have enjoyed serving you. Please come back again. You may pay the cashier."

In the second scenario, the server is expected to collect payment for the meal. The check is brought to the person paying the bill and is presented face down and then the server departs. The guest leaves payment plus a tip and leaves. If the guest does not have the proper amount, an amount greater than the check total is left and the server deposits the right amount with the cashier and brings back the change on the tray and leaves it with a "thank you." The guest picks up the change and normally leaves a tip. Servers can encourage a good tip by bringing guests' change in some single dollar bills instead of only larger bills.

It is common to bring a receipt torn from the check for the guest. Servers should never manipulate the receipt amount to be larger than the actual bill, as this is a form of fraud.

Payment today is often made by cash or credit card. However, if payment is by personal check, the server usually must get approval for acceptance from an approved authority. Always read checks to see that they are completed accurately. Most operations ask for identification from the guest.

FIGURE 4.7 Presenting the check is often the last impression that guests will have of their server. Courtesy Action Systems, Inc.

Credit cards are much more common. Most are readily accepted with no identification because payment is guaranteed by the bank or credit card company. Always check the card for a valid date, and get authorization from the credit card company. The guest must sign the credit card receipt; the name and signature must match those on the card. Tips can be added to the receipt. The tip is then paid in cash to the server by management, which is reimbursed when the charge is paid.

It is unprofessional for a server to show in any way that a tip is expected. It is also unprofessional to show disappointment in the amount of the tip. Tips are given to show appreciation of good service. A tip lower than expected might be showing that the service was less than expected. Servers should know also that some guests are unfamiliar with American tip practices. In Europe, for example, tips (gratuities) are often included automatically in the check total. This is often true in the United States with larger groups.

Guest checks should be used for all sales transactions by all servers, bartenders, or others who make sales. Guest checks should be ordered only by the management, kept in a locked secure place, and issued only in recorded lots. Checks supplies should be frequently audited to ensure that none are missing.

Traditional cash register systems require the register operator to open the register to receive and dispense money. Enhanced point of sale systems reduce or eliminate this need, and may allow several order-entry terminals to feed orders to the kitchen, central register, and inventory system. When a POS computer is used, all payment is recorded automatically. If a payment is not recorded, the check remains active. Management can thus see from time to time which checks are still out and for how long. Walkouts can be discovered more quickly.

Many restaurants now use touch-screen POS systems (point-of-sale systems) that allow servers to close out their own checks and get them quickly to guests. These systems also process credit card purchases through computer-system links with national credit card companies.

Before guests leave, servers should be sure to thank them again and invite them to return. This lets them leave with a good feeling about the operation and an incentive to return.

CLOSING

When the serving period has ended, there are closing duties. Soiled linen needs to be counted, bagged, and placed in proper storage. All unused linen should be folded and stored with other clean linen. Unused clean flatware and other similar items should be returned to proper storage. Condiments should be wiped-clean and stored properly. Salt and pepper shakers, sugar bowls, and other similar items may be placed on trays to take to a work station to be replenished. Butter should be covered and stored under refrigeration. The work station should be placed in order. Tables needing fresh linen should receive it, and tables should be reset for the next meal, with clean glasses and flatware. (Some operations do not want overnight setting.)

There will be sidework that must be done. Usually management draws up a list of these tasks so servers are reminded about what needs to be done.

Closing after a serving period varies according to whether there is another meal period coming or it is the end of the day. It is important that those who close for the night see that those who come in to start the morning shift are not unduly hampered because the evening group did not properly prepare for the next meal.

FORMAL DINING

Formal dining is characterized by a number of factors, including:

- The dress code is usually more strict and formal.
- The food and service are usually quite elaborate.
- Menus are also quite elaborate.
- The decor is elegant.
- More servers are used.
- The atmosphere is reserved, quiet, and peaceful.
- The price will reflect the cost of these extras.

Generally speaking, the basic service mechanics mentioned for casual dining are also applicable in formal dining, but their execution is more elaborate. For example, butter pieces in casual dining are usually squares, while in formal dining they might be in the shapes of rosettes or flowery curls, requiring more delicate handling by servers.

When French service is used, much of the service is from the *guéridon*. American and Russian service are also used.

In formal service, wine is featured much more as a meal accompaniment; a sommelier is usually on staff. Wine service is also more elaborate and formalized. All servers in fine dining must be well trained, and work might be specific to service positions. Thus, a chef de rang's tasks revolve mostly around the table, while the commis du rang will leave the table to bring food from the kitchen and do most of the serving. Captains may do special work such as deboning a fish or preparing Crêpes Suzette.

THE BUSPERSON'S ROLE

After guests have been seated and menus have been given out, often the next person to make contact with guests is the busperson. Buspersons might be young, but some like the work and stay in it for a lifetime. The position can be professional and lead to many job satisfactions. Often, besides a minimum wage, the busperson receives 15 percent of the food server's gratuity. In other food services, gratuities are pooled and distributed equally between all service personnel. Also, jobs often are not plentiful and the foodservice industry usually provides one. Some just like the work and stay in it.

The busperson's first responsibility is to provide water, butter, and perhaps bread after guests are seated and given menus. Bread baskets should be lined with a napkin because it is more sanitary, keeps the bread warm for a longer time, and looks appropriate and correct. Butter should be served cold but not on ice. (Once the butter softens and the ice cubes melt, the butter is apt to look messy and unappetizing.) Most often, water is poured at the table, but water in glasses can be brought to the table on a cocktail tray. (This can be heavy when serving a party of six or more. The procedure for handling a heavy tray is discussed earlier in this chapter.) There are many other duties required of buspersons, including the following:

- Bring in foods from the kitchen.
- See that ice and water are always at hand.
- Assist food server in removing soiled items. Always separate china, glassware, and flatware. Soiled items should be stacked according to shape and size to allow more room and give proper support to stacks. (This allows more to be stacked on the tray and saves on trips. It also helps the dishwasher.)
- Provide any supplementary service items needed by guests.
- Assist servers in beverage service.
- Refill coffee and tea orders.
- Ensure all condiments and service supplies, such as cream, sugar, lemon, teaspoons, cups, and saucers are readily available.
- Help maintain linen, equipment, and serviceware in an orderly manner in the various storage areas.
- Be available at all times for guests' special requests.
- After guests' departure, reset tables.

Here are some guidelines for doing the busperson's job effectively:

- Keep all equipment organized (a place for everything and everything in its place).

- Avoid overstacking items to guard against breakage and accidents.

- Always keep safety in mind; act immediately when there is broken china, glass, or spilled liquids on the floor.

- Walk, don't run. Perform tasks in a systematic manner.

- Try not to travel empty-handed. There is usually something to be carried in or out of the dining room or to work areas.

- Do not engage in long conversations with guests unless encouraged by guests.

- Good communication skills help make the job flow more smoothly and easily. Work to have open communication with other serving personnel and kitchen workers.

- At the end of a shift, leave the stations immaculate. Wipe down all condiment containers, bread warmers, cutting boards, bus pans, and carts, and make certain that all soiled linen is counted and properly bagged. Act immediately when you notice that the restaurant is running low on cleaning and paper supplies, equipment, or serviceware. Some operations like to have tables set up and prepared for the next shift. Others do not. Whether this is to be done or not is a management decision.

Throughout the course of the meal, the busperson should constantly remember one of the most crucial components of service—anticipating guests' needs. Service cannot be of good quality if guest needs are not anticipated. Patrons can become exasperated if during the meal they have to continuously ask for more water, bread, and butter. The novice has to focus attention on the table until, after a little practice and experience, it will become second nature to spot these needs, even from a distance. The busperson's approach should be immediate and courteous.

CHAPTER SUMMARY

Some general rules and procedures used in all types of operations include serving water and ice, carrying trays, handling china and glassware, and handling flatware.

Greeting and seating guests is the first step in good service. This task is very important since it gives a good impression to guests as to what is to follow. An important point in this first step in service is that servers should see that their station is ready to serve guests. This includes proper table setting, putting glasses upright ready for use, and so on. The seating of guests should not be a random function; those who seat guests need to make quick and intuitive guesses as to where to place guests.

Servers should greet guests with a smile and a welcome that lets the guests know that the server is happy to serve them. It is proper for the server to introduce himself or herself, hand out menus, and to help them make up their minds. Different operations present menus to guests differently. It is crucial that servers know the menu and are able to interpret it and describe items for guests. Often guests have questions or need help in making their selections, and the server is responsible for explaining what menu items are and how they are made. Servers should also be adept and comfortable with suggestive selling, not only to increase check totals and tips, but also to please guests.

Servers should use some system to write up orders so they know which guests placed which orders. Mechanized devices and computers transfer orders automatically to the kitchen and record sales. Order taking is made much easier and quicker when servers use abbreviations.

In noncomputerized operations, servers call out orders, place orders on a spindle or wheel, or give orders to an aboyeur or announcer.

The serving of the order is the culmination of all efforts of service and production. The main item of each course should be placed at the six o'clock position. Most items are served using the left hand on the guest's left, except beverages, which are served using the right hand at the guest's right.

Some of the essential rules and procedures for serving breakfast and lunch are covered. In dinner service, there often is a specific sequence of courses. Courses will be placed by servers or guests might serve themselves from serving dishes. Special considerations are discussed for booth service. Items should be cleared properly from tables and the table crumbed.

The server usually lays the check face down on the table near the person who is to pay it. Knowing who is to get the check is important because servers can cause some embarrassment if they do not know. If the server is to collect, the check is presented on a small tray or plate. The server receives payment and brings back any change along with a receipt. The guest then leaves the tip on the tray or plate. Credit card payment is common today. The server should always be sure to thank guests and invite them back.

Service does not end when guests leave. There is much to be done to be ready for the next service at that table. It must be reset, and the area made presentable. When closing out the meal, there are other things that must be done so as to be ready for the next meal to come. If the operation is to close for the night, other tasks must be done.

Formal service is characterized by how guests dress, the kind of place in which it occurs, special kinds of foods and menus, table preparation and service, and other factors. French service using the guéridon is common, but American and Russian service are seen. A few special rules and procedures for formal service are discussed.

The importance of the busperson in accomplishing service cannot be understated. Their tasks help make the meal flow smoothly. Servers often share tips with buspersons.

The busperson's role can be summed up in the saying, "In every way, support the server."

KEY TERMS

aboyeur	guest check	serviette
captain	guest-check system	spindle method
food covers	pivot system	touch screen
gratuities	POS system	tray jack
greeter	preset keyboard	

CHAPTER REVIEW

1. Where are heavy items placed when loading a tray? Where are lighter items placed?

2. What precaution must be taken when loading both hot and cold items onto a tray?

3. Why are the surfaces of trays often covered with cork? If a tray is not covered with cork, what can be done to give a similar effect?

4. Who normally first greets guests?

5. What is an appropriate way for a server to introduce herself or himself to guests at a table?

6. Why is it good for a server to help guests by suggestive selling? How can suggestive selling help the server?

7. If a guest orders a steak medium rare, how would you write it as an abbreviation?

8. Describe how a computer is used in placing orders. What else does a POS computer do?

9. How are items stacked properly on a tray or bus pan?

10. How should you present a check if the guest is to pay a cashier? If the guest were to pay the server?

Case Studies

PUTTING ON A BANQUET

The food and beverage manager of a large country club has a banquet in a room 120 feet by 100 feet. Using banquet tables that each seat eight guests, up to 1,000 guests can be served banquet style. A club president wants a banquet for approximately 800, plus or minus 5 percent.

The president wants the meal to be a first course, main meal with a salad, and dessert. He specifies the foods for each course. The food and beverage manager has a suggestion. After the main meal, omitting the dessert, the group would have its program, after which the guests would leave their tables and go to the large reception room next to the banquet room for dessert. The desserts would be displayed on four large tables, and the guests could select what and as much as they wish. They would eat standing up while talking to others. Coffee would be served at other tables nearby. He tells the president that this will allow him to lower the price of the banquet by a dollar per person. (He can afford to do this because it allows him to dismiss most of his service staff and keep only a skeleton crew to handle this dessert and coffee course.)

The president is doubtful. He is afraid of congestion and thinks that many of his club members will not like the arrangement. The food and beverage manager assures the president that he has not received complaints from this arrangement in the past. What other positive factors should the manager mention to convince the president that this is the way to go?

HANDLING A PERSONNEL PROBLEM

A large restaurant in a busy metropolitan area serves three meals a day. At lunch, it caters to shoppers, businesspeople, and high-income diners, mostly from surrounding hotels. It is a highly successful and thriving operation.

A large enrollment of downtown students at a business college near the restaurant has proven to be an excellent source of wait staff, both male and female. Careful selection is made to get neat, professional appearing, able female waitresses and male servers. Since the restaurant does a big business, the wait staff is large.

To fill an opening, a male waiter is hired. He's 23 years old with a dynamic personality. It is soon apparent that he is very lively and talkative. He immediately becomes of interest to a number of the female staff. He responds positively to this and becomes the envy of many of the male staff. In fact, quarrels and near fights break out. Some of the female waitresses also compete over him. What was a harmonious staff working together becomes a caldron of disharmony. It, of course, affects the service, and management begins to get more complaints than usual of poor service.

Management could correct the situation by letting the new hire go, but this may not necessarily rid them of the problem. Friction has developed that this would not correct. Besides, the new hire has developed into their best server. In the short time he has been there, he has developed a clientele, and patrons are asking for his tables. In fact, he's building business for the restaurant. Describe how you would handle this personnel problem.

BAR AND BEVERAGE SERVICE *

Outline

---

* Authored by Lendal H. Kotschevar and Valentino Luciani.

Learning Objectives

After reading this module, you should be able to:

- Know enough to serve and recommend beverage alcohol and nonalcohol beverages to guests based on informed knowledge of beverages.

- Correctly follow legal and ethical procedures for serving alcoholic beverages.

INTRODUCTION

For thousands of years, people have concocted all kinds of alcoholic beverages. Many of these early brews were made from fermented milk, berries, and fruits. Ciders were made from every type of fruit known, and countless concoctions were created by mixing water with essences of herbs, seeds, and spices. Far older than written histories are cave pictographs showing humans drinking beverages in celebration. A several-thousand-year-old stone tablet was found on Mount Ararat, near where Noah's ark is thought to have landed, containing a recipe for making beer from grain. Another fermented beverage (tequila) was made from the agave plant, and honey mixed with fermented liquid was used to make mead. Ciders were poured into open containers and allowed to stand until they "moved" by showing bubbles on the surface. The fermented juice of grapes was known to many early civilizations as far back as 8,000 to 10,000 years ago.

Coffee and tea were also consumed by early civilizations in southern Asia, where coffee was first discovered. Coffee, grown in the Middle East, Africa, and South America, has long been thought to have medicinal properties. However, Europeans in the eighteenth century found that when too much was consumed, it led to indigestion, depression, and states of irritability and anxiety. For these and other reasons, Pope Clement VIII declared coffee an infidel drink and forbade its use. (Later, another pope was tempted to taste it, did so, and found it much to his liking, and so he "baptized" it, thereby ridding it of its satanic properties.) In the United States, coffee was drunk as early as the 1660s. Today it is the most widely consumed beverage.

The Chinese were the first to drink tea made from the leaves and buds of a semitropical bush related to the camellia. It later became popular in Europe; tea has never been as popular in the United States as coffee is. Nevertheless, it is consumed in significant quantities.

Although Coca-Cola was first made in the 1880s, carbonated beverages were not mass produced until the 1920s and 1930s. Root beer, ginger beer, and ginger ale were the first, but with the introduction of cola, the popularity of carbonated beverages increased. Today cola drinks are popular all over the world. Americans drink a tremendous amount of carbonated beverages, and the amount per capita is increasing.

Specialty drinks with spirits, especially single-malt scotches and martinis, have made a comeback in this decade. Wine, especially Chardonnay, White Zinfandel, Cabernet Sauvignon, and Pinot Grigio, has become very popular in the United States.

Premium and specialty beer sales grew in popularity throughout the 1990s and remain strong sellers today. Specialty beers from both large breweries and microbreweries have gained popularity for their distinct flavors. Many restaurants and bars are capitalizing on beer's increasing popularity by making more varieties available, promoting them through beer-of-the-month clubs, training employees in product knowledge, introducing homemade beers through a brewpub concept, and suggesting beers with food. According to one recent study, the average beverage operation carries up to

FIGURE 5.1 The consumption of alcohol in social settings has a long tradition. Courtesy Corbis Digital Stock.

twenty bottled brands of beer and offers five brands of tap beer. Beer is by for the most popular alcoholic beverage. In 2003 it made up more than 50 percent of all alcohol sales.

SOME IMPORTANT FACTS ABOUT BEVERAGE ALCOHOL

The formation of alcohol is the result of an action brought about by yeast, which breaks down carbohydrates, freeing carbon dioxide, which adds to the brew a residue liquid called ethyl alcohol. It is a depressant and intoxicant. Alcohol is measured in people's systems as blood alcohol content, or BAC. Most people's liver can only break down about one ounce of alcohol per hour. Exceeding that amount in an hour can lead to dizziness, nausea, light-headedness, and more serious conditions. A BAC of as low as 0.05, or one-half drop of alcohol per thousand drops of blood, can begin to reduce inhibitions and reasoning, and slow down reactions. At 0.08 BAC, the legal limit in all fifty states for blood alcohol levels indicating intoxication a person might have slurred speech and blurred vision. At 0.15 there is a loss of muscle control, and alcohol can now act as a poison, causing vomiting and nausea. At 0.30 to 0.40, one passes out—a good thing, because from 0.40 to 0.50, the deep part of the brain is affected and one loses essential bodily functions, such as breathing and beating of the heart, leading to death.

Although some health risks are associated with overconsumption of alcohol, moderate consumption has been shown to have beneficial effects. It has been linked to lower risk of heart disease and lower blood pressure. Social drinking can lead to relaxation and conviviality. It can stimulate the appetite. Because it relaxes, it is often given to individuals just for that purpose. It expands the capillary system and makes the body feel warmer. It can help one sleep. There is evidence to show that those who drink alcohol moderately have fewer heart attacks than those who don't.

Alcohol Content and Proof

The federal government requires that the alcohol content of beverage alcohol be stated on the label of the container. In the United States it is stated in different ways. One is by weight, which we call proof. A spirit labeled 60 proof contains 30 percent alcohol by weight; one labeled 100 proof contains 50 percent alcohol by weight. The proof is double the alcohol content by weight. We do not indicate the alcohol content of wine and beer by weight, but by volume. This overstates the amount by weight of alcohol, because a liter of pure alcohol weighs 800 grams while a liter of water equals 1,000 grams. Thus, the ratio is 80:100 or 80 percent to 100 percent. In other words, a beer of 6 percent and a wine of 14 percent are respectively 4.8 percent and 11.2 percent alcohol ($0.06 \times 0.80 = 0.48$ and $0.14 \times 0.80 = 0.112$ or 11.2%). Other countries have different methods of labeling alcohol. The equivalent of an ounce of pure alcohol is two 12-ounce cans of beer, an 8-ounce glass of wine, $2\frac{1}{2}$ ounces of 80-proof spirit, and 2 ounces of 100 proof spirit.

Aging

Some alcohol beverages, such as spirits and wine, are improved by age. Beer does not improve; in fact, it should be consumed as soon as possible after production. Wines age while in the cask and also after bottling. Spirits age only in the cask; after bottling there is little change. The date a spirit was made, indicated often on the label, can be a guide to how long is has been in the bottle. Some alcohol must be aged for certain periods of time to be called by a specific name; a *bottled-in-bond* spirit must be aged four years in a government warehouse. Servers dispensing beverage alcohol need to know what aging means in the various beverages they serve. Age can be an indication of quality, and guests might want to know the age to know the quality of the item ordered.

KNOWING SPIRITS

Servers should know a great deal about the kinds of beverage alcohol they serve, so they can inform guests on what they are as well as how to serve them properly. The following sections will give you good basic information, but they are in no way complete. A server who wishes to be completely informed should take a special course in knowing and serving beverage alcohol.

Spirits are produced by the fermentation of grains, fruit, plants such as agave, sugar cane, and other products. After fermentation the brew is distilled at or above 160°F (71°C). The alcohol vaporizes, leaving the water in the brew. When this vapor is condensed it is a liquid made up of mostly alcohol. However, the alcohol carries over with it flavoring and other ingredients and so a number of alcohols take on the flavor of the products from which they were made. Others have flavors added to them after distillation. (See Figure 5.2.)

Spirits in the United States cannot be less than 80 proof; many are higher. However, cordials can be less.

A spirit labeled as bonded must be produced from a single distillation at 160 proof or less, be bottled at 100 proof, and be unblended, which means it is a straight liquor.

Whiskey

There are straight and blended whiskeys. Straight means that the spirit is from one distillation and has not been blended with grain neutral spirits. A blended whiskey is

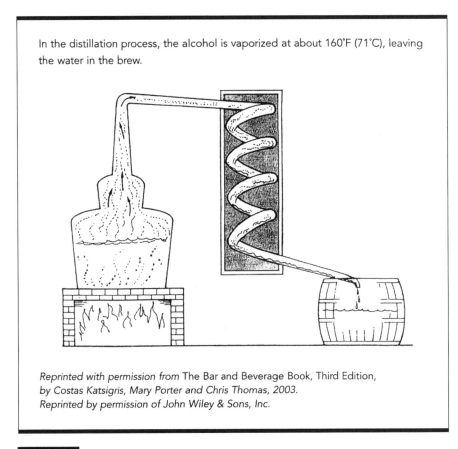

In the distillation process, the alcohol is vaporized at about 160°F (71°C), leaving the water in the brew.

Reprinted with permission from The Bar and Beverage Book, Third Edition, by Costas Katsigris, Mary Porter and Chris Thomas, 2003. Reprinted by permission of John Wiley & Sons, Inc.

FIGURE 5.2 The distillation process.

a straight whiskey blended with other batches of whiskey or grain neutral spirits. This ensures that all the whiskey from a particular brand has the same flavor and quality.

Bourbons must be made from at least 51 percent corn as the fermentable material and normally be aged four years in charred oak barrels at 125 proof. Kentucky bourbon must come from that state, but many bourbons come from other states. Rye whiskey is distilled from a mash containing not less than 51 percent rye as the fermentable material. It is like bourbon but is heavier in flavor. It must be aged at least two years in charred oak barrels. Corn whiskey must be made from a mash containing at least 80 percent corn. Canadian whiskeys are blended and can be made from rye, corn, or barley. They are lighter bodied than American whiskey, and with the trend toward lighter spirits this has made them heavy competitors of American whiskey. Canadian whiskey is made from liquors aged at least three years.

Scotch whiskey (or whisky, as it is spelled in Scotland) is made from malt or grain. Scotch's smoky flavor comes from drying sprouted barley over peat fires. American scotch must be 80 to 86 proof and aged at least four years.

Irish whiskey is made from barley but the sprouted grain is not dried over peat and, thus, has no smoky flavor. It is usually 86 proof and aged at least seven years; it has a heavier body than scotch.

Liqueurs (Cordials)

Liqueurs, also called cordials, are distilled spirits that have been treated with special flavoring ingredients. Many different ingredients are used to make a wide assortment of these beverages. Fruit, seeds, herbs, spices, honey, and other products are used for flavor extraction. Many cordials are quite sweet, which is an important distinguishing feature differentiating them from other spirits. Some cordials have been made for centuries. One of these cordials, Benedictine, is made from a secret, old recipe of the Benedictine monks. Usually, cordials are classified by their flavoring ingredient. Some popular liqueurs, or cordials, are Amaretto, Creme de Casis, Rock and Rye, Sambuca, Blackberry Liqueur, Peppermint Schnapps, Curacao, Maraschino, and Wisniak.

Gin

Gin is made from a spirit that would end up as a grain neutral spirit, except that usually in the last distillation, the distillate is allowed to come in contact with a gin head containing flavoring substances (botanicals) such as juniper berries, cassia bark, or cardamom. Holland gin is flavored only with juniper berries and is quite heavy in body and flavor. This makes it undesirable for making mixed drinks. London or English gin, also called dry gin, is lighter in flavor and body. It is a good mixing gin. Most American gins are similar to English gins. Few gins are aged; if they are, they take on a golden color and are called golden gin. Tanqueray, Booth's, Beefeaters, and Bombay are quite popular brands of gin.

Vodka

The federal government defines vodka as "neutral spirits, so distilled or so treated after distillation with charcoal and other materials, as to be without distinctive character, aroma, or color." Vodkas are typically between 80 and 100 proof, and they are not aged. Many countries around the world produce fine vodkas, such as Absolut (Sweden), Grey Goose (France) Stolichnaya (Russia) and Skyy (United States). Vodkas have enjoyed an increase in popularity due to the production of flavored vodkas using citrus, berries, and spices. Flavored vodkas such as Limonnaya, made from lemon peel, and Starka, made from brandy, vanilla, honey, and apple and pear tree scents, are uniquely flavored vodkas.

Tequila

Tequila is a distilled spirit made from the core of a blue agave plant. The starches in the agave plant's core are turned to sugar through a roasting process. The juices are then extracted and placed in formatting tanks. Yeast is added to the tank, enabling the sugar to convert to alcohol. Tequila alcohol content is between 70 and 110 proof. A worm in a bottle of tequila is thought by many to be part of the tequila-making process. This, in fact, is a myth and is mostly a marketing ploy.

Rum

Fermented sugarcane or molasses are the sources of rum. Light-bodied rums (also called silver or dry rum) are quite smooth and have a light body and slightly sweet flavor. These rums are produced in Puerto Rico, the Virgin Islands, Cuba, Dominican Republic, and Haiti. Light rums usually have a white or silver label; they are usually aged one year. If aged, the label states anejo (old) or muy anejo (very old). The heavy-bodied rums, made in Jamaica, Barbados, Martinique, and Trinidad, are darker in color and richer in flavor. The label is usually tan or brownish. Bacardi, Ron Rico, and Rhum Saint James are all popular brands of rum.

Brandy

Any spirit distilled from a mash of fruit or fruit derivatives can qualify as brandy. However, only a distillate made from grapes can be called brandy; those from other fruits must be labeled by the name of the item used, such as Apricot Brandy. Cognac is a brandy that comes from the Cognac region in France; only brandy from this area may be called Cognac. Armagnac comes only from that French region. Calvados, an apple brandy, comes from Normandy.

Most brandies are aged, some for very long periods. Most brandies are 80–100 proof. Brandy labels often contain words, letters, or stars that indicate certain things; for example, VS or three stars means the brandies in the blend are less than $4\frac{1}{2}$ years old, Vieux or Grand Reserve means most of the brandies in the blend are 20 to 40 years old and the youngest is more than $5\frac{1}{2}$ years old.

Grain-Neutral Spirits

Many alcoholic beverages are made from grain-neutral spirits, a plain, unflavored liquid made of pure alcohol plus water in varying degrees of proof. If it is not made from grain, the neutral spirit cannot be called *grain*. A grain-neutral spirit is the alcohol used to make cordials, gin, vodka, blended whiskeys, and other products. If a label says "Blended Scotch" or "Blended Bourbon," then the straight—unblended—item has been diluted with grain-neutral spirits that have no flavor. The flavor is provided by the addition of the other distilled product.

KNOWING WINE

Wine is made by fermenting fruit. In the process the yeast changes the sugars in the fruit to alcohol and carbon dioxide, while at the same time extracting the flavor of the fruit. Wines are not distilled. Aging can improve the flavor of some wines. Certain wines are aged a year or more in the cask before they are bottled. White wines age well, usually up to about six years, but some age longer. Red wines can age for many decades, but the change in flavor, color, and body, from the earliest to the latest wines, is usually dramatic. The alcohol content of wines can run from about 6 percent up to 20 percent or more. If above 14 percent, the wine usually has had a spirit added to it.

Types of Wine

Wine can be categorized into three types: table wines, sparkling wines, and fortified wines. Table wines are nonbubbling, or still. The CO_2 gas (carbon dioxide) that is a byproduct of fermentation is allowed to escape. Table wines usually have an alcohol range of 8 to 15 percent and are sold in restaurants and bars by the bottle, carafe, and glass.

Sparkling wines bubble because yeasts and sugar are added to still wine, causing a second fermentation in the bottle. These bubbling wines can be white, red, or rosé (blush), and usually contain 8 to 15 percent alcohol by volume plus CO_2. The most well-known type of sparkling wine is Champagne. For European wines, the name *Champagne* can only be used for sparkling wines made in the Champagne district of France. This district is in the northeastern corner of France and has a shorter growing season. Thus, the grapes are picked with higher acidity, which lends Champagne its distinct taste.

The following terms describe Champagne from the driest to sweetest:

■ *Brut*—Driest

■ *Extra dry*—Less dry

■ *Sec*—More sweet

■ *Demi-sec*—Sweetest

Brut and extra-dry are the Champagnes to serve throughout the meal. Sec and demi-sec are served with desserts and wedding cake.

Fortified wines are those with added alcohol, usually brandy. All wines with 15 percent alcohol or more have been fortified. Most fortified wines have an alcohol content of 17 to 22 percent. These wines come in two varieties: apéritif wines and dessert wines. Apéritif wines are flavored with herbs and spices, and are usually served before a meal. Vermouths from Italy and France are one type of apéritif; they can be sweet or dry. Dessert wines such as port, sherry, and Madeira, are typically sweet, rich, and heavy, so they are commonly served after dinner. The primary difference between port and sherry is that the brandy is added during fermentation with port for sweetness, and after fermentation with sherry.

Grape Varieties

Red wine is made from grapes with red, black, or purple skins. These grapes have been fermented with their skins on, giving their color and tannin—the strong, slightly bitter flavor that makes the mouth pucker—to the wine. Red wines possess many hues—the exact shade is determined by the type of grape, the time the grape skins are left in the fermenting brew, and age of the produced wine. They tend to be heartier, heavier, and more flavorful than whites and rosés. In addition, red wines are almost always dry, or lacking in sweetness.

White wine can be made from red, green, or white grapes. The juice is extracted and separated from the skins. The result is then fermented into wine. White wines are lighter in color, flavor, and body than reds, and generally have a shorter life span. They range in style from very sweet to very dry, and range in color from pale yellow to gold; some may have a greenish tinge.

Blushes or rosés are pink and range in color from very pale to nearly red. They have a fruity flavor and are light and fresh; some have a slightly sweet taste. Thus, they resemble white wines more than reds. Blushes can be produced by fermenting grape skins for a shorter duration or blending red and white grapes. Some rosés are even called white, such as the white Zinfandel and white Pinot Noir wines from California. Figure 5.3 shows various grapes.

Different grapes produce many different types of wine.

Grape	Color	Body	Sweetness	Flavor Intensity	Region/Country of Origin
Barbera	red	medium to full	dry	medium to intense	California, Italy
Cabernet Sauvignon	red	medium to full	dry	medium to full	California, Bordeaux (France), Australia
Chardonnay	white	medium to full	dry	medium to full	California, Burgundy (France), Chablis (France), Champagne (France), Italy, Spain, Bulgaria, Australia, New Zealand
Chenin Blanc	white	medium	slightly sweet	medium	California, Loire Valley (France)
Gamay	red	light to medium	dry	delicate	Beaujolais (France)
Gewurztraminer	white	medium	dry	spicy, full	California, Alsace (France), Australia, New Zealand
Grenache	red	light to medium	dry	light to medium	California, Rhÿne Valley (France), Spain, Australia
Merlot	red	light to medium	dry	soft, delicate	California, Italy, Bordeaux (France)
Muller-Thurgau	white	soft to medium	sweet	mild to medium	Germany
Muscat	black or white		medium to sweet	medium to full	Italy, Alsace (France), Bulgaria
Nebbiolo	red	full	dry	intense	Italy
Pinot Blanc	white	light to medium	dry	light	California, Italy, Alsace (France), Champagne (France)
Pinot Noir	red	medium to full	dry	medium to full	California, Burgundy (France), Oregon, Champagne (France), Australia
Riesling	white	light to medium	slightly sweet	delicate	Germany, Alsace (France), Australia, California, Washington, Oregon
Sangiovese	red	medium to full	dry	medium to full	Italy
Sauvignon Blanc	white	medium	dry	medium	California, Bordeaux (France), Loire Valley (France), Chile
Sémillon	white	light to medium	dry	medium	California, Bordeaux (France)
Silvaner	white	light	dry	light	Alsace (France), Germany
Syrah, Shiraz	red	medium to full	dry	intense	Rhÿne Valley (France), Australia
Trebbiano	white	light to medium	dry	light to medium	Italy
Zinfandel	red	medium to full	dry	medium to intense	California

Reprinted with permission from The Bar and Beverage Book Third Edition, *by Costas Katsigris, Mary Porter, and Chris Thomas, © 2003. Reprinted by permission of John Wiley & Sons, Inc.*

FIGURE 5.3 Grape varieties.

How Wines Are Named

In the United States, wines are named in three ways:

1. By the predominant variety of grape used (varietal)
2. By broad general type (generic)
3. By brand name

Imported wines may also be named by their place of origin. For a varietal wine, the name of the grape is the name of the wine, and that grape will give the wine its predominant flavor and aroma. Well-known examples include Cabernet Sauvignon, Chardonnay, Chenin Blanc, and Zinfandel. These terms were introduced to differentiate American wines from European wines. Varietals are very popular in this country. Legally, a varietal wine must include at least 75 percent of the dominant grape.

A generic wine is an American wine of a broad general type, such as burgundy or chablis. Their names are borrowed from European wines that come from well-known districts, which have a resemblance to the original. Federal law requires all American generics to include a place of origin on the label (such as California, Washington, Napa Valley). The best of the generics are pleasant, uncomplicated, affordable wines that operations often serve as house wines. As Americans have learned more about wine, they have come to recognize varietal names. Many wineries are using the terms *red table wine* or *white table wine* for these blends.

A brand-name wine may be anything from an inexpensive blend to a very fine wine with a prestigious pedigree. A brand name, also called a proprietary name, or in France, a *monopole,* is one belonging exclusively to a vineyard or a shipper who produces and/or bottles the wine and takes responsibility for its quality. A brand name alone does not tell you anything about the wine. The reputation of the producer should be your guide.

Tasting Wine

When tasting wine, a stemmed glass should be used, held by the foot or stem—never by the bowl, which would convey the heat of the hand to the wine. The same amount of wine should be poured each time (no more than half full) so that valid comparisons can be made.

There are generally considered to be five steps involved in the wine tasting experience.

1. It all begins with color. Holding the wine up to the light will help to show color, clarity, brilliance, and viscosity. Some terms that may describe a wine's appearance are:

2. The next step is to swirl and smell the wine. Swirling helps the wine to contact the air, which develops its bouquet. Do not swirl sparkling wines, as this would release all the bubbles.

3. Smelling should be done with the nose inside the glass, taking deep breaths. Swirling and smelling can be done several times. If the scent is fruity or flowery, it is called an aroma—aroma reflects the scent of the young wine. As the wine ages, the aroma becomes the bouquet. The bouquet is the fragrance imparted by the winemaking and aging process. Descriptive words for the smell of wine include perfumed, woody, young, baked, complex, closed, acrid, corky, moldy, skunky, minty, vegetal, and grassy. Many other familiar fragrances may be detected, including fruit, flower, and spice smells.

4. Actual tasting determines not only flavor, but a multitude of sensations including body, sweetness, acidity, and tannin. Tasting terms include syrupy, cloying, hot, biting, raw, harsh, mild, fat, nervous, round, firm, clumsy, flabby, velvety, soft, and generous. Also, the fruits, nuts, and spices and other flavors that were smelled can now be tasted. The wine can be either swallowed or spit out after tasting.

5. The impression left in the mouth is called the finish. Light, crisp wines will finish clean; great, complex wines will have a lingering finish. This is the evaluation period of a wine tasting.

Pairing Wine with Food

To match wines with food, you first need to taste the wines and foods in your operation so you can describe them enthusiastically and make recommendations. People's individual tastes vary, so nothing is cast in stone, but there are also some general rules you can follow.

Appetizers—Dry to medium dry, light-bodied acidic white wines are usually good choices with appetizers, because they have refreshing quality that tends to stimulate the appetite. Sparkling wines are great combinations with many hors d'oeuvres.

Fish and seafood—Dry white wine (Chardonnay, Sauvignon Blanc) usually pairs best with seafood because the wine's crispness allows the food's subtler flavors to surface. Light-bodied red wines with little tannin (Gamay Beaujolais) are delicious with firm-fleshed fish such as swordfish.

FIGURE 5.4 The knowledge of how to pair particular wines with food selections will add to the dining experience. Courtesy PhotoDisc/Getty Images.

Poultry and pork—Preparation, tastes, textures and appearances can vary. Carefully consider the sauce when pairing the right wine—a white, blush, or red may all be appropriate.

Veal—Leanness and delicate flavor is complemented by lighter red wines, well-aged red wines, or dry white wines.

Beef and lamb—Both are higher in fat and require wines with sufficient tannin to cut through full flavor. Complex red wines (Cabernet Sauvignon, Merlot) are good choices. Seasoned or marinated meats need a younger red (Pinot Noir).

Ham—Cured ham takes careful matching due to the saltiness or sweetness of meat. If the ham is glazed, a fruity rosé or blush (White Zinfandel) can be a nice match.

Figure 5.5 lists some more specific wine and food pairings.

KNOWING BEER

In today's bar and beverage operations, beer is the largest-selling beverage alcohol. In the United States, the first beer reference is from a Mayflower diary of 1622. The ship's captain had not planned to dock at Plymouth Rock, but he did when informed their beer was running out. They found they liked it there and stayed.

Certain foods are paired well with specific types of wine.

PASTA
Fettuccine Alfredo	Frascati, Sauvignon Blanc
Lasagna	Chianti, Cabernet Sauvignon
Spaghetti primavera	Soave, Sauvignon Blanc

FISH/SEAFOOD
Fish, grilled or broiled	Chardonnay, Sauvignon Blanc
Fresh shellfish	Sauvignon Blanc, Johannesburg Riesling
Fried catfish	White Zinfandel

POULTRY
Barbecued chicken	Gamay Beaujolais
Sweet and sour chicken	White Zinfandel, Johannesburg Riesling
Chicken with light cream sauce	Chardonnay, Johannesburg Riesling

BEEF
New York strip steak	Cabernet Sauvignon, Merlot
Beef Stroganoff	Merlot, Pinot Noir
Filet mignon with béarnaise sauce	Cabernet Sauvignon, Merlot

PORK/VEAL/LAMB
Roast pork	Chardonnay, Gamay Beaujolais
Grilled pork chops	Gamay Beaujolais, Zinfandel
Veal parmigiana	Zinfandel, Chardonnay

LIGHT ENTREES
Fruit salad	Johannesburg Riesling
Quiche Lorraine	Sauvignon Blanc, Chenin Blanc
Chicken Caesar salad	Sauvignon Blanc, Chardonnay

FIGURE 5.5 Guidelines for pairing wine and food.

Beers are made from barley, yeast, water, and hops. Other grains such as rice and wheat are sometimes used. Malt made from sprouted barley is the grain most commonly used. Sprouting turns the barley's starch into a sugar called maltose. The sweetness of the malt is largely lost as the sugar changes to carbon dioxide and ethyl alcohol. However, in some beers the sweetness of the malt remains, such as in porter and stout.

Special yeasts are needed to produce different kinds of beers. Beer is more than 90 percent water, and brewers often claim the excellence of their beer stems from the water used.

Hops give a pleasant bitter flavor to beer along with additional flavor. The most popular style of beer in the United States is pilsner, made by the lager method, which requires a long period of cold fermentation. Fermentation proceeds slowly from the bottom, so lagers are called bottom-fermented beers. Some other beers are top-fermented, which require only about three days to ferment. Ales, stouts, and porters are top-fermented.

Most lagers contain about 4 percent alcohol by volume. Ales may have a slightly higher alcohol content. Porter, stout, and bock beer have higher alcohol contents (about 6 percent) and are heavier in body, richer in flavor, darker, and sweeter than lagers. Malt liquor is highest of the beers in alcohol content.

Light beers are becoming increasingly popular due to their low-calorie content, which is about 100 calories per 12-ounce serving, as opposed to 140 to 175 for other beers.

Brewers are constantly striving for new types of beer that will attract the market. Steam beers, dry beers, and ice beers are recent successful entries into beer jargon. (See Figures 5.6 and 5.7.)

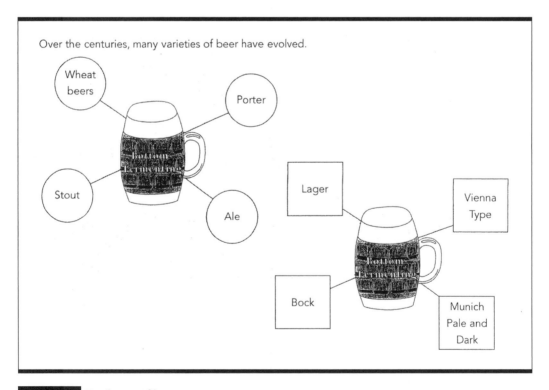

Over the centuries, many varieties of beer have evolved.

FIGURE 5.6 Family tree of beers.

Some beers are best consumed with certain types of food.

Food	Beer
Salads	Pilsner
Light appetizers	Lager, amber
Seafood	Lager
Spicy food, soup	Ale
Beef, game, other meats	Dark ale
Desserts	Stout, bock, double-bock, barleywines

FIGURE 5.7 Guidelines for pairing beer and food.

KNOWING NONALCOHOLIC BEVERAGES

Coffee

Coffee has long played a major role in food service. The coffee tree (Coffea Arabica) is a tropical evergreen shrub native to Africa. The coffee shrub produces several types of beans, of which the Robusta and the Arabica are the best known. The word *coffee* seems to have originated from the Ethiopian region of Kaffa, although both the Turks and the Arabs claim to have named it first. The French botanical scholar and explorer Jean de la Roque, in his book *Voyage de l'Arabie Heureuse,* published in 1666, reports that the Turks made the beverage popular in the Middle Ages and called it cahveh. De la Roque was the first person to introduce coffee to Europe by bringing from his voyages coffee beans and brewing the first cup of coffee (Marseilles, France, 1644). The first coffee houses on records are found in the Taktacalah quarter of old Constantinople (now Istanbul).

Roasted coffees are sold as one type or blended. Light roasting produces a mild flavor, while long roasting creates a dark, stronger coffee. After roasting, the beans are ground. The fineness of the grind has much to do with the extraction time, or the length of time the water and the grinds are in contact. The extraction time for fine grinds is two minutes, after which used grinds should be removed to prevent the bitter remnants of the coffee from harming its flavor.

Coffee flavors are carried in bean oils. These oils are extremely fragile and oxidize very easily. To prevent off-flavor development within three days, ground coffee must be kept in a vacuum-sealed container or at freezing temperature. Whole-bean coffee keeps its flavor for about two weeks at room temperature. Some operations buy freshly roasted whole bean coffee and grind each batch independently to produce the finest quality coffee.

In the last two decades, decaffeinated coffee has become increasingly popular, so much so that in many foodservice operations patrons request it by a ratio of two to one. Decaffeinated coffee contains only 3 percent of the original caffeine. The caffeine is extracted by soaking the beans in hot water for several hours and by transferring them to a separate tank where they are treated with a solvent that absorbs the caffeine. Trichlorethylene and methyline chloride are the solvents most often used. However, the best method is by only water extraction, called the *European method*.

In the sequence of meal service, coffee is often served last and, thus, is charged with the responsibility of leaving the last impression to guests. In table service, unless requested earlier, coffee follows the entree, usually with or after the dessert. Before coffee service, the table should be cleared of all soiled items and unnecessary tableware. If the table has a tablecloth, it should be crumbed. In a coffee shop or family-style restaurant coffee is typically served in six-ounce cups. Coffee should be served hot—above 160°F (71.1°C)—to give the best flavor. Scrupulously clean equipment, good coffee and water, and proper brewing methods are required to make good coffee and, where servers are charged with its making, the principles for clean equipment and proper brewing should be observed. Coffee flavors are extracted best at about 205°F (96.1°C). Most operations today use a 10- or 12-cup coffee brewer, which permits service from the brewing pot. Decaffeinated coffee, espresso, cappuccino, caffé latté, café au lait, and other coffee drinks have become very popular and profitable.

Before serving coffee, use a serviette to wipe off the spout or mouth of the container. Alert guests that pouring is about to begin so they are aware of it and do not make a sudden movement that causes spillage and perhaps burning. The spout or container pouring edge should be from one to two inches above the rim of the cup and pouring should be done slowly and attentively. Many servers prefer to place the milk or cream container and sugar container on the table before pouring, but it can be done immediately afterward. They should be placed to the right of the cup. When serving at a table where there is more than one guest, it is proper to position them at the table center so it is easy for guests to help themselves.

If the coffee is poured from a pot carried on a cocktail tray, the server, while pouring, must make certain that the tray is always level and balanced. When carrying a pot by hand, as when refilling a cup, it is recommended that an underliner be held on the other hand. Without it, there is always a risk of a drop or two falling on the table or onto a guest. All beverages are poured from the right and cleared from the right. The cup's handle should be placed at the three o'clock position with the teaspoon to the right of the saucer, pointed upward. While such positioning might seem trivial, to

FIGURE 5.8 Coffee should be poured from the right, with the handle at the three o'clock position. Courtesy PhotoDisc, Inc.

discerning guests it indicates consideration of the finer details of service. It usually takes the same amount of time and effort to place things properly as it does to place them incorrectly.

Hot Chocolate

Chocolate is derived from the bean of the semitropical cacao tree. This bean is roasted and broken into small pieces called nibs. The nibs are ground and the resulting product is bitter chocolate, a substance containing more than 50 percent cacao butter. Treating chocolate with alkali gives it a lighter appearance and smoother texture. It is called *Dutch* because it was first done in Holland.

Cocoa is produced after extracting some of the cacao butter (fat) from chocolate. A cocoa labeled *breakfast* contains 22 percent or more of cacao butter. Hot chocolate in most operations is a blend of cocoa, sugar, milk, and other ingredients.

To make hot chocolate from a mix, enough powder for one serving is placed into a cup, hot water is added, and the mixture is stirred. Whipped cream, shredded chocolate, and cinnamon may be served as toppings. The service of hot chocolate is patterned closely to that of coffee and tea.

Tea

Tea is an aromatic beverage obtained by infusion of tea leaves with boiling water. The word *tea* originated from the Chinese T'e. In the United States, tea has been widely consumed since the advent of the pilgrims. A historical event much related to tea consumption, the Boston Tea Party, was a factor leading up to the revolutionary war. To obtain a fine-quality tea, blends of different type of leaves are often used. The preferred teas are those made with leaves grown in higher altitudes.

In processing, all teas have their leaves first rolled to release juices and develop flavor. The next steps vary according to the type of tea to be made. Green tea is not oxidized; in fact, it is often steamed or otherwise treated to prevent any change. It goes directly into drying after rolling. Oolong tea is lightly oxidized and black tea is fully oxidized and then both are dried. In the United States, an average of two pounds of tea per person is used each year. The best tea comes from the higher elevations.

Hot tea should be brewed in freshly boiled water above 185°F (85°C) for up to ten minutes. The custom of putting a tea bag into a cup and then pouring hot water over it and bringing the cup to the guest is not recommended. The tea should be put into a preheated stainless steel or ceramic pot and have boiling water poured over it. This pot should hold at least a pint so enough heat is produced to provide good extraction. After five minutes, the proper amount of extraction occurs, and guests should then remove the tea to prevent overextraction. The handle of the pot should point toward the guest's right. It is good service to also provide a pot of plain, freshly boiled water so the guest can brew the strength of the tea to that desired. Some guests prefer to add the bag to the tea while others wish the server to do this. Few desire cream for their hot tea but some like milk, while others just like a bit of lemon. The basic service procedures are the same as for coffee. In fine service, the milk or lemon is brought to the table on a plate lined with a doily. This is placed slightly above and to the right of the cup. Some operations offer exotic blends of brewed teas with added flavors such as spices, honey, herbs, fruits, or other flavorful ingredients.

Iced tea is usually made from orange pekoe black tea. The strength should be about double that of regular tea because of the dilution from ice. There is a danger of clouding in making tea of such strength when it chills. It also can cloud when tea is poured over ice. The reason is that chilling tends to precipitate the tannins in the tea, causing the clouding. For this reason, iced tea is usually newly brewed each day and is not refrigerated.

Iced tea is served in a tall glass with ice and a teaspoon. Sugar, brown sugar, regular sugar, or an artificial sweetener should be brought to the table prior to the service of the tea. Lemon is often served with the tea, preferably in wedges brought to the table on a small plate lined with a doily. Some operations find that using instant powdered iced tea pleases guests. Often the tea is in a portion package and the server only needs to add this to some cold water and ice to have iced tea.

HOSPITALITY BEHIND THE BAR

Excellent bar service relies on good organization, efficient control systems, and talented and knowledgeable staffing. A good bartender knows everything about what

FIGURE 5.9 Many casual and fine-dining restaurants offer a selection of teas.

is for sale, how and when to suggest drinks, how to tell a joke or a good story, and how to serve responsibly. The bar can even become an information desk, especially in airports, train stations, and stadiums. The skills required of bartenders are many and varied.

Bartenders should come to work in a neat, clean work uniform. Before the shift, the bartender should check to see that everything is in order, neat, and clean. An inventory is usually taken of the storeroom before opening. Items are stored in their proper places. Supplies for the shift should be seen to be adequate. If an electronic liquor gun is used, the bartender should check where the liquor is stored to see that supplies are adequate and the system is connected correctly. Bar bottles should be checked to see that pouring caps are on, cordial corks are not sticky, and so forth. A sufficient supply of glassware should be on hand.

Offering food when serving alcoholic beverages is not only good hospitality but an important part of responsible service. In general, food slows the absorption of alcohol into the bloodstream. Furthermore, guests who are relaxing and having food may not drink as much or as quickly. This delay gives the liver more time to break down the alcohol in the person's blood. Food also helps protect the stomach from alcohol irritation. The foods that work best at slowing alcohol absorption are fatty and high-protein foods. These foods tend to take a while to digest, thereby keeping beverage alcohol in the stomach. Some examples include beef tacos, cheese, chicken wings, crackers and dip, fried foods, meatballs, and pizza.

A friendly bartender can be a bar's biggest asset. Courtesy Corbis Digital Stock.

Advance preparation—mise en place—is one key to good bar service when things get rushed. Good organization and rhythmic preparation helps when a busy period hits the bar. In most times the bartender or bartenders are alone to handle business but it is good to have someone who can step in and help in times of stress.

Bartenders use house liquors or well stock to fill drink orders when no brand is specified. Well liquors are typically kept on lower shelves or in a well along the bar. Operations also offer call stock, brands that guests ask for especially rather than the regular well stock. Often these are premium brands and the charge for them is greater than for the well stock.

When mixing drinks in front of guests, the bartender places the glasses on the bar and mixes the drinks in a mixing container or pours from bottles. The bartender then puts down bar napkins, places each filled glass on a napkin, then gently slides each glass to the proper guest. Straws, stirrers, garnishes, or other accompaniments should be placed as the drink is put in place. Except for rind twists, garnishes should not be touched with the fingers, but put into place by using a decorative bar sword (a plastic toothpick in the shape of a sword) or toothpick.

Many guests do not like to see a bartender use a liquor gun to mix drinks because there is no flexibility in drink strength. Most operations allow bartenders to use free pouring, but this method makes it difficult to control portions and costs. Many bars portion drinks using jiggers that measure consistent amounts. When pouring with a jigger, place the glass on the bar in front of the guest and hold the jigger directly over it. Pour the liquor into the jigger, then dump it into the glass.

Standardized recipes that give the amount of alcoholic beverage, method of preparation, glassware to use, and garnish establish a strong foundation for customer satisfaction and profit. Customers should not be able to tell which bartender made their drink. Every drink must be the same. Method of service should also be standardized, and here also customers should not be able to identify which server served their drink.

SERVING SPIRITS

Serving Straight Drinks

The term straight used with alcohol beverages means the spirit is served alone; nothing is added. If ice is served, the drink is termed on the rocks. Spirits, wines, and beers are usually served straight, although they also can be served blended with other ingredients. Straight spirits are typically served in an old-fashion glass (7-ounce) but also can be brought to the table in a smaller glass. Some operations like to bring either water, mineral water, or plain soda to the table with a straight spirit drink which, if the guest uses, makes it no longer a straight drink.

Serving Mixed Drinks and Cocktails

The term mixology refers to the art of mixing drinks. A mixed drink is any drink in which one beverage is mixed with one or more alcohol or nonalcohol ingredients. Mixed drinks include cocktails, highballs, tall drinks, frozen drinks, and coffee drinks. Many drinks have standard garnishes that are as much a part of the drink as the rest of the ingredients.

There are four basic mixing methods:

1. **Build**—Mix step by step in the serving glass, adding each ingredient one at a time. Built drinks include highballs, fruit-juice drinks, tall drinks, hot drinks, and drinks where one ingredient is floating on top of another.

2. **Stir**—Mix the ingredients by stirring them with ice in a mixing glass and then straining the drink into a chilled serving glass. The purpose of stirring is to mix and cool ingredients quickly with minimal dilution from the ice. Ingredients that

blend together easily are stirred cocktails made of two or more spirits, or spirits plus wine.

3. **Shake**—Mix by shaking with a hand shaker or by mixing on a shake mixer (mechanical mixer). Shake drinks are made with ingredients that do not readily mix with spirits: sugar, cream, egg, and sometimes fruit juice.

4. **Blend**—Mix in an electric blender. You must blend any drink that contains solid food or ice. Strawberry daiquiris and frozen margaritas are blended. Although some bars blend drinks when they could easily shake or mix them, the blender is not nearly as fast as the mechanical mixer, and it does not make as good a drink as the hand shaker.

It is nearly impossible for one to know all of the various mixed drinks available today. Servers and bartenders should know the drinks usually requested by guests. If others are ordered, the bartender can look them up in a recipe book which should be kept at the bar. Bartenders should not guess or depend upon their memories, but should check. An improperly prepared drink not only displeases a guest but also results in a loss of ingredients when the drink is rejected and a replacement has to be made.

Serving Cordials/Liqueurs

Cordials, or liqueurs, are typically enjoyed before and after a meal as highly flavorful aperitifs and digestifs. Sweet cordials are a wonderful ending to a meal.

Liqueurs are usually served in small stemmed glasses that hold from 1 to 1 1/2 ounces or with ice in a larger bowled glass called a brandy snifter. In some fine dining restaurants, the cordial glass is served on a small plate with a doily and placed in front or slightly to the right of the guest. Often a well-appointed cordial cart is brought to the table by the captain or the server, thus enabling the guest to select among the various brands featured on the cart.

SERVING WINE

Knowing how to serve wine can lead to increased sales for the operation and increased tips for the servers. Service need not be pretentious, but nothing can be more elegant during a meal than the opening and serving of a bottle of wine. Although wine is an excellent accompaniment to many foods, more and more guests are ordering it in place of other alcohol drinks. Today wine is served not only in food services but in practically every bar or other operation selling beverage alcohol.

Servers are also salespersons, and for them to do their best job in selling wines they should receive training on what wines are, their proper storage and service, and how to suggest wines that guests might like. This takes a considerable amount of knowledge, as well as serving skill. Wine and food have a long and historic association. Because of the wide variety of wines available, nearly every food can be paired with a wine that brings out its best qualities. Tradition held that red wines went with red meats, while white wines complemented poultry and fish, but this is no longer a set rule. The wine a person prefers is the proper wine.

Many find chilling a dry or medium-dry white wine increases its crispness, but overchilling can result in loss of bouquet and taste. White wines are best when served at 45°F to 55°F (7.2°C to 12.8°C) and reds at about 70°F (21.1°C). Wine is often served in chilled marble "coolers" placed on the table instead of a wine bucket. To chill wine quickly in an ice bucket, place a bottle in a, bucket filled half with ice and half with water. It takes about 15 minutes to bring a bottle of wine to about 50°F (10°C). If a wine bucket is filled with only ice, it is difficult to force the bottle down to the bottom; it also cools more slowly. When removing a bottle from the bucket, wipe it thoroughly. After guests have finished a beverage, remove the empty glasses promptly.

Some wines develop sediment and should be decanted. Sediment can be left in the bottle by gently opening a bottle and then carefully pouring the wine slowly into a decanter from which the wine will be served. Some place a very short burning candle under the neck until they see the appearance of sediment.

In some operations a sommelier (wine steward) will give out the wine list, take the order, bring the glasses, and serve the wine. However, in most operations the server must do this. If guests have questions about what wine to order, the server should inquire about their tastes and preferences. When given the type of entree(s) ordered and specific price range requested, the server may suggest a number of appropriate wines to accompany the meal.

Follow the pivot system and use abbreviations when taking orders. After serving wine from a bottle, watch the table and be there before guests have to reach for the bottle and serve themselves. Be prompt in asking to bring another bottle after one is emptied or even before, if the bottle is nearly empty.

There are many glasses (practically all stemmed) designed for holding various kinds of wine; in some fine dining operations all of them will be used. This provides elegant service, but is costly and not necessarily appreciated by some guests. Many operations avoid the necessity for having a large inventory of expensive, stemmed glass-ware by using an all-purpose wine glass for all wines, including Champagne. However, Champagne and other sparkling wines are more often served in either a fluted glass

FIGURE 5.11 Some fine-dining establishments have a sommelier to recommend and serve wine selections. Courtesy PhotoDisc/Getty Images.

holding about five ounces, or an aperitif or dessert glass holding three to four ounces. (See Figure 5.12.)

Servers should note that guests perceive the service of wine often as equal in importance to that of food; some even more so. In taking the wine order, the server should not make any adverse comment about the quality of the wine selected, the

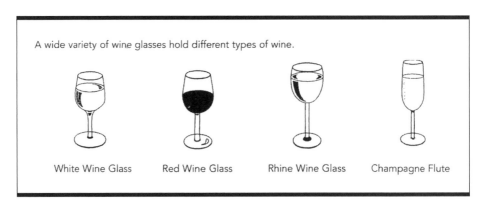

A wide variety of wine glasses hold different types of wine.

White Wine Glass   Red Wine Glass   Rhine Wine Glass   Champagne Flute

FIGURE 5.12 Wine glasses.

FIGURE 5.13 Servers should be able to quickly and efficiently open a wine bottle. Courtesy PhotoDisc/ Getty Images.

guest's pronunciation of the wine name, or anything else that might indicate a lack of knowledge on the part of the guest. The bottle should be brought to the table and presented unopened to the orderer, and held from the bottom with an opened hand while being held by the neck with the other hand. It is proper to hold a serviette or napkin behind the bottle about halfway around. This presentation is done so the orderer can check to see if what is being offered is what was ordered. Hold the label so it is at eye level, and give plenty of time so the guest can note the label's contents and make any comments desirable to the other guests. Handle bottles with care, being careful not to shake them, especially vintage reds, since this might disturb the sediment and cloud the wine.

To open a bottle, rest the bottle on the side of the table between the person ordering the wine and the guest on the right, or turn to a nearby cart and open the bottle there. Cut the top foil away with the blade of the corkscrew, leaving the bottom foil around the neck. The cutting of the foil should be neat and quick. Wipe the top neck of the bottle and the top part of the cork with a napkin or serviette. Insert the opener into the center of the cork. Avoid placing the opener on the side of the cork; this makes it difficult to get a clean, smooth pull. Remove the cork.

The next step is to bring the bottle to the right of the person ordering and pour approximately one ounce into this person's glass, so it can be tasted and approved or disapproved. As the server ends pouring, the bottle should be given a slight, gentle twist with a short, quick movement of the wrist to prevent dripping. Next, remove the cork from the corkscrew and set it on a folded serviette or small plate to the right of the taster. Some may choose to smell the cork for the appropriate aromas and bouquets; it also should be felt, as a dry cork can indicate improper storage.

Serve the other guests in a clockwise manner, ending with the orderer. Some operations serve women before men. Fill glasses with still wine to about two-thirds full; sparkling wines tend to bubble up quickly when poured, leaving a bit of foam. A short pause in pouring allows this foam to subside and the glass may then be filled to the desired level. After pouring, place the bottle of white or sparkling wine into a wine bucket or insulated cooler (without ice) at table-side; rest opened red wines to the right of the orderer. Place older reds in a wine basket that holds the bottle on a slant so the lees are not disturbed.

SERVING SPARKLING WINE

When serving Champagne and other sparkling wines, it is very important to know the correct method of opening a bottle. A flying cork can sometimes be a dangerous missile. Make sure the bottle is chilled and has not been disturbed before opening it. The following steps outline the correct procedure for opening a bottle of champagne.

1. Cut the foil around the top of the bottle.
2. Place hand on top of the cork, never removing it until the cork is pulled out completely. Take off the wire.
3. Wrap a towel around the bottle for safety and spillage. Remove cork gently, slowly turning the bottle in one direction and the cork in another. Ease the cork out gently rather than jerking it out or letting it shoot out from the bottle. Gentle removal does not disturb the wine and keeps the liquid from gushing out.
4. Pour the sparkling wine into the appropriate glassware.

SERVING BEER

Beer may be served in a pitcher, in mugs, in a variety of glasses, or in a bottle accompanied by a glass. When serving, be sure to wipe the bottle before bringing it to the table. When a beer is poured at the table, place the glass or stein on the table to the right of the guest. If the server pours for the guest, he should pour carefully, not down the side of the glass, but in the center so about an inch of foam appears; it is proper to have the foam come to the rim. Some guests prefer to pour their own and will indicate so to the server. An alert server will remember this; if the guest is served again, the server will know that this guest prefers to pour his or her own. The amount of beer in different glasses varies, but 10- and 12-ounce glasses are common. Since there should be a collar of foam, the actual amount is not that of the full glass.

As the server finishes pouring from a bottle, the bottle should be given a slight twist with a quick movement of the wrist to stop drops from falling after pouring stops, Serving beer from a can is not recommended. However, the server can pour from a can into a glass, then place the can next to the poured glass for the customer.

Servers should serve draft beer within thirty seconds of its drawing. The beer looks unappealing if served flat; the foam should be between 1 1/2; and 2 inches high. Draft beer ordinarily comes from a keg kept in a refrigerated area at about 40°F (4.4°C). It is carbonated as it comes out of the spout. Draft beer is very perishable because it has not been pasteurized to destroy harmful organisms. Canned or bottled draft beer is filtered through extremely fine filters to remove these organisms. This makes it unnecessary to pasteurize the product, which would spoil the draft taste.

SERVING NONALCOHOLIC DRINKS

Milk is usually served chilled and seldom with ice unless requested. The glass used is normally a tall highball, but goblets or plain 8-ounce glasses can also be used. Buttermilk, chocolate milk, and other complete milk drinks will be served in the same manner as milk. In the more casual dining operations, milk may be brought to the table in its paper carton resting on a small plate. Milk is often served to children in a plastic cup, with a lid and a straw.

Milkshakes, malted milks, and other milk and ice cream mixtures are served in tall, thick glasses topped often with whipped cream and a cherry. A straw and ice cream spoon should be served with them.

Juices are often served in a 6-ounce glass, but some large portions may be served in an 8- or 10-ounce glass. A highball glass may also be used. They should be served chilled but seldom are iced. In some operations servers pour their own juices; if so, attention must be paid to see the liquids are properly handled and refrigerated; they are highly perishable.

Although bottled waters have been around for a long time, they have increased in popularity in the last decade. They may be poured from the container and brought to the table or the opened bottle may be brought to the table and poured there by the server. Usually the glass used is the tumbler type; other shapes and sizes of glassware are used, depending upon the desires of the operation. When serving from a bottle at the table, it is proper to place the glass with ice on the table and pour by filling about a half of the glass. Sometimes a guest may request more and the server pours the glass to about three-fourths full. As with water, most guests dislike handling a glass filled nearly to the rim. In upscale operations the glass is placed on a small plate lined with a doily.

Carbonated beverages are often served to diners throughout the entire meal. Some guests will order sodas without caffeine and diet sodas. Some operations garnish certain drinks with a slice of lemon or other fruit. The service of carbonated beverages is the same as for bottled waters. If carbonated drinks are served from a soda gun they must be ordered from the bar. In some operations, servers operate a fountain themselves.

SERVING ALCOHOL RESPONSIBLY

One has a greater chance of avoiding legal and criminal action and successfully handling problems related to alcohol beverages if there is a responsibly planned and continuously reviewed set of policies and procedures for every aspect of alcoholic beverage service. The following policies and procedures, in addition to those management thinks are important, should be in place:

1. Written policies and procedures include never serving a person alcohol to a point of intoxication, or serving an already intoxicated person, or serving minors.

2. Have good training program in alcohol service and in seeing those engaged in alcoholic beverage service are well trained in it, including disciplinary procedures for those who disobey them.

3. Eliminate certain marketing ideas, like 2-for-1s, and oversized drink promotions.

4. Check every young guest's ID to ensure minors are not served alcoholic beverages.

5. Offer food and nonalcoholic beverages.

6. Ensure that intoxicated guest do not drive away from the establishment. Call the police if one refuses assistance and does drive away.

7. Record all incidents in a log book.

The service of beverage alcohol is big business to the foodservice industry, but today their service to the public entails much more responsibility than it did in the past. This is because of numerous court decisions that have increased the liability of those engaged in serving alcohol to the public. Today those serving alcohol can be charged with responsibility for any mishap that might come to someone who becomes intoxicated from drinks served by them. The business in which the drinks are served can also be charged. If a person becomes intoxicated from drinks served in an operation and injures others because of the intoxication, both the server and the operation could be charged with what is called third-party liability. Heavy fines and even prison sentences are now possible.

Because of this greater responsibility, many states now require that those who serve alcohol take a course in alcohol awareness. These courses typically include training in the possible consequences of overserving, how to recognize signs of intoxication, how to tell guests they can no longer be served alcohol, and what to do in case someone arrives or becomes intoxicated. Servers must look for attitude changes, body language, speech, disruptive behavior, and any other deviation from normal behavior. The server, with support from a manager, must be trained to assess each situation and decide what action to take.

Alcoholic beverage service laws and their enforcement differ from area to area. The first rule of responsible alcohol service is to know and obey the laws that apply to the establishment. Currently, no federal agency sets standards for all beverage alcohol service, as the Food and Drug Administration (FDA) does for food safety and sanitation. Agencies such as police departments, departments of transportation, beverage alcohol commissions, and beverage alcohol and substance abuse associations can enforce local laws.

Most states use the BAC (blood alcohol concentration) test to determine intoxication. (See Figure 5.14.) A BAC of 0.08 or more is considered intoxication in all states—this means that there are at least 0.08 drops of pure alcohol for every 1,000 drops of blood. A 150- to 180-pound person adds 0.02 to 0.03 BAC for every drink consumed—a drink is considered either two ounces of 80 proof spirit, 12 ounces of regular beer, or three ounces of 14 percent wine. About six ounces of 6 percent white wine would be about the same; this is why so many customers now ask for white wine—the alcohol content is lower. Four or five drinks brings about intoxication. A person below 150 pounds builds up a BAC of 0.04 for every drink, so three is a maximum. The normal body destroys about 0.04 BAC per hour. Thus, serving a 175-pound man five drinks in an hour should put the man in the red zone. (One system of monitoring intoxication puts a person with a low BAC in the green zone, one approaching intoxication in the yellow zone, while one who is in danger of being or is intoxicated is said to be in the red zone.) The reason the man having five drinks in an hour is in the red zone is that if each drink contributes 0.025 BAC, he has had enough alcohol to build a BAC of 0.125 (1×0.025), but his body has probably destroyed 0.04 BAC and so he should have a BAC of 0.085 ($0.125 - 0.04$). This is close enough to 0.10 for the server to take cautionary measures.

BAC, or blood alcohol level, indicates how intoxicated a person is.

Body Weight	Number of Drinks* during a two-hour period									
100 lbs	1	2	3	4	5	6	7	8	9	10
120 lbs	1	2	3	4	5	6	7	8	9	10
140 lbs	1	2	3	4	5	6	7	8	9	10
160 lbs	1	2	3	4	5	6	7	8	9	10
180 lbs	1	2	3	4	5	6	7	8	9	10
200 lbs	1	2	3	4	5	6	7	8	9	10
220 lbs	1	2	3	4	5	6	7	8	9	10
240 lbs	1	2	3	4	5	6	7	8	9	10
	Be Careful Driving BAC to 0.05%			Driving May Be Impaired 0.05–0.09%**			Do Not Drive 0.10% and up		

BAC—Blood Alcohol Concentration

 * One drink is 1 1/4 oz of 80-proof liquor, 12 oz. of beer, or 3 oz. of 14% wine.
** In all states, legal intoxication is 0.08%.

This chart provides averages only. Individuals may vary and factors, such as food in the stomach, medication, and fatigue, can affect your tolerance.

Courtesy of the National Restaurant Association.
Source: Distilled Spirits Council of the United States, Incorporated.

FIGURE 5.14 BAC chart.

Carefully check IDs. Many establishments check IDs of anyone who looks younger than 30. Clubs or bars patronized by young people often check everyone's ID. In either case, be sure that IDs are valid and depict the person presenting the ID. Minors frequently obtain alcoholic beverages by presenting someone else's ID or a fake one. Set up a complete ID-checking station at each entrance and staff it with employees trained in this task.

To verify customer identification if customer requests an alcoholic beverage, take these steps:

1. Ask for identification from customer.

2. Examine identification.
    - Verify photo is that of customer.
    - Verify date of birth.
    - For identifications in question, compare to ID guidebook:
        Problem Possibility:
          Customer does not look like photograph.
        Problem Response:
          Obtain other form of identification.
        Problem Possibility:
          Customer does not have any identification.
        Problem Response:
          Politely refuse to serve alcohol.
        Problem Possibility:
          Customer does not have a driver's license.
        Problem Response:
          Examine other acceptable form of identification.
        Problem Possibility:
          A dispute of validity of the identification of a customer arises.
        Problem Response:
          Contact management and brief manager or head waiter on situation.

3. Thank customer and return identification.

4. Check everyone in the party who is questionable.

State liquor codes govern liquor licenses. One should establish a good relationship with law enforcement and regulatory agents in your area by adhering to your state liquor code and practicing good business ethics. Disobeying liquor code regulations is a criminal violation that can result in fines, imprisonment, and suspension or loss of your liquor license.

Each area's liquor code covers a variety of regulations, but the key issue is who not to server. In most areas it is illegal to server alcoholic beverages to the following people:

- Minors under 21 (All guests must be able to show proper picture identification establishing their age.)

- People who are already intoxicated

There is no penalty for refusing to serve someone you merely suspect is a minor or an intoxicated person. You have the right to protect your guests, yourself, and your establishment's liquor license.

CHAPTER SUMMARY

Beverage service requires specialized knowledge. Beverage alcohol has enjoyed a long and distinguished history, and has played an important role in human religious, social, and philosophical development. Today, restaurants and hotels may find a third to half of their net profit comes from beverage alcohol service.

Alcohol is produced by the fermentation of a carbohydrate, which is changed by the process into alcohol and carbon dioxide. The amount of alcohol is stated in terms of proof, which is twice the percentage of its pure alcohol. The alcohol content of wines and beers is stated in percent of volume. Because alcohol is lighter than water, it takes more to make the same weight as water. Thus, a spirit of 12 proof, which is twice its real alcoholic content or it is actually 6 percent by amount or weight, has less alcohol than a wine or beer of 6 percent in volume. Put this way, if it is a jigger of alcohol versus a jigger of water, the jigger of water is greater than the jigger of alcohol. It takes just a bit more alcohol to make the same weight. Thus, a wine or beer of 6 percent by volume has less alcohol than a spirit of 6 percent by weight.

Spirits include whiskeys, gins, brandies, vodkas, rums, and grain-neutral spirits. Grain-neutral spirits are used as the base of cordials, vodkas, gins, and for blending into whiskies.

Wines are categorized into three types: table wines, sparkling wines, and fortified wines. Tables wines are still. Sparkling wines, including Champagne, are bubbling with carbon dioxide. Fortified wines have added alcohol, usually brandy. Fortified wines include apéritifs, vermouths, port, sherry, and Madeira.

Red grape varieties include Barbera, Cabernet Sauvignon, Gamay, Grenache, Merlot, Nebbiolo, Pinot Noir, Sangiovese, Syrah (or Shiraz), and Zinfandel. White grape varieties include Chardonnay, Chenin Blanc, Gewurtztraminer, Muller-Thurgau, Muscat, Pinot Blanc, Riesling, Sauvignon Blanc, Semillon, Silvaner, and Trebbiano. Wines may be named for their predominant grape, generic type, or brand name.

The five steps of tasting wine are looking, swirling, smelling, tasting, and finish. Although there are general guidelines for pairing particular wines with foods, the most important consideration in a restaurant is the guest's preference.

Beer is made from grains, yeast, hops, water, and and a fermentable product called an adjunct. Types of beer include lagers, pilsners, ales, stouts, porters, malt liquor, bock beer, light beers, steam beer, dry beer, and ice beer.

Coffee, tea, and hot chocolate service are very much the same. Servers must use precaution when serving these hot beverages. The two best known coffee bean varieties are Robusta and Arabica. Well-brewed coffee should be served at about 160°F (71.1°C) and held no longer than one hour. Popular coffee drinks include espresso, cappuccino, caffé latte, and café au lait. Teas come in a variety of colors and flavors, and are best served in a pot. Servers should know the appropriate garnish for the wide variety of hot beverages available.

Bar service requires many skills of bartenders besides the ability to mix and serve drinks. Speed, precision, service skills, and attention to good sanitation are equally important. Basic knowledge behind the bar includes the ability to mix a wide variety of drinks, as well as knowing the difference between well liquors and call brands.

Spirits may be served straight up, on the rocks, mixed with one mixer, or as a cocktail. Drinks may be built, stirred, shaken, or blended. Brandy is traditionally served in a snifter.

Review the steps of serving wine carefully. The guest dining experience depends greatly on the impression left by the server's grace and speed in presenting, opening, and pouring wine. The server must be able to suggest wines and answer questions about any wine on the list. Extra care is required when serving sparkling wine so that the cork does not fly out of the bottle.

Beer must be served with a healthy head, which is accomplished only by pouring from the bottle or draft-beer system at the correct angle.

The legal climate surrounding alcohol service has changed drastically in the last decade as third-party liability has become more common. All servers of alcohol must be trained in responsible service, which includes knowing how alcohol affects the body in terms of blood alcohol content (BAC), how to monitor and control guests' drinking, and what to do when a guest becomes intoxicated and tries to drive away. Remember that a full training program in this area is required in most states, and thorough training helps protect an operation in case of a third-party lawsuit.

KEY TERMS

alkal	black tea	bottom fermented
anejo/muy anejo	blended	bouquet
apéritif	blood alcohol content (BAC)	brand-name
Arabica	blushes	brut
armagnac	bock beers	cacoa tree
aroma	bonded	cahuch

call stock	Jean de la Roque	rosé
calvados	jiggers	sediment
Champagne	Kaffa	sparkling wines
clouding	lager method	spirits
Coffee Arabica	light-bodied rums	still
cognac	liqueurs	stout
Cordials	malt liquor	sommelier
demi-sec	maltose	straight
dessert wines	methyline chloride	Taktacalah
ethyl alcohol	mixology	tannin
extraction time	nibs	T'e
fermentation	on the rocks	tea
finish	oolong tea	third-party liability
fortified	pilsner	top fermented
generic	porter	trichlorethylene
Grand Reserve	proof	varietal
green tea	proprietary name	Vieux
hops	red, yellow, and green zones	VS
	Robusta	well stock

CHAPTER REVIEW

1. How does aging affect spirits, wine, and beer?

2. What is BAC? At what level of BAC do most states say one is intoxicated? About how much alcohol does the ordinary person break down per hour?

3. If a spirit is 80 proof, what is its alcohol content?

4. How is bourbon different from other types of whiskey?

5. What is used to make rum?

6. How high should wine glasses be filled?

7. List the qualifications you would want in hiring a bartender.

8. What is well stock? What is a call brand?

9. A party of six comes in for service, two of whom appear to be minors. What should the server do?

10. Describe how to pull the cork out of a bottle of wine.

11. Taste a Scotch, an Irish whiskey, a bourbon, and a rye. Write one word to describe the flavor of each.

   (1) Scotch: _____

   (2) Irish whiskey: _____

   (3) Bourbon: _____

   (4) Rye: _____

12. Taste each of the following spirits, and write one word to describe the flavor of each.

    (1) Sambuca: _____

    (2) Curacao: _____

    (3) Gin: _____

    (4) Vodka: _____

    (5) Rum: _____

    (6) Cognac: _____

    (7) Tequila: _____

13. Set up four plates of food: one salty, one with red meat, one with fish, and one with a cream sauce. Taste each food along with a sip of each of the following wines. Describe the flavor of each combination.

    (1) Sparkling wine:_____

           Salt: _____

           Meat: _____

           Fish: _____

           Cream: _____

    (2) Cabernet Sauvignon: _____

           Salt: _____

           Meat: _____

           Fish: _____

           Cream: _____

    (3) Chardonnay: _____

           Salt: _____

           Meat: _____

           Fish: _____

           Cream: _____

    (4) Merlot: _____

           Salt: _____

           Meat: _____

           Fish: _____

           Cream: _____

    (5) Pinot Noir: _____

           Salt: _____

           Meat: _____

           Fish: _____

           Cream: _____

14. Set up four plates of food: one salty, one with red meat, one with fish, and one with a cream sauce. Taste each food along with a sip of each of the following beers. Describe the flavor of each combination.

    (1) Stout: _____

           Salt: _____

           Meat: _____

Fish: _____

Cream: _____

(2)   Porter: _____

Salt: _____

Meat: _____

Fish: _____

Cream: _____

(3)   Weiss: _____

Salt: _____

Meat: _____

Fish: _____

Cream: _____

(4)   Pilsner: _____

Salt: _____

Meat: _____

Fish: _____

Cream: _____

(5)   Pale ale: _____

Salt: _____

Meat: _____

Fish: _____

Cream: _____

15.   Invent a new coffee drink that contains at least three ingredients, including a garnish. Write the recipe here.

_____

_____

_____

_____

_____

_____

_____

_____

_____

_____

_____

_____

_____

_____

_____

_____

_____

_____

Case Studies

THE IDEAL SERVER

You are to present your ideas to the class on what you feel is the ideal server. Write a list of the things you feel are important. Be sure to include ideas on serving people with various handicaps, handling alcohol problems, and mollifying difficult guests who try to raise an argument.

THE AWARD PROBLEM

The manager of a white tablecloth restaurant decides to give an award to the server who sells the most wine in a two-week period. She decides to give different points for various priced wines with the server with the highest score winning $500. She publishes the following price and point schedule for the contest:

WINE PRICE	POINTS
Under $10.00	10
$10.01–$15.00	15
15.01–20.00	20
20.01–25.00	25
25.01–30.00	30
30.01–35.00	35
35.01–40.00	40
40.01–45.00	45
45.01–50.00 and over	50

The contest was a spirited one and enjoyed by all the servers. There was much camaraderie and general good will developed by the servers. Mary Jones was declared the winner with 134 bottles of wine sold and 2,808 points. Joe Tobias was a close runner-up, with 122 bottles sold for a total of 2,788 points. The rest of the server staff did fairly well, but these two were the leaders. When the manager found the contest boosted sales by 12.1 percent, she considered the contest very worthwhile.

A few days later, Joe Tobias made his own check of his total bottle sales and points. He found he sold 126 bottles of wine with total points of 2,815. He called management's attention to what he believed was a mistake in the calculations. The manager checked the figures herself and found that the person who made the original calculations had indeed made a mistake. Tobias was the winner.

What should management do? Nothing? What would be the results if this were done? Should she ask Mary Jones for the $500 back and give it to Joe? Should she instead call it a tie and also give Joe $500? Is this a good or bad way to solve the problem? Explain your reasoning.

The manager realizes she has a morale problem here. The wrong decision could destroy staff morale and the chances of ever running a successful contest again.

Critique this contest on the basis of using this point system for deciding the winner. Was there an easier and simpler way? Was it a good idea to give only a first prize? What would you have done? Why?

Set up your own rules for running such a contest.

MANAGEMENT'S ROLE
IN SERVICE*

Outline

---

* Authored by Lendal H. Kotschevar and Valentino Luciani.

Learning Objectives

After reading this chapter, you should be able to:

■ Describe management functions necessary to a successful operation.

■ Explain how motivating and training servers helps an operation deliver excellent customer service.

INTRODUCTION

Good service comes not only from servers, but also from managers. Managers bear a great responsibility for establishing service standards, motivating servers, scheduling servers, training servers, and providing them with the equipment, tools, and environment they need to do their job well. The establishment of good service is a partnership task between managers and servers working as a team to deliver it.

To have good service, management must set high service standards, communicate them to employees, see that they are met or exceeded, and support employees in their efforts through training and recognition. Unless this is done, servers are apt to establish their own standards and practice them. This may not give the best in service.

ESTABLISHING SERVICE STANDARDS

Standards can be defined as specific rules, principles, or measures established to guide employees in performing their duties consistently. With standards, management can measure and evaluate employee performance and operation performance toward pleasing guests.

Service standards include service policies and service mechanics models, such as how to pour water, how to deliver food to the table, how to set up a table, or how to prepare a service station. Management establishes service standards based on the type of operation and the quality of service management wants to achieve. In a fine-dining environment, the service standards for wine service are usually more extended and elaborate than they are in an informal, family-style operation (see Chapter 5).

The first step in managing and delivering quality service is to set up and communicate service standards. Setting service standards involves seven distinct steps by managers:

1. Set standards and describe them in detail.

2. Establish policies and procedures for accomplishing these standards. A *policy* is a plan or course of action to meet a standard. A *procedure* is the manner in which that plan is implemented.

3. Provide the necessary space, equipment, and environment to achieve standards.

4. Provide adequate training and guidance to servers and ensure that standards are met.

5. Review with employees periodically, so they know and understand how standards performance will be measured.

6. Train employees to perform specific tasks to meet standards. Follow up with checklists, sidework, tasks lists, and job descriptions.

7. Encourage and seek out employee feedback so management can be aware of problems that need correction.

Experienced managers are unanimous in reporting that the establishment of standards is a relatively simple task. The most difficult task is to train employees in those standards and then see that they follow them consistently day after day. Often, management establishes the standards and then delegates to secondary management the task of seeing that they are followed.

Standards vary, from the elegant service required in a fine-dining establishment to that appropriate for casual dining facilities. This book discusses typical full-service standards, but every operation must interpret these to suit its guests. In other words, what is correct and what is not correct will depend on the operation and situation. Specific standards have to be built for each operation, and it is management's responsibility to establish them.

MANAGEMENT FUNCTIONS

Good service occurs when operations are well managed. A poorly run organization is unsettling to employees and leads to poor productivity and work performance. Seeing that an operation is properly run is a management responsibility and revolves around managers performing five management functions: planning, organizing, staffing, leading, and controlling.

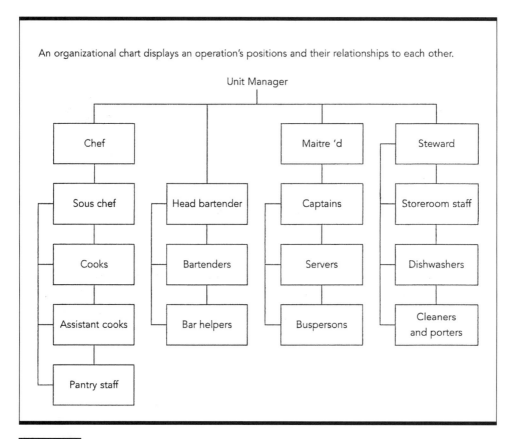

An organizational chart displays an operation's positions and their relationships to each other.

FIGURE 6.1 A sample organization chart.

Planning

The planning task starts with establishing a mission and goals for the organization and its people. This should be done with input from all employees, including servers. After all, who knows customers better than the people who serve them every day? All employees must have a stake in organizational goals or they won't be realized. Once goals are set, managers must see that realistic plans are developed, followed, and revised so these goals are met.

Organizing

Organizing applies to all of an organization's processes and resources, including its people. An organizational chart shows an operation's positions and their relationships to each other, including who reports to whom. (See Figure 6.1.) When responsibility and authority in an organization flow from the top down, it is known as a line organization. In practice, a hostess may be responsible for servers and to an assistant manager, who reports to a manager. A number of head waiters may be responsible to the hostess, and each head waiter may have a group of servers responsible to him or her. Large hotels tend to use a complex line organization, from food and beverage managers, to maitre d', to dining room captains, to chefs de rang (food servers), to commis (assistant servers), to buspersons. An important factor in line organization is that people should have to report to only one immediate superior. Reporting to more than one person and circumventing proper communication channels can cause needless frustration and miscommunication. For example, *unity of command,* as defined by management theory, ensures that all employees throughout the operation follow the same policies and regulations.

If a number of employees have a problem with their supervisor, they should be encouraged to talk to another person with authority to effect results.

Many organizations are replacing line organization with an approach called *team effort.* One version of this is the reverse pyramid in which the manager is at the bottom of the pyramid, supervisors are in the middle, and front-line employees are on the top. In this model, managers are seen as serving front-line employees so they can better serve customers (see Figure 6.2).

An important component of organization is delegation. Responsibilities and tasks can be delegated to employees, but the delegator does not escape responsibility for seeing that the job is done properly. An important part of delegating responsibility is also to give an employee authority to accomplish the work. Without authority, employees' hands are tied.

Proper delegation can work to the advantage of management:

- It can help the manager perform better on the job.
- It can be instrumental in establishing a definite sense of pride in the employee charged with the new responsibility.
- It can save managers time by freeing them from some tasks that will allow them to give that time to other important tasks.

Proper delegation requires the following:

- The delegatee must know how to do the delegated tasks.
- The person being delegated to do a task must be willing to do it.
- The person delegating assignments must provide the resources and all the assistance needed to do the job. The delegatee must be given the authority to do the tasks. If this is not given, usually the delegation tasks are not done or are improperly done.

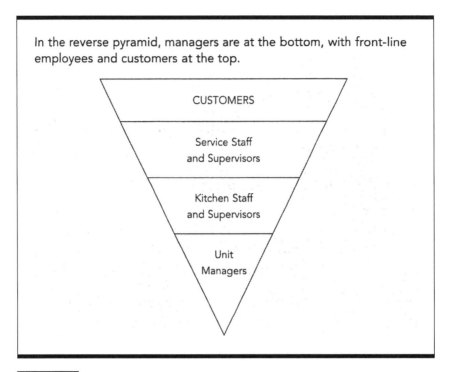

In the reverse pyramid, managers are at the bottom, with front-line employees and customers at the top.

CUSTOMERS

Service Staff
and Supervisors

Kitchen Staff
and Supervisors

Unit
Managers

FIGURE 6.2 A sample reverse pyramid organization chart.

Staffing

Hiring qualified employees is the first step in creating an excellent service staff. Hiring an employee that knows what is expected and will meet operation standards is more important than hiring an employee that simply acknowledges the specific duties of the job. Just because an employee has done the job before does not mean they will meet the hiring operation's standards. The person doing the hiring must ascertain whether those seeking positions have the necessary abilities and attitudes for the job, and reject those that do not have the necessary attributes.

One builds a staff by first determining what tasks must be performed to achieve the desired goal and then allocating positions so that these tasks are performed. After this, job specifications are written up, indicating what the person in each position does. Figure 6.3 is an example of a job description written up for a server. The next step is to hire people who can adequately fill these positions.

A staff consists of a group of individuals who are working together toward a common goal. A number of specialized positions are needed to perform the various

---

Job descriptions indicate the necessary requirements for each position in the organization.

Job Title	Server
Job Summary	Serves guests in all ways to ensure maximum sales and profits
	Coordinates service of meals to customers to ensure 100 percent satisfaction, including troubleshooting and resolution of all complaints
	Acts as primary bridge of communication between the operation's management and its customers
Job Objectives	Greets guests warmly and sincerely
	Informs guests of specials, signature items, and specialties of the operation
	Suggests menu items to guests and answers questions about the menu
	Works with guests to solve all service-related problems
	Keeps manager informed of potential and actual service problems
	Gives guests' orders to the chef and other kitchen employees accurately and in a timely manner
	Expedites orders and verifies that they are correct and complete before serving guests
	Serves all menu items to customers in a timely and courteous manner, according to the management's dictates
	Provides continuous service to customers throughout the meal
	Totals customer checks with 100 percent accuracy and presents checks to customers
	Thanks all customers for their patronage and invites them back

---

FIGURE 6.3 Job description for a server.

tasks. In food service there will be a culinary staff, a server staff, a managing staff, and perhaps others. Within each staff will be various positions. For example, within the service staff the positions are a host or hostess, servers, buspersons and others. Each staff works together as a team to perform its functions, and the various staffs then blend their efforts together to achieve their goal. All servers should realize this and make themselves a part of the team. If they do, it will make their job a better one. Individuals working alone are without help. Being a member of a team helps to carry one along much more easily and smoothly.

Leading

An operation cannot succeed without effective leadership. To be a good leader, one must know what the goal of the operation is and then take firm and adequate steps to reach that goal. Good leaders must command respect and good will, as well as success and profits. Good leadership motivates workers to do their best, and sees that workers are treated fairly and are given a chance to reach their goals.

Leadership styles run the gamut, from strict authoritarians to passive leaders. The recommended style today is a mixture of these, called participative leadership. In this style of leadership, the manager is a part of a team working with the employees toward a common goal. Traditionally, hospitality industry leaders have been authoritative, or dictatorial. There are reasons for this: (1) The nature of the industry was extremely competitive, with little time to promote a team atmosphere; (2) Managers had little time to train employees and had to set up tight control measures to see they were followed; (3) Because of the high employee turnover in the industry, managers were not able to build teams among their staff. As the labor market and the industry changed, managers found they had to change their management style to survive.

While authoritative leaders rule with little or no employee input and use fear of discharge or punishment to motivate action, participative leaders act as coaches to lead teams to success. Such leaders seek out ideas and opinions of workers and often follow them, giving employees a feeling of value and respect. They work alongside employees when necessary, creating a feeling of fellowship and the sharing of responsibilities.

Participative leaders still must ensure that standards are met and that rules are applied consistently and fairly. Participative leaders, rather than reprimanding and punishing, point out problems to employees and help correct them. This is why standards are so important, so that employees understand what is expected. It is important to specify the corrective action when pointing out mistakes, and to be as positive as is appropriate. Managers should correct the words, actions, or attitudes, not the employee personally. Counseling sessions should be held in private without any tones of anger or threats. They should be done more to make the employee feel they are being offered help rather than criticized.

Controlling

Controls lead an operation toward achieving its goals. Without controls, operations lose money and workers become frustrated and unhappy. Establishing standards and procedures for meeting them is key. Examples of service controls include the following:

- Greeting guests within one minute of being seated
- Serving lunches in less than fifteen minutes
- Receiving fewer than ten guest complaints per month
- Knowing the specific steps to take when guests complain

Servers and managers should check continuously to see that deviations from standards are avoided or corrected.

MOTIVATING SERVERS

Management is responsible for seeing that employees are motivated and that they work in a motivating environment. To ensure good service, managers must develop a staff of servers that want to do the best possible job and do it consistently. Developing a motivated staff is not easy and management should make it one of its most important goals.

People are motivated to work by a number of factors. Primarily are the basic needs for food, housing, transportation, and so forth. Next comes the need to work in an environment that is safe and secure. Following this are social and environmental needs; people want to feel in any job situation that they belong and they are an accepted member of a group. A number of people also are motivated to work just to get a change in environment—elderly people may work because they are lonesome and bored with their home surroundings. Next comes the need to satisfy self or ego needs—people may like the independence of having their own income or just want the pride of having a job. And lastly, one may work to realize self-actualization or achievement needs—a teenager may become a busperson not only to have an income but to assert maturity.

It is a mistake to think that everyone is motivated in their work by all these needs. Some workers barely rise above basic security and safety needs, while others are motivated by all of them. Teenagers have different needs than more mature adults, and elderly workers often have different needs than those in other age groups.

Managers should not only try to satisfy the needs that workers have, but should also seek to extend them to higher levels. It will result in more satisfied employees. Every individual also has pet needs. If management can satisfy these, a more satisfied worker is made.

Hiring Motivated Servers

As indicated previously, hiring is the first step to achieving motivated employees. Often the motivated employee can be detected in the interview by certain personality traits:

- A genuine interest and respect for people
- A warm and outgoing attitude toward life
- A sincere wish for the job
- Habits that will not interfere with the job
- A willingness to accept an entry-level position if they have little or no experience
- A positive job record
- Poise and confidence
- An ability to solve problems and make good decisions
- A pleasing appearance
- Experience working in good operations, if applicable
- Positive reasons for working other than income
- Willingness to grow in the job and eventually be promotable
- Good self-direction and self-reliance

People must possess self-motivation to work hard and serve people enthusiastically. The following interview questions might help in evaluating an applicant's capability of becoming a well-motivated server.

1. What was the biggest challenge you had in your current/last position? How did you meet that challenge?
2. What are your strengths? What are your weaknesses?
3. Have you ever had problems following instructions?

4. What type of goals have you set for yourself?

5. What do you see yourself doing five years from now?

6. Do you consider yourself a person that performs service duties with enthusiasm and dedication?

7. Do you like to deal with and be around people?

8. What do you expect from your coworkers?

9. What do you expect from your supervisors?

10. Can you point out how you introduced a new idea that improved your work or the work of others? How did it make you feel?

11. How would you handle a guest who is irate because the order was served late and the food was cold?

There are laws that restrict what one can ask while interviewing people for jobs. These relate to questions about things that are not job related. For example:

1. Have you ever been arrested or accused of stealing?

2. Do you have a green card?

3. How long have you lived at this address?

4. Are you the wage earner in your family?

5. Are you married? What does your spouse do?

6. How many children do you have or plan to have?

7. How old are you?

8. What would you say your credit rating is?

Creating a Motivating Environment

One of the most important things managers must do to motivate employees is to see that a respectful, pleasant environment prevails. This helps servers feel both secure and appreciated, as well as motivated to give good service. One highly successful manager has said, "I treat my employees as I treat my customers; both are valued." A positive environment fosters team work and cooperation among servers. This is essential in the often pressure-filled, fast-paced, and demanding profession of serving.

To ensure good service, one must develop a staff of servers who want to do the best possible job, and do so consistently. One must create a feeling of respect and commitment between team members, with managers participating in this team. Establishing standards and enhancing jobs such as empowering workers, or doing all one can to make the work easier are good motivators. Encouraging open communication, including servers in goal setting, treating employees fairly and with respect, and creating awards for good performance are others.

Some managers do things that destroy motivation:

- Assigning extra work without adequate compensation in praise, promotion, or other recognition.
- Demonstrating unfair or nonuniform treatment or aggressive, abusive, cold, inconsistent, or stand-offish behavior.
- Failing to provide good communication, supplies, tools, or other standard conditions.
- Ridiculing or using sarcasm instead of constructive criticism.
- Oversupervising and showing a lack of independence and trust.
- Failing to follow up on problems mentioned by servers.
- Being indecisive or unwilling to support servers.
- Making decisions, without consulting servers, that might interfere with their being able to adequately do their jobs.
- Having too many bosses.

Empowering Employees

Empowerment is a management tool in which employees are given the power to make decisions that achieve higher standards of service. This power includes the authority and responsibility to make things happen. For example, instead of a server having to go to a superior to approve a meal deduction, the server is empowered to make the decision in order to correct the problem. Servers may be given some guidelines so they know what is and is not appropriate. Empowerment benefits servers, who are likely to feel more personal commitment to serving guests well. Empowered employees likewise benefit employers. Problems solved more quickly are better served. Dissatisfied customers are helped more quickly, and situations are resolved.

Rewards as Motivators

There are many ways management can let employees know when they are doing a good job and thus motivate them toward doing an even better one. Positive feedback and recognition of a job well done are very valuable. Monetary rewards and prizes may also be given. Many operations have an employee-of-the-month and employee-of-the-year award. Recognition of servers to guests is very powerful. Some operations offer servers bonuses after a certain length of employment. Others use extra vacation days, dining credits, concert tickets, amusement park passes, and trips to reward excellence performance. Achievement is traditionally rewarded with advancement.

Rewards should be open to all in the same category, and all must be given complete information on what is required to get the reward. Monitor the program and evaluate it; does the program achieve its desired objective? Give the award as soon as possible after it has been won and tell them exactly why they qualify. Make the award worthwhile. The award program should be respected by the servers.

Things like offering adequate health care for servers and their dependents, giving educational assistance or assistance in personal problems, and even day care assistance for children can be good motivators to keep servers on the job. Whatever the incentive, managers should give them consistently and tie them to concrete behaviors. Special favors will undermine any incentive plan.

Remember that respect and loyalty cannot be purchased. It must be earned through sincere actions. Servers will see through attempts to be manipulated. Unless incentives are given appropriately, they will act as demotivators rather than motivators. Money alone rarely satisfies employees. In a survey taken of what employees want, the following motivators were mentioned frequently:

- Job security
- Good working conditions
- Appreciation
- Job satisfaction
- Good wages
- Acceptance
- Dignity and respect
- Good benefits

Note that only two (good wages, benefits) of the eight items are monetary; the other six deal with psychological factors that can cost little or nothing.

FIGURE 6.4 Rewards are great motivators for employees and can help promote job satisfaction. Courtesy Corbis Digital Stock.

Unless servers get a sense of gratification from doing a good job, they lose interest. The work must have meaning to them and it must help them reach their own personal goals. Managers need to know that they cannot reach their goals unless employees reach theirs.

Evaluations as Motivators

The formal way of giving employees feedback on how well they are doing is the performance evaluation, or appraisal. Managers should make it clear that the purpose of evaluations is to help the employees develop and improve. It is important that servers know that evaluations are positive, not negative. Evaluations should let employees know their opportunities for advancement.

The evaluator should look at customer comments, dollars produced, tips, covers served, and other factors to make the evaluation. Other intangible factors, such as attitude, teamwork, and punctuality, should also be included. A performance record should be kept.

Appraisals can be helpful to management in giving information on employees attitudes, goals, needs, and concerns. The information gained can also be helpful in giving advancement, pay increases, rewards, and what management must do to further the employee's pursuit of goals.

A good appraisal leaves employees more sure about how well they are doing and what has to be done to improve. The things that need to be done for advancement, better pay, or other benefits can be learned.

SCHEDULING SERVERS

Proper scheduling can be a good motivating factor. It is essential that all workers be treated fairly in scheduling. Some operations have a scheduling system that rotates servers among the different stations because some stations are easier to work or give better tips than others. Requests for special days off or certain hours should be given consideration and allowed, if possible.

Managers are responsible for seeing that adequate, competent servers are scheduled at the right times. If too little help is on the floor, good service is impossible. If underscheduling is consistently done, servers will slow down and management will create a very difficult problem for itself (see Figure 6.5).

The number of covers in a station should be assigned according to the stations' distance from the kitchen. Team service allows at least one server per station to attend to guests while others do other work. Experienced buspersons also help in placing orders and delivering food and beverages.

	Monday	Tuesday	Wednesday	Thursday	Friday	Saturday	Sunday
Jenn	Off	10 a.m.–3 p.m.	Off	10 a.m.–4 p.m.	10 a.m.–3 p.m.	10 a.m.–4:00 p.m.	11 a.m.–7 p.m.
Terry	Off	11 a.m.–7 p.m.	10 a.m.–4 p.m.	10 a.m.–3 p.m.	Off	11 a.m.–7 p.m.	10 a.m.–3 p.m.
Damon	Off	10 a.m.–4 p.m.	10 a.m.–3 p.m.	Off	10 a.m.–4 p.m.	10 a.m.–3 p.m.	10 a.m.–4 p.m.
Kate	Off	Off	4 p.m.–close	3 p.m.–close	3 p.m.–close	4 p.m.–close	3 p.m.–close
Carlos	Off	3 p.m.–close	11 a.m.–7 p.m.	4 p.m.–close	11 a.m.–7 p.m.	Off	4 p.m.–close
Lisa	Off	4 p.m.–close	3 p.m.–close	11 a.m.–7 p.m.	4 p.m.–close	3 p.m.–close	Off
Deb	Off	3 p.m.–10 p.m. →				→	Off
Kyiel	Off	Off	4 p.m.–close	10 a.m.–4 p.m.	4 p.m.–9 p.m.	4 p.m.–9 p.m.	4 p.m.–9 p.m.
Shawn	Off	11 a.m.–7 p.m.	10 a.m.–3 p.m.	6 a.m.–11 a.m.	3 p.m.–close	Off	5 p.m.–close
Rosa	Off	10 a.m.–4 p.m.	Off	2 p.m.–9 p.m.	10 a.m.–4 p.m.	11 a.m.–6 p.m.	4 p.m.–10 p.m.
Dan	Off	4 p.m.–close	10 a.m.–3 p.m.	Off	11 a.m.–6 p.m.	5 p.m.–close	11 a.m.–6 p.m.
Yi	Off	2 p.m.–8 p.m.	10 a.m.–4 p.m.	4 p.m.–close	Off	5 p.m.–close	10 a.m.–3 p.m.

FIGURE 6.5 Sample server schedule.

Managers should take advantage of computer software programs that can help in planning better station assignments, scheduling, analyzing payroll, and monitoring service.

DINING ROOM ARRANGEMENT

The dining area must be planned properly to allow for good service. Aisles through which servers must move while carrying heavy trays must be wide enough to allow for safe and good passage. Often managers are tempted to add too many tables, cutting down on space for servers. This is one good way to achieve poor service. Twelve square feet per guest is the minimum for regular table service and 20 square feet per guest is required for counter service. Club and luxury dining areas often have more than 12 square feet per guest. Banquet service requires less. Distances between tables should be 4 to 5 feet so that aisle space between servers is not restricted. The table should allow at least 24 inches of linear space per cover. Thus, a table for four should be at least 30 inches square.

Managers should see there is adequate room for tray stands, service stations, and other service equipment. One to four servers typically use one service station; the fewer the better. If possible, water should be piped to the station. In fine-dining operations, a carving station may be placed among tables for carving, deboning, and other activities. Mobile service or carving stations may be used. These can save space and give more flexibility in arranging tables.

Tray stands, service stations, and other things needed to give good service should be kept in order and be sufficient in number.

KITCHEN ARRANGEMENT

Managers will assist servers by seeing that a smooth-flowing kitchen arrangement is set up. Unnecessary backtracking leads to delays, accidents, and frustration. A melee of workers going in all directions during busy periods makes things hectic for everyone, including cooks. A smooth, one-way flow, with pick-up arranged in sequence of courses, is best. This might be difficult to achieve since one section may be responsible for several courses. (A pantry might serve cold appetizers and salads while the grill area prepares only grilled items.) In these operations, sections should be placed apart from each other so as not to interfere with flow. Mobile equipment can be used to move items between stations, reducing server travel.

It is essential that food be delivered to guests with the proper appearance and temperature. Guests should not have to wait long for food. Efficient traffic patterns help ensure satisfied guests.

TRAINING SERVERS

A wise manager would never send an untrained, inexperienced server out to work a station alone. Servers must be trained in what to do, how it is to be done, and the professional standard expected. Although managers are responsible for seeing that servers are properly trained, the training function can be delegated to others who can do a good training job, who themselves must be taught to give good training.

Although service training can be costly, poor service is more costly in terms of lost guests and profits. Here are some of the benefits of good training:

- Improved service and increases number of satisfied guests
- Improved productivity, reducing both employee turnover and labor costs
- Reduced waste, accidents, and breakage
- Opportunities for skilled, knowledgeable, confident servers to grow and advance
- Lower frustrations
- Reduced turnover

Training should be an ongoing program in all operations, because one never stops learning. Training should improve knowledge, skills, and attitudes.

The Effective Trainer

A good trainer knows people, how to teach them, and how to motivate them to learn. Good learning can only take place when the trainer knows what must be taught and can teach this to the trainees. Before one starts to teach, one should have a lesson plan. This helps the trainer to stay on the objective and not stray, helps keep the program on time, and organizes the training session. Trainers need to be good leaders and must be able to control the learning session. They should be adept in building a feeling of trust and confidence with those they teach. A good trainer is a good listener as well as speaker. Students should be stimulated to ask questions and become involved in the training session. The learning given should have meaning to the student. Besides indicating the what, how, and when for jobs, the why should also be given. A student knowing why is more apt to make the learning permanent than just hearing the what, how, and when. Trainers should not be afraid to repeat; repetition reinforces learning. They should also seek feedback on how well the student has learned.

Trainers should know the jobs they teach thoroughly and be able to communicate such knowledge to others. Not everyone can be a good teacher. One must have a personality for it and like to do it. Persons who are to train others should be trained for it. Although teaching may come naturally, one can improve on that natural ability by knowing some of the techniques of teaching.

The trainer should plan detailed training and orientation sessions. Giving a pretest enables trainers to identify in what areas employees need the most training. Never assume that a server, even those with extensive experience, knows everything. It is a good idea to test servers after a training session, and then periodically test following the session. This ensures application of training on the job.

The Training Session

Lecturing, group discussion, role-playing, show-and-tell, and on-the-job training (OJT) are some of the ways used to train servers.

Lecturing is good when the material to be covered is short and not too technical. It is good for imparting broad and overall information. Any lecture session should be short. Listeners quickly tire of just listening. It is best to use lecturing with the other techniques of teaching.

In planning the format and preparing the material for a learning session, the trainer will greatly benefit by keeping in mind that trainees remember:

15% of what they hear
30% of what they see
50% of what they hear and see
85% of what they practice

Group discussions provide motivation, interest, and subject retention for those being trained. They can be stimulating and very beneficial in getting learner interaction. The trainer must first identify the discussion objective, relate the topic to the learning objective, and manage the discussion. Trainers should try to get the discussion started and then stay out of it, only helping from time to time to direct the discussion.

Role-play allows servers to see and practice what is to be learned. It gives servers a chance to review and criticize, and helps to change or strengthen attitudes, skills, or knowledge. The active participation teaches one to work with others. The first step in role play is to give the trainee a situation relating to their position, and then allow the trainee to work his/her way through it. Role-playing is best used where active, physical effort is needed, coupled with the demonstration of some skill and knowledge. The proper way to perform may be explained by the trainer and then the student or students allowed to go perform the task. A critique should follow. Effective learning occurs if the others in the class join in the critique.

A show-and-tell method gives students a chance to hear and see how something is done, perform it, and then see where improvement is needed from the trainer and perhaps others in the class. Such feedback reinforces learning. Show-and-tell usually is used in classroom situations.

Usually there are four steps in show-and-tell:

1. Tell the server how to do the task.
2. Show what is to be done, how to do it, and why.
3. Have the server repeat the task, verbally explaining what is done and why.
4. Have the trainer and/or the class review the performance.

Observation and on-the-job training (OJT) usually occurs in the workplace under real conditions. It can be quite successful if done correctly. Observation allows trainees to follow the trainer through the tasks so they can see how they are correctly performed, and then under a real situation go through the same tasks. The trainer observes and later provides feedback in private. OJT must be done carefully so as not to lower the quality of service to guests. Trainers should be competent to train and know the correct ways work is to be done. Too often the trainee learns, but learns the wrong way because the trainer did not know how to do it.

The Training Space, Tools, and Equipment

Some operations have wisely established their own training manuals. These usually cover such areas as greeting guests, giving menus, taking orders, and sequence of service. Mise en place (work done to get ready for guests' arrival) information should cover linen arrangement, table setup, sanitation and safety practices, and stacking service stations. Menus and preparation that servers need to complete orders should be included. Selling techniques should be discussed and employees trained to use them. Job descriptions should indicate servers' tasks and responsibilities. They are good learning materials because they describe all the tasks done.

FIGURE 6.6 On-the-job training is a valuable method for instructing new employees. Courtesy Action Systems, Inc.

Externally produced training booklets, videos, software packages, CD-ROMs, and posters are available from professional associations and publishers. They are usually of high quality, having been prepared by authorities on various service topics.

Training models and formats vary according to the size and type of operation. Among the most common are: programmed learning by exercises, on site demonstrations, classroom activities, co-op programs, apprenticeships, and on-the-job-training.

RESERVATIONS

Management is responsible for establishing the reservation system and seeing that it operates as desired. Often employees operate the reservation system and sometimes the employee may be a server.

The reservation taker should show warmth and cordiality in taking the reservation. This person provides the first impression of the operation, and this is important. Follow the greeting with the name of the operation, perhaps adding, "How may I help you?" The conversation should be short and precise. Check the reservation book before confirming a reservation, noting the date, time, and party number. At the end of taking any reservation, the taker should thank the caller.

Some reservation takers tell guests to please inform them if plans change. No-shows can create problems. It is advisable to ask for a number where one can reach the guest, especially in the case of a large party. This number may be called on the day of the reservation to be sure the party is still planning to come. Some operations take a credit card number and may charge for a no-show. Sometimes a request for a reservation is made too far in advance. A note can be made of this, and the guest can call at a later date. The seating preference should be noted, especially smoking or nonsmoking, if the restaurant has a smoking section. Other things to note on the reservation book are occasion, special menu request, and any special needs.

It is important that reservations be arranged to get the best turnover possible. It is usual to stagger reservations to avoid having everyone come in at one time. This avoids overloading kitchen and service staffs. Some operations refuse to take reservations because of no-shows and cancellations. They usually have enough walk-in business to make the operation successful, and a reservations system would be a burden rather than a help.

To establish a reservation system, first determine the number of tables and the number of seats available, and if tables will be moved to include different sized groups. From this, set up a reservation chart. (See Figure 6.7.) Usually a table is filled at dinner time for $1\frac{1}{2}$ hours for a table of one or two, but for larger groups the time is longer. Of, course, the meal has much to do with it. Breakfasts have a fast turnover, lunch has a little longer, and dinner has the longest stay. However, a breakfast group having a meeting, or a meeting for some other purpose, may hold for two or more hours. An understanding about how long tables will be filled will give the reservation person an idea of the timing of reservations.

It is not unusual to overbook by about 10 percent of the dining room capacity. This is done to take care of no-shows, cancellations, and a slow walk-in night. This can, at times, lead to problems of having too many guests arrive with no tables to receive them. When this happens, the following is suggested:

1. Be consistent in handling situations.
2. Ask the party to please wait a few minutes, saying they will be seated as soon as possible. Telling a little white lie that the guests at the table are staying a little longer than expected is all right. If the wait is long, perhaps invite the group into the lounge for a before-dinner beverage. Or, say you are sorry, but to make up for the delay you will serve the party a complimentary bottle of wine.

A reservation chart details where different tables and sections are located in the dining room.

LUNCH RESERVATIONS FOR JOHN PURDUE ROOM

Name	Number in party	Phone	Your initials	Smoking/ no-smoking	Special requests
11:30					

Name	Number in party	Phone	Your initials	Smoking/ no-smoking	Special requests
11:45					

FIGURE 6.7 Sample reservation chart.

3. Give the time of wait if possible, but be sure the time is as accurate as you can make it. Do not say, "It will be just a moment," if you know it will be longer. Nothing causes more frustration than being given a time and then having it be far off. A slight difference is not important. If one cannot give an accurate time, tell the party, "Your table will be ready as soon as the party seated there leaves."

4. When approaching several groups waiting to be seated, pleasantly tell the group or groups whose tables are ready, and then reassure the other groups that they have not been forgotten.

5. A seat card prepared for the specific needs of the establishment can be a very helpful tool. Upon seating the guests, the host, hostess, or maitre d' will give the card to the server. The card contains all the information the server needs to know in order to follow up during the course of the meal: name of the host, table

number, time seated, eventual time frame, special celebration, special requests, dietary needs, and so on.

A typical seating card might read:

Mr. and Mrs. H. Johnson–2

Time in: 7:30 p.m.

Table #8

Server: David

Notes: Anniversary cake, Mrs. J. allergic to seafood

There are many other things management must do to see that good service occurs. Often, these duties do not directly influence service, but do so in an indirect way.

A manager is responsible for seeing that good employee records are maintained, that tips are paid to employees and recorded, that vacation time is appropriately planned, and that employee activity programs, such as the establishment of a ball team, a dance, or other events are fully encouraged and supported. Management should work to make the whole operation one cohesive family. It not only leads to more motivated employees, but to the profit of the operation.

CHAPTER SUMMARY

Managers are responsible for good service and should help their employees achieve it. One of the things that can help develop good service is a well-run operation. A poorly run operation frustrates employees. To run well, a management must properly practice the five functions of management—planning, organizing, staffing, leading, and controlling.

It is management's job to see that servers are motivated to achieve high standards of service. A part of this comes in the hiring, but management has available many motivating rewards it can use, and many of these cost nothing. A warm environment, and fair and helpful treatment can motivate employees. Management should be a member of a team that wants to achieve. Participative management is usually the most successful.

Management is responsible for proper scheduling so servers know where to be when needed. This is management's job. Management is also responsible for seeing that the dining room and kitchen arrangements are set up to encourage good service.

Training is essential for good service, even with experienced servers. Training programs should be set up so servers know their work and possess the skills required. Training is management's responsibility and should be ongoing.

Complaints are often handled by servers, but sometimes management must step in and handle difficult ones. Knowing how to handle complaints is essential to prevent dissatisfied customers. Complaints can often be avoided by recognizing when the potential for one exists. For this reason, it is strongly recommended that managers and supervisors spend time with the service staff discussing how anticipating customer needs leads to better service.

Reservation programs are also the responsibility of management but at their establishment others may do the reservation taking, and sometimes these people are servers. The reservation taker should get complete information such as date, time, number in party, and other information desired by the operation. Some operations refuse to take reservations because of no shows, cancellations, and other problems relating to a reservation system. The reservation taker should show warmth in taking the reservation and should thank the caller when the reservation taking is finished.

RELATED INTERNET SITES

*B*ureau of Labor Statistics
The occupational outlook for foodservice managers provides an insightful discussion about the intricacies of the food service industry, as well as expected salaries for various segments.

www.bls.gov/occ

KEY TERMS

delegation	line organization	service controls
empowerment	participative leadership	show-and-tell
five management functions	reverse pyramid	standards
job descriptions	role-play	

CHAPTER REVIEW

1. Why are standards important to good service? Who should establish them?

2. Describe line organization. What are some advantages? What other type of organization is used today instead?

3. What are the characteristics of a participative leader?

4. Create a list of questions you would ask a person applying for a job. Are the questions lawful? That is, do they violate a person's privacy?

5. Name several faults in dining room arrangement that can cause problems for servers. Name some in kitchen arrangement.

6. What are some benefits of having a good server training program?

7. What information should one get from a guest in making a reservation?

8. What should the host or hostess do if two parties arrive at the same time, with reservations, and there is only one table available?

9. One server is so busy with a large party that she hasn't been able to approach a table that was seated five minutes ago to take the order. What can the other servers do to help?

10. There are a number of duties that managers must perform to ensure that good service occurs. Name some of these.

Case Studies

MEETING COMPETITION

Ralph Martin has, for a number of years, operated a successful family restaurant in a large shopping center. However, he finds that in the last few years new operations have come into the area and reduced his business. If the trend continues, he will soon be operating a losing restaurant.

Two of his competitors are fast-food operations. Another is a family restaurant like his, but with newer decor and menu. This operation serves a quicker food menu with more emphasis toward meeting guests' nutritional concerns. This family food competitor recently introduced an early-bird menu to attract budget-minded customers and the elderly who like slightly smaller servings at lower prices and enjoy eating earlier.

Martin wonders what his options are. During his years of operating his restaurant, he has been able to save enough to retire. Should he look for a buyer, sell out, and retire? Despite his savings, he feels that he has a few good years of active business life left in him, and that he will miss the busy life of running a restaurant. He is rather doubtful that he would like retired life right now. He would like to set aside a little larger nest egg, to afford more travel when he is retired. In addition to everything else, his competitive nature is not happy letting another business best him in a game in which he has been successful for years.

What should he do? Should he revise his menu? Are there any ways you can think of meeting the competition that would make his operation stand out as different from others? His staff belongs to a union, and over the years he has done so well that he has let his employees' wages get higher then the norm. Should he call his workers and the union together to discuss the problem? Should he contemplate the renovation of his facilities and introduce a more modern menu? What's the risk of spending so much money in renovating? Might it fail to do the trick?

Write up your assessment of where you think his main problems are and how he can try to solve them. Can you find adequate and good reasons for bowing out that might be of greater weight than those given for his staying in business?

PROJECTING COSTS FOR A NEW OPERATION

Jonathan Olinas, a successful operator of cafeterias, feels that there is a good opportunity to start a cafeteria in a thriving shopping center in a newly established business district. It will cater to shoppers and families. The income level of the families surrounding the shopping center is above average.

He estimates probable revenue and is pleased with what he sees as income by estimating numbers of shoppers and estimating probable income from that source based on demographics. He does the same in estimating family patronage and income from that source. There is a probable source of income from take-out, which he estimates as well. He is encouraged with what he finds.

He then does a study and comes up with the following estimate of costs:

Food and beverage cost	38.1%
Payroll and benefit costs	39.0
Operating expenses	5.8
Advertising and marketing	2.2
Repairs and maintenance	1.5
Rent	6.1
Taxes	0.6
Insurance	0.7
Depreciation	2.5
Administrative and general	3.8
Miscellaneous expenses	2.8
	103.1%

Of course he is disappointed. He wants to make a 4 percent to 5 percent profit.

What would you advise him to do? Give up the idea, or make changes that will bring costs into line? Reducing the costs by 7 percent to 8 percent is a challenge. Make suggestions for decreasing expenses and then describe how you would go about implementing the changes. Your changes should be realistic, backed with possible ways of how he is going to do it.

HIRING

Antonia Smith is the operator of three upscale restaurants. She needs servers who are above average in their skills, are able to please guests, are highly presentable in their dress and appearance, and can learn how to serve guests of upper-scale dining. Tips are good and a number of her wait staff make a satisfactory living by just working as servers. She hires many college or university students. She finds they are bright, flexible, and quickly fit into her system of service. However, it is difficult to fill her server needs from this source, and she finds she is being forced to take servers who do not come up to the standards she believes she needs for her type of operation.

A person in her office is assigned to interview and select staff. This person is well educated and very capable of selecting a high-class employee, the kind she needs. However, in several instances this interviewer got her into trouble with authorities because of questions asked in interviewing applicants for jobs.

Set up a guide for this interviewer to follow in interviewing. Also, describe how she can attract more servers who are college or university students. Would putting a student representative on the campuses be a good idea? What kind of advertising might be effective? Would a cash reward for bringing in employable candidates be helpful? Address these questions and describe other ways you think Antonia Smith could recruit the staff she needs.

TABLE ETIQUETTE*

Outline

Learning Objective

After reading this chapter, you should be able to:

■ Describe the etiquette rules concerning special foods.

INTRODUCTION

The way customers are served food and drink often greatly influences how they proceed in eating and drinking it. The proper items for their consumption must accompany them, and placement and other factors must be correct. Because of this,

---

* Authored by Lendal H. Kotschevar and Valentino Luciani.

servers should know the basics of service and dining etiquette so guests can enjoy their meal.

The failure of a server to serve properly may cause a guest to feel uncomfortable and not enjoy a meal. Serving properly includes not telling a guest how to eat and drink. The adage, "To possess good manners is to not tell others what good manners are" holds true. Saying to a guest, "I brought you a bowl for your clam shells," lets the guest know what to do without embarrassment. If a guest looks uncomfortable, astute servers can help lead the guest through the meal. It is every server's duty to help prevent the guests from feeling embarrassed or uncomfortable because of etiquette, and every manager's duty to see that servers are trained in proper etiquette and service.

A HISTORY OF TABLE ETIQUETTE

People have gathered to dine together for thousands of years. Undoubtedly, certain rules of decorum arose in various cultures suited to the needs of that culture. However, we find no written record of these rules until near the end of the Middle Ages (454 A.D.–1474 A.D.) in Europe. In 1474, a treatise titled *De honesta voluptate et valetudine*, "Health and enjoyment within decency," written by Platina da Cremona (whose actual name was Bartolomeo de Sacchi) appeared. It proved to be a popular work on the art of good living and manners. In 1507, a manual titled *Il Cortegiano, The Courtier*, by Baldassare Castiglione, dealt largely with proper conduct in public but also covered dining. It immediately became the accepted authority. Even some educational institutes used it as a text for teaching ethical behavior and morality. Although *The Courtier* won wide acclaim with aristocrats and educators, the most popular work on the subject appeared in 1555, a work titled *Galateo* by Giovanni Della Casa. This short, unpretentious work quickly became the authority on good manners, and in a few years was translated into every language in Europe. The author delivers his message in an imaginary conversation between an old wise man and his young nephew who is getting ready to confront the realities of life. The brief narration centers on the teachings of this old master, who is concerned about eventual social errors the youth might commit. The advice is specific and practical:

> While seated at the table it is against good rules to scratch oneself. A person has to prevent the practice of spitting and if it has to be done, then it must be done in a decorous manner. I have heard of nations where people are so well behaved that [they] never spit. We should avoid taking food with avidity; it will help avoid hiccups or any other unpleasant sequence. It is ill-mannered to rub a napkin or a finger against the teeth and to wash the mouth

with wine and spit. It is also improper to take small items like toothpicks from the table and hold them in the mouth looking like the beak of a bird that is building a nest, or holding them over the ear like a barber. Some gentlemen seat on [sic] the table already with toothpicks placed in the clothing around their neck. Going that far I wonder if they should come to the table with spoons tied around their neck!! It is incorrect to lean all over the table and eat so much food in one time that both sides of the mouth and both cheeks look swollen. . . .

Other early notable works on table etiquette are *A Treatise on Manners* written by Erasmus in 1526, and a collection of the principles on proper table etiquette by Robert de Blois, which appeared in the middle of the sixteenth century. In 1765 Antoine Le Courtin authored the *Traite de Civilite* in which he summarized all of the previous writing and offered some advice of his own according to the needs of the time. There are also interesting accounts in Japanese, Chinese, and Arabic literature on the rules of good behavior when eating. Many of the customs in these cultures differ greatly from the Western cultures.

PRINCIPLES OF PUBLIC DINING ETIQUETTE

Our rules for dining etiquette grew out of what is practical, makes for good social functioning, considering others, accommodating people in social situations, and facilitates the art of eating and dining. They were not formed by one authority but evolved from common usage of dining practices and social relations. Authorities have collected, summarized, and published them, but people themselves formed them.

Rules of etiquette are not set; they change constantly as society changes. Today's rules are less formal than they were during England's Victorian era. There is also increased awareness that customs and etiquette differ from culture to culture. Rules differ from occasion, time, place, and company. Two senators might treat each other quite differently on the U.S. Senate floor than they would on the street. Today, we have accepted norms for eating out in public, but they are not rules that cannot be violated. Servers should learn the rules and follow them when appropriate, while realizing that all rules depend on the situation at hand.

Pre-Service Etiquette

Some food service operations take reservations. In general, the employee taking the reservation should get the party's name, request for a smoking or nonsmoking section

FIGURE 7.1 Children can learn proper table etiquette by following adult examples. Courtesy PhotoDisc, Inc.

if appropriate, number in the party, arrival time and date, and any special arrangements or requests. When guests with reservations arrive, if there is a wait, apologize for it, say how long the wait will be, and where they should wait. Some operations won't seat a party until all of the party is present. Others will hold a reservation for only 15 minutes. Some operations call the person who made the reservation on the day it is to be honored to remind the guest of the reservation time. There are operations that make a charge against a guest's credit card for a no show. Coats should be checked so that the table and seats are clear for the guest. The maitre d', host, or hostess should ask guests for their seating preference before leading them to a table. If a preferred table is unavailable, tell the guests how long a wait will be and what their options are.

When guests have seated themselves, the server may place napkins on guests' laps or allow guests to do this themselves. It is considered improper for guests to tuck the napkin under the chin or in any piece of clothing, although it can be discreetly fastened under a belt to prevent the napkin from falling. Do not give the napkin a violent shake to open it. Napkins should be placed on the table so guests can pick them up by the closest edge and unfold them easily.

One of the first things the server will do is ask the guests for their drink order. It is considered impolite to urge guests to drink an alcohol beverage if a guest prefers not to drink alcohol. The server should suggest a nonalcoholic beverage.

Servers should announce specials and their prices clearly and slowly. Giving some time between specials helps guests evaluate each one. The delay, however, should not be too long.

Sometimes guests wish to share each other's orders. Let guests know that they should ask the server to have this done in the kitchen and avoid doing it at the table. Guests may desire to taste someone else's food. The person with the food can place a small amount on a plate passed by the other person. Or, the person with the food may pass over the whole plate while the other takes what is desired and passes the plate back. Take-home containers are acceptable except at formal meals and banquets.

It is considered rude for any guest to whistle, clap, snap fingers, strike a glass or cup, stamp feet, or make other noises to attract a server. Turning toward the server and raising one's hand should be a sufficient gesture to indicate the server's attention is desired. If the server is close by, one also might call, "server," in a soft voice to get the server's attention.

Sometimes a guest is served something that one must avoid because of an allergy or dislike. The proper thing for a guest to do is to not mention the problem but to avoid the item and eat the others. If something must be removed from the mouth, it can be brought to the front gently and put onto a fork or spoon and then placed down on a plate. It is also all right to move the item from the lips with the fingers, such as a fish bone. Inedible items should not be spit out, but also removed as unobtrusively as possible and put onto a plate. If a guest sees something inedible on any food, it should be called quietly to the attention of the server to be removed. If an item is dropped, one should use a fork or spoon to pick it up and then put it on a plate to be removed with the plate. A large spill requires the attention of the server, who must clean it up and then cover it with a clean napkin.

Guests should not reach, but should ask to have things passed. It is helpful if a guest holds a dish for another while the other is helping herself or himself from it. When taking something solid from a dish, it is helpful if one can use the Russian technique, using the spoon and fork to lift and carry the item to the plate. In passing items with a handle, pass with the handle pointed toward the person receiving the item.

Butter and other items often are served in small containers. Guests should remove the cover, take pats of butter with the knife or fork provided, place on the butter plate, and replace the cover. The same is done with jellies, jams, and other solid or semisolid items. Servers should remove and replace empty containers as soon as possible.

It is proper to wait until all have been served before eating, but in large groups this could mean that some food will get cold. In this case, one should eat when served. Often the guest not yet served will try as much as possible to urge others to eat as soon as served. Servers should serve all guests in the party at the same time. Servers might wait until all guests are finished with one course before clearing soiled dishes. However, it is not improper to clear one guest's plate, while another is still eating. Some guests do not like to sit with their soiled dishes in front of them. If in doubt, the server should always ask, "May I take your plate?"

Tableware

Especially in formal dining, eating utensils are given precise placement on the table for specific uses. Knives and spoons are placed to the right of the guest, while forks are to the left. In the United States people cut their food then transfer the fork from the left to the right hand, a process sometimes described as zig-zag method. Europeans do not use this zig-zag method. After cutting they leave the fork in the left hand to bring the food to the mouth.

The fork should be held at a 40-degree angle with the tines pointing down, holding the food to be cut, with the thumb under and the second finger giving support on the right side of the handle. The index finger should be placed on top of the back of the fork's handle, pushing down. It is acceptable to use the fork to push food toward a sauce before eating it. Only small amounts of food should be taken at a time.

Some people like to emphasize their conversation by using their hands and arms. Servers should watch for this to prevent spillage and burns. Servers should indicate that service is coming so the guests may be warned. Guest should avoid pointing with utensils or waving them about, especially if there is food on the item.

When the menu is preset, such as at a banquet, tables will be set with all the flatware needed. At a formal meal, guests might sit down to as many as twelve pieces of flatware and wonder, "Which do I use first?" "What piece goes with what course of food?" Most people feel too embarrassed to ask. As a rule, the first utensil used is the one placed at the outer right or outer left and then the order of use is inward, so that just before the last (dessert) course is served, only the dessert spoon and fork are left (which can be at the top of the cover and not to the left or right). Sometimes, however, the first utensil to use is placed with the food item. Thus, a shrimp cocktail might be placed in front of a guest with the small cocktail fork on the plate. In glassware, one also follows the rule, outer to inner.

Sometimes guests are confused as to whether one should use the right or left outer item. Servers should help guests to know which to use. Although it is usual to place flatware in sequence of outer right or left in as courses proceed, there can be an exception, as in the case where the teaspoon may be placed on the outer right with the soup spoon inside next to it. The first course is a soup. One then does not use the teaspoon but picks up the soup spoon and uses that.

When a guest is finished eating, the knife and fork can be placed on one side of the plate, both pointing the same direction. A more traditional way is to leave the two utensils crossed in the middle of the plate. It is wrong to place used flatware on the table. All items should rest on plates. It is also wrong for servers to expect guests to reuse flatware. Fresh, clean items should be brought with each new course.

When drinking from a glass, the fingers should not be allowed to touch the rim. Goblets and stemmed glassware should be handled by the stem.

Etiquette for Specific Foods

Many foods require specific treatment to eat properly. Certain utensils, dishes, and other items may be required to proceed correctly along with special kinds of service. (See Figure 7.2.) A lobster bib, finger bowl, or special piece of flatware may be used. Some foods must be accompanied by special condiments or sauces. Servers should know the specific needs of these different foods so people can eat them properly. It may also be that by just serving things right servers can do much to aid guests in eating a food item properly, even if they're eating it for the first time.

If a guest does not know how to eat a food, it is not wrong to ask. However, if the guest prefers not to, he or she should wait and see what the others do, and then follow.

Finger Foods Often at receptions, cocktail parties, and other social events, guests eat and drink standing up. Guests must sometimes have the skills of an acrobat to hold, eat, and drink. Party planners should have tables and chairs situated so guests can sit and eat. Another way is to have a number of small stands on which guests can set their beverages while eating. If no tables are available, there should be plenty of small bus stands on which guests can place their empty items. Guests do not like to walk too far to dispose of these items and, if tables are not supplied, plates and glasses will be found on top of armchairs, plant containers, bookshelves, and other places where they should not be.

Moist or greasy foods soil guests' fingers, so plenty of napkins should be available. In some cases, servers might offer guests finger bowls, or small cloths dipped in hot water and then wrung dry.

Some foods are served very hot. If they are, servers should warn guests that they have just come fresh from the kitchen and to wait before biting into them. If such foods

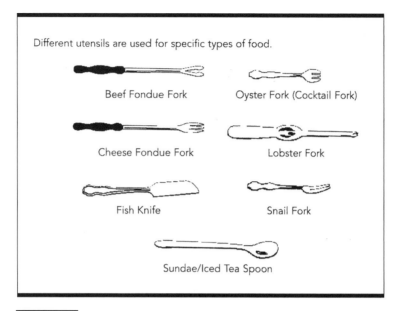

Different utensils are used for specific types of food.

Beef Fondue Fork

Oyster Fork (Cocktail Fork)

Cheese Fondue Fork

Lobster Fork

Fish Knife

Snail Fork

Sundae/Iced Tea Spoon

FIGURE 7.2 Special Utensils.

come with a small pick in them, they are easier to handle. Such picks also avoid soiling the fingers.

The plate most used at cocktail and receptions is the five-inch bread-and-butter plate, with or without a doily. Guests may pick these up and serve themselves from a buffet, or the food items will be passed by servers moving through the group. (Russians in the nineteenth century called the trays on which such foods were carried on *flying platters* because they were carried above guests' heads.)

Dips and sauces are often served at parties. After an item is dipped once, it should not be dipped again. Guests must take care to avoid spillage.

At picnics, foods such as hot dogs, hamburgers, submarines, dagwoods, and tacos may be served. It is often helpful to serve such foods wrapped in a napkin to hold them together and avoid spillage. The same is true of many desserts, such as frozen ice cream sandwiches.

Beef and pork ribs can and should be eaten with the fingers. When covered with sauce, ribs are very sticky, so extra napkins or a moist small towel should be provided. Other barbecued meats may also be considered finger foods and should receive similar service. A finger bowl should be served at the end of eating these items, if the operation uses them.

If shish kebob or other skewered item is served, it is proper to lift the skewer by its handle and push the pieces of food onto the plate with a fork. The skewer can be set aside on a plate.

Soups Soup are served in a bowl or a cup. If the cup has two handles, the guest can lift the cup when only a small amount is left. This works only for thin soups. Drinking from a bowl is considered uncouth, as is blowing on the soup to cool it. Instead, take some hot soup in the spoon and hold it until it cools. Croutons should be served with a spoon when serving; never use the hands. It is better to eat crackers separately with soup, but it is not improper to break them up and scatter them over the soup.

Soup spoons are larger than other spoons. To use a soup spoon properly, move it across the bowl away from yourself. To get the last spoonful, it is not improper to tip the bowl and let the soup run into the far side where it can be spooned up. When finished, the spoon is left in the bowl, not on the table.

Breads Bread is usually served as rolls, in slices, or in whole loaves. Loaves should be served on a cutting board with a serrated knife and a napkin with which to hold the loaf while cutting.

Vegetables Vegetables are normally easy to handle, but a few can represent a challenge in eating. Corn on the cob is one. After adding seasonings, the cob can be held with one hand, both hands, or small cob holders stuck in the ends. Artichokes are eaten by pulling the leaves off one at a time, dipping the tender end into a sauce, and removing the soft flesh with the teeth. The leaf is then placed on a plate, which should be provided. The heart, or core, contains a layer of thistles over it. The diner can scrape these away and then eat the heart using a knife and fork. Asparagus can be picked up and eaten with the fingers, but it is more proper to use a fork and knife.

A vegetable may be served with its sauce on the plate, or the sauce may be brought to the table in a sauce boat. The server should ask guests if they want sauce and how much, or leave the boat so guests can add more if desired.

Salads When eating salads, a knife may be used to cut large leaves, vegetables, and meats. Sometimes the salad is served as the first course. If guests prefer to eat it with their main meal, the server should move the salad to the guests' left. Some guests will eat some of the salad as the first course and then ask the server to leave it to be finished with the main course. The server should then move the salad to the left. If guests ask for salad dressing on the side, the server should bring it in a small container and place it on the side of the salad or on a small plate.

Pasta Some people prefer to eat long pastas by twisting a small amount of strings around the fork and supporting it with a large spoon. Or the fork can be placed down almost vertically onto the plate and twisted until the desired amount is obtained. Others may choose to take a certain amount and bring it to the mouth without twisting. This might be more difficult considering that by rolling the pasta around the fork the size of the bite becomes smaller, more compact, and easier to eat.

Fish and Shellfish Seafood can be tricky to eat properly. Some fish must be boned. Crustaceans must be removed from their shells. Often, guests avoid ordering these items, but servers can help them to overcome the difficulty and enjoy something that they really like.

Fish have a central bone structure to which most other bones are attached. The fins also carry bones. Often these are removed by filleting. However, if this is not done, these must be removed after service. Fin bones are easily removed by placing a knife or fork under the flesh surrounding the fin and removing it. By placing a fork or knife along the back and lifting, the flesh on top of the central bone structure can be exposed and this bone lifted out. In some small fish, small bones remain which must be watched for while eating. Often a fine-dining restaurant will have the chef de rang, captain, or maitre d' remove the bones, relieving the guest of this process.

In fine-dining operations, a fish fork and knife are provided. Although the knife can be distinguished easily from a dinner knife, a fish fork can easily be mistaken for a salad fork. Lemon wedges or halves are customarily served with fish or seafood. Special attention should be paid when squeezing lemon. If a wedge is served, the fork tines should be inserted in the center and the pressing should be light while holding the wedge between the index finger and thumb. It is recommended to place the hand as a cover so as to prevent the seeds and juice from squirting other guests. Some operations offer lemon halves wrapped in cheesecloth lined with a rubber band to facilitate neat squeezing. Drawn butter may be served with fish or seafood. It is proper to dip items in the butter, letting any drip fall onto the dinner plate.

Oysters and clams are often served raw on the half shell, often loosened from the shell for guests' convenience. They usually come on a plate set in a circle resting on a bed of ice with an oyster fork. A cocktail sauce will usually be in a small container in the center. Lemon or warm lemon butter or other sauce may be served with them. Some guests also like to have a hot sauce in addition. It is improper to cut raw clams or oysters. They should be eaten whole. One can dip them into the cocktail sauce, or take a bit of sauce with a fork and drop it on the clam or oyster. It is acceptable to crush oyster crackers into cocktail sauce.

Steamed clams and mussels are often served in a large bowl along with an oyster fork, sauce, warm lemon butter, oyster crackers, and some of the liquor obtained in steaming. One can pick up the shell and remove the meat with a fork or leave the shell in the bowl and remove it from there. The former method is preferred. It is not improper to lift the shell and remove the meat with the fingers, but this especially messy. The item is then dipped into the sauce or lemon butter. An empty bowl should be brought to the table for the empty shells. It is usual to follow steamed clams and mussels with a finger bowl.

The most difficult task in eating crustaceans such as lobster and crab is removing the meat. Shrimp and lobster tail are easier to handle, as their shell comes off little effort. To eat a whole or half lobster, hold the claw with a firm grip, preferably wrapping it in a napkin or holding it with tongs, or better yet, cracking it before serving. With the other hand, crack the shell in various places using a cracker, which should be provided. Insert a cocktail fork or pick and gently pull the meat out of the shell. It is not improper to remove the legs and gently suck on them. The roe or coral (eggs) of a female lobster is prized and can be eaten along with the meat. Warm drawn or lemon butter is usually served in a small dish or a plate. The server should place an extra plate or bowl at the right side of the guest for empty seafood shells. A lobster bib is appropriate not only for lobster but for any seafood item that must be shelled, but the server should give the guest the option of wearing one or not. A finger bowl with a thin slice of lemon should be provided after eating lobster.

If shrimp in a cocktail are large, there may be a problem eating them, since it is not correct to pick up the shrimp with a cocktail fork, bite off a bit and put the shrimp back. If they are hung around the outside edge of the cocktail glass, they may be removed with the cocktail fork and set onto the plate. They can then be cut with a fork and the pieces dipped into the sauce in the glass. If they are in the glass, it is proper for one to hold the glass and cut the large shrimp into bite-sized pieces. If sushi or ceviche is served containing large pieces of fish and seafood, it is proper to cut them into bite-sized pieces.

Desserts In fine-dining establishments, the dessert fork and spoon are set together above the cover pointing in different directions. In many other establishments, these utensils are brought with the dessert. Some desserts can be eaten either with a fork or a spoon. The server should bring both utensils so the guest can use either.

Fruit is sometimes served as a dessert, usually sliced or cut somehow for easier eating. If this is done, guests will use a fork for some fruits such as a piece of melon and a sharp fruit knife for whole fruits such as apples, peaches, pears. A plate should be available for a diner to leave peels, cores, and so on. A small sharp knife should be on the plate. It is not wrong for guests to pick up a fruit like an apple and eat it holding it in the hand. This is called *eating hand fruit*.

At the end of a meal when one is ready to leave, one should catch the attention of the server and ask for the check.

TIPPING

The question of tipping is new for every meal. Tips should be based on the bills total *before* tax. A 10 percent tip is the least one should tip for adequate service. Below 10 percent indicates to the server displeasure with the service. Fifteen percent is the normal tip for satisfactory service, although some tip more than that. The tip many be higher than 20 percent for unusually good service. If servers are to split a tip, the tipper should indicate the division. Fifteen to 20 percent of the nontax total is often given the captain, but some just slip them a $10 or $20 bill. Remember that people from outside the United States are not used to tipping.

The usual tip for valet parking is one or two dollars, but in some instances it might be higher.

Maitre d's also can be tipped; in fine-dining establishments they will expect it, particularly if an extra service is provided. An attentive server should not have to be asked for the bill.

DINING ETIQUETTE OF VARIOUS CULTURES

Rules of dining etiquette are not universal. Cultures have vastly different dining rules; from cultures that use no utensils to cultures that use many sets of utensils to accompany various courses. What's more, dining rules are not always consistent within a culture. Different food sources, living conditions, and differences among people of a country make for different dining practices.

Ethnic dining in this country has become an integral part of the foodservice industry. The most common cuisines are Italian, Chinese, and Mexican and more establishments are offering Indian, Japanese, Middle Eastern, and other ethnic foods. The following synopsis details some of the most important differences associated with the food and service of various ethnic cuisines.

Traditional Jewish Service

Jewish dietary practices are interwoven with their faith. Jewish religious law dictates food selection, preparation, and service. Jewish holidays and religious events are often by marked with the service of special dishes.

Kosher literally means fit or proper, and refers to a set of dietary rules called *Kashrut*. These laws are biblically based, and their application has been determined by rabbinic interpretation.

Mammals must have split hooves and chew their food. Only a specific list of birds are considered Kosher. Both birds and mammals must be slaughtered in a specific manner, called *shechita*, by a trained Jewish slaughterer called a *shochet*. Furthermore, the meat must be *Koshered*, or soaked and salted in a specific manner to remove all blood.

Only fish with both fins and scales are kosher. This excludes shellfish. Fish do not need to be killed in any specific manner.

Dairy products and meats cannot be cooked or served together. There are separate cooking utensils and serving dishes, for meat and dairy. During the Passover holiday, no dish, utensil, plate, or other item that has touched a leavened product can be used for food preparation or service. Some foods are called neutral (*parve*), such as fish, eggs, vegetables, and fruits, and can be served with either meat or dairy.

No cooking is permitted on the Sabbath, so food must be eaten cold or prepared ahead and kept warm. In many foodservice operations, boilers furnishing the heat in steam tables can be used to keep food warm.

A blessing is said before the meal begins. On the Sabbath and holidays, there is always a special blessing said over bread, usually *challah*, a braided egg-bread.

European Dining Etiquette

For the most part, dining etiquette in Europe is similar to the etiquette in the United States.

Traditionally, European dining was more formal than American dining, but even Europe is becoming more fast-paced and casual.

Chinese and Japanese Dining

Although there are many differences between Chinese and Japanese dining etiquette, both emerged thousands of years ago in common. Chopsticks are used in both Chinese and Japanese dining. Some common food items found in both cultures are rice, wheat, soy sauce, and tofu (bean curd). However, the separation of these cultures for so many years has produced many differences in Chinese and Japanese dining etiquette.

Chinese Dining Chinese dining is an adaptation of family dining, where food is brought to the table in serving dishes and guests help themselves. Often the foods are placed on a circular movable platform set in the middle of the dining table. Guests rotate this to get to the various dishes. The main plate is usually about the size of a salad plate, and portions are small. There is also a rice and a soup bowl. A rice wine may be served in small cups. There is typically no water or other liquid on the table because soups supply the liquid. Tea is sometimes served. Chopsticks are the main eating utensil, and a special soup spoon is used for the soups. Foods are usually cooked in bite-sized pieces so they can be picked up with chopsticks. If the piece of food is larger than a bite, the plate may be raised, and the piece picked up with the chopsticks for a bite. It is not considered impolite to raise the rice bowl to the mouth to guide the rice in with the chopsticks.

Traditionally, the host sits with his back to the door, with the main or honored guest opposite him. This custom springs from an old legend, where an emperor was visiting a friend. The emperor had many enemies, and he was in constant fear of being murdered by them. To relax him during meals, the host sat with his back to the door and placed the emperor opposite him so he could see who entered. The strategy worked. Enemies did come in, but were seen as they entered. The emperor was always ready for them. Today, the tradition holds.

Next to the main honored guest may be other guests seated in turn around the table toward the host. It is considered an insult to the main guest to have the grain of the wood running toward him; it must run toward other guests.

Japanese Dining The Japanese take great care in the presentation of their food. Meat, vegetables, fruits, and other items are cut and served attractively. The color and shape of the dish on which the food is served—one dish for each food item—must suit the food. Placement of the food on the dish is precise and decorative. Glass dishes are often used in the summer, green porcelain in the spring, heavy stoneware in the winter, and basket-shaped dishes tinted with the color of autumn leaves in the fall.

Traditional Japanese dining is quite formal. One is expected to use the best manners, giving deference to others at the table. The meal is usually served all at once. One should start a meal by taking a grain or two of rice and then a small sip of soup. It is considered bad taste to have any cutting utensil on the table, so all food should be served in bite-sized pieces. Soups and beverages are sipped from their dishes.

Traditionally, the Japanese do not sit at tables or chairs to eat. Instead, they kneel on a *tatami*, or mat, and the food is served on a small, raised stand in front of them. For a group, a large, low table may be used instead of the individual stands. The host faces guests, and no one is ever seated on the ends. Some Japanese restaurants provide tables that sit above a shallow opening in the floor so guests can sit on the floor and let their legs hang down in the opening.

Often a dining area will have a *tokonama*, or a scroll on the wall. In front of this sits a low table with a Japanese flower upon it. The honored guest is invited to sit in front of the tokonama. However, the guest should refuse this honor, and only accept the invitation upon the host's insistence.

Many restaurants provide small ceramic holders for chopsticks. In places where these are not used, the chopsticks will usually come wrapped in paper. One should use the paper wrappings to rest the chopsticks. Pickles are typically served at the end of the meal.

Indian Dining

Indians are largely vegetarians. Some use no eating utensils, but eat with their right hand. The food is usually ladled out of bowls onto plates. Many people sit on the floor to eat, and no one wears shoes in the dining room. Food services have places outside where those going to eat can wash their hands. The upper classes usually eat with knives, forks, and spoons. Rice is eaten usually instead of potatoes. They avoid pork and most (of Hindu faith) do not eat beef.

Middle Eastern Dining

In dining the peoples of Middle Eastern countries, most of whom are Muslim, follow traditional religious influences, food resources, and social customs. It is customary to wash the hands before and after eating. One eats only with the right hand, and often no eating utensils are used. As many as thirty different dishes may be served in small quantities, with cold foods coming first. Guests serve themselves. Pita bread is commonly used to help lift the food to the mouth. When meat is eaten, it is usually followed with rice. If a knife and fork are used, these should be left in a crossed position on the plate when finished.

Guests are honored by being seated to the right of the host. Traditionally, pillows are placed in a circle around a table, and guests sit cross-legged on a pillow on a rug while eating.

CHAPTER SUMMARY

The tradition of table etiquette in Western countries has evolved since the Middle Ages in Europe. Writers have collected and published established customs but the customs themselves have developed over time by common adoption. Etiquette differs greatly from culture to culture, and from occasion, time, and company. At its core, etiquette is based on being considerate of other people and ensuring pleasant social interactions.

In a seated-service, white tablecloth operation, dining etiquette plays a much more important role then in the casual drop-in operation. Preservice etiquette includes taking reservations, providing a coat check, and allowing for seating preference. Once the guests are seated, servers must ask guests for a drink order, and announce specials and their prices.

It is helpful when a server knows how one should eat a food and what proper manners are when eating. Servers must know how to help guests in various situations, including allergies, inedible foods, passing dishes, and when to eat. It is important for servers to know what is needed in service so people can enjoy eating in public without embarrassment.

Utensils are always given precise placement on the table. Up to twelve pieces of flatware may be set. For flatware and glassware, the general rule of outer to inner should be used. It also helps for the server to know which supplementary utensils are needed for each of the specific items. When a guest is finished eating, the knife and fork can be placed on one side of the plate, facing the same direction, or placed in the middle of the plate, the rim of the plate acting as a frame.

Some foods require special utensils, condiments, or sauces to be eaten correctly. At functions where there are no tables and guests stand to eat and drink, small stands may be available for guests to place their beverages upon while eating. Napkins and small picks are often served with greasy foods, or foods that are hot, to make the foods easier to handle and to prevent soiling. If dips and sauces are served at parties, guests may dip the item only once.

Soups, vegetables, and seafood all require special methods or additional utensils when eating. Soups are served in either a bowl or a cup. The soup spoon is larger than other spoons and should be moved across the bowl away from the diner. Vegetables like corn on the cob can be held with both hands, or preferably with attached cob holders.

Seafood can be very tricky to eat properly. Some fish must be boned, while crustaceans must be removed from their shells. Lemon, drawn butter, and cocktail sauce are often served with fish and shellfish.

At the close of the meal, the appropriate tip should be left for the server, and should be based on the total bill before tax. A tip between 15 to 20 percent is traditional, and if necessary, should be split to suit the service. In high-scale operations, it is typical to tip the captain and possibly the maitre d'.

KEY TERMS

etiquette	Russian technique	zig-zag method
finger bowls	*Traite de Civilite*	
Galateo	*A Treatise on Manners*	

CHAPTER REVIEW

1. Why is it important for a server to know proper table manners?
2. How did the rules for proper eating develop? Do they change over time? Are they inviolate?
3. A guest orders broiled lobster. What should be served with it?
4. What is a finger bowl used for? What is its proper service? When should it be served?
5. How should guests place flatware on the plate when they are done eating?
6. There is a rule saying that one never places the elbow or elbows on the table. There is another rule saying that guests should not use the fingers to bring food to the mouth. Can either of these be violated? Under what circumstances?
7. A guest asks for a large tablespoon along with a fork to eat spaghetti. Is the guest wrong in asking? Why or why not?
8. How does a guest displeased with the service indicate this in the tip? What is a low tip percentage? What is a typical tip percentage?
9. What should a server do if a guest spills something?
10. After the guests are seated, what is the first question the server should ask them?
11. Answer the following guest questions:
    - (a) "What are these little finger bowls for?"
    - (b) "Is it okay if we share something?"
    - (c) "Is it rude to start before everyone at this banquet is served?"
    - (d) "Which fork do I use for the salad?"
    - (e) "How do I eat these snails?"
    - (f) "Where do I put the mussel shells after I eat the mussels?"
    - (g) "Can I use my fingers to eat these ribs?"
    - (h) "What's the best way to get the last of the soup out of this bowl?"
    - (i) "What's the best way to pick up spaghetti?"
    - (j) "What is the proper way to eat these raw oysters on the half shell?"

Case Studies

SERVING FISH AND SEAFOOD

John is an experienced server and secures a job in an upscale fish and seafood restaurant, the top restaurant in Boston of its kind. Besides ordinary knives and forks, it serves with its fish and seafood items the correct utensils, dishes, and tableware. He comes to the restaurant one day ahead to see the service and learn the proper dishes and utensils that go with the various fish and seafood items. What must he learn about serving lobster, oysters or clams on-the-half-shell, snails, whole fish that the server must debone for the guest, and so on? Write up what he records about serving these items.

THE TIPPING PROBLEM

Mary is a good waitress and makes good money in tips. She serves a group of people. They want individual checks. The bill of one person comes to $19.50 plus a 15 percent tax or for a total bill of $21.43. The person pays by credit card. When the time comes for this individual to add the tip and give Mary a signed sales slip, she adds $2.15, or about 10 percent of the total bill. As noted, Mary is a good server and gave this table excellent service. What's wrong in what the individual did?

CONCEPT, LOCATION, AND DESIGN*

Outline

Learning Objectives

After reading and studying this chapter, you should be able to:

- Recognize the benefits of a good restaurant name.

- Explain the relationship between concept and market.

- Explain why a restaurant concept might fail.

- Discuss some qualities of successful restaurant concepts.

- Identify factors to consider when choosing a restaurant's location.

- Identify factors to consider when developing a restaurant concept.
- List restaurant knockout criteria.

---

* Authored by John R. Walker and Donald E. Lundberg.

RESTAURANT CONCEPTS

The objective in planning a restaurant is to assemble, on paper, the ideas for a restaurant that will be profitable and satisfying to the guest and owner/operator. The formulation of these ideas is called the *restaurant concept*, the matrix of ideas that constitutes what will be perceived as the restaurant's image. The concept is devised to interest a certain group of people (or groups of people), called a *target market* or *niche*. Marketing is the sum of activities intended to attract people to the restaurant. This includes determining what group or groups (target markets) are most likely to react favorably to the concept.

In this section, we discuss restaurant concepts. Later sections discuss the relationships between concept, business plan, site selection (restaurant location), and marketing. Concept, location, ambiance, and marketing are interdependent. Concept development applies to any foodservice operation, from a hot dog stand to a luxury restaurant, from quick-service to theme restaurants.

The challenge is to create a restaurant concept that fits a definite target market, a concept better suited to its market than that presented by competing restaurants, and to bring it into being. This is known as being *D&B*—different and better. The restaurant business is intensely competitive. There is always a better concept coming on stream—better in atmosphere, menu, location, marketing, image, and management. If a restaurant is not competitive, another restaurant down the street, across town, or next door will take away its customers.

This challenge does not mean that a new restaurant must be built. Plenty of existing restaurants and other buildings can be taken over. The challenge is to develop and install a new concept, acknowledging the possibility that it may be necessary to modify it as competition and other conditions change.

> The best concepts are often the result of learning from mistakes. Just when you think you have your concept figured out, guess what? You don't. Also, just when you think it's hopeless, a light's going to come on, a rainbow is going to appear, and the concept will be reborn. And it may not be the one you started out with. Restaurants are essentially about food and service. The success of your concept is going to depend on both.[1]

Every restaurant represents a concept and projects a total impression or image. The image appeals to a certain market—children, romantics, people celebrating special occasions, fun types, people seeking a formal or a casual venue. The concept should fit the location and reach out to appeal to its target market(s). In planning a restaurant concept, location, menu, and decor should intertwine. When a concept and image lose appeal, they must be modified or even changed completely.

Concept comprises everything that affects how the patron views the restaurant: public relations, advertising, promotion, and the operation itself. Concept frames the public's perception of the total restaurant. It includes the building, its curbside appeal, its exterior decor. Does the restaurant invite people to venture in, or is it neglected and dirty in appearance? Decor, menu, and style of operation are part of the concept. Concept includes the personality of the owner, the appearance of the dining room staff, the music, and the tone of the place. Particularly important are the menu and the food and its presentation. Symbols, as seen in the sign, logo, colors, upholstery, and lighting, are aspects of concept. The right music reinforces the concept. The concept provides the framework on which to hang the image.

Don't open a restaurant unless you:

1. Have experience in the restaurant business, especially in the segment in which you plan to operate.

2. Don't mind giving up your evenings and long weekends—not to mention mornings and afternoons.

3. Are able to accept personal risk. Have money to lose—oops! we mean capital to start a high-risk business.

4. Have a concept in mind and menus developed.

5. Have completed a detailed business plan.

6. Have personal and family goals established for the next several years.

7. Have the patience of a saint and two active thyroid glands!

8. Have identified a quantifiable need in the market for the type of restaurant you are considering opening.

9. Have an exit plan—the restaurant business is easy to enter but potentially costly to exit.

10. Can afford a lawyer and an accountant experienced in the restaurant business.

SEQUENCE OF RESTAURANT DEVELOPMENT: FROM CONCEPT TO OPENING

From the time a concept is put together until a location is obtained, architectural drawings are made, financing is arranged, the land is leased or purchased, approvals for building are secured, construction bids are let, a contractor is selected, and—finally—the building is put in place, can take two or more years. The sequence of

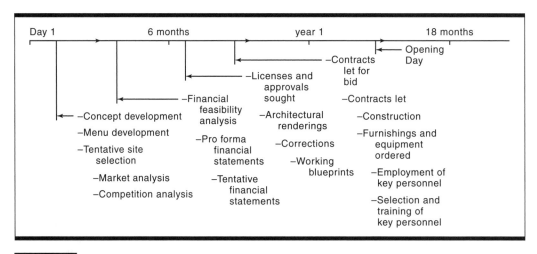

FIGURE 8.1 Time line showing the sequence of restaurant development.

events (Figure 8.1) may include the following:

1. Business marketing initiated
2. Layout and equipment planned
3. Menu determined
4. First architectural sketches made
5. Licensing and approvals sought
6. Financing arranged
7. Working blueprints developed
8. Contracts let for bidding
9. Contractor selected
10. Construction or remodeling begun
11. Furnishings and equipment ordered
12. Key personnel hired
13. Hourly employees selected and trained
14. Restaurant opened

In some cases, the time may be reduced, especially when taking over an existing restaurant or altering an existing building. Restaurant chains with preplanned restaurant concepts generally reduce the time line by 6 to 12 months.

Planning Services

The person building a restaurant should employ an architect experienced in restaurant design. The architect, in turn, may hire a restaurant consultant to lay out the kitchen and recommend equipment purchases.

The builder may employ one of the relatively few restaurant consultants or can turn to restaurant dealers who double as planners or employ planners. The consultant works for a fee or a percentage of cost. The dealer may also charge a fee, but is likely to reduce or eliminate it if the equipment is purchased from him or her.

The best guide in selecting a planner/consultant is that person's experience and reputation. Remember that any kitchen can be laid out in a variety of ways and still function well.

The consultant/planner will require a signed design agreement, including agreed-upon fees. The agreement spells out what services will be completed by the designer and usually includes the following:

- Basic floor plan
- Equipment schedules
- Foodservice equipment electrical requirements
- Foodservice plumbing requirements
- Foodservice equipment
- Foodservice equipment elevations
- Refrigeration requirements
- Exhaust air extraction and intake requirements
- Seating layout

Common Denominators of Restaurants

In formulating a restaurant concept, the planner considers the factors common to all kinds of restaurants. An analysis of these common denominators may suggest a concept that is a hybrid of two or more classifications. Fast-food restaurants take on the character of coffee shops, vending operations may offer limited service, cafeterias take on the appointments of luxury restaurants, and so on.

Common denominators of restaurants can be compared: the human needs met by the restaurant, menu prices, degree of service offered, space provided for each customer, rate of seat turnover, advertising and promotion expenditures, productivity per employee, labor cost, and food cost.

The planner picks and chooses from among the common denominators to come up with a concept believed to be most appealing to a particular market.

UTILITY VERSUS PLEASURE

What is the purpose of a particular restaurant? Is it there to provide food for nutritional purposes or for pleasure? Up to 75 percent of the meals eaten away from home are for utilitarian purposes, while the other 25 percent are for pleasure. The distinctions are not clear-cut. Depending on the individual, the quick-service experience may be thrilling or boring. For the child, McDonald's may be full of excitement and fun. For a sophisticate, McDonald's can be a drag. The family that visits a Burger King or a Wendy's may find the experience as exhilarating as depicted in the TV commercials. For them, the utilitarian restaurant is a fun place, perhaps more pleasurable than an ultraexpensive French restaurant. McDonald's (and some other fast-food restaurants) has further blurred the line by adding play areas and party rooms. This is a far cry from Ray Kroc's original plan to keep McDonald's entertainment free to encourage quick turnover.

As a general rule, however, pleasure dining increases as service, atmosphere, and quality of food increase. Presumably, pleasure also increases as menu price increases. Many factors intrude on such straight-line correlation.

DEGREE OF SERVICE OFFERED

As seen in Figure 8.2, restaurant service varies from none at all to a maximum in a high-style luxury restaurant.

As menu price increases, so, usually, does service—the higher the price, the more service provided. At one end of the spectrum, the vending machine is completely impersonal—no service at all. At the other end, the luxury restaurant, a captain and two buspersons may attend each table. Service is maximal. The customer pays for the food but also for the ambiance and the attention of service personnel. It is interesting to compare the productivity and profitability of a luxury restaurant with those of a casual or popular-concept restaurant. The casual restaurant can quickly train personnel replacements and pay relatively low wages. The French restaurant relies on years of experience and polished skills. It is also relatively inefficient. The chain restaurant relies on system and replication, the French on individuals. The chain markets its restaurants; the French restaurant attracts limited patronage with ambiance, personality, word of mouth, and public relations.

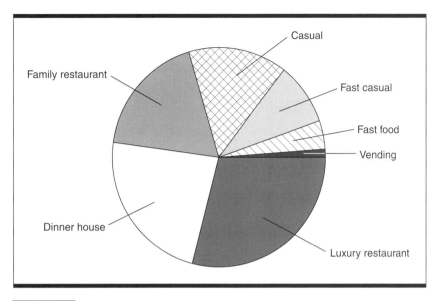

FIGURE 8.2 Different kinds of restaurants require different levels of service.

Restaurant service breaks down into seven categories: vending, quick service, fast casual, casual, family restaurant, dinner house, and luxury restaurant. Figure 8.3 shows that different kinds of restaurants have different seat turnover levels.

The degree of service offered probably correlates with menu price and pleasure—at least, that is the expectation of the diner. Here again, there are many exceptions, and as the expectations are purely psychological, a number of factors can intrude on the correlation.

TIME OF EATING AND SEAT TURNOVER

Utilitarian eating is often accomplished in double-quick time, while the customer of a luxury restaurant who spends $75 to $100 per person for an evening out may savor every minute of the total experience, plus the pleasure of anticipating the dining experience and the pleasure of remembering it. Telling one's friends about the truffled turkey can be worth the price of the meal, a conversation piece adding luster to the dinner. At the other end of the spectrum, the stand-up diner in New York City can hardly be expected to be enthralled by the experience.

The seat turnover and speed of eating correlate with the restaurant classification, but not perfectly (Figure 8.3). In some restaurants, the family style can offer speedy service and fast turnover, and still provide an enjoyable atmosphere for its customers.

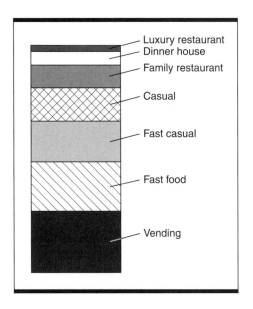

Luxury restaurant
Dinner house
Family restaurant
Casual
Fast casual
Fast food
Vending

FIGURE 8.3 Different kinds of restaurants have different seat turnover levels.

Turnover is also highly correlated with the efficiency of the operation; turnover in two restaurants of exactly the same type can vary widely because of layout and management.

Square Foot Requirements

Figure 8.4 suggests the amount of space per customer needed by each type of restaurant. The restaurant customer, in effect, rents space for dining. The drive-through restaurant provides no dining space at all; the customer's automobile is the dining room. Coming up the scale a bit, the customer may walk to a counter and receive some service. The coffee shop provides counter and booth seating and a nominal kitchen, while the luxury restaurant needs upholstered chairs and 15 to 20 feet of space per patron, plus the kitchen equipment to handle the more extensive menu.

The square-foot requirements and the turnover in patrons per seat per hour are listed in Figure 8.5.

Menu Price and Cost per Seat

Menu pricing correlates highly with the degree of service offered, the time of eating, the labor cost, the amount of space offered the customer, and the cost of the restaurant itself.

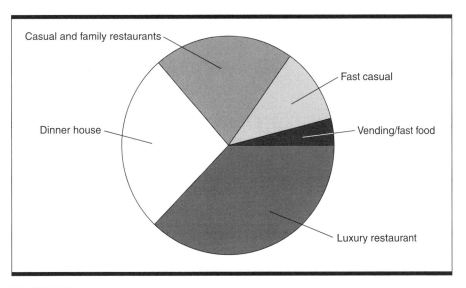

FIGURE 8.4 Different kinds of restaurants have different space-per-customer requirements.

It might be expected that the cost per seat of a restaurant varies directly with the other factors mentioned. This is true to an extent, but there are wide variations. Some of the chain dinner houses cost at least $15,000 per seat, whereas a small neighborhood restaurant may cost $5,000. Some of the quick-service restaurants are very costly per seat, much more so than the family restaurant. Cost per seat thus does not correlate well with the restaurant classifications presented.

	Dining Room (square feet per seat)	Turnovers in Patrons (per seat per hours)
Fast casual	10–12	1.75–3.0
Dinner house	15–17	1.25–1.75
Deluxe restaurants	13–18	0.5–1.25
Casual restaurants	11–15	1–2.5

Source: Adapted from Arthur C. Avery, *Commercial Kitchens* (New York: American Gas Association, 1989).

FIGURE 8.5 Square-foot requirements and turnover rates.

The Correct Number of Seats

Theoretically, a given location will support a given number of seats with a particular concept. A 120-seat restaurant may be right for location *x*, while a 240-seat restaurant would be wrong. Restaurant chains go through a period of evolution to arrive at the right size to suit their concept. Companies such as McDonald's, Denny's, and Pizza Hut have developed as many as three sizes of restaurants to fit different locations.

Surveys show that 40 to 50 percent of all table-service restaurant customers arrive in pairs; 30 percent come alone or in parties of three, 20 percent in groups of four or more. To accommodate these parties, consultants recommend tables for two that can be pushed together. Booths for four, while considered inefficient for some restaurants, are ideal for family places. Larger groups can be accommodated at several small tables placed together, in booths for six, or at large round tables. The floor space required per seat will vary according to the restaurant's service or atmosphere. Luxury and table-service restaurants require 15 to 20 square feet per seat; coffee shops and luncheonettes should allot about 12 to 17 square feet for each seat, while cafeterias need just 10 to 12 square feet per seat or per stool.

For the beginning restaurateur, it is probably better to build too small than too large. If the restaurant is excessively large for the location, it will be only partially filled. A crush of customers creates ambiance and excitement.

Some restaurants are too large for their markets. Better to shut down some rooms, if possible, so that customers can be seated with other customers. Few people like to sit in a large room with only a handful of other people present.

ADVERTISING AND PROMOTION EXPENDITURES

In advertising and promotion, expenditures may vary according to the type of restaurant. Figure 8.6 shows the percentage of sales spent on advertising and promotion among types of restaurants. The vending machine operator spends little or nothing in advertising. Quick-service restaurants are likely to spend 4 to 5 percent of their income on advertising, more than is spent by the casual, fast casual, or family restaurant, or the dinner house. At the far end of the spectrum, the restaurant featuring fine food may spend heavily on public relations. Promotion may take the form of entertaining food columnists, the proprietor's being seen at the right places at the right times and with the right people, and the cost of paying a public relations firm for keeping the restaurant in the news.

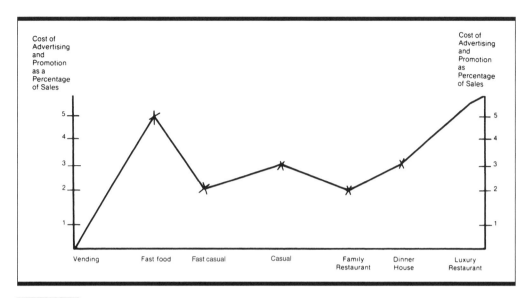

FIGURE 8.6 Advertising and promotion expenditures.

LABOR COSTS AS A PERCENTAGE OF SALES

Productivity per employee correlates highly with the various elements, moving from a high point at the quick-service end of the classification scale to a low point in a luxury restaurant or at a country club. Here, too, there are exceptions, depending on management skill, the layout of the restaurant, and the menu.

As might be expected, labor costs vary inversely with productivity, as shown in Figure 8.7. Quick-service restaurants operate at comparatively low labor costs. Labor costs are covered in more detail in Chapter 10.

PLANNING DECISIONS THAT RELATE TO CONCEPT DEVELOPMENT

Who Are the Target Markets, the Customers? Children, teenagers, young married couples, families, businesspeople, retirees, low-income people, high-income people, the adventurous, the sophisticated—anyone who is hungry could be your target market.

Buy, Build, Lease, or Franchise? Building is usually the most time-consuming of these options and can require two or more years from concept to completion. Arranging for financing, employing an architect, buying the land, getting the necessary approvals, and formulating contingency plans all eat up time and money. In franchising, the problem

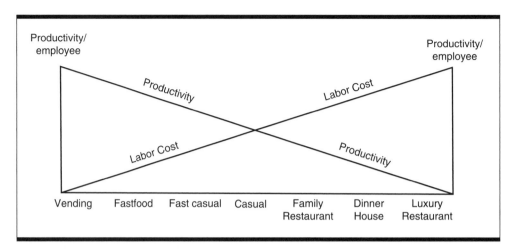

FIGURE 8.7 Productivity per employee.

is to pick the right operation and to recognize that most major decisions have already been made and will continue to be made by others.

Food Preparation from Scratch or from Convenience Items? How much of the food will be prepared on the premises? How much will be purchased ready for heating? How many of the menu items will be prepared from mixes, soup bases, and other convenience food items? Some restaurants prepare everything possible from fresh ingredients. Others prepare everything possible from convenience items and have a definite policy of cutting preparation time to the minimum. Most restaurants make some items and buy others. Chain operations often produce some foods in a commissary, then have them delivered for final preparation at the various unit restaurants. Even upscale restaurants usually purchase most of their desserts and pastries.

A Limited or an Extensive Menu? Will the location and the concept support a limited menu, or does the concept call for an extensive menu requiring a large population base to support it?

How Much Service—Limited or Full? The operator can pick from a wide range of service degrees, from vending to walk-up, carry-out, cafeteria, drive-through, and on up to luxury full service. Which best fits the concept and market?

Young Part-time Employees or Older Career Employees? Much of today's foodservice industry is staffed by teenagers, people in their early twenties, and people who receive minimum or slightly above minimum wage. Some restaurants employ a range of age groups and depend on career employees rather than part-timers. Most restaurants offer at least some part-time positions.

Paid Advertising or Word-of-Mouth Advertising? How will the target markets be reached—paid advertising, public relations, promotions, or largely by word of mouth? A number of successful restaurants have a definite policy of no paid advertising. Others rely heavily on paid advertising, still others on promotion or a combination of advertising and promotion, particularly the use of coupons.

Grand or Quiet Opening? Will you open with a bang and fanfare or open quietly on Monday morning and allow the crew to ease into volume operation?

Electricity or Gas? This decision is not an either/or proposition—some pieces of equipment can be gas fired, others wired for electricity—but the decision is an important one because installation is only part of the total cost. What is the cost of operating gas versus electric equipment, and what are the advantages of each type? Regional utility rates are a factor. In some locations, electricity is cheap; in others, expensive.

PROFITABILITY

Now for the famous last-but-not-least factor—profitability. Without a doubt, the most profitable restaurants are in the quick-service category. The larger quick-service purveyors have produced dozens of millionaires and more than a few multi-millionaires. A number of franchisees have acquired chains within the chain, multiple units clustered within an area. With predominantly minimum-wage personnel, high sales volume, the use of systems, and excellent marketing, the quick-service business is the all-out winner. Oddly enough, few restaurant-management students opt for quick-service management, believing it lacks the variety, glamour, and opportunity for self expression found in restaurants offering more service and style. The professional restaurateur sees the restaurant as an ego extension. The investor usually cares most about profitability and what it takes to maximize profits.

THE MISSION STATEMENT

A mission statement drawn up by the restaurant owner can encapsulate the owner's objectives for the business. The statement may be brief, such as the one for Creative Gourmets, a catering company based in Charleston, Massachusetts: "Excellence

Through Caring."[2] Or it could be much more encompassing, as in Chili's Grill and Bar, whose home office is in Dallas:

> We aim to be a premier growth company with a balanced approach toward people, quality, and profits; to cultivate customer loyalty by listening to, caring about, and providing customers with a quality dining experience; to enhance a high level of ethics, excellence, innovation, and integrity; to attract, develop, and retain a superior team; to be focused, sensitive, and responsive to our employees and their environment; and to enhance long-term shareholder wealth.[3]

A mission statement can be explicit about the market(s) served, the kinds of food offered, and the atmosphere in which the food will be served. The ethical standards to be followed can be stated as part of the mission statement or written as a separate code of conduct. The goals to be followed in relating to patrons, employees, vendors, and the community can be included. Restaurants Unlimited, a dinner-house chain based in Seattle, states something of the moral character of the company, the way it views the guest and the employees:

> To build a growing, financially successful business through increasing sales and excellent profits. This is achieved by living these values. We act Guest First. We deliver high-quality food every time at reasonable prices. We give great service and engage each guest. We hire the best and care about them. We are clean![4]

Several advantages accrue to the restaurant owner/management that takes the time to spell out a mission statement. The exercise forces owners to think through and put in writing an explicit statement about what the restaurant is all about, a statement that is sharp and to the point and can focus the energies of management and employees and set forth the responsibilities of the enterprise in its relations with patrons, employees, vendors, and the public.

Mission statements can include input from employees. Discussions with employees can mobilize their thinking about the restaurant's purpose and reason for existence. There should be no hesitation about stating the profit motivation and such goals as cleanliness, customer service, and customer delight.

A code of ethics may strike some people as naive. Codes of ethics place a burden on restaurant owners and managers to live up to the code, remind them that ethical behavior begins at the top, and presume a commitment to following the highest standards in personal cleanliness, food protection, service, and employee relations. One clause can address striving to price food to provide fair value and fair profit to investors. It does no harm to state that the restaurant expects employees and vendors to be scrupulously honest and pledges to do the same.

Some business writers say that a mission statement contains four elements:

1.   The purpose of the enterprise

2.   Its business strategy

3.   The behavior standards it will follow

4.   The values that the management and employees will hold foremost[5]

A mission statement is a useful part of the work plan needed to support a loan application from the Small Business Administration, bank, or other loan source.

REFERENCES

1. Al DaCosta, FCSI, Cohn DaCosta International, "So You Want to Own a Restaurant?" *The Consultant* (Fall 1998): 57.

2. "Best-Run Companies," *Restaurants and Institutions* (May 29, 1989).

3. Courtesy Chili's Grill and Bar.

4. Courtesy Restaurants Unlimited.

5. Andrew Campbell and Sally Yering, "Creating a Sense of Mission," *Long-Range Planning*, 24, 4 (August 1991): 10–20.

FINANCING AND LEASING*

Outline

Sufficient Capital

Preparing for the Loan Application
  Budgeting

Forecasting Sales

Income Statement

Learning Objectives

After reading and studying this chapter, you should be able to:

- Forecast restaurant sales.

- Prepare an income statement.

- Prepare a financial budget.

- Identify requirements for obtaining a loan in order to start a restaurant.

- Discuss the strengths and weaknesses of the various types of loans available to restaurant operators.

- List questions and the types of changes a lessee should consider before signing a lease.

- Know what it takes to acquire a loan in order to start a restaurant.

---

* Authored by John R. Walker and Donald E. Lundberg.

- Discuss the strengths and weaknesses of the various types of loans available to restaurant operators.
- Explain the nuances of restaurant leases.

Once the concept, location, and menu are chosen, the next step is financing the restaurant. Where does the money come from? Many restaurants have been started by borrowing money on property, including the family home. Others have been started with a loan from a relative, a friend, or a group of friends. An experienced restaurant operator may have a lawyer put together a partnership with the operator as managing partner and investors as limited partners. Still other restaurants are financed by groups of investors who form a corporation to buy or build and operate a place. Forming a corporation is simple and can be done quickly and at relatively low cost. The corporation becomes a legal entity that can take on debts and guarantee loans. To do so, however, a corporation must be creditworthy, just as an individual must. It must pay taxes, just as any individual with income must do, which can mean double taxation for the owner. The corporation pays a corporation tax, and the individual owners receiving income from the corporation pay individual income tax as well. But there are ways to avoid double taxation, as we shall see in this chapter.

SUFFICIENT CAPITAL

Many would-be restaurateurs try to start restaurants with only a few thousand dollars in capital. Such ventures usually fail. Although the number-one factor in restaurant failure is said to be lack of management, lack of finance and working capital is a close second. No one knows the real rate of failure in the restaurant business because so many restaurants merely fade away, the owners taking severe losses and selling for what they can get. Dun and Bradstreet, the major firm that reports business failures, has no way of assessing the number of fadeaways. Often, a restaurant opens, but the owners lack the working capital needed to keep it alive more than a few months.

Ruth Fertel, founder of the Ruth's Chris Steakhouse chain, mortgaged her house in 1965 to raise the money to start her first restaurant. This was against the will and wisdom of her brother, lawyer, and banker. She was warned that she would not be able to handle the hard work and that she would lose her home because she didn't have any experience in the business.

To accumulate enough assets to start a restaurant without borrowing is difficult. To borrow money wisely and to know how to get loans is a major part of a businessperson's acumen.

In financing any business, astute businesspersons are concerned with risking somebody else's money rather than their own. Many individuals struggle and scheme for years to come up with a way of doing this. Some people have a knack for interesting other people in putting up their money for a venture that the promoter controls.

Few persons entering the restaurant business have the total capital necessary to enter as a complete owner, debt free. Such a course of action would mean owning the land, the restaurant building, and its equipment and furnishings, plus having working capital—that is, a standby amount of cash to open the restaurant and to get through possibly several unprofitable months of operation.

Experienced businesspersons seek to rent or lease the building and land and to search for a loan for the furnishings, equipment, and necessary start-up expenses. Ownership of the land on which the restaurant sits is usually left to a long-term investor. The same may be true for the restaurant building. Rather than using capital for the ownership of the real property, restaurant operators believe their expertise is their investment. They usually want to conserve capital or use it in the most productive way possible. Also, they want to face limited personal risk, should the business fail.

In buying or selling a restaurant, there is a simple rule to follow, say the experts: When you sell, get as much cash as possible. When buying, put as little cash down as possible.

Where does one get the money for a restaurant? Commercial banks are common sources of funds, but the borrower must remember that the lending officers in the banks are only paid employees, not owners, and are also limiting their risks. They take minimal risks because their performance is largely judged by good loans. Lending officers tend to be ultraconservative.

Ordinarily, unless the individual has established a line of credit, the bank wants at least 40 percent (and usually more) of the total needs to be invested by the individual or corporation. This can be a considerable amount. The bank also wants collateral (assets that the bank can take should the loan not be repaid) to be pledged.

Loans are made for varying periods of time:

- A *term loan* is one repaid in installments, usually over a period longer than a year.

- *Intermediate loans* are made for up to five years.

- *Single-use real estate loans* typically run less than 20 years.

A construction loan is made in segments during the course of construction and is usually a term loan. The borrower should be clear as to when segments of a construction loan will be available—that is, before or after each phase of construction is completed. Borrowers often ask for a construction loan larger than the actual amount required, and, if granted, use the balance as working capital. (Never pay a contractor all of the money required up front.)

PREPARING FOR THE LOAN APPLICATION

Obtaining the necessary amount of money to get into a restaurant is never easy—unless your friends or relatives are loaded and prepared to back you. Aspiring restaurateurs have bought the furniture and fixtures of an existing restaurant for $30,000. This money is paid to the previous person leasing the property, for the work they had done to set up a restaurant, including the kitchen, storeroom, toilets, dining area, plumbing, and electrical.

This $30,000 was paid after a due diligence—that is, a thorough check to assure that everything works and that the health department or some other agency isn't about to shut the place down for some infringement of their regulations. The kitchen and all its equipment—stoves, ovens, grills, broilers, fryers, refrigerators, mixers, tables, shelves, storerooms—and the tables, chairs, booths, and bar out front are all part of the FF&E—furnishings, fixtures, and equipment. Obviously, it would cost considerably more to make alterations to the building to accommodate a restaurant.

Larger restaurants will naturally cost more to get into, and it's just a matter of finding a location and price that are right for you. Likewise, better locations cost more. For example, you might pay $65,000 for a run-down restaurant in a good location.

Danny Meyer got into Union Square Café in 1985 for $75,000; he was smart enough to start a restaurant in an area that was on the upswing!

Given that one of the main reasons for restaurant failure is a lack of funds, it is critical to address three important financial questions from the get go:

1.   How much money do you have?
2.   How much money will you need to get the restaurant up and running?
3.   How much money will it take to stay in business?

A personal financial statement can answer the first question. Figure 9.1 shows the headings for the various assets and liabilities of a personal financial statement.

Figure 9.2 addresses how much money will be needed. The start-up costs need to be accurately assessed, because they must be paid for out of revenues once the restaurant is open. From the signing of the lease until opening day there is often a gap of a few weeks or months. You will need money to live on, and there will also be expenses for

---

PERSONAL FINANCIAL STATEMENT
_____, 200__

ASSETS

Cash on hand	_____
Savings account	_____
Stocks, bonds, securities	_____
Accounts/notes receivable	_____
Real estate	_____
Life insurance (cash value)	_____
Automobile/other vehicles	_____
Other liquid assets	_____
TOTAL ASSETS	_____

LIABILITIES

Accounts payable	_____
Notes payable	_____
Contracts payable	_____
Taxes	_____
Real estate loans	_____
Other liabilities	_____

FIGURE 9.1 Personal financial statement.

Source: http://www.sbaonline.sba.gov/starting/checklist.html

Start-up cost estimates

Decorating, remodeling   _____

Fixtures, equipment   _____

Installing fixtures, equipment   _____

Services, supplies   _____

Beginning inventory cost   _____

Legal, professional fees   _____

Licenses, permits   _____

Telephone utility deposits   _____

Insurance   _____

Signs   _____

Advertising for opening   _____

Unanticipated expenses   _____

     TOTAL START-UP COSTS   _____

FIGURE 9.2 Start-up cost estimates.

Source: Adapted from http://www.sbaonline.sba.gov/starting/checklist.html

the restaurant. Figure 9.3 will help allocate costs for those weeks/months from lease signing to opening. Hopefully, there will be no delays and the opening will be on time. These expenses continue once the restaurant is open but will then be on the income statement.

Logically, the next step in planning the restaurant is to do a budget.

Expenses for one month

Your living costs   _____

Employee wages   _____

Rent/lease   _____

Advertising   _____

Supplies   _____

Utilities   _____

Insurance   _____

Taxes   _____

Maintenance   _____

Delivery/transportation   _____

Miscellaneous   _____

FIGURE 9.3 Expenses for one month.

Source: http://www.sbaonline.sba.gov/starting/checklist.html

Budgeting

The purpose of budgeting is to "do the numbers" and, more accurately, forecast if the restaurant will be viable. Sales must cover all costs, including interest on loans, and allow for reasonable profit, greater than if the money were successfully invested in stocks, bonds, or real estate. Financial lenders require budget forecasts as a part of the overall business plan. The first step in the budget process is to forecast sales. The next is to allocate costs to the forecasted sales, allowing for a fair profit margin. This must all be done in relation to the competitive price-value-quality equation.

In establishing an accounting format to project sales and operational costs of a restaurant, the following basic categories are useful:

- Sales
- Cost of sales
- Gross profit
- Budgeted costs
- Labor costs
- Operating costs
- Fixed costs

Forecasting Sales

Sales forecasting for a restaurant is, at best, calculated guesswork. Many factors beyond the control of the restaurant, such as unexpected economic factors and weather, influence the eventual outcome. Without a fairly accurate forecast of sales, however, it is impossible to predict the success or failure of the restaurant because all expenses, fixed and variable, are dependent on sales for payment. Predicting sales volume, while not easy, can be done with a high degree of accuracy if a budget forecast is completed.

Sales volume has two components: the average guest check and guest counts. The average guest check is the total sales divided by the number of guests. Menu prices plus beverage sales partly determine the amount of the average check. The guest count is simply the total number of guests patronizing the restaurant over a particular period.

The first step is to estimate the year's projected guest count. This is done by dividing the year into one 29-day and twelve 28-day accounting periods, then breaking these down into four 7-day weeks. It is better to keep separate records for each meal,

Budget Forecast of Restaurant Sales, Period_____ Week_____ 20XX

Day	Forecast No. of Guests	Actual No. of Guests	% + or (-)	Forecast Amount of Average Check	Actual Amount of Average Check	% + or (-)	Forecast Amount of Food Sales	Actual Amount of Food Sales	% + or (-)	Forecast Amount of Beverage Sales	Actual Amount of Beverage Sales	% + or (-)	B	L	D	Total Forecast Sales	Total Actual Sales	% Total Actual for Sales (-)
Mon																		
Tues																		
Wed																		
Thur																		
Fri																		
Sat																		
Sun																		
Week's Total																		

Note: B = Breakfast; L = Lunch; D = Dinner.

FIGURE 9.4 Budget forecast of restaurant sales for one week.

Budget Forecast of Restaurant Sales, Period _____ — 28 Days, Date _____ 20XX

Period	Forecast No. of Guests	Actual No. of Guests	% + or (−)	Forecast Amount of Average Check	Actual Amount of Average Check	% + or (−)	Forecast Amount of Food Sales	Actual Amount of Food Sales	% + or (−)	Forecast Amount of Beverage Sales	Actual Amount of Beverage Sales	% + or (−)	B	L	D	Total Forecast Sales	Total Actual Sales	% + or (−)
1																		
2																		
3																		
4																		
5																		
6																		
7																		
8																		
9																		
10																		
11																		
12																		
13																		
Annual Total																		

Note: B = Breakfast; L = Lunch; D = Dinner.

FIGURE 9.5 Sales forecast for the year.

because the sales and therefore staffing levels will need to be compatible. Keeping a sales history from day one is recommended (see Figure 9.4).

After the four weekly forecasts are complete, they are totaled on the period-one sheet. The remaining 12 accounting period sheets are then completed, giving the total sales forecast for the year (Figure 9.5).

	Amount	Percentage
Sales		
Food		
Beverage		
Others		
Total sales	_____	100.00
Cost of Sales		
Food		
Beverage		
Others		
Total cost of sales	_____	
Gross profit	_____	
Other income	_____	
Total income	_____	
Controllable Expenses	_____	
Salaries and wages		
Employee benefits		
Direct operating expenses[a]		
Music and entertainment		
Marketing		
Energy and utility		
Administrative and general		
Repairs and maintenance		
Total controllable expenses	_____	
Rent and other occupation costs		
Income before interest, depreciation, and taxes		
Interest		
Depreciation		
Net income before taxes	_____	
Income taxes	_____	
Net income	_____	

[a]Telephone, insurance, accounting/legal office supplies; paper, china, glass, silver, menus, landscaping, detergent/cleaning supplies, and so on.
Source: Adapted from Raymond S. Schmidgall, *Hospitality Industry Managerial Accounting*, 2nd ed. (East Lansing, Mich.: Educational Institute of the American Hotel and Motel Association, 1990), 94.

FIGURE 9.6 **Sample income statement.**

The totals from each of the accounting periods add up to a yearly total sales forecast. The results may be checked by discussing with other restaurant personnel and credit card representatives to gain an estimate of sales at a similar restaurant. With experience, the margin of error in estimating a restaurant's total sales generally decreases.

The sales forecast for the first few months should consider the facts that it takes time for people to realize that the restaurant is open and that a large number of people are usually attracted to a new restaurant.

Once weekly, monthly, and yearly sales figures are estimated, the cost of sales is determined. It is then possible to allocate fixed and variable costs to reveal a predicted profit (or loss) figure.

Income Statement

The purpose of the income statement (Figure 9.6) is to provide information to management and ownership about the financial performance (profitability) of the restaurant over a given period of time. Information on sales and costs is provided in a systematic way that allows for analysis and comparison. The net income (or loss) is shown after expenses are deducted from sales.

The income statement begins with sales of food, beverage, and other sales (which could be take-out, catering, cigars, cigarettes, tobacco, telephone, etc.). The cost of goods sold is deducted from total sales. This leaves a gross profit, which is sales minus cost of goods sold.

From the gross profit, the remaining controllable variable and fixed costs must be deducted before taxes are paid and profits distributed.

RESTAURANT OPERATIONS AND CONTROL*

Outline

Restaurant Operations

Front of the House

Control

Liquor Control

Controllable Expenses

Labor Costs

Learning Objectives

After reading and studying this chapter, you should be able to:

- Describe back-of-the-house operations.

- Describe front-of-the-house operations.

- Identify ways to control food, beverage, and labor costs.

- Discuss methods of guest check control.

RESTAURANT OPERATIONS

Restaurant operations are split between the back and front of the house. In the back of the house are the areas that include purchasing, receiving, storage, issuing,

---

* Authored by John R. Walker and Donald E. Lundberg.

food preparation and service, dishwashing area, sanitation, accounting, budgeting, and control. The back of the house is sometimes called the "heart" of the operation. A successful restaurant operation depends on the back of the house functioning smoothly. The kitchen is the center of production and must be run properly, producing an excellent food quality and presentation and meeting costing goals.

The chef, having set the menu for the day—this might be either a permanent menu with specials or a daily menu—will have checked inventory at the close the night before to ensure sufficient food quantities for the anticipated orders of the next meal period, and completed a purchase order that was given to an office assistant or owner/manager to place with vendors. The chef made out a production sheet for each station, detailing all the tasks necessary to bring the food quantities up to par stock of prepared items and to complete the preparation on time. As the prep cooks arrive, they are given their assignments and begin to prepare the various menu items for the anticipated number of guests according to the standardized recipes. Most of the prep work is done during the early morning and afternoon.

The chef makes sure that all menu items are prepared in accordance with the standardized recipes and that the line is ready for service. During service, either the chef or a manager may act as a caller—in an attempt to control the ordering and expediting of plates at *the pass*. All hand-written orders must be easily read or come through on the kitchen printer so that the kitchen cooks can put up the right plates at the right time. During service everyone is focusing on timing and presentation. The food must be at the right temperature, yet not be overcooked; flavorful, but not overpowering.

After the service, the food is properly put away and the cleanup is done, the par stocks for all stations for the next service are checked, orders are made, and production schedules for all stations are done. As you well know, it's a never-ending challenge that is so fascinating to all who love the restaurant business. It sounds easy, but ask those who know and you may get a different story. Don't forget to thank the crew for a great shift!

FRONT OF THE HOUSE

F *ront of the house* refers to the hosts, bartenders, servers, and bussers. There is an opening manager and a closing manager. If necessary, each area of the restaurant will have an opener, a swing shift person, and closers, so as to spread the staff to cover the shift in the most effective manner. However, guests often call for reservations or

NO Thanking a crew member for a great shift. Courtesy Anna Maria Oyster Bar.

directions and receive a first impression of the restaurant by the way they are treated. Guests also receive a first impression known as *curbside appeal*—or, would you even stop or get out of the car? The visual appeal of the building and parking area are important to potential guests. Is the pathway to the entrance door clean, or are there cigarette butts littering the sidewalk? Are the doors clean, or do they have fingerprints all over them? Is the host's greeting welcoming? Each of these adds up to that important first impression of a restaurant.

The first thing restaurant managers do is to forecast how many guests are expected and share that information with the kitchen. A guest count is arrived at by taking the same day last year and factoring in things like today's weather, day of the week, and so on. Figure 10.1 shows a *daily flash report* for a large-volume restaurant. Notice the daily sales for the month of October and the sales for the same day last year. Keeping accurate records is vital in the restaurant business. Having last year's sales is helpful in planning for this year. This report also has the number of guests and the average check, together with month-to-date sales and variances. The forecast is also used for staffing levels to ensure an appropriate level of service. Different restaurants have different table configurations. In the high-rent district, tables are often 24 inches square and about the

As Of 09/30	Sales To Date 2002 3,852,448.64			Sales To Date 2003 4,105,336.69			MTD 2002	MTD 2003	Daily Flash MTD Variance 2002-2003	YTD 2002	YTD 2003	YTD Variance 2002-2003
	Daily Sales	Retail	GST/$ CH	Daily Sales	GST/$ CH	Retail						
01-Oct	5,048.39	88.99	357/14.39	5,923.31	341/18.81	490.58	5,048.39	5,923.31	874.92	3,857,497.03	4,111,260.00	253,762.97
02-Oct	7,416.94	142.70	505/14.96	8,412.06	597/14.87	465.63	12,465.33	14,335.37	1,870.04	3,864,913.97	4,119,672.06	254,758.09
03-Oct	10,436.67	268.89	648/16.52	18,958.86	1089/17.75	374.78	22,902.00	33,294.23	10,392.23	3,875,350.64	4,138,630.92	263,280.28
04-Oct	16,149.93	558.73	1048/15.94	20,744.17	we/1344/15.81	513.93	39,051.93	54,038.40	14,986.47	3,891,500.57	4,159,375.09	267,874.52
05-Oct	19,897.08	673.68	we/1348/15.26	13,074.03	we/896/14.96	333.77	58,949.01	67,112.43	8,163.42	3,911,397.65	4,172,449.12	261,051.47
06-Oct	13,655.00	431.06	we/900/15.65	8,807.25	598/15.19	281.35	72,604.01	75,919.68	3,315.67	3,925,052.65	4,181,256.37	256,203.72
07-Oct	9,439.82	542.42	595/16.77	10,037.79	669/15.73	488.29	82,043.83	85,957.47	3,913.64	3,934,492.47	4,191,294.16	256,801.69
08-Oct	8,714.72	335.88	648/13.96	9,979.03	641/16.13	364.62	90,758.65	95,936.50	5,177.95	3,943,207.19	4,201,273.19	258,066.00
09-Oct	10,105.22	157.95	696/14.74				100,863.77					
10-Oct	9,042.58	442.49	637/14.89				109,906.35					
11-Oct	16,940.07	785.41	1126/15.74		we		126,846.42					
12-Oct	19,019.89	667.20	we/1254/15.69		we		145,866.31					
13-Oct	15,433.36	545.95	we/1026/15.57				161,299.67					
14-Oct	8,469.89	386.68	hr/550/16.11				169,769.56					
15-Oct	5,073.38	554.68	r/355/15.85				174,842.94					
16-Oct	9,241.20	452.89	603/16.07				184,084.14					
17-Oct	11,505.97	540.74	723/16.66				195,590.11					
18-Oct	17,775.63	609.30	1198/15.34		we		213,365.74					
19-Oct	18,692.93	453.42	we/1113/17.21		we		232,058.67					
20-Oct	12,137.37	301.73	we/850/14.63				244,196.04					
21-Oct	9,338.07	320.65	635/15.18				253,534.11					
22-Oct	9,752.52	397.92	679/14.94				263,286.63					
23-Oct	9,011.51	590.73	599/16.03				272,298.14					
24-Oct	12,925.34	615.76	708/19.12		we		285,223.48					
25-Oct	17,504.63	783.48	964/18.97		we		302,728.11					
26-Oct	18,790.51	570.62	we/1315/14.72				321,518.62					
27-Oct	13,365.76	354.40	we/960/14.29				334,884.38					
28-Oct	12,104.74	349.72	781/15.74				346,989.12					
29-Oct	8,119.43	316.84	556/15.17				355,108.55					
30-Oct	7,016.80	149.89	466/15.37				362,125.35					
31-Oct	6,425.25	281.74	425/15.78				368,550.60					
Total	388,550.60	13,672.54		95,936.50		3,312.95						

	2001	2002	2003	Average		2001	2002	2003	Average
JAN	265,910.27	277,170.15	267,633.02	270,237.81	JUL	427,282.31	447,676.15	487,680.15	454,212.87
FEB	465,575.02	393,856.56	406,657.17	422,029.58	AUG	371,443.39	372,076.64	388,821.95	377,447.33
MAR	517,305.12	619,728.81	656,074.68	597,702.87	SEP	225,733.12	266,581.66	287,659.20	259,991.33
APR	563,230.27	564,188.03	639,666.97	589,028.42	OCT	307,391.00	368,550.60	0.00	225,313.87
MAY	471,499.80	482,067.26	556,313.22	503,293.43	NOV	328,428.24	321,977.07	0.00	216,801.77
JUN	428,233.94	429,103.38	414,830.33	424,055.88	DEC	294,560.80	270,770.83	0.00	188,443.88
SUBTL	2,711,754.42	2,766,114.19	2,941,175.39		PTD TOTAL	4,666,593.28	4,813,747.14	4,105,336.69	

FIGURE 10.1 A daily flash for a large restaurant showing daily sales for the month of October, the number of guests and average check, month-to-date and year-to-date sales, and variances and sales for the same date last year.

same distance from each other—waiter, there's an elbow in my soup! The best tables are those that can go from a deuce to a foursome with flaps or quickly become a six-top, when spread open. Servers can then arrange for parties of various numbers, without too much trouble. The restaurant is set, the tables laid, the bar is stocked and ready. Then the front of the house staff have a quick-service meeting to go over the specials of the day and perhaps a training detail. This is followed by a family-style meal for all front-of-house staff. Then it's action stations!

Hosts greet guests and seat them by rotation in sections, so as not to overwhelm any one server. The hosts generally give guests menus and inform them that Alicia will be your server. Occasionally, guests will be asked to wait—hopefully, only a few minutes. This is also done to help space out the orders, which helps avoid the kitchen getting too slammed! The server introduces himself or herself, explains the beverage specials, and takes and brings the beverage order while the guests are deciding what to have from the menu. Specials of the day are explained and any questions are answered. Servers need to be knowledgeable about the menu so as to describe and "suggestively sell" dishes. Once the order is taken, it is given or sent to the kitchen, the appropriate cutlery is checked for each guest, soup spoons either being added or removed as the case may be. The busser or server may bring bread or similar items to the table, followed

Gary spending time with a regular guest at the Anna Maria Oyster Bar. Courtesy Anna Maria Oyster Bar.

by the server bringing the beverage order and serving it. Appetizers are brought to the table and served—each to the correct person, without having to ask "who's having what." As this table is enjoying the meal, the server keeps an eye on the guests but also takes care of three or four other tables. Entrees are served and cleared, the table is cleaned, the dessert cutlery is brought down to the side of the guest (if it's on the table), and dessert menus are given to the guests. Coffee and after-dinner liquors are also suggested. Eventually, the check is requested and presented.

The manager makes sure everything goes smoothly, by helping guests and staff in any way that will make for a more enjoyable dining experience. Managers need to spend time with guests, ensuring that they return soon with their friends.

Danny Meyer describes his restaurants as machines. The cleaning takes place overnight. At 6 A.M. the lunch cooks arrive. Deliveries are received, the cooks cook, and the bakers bake. Managers arrive at 8:30 and servers at 10:15. In between, the chef and sous chef may be shopping for fresh produce. Once the set-up is complete at 11 A.M., all servers and cooks have a family lunch. During this time they go over the service notes and lunch specials. At 11:30, the final touches are completed—uniforms checked, the seating chart finalized. After lunch, there is a managers' meeting to review the lunch and prepare for dinner. The dinner cooks arrive at 2:30 and the dinner servers at 4:30. They all have a family meal at 5 P.M. The specials and any particular service details are discussed, and the evening dinner service begins. Managers also have a debriefing after the service and record all-important points in the logbook. Managers and chefs watch the clock to be sure that as the restaurant gets quieter, staff are thanked for their shifts and get off the clock. Sounds simple, doesn't it? When you think of the number of guests served at a restaurant like Union Square Café, your respect for Danny Meyer and his partners greatly increases.

Operationally, the owner/manager goes through the elements of management to constantly deal with the many challenges of running a restaurant and meeting or exceeding the goals set. The elements of management are planning, organizing, communicating, decision making, motivation, and control. Goals are set for each *key result area* (KRA). For example, sales goals include the number of guests per meal every day and the average check. Planning also includes working with the chef/cook to determine the amount of each menu item to prepare and the specials to add to the menu.

Several restaurants use the *Red Book* to assist in managing the restaurant—it aids from planning to control. Important information like sales, specials, any short orders from suppliers, who's quit, who's fired, who's hired, and any occurrences from the shift are recorded. Another aspect of planning is that the chef gets a dollar amount for a combination of hourly labor, food, and kitchen supplies purchases, an example being 38.5 percent. This and other aspects of planning link to all the other elements of management.

Schedules and checklists help organize the restaurant. A "lead sheet" lists staff on both shifts so you can easily see who's on duty. There is also a list of staff and phone numbers plus part-timers on call. There is a preshift meeting to go over any service details and the specials. For motivation, restaurants might have sales contests to see who can sell the most of a particular item, usually wine or cocktails. Prizes vary from DVDs to televisions. It's amazing to see how pumped some staff members get over such competitions. An example of control is to keep the cost of goods sold below 52 percent and give managers a bonus on the results. The good thing about pegging this bonus on the total cost of goods sold is that it ties the back and front of house together. So managers are watching for waste, portion control, and so on.

Some restaurants use the services of a *shopper* who makes a reservation at the restaurant, arrives, and has a meal like any other guest—albeit anonymously. The shopper completes a report on the restaurant. A sample of a shoppers' report is shown in Figure 10.2 . Notice how it covers all areas of the restaurant and service. Other forms offer a scale of 1 to 5, for example, for the shopper to score the restaurant and express an overall percentage result.

CONTROL

In the restaurant business, you first have to know how to steal the chicken before you can stop someone else from stealing the chicken. There is so much food and beverage in a restaurant that, unless management and owners exert tight control, losses will occur. If portion control is not used, you might as well put a few dollars on each plate as it goes out of the kitchen. "Control is like saying, how do you eat an elephant—you take a lot of little bites." Stephen Ananicz, chief operating officer of the Childs restaurant group, offers this advice: "Don't 'manage' to cut costs—manage to build revenue." Buy the best product and use standardized recipes and weigh and measure frequently. When checking in produce and dry goods, the worst thing you can do is to allow someone to sign for it, or even to just look at the boxes. There might be rotten stuff packed at the bottom. Really check the expensive items to see that they are what you ordered—quantity, quality, and weight. So pull things out and really check that you get what you're paying for. Don't over or under order—order a realistic expectation for the number of guests and the choices of menu items they are likely to make. Do a daily inventory of high-priced items like meats.

LOCATION ID	Location Name		
FILL ID	Date		9/17/03
EVALUATOR ID	Day		Wednesday
Location Address	Arrival Time		6:10pm
City, State	Departure Time		7:30pm
Phone	Total Amount Spent		**$61.18**
	Guest Demographic	#Adults 2 #Males 1	
		#Kids 0 #Females 1	

PHONE CALL	YES	NO	**Comments**
Was the phone answered within 3 rings?	☒	☐	Terri answered after two rings.
Was the greeting appropriate?	☒	☐	Cheerful voice!
Was the person friendly?	☒	☐	
Was your question answered without hesitation?	☒	☐	All questions were answered.

ENVIRONMENT–Initial Impression

Was the parking lot free of debris?	☒	☐	
Was the exterior of the building in good repair?	☒	☐	
Was the landscape well maintained?	☒	☐	
Was the entrance clean and free of debris?	☒	☐	
Was the waiting area clean?	☒	☐	
Were the windows and doors clean?	☒	☐	
Were all of the light bulbs functional?	☒	☐	
Were the light fixtures, fans and rafters dust free?	☒	☐	
Were the floors clean?	☒	☐	

ENVIRONMENT–Table Preparation

Was the seating area neatly arranged?	☒	☐	
Was the tabletop clean?	☒	☐	
Were the chairs clean?	☒	☐	
Were the menus clean and grease free?	☒	☐	
Were the utensils clean?	☒	☐	
Were the condiment containers full and clean?	☐	☐	There were no condiments at the bar.
Were the ashtrays clean and empty?	☐	☐	☒ N/A

ENVIRONMENT–Atmosphere

Was the atmosphere appropriate?	☒	☐		
How was the music sound level?	☒ Perfect	☐ Too Loud	☐ Too Soft	
How was the lighting level?	☒ Perfect	☐ Too Bright	☐ Too Dark	
How was the restaurant temperature?	☒ Perfect	☐ Too Hot	☐ Too Cold	

ENVIRONMENT–Restroom

Which restroom did you visit?	☒ Mens	☒ Ladies	
Was it odor free?	☒	☐	
Was the area clean?	☒	☐	
Was toilet paper available?	☒	☐	
Were paper towels available?	☒	☐	One paper towel holder was empty, but the other one had paper.

FIGURE 10.2 Restaurant shopper's report. Courtesy Anna Maria Oyster Bar.

Restaurants can use programs like Chef Tec, which shows the actual food cost compared with the ideal food cost. This is known as *food optimization*. It works like this: Take every item on the menu and cost it out by ingredients. At the end of the day, run a *product mix*, which tells how many items were sold, multiply each menu

SERVICE

Hostess/Host–Appearance   Name   **Carry**

Description (required) Gender: **F** Hair Color: **Blonde** Hair Length: **Shoulder** Height: **5'1''** Weight: **100**

	YES	NO	Comments
Was her/his overall appearance neat?	☒	☐	Black Top and Tan Slacks
Was she/he friendly?	☒	☐	

Hostess/Host–Service

	YES	NO	Comments
Were you immediately greeted?	☒	☐	She was seating a customer and we asked if we could sit at the bar and she said "Yes! certainly."
Was the greeting warm and friendly?	☒	☐	
Were you given an estimated waiting time?	☐	☐	☒ N/A
If YES, what time period was given?		Minutes	
If YES, were you seated within the time period given?	☐	☐	☒ N/A
Were you offered a choice of seating?	☐	☐	N/A
Were you escorted to your table?	☐	☐	N/A
Were you given menus when seated?	☐	☐	N/A
Were children given a menu and crayons?	☐	☐	☒ N/A
Were you told who your server would be?	☐	☐	N/A

Server–Appearance   Name   **Jim**

Description (required) Gender: **M** Hair Color: **Salt/Pepper** Hair Length: **Short** Height: **5'7''** Weight: **145**

	YES	NO	Comments
Was her/his overall appearance neat?	☒	☐	Tropical Shirt and Tan Shorts
Was she/he friendly?	☒	☐	

Server–Service

	YES	NO	Comments
Were you greeted within a reasonable time?	☒	☐	
Was the greeting warm and friendly?	☒	☐	
Were your utensils delivered before your food?	☒	☐	
Were your beverages served in a timely manner?	☒	☐	If NO, how long?
Was your appetizer served in a timely manner?	☒	☐	If NO, how long?
Were your entrees served in a timely manner?	☒	☐	If NO, how long?
Was your dessert served in a timely manner?	☐	☐	If NO, how long? N/A
Was your order correct?	☒	☐	
Was your satisfaction verified within 2 minutes of receiving your order?	☒	☐	
Was your satisfaction verified once more during your meal?	☒	☐	
Were your non-alcoholic drinks refilled without question?	☒	☐	
Was your table cleared as needed?	☒	☐	
Were you offered a to-go container?	☐	☐	Not Needed
Were your items placed in the to-go container for you?	☐	☐	N/A
Was your check presented in a timely manner?	☒	☐	
Was your check correct?	☒	☐	
Was your check processed in a timely manner?	☒	☐	
Was your receipt returned and change counted back?	☒	☐	

FIGURE 10.2 (Continued)

	YES	NO	Comments
Server–Suggestive Selling			
Were you offered specific drinks?	☐	☒	
If you ordered beer, was a pitcher suggested?	☐	☐	☒ N/A
Did the server suggest specific appetizers?	☒	☐	Jim told us to check out the Specials on the Shrimp Menu.
Did the server suggest specific entrees?	☒	☐	Jim did a great job of making suggestions
Did the server suggest specific side items?	☒	☐	and of answering questions about the
Did the server suggest coffee?	☒	☐	different menu items.
Did the server suggest dessert?	☒	☐	
The Team–Teamwork			
Did the team members ID younger patrons?	☒	☐	
Did the team work together to get food served?	☒	☐	
Did the team work together to keep tables cleared?	☒	☐	
Did the team interact and contribute to the atmosphere?	☒	☐	
Were all of the team members friendly?	☒	☐	
Were you thanked for your visit?	☒	☐	
Were you invited to return?	☐	☒	No one present at the door when we left.

The Manager   Name   **Not Observed**

Description (required) Gender: Hair Color: Hair Length: Height: Weight:

	YES	NO	
Was the Manager visible in the dining area?	☐	☒	
Did the Manager greet you at any time?	☐	☒	
Was the Manager interacting with customers?	☐	☒	We did not see anyone acting in a management position.

PLEASE LIST ADDITIONAL TEAM MEMBERS THAT INTERACTED WITH YOU DURING YOUR VISIT.

Position   Name
Description (required)   Gender: Hair Color: Hair Length: Height: Weight:
Comments
Position   Name
Description (required)   Gender: Hair Color: Hair Length: Height: Weight:
Comments
Position   Name
Description (required)   Gender: Hair Color: Hair Length: Height: Weight:
Comments

PLEASE LIST AND RATE ITEM ORDERED, EVEN IF THEY ARE NOT REIMBURSABLE

MENU

	Ratings	1–Poor Presentation	2–Good Taste	3–Great Temperature	List Receipt Price	Would you order again?
Beverages						
2–Vodka Tonic		☐1☐2☒3	☐1☐2☒3	☐1☐2☒3	8.50	☒Yes☐No
2–Coffee		☐1☐2☒3	☐1☐2☒3	☐1☐2☒3	3.38	☒Yes☐No
		☐1☐2☒3	☐1☐2☒3	☐1☐2☐3		☐Yes☐No
Appetizers						
2–Coconut Shrimp		☐1☐2☒3	☐1☒2☐3	☐1☐2☒3	11.98	☒Yes☐No
		☐1☐2☐3	☐1☐2☐3	☐1☐2☐3		☐Yes☐No
		☐1☐2☐3	☐1☐2☐3	☐1☐2☐3		☐Yes☐No

FIGURE 10.2 (Continued)

Entrees					
Grouper, Dinner Portabella	☐1☐2☒3	☐1☐2☒3	☐1☐2☒3	13.99	☒Yes☐No
Grouper, Dinner Fried	☐1☐2☒3	☐1☐2☒3	☐1☐2☒3	11.99	☒Yes☐No
	☐1☐2☐3	☐1☐2☐3	☐1☐2☐3		☐Yes☐No
Side Items					
Red Potatoes/Garlic Carrots	☐1☐2☒3	☐1☐2☒3	☐1☐2☒3	incl.	☒Yes☐No
Red Potatoes/Cole Slaw	☐1☐2☒3	☐1☐2☒3	☐1☐2☒3	incl.	☒Yes☐No
	☐1☐2☐3	☐1☐2☐3	☐1☐2☐3		☐Yes☐No
Desserts					
	☐1☐2☐3	☐1☐2☐3	☐1☐2☐3		☐Yes☐No
	☐1☐2☐3	☐1☐2☐3	☐1☐2☐3		☐Yes☐No

Receipt Total	$53.18
Gratuity Amount	$8.00
Total Amount Spent	**$61.18**
Check Number	20032
Server #	Jim
For Office Use Only–Reimbursed Amount	**$54.27**

FIGURE 10.2 (Continued)

item by the number sold, and that will give you what food should have cost for the day. Chef Tec will also cost, scale, and store recipes; write recipe procedures using cut and paste, customizable fonts, colors, and a culinary spellchecker; instantly analyze recipe/menu cost by portion and yield; attach photos, diagrams, videos, or company logos to recipes; print kitchen-readable recipes; calculate costs based on highest or most recent prices paid for ingredients; save recipes in HTML; and share data via the Internet.

For inventory control, Chef Tec can preload an inventory list of 1,900 ingredients, import purchases from vendors' online ordering systems; track vendor pricing from purchasing bids, compare vendor pricing from purchases or bids, instantly see the impact of a price increase on recipes, automate ordering with user-set par levels, and generate customized reports detailing purchases, bids, and credits. Nutritional analysis is also a part of the program.

The food cost percentage should be calculated at least monthly. The formula for doing the food cost percentage is

$$\frac{\text{cost}}{\text{sales}} \times 100$$

So, if an item cost $1.00 and sold for $4.00, the food cost percentage is $1.00 \div 4.00 = .25, \times 100 = 25$ percent. It works like this:

Opening inventory	500.00
+ Purchases	200.00
	700.00
− Complementary & staff meals & spoilage	50.00
− Closing inventory	400.00
= Cost of food sold	250.00

The cost of food sold divided by food revenue ($1000.00) = the food cost percentage. So here, $250.00 divided by $1000.00 = .25 × 100 = a food cost of 25 percent. All you have to do is remember cost ÷ sales × 100, and opening inventory + purchases − any deductions − employee meals.

Taking the actual inventory can be a pain, but if the storeroom and coolers or refrigerators are clean and tidy and you have a list of all the items typed out or, better yet, entered into the computer or handheld device, it will be much easier and quicker. Make sure that the items are listed as they appear on the shelves. Experienced operators take spot inventories of expensive items and do a quick check on the number of sales of that particular item to see that there is no pilferage.

LIQUOR CONTROL

Control of liquor is critical to the success of the restaurant. There is too much opportunity for abuse and theft. The cycle begins with management deciding which brands to have for the well or house, then setting a par stock of beverages to have on hand. Management also decides on the selling price and mark-up for beer, wine, and liquor. This will set the standard for the beverage cost percentage. Once the standard is set, there is something to measure actual performance against. Remember that the normal pouring cost for beer is 24 to 25 percent. Thus, if a beer cost 60 cents, then it should sell for $2.40. Now, the pricing level and mark-up is your choice. It could be that you want to sell domestic beer at $2.75 or $2.95. If it still costs 60 cents, then the pouring cost percentage will go up and you will make more money. You will best know the price points for your guests.

Wine should have a pouring cost of 26 to 30 percent. So, for a 30 percent cost, if a bottle of wine cost $10.00, the selling price is $33.30. If you wanted a 33 percent pouring cost on wine, then the selling price would be $30.00 or, better yet, $29.99.

Liquor pouring costs should be 16 to 20 percent of sales. Thus, for a 20 percent pouring cost if a shot of premium Johnnie Walker Gold cost 83.33 cents, it would need to sell for $4.16, or a rounded figure. The size of the bottle and the measure poured will also influence the pouring cost percentage. For example, if the Scotch comes in a quart bottle and you are using a 1.5-ounce measure, then you would expect to get 21 measures out of the bottle. Some bottles are liters and will need to be computed into U.S. measures. Mixed drinks really complicate things because they use a base liquor plus a small amount of two or three other liquors. Fortunately, the popular cocktails can be recorded in the POS system and costed out accordingly. The number of mixed drinks is recorded and the correct amount of liquor allocated to the cost of each drink is charged, so that when the cost of beverages is calculated, it will include the correct amount.

Combined, the beverage pouring cost should be 23 to 25 percent of beverage sales. In order to obtain this pour cost percentage, restaurant operators get to make their own rules on pouring. We will insist that all drinks are poured using the pour spout or a jigger—no free pouring, and nothing is served unless there is a check. Management needs to observe the bar—this can be done with a camera and spotters if necessary.

The beverage inventory must be secure at all times. The storage area must be kept locked, with only one key available to the manager. New bottles should only be issued only when the old bottle is returned. All bottles should have an indelible stamp of the restaurant on them, and the liquor bottles must have the state tax stamp when sold by the wholesaler or distributor—it is a different color from the stamp on bottles sold in retail stores.

Beverage inventory is done by "eyeball," measuring bottles of liquor in tenths. The amount is recorded either on a sheet or directly into a program on a computer or handheld. The total value of liquor is added and recorded. Wine and beer bottles are counted and priced. Then a total beverage inventory value is arrived at. This is then expressed as a percentage of beverage sales—not total sales! A similar formula is used:

Opening inventory	$1,000	
Plus purchases	500	
		1,500
Less complementary & spillage	50	
Less closing inventory	750	
		800
= Cost of goods sold		700

If we assume beverage sales were $2,800, then the beverage cost percentage would be 25 percent.

Gary managing the percentages. Courtesy Anna Maria Oyster Bar.

As with the food purchasing, have the bartender make out an order and turn in the empty liquor bottles when requesting new ones. A copy of the order should go to the person receiving the beverage delivery. (You should not rely on the delivery person's sheet but on your own order.) A manager must carefully check everything into the secure storeroom, and issues must be made only when a proper requisition is given in exchange for the bottles.

Figure 10.3 shows the projected food and beverage sales and costs, the actual sales and costs, and the variance for a volume restaurant. Notice how it is more difficult to achieve the percentages when the sales drop as they did in August. The skill of management is to manage to get the percentages in times of lower sales.

CONTROLLABLE EXPENSES

Controllable expenses is the term used to describe the expenses that can be changed in the short term. Variable costs are normally controllable. Other controllable costs include salaries and wages (payroll) and related benefits; direct operating expenses, such as music and entertainment; marketing (including sales, advertising, public relations, and promotions); heat, light, and power; administration; and general repairs and

Optimum Costs				
	04/30/2003	05/31/2003	06/30/2003	07/31/2003
Restaurant 1				
Food				
Sales	253,943.77	254,048.06	197,163.00	240,348.79
Cost	70,624.89	70,848.51	56,608.45	68,858.42
%	27.81%	27.89%	28.71%	28.65%
Actual Sales	372,505.78	298,191.75	236,082.62	269,029.44
Actual Costs	113,267.63	97,768.77	76,762.95	87,325.46
Actual %	30.41%	32.79%	32.52%	32.46%
Variance	2.60%	4.90%	3.80%	3.81%
Liquor				
Sales	81,736.01	70,985.71	47,267.47	58,580.56
Cost	13,081.09	11,537.95	7,667.29	9,670.63
%	16.00%	16.25%	16.22%	16.51%
Actual Sales	83,531.47	69,673.86	49,798.18	61,300.67
Actual Costs	13,683.82	13,059.45	8,669.18	11,438.24
Actual %	16.38%	18.74%	17.41%	18.66%
Variance	0.38%	2.49%	1.19%	2.15%
Beer				
Sales	32,687.61	26,292.40	18,474.87	24,519.25
Cost	8,222.21	6,454.98	4,482.31	6,115.70
%	25.15%	24.55%	24.26%	24.94%
Actual Sales	33,373.99	26,963.20	20,221.85	24,975.13
Actual Costs	8,371.40	7,612.03	5,701.85	6,005.33
Actual %	25.08%	28.23%	28.20%	24.05%
Variance	-0.07%	3.68%	3.93%	-0.90%
Wine				
Sales	28,264.48	23,012.59	14,514.90	16,206.65
Cost	7,299.89	6,294.22	3,761.61	4,237.88
%	25.83%	27.35%	25.92%	26.15%
Actual Sales	28,982.50	23,279.45	16,569.78	16,741.21
Actual Costs	8,027.93	5,474.96	3,759.38	4,856.56
Actual %	27.70%	23.52%	22.69%	29.01%
Variance	1.87%	-3.83%	-3.23%	2.86%

FIGURE 10.3 Projected and actual food and beverage sales cost.

maintenance. The total of all controllable expenses is deducted from the gross profit. Rent and other occupation costs are then deducted to arrive at the income before interest, depreciation, and taxes. Once these are deducted, the net profit remains. Figure 10.4 is a sample income statement showing controllable expenses.

	Statement Period				
	Projected Amount (Thousands)	Percentages	Actual Amount	Percentages	Variance
Sales					
Food (Schedule D-1)	750.0	75.0			
Beverage (Schedule D-2)	250.0	25.0			
Total sales	1,000.0	100.0			
Cost of Sales					
Food	232.5	31.0			
Beverage	55.0	22.0			
Total cost of sales	287.5	28.8			
Gross profit	712.5	71.2			
Other income (Schedule D-3)	4.5	0.5			
Total income	717.0	71.7			
Controllable Expenses					
Salaries and wages (Schedule D-4)	240.0	24.0			
Employee benefits (Schedule D-5)	40.0	4.0			
Direct operating expense* (Schedule D-6)	60.0	6.0			
Music and entertainment (Schedule D-7)	10.0	1.0			
Marketing (Schedule D-8)	40.0	4.0			
Energy and utility (Schedule D-9)	30.0	3.0			
Administrative and general (Schedule D-10)	40.0	4.0			
Repairs and maintenance (Schedule D-11)	20.0	2.0			
Total controllable expenses	480.0	48.0			
Rent and other occupation costs (Schedule D-12)	50.0	5.0			
Income before interest, depreciation, and taxes	187.0	18.7			
Interest	15.0	1.5			
Depreciation	23.0	2.3			
Total	38.0	3.8			
Net income before taxes	149.0	14.9			
Income taxes	50.0	5.0			
Net Income	99.0	10.7			

*Telephone, insurance, accounting/legal office supplies; paper, china, glass, silvers, menus, landscaping, detergent/cleaning supplies, and so on.
Source: Adapted from Raymond S. Schmidgall, *Hospitality Industry Managerial Accounting*, 2nd ed. (East Lansing, Mich.: Educational Institute of the American Hotel and Motel Association, 1990), 94.

FIGURE 10.4 Income statement showing projected and actual controllable expenses.

LABOR COSTS

In most full-service restaurants, the largest variable cost is labor. Depending on the type of restaurant and the degree of service provided, labor costs may range from approximately 16 percent of sales in a quick-service restaurant to 24 percent in a casual operation and up to about 30 percent in an upscale restaurant.

Projecting payroll costs requires the preparation of staffing schedules and establishing wage rates. Staffing patterns may vary during different periods of the year, with changes occurring seasonally or when there are other sales variations. These changes are identified and categorized on a schedule form used to project any single week's payroll activities and to compare them with customer count/sales projections.

Restaurant operators should make a budget at the beginning of the month; break it down to a daily dollar amount, then to hours in the kitchen. Hosts and servers are likely to be at minimum wage, so it's the kitchen where it is important to keep control with an hourly wage of $9 to $14 per hour. Do a labor pro-forma—write out a schedule without names:

3 prep cooks
2 cooks
1 pantry
1 dishwasher   × 7 hours × their average wage = cost per shift

Software programs can give a cost of labor, but you can also work it out. A rule of thumb is 9.2 percent for front-of-the-house labor costs as a percentage of sales and 13 percent for the back of the house. Front of the house staff planning goes like this: If you have 25 tables and want 4 table sections, then $4 \times 6 = 24$, so you need 6 servers to cover the tables every day.

If you are open seven days a week and each server works a four-day workweek, you can calculate how many total shifts/week, or how many servers, are needed to cover every shift. The math looks like this:

7 days/week × 6 servers/day = 42 servers/week, or 42 shifts
42 shifts ÷ 4 shifts/week = 10.5 shifts/week

You can't hire half a person, but you can hire one person part time, so .5 shifts/week is acceptable. But this is based on 25 tables, and they had better be filled! Otherwise, the servers will be standing around. If you know that you will not be using all 25 tables, then downsize the staffing level accordingly. Don't forget the bussers: you need three or four per busy shift—less on quieter ones.

In the bar, depending on the volume of business, if you are open for lunch and are busy, you need one bartender and one or two at night. It's a good idea to crosstrain a couple of servers to assist in the bar if necessary and to cover days off. The host desk also needs covering for each shift. Calculating for lunch and dinner seven days a week and including days off, that can mean three or four people. In all areas, certified trainers will help new servers and other workers, get up to speed. These trainers receive additional compensation for their efforts. Training definitely helps reduce labor turnover. A form such as Figure 10.5 can be used both for projecting expected payroll amounts for any future period and for comparing these projections at a later time for cost-control purposes.

In some cases, it may be desirable to complete this effort for each of the 52 weeks in the coming year. More often, some standardizing can accommodate expected variations, and three or four standard weeks can be established and used as a basis for shorter calculations. (Many weeks develop a pattern and can be duplicated.) The more accurate the breakdown, the more precise the result.

Figure 10.6 illustrates a summary of expected staffing and resulting payroll costs, utilizing a breakdown into four categories of restaurant staffing: management and administration, production, service and cashiers, and sanitation. The breakdown allows for planning by activity as well as for control of both employee hours and payroll dollars.

Payroll and related costs fall into two categories: variable (percentage ratio to payroll) and fixed (dollar amount per employee on the payroll). Variable items include those mandated by law: Social Security (FICA), unemployment insurance (state and federal), Workers' Compensation insurance, and state disability insurance. The fixed items usually mean employee benefits and include health insurance (an amount per employee per month), union welfare insurance (also an amount per employee per month), life insurance, and other employee benefits.

Employee meals can be treated as payroll costs or as part of food cost and wages. It is more common to find employee meals treated as food cost for a restaurant operation. Operators need to establish a value for employee meals, but they are treated as a nontaxable benefit by the IRS.

> Wendy's, in one cost-cutting mode, trimmed unit payrolls by 30 hours per week. This was achieved by finding a different way to pan meat and by weighing cash on scales so no one has to count it. Another labor-saving method is using a Jacuzzi-like power washer to scrub pots, pans, and condiment pumps.
>
> Streamlining was attained by reducing the average time for drive-through service from 160 to 100 seconds. That jump in efficiency enabled stores to crank another 30 to 40 cars through the line at peak periods. Window sales increased from 56 to 63 percent of sales.
>
> *Source:* Peter Romeo, "Less Is More: Wendy's Initiatives Cut Labor, Boost Sales," *Restaurant Business* 98, no. 21 (1 November 1999): 13–14.

JOB TITLE	RATE	HOURS PLANNED							WEEKLY TOTAL		SUMMARY
		SAT.	SUN.	MON.	TUES.	WED.	THURS.	FRI.	HOURS	AMOUNT	
											PROJECTED SALES
											ESTIMATED PAYROLL
											PAYROLL RELATED
											TOTAL PAYROLL
											% TO SALES
											DATE PREPARED
											PREPARED BY
TOTAL HOURS											APPROVAL
PROJ. CUST. COUNT											
PROJ. CHECK AVER.											
ESTIMATED SALES	$	$	$	$	$	$	$	$	$		

UNIT NAME   UNIT NUMBER

FIGURE 10.5 Form for projecting expected payroll amounts.

235

The average check for lunch is $9.00 and dinner $16.00

I. Management and Administration

1	General Manager		$ 50,000 + Bonus
2	Assistant Managers (open & close)		48,000
1	Office Clerical		20,000
			118,000

II. Production

1	Kitchen Manager		35,000 + Bonus
7	Line Cooks	@ Avg. 9.50 per hour	138,320
3	Dishwashers	@ 6.00 per hour	37,440
4	Prep Cooks	@ 7.00 per hour	58,240
			$269,000

III. Service

3	Hosts @ 6.00 per hour		37,440
20	Servers and Bussers @ 6.00 per hour		249,600
3	Bartenders @ 6.00 per hour		37,440
3	Cashiers @ 6.00 per hour		37,440
			$360,920

IV. 1 Sanitation @ 6.25 $ 13,000

Recapitulation

I	Management and Administration	118,000
II	Production	269,000
III	Service	360,920
IV	Sanitation	13,000
	TOTAL	$760,920

FIGURE 10.6 Projected payroll costs for a hypothetical casual restaurant of 175 seats with sales volume of $2.75 million.

When determining the number of staff to schedule for a restaurant, take the number of seats and decide how many tables/seats to give each server. Take expected sales into account—on a Monday lunch, sales may be $3,000, but on a Friday, $6,800. So, obviously, more staff are needed for Friday. In the kitchen, the various stations need to be covered: pantry; boxes (stoves, convection ovens, and steamers, so named because they look like boxes); grill/sauté; fryer/breader; wheel person; expediter; and dishwasher. In the volume restaurant described here, everyone must pull together—if one section gets behind, everyone is in trouble. The wheel person has to really have it together. This person might never even cook a thing, but must coordinate the food coming from all the stations and double-check that plates are correct by the order. It is easier when the order goes from the servers' POS directly to each station—this saves someone having to bark out the orders at the pass. Figure 10.7 shows an actual versus projected payroll for a week. Notice the projected and actual sales and projected and actual costs for back and front of house, as well as the total per day and week to date.

Payroll: Actual vs Projected
Week of: May 26–June 01, 2003

	26 MON	27 TUE	28 WED	29 THUR	30 FRI	31 SAT	1 SUN
Projected Sales	$3,000	$4,500	$4,600	$4,600	$6,800	$5,400	$5,200
WTD Prjctd Sales		$7,500	$12,100	$16,700	$23,500	$28,900	$34,100
Actual Sales	$3,673	$4,307	$3,773	$5,148	$6,851	$5,103	$4,527
WTD Actual Sales		$7,980	$11,753	$16,901	$23,752	$28,855	$33,382
Daily + or - %	22.44%	-4.29%	-17.98%	11.91%	0.75%	-5.49%	-12.94%
Actual vs Proj Sales	$673	($193)	($827)	$548	$51	($297)	($673)
WTD + or -		$480	($347)	$201	$252	($45)	($718)
Weekly + or - %	22.44%	6.40%	-2.87%	1.20%	1.07%	-0.16%	-2.11%
B O H							
Projected BOH Labor	$398	$440	$470	$467	$640	$561	$515
WTD Prjctd BOH		$838	$1,308	$1,775	$2,415	$2,976	$3,491
Actual BOH Labor	$438	$492	$446	$460	$616	$503	$474
Daily BOH Labor %age	11.93%	11.42%	11.82%	8.94%	8.99%	9.85%	10.46%
WTD Actual BOH		$930	$1,376	$1,837	$2,453	$2,956	$3,429
Daily + or - %	10.14%	11.80%	-5.11%	-1.44%	-3.73%	-10.35%	-8.05%
Actual vs Proj BOH	$40	$52	($24)	($7)	($24)	($58)	($41)
WTD + or -		$92	$68	$62	$38	($20)	($62)
WTD BOH Labor %age		11.66%	11.71%	10.87%	10.33%	10.24%	10.27%
FOH							
Projected FOH Labor	$246	$248	$284	$275	$458	$310	$307
WTD Prjctd FOH		$494	$778	$1,053	$1,511	$1,821	$2,128
Actual FOH Labor	$291	$312	$283	$275	$380	$309	$316
Daily FOH Labor %age	7.92%	7.25%	7.50%	5.35%	5.55%	6.05%	6.99%
WTD Actual FOH		$603	$886	$1,161	$1,542	$1,850	$2,167
Daily + or - %	18.18%	25.85%	-0.34%	0.18%	-16.96%	-0.42%	3.08%
Actual vs Proj FOH	$45	$64	($1)	$0	($78)	($1)	$9
WTD + or -		$109	$108	$108	$31	$29	$39
WTD FOH Labor %age		7.55%	7.54%	6.87%	6.49%	6.41%	6.49%
Total Labor							
Total Projected Labor	$644	$688	$754	$742	$1,098	$871	$822
WTD Prjctd Labor		$1,332	$2,086	$2,828	$3,926	$4,797	$5,619
Actual Total Labor	$729	$804	$729	$736	$996	$812	$790
WTD Actual Labor		$1,533	$2,262	$2,998	$3,994	$4,806	$5,596
Actual vs Proj Total	$85	$116	($25)	($6)	($102)	($59)	($32)
WTD + or -		$201	$176	$170	$68	$9	($23)
Projected %	21.47%	15.29%	16.39%	16.13%	16.15%	16.13%	15.81%
WTD Prjctd %		17.76%	17.24%	16.93%	16.71%	16.60%	16.48%
Actual %	19.85%	18.67%	19.32%	14.29%	14.55%	15.90%	17.45%
WTD Actual %		19.21%	19.25%	17.74%	16.82%	16.66%	16.76%

FIGURE 10.7 Payroll: actual versus projected.

MANAGERS' BONUS AUGUST 2003			JULY 28 - AUG 24, 2003	
		COGS Bonus Scale		

Volume +55,000 per week		**Volume** 40-55,000 per week		**Volume** <40,000 per week	
<50.0%	$1,000	<51.0%	$1,000	<52.5%	$1,000
<51.0%	$750	<52.0%	$750	<53.5%	$750
<52.0%	$500	<53.0%	$500	<54.5%	$500
<53.0%	$250	<54.0%	$250	<55.5%	$250
<54.0%	$100	<55.0%	$100	<56.5%	$100
+54%	$0	+55%	$0	+56.5%	$0

2003 Total Volume	$146,448.00	Wkly. Avg	$36,612.00	
2003 Food Volume	$127,409.76	87.00%		
2003 Bev Volume	$18,306.00	12.50%		
2003 Retail Volume	$732.24	0.50%		
Food Purchases	$52,714.00	41.37%	36.00%	
Supplies	$0.00	0.00%	0.00%	
Total Food Purchases	$52,714.00	41.37%	36.00%	
Bar Purchases	$5,190.00	28.35%	3.54%	
Total Purchases	$57,904.00	39.54%	39.54%	
Labor	$24,987.00		17.06%	
Total Cost of Goods S	$82,891.00		56.60%	
		Total Bonus:		$0.00

Bonuses Paid				
	John	$0.00	DJ	$0.00
	Fred	$0.00	Jenn	$0.00
	Gary	$0.00	Shawn	$0.00
			Sean	$0.00

Total	$0.00		Date Paid	
Authorized				

FIGURE 10.8 Managers bonus. Unfortunately no one received a bonus this month.

One successful restaurant has begun a manager's bonus for each of its four restaurants. The managing partner and four managers are each eligible for a monthly $1,000 bonus based on meeting or exceeding performance goals. Figure 10.8 shows the cost-of-goods-sold (COGS) bonus scale expressed for three different sales volume levels. In the month of August, the total cost of goods sold came to 56.60 percent and sales were $36,612, so no bonuses were given.

If we look at the right-hand column, we can see at the bottom of that column + 56.5% = $0. If the COGS had been, say, 56.5 percent, then each manager would have received $100. In this restaurant's case, discussion is taking place about whether to include training in the labor costs. In a seasonal restaurant and a more transient labor market than others, staff turnover is an issue—of course, it can be argued that management/leadership should minimize labor turnover. What do you think?

P A R T

2

MANAGEMENT AND SUPERVISION/CAREER DEVELOPMENT

T he chapters on Management and Supervision start on page 241, and the chapters on Career Development start on page 631.

THE SUPERVISOR AS MANAGER*

Congratulations for joining this course, and welcome to supervision, the practical application of human resource leadership in the hospitality industry. You are now a boss, or soon will be. Being a new supervisor is exciting; there will be challenges, opportunities, and rewards. Your company has invested its trust in you and has expectations of your performance. But how do you feel? Well, you wouldn't be alone if you felt some apprehension because you are responsible not only for your work, but

---

* Authored by Jack E. Miller, John R. Walker, and Karen Eich Drummond.

also for the work of others. We hope you get off to a great start with this book and wish you success in your career.

The team members that you will be supervising will probably take a wait-and-see attitude until they get to know you. Actually, their concerns will likely exceed yours because you're the boss and they are awaiting your first moves. A good approach for a new supervisor is to talk to the previous supervisor and your boss, since they best know the details of the job and the people you will be supervising. Of course, there is a caution: What if the previous supervisor was no good or had biases? That's why you check carefully with your new boss to get his or her perspective.

Another wise move is to review the files of the employees you will be supervising. By looking over their file and evaluations, you should be able to gain a better understanding of your new employees. The best way to start your first day as a new supervisor is to have your boss introduce you in a formal capacity followed by a chance for informal interaction.

Ever wonder about the impact that supervisors have on the success of a hospitality company? Here is an example: On Restaurant Row in one city, one family restaurant has had 12 different busboys in two months. In the restaurant next door, the food is superb one week and terrible the next. The bar on the corner cannot find a decent bartender, much less keep one. Across the street, one restaurant had a near-riot in the kitchen resulting from an argument between the cooks and servers. The Italian restaurant two doors down is losing customers steadily because its service is so poor. But the oldest restaurant on the block is packing them in night after night, with staff who have been there for years.

Across town, students at the local community college would rather eat at the local fast-food restaurants than in the school's cafeteria, where the pizza and burgers leave much to be desired. On the outskirts of the city, students at the state university rave about the quality of the food and the tremendous choices they have. Many of the students look for jobs working for the university foodservice.

In many of the city's hotels, the employee turnover rate is fantastically high. Every seven days we turn thousands of employees in this industry. We don't have a "labor" crisis. We have a turnover crisis.[1] Service is poor and guests complain, but then that's just part of the game, isn't it? Yet several hotels in town have few staffing problems and happy guests.

Throughout the city a common cry in the hospitality industry is that you just can't get good people these days. People don't work hard the way they used to, they don't do what you expect them to, they come late and leave early or don't show up at all, they are sullen and rude, they don't always speak English—the complaints go on and on. The rotten help you get today must cause all the problems.

Is this true? If it is true, what about those establishments where things run smoothly? Can it be that the way in which the workers are managed has something to do with the presence or absence of problems? You bet it does! And that is what this book is all about. In this chapter we explore the management aspect of the supervisor's job. It will help you to:

- Describe the primary role of a supervisor in the hospitality industry.
- Explain the different levels of supervision, and identify first-line supervisors on an organizational chart.
- Define the terms *authority* and *responsibility*.
- Explain the difference between exempt and nonexempt employees.
- Outline the supervisor's obligations and responsibilities to owners, customers, and employees.
- Describe briefly the important functions of management.
- Explain the challenge of applying common management theories in the hospitality work environment.
- Compare and contrast the major theories of people management as they relate to hospitality employees.
- List examples of technical, human, and conceptual skills used by hospitality supervisors.

THE SUPERVISOR'S ROLE

In the hospitality industry almost everything depends on the physical labor of many hourly (or nonmanagerial) workers: people who cook, serve tables, mix drinks, wash dishes, check guests in and out, clean rooms, carry bags, mop floors. Few industries are as dependent for success on the performance of hourly workers. These employees make the products and they serve the customers—or drive them away.

How well these workers produce and serve depends largely on how well they are managed. If they are not managed well, the product or the service suffers and the establishment is in trouble. It is the people who supervise these workers who hold the keys to the success of the operation.

A supervisor is any person who manages people who make products and/or perform services. A supervisor is responsible for the output of the people supervised—for the quality and quantity of the products and services. A supervisor is also responsible for meeting the needs of employees and can ensure the production of goods and services only by motivating and stimulating employees to do their jobs properly. Today's employees are different than they were 10 to 20 years ago; they no longer give their allegiance to the supervisor automatically in exchange for a paycheck. Instead, they give their supervisor the right to lead them. Usually, a supervisor is the manager of a unit or department of an enterprise and is responsible for the work of that unit or department. In large enterprises there are many levels of supervision, with the people at the top responsible for the work of the managers who report to them, who in turn are responsible for the performance of those they supervise, and so on, down to the first-line supervisor who manages the hourly workers. First-line supervisors and unit managers are the primary focus of this book. Figure 11.1 shows the levels of employees in a large company.

No one is more responsible for a business's success than the manager. It takes a lot of savvy to manage a bar or restaurant well, and not just anyone can pull it off. There are some qualities that make up the all-pro manager. For example, all-pro managers not only have a working knowledge of the business they operate but also possess a sound grasp of business in general. A good manager knows his or her market, knows the competition and what they are doing, and responds accordingly. Other all-pro manager traits include a desire to lead, maturity/stability, a good money sense, possession of street smarts, and legal knowledge.

Organizational charts for a large hotel and a large restaurant are shown in Figures 11.2 and 11.3. An organizational chart shows the relationship among and within departments. Line functions (associates directly involved in producing goods and services) and staff functions (the advisers) are spelled out. The human resources (or personnel) and training departments are examples of staff who advise line departments, such as the food and beverage department, on matters including hiring, disciplining, and training employees.

Using the organization chart, you can also see the various levels of management, with authority and responsibility handed down from the top, level by level. Authority can be defined as the right and power to make the necessary decisions and take the necessary actions to get the job done. Responsibility refers to the obligation that a person has to carry out certain duties and activities. First-line supervisors represent the lowest level of authority and responsibility, and hourly workers report to them.

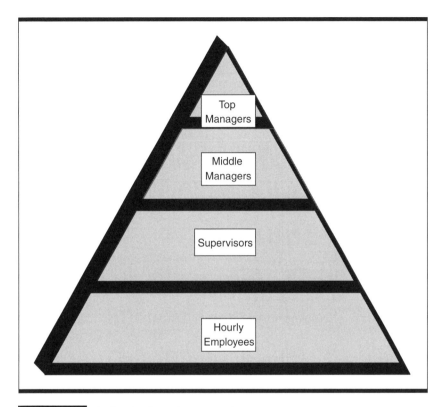

FIGURE 11.1 The levels of employees in a large company.

Many supervisors—station cooks, for example—also do some of the work of their departments alongside the workers they supervise. Thus, they are typically in close daily contact with the people they supervise and may even at times be working at the same tasks. They are seldom isolated in a remote office but are right in the middle of the action. They are known as working supervisors (but as we shall see later in the text, these supervisors may not qualify as exempt employees).

Each supervisor's job is probably described in terms of a job title and the scope of the work required rather than in terms of the people to be supervised. An executive chef, for example, is responsible for all kitchen production. An assistant executive housekeeper in a hotel is responsible for getting the guests' rooms made up. A food and nutrition supervisor in a hospital may be responsible for overseeing the service of patient meals. A restaurant manager or a unit manager in a food chain is responsible for the entire operation. Thus the focus is placed on the work rather than on the workers. But since the work is done by people, *supervision is the major part of the job*.

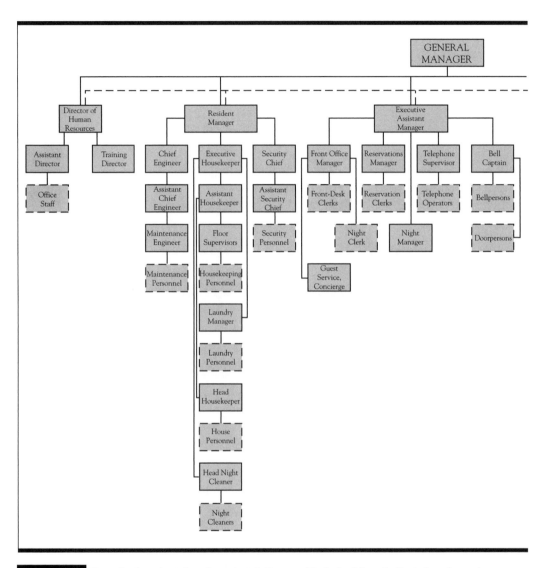

FIGURE 11.2 Organization chart for a large hotel. Boxes with dashed lines indicate hourly workers. Dashed reporting lines indicate staff (advisory) positions.

As a supervisor, you depend for your own success on the work of others, and you will be measured by their output and their performance. *You will be successful in your own job only to the degree that your team members allow you to be,* and this will depend on how to manage them. This will become clearer as you explore this book.

Other organizational terms with which you need to become familiar include exempt employees and nonexempt employees. Hourly employees are considered non-exempt employees because they are not exempt from federal and state wage and hour

FIGURE 11.2 (Continued)

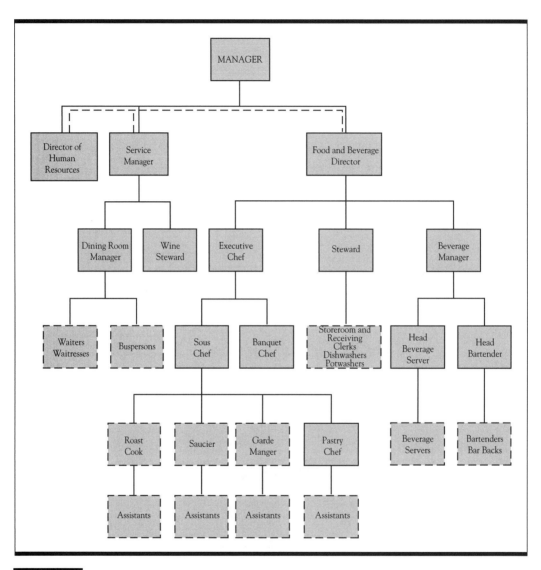

FIGURE 11.3 Organization chart for a large restaurant. Boxes with dashed lines indicate hourly workers. Dashed reporting lines indicate staff (advisory) positions.

laws. In other words, they are covered by these laws and are therefore guaranteed a minimum wage and overtime pay after working 40 hours in a workweek. Supervisors are considered exempt employees; they are not covered by the wage and hour laws and therefore do not earn overtime pay when certain conditions are met: when they spend 50 percent or more of their time managing, when they supervise two or more employees, and under federal law when they are paid $1,000 or more per month (or more if the state imposes a higher standard).

OBLIGATIONS AND RESPONSIBILITIES OF A SUPERVISOR

When you begin to supervise the work of other people, you cross a line that separates you from the hourly workers—you step over to the management side. In any work situation there are two points of view: the hourly workers' point of view and management's point of view. The line between them is clear-cut; there are no fuzzy edges, no shades of gray. When you become a supervisor, your responsibilities are management responsibilities, and you cannot carry them out successfully unless you maintain a manager's point of view. Now, you will be a part of setting the standards rather than seeking to attain performance goals set by others. You will be held accountable for achieving department goals and keeping your team motivated and productive.

In order to maintain a reputation of excellence, you should realize the importance of being responsible for:

1. Achieving or exceeding the expected results, on time and on budget, planning = determining priorities; organizing = scheduling; motivating = creating a positive work environment; controlling = monitoring and taking corrective action if deviations are outside acceptable limits.

2. Communicating effectively.

3. Building a winning team.

4. "Walking your talk" as a leader, setting a good example, plus you should be able to do the work of those you supervise.

5. Creating a positive work environment.

6. Motivating your team.

7. Working efficiently and effectively with your manager and peers.

8. Coaching and mentoring your team.

9. Getting the resources necessary for your team to do the job.

10. Treating all team members fairly and equally.

Now is a good time to reflect on your past supervisors and see how you would describe them. What made them good or bad supervisors? You could take a supervisor's assessment to check on your supervisory skills. Figure 11.4 illustrates a typical supervisor's assessment.

Supervisor's Assessment

	1 Great Need for Improvement	2 Need for Improvement	3 Acceptable	4 Good	5 Excellent
1. You know the company's mission and department goals.					
2. You know the tactics to meet goals.					
3. You would include associate input into formulating goals.					
4. You know the policies and procedures.					
5. You are fair, consistent, and treat everyone the same.					
6. You give praise for job well done.					
7. Your associates clearly understand what is expected of them.					
8. You are a good example.					
9. You have enthusiasm for your work.					
10. You are a good listener.					
11. You are a good coach / trainer.					
12. You respect your associates.					
13. You are a good communicator.					
14. You are a good decision maker.					
15. You are passionate about the success of your team / department.					
16. You are a good delegator.					
17. Your team gets the job done on time and on budget.					
18. You are a good motivator.					
19. You give positive reinforcement.					
20. You represent your associates well with management.					

For best results, compare the supervisor's score with one from the boss and an established score from the associates who are being supervised.

FIGURE 11.4 For best results, compare supervisor's score with one from the boss and an established score from the associates who are being supervised.

The Supervisor in the Middle

As a hospitality supervisor, you have obligations to the owners, the guests, and the employees you supervise, which puts you right in the middle of the action (Figure 11.5). To your employees, you represent management: authority, direction, discipline, time off, more money, and advancement. To the owners and your superiors in management, you are the link with the workers and the work to be done; you represent productivity, control of food cost and labor cost, quality control, and guest service; you also represent your people and their needs and desires. To the guests, your output and your employees represent the enterprise—if the food is good, it's a good restaurant; if the doorperson and the desk clerk and the server in the coffee shop provide high-quality service, it's a good hotel. No matter how modest your area of responsibility, it is a tough assignment.

Many new supervisors are promoted from hourly jobs and suddenly find themselves supervising people with whom they have worked side by side for years. You

Supervisors have obligations and responsibilities to guests, employees, and employers. Courtesy of PhotoDisc/Getty Images.

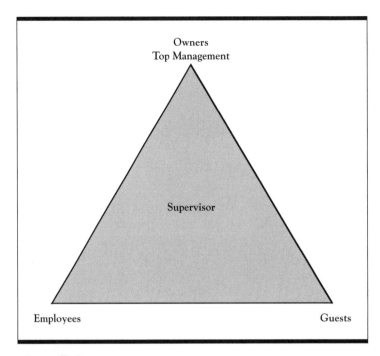

FIGURE 11.5 The supervisor is right in the middle of everything and everybody—the link between top management and employees and guests.

worked together, drank beer together, griped about the company together, conspired together to keep from working too hard. Now you find yourself on the other side of that line between management and workers. Now you may be carrying out policies you used to complain about. You may have to work your entire crew on Christmas Day. You may have to discipline your best friend.

It is lonely on that side of the line, and the temptation is great to slip back to your buddies, to the old attitudes, the old point of view. We call this boomerang management—going back to where you came from—and it doesn't work. You've got to maintain a manager's point of view; you've got to stay in charge. There is no compromise. You can empathize with your workers; you can listen and understand. But your decisions must be made from management's point of view. Your employer expects it, and your people expect it. If you try to manage from your workers' point of view, they will take advantage of you. They really want you to manage.

Now, let's look in more depth at the supervisor's obligations to the big three: owners, guests, and employees.

When you become a supervisor, your responsibilities are management responsibilities, and you cannot carry them out successfully unless you maintain a manager's point of view. Courtesy of Sodexho.

Obligation to Owners

Your primary obligation to the owners is to make their enterprise profitable. They have taken the risk of investing their money, and they expect a reasonable return on that investment. The major part of your responsibility to them is to run your part of their business to produce that return. That is what they are interested in; that is what they have hired you to do.

They also want you to run things their way. If they tell you how they want it done, you have an obligation to do it that way, even though you see better ways to do it. They are paying you to do it their way, and you have an obligation to do anything they require that is morally and legally correct.

Suppose that the owners have a system for everything. They don't want you to change anything; they want you to oversee their system. Suppose you don't agree with it. Suppose you think they don't put enough french fries on each plate; you think the customer should have more, and so does the customer. Do you add a few fries to each order? No! You leave the system as it is and you oversee it—you see that your people follow it.

Suppose you see a better way of doing something. You don't take it upon yourself to make a change. You go back to the owner or to your supervisor and you explain your idea and why it would be better. The two of you must agree on what changes, if any, you are going to make.

Suppose the people who hire you don't tell you how they want things done. This happens all too often in the restaurant business; they hire you and put you to work without telling you what to do. They may have definite expectations of you, but they do not verbalize at least 50 percent of what they ought to; they expect you to know what they want. You must find these things out for yourself—ask questions, get things straight. What are the guidelines and procedures? What authority do you have? Where, if anywhere, do you have a free hand? Since you must manage, as they want you to manage, it is your obligation to find out what they want and be sensitive to their expectations. Because of your daily interactions with customers and employees, you also have an obligation to communicate their desires to the owners.

Suppose that you are hired to run a hospital kitchen. Although there may be no profit involved, your obligation to follow the system is absolute, because the health of the patients is at stake. Patient health is the purpose of the hospital, and food is a basic element in patient care. Every recipe must be followed to the letter and to the quarter ounce. Every grain of salt is important. Every sanitation procedure is critical. You must not change a thing without having the authority to do so.

Obligations to Guests

Your second obligation as a supervisor is to the guests. They are the reason a hotel or restaurant exists, and they are the source of its profits. They come to your enterprise by choice. If they are treated well, they may continue to come. If they are not, you will probably never see them again. The importance of customer service seems obvious, yet poor service is all too common, and it is one of the big reasons for failure in the hospitality industry. Most of the people who never come back are responding to poor service or to the fact that an hourly employee was insensitive to their needs.

Consider the following scenario. You are a customer arriving at a hotel after a long and tiring trip, and you tell the desk clerk you have a reservation. She runs your name through her computer and says, "No, you don't have a reservation." How do you feel? You are frustrated and angry because you know you made a reservation. "Well," you ask, "do you have any rooms?" "Yes," she says, "we have rooms, but you don't have a reservation." Now you are not only frustrated and angry but you are beginning to feel rejected. "Well," you say, "may I have a room?" She lets you (*lets you*) have a room. As you start off with your bags, huffing, she says—as though to a bad child—"But you didn't have a reservation!" Will you stay at that hotel again? Not if you can help it.

That desk clerk obviously had not been trained by her supervisor in guest relations. Furthermore, chances are good that she picked up her attitude and behavior from the supervisor. It is very easy, when your mind is on a million other things, to blame the guests for being demanding and unreasonable, and you often feel that if it weren't for the guests, you could get twice as much work done in half the time. You forget that if it weren't for the guests, you would have no work to do. As a manager you must fulfill their needs and desires, and that also means training your people to assume this obligation. Never forget that your employee is a direct reflection of you.

In a hotel or restaurant, guests usually encounter only hourly workers. Hotel guests see the desk clerk, the bellperson, the server in the restaurant, and the housekeeper, who is sure to be cleaning their room when they get back after breakfast. Restaurant patrons see the host or hostess, servers, and perhaps a bartender or cashier. These hourly workers represent you, they represent the management, and they convey the image of the entire establishment.

As a supervisor you have an obligation to these guests to see that your workers are delivering on the promises of product and service that you offer—giving the guests what they came for. And you should be visible in person—customers like to feel that the manager cares, and your workers work better when you are present and involved in the action.

In a hospital or nursing facility kitchen, you have an obligation to the patients to see that they get the kind of food the doctor ordered and that it is not only nourishing and germ-free but that it looks good and tastes good. The food cannot help the patients recover if they don't eat it.

For many people in hospitals, food may be the most important part of their day. They lie in bed with nothing to do, and breakfast, lunch, and dinner become major events. You have an obligation to those patients to speed their recovery by giving your best effort to making their meals a pleasure.

As a supervisor in a school cafeteria, you have an obligation to the students. As a supervisor in a U.S. Army or Navy kitchen, you have an obligation to your country. Wherever you work, you have an obligation to the consumer of the product your workers prepare and to the user of the services your people provide.

Obligations to Employees

Your third obligation as a supervisor is to the people you supervise. It is up to you to provide these employees with an environment in which they can be productive for you. This is something you need, because you are directly dependent on them to make you successful. You certainly can't do all the work yourself.

The most important value for most employees is the way the boss treats them. They want to be recognized as individuals, listened to, told clearly what the boss expects of them and why. If they are going to be really productive for you, they want a climate of acceptance, of approval, of open communication, of fairness, of belonging. With most workers today, the old hard-line authoritarian approach simply does not work. You owe it to your workers and to yourself to create a work climate that makes them willing to give you their best.

A poor work climate can cause high labor turnover, low productivity, and poor quality control and can ultimately result in fewer customers—problems that are all too common in restaurants, hotels, and hospitals. It is easy for employers to blame these problems on "the kind of workers we have today" and to look at these workers as a cross they have to bear. There is an element of truth here: It is difficult to get people who will do a good job day after day after day in repetitive jobs—washing pots in a hot kitchen, handling heavy luggage, busing dirty dishes, mopping the same dirty floors, making the same beds, cleaning the same toilets, walking the same empty corridors all night as a security guard.

The fact is, though, that two enterprises hiring from the same labor pool can get radically different results according to the work climate their supervisors create. You can see this in multiunit operations: There is always one unit that is consistently better than the others—one that is cleaner, has a better food cost, has a better labor cost, and has more satisfied customers. It is always the manager who makes this difference, and usually this manager has created a climate in which the workers will give their best.

So Who's Number One?

There's an expression in the hospitality industry that goes like this: "If you [the manager] take care of the employees, the employees will take care of the guests, and the profits will take care of themselves." As a supervisor, your number one concern is your employees. You need to be committed to serving the employees who serve the guest, because the way you treat your employees will be reflected in how they treat the customer. When you treat employees the way you want them to treat customers (with consideration, respect, and so on), employees then tend to provide high-quality service. This keeps customers happy and increases the chances of return visits, meaning more business and more money spent. This, in turn, helps build profits and keeps the owners happy. Studies involving various companies show that those who value their employees highly (by providing training, rewards, and so on) have higher customer satisfaction and profitability.

Randy Garutti, at 28 and general manager of New York's Union Square Restaurant, says that with 110 employees, ranging in age from 18 to 40-something, his biggest challenge is in creating an atmosphere in which people want to work. He places his employees before the guests because if the employees are happy so will the guests be happy.[2]

Check Your Knowledge

1.   What is the primary role of a supervisor?

2.   Briefly discuss the obligations that a supervisor has to his or her employees.

FUNCTIONS OF MANAGEMENT

Are first-line supervisors really managers? Yes, indeed. A manager is a person who directs and controls an assigned segment of the work in an enterprise. Although supervisors often do not have the title manager, although midlevel managers and top executives in large enterprises may not regard them as part of the management team, supervisors have crossed that line from the workers' side to the management side, and they perform the functions of management in their area of control. So we need to examine the functions of management.

Theoretically, there are four or five main functions and up to 20 major activities that a manager performs. Here are some of the more important ones:

- **Planning:** looking ahead to chart goals and the best courses of future action; involves, for example, determining who, what, why, when, where, and how work will be done

- **Organizing:** putting together the money, personnel, equipment, materials, and methods for maximum efficiency to meet an enterprise's goals, such as developing employee work teams

- **Staffing:** determining personnel needs and recruiting, evaluating, selecting, hiring, orienting, training, and scheduling employees

The work environment is one of the most important aspects of supervision.

- **Leading:** interacting and guiding employees about getting certain goals and plans accomplished; involves many skills, such as communicating, motivating, delegating, instructing, supporting, developing, and mentoring employees

- **Controlling** and **evaluating:** monitoring and evaluating results in terms of goals and standards previously agreed upon, such as performance and quality standards, and taking corrective action when necessary to stay on course

- **Coordinating:** meshing the work of individuals, work teams, and departments to produce a smoothly running operation

- **Problem solving** and **decision making:** using a logical process to identify causes of and solutions to problems or to make decisions

- **Representing:** representing the organization to customers and other people outside the enterprise

Does this list seem remote and unreal to you? It does to many people who run hotels and foodservice operations, and there is nothing like management experience to upset management theory. A busboy quits, the dishmachine breaks down, two servers are fighting in the dining room, the health inspector walks in, an official from the liquor control board is coming at 2:00 this afternoon, and someone rushes up and tells you there's a fire in the kitchen. How does management theory help you at a moment like this?

The Reality

There is nothing wrong with management theory; it can be useful, even in a crisis. The problem is how to apply it. In the circus we call the hospitality industry, nothing comes in neat and tidy packages. Managers seldom have control over the shape of their day. The situation changes every 20 to 48 seconds; you blink and the unexpected usually happens. In a foodservice operation, you are manufacturing, selling, and delivering a product, all within minutes. In a hotel you may have 5,000 customers one day and 500 the next. You deal with your superiors, you deal with your subordinates, and you deal with your guests, all coming at you from different directions. Salespeople, deliveries, inspectors, customer complaints, and applicants for jobs interrupt you. You are likely to have only a few seconds available when you make many important decisions. Figure 11.6 shows the interactions of a supervisor.

In such circumstances managers usually react to situations rather than acting on them according to a preconceived plan plotted out in the quiet of an office. Managing becomes the ability to adjust actions and decisions to given situations according to the demands of those situations. It is a *flex style of management*, calling upon theory, experience, and talent. It is a skill that cannot be taught but has to be developed in supervised experience on the job. It means doing what will be most effective in terms of the three elements involved: *the situation, your workers*, and *yourself*. It means developing techniques and applying principles of management in ways that work for you.

The fact is that most textbooks on management were written to be read by MBA students headed for middle-management jobs in large corporations, and they do not often address the problems of the small individual enterprise, the supervisor of hourly workers, and the nitty-gritty of managing production and service. They also don't always address the art of managing people. According to a survey by the Center for Creative Leadership, a research firm in Greensboro, North Carolina, poor interpersonal skills represent the single biggest reason that managers fail. Managers who fail are often poor listeners, can't stimulate their employees, don't give and take criticism well, and avoid conflict. Managers need to learn how to manage people, just as you do, through supervised experience on the job. They must learn how to convert classroom theories into practical applications that are accepted by the people they supervise. No one can teach you; it is theory, then practice, then experience.

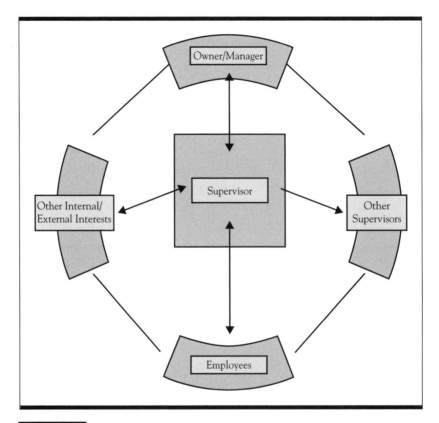

FIGURE 11.6 The interactions of a supervisor.

As a flex-style manager reacting to constantly changing situations, your on-the-spot decisions and actions are going to be far better if you, too, can draw on sound principles of management theory and the accumulated experience of successful managers. In this book we introduce you to those principles and theories that can help you to work out your own answers as a supervisor in a hotel or foodservice setting. They can provide a background of knowledge, thoughts, and ideas that will give you confidence and a sense of direction as you meet and solve the same problems that other managers before you have met and solved.

THEORIES OF PEOPLE MANAGEMENT

The development of management as an organized body of knowledge and theory is a product of the last hundred years. It was an inevitable outgrowth of the Industrial

Revolution and the appearance of large enterprises needing skilled managers and new methods of running a business.

Scientific Management

One of the earliest developments affecting the management of people was the scientific management movement appearing around 1900 and stemming from the work of Frederick Taylor. Taylor's goal was to increase productivity in factories by applying a scientific approach to human performance on the job. Using carefully developed time-and-motion studies, he analyzed each element of each production task and by eliminating all wasted motions, arrived at the "one best way" to perform the task. In the same way he established a "fair day's work," which was the amount of work a competent worker could do in one workday using the one best way.

The system Taylor developed had four essential features:

1. Standardization of work procedures, tools, and conditions of work through design of work methods by specialists

2. Careful selection of competent people, thorough training in the prescribed methods, and elimination of those who could not or would not conform

3. Complete and constant overseeing of the work, with total obedience from the workers

4. Incentive pay for meeting the fair day's work standard—the worker's share of the increased productivity

Taylor believed that his system would revolutionize labor–management relations and would produce "intimate, friendly cooperation between management and men" because both would benefit from increased productivity. Instead, his methods caused a great deal of strife between labor and management. Workers who once planned much of their own work and carried it out with a craftsman's pride were now forced into monotonous and repetitive tasks performed in complete obedience to others. Taylor believed that higher wages—"what they want most"—would make up for having to produce more and losing their say about how they did their work. But his own workers, with whom he was very friendly, did everything they could to make his system fail, including breaking their machines. The craft unions of that day fought Taylor's system bitterly, and relations between management and labor deteriorated. Productivity, however, increased by leaps and bounds, since fewer workers could do more work.

Another innovator, Frank Gilbreth, carried forward the search for the one best way of performing tasks, or work simplification. Using ingenious time-and-motion study techniques, he developed ways of simplifying tasks that often doubled or tripled what a worker could do. His methods and principles had a great impact in foodservice kitchens, where work simplification techniques have been explored extensively and widely adopted.

Taylor's innovations began a revolution in management's approach to production. His theories and methods were widely adopted (although the idea that the worker should share in the benefits of increased productivity seldom went along with the rest of the system). A whole new field of industrial engineering developed in which efficiency experts took over the planning of the work. In this process the workers came to be regarded as just another element of the production process, often an adjunct to the machine. Their job was to follow the rules, and the supervisors saw to it that they did, and this became the prevailing philosophy of people management.

Profile

JIM SULLIVAN

Courtesy of Jim Sullivan.

I like what I do. Every year I arrange dozens and dozens of service and sales-building seminars for successful companies around the world. I also help overhaul and redesign manager and server training manuals and programs for a variety of successful chains and independent restaurants. And in doing so, I get to assimilate a wide variety of best practices relating to customer service, employee retention, same-store-sales building, cost controls, and creative management. I also see subtle patterns, trends, and evolutions occurring in hospitality management theory and practice. In case you hadn't noticed, a sea change of behavior is in full swing right now. I'd like to outline and possibly debunk nine customer service myths that used to hold water in our industry and now are losing value as operating principles. Do you agree or disagree with the following points and counterpoints? The way you think about each one may provide a road map for your operation's success in the new century.

No. 1: "The customer comes first." Really? Today you need good employees more than they need you. As Wally Doolin, chief executive of TGI Friday's parent, Carlson Restaurants

Worldwide, pointed out at the recent Multi-Unit Foodservice Operators confab: "Our employees are our first market." Amen. So, instead of ranking relationships between customers and employees, we should focus on establishing equity instead. In other words, never treat a customer better than you do an employee. Service, like charity, begins at home, and if you're not investing in serving your team as well as you serve your customers, you're headed for trouble, pure and simple.

No. 2: "A satisfied customer comes back." Customer "satisfaction" is meaningless. Customer loyalty is priceless. People don't want to be "satisfied" as customers. Heck, Kmart can "satisfy" customers, for crying out loud. They want fun, flair, and memorable experiences. A satisfied customer doesn't necessarily ever come back. As the noted New York restaurateur Danny Meyer says, "Give your guests what they remember and give them something new each time they visit."

No. 3: "We've got to focus on the competition." That's right. But what you may not realize is that your competition is the customer, not other restaurants. So stop looking across the street and focus on the face above the tabletop or at the counter.

No. 4: "Comment cards and 'secret' shoppers accurately measure service." Measuring customer satisfaction in your restaurant merely by tallying mystery-shopper scores and comment cards is like judging chili by counting the beans. Measure what matters: Same-store sales increases, higher customer traffic, and lower employee turnover are just as important—if not more so. Mystery shopping is effective, but only if it measures the good as well as the bad and the "shoppers" are people with hospitality experience who know the subtleties to look for. Focus on creating internal quality for your staff first, and they will build a happy customer. A happy customer buys more.

No. 5: "People are our most important asset." That old adage is wrong. The right people are your most important asset. The right people are not "warm bodies." The right people are those servers, cooks, hostesses, or managers who exhibit the desired team and customer service behavior you want, as a natural extension of their character and attitude, regardless of any control or incentive system. Hire the personality; train the skills. Where do you find them? See No. 6.

No. 6: "There's a labor crisis." According to the National Restaurant Association and the Bureau of Labor Statistics, every seven days we turn over 250,000 employees in this industry. Yikes. But where do they go? Is it to other industries or other restaurants? Get straight on this:

We don't have a "labor" crisis. We've got a turnover crisis. So the tough question you have to ask yourself about your operation is not, "Are there enough people available to work?" but rather, "Are there enough people available to work who want to work for us?" Make your operation a fun, reputable, and caring place to work.

No. 7: "Invest first in building the brand." Sorry, I disagree. Invest first in people, second in brand, third in bricks and mortar. Mike Snyder, president of Red Robin International Inc., summed it up this way. He said, "Give me a Weber [barbecue] and a tent in a parking lot along with the best service-oriented people who take care of the customers and each other, and I'll beat the roof off the restaurant with the multimillion-dollar physical plant every shift."

No. 8: "Information is power." Know the difference between "information" and "communication." Those two words often are used interchangeably but in fact mean two different things. Information is "giving out"; communication is "getting through." Training is your secret weapon, but I suspect that much of your training informs more than it communicates. Besides, the belief that information is power leads managers to hoard it, not share it, and that's backward thinking. Sharing information not only enlightens but also shares the burden of leadership and engages the creativity and solutions of the entire team.

No. 9: "We need new ideas to progress." Why do companies always want new ideas? I'll tell you why: Because "new ideas" are easy. That's right. The hard part is letting go of ideas that worked for you two years ago and are now out of date. So before you and your team brainstorm dozens of new ideas that get listed on flip charts, give everyone a warm, fuzzy feeling, and that never are implemented, allow me to suggest a different angle. The newest and most innovative thing you can do for your business may be to master the "basics" that everyone knows and no one executes consistently. I'm referring to caring behavior, service with flair, and employee appreciation. Because, unlike Nehru jackets and the Backstreet Boys, the basics of great service never go out of style.

In summary, remember that there is no silver bullet for guaranteeing great service and a great team. Maybe Darrell Rolph, chief executive of Carlos O'Kelly's, says it best: "Keep it fresh, keep it focused, and remember to say thank you."

Everything is systematized, and the worker is simply taught to run the machines, follow the rules, and speak given phrases. When the bell rings, the worker turns the hamburgers on the grill. To make a pancake, the worker hits the batter dispenser one time. There is no room for deviation.

Such standardization has many benefits to the enterprise. It maintains product consistency from one unit to the next. It allows the use of unskilled labor and makes training quick, simple, and inexpensive. It is well suited to short-term workers on their first jobs. But such complete standardization may not work so well in other settings or for other types of workers. When there is no room for deviation, there is no opportunity for originality, no relief from monotony. Enterprises less completely geared to high turnover may have problems with training and morale.

You can also see scientific management at work in the standardized recipe, the standardized greeting, the standardized hotel registration procedures, and the standardized making of a hospital bed. But scientific management as a whole is practiced in restaurants and hotels far less than it could be. We have the methods and techniques, but we seldom use them. We may have standardized recipes, but except in baking, many cooks never look at them. We may standardize procedures, but we seldom enforce them. We hire in panic and in crisis; we take the first warm body that presents itself and put it to work. We use the magic apron training method: We give the new employee an apron and say "Go." We assume that anyone knows how to do some of our entry-level jobs. We hang on to inefficient workers because we are afraid that the next ones we hire will be even worse. As for overseeing their work, who has time to do that?

Probably the very nature of the hotel and food businesses makes them unsuitable for totally scientific management. Still, there are important elements of the method that can be used to increase productivity, achieve consistent results, make customers happy and patients well, increase profit, and make a manager's life much easier, all without making workers into human machines.

Human Relations Theory

In the 1930s and 1940s, another theory of people management appeared—that of the human relations school. This was an outgrowth of studies made at the Hawthorne plant of Western Electric Company. Researchers testing the effects on productivity of changes in working conditions came up with a baffling series of results that could not be explained in the old scientific management terms. During a prolonged series of experiments with rest periods, for example, the productivity of the small test group rose steadily whether the rest time was moved up or down or was eliminated altogether. Furthermore, workers in the test group were out sick far less often than the large group of regular workers, and the test group worked without supervision. It became obvious that the rise in productivity was the result of something new, not the economic factor of a paycheck or the scientific factors of working conditions or close supervision.

Elton Mayo, the Harvard professor who conducted the experiments, concluded that a social factor, the sense of belonging to a work group, was responsible. Other people had other theories to explain the increased productivity: the interested attention of the researchers, the absence of authoritarian supervision, participation in the planning, and analysis of the experiments. People are still theorizing about what human relations theory can do for you. We explore this in later chapters.

Participative Management

Participative management was the real meaning of the Hawthorne experiments, but everyone agrees that the experiments shifted the focus of personnel management to the people being managed. Now enter the human relations theorists, who stressed the importance of concern for workers as individuals and as members of the work group. "Make your employees happy and you will have good workers," they said. "Listen to your people, call them by name, remember their birthdays, help them with their problems." This was the era of the company picnic, the company newspaper, the company bowling team, the company Boy Scout troop. Human relations practitioners flourished especially in the 1940s, during World War II and after, and many of their theories are still at work, maintaining a healthy focus on the importance of the individual.

But happiness, it turns out, does not necessarily make people productive. You can have happy workers who are not producing a thing: There is more to productivity than that. Yet we do need nearly everything the human relations theorists emphasized. Supervisors do need to know their workers, to treat them as individuals, to communicate and listen, to provide a pleasant working environment, and to encourage a sense of belonging. But we need still more. It isn't happiness that will make your workers produce; it is your own ability to lead your people. Some of the human relations techniques, such as listening and communicating and treating people as individuals, can make you a better leader, and this is the biggest thing that human relations theory can do for you. We explore this in later chapters.

Building on the new interest in the worker, a trend toward participative management developed in the 1960s and 1970s. In a participative system, workers participate in the decisions that concern them. They do not necessarily make the decisions; this is not democratic management by majority vote. The manager still leads and usually makes the final decision, but he or she discusses plans and procedures and policies with the work groups who must carry them out, and considers their input in making final decisions. In taking part in such discussions, workers come to share the concerns and objectives of management and are more likely to feel committed to the action and to being responsible for the results.

In the foodservice industry you can see the influence of scientific management in some fast-food operations. Courtesy of Action Systems, Inc.

Participative management as a total system is probably not suited to the typical foodservice or lodging enterprise. Nevertheless, certain of its elements can work very well. Discussing the work with your people, getting their ideas, and exchanging information can establish a work climate and group processes in which everybody shares responsibility to get results. You might call it *management by communication.*

Humanistic Management

What is likely to work best in the hotel and foodservice industries is selective borrowing from all three systems of management: scientific, human relations, and participative. We need to apply many of the principles of scientific management: We need standardized recipes, we need to train workers in the best ways to perform tasks, and we need systems for controlling quality, quantity, and cost. But one thing we do not need from scientific management is its view of the worker as no more than a production tool. Here we can adapt many features of the human relations approach. If we treat workers as individuals with their own needs and desires and motivations, we can do a much better job of leading them and we are far more likely to increase productivity overall. From participative management we can reap the advantages of open communication and commitment to common goals, so that we are all working together. The successful manager will blend all three systems, deliberately or instinctively, according to the needs of the situation, the workers, and his or her personal style of leadership. We call this humanistic management.

Like Frederick Taylor and all the theorists since, today's supervisor is concerned with productivity: getting people to do their jobs in the best way, getting the work done on time and done well. This is an age-old problem: When Pope John XXIII was asked how many people worked for him, he answered, "About half of them." It is sad but human that many people will do as little work as possible unless they see some reason to do better. Often they see no reason.

This is where leadership comes in: the supervisor interacting with the workers. Look at it as a new form of ROI, not *return on investment* but *return on individuals*. As a supervisor you will succeed only to the degree that each person under you produces; you are judged on the performance, the productivity, and the efficiency of others. The only means for your success is a return on each person who works for you. As a leader you can give them reasons to do better. Use your I's: imagination, ideas, initiative, improvement, interaction, innovation, and—why not?—inspiration. It is the personal interaction between supervisor and worker that will turn the trick.

MANAGERIAL SKILLS

Management at any level is an art, not a science providing exact answers to problems. It is an art that can be learned, although no one can really teach you. You do not have to be born with certain talents or personality traits. In fact, studies of outstanding top executives have failed to identify a common set of traits that add up to successful leadership, and experts have concluded that successful leadership is a matter of individual style. There are, however, certain managerial skills essential to success at any level of management: technical skill, human skill, and conceptual skill. At lower levels of management, technical and human skills are most important because managers

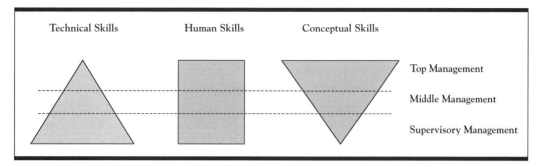

FIGURE 11.7 Levels of technical, human, and conceptual skills required by top, middle, and supervisory managers.

here are concerned with the products and the people making them. Conceptual skill is necessary, too, but not to the same degree. In top-management positions in large corporations, conceptual skill is all-important, and the other skills come into play less often (see Figure 11.7).

All these skills can be developed through exercise, through study and practice, through observation and awareness of oneself and others. We will look at them as they apply to supervisors in foodservice and hospitality enterprises. Then we add to the list of skills a fourth essential for managerial success: some personal qualities that will enable you to survive and prosper.

Technical Skills

The kind of technical skill useful to you as a supervisor is the ability to do the tasks of the people you supervise. You may not have their proficiency—you may not be able to make a souffle or operate a hotel telephone system—but you should know what these tasks involve and in a general way know how they are carried out. You need such knowledge to select and train people, plan and schedule the work in your department, and take action in an emergency. Most important, your technical skills give you credibility with your workers. They will be more ready to accept and respect you when they know that you have some competence in the work you supervise.

If you have been an hourly worker, you may already have the technical skills you need. Many supervisors pick up these skills from their workers on the job. In large organizations some supervisors are required to go through the same skills training as the workers.

Human Skills

The skill of handling people successfully is really the core of the supervisor's job. Such skill has several ingredients and it is not achieved overnight.

First in importance is *your attitude toward the people who work for you*. You must be able to perceive and accept them as human beings. If you don't—if you think of them as cogs in the wheels of production, or if you look down on them because you are the boss and they scrub floors for a living—they will not work well for you or they will simply leave. *They will not let you succeed.*

A second ingredient of human skills is *sensitivity*, the ability to perceive each person's needs, perceptions, values, and personal quirks so that you can work with each one in the most productive way. You need to be aware that Jose still has trouble with English, and that Rita will cry for days if you speak sharply to her but Charlie won't do anything at all unless you almost yell. You need to realize that when Jim comes in looking like thunder and not saying a word, he's mad about something and you had better find a way to defuse him before you turn him loose among the customers. You need to be able to sense when a problem is building by noticing subtle differences in employee behavior.

A third ingredient is *self-awareness*. Have you any idea how you come across to your workers? You need to be aware of your own behavior as it appears to others. For example, in your concern for quality, you may always be pointing out to people things they are doing wrong. They probably experience this as criticism and see you as a negative person who is always finding fault. If you become aware of your habits and their reactions, you can change your manner of correcting them and balance it out with praise for things well done.

You also need to be aware of your own perceptions, needs, values, and personal quirks and how they affect your dealings with your associates. When you and they perceive things differently, you will have trouble communicating. When you and they have different needs and values in a work situation, you may be working at cross-purposes.

Human skills come with practice. You have to practice treating people as individuals, sharpening your awareness of others and of yourself, figuring out what human qualities and behaviors are causing problems and how these problems can be solved. This is another instance in which the flex style of management figures: responding to your people, yourself, and the situation. It is a continual challenge because no two human situations are ever exactly alike. The ultimate human skill is putting it all together to create an atmosphere in which your people feel secure, free, and open with you and are willing to give you their best work.

Conceptual Skills

Conceptual skills require the ability to see the whole picture and the relationship of each part to the whole. The skilled comes in using that ability on the job. You may need to arrange the work of each part of your operation so that it runs smoothly with the other parts—so that the kitchen and the dining room run in harmony, for example. Or you may need to coordinate the work of your department with what goes on in another part of the enterprise. For example, in a hotel the desk clerk must originate a daily report to the housekeeper showing what rooms must be cleaned, so that the housekeeper can tell the cleaning associates to draw their supplies and clean and make up the rooms. When they have made up the rooms, they have to report back to the housekeeping department so that the rooms can be inspected and okayed, and then the housekeeping department has to issue a report back to the desk clerk that the rooms are ready for occupancy. If you are the front office manager, you must be able to see this

You need to establish person-to-person relations with individual workers. Call them by name; get to know them as people—their families, their hobbies, and so on. They must be able to accept you as a human being, too, so they can look you in the eye and not be afraid of you. They will listen better to your instructions, and they will do better work if you act like a person as well as a boss. Courtesy of Sodexho.

process as a whole even though the front desk cares only about the end of it—are those rooms ready? You must understand how the front desk fits into a revolving process that affects not only housekeeping and cleaning personnel but laundry, supplies, storage, and so on, and how important that first routine report of the desk clerk is to the whole process, to everyone involved, to customer service, and to the success of the enterprise.

In departments where everyone is doing the same tasks, conceptual skill is seldom called on, but the more complicated the supervisor's responsibilities, the greater the need for conceptual skill. A restaurant manager, for example, has a great deal of use for conceptual ability since he or she is responsible for both the front and the back of the house as well as the business end of the operation.

Consider what happened to this new restaurant manager. Things got very busy one night, and a waitress came up to him and said, "We can't get the tables bused." "Don't worry about it," he said, and he began to bus tables. Another waitress came to him and said, "We can't get the food out of the kitchen quick enough to serve the people." "Don't worry about it," he said, "I'll go back there and help them cook the food." While he was cooking, another waitress came in and said, "We can't get the dishes washed to reset the tables." "Don't worry about it, I'll wash the dishes," he said. While he was washing the dishes, another waitress came in and said, "We can't get the tables bused." And so it went: the tables, the food, the dishes, the tables, the food. At this point the owner came in and said, "What the hell are you doing?" "I'm washing the dishes, I'm busing the tables, I'm cooking the food, and before I leave tonight I'm gonna empty the garbage," said the manager with pride. *"Look at this place!"* the owner shouted. "I hired you to manage, not to bus tables and cook and wash dishes!"

That manager had not been able to see the situation as a whole, to move people about, to balance them out where they were needed most: to manage. He had boomeranged back to doing the work himself because it was easier than managing, more familiar than dealing with the whole picture. Supervisors who are promoted from hourly positions often have this problem. When they finally learn to look at the whole picture and deal with the whole picture, they have truly attained the management point of view.

Check Your Knowledge Define the following terms: scientific management; humanistic management.

Personal Skills and Qualities

In addition to managing others, *supervisors must be able to manage themselves*. This, too, is a skill that can be developed through awareness and practice. It means doing your best no matter what you have to cope with, putting your best foot forward and your best side out, keeping your cool. It means setting a good example; it means self-discipline. You cannot direct others effectively if you cannot handle yourself. It also means having self-control and supporting your own supervisor even when you personally disagree with a decision or action.

Managing yourself also means thinking positively. According to Manz, two different patterns of thinking are opportunity thinking and obstacle thinking. When faced with a challenging situation, opportunity thinkers concentrate on constructive ways of dealing with the circumstances, whereas obstacle thinkers focus on why the situation is impossible and retreat. Let's say that you are a supervisor and your evening dishwasher calls in sick. If you are an opportunity thinker, you'll look at the work schedule to see who else may be able to fill in and take steps to contact them. If you are an obstacle thinker, you'll think there's nothing you can do except ask the staff to switch to disposable dishes, even though you know it costs a lot more and the food doesn't look as good. Work on being an opportunity thinker, and if you make mistakes, learn from them and don't make yourself miserable. Everyone makes mistakes, even the people at the top of the organization chart. Guilt and worry will wear you down; self-acceptance and self-confidence will increase your energy.

Your own moods will affect your workers, too; they can run right through your whole department. Your employees watch you more carefully than you think; they can tell if your day is going fine or if you just had a frustrating meeting with your boss. When you get right down to it, your employees need a boss with a consistently positive outlook and attitude on the job.

You need to build a good, *strong self-image*. You have obligations to yourself as well as to others. Give yourself credit when you are right; face your mistakes when you are wrong and correct them for the future. You need to know yourself well, including your strengths and weaknesses, to work out your personal goals and values as they apply to your job, to know where you stand and where you are going.

In addition to having faith in your own ability to reach goals, you need to *believe that employees will perform effectively when given a reasonable chance*. You need to realize that you are also responsible for developing your employees through techniques such as coaching and counseling.

Another pair of useful personal qualities are *flexibility* and *creativity*. No hospitality manager can survive for long without flexibility, the ability to respond effectively to constantly changing situations and problems, to adapt theory to the reality of the moment, to think creatively because there are no pat answers. You must be able to respond to changes in the industry, too; yesterday's solutions will not solve tomorrow's problems. These again are skills that you can learn and practice; you do not have to be born with them.

Finally, being a supervisor requires *high energy levels and the ability to work under great pressure*. The time pressure in the hospitality field is unlike that in many other businesses; the meals must be served in a timely fashion; the rooms have to be ready in time for the next guest; the diabetic hospital patient needs his snacks at 2:00 P.M. and 8:00 P.M., period. Much stamina is needed to deal with these pressures.

You need to make a conscious and deliberate decision to be a manager. Here are three questions you must answer:

1. *Do you really want it?* Is there something about being a manager in this hospitality business (or wherever you are) that provides the responsibility, the challenge, and the fulfillment you want from the work you do?

2. *What is the cost?* Without tips or overtime pay, you'll probably make less money than some of your workers do. The hours are long, you'll work on weekends when everyone else is playing, the responsibility is unremitting, and the frustration level is high. You are squarely in the middle of all the hassle: Your employer is telling you, "I want a lower food cost, I want a lower labor cost, and I want this place cleaned up." Your workers are saying, "I can't be here Friday night, that's not my job, get somebody else to do it, I want more money." The customers are saying, "The food is cold, your service is slow, and your prices are too high." And your family is saying, "You're never home, we never get to go out together, you don't have time to help us with our homework, what do you mean fix you a cheese sandwich after you've been down there with all that food all day?" You work with people all day long, and yet it is a lonely job.

3. *Is it worth the cost?* Is the work itself satisfying and fulfilling? Will you learn and grow as a professional and as a person? Are you on the path you want to be on? Do you want to be a manager enough to pay the price?

If your answer is yes, then pay the price—pay it willingly and without complaint, pay it gladly. This may be the most important quality of all—to have the maturity to decide what you want and accept the tough parts with grace and humor; or to see it clearly, weigh it carefully, and decide you are not going that way after all. One successful manager is Tim Stanton, a joint venture partner with Outback Steakhouse, who is described by a colleague as being incredibly driven and extremely motivated, detail-oriented, passionate about food quality, and demanding but fair.[3]

TIPS FOR NEW SUPERVISORS

As we are beginning to realize, being a new supervisor can be a daunting task but it can also be a stimulating and rewarding time of personal accomplishment. New supervisors need to be prepared, particularly in the hospitality industry where we need to "hit the ground running."

The following are some tips that you may find useful:

- Start as you mean to continue—meaning set your standards and keep them.
- Develop a game plan with your boss of what you and your employees are to achieve and the best ways to go about it.
- Be you—don't try and be someone else now that you have some authority. Be objective, treat everyone the way you would like to be treated.
- Praise the good work that you and your team have done in the past.
- Your employees have needs—ask how you can help them do a better job.
- Begin getting a "feel" for the workplace by listening and asking questions. You may see changes that should be made but don't rush into making hasty decisions from the get-go. It's much better to solicit the ideas and questions from your team.
- Be positive, upbeat, and be ready to share the knowledge of your team and encourage everyone's participation.
- Outline the team's strengths, accomplishments and the challenges ahead. Explain that this will be a we-and-us, not an I-and-you situation, because as a team more can be accomplished and obstacles can be overcome.
  - Know the company's vision, mission, goals, and strategies.
  - Know the company's philosophy and culture.
  - Check the organization chart for reporting relationships.
  - Check the budget—what are your budgeting responsibilities, what percentage is discretionary, and what can be moved from one item to another?
  - Know the policies and procedures but don't be afraid to say "I need to check on that and get back to you"—but do so.
  - Set a good example: arrive early, dress appropriately, and do not do personal business on company time. Remember, your behavior, attitude, and work habits will influence your team.

Before you became a supervisor you were in a position where you were aware of the department's goals and your own responsibilities but you were an individual whose main concern was a contribution or doing your part toward the success of the department. Now however, you are responsible for the work of others and a productive team. Now is the time to determine your priorities and plan the work to be done.

The types of behavior that good supervisors and managers exhibit are described in an article by Jim Sullivan as: earns the organization money; tells the truth; keeps promises; excels at conflict resolution; teaches; evaluates then acts; makes people want to work for them; runs business as if it's theirs; is enthusiastic; and makes pre-shift huddles mandatory.[4]

As we progress through this book we will learn more about these an other types of successful supervisor behavior. In the next chapter we examine supervisory leadership.

KEY POINTS

1. A supervisor is any person who manages people making products or performing services. A supervisor is responsible for the quality and quantity of the products and services and for meeting the needs of employees. Only by motivating and stimulating the employees to do their jobs properly will supervisors ensure that high-quality products and services are produced.

2. Using an organization chart, you can see line and staff functions as well as how authority and responsibility are handed down from the top level of management to the first-line supervisors.

3. As a supervisor, your own success depends on the work of others, and you will be measured by their output and their performance. You will be successful in your own job only to the degree that your workers allow you to be, and this will depend on how you manage them.

4. As a hospitality supervisor, you have obligations to the owners, customers, and employees. To your employees, you represent management. To the owners and your bosses, you are the link with the workers and the work to be done; you represent productivity, cost control, quality control, and customer service. You also represent your people and their needs and desires. To the customers, your output and your employees represent the company.

5. As a supervisor, you've got to maintain the management point of view. You can't go back to where you came from (boomerang management).

6. As a supervisor, if you take care of the employees, the employees will take care of the customers, and the profits will take care of themselves. Your principal concern is your employees.

7. Some of the most important management activities you will be involved in are planning, organizing, staffing, leading, controlling or evaluating, coordinating, problem solving and decision making, and representing.

8. Managing is the ability to adjust actions and decisions to given situations—it is a flex style of management, calling upon theory, experience, and talent. It is a skill that cannot be taught but has to be developed on the job.

9. The successful manager will blend principles of scientific management, human relations, and participative management, according to the needs of the situation and the employees, into a style referred to as humanistic management.

10. For success, managers need technical skills, human skills, conceptual skills, and certain personal skills.

KEY TERMS

authority	humanistic management	problem solving
boomerang management	leading	representing
conceptual skill	line functions	responsibility
controlling	manager	scientific management
coordinating	managerial skills	staff functions
decision making	nonexempt employees	staffing
evaluating	obstacle thinkers	supervisor
exempt employees	opportunity thinkers	technical skill
first-line supervisor	organizational chart	work climate
hourly workers	organizing	work simplification
human relations	participative management	working supervisor
human skill	planning	

REFERENCES

1. Personal conversation with Jim Sullivan, July 16, 2004.

2. Erica Duecy, "The NRN 50 General Managers," Randy Garutti, *Nation's Restaurant News.* Vol. 38, no 4. January 26, 2004.

3. Ibid p. 134–135.

4. Jim Sullivan, "It Takes More than Tenure to Be a Great General Manager," *Nations Restaurant News.* May 31, 2004. Vol. 38, Iss. 22, p. 16.

C
H
A
P
T
E
R

12

THE SUPERVISOR AS LEADER*

I f you were to ask any hospitality leader what his or her greatest challenge is, the likely answer would be finding and keeping great employees motivated. Given the high turnover in the hospitality industry and the resultant cost, we begin to understand some of the leadership challenges that supervisors face.

The idea that a supervisor must be a leader comes as a surprise to people who have never thought about it before. The term *leader* is likely to be associated with politics or religious movements or guerrilla-warfare situations in which people voluntarily become followers of the person who achieves command. Although it is not necessarily true, it is generally assumed that the one who is followed is a "born leader" whose influence is

---

* Authored by Jack E. Miller, John R. Walker, and Karen Eich Drummond.

based at least partly on charisma or personal magnetism. A definition of leadership is: "The ability to articulate a vision, to embrace the values of that vision, and nurture an environment where everyone can reach the organizations goals and their own personal needs."[1]

Leadership begins with a vision, a mission, and goals. Vision is the articulation of the mission of the organization in such an appealing way that it vividly conveys what it can be like in the future. Vision instills a common purpose, self-esteem, and a sense of membership in the organization. The mission statement describes the purpose of the organization and outlines the kinds of activities performed for guests. Mission statements normally have three parts: First, a statement of overall purpose, second, a statement explaining the values employees are expected to maintain in the daily decision-making process, third, a declaration of the major goals that management believes is essential to attain the goals. Goals should be relevant to the mission, specific and clear, challenging yet achievable, made in collaboration with employees, and written down with the strategies and tactics of how to meet the goals. The importance of vision, mission, goals, strategy, and tactics is critical to the success of the company, and much of the crucial work is done by supervisors.

In a work situation, the supervisor is in command by virtue of being placed there by the company and its superiors. In the hospitality industry the term *supervisor* refers to a manager at a lower organizational level who supervises entry-level or other employees who themselves do not have supervisory responsibilities. The workers are expected to do what the boss tells them to do—that's just part of the job, right?

But if employees simply do what they are told, why is labor turnover so high, productivity so low, and absenteeism so prevalent? Why is there conflict between labor and management? The truth of the matter is that the boss is in charge of the workers, but that does not guarantee that the workers will put all of their efforts into the job. This is where leadership comes in.

In this chapter we explore the kinds of interactions between a supervisor and the workers that relate to the building of leadership in work situations. It will help you to:

- Identify typical hourly jobs in foodservice and lodging establishments.
- Outline the demographics of the labor pool typically hired for hourly jobs in the hospitality industry.
- Explain the concept of leadership.
- Describe the characteristics of leadership.
- Compare and contrast the concepts of formal authority and real authority.

- Compare and contrast Theory X and Theory Y management styles.

- Describe and give examples of leadership styles—autocratic, bureaucratic, democratic, and laissez-faire, situational, transactional, transformational.

- Outline leadership practices.

- Develop your own leadership style.

YOU AND YOUR PEOPLE

More than one out of every eight Americans now working have worked in a McDonald's since the first one opened over 50 years ago in California. It seems an incredible statistic, but keep in mind that 8 percent of American employees work in foodservice, and many young people find their first job in foodservice or a hotel. You may already have worked in a hospitality operation yourself.

The hospitality industry is composed of 70 percent part-time, short-term people. They are "only working here until"—until they get out of high school, until they get out of college, until they have enough money to buy a car, or until an opening comes up someplace else. It is not uncommon to hear a young hourly employee say, "I'll keep this job until I can get a real job," for what they often mean is that they plan to switch from an hourly to a salaried position.

The Jobs and the Workers

Hotels and restaurants are dependent on large numbers of people to fill low-wage entry-level jobs that have little interest and no perceived future. Washing pots, busing tables, dishing out the same food every day from the same steam table, lifting heavy bags, mopping dirty floors, cleaning rest rooms, straightening up messy rooms left by unheeding customers every single day can become very tiresome. Workers take these jobs either because no special skill, ability, or experience is required, or because nothing else is available.

Some of these people consider the work demeaning. Even though they are doing demanding work that is absolutely essential to the operation, management often looks down on them. They are frequently taken for granted, ignored, or spoken to only when reprimanded. Given the nature of the work and the attitudes of management and sometimes of other workers, it is no wonder that turnover is high.

Another level of hourly worker is the skilled or semiskilled: the front desk clerk, the cashier, the bartender, the cook, the waiter and waitress. These jobs are more appealing, the money is better, and there is sometimes a chance for advancement. Yet here, too, you often find temporary workers—students, moonlighters, people who cannot find anything in their own fields—people working there *until*.

Many employers assume that their employee will not stay long, and most of them do not. According to a National Restaurant Association's Restaurant Industry Operations Report, the turnover rate for hourly workers in full-service operations is 100 percent. That means that your typical full-service restaurant will lose every one of its hourly employees during one year and have to fill every position. If we were to ask workers to explain why they left their jobs, the most frequently cited reasons would likely be more money, a better work schedule, and more enjoyable work.

There is really no valid stereotype of today's hospitality worker. The industry employs people of all ages and backgrounds. In fact, an already diverse workplace is becoming more diverse than ever. This is due in part to the fact that new workers entering the workforce are overwhelmingly non-Caucasian ethnic minorities, immigrants, and women.

Approximately half of the foodservice workforce, as well as a big presence in hotels, are employees from 18- to 40-something years old, a group referred to as Generation X (those born between the late 1960s and 1980) and Generation Y (those born in the 1980s or 1990s. There are 70 millon Generation Y'ers). X'ers and Y'ers will work hard, but they will also make certain demands. They want to do work that they consider worthwhile as well as work they enjoy doing. The employees want their supervisors to let them be more involved by listening to them and by allowing them to participate in decision making. Not surprisingly, employees do not want supervisors to bark orders in a militant fashion, they want training and expect management to invest time and money in their training and development.

At least 60 percent of both foodservice and hotel workers are women. There are more women working now than ever before and they are not necessarily satisfied with traditional women's jobs. There are many female bartenders, cooks, and chefs, as well as many other management positions now filled by women.

The fastest-growing ethnic groups in the United States are Hispanics, people of Asian origin, and African-Americans, so it is not surprising to see many of these people in hospitality jobs. Did you know that Hispanics have been the biggest minority in foodservice since 1993? Did you also know that one out of six foodservice workers speaks a language other than English at home? We discuss diversity of the hospitality workforce in more detail in Chapter 13.

As we noted in Chapter 11, many of today's workers tend to have a higher expectation level and a lower frustration tolerance than workers of past generations. They expect more out of a job than just a paycheck. Most are not tied by need to jobs they don't like; in good times, hospitality jobs are usually plentiful, and unemployment insurance tides workers over during a move from one job to another. Availability of jobs, of course, varies with economic conditions and from one area to another. But even needing that paycheck does not guarantee that a person will work well on the job. That is why it is necessary to have supervisors and managers.

A lack of leadership is a problem in our industry. Part of the problem is that we're not talking about leadership in our meetings at a unit level. We, as managers, need to realize that people don't want to be managed; they want to be led.

Source: Erica Duecy, "Quality leaders key to serving up excellence everyday" *Nations Restaurant News*, Vol. 38, No. 24, p. 88, June 2004.

CHARACTERISTICS OF LEADERS

If we were to examine great leaders of the past we would likely come up with a list of characteristics and traits like this from the *U.S. Guidebook for Marines.*

Bearing, courage, decisiveness, dependability, endurance, enthusiasm, initiative, integrity, judgment, justice, knowledge, loyalty, tact, and unselfishness. Of these, a marine would likely say that integrity is the most important. Integrity to a marine means to do something right even if nobody is aware of it.

Several studies have shown that effective leaders have six traits that distinguish them from nonleaders: drive, the desire to influence others, honesty and moral character, self-confidence, intellegence, and relevant knowledge (Figure 12.1).

A person's *drive* shows that he or she are willing and able to exert exceptional effort to achieve a goal. This high-energy person is likely to take the initiative and be persistent.

Leaders have a *desire to influence others*. This desire is frequently seen as a willingness to accept authority. A leader also builds trusting relationships with those supervised, by being truthful. By showing consistency between their words and actions, leaders display *honesty and moral character*.

Leaders have *self-confidence* to influence others to pursue the goals of the organization. Employees tend to prefer a leader who has strong beliefs and is decisive over one who seems unsure of which decision to make.

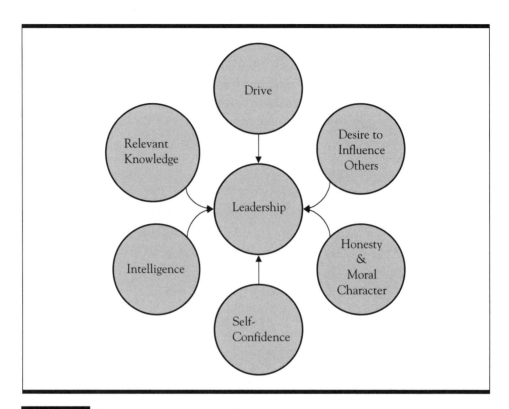

FIGURE 12.1 Characteristics and traits of effective leaders.

Influencing others takes a *level of intelligence*. A leader needs to gather, synthesize, and interpret a lot of information. Leaders create a vision, develop goals, communicate and motivate, problem-solve, and make decisions.

A leader needs a high level of *relevant knowledge*, technical, theoretical, and conceptual. Knowledge of the company, its policies and procedures, the department, and the employees are all necessary to make informed decisions.[2]

Effective leaders are able to influence others to behave in a particular way. This is called power. There are four primary sources of power:

1. *Legimate power*, which is derived from an individual's position in an organization

2. *Reward power*, which is derived from an individual's control over rewards

3. *Coercive power*, which is derived from an individual's ability to threaten negative outcomes

Approximately half of the foodservice workforce, as well as a big presence in hotels, are employees from 18 to 38 years old. Courtesy PhotoDisc/Getty Images.

4.   *Expert power*, which is derived from an individual's personal charisma and the respect and/or admiration the individual inspires

Many leaders have a combination of these sources of power to influence others to goal achievment.[3]

THE NATURE OF LEADERSHIP

You are going to be a leader. Now, you may wonder, "What is a leader, and how is it any different from being a manager?" These are good questions. As a part of the management staff, one is expected to produce goods and services by working with people and using resources such as equipment and employees. That is what being a manager or supervisor is all about. As discussed in Chapter 11, an important managerial function is to be a leader. A leader can be defined as someone who guides or influences the actions of his or her employees to reach certain goals. A leader is a person whom people follow voluntarily. What you, as a supervisor, must do is to direct the work of your people in a way that causes them to do it voluntarily. You don't have to be a born leader, you don't have to be magnetic or charismatic; you have to get people to work for you willingly and to the best of their ability. That is what leadership is all about.

Although it is true that many leadership skills are innate and that not all managers make great leaders, it is also true that most managers will benefit from leadership training. Moreover, natural leaders will flourish in an environment that supports their growth and development.

There are seven steps to establishing a foundation for leadership development:

1. Commit to investing the time, resources, and money needed to create a culture that supports leadership development.

2. Identify and communicate the differences between management skills and leadership abilities within the organization.

3. Develop quantifiable measurables that support leadership skills. These include percentage of retention, percentage of promotables, and percentage of cross-trained team members.

4. Make leadership skills a focus of management training. These include communication skills (written, verbal, nonverbal, and listening), team-building skills (teamwork, coaching, and feedback), proactive planning skills (transitioning from managing shifts to managing businesses), and interpersonal skills (motivation, delegation, decision making, and problem solving).

5. Implement ongoing programs that focus on leadership skills, such as managing multiple priorities, creating change, and presentation skills.

6. Know that in the right culture, leaders can be found at entry level.

7. Recognize, reward, and celebrate leaders for their passion, dedication, and results.

In theory, you have authority over your people because you have formal authority, or the right to command, given to you by the organization. You are the boss and you have the power, the ability to command. You control the hiring, firing, raises, rewards, discipline, and punishment. In all reality, your authority is anything but absolute. Real authority is conferred on your subordinates, and you have to earn the right to lead them. It is possible for you to be the formal leader of your work group as well as have someone else who is the informal leader actually calling the shots.

The relationship between you and your people is a fluid one, subject to many subtle currents and cross-currents between them and you. If they do not willingly accept your authority, they have many ways of withholding success. They can stay home from work, come in late, drag out the work into overtime, produce inferior products, drive your customers away with rudeness and poor service, break the rules, refuse to do what you tell them to, create crises, and punish you by walking off the job and leaving you in the lurch. Laying down the law, the typical method of control in hospitality operations, does not necessarily maintain authority; on the contrary, it usually creates a negative, nonproductive environment.

What it all adds up to is that your job as a supervisor is to direct and oversee a group of transients who are often untrained, all of whom are different from each other, and many of whom would rather be working somewhere else. You are dependent on them to do the work for which you are responsible. You will succeed only to the degree that they permit you to succeed. It is your job to get the workers to do their best for the enterprise, for the customers, and for you. How can one do this?

As a distinguished leadership expert noted, "Managers are people who do things right, and leaders are people who do the right things." Think about that for a moment. In other words, managers are involved in being efficient and in mastering routines, whereas leaders are involved in being effective and turning goals into reality. As a supervisor and leader, your job is to do the right things right, to be both efficient and effective. An effective supervisor in the hospitality industry is one whom, first, knows and understands basic principles of management, and second, applies them to managing all the resource operations.

In the hospitality industry we use a technique referred to as MBWA, *management by walking around*, spending a significant part of your day talking to your employees, your guests, and your peers. As you are walking around and talking to these various people, you should be performing three vital roles discussed in this book: listening, coaching, and troubleshooting.

Check Your Knowledge

1. What is a leader?
2. What is the difference between formal and informal authority?
3. What is real authority?

LEADERSHIP STYLES

The term *leadership style* refers to your pattern of interacting with your subordinates: how you direct and control the work of others, and how you get them to produce the goods and services for which you are responsible. It includes not only your manner of giving instructions, but the methods and techniques you use to motivate your workers and to assure that your instructions are carried out.

There are several different forms of leadership style: autocratic, bureaucratic, democratic, and laissez-faire being the most popular styles today (Figure 12.2). Before choosing a style of leadership, one must identify the pros and cons of each and then decide if it will be the most effective style in the hospitality industry.

Autocratic leadership style can be identified with the early, classical approach to management. A supervisor practicing an autocratic style is likely to make decisions without input from staff, to give orders without explanation or defense, and to expect the orders to be obeyed. When this style of leadership is used, employees become

Forms of Leadership Style			
__Autocratic__	__Bureaucratic__	__Democratic__	__Laissez-Faire__
Sees themself as sole decision maker	Strictly by the book	Almost a reversal of autocratic	Hands-off approach
Shows little concern about others' opinion	Relies on rules and regulations	Wants to share responsibilities	Turns over control; delegates authority
Focuses on completing goals	Act like they are a police officer	Collaborates opinions when decision making	Works well when employees are self-motivated
Dictates tasks to be accomplished	Appropriate when employees are permitted no discretion	Is a concerned *coach* of the team	Little application in the hospitality industry

FIGURE 12.2 The pros and cons of each leadership style.

dependent on supervisors for instructions. The wants and needs of the employees come second to those of the organization and the supervisor.

In bureaucratic leadership style, a supervisor manages "by the book." The leader relies on the property's rules, regulations, and procedures for decisions that he makes.

To the employees, their leader appears to be a "police officer." This style is appropriate when the employees can be permitted no discretion in the decisions to be made.

Democratic (also called *participative*) leadership style is almost the reverse of the autocratic style discussed previously. A democratic supervisor wants to share decision-making responsibility. They want to consult with the group members and to solicit their participation in making decisions and resolving problems that affect the employees. The employer strongly considers the opinions of employees and seeks their thoughts and suggestions. All employees are informed about all matters that concern them. One could compare a democratic supervisor to a coach who is leading his or her team.

Laissez-faire (also called *free-reign*) leadership style refers to a hands-off approach in which the supervisor actually does as little leading as possible. In effect, the laissez-faire supervisor delegates all authority and power to the employees. The supervisor relies on the employees to establish goals, make decisions, and solve problems. At best, the laissez-faire style has limited application to the hospitality industry.

The Old-Style Boss

In the hospitality industry, the traditional method of dealing with hourly workers has generally been some variation of the command-obey method combined with carrot-and-stick techniques of reward and punishment. The motivators relied upon to produce the work are money (the carrot) and fear (the stick)—fear of punishment, fear of losing the money by being fired. All too often, the manner of direction is to lay down the law in definite terms, such as cursing, shouting, and threatening as necessary to arouse the proper degree of fear to motivate the worker.

People who practice this autocratic method of managing employees believe that it's the only method that employees will understand. Perhaps that is the way the supervisor was raised, or perhaps it is the only method the supervisor has ever seen in action. In any case, it expresses their view of the people involved that "workers these days are no good."

Some workers are simply bad workers. However, cursing, shouting, and threatening seldom helps them improve. Many workers do respond to a command-obey style of direction, but those workers often come from authoritarian backgrounds and have never known anything else. This style is traditional and military; the style of dictatorship in countries from which some immigrants come. However, for your average American employee, it does not work. It may be enough to keep people on the job but not working to their full capacity.

When coupled with a negative view of the worker, this style of direction and control is far more likely to increase problems than to lessen them, and to backfire by breeding resentment, low morale, and adversary relationships. In extreme cases, the boss and the company become the bad guys, the enemy, and workers give as little as possible and take as much as they can. In response, close supervision and tight control are required to see that nobody gets away with anything. In this type of atmosphere, customer service suffers and patrons go somewhere else.

We are also learning more about what causes workers to work productively, including many of the things we have been talking about, such as positive work climate, person-to-person relations, and other people-oriented methods and techniques. At this point, let us look at some current theories of leadership and see how—or whether—they can be applied in hotel and foodservice settings. These theories emerged in the 1950s and 1960s, following the discovery that making workers happy does not necessarily make them productive. The theories are based on what behavioral scientists, psychologists, and sociologists tell us about human behavior. They explore what causes people to work productively and how this knowledge can be used in managing employees.

Theory X and Theory Y

In the late 1950s, Douglas McGregor of the MIT School of Industrial Management advanced the thesis that business organizations based their management of workers on assumptions about people that were wrong and were actually counterproductive. He described these faulty assumptions about the average human being as Theory X:

1.   They have an inborn dislike of work and will avoid it as much as possible.
2.   They must be "coerced, controlled, directed, threatened with punishment" to get the work done.
3.   They prefer to be led, avoid responsibility, lack ambition, and want security above all else.

McGregor argues: "These characteristics are not inborn." He believed people behaved this way on the job because they were treated as though these things were true. In fact, he stated, "This is a narrow and unproductive view of human beings," and he proposed Theory Y:

1. Work is as natural as play or rest; people do not dislike it inherently.

2. Control and the threat of punishment are not the only means of getting people to do their jobs. They will work of their own accord toward objectives to which they feel committed.

3. People become committed to objectives that will fulfill inner personal needs, such as self-respect, independence, achievement, recognition, status, and growth.

4. Under the right conditions, people learn not only to accept responsibility, but also to seek it. Lack of ambition, avoidance of responsibility, and the desire for security are not innate human characteristics.

5. Capacity for applying imagination, ingenuity, and creativity to solving on-the-job problems is "widely, not narrowly, distributed in the population."

6. The modern industrial organization uses only a portion of the intellectual potential of the average human being.

Thus, if work could fulfill both the goals of the enterprise and the needs of the workers, they would be self-motivated to produce, and consequently, coercion and the threat of punishment would be unnecessary.

Theory X fits the old-style hospitality manager to a T, and it is safe to say that this pattern of thinking is still common in many other industries as well. However, behavioral science theory and management practice have both moved in the direction of Theory Y. Theory Y is a revised view of human nature with emphasis on using the full range of workers' talents, needs, and aspirations to meet the goals of the enterprise.

A popular way of moving toward a Theory Y style of people management is to involve one's workers in certain aspects of management, such as problem solving and decision making. Usually, such involvement is carried out in a group setting: meetings of the workers for the specific purpose of securing their input. The degree of involvement the boss allows or seeks can vary from merely keeping the workers informed of things that affect their work to delegating decision making entirely to the group.

The participative management style, mentioned in Chapter 11, results when workers have a high degree of involvement in such management concerns as planning and decision making. Enthusiasts of a participatory style of leadership believe that the greater the degree of worker participation, the better the decisions and the more likely they are to be carried out. However, others point out that the degree of participation that is appropriate for a given work group will depend on the type of work, the people involved, the nature of the problem, the skill and sensitivity of the leader, and the pressures of time—the situational leadership approach, to be discussed shortly. The degree to which the boss involves the workers may also vary from time to time, depending on circumstances. You are not going to make a group decision when a drunk is making a scene in the dining room or when a fire alarm is going off on the seventh floor.

Situational Leadership

In the situational leadership model developed by Kenneth Blanchard and Paul Hersey, leadership behaviors are sorted into two categories: directive behavior and supportive behavior. *Directive behavior* means telling an employee exactly what you want done, as well as when, where, and how to do it. The focus is to get a job done, and it is best used when employees are learning a new aspect of their jobs. *Supportive behavior* is meant to show caring and support for your employees by praising, encouraging, listening to their ideas, involving them in decision making, and helping them reach their own solutions. This method is best used when an employee lacks commitment to do a job.

By combining directive and supportive behaviors, Hersey and Blanchard came up with four possible leadership styles for different conditions. When an employee has much commitment or enthusiasm but little competence to do a job, a directing style is needed; this is high on directive and low on supportive behaviors. Suppose that you have a new employee full of enthusiasm who knows little about how to do the job. A directing style is appropriate: You train the new employee by giving multiple instructions, you make the decisions, you solve the problems, and you closely supervise. Enthusiastic beginners need this direction. A directing style is also appropriate when a decision has to be made quickly and there is some risk involved, such as when there is a fire and you need to get your employees out of danger.

As new employees get into their jobs, they often lose some of their initial excitement when they realize that the job is more difficult or not as interesting as they originally envisioned. This is the time to use a coaching style, with lots of directive behaviors to continue to build skills and supportive behaviors to build commitment. In addition to providing much direct supervision, you provide support. You listen, you encourage, you praise, you ask for input and ideas, and you consult with the employee.

As employees become technically competent on the job, their commitment frequently wavers between enthusiasm and uncertainty. In a situation like this, the use of a supporting style that is high on supportive behaviors and low on directive behaviors is required. If an employee shows both commitment and competence, a delegating style is suitable. A delegating style of leadership is low on directive and supportive behaviors because you are turning over responsibility for day-to-day decision making to the employee doing the job. These employees don't need much direction, and they provide much of their own support.

Using this view of situational leadership, you need to assess the competence and commitment level of your employee in relation to the task at hand before choosing an appropriate leadership style (Figure 12.2). As a supervisor, your goal should be to build your employees' competence and commitment levels to the point where you are using less time-consuming styles, such as supporting and delegating, and getting quality results.

Transactional Leadership

Transactional leaders motivate workers by appealing to their self-interest. In other words, workers do their jobs and give their compliance in return for rewards such as pay and status. Transactional leaders stress communication of job assignments, work standards, goals, and so on, in order to maintain the status quo.

Transactional leaders motivate workers by appealing to their self-interest. Courtesy of Sodexho.

James McGregor Burns wrote a significant book entitled *Leadership*. In the book Burns describes leadership as falling within two broad categories: transactional and transformational. Transactional leadership seeks to motivate followers by appealing to their own self-interest. Its principles are to motivate by the exchange process. Transactional behavior focuses on the accomplishment of tasks and good employee relations in exchange for desirable rewards.

Transactional leadership behavior is used to one degree or another by most leaders. However, as the old saying goes, "If the only tool in your toolbox is a hammer . . . you will perceive every problem as a nail." Transactional leadership seeks to influence others by exchanging work for wages, but does not build on the employee's need for meaningful work or tap into their creativity. The most effective and beneficial leadership behavior to achieve long-term success and improved performance is transformational leadership.[4]

Profile

LAURA HORETSKI

Courtesy of Laura Horetski

I was asked what leadership means to me as the front office manager of a major hotel chain. When you look at the definition of a leader, it states, "one who leads or guides." And we've all heard the phrase "lead by example." I don't think that is enough. There are at least seven qualities of leadership that I can think of that make a good leader.

A good leader is someone who is not afraid to get his or her hands dirty. Someone who will do the same job, duty, or task alongside subordinates, peers, and supervisors, while keeping a positive attitude. This helps build and gain respect. Besides, how else can you expect someone to do the job you ask him or her to do if you do not know how or are not willing to do it yourself?

A person who listens, not just hears. Pay complete attention to what the person is saying. Look them in the eyes, acknowledge them and don't interrupt. Ask questions of clarification, reiterate what they are saying, and ask the person if you understand them correctly. But listening doesn't stop there. You need to follow through on the conversation and do what you said you would do. Build integrity and trust.

Make good business decisions but show compassion when needed. The bottom line is the bottom line. You don't have to be cruel to accomplish tough results. Be honest, state the facts, ask for suggestions, and make the best decision. A lot of times things look good on paper but don't really work in reality. Sometimes those who are on the front lines and performing the job everyday give the best answers. Not only do you get the answer you may be looking for, you also build confidence and develop future managers and supervisors.

Treat others fairly, including yourself. Favoritism has no place at work. Is it hard not to solely rely on those who are the strongest? Absolutely. But as a leader it's your job to encourage and improve your super performers. Favoritism also provides an impartial playing field for everyone. Learn to delegate to improve teamwork and lighten the load for everybody.

Learning never stops. I try to learn something new every day, sometimes without even seeking it out. You also need to be open to learning from subordinates, peers, and supervisors. There is no one person who has all the answers. The workforce is always changing in every aspect and you need to be able to adapt. It's important to stay fresh and current. Think outside the box; there's usually more than one way to accomplish a goal. If the way you tried doesn't work, you've learned, and it's what you take from the experience that's important.

Develop those under you. The fastest way to move up is to train someone to take your job. This is one of the best ways to show leadership. Too often, people are afraid of "losing their jobs" because someone else knows how to do their job. This is not the case. This frees up time for you to develop your skills in another position you are interested in, while developing your successor.

Finally, you need to be able to admit that you've made mistakes. As I said earlier, no one person has all the answers. You're going to stumble, trip, and even fall. But those who are honest and admit their failures will gain the respect of others and will learn the most. There's a saying, "No question is a dumb question." I say, "No mistake is a mistake."

I have had many teachers throughout my career and I have taken pieces of their leadership style along with me. You are never done learning how to lead. Each circumstance has its own manner in how to approach it. Above all else, a good leader is fair and ever changing.

Above all, have fun!

Transformational Leadership

Transformational leadership is about finding ways of long-term higher order changes in follower behavior. It is the process of gaining performance above expectations by inspiring employees to reach beyond themselves and do more than they originally thought possible. This is accomplished by raising their commitment to a shared vision of the future. As illustrated in Figure 12.3, instead of using rewards and incentives to motivate employees, transformational leaders do the following:

1.   Communicate with and inspire workers about the mission and objectives of the company.
2.   Provide workers with meaningful, interesting, and challenging jobs.
3.   Act as a coach and mentor to support, develop, and empower workers.
4.   Lead by example.

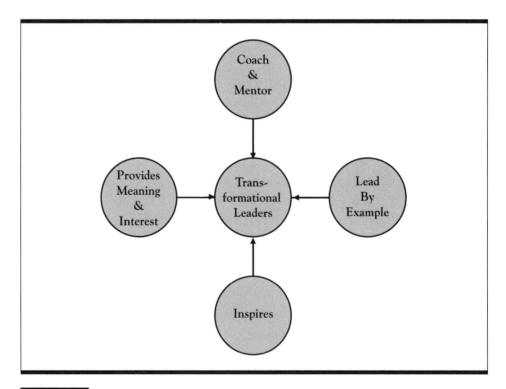

FIGURE 12.3 Transformational leaders.

By appealing to workers' higher-order needs, transformational leaders gain much loyalty that is especially useful in times of change. Transformational leaders generally have lots of charisma. One of the most transformational leaders was Dr. Martin Luther King Jr. Dr. King dedicated his life to achieving rights for all citizens by nonviolent methods. In 1964, Dr. King won the Nobel Peace Prize and is perhaps best remembered for his "I Have a Dream" speech. Delivered in front of the Lincoln Memorial in the summer of 1963, Dr. King inspired his listeners to feel that history was being made in their very presence.

A more recent and hospitality example of a transformational leader was Horst Schultze, who developed Ritz-Carlton hotels and lead them to win the Malcolm Baldrige National Quality Awards. Another was Herb Kelleher of Southwest Airlines. Kelleher set a vision and was able to communicate so well to all employees that they went the extra mile to ensure the companies and their own success.

Practices of Leaders

Leaders vary in their values, managerial styles, and priorities. Peter Drucker, the renowned management scholar, author, and consultant of many years, discussed with hundreds of leaders their roles, their goals and their performance. Drucker observes that regardless of their enormous diversity with respect to personality, style, abilities and interest, effective leaders all behave in much the same way:

1. They did not start out with the question, "What do I want?" They started out asking, "What needs to be done?"

2. Then they asked, "What can and should I do to make a difference?" This has to be something that both needs to be done and fits the leader's strengths and the way she or he is most effective.

3. They constantly asked, "What are the organization's *mission* and *goals*? What constitutes *performance* and *results* in this organization?"

4. They were extremely tolerant of diversity in people and did not look for carbon copies of themselves. But they were totally—fiendishly—intolerant when it came to a person's performance, standards, and values.

5. They were not afraid of strength in their associates. They gloried in it.

6. One way or another, they submitted themselves to the *mirror test*—that is, they made sure the kind of person they saw in the mirror in the morning was the kind of person they wanted to be, to respect, and to believe in. This way they

fortified themselves against the leader's greatest temptations—to do things that are popular rather than right and to do petty, mean, sleazy things. Finally these leaders were not preachers, they were doers.[5]

Empowerment

Empowerment, which is also discussed in Chapter 17, is a technique used by participative leaders to share decision-making authority with team members. Empowerment means giving employees more control over their decisions, resources, and work. When decision-making power is shared at all levels of the organization, employees feel a greater sense of ownership in, and responsibility for, organizational outcomes.[6] The relationship between employees and the company is more of a partnership, where the employee feels responsible for their jobs and have a share of ownership in the enterprize. Empowered employees take responsibility and seek to solve problems, they see themselves as a network of professionals all working toward the same goals.

An example of empowered employees making a difference happened at Hampton Inns after they began a program of refunds to guests who were dissatisfied with their stays. The refund policy created far more additional business than it cost, but a surprise bonus was the increased morale when employees—everyone from front-desk associates to housekeepers—were empowered to give refunds. With greater participation and job satisfaction, employee turnover fell by more than half.[7] Empowerment has strong links to Total Quality Management, which is discussed at length in Chapter 17.

DEVELOPING YOUR OWN STYLE

Applying theory to reality is going to be something you work out for yourself. No one can teach you. Since even the theorists disagree among themselves, the choice is wide open. But don't throw it all out; a lot of what the behavioral scientists are saying can be very useful to you. There does seem to be general agreement, supported by research and experience, that the assumptions Theory X makes about people are, at best, unproductive and at worst counterproductive, if not downright destructive. However, an authoritarian style of leadership can be effective and even necessary in many situations, and there is actually no reason why it cannot be combined with a high concern for the workers and achieve good results.

As for Theory Y, probably two-thirds of the workforce has the potential for a Theory Y type of motivation—that is, working to satisfy such inner needs as self-respect, achievement, independence, responsibility, status, and growth. The problem with applying this theory in the hospitality industry is really not the workers. It is the nature of the work, the number of variables you have to deal with (including high worker turnover), the unpredictability of the situation, the tradition of authoritarian carrot-stick management, and the pressures of time. The pace and pattern of the typical day do not leave much room for group activity or for planning and implementing changes in work patterns to provide such motivation. Furthermore, your own supervisor or your company's policies may not give you the freedom to make changes. In conclusion, Theory Y does not always work for everyone.

However, it is remarkable what is possible when an imaginative and determined manager sets out to utilize this type of motivation and develop this type of commitment. We will have a lot more to say about motivation in Chapter 14.

The best style of leadership, for you, is whatever works best in terms of these three basics: your own personality, the workers you supervise, and the situations you face. It should be a situational type of leadership, just as your management style must be a flex style that reacts to situations as they arise.

> Success in life is measured by what we have overcome to be what we are and by what we have accomplished. How we are is more important than what position we have.

You may give an order to Peter, but say "please" to Paul. You may stop a fight in the kitchen with a quick command when server Linda and server Chris keep picking up each other's orders, and then later you may spend a good hour with the two of them helping them reach an agreement to stop their running battle. You may see responsibilities you could delegate to Evelyn or John. You may see opportunities to bring workers in on solving work problems, or you may solve them yourself because of time pressures or because the problems are not appropriate for group discussion.

You can borrow elements and techniques of Theory Y without erecting a whole system of participative management. If something does not work for all three of you—yourself, the workers, the situation—don't do it.

What you need most in finding what works best is *awareness*: awareness of yourself and the feelings, desires, biases, abilities, power, and influence you bring to a situation; awareness of the special needs and traits of your various workers and awareness of the situation, the big picture, so you can recognize what is needed, conceptual skills and human skills.

Much attention has been focused on corporate leadership and the associated scandals including misuse of power, embezzlement, lack of moral and ethical behavior, lying, and other forms of improper behavior that has shaken the public's confidence in corporate leadership. Add to this the huge salaries many of these leaders are (and were) paid—even if their company did poorly, they still received a large salary increase. Events such as these have caused public opinion to persuade corporate leadership to become more ethical and moral in their behavior and to make better decisions.

As a leader you will need to have a vision that is realistic, credible, and one which everyone in the organization (or department) can rally around. Your vision—to be the best, or to be the most popular—needs to be complemented by the company purpose and mission statement. It needs to be ambitious and inspire enthusiasm. Leaders make things happen because they have developed the knowledge, skills, and attitude to positively motivate others to reach common goals.

Leadership is also about change. As a new supervisor or a supervisor in a new location, you will see an obvious need for change. Remember there is a six-step method of making changes. *First*, state the purpose; *second*, involve others; *third*, test the plan before you implement it company wide; *fourth*, introduce the change; *fifth*, maintain and reinforce the change; and *sixth*, follow up.[8]

The best style of leadership is to be yourself. Trying to copy someone else's style usually does not work—the situation is different, you are different, the shoe does not fit.

Today the hospitality leaders are expected to be leaders who have the communication skills to mobilize the energy and resources of a management team. Leaders are expected to be visionaries, who see the future clearly and articulate the vision so that others can follow.

ETHICS

Although there are many definitions of ethics, ethics can generally be thought of as a set of moral principles or rules of conduct that provide guidelines for morally right behavior. To give you an idea of how ethics are involved in your job as a hospitality supervisor, let's look at three scenarios.

1. You've completed interviewing a number of candidates for a security position. One of the top three candidates is a relative of a supervisor in another department with whom you are close friends. You've been getting pressure from your friend

to hire this candidate, and you don't want to alienate him, so you hire his relative even though one of the other candidates is more suited for the job.

2. Business at the hotel could be better on weekends, so you advertise 25-percent discounts on rooms. To keep profitability high, you inflate the room rate before taking the discount.

3. As purchasing manager, you know that the policy is not to accept free gifts from vendors. But one day when you are out to lunch with a vendor, he offers you free tickets to a major league baseball game and you accept them. You can't wait to take your son to the game.

As you can see from these examples, moral principles and standards of conduct are just as necessary in the workplace as they are in your personal life. There are ethical considerations in many of the decisions that you will make, from personnel management issues to money issues to purchasing and receiving practices. Unfortunately, the hospitality industry as a whole has not written its own code of ethics, but you will find that some operations have written their own.

Why is a code of ethics needed for hospitality operations? Just look at the temptations: stockrooms full of supplies that can be used at home and are often loosely inventoried, any kind of alcoholic beverage you want, empty hotel rooms, gambling, high-stress jobs, irregular hours, pressures to meet guests' needs. It can be easy to lose a sense of right and wrong in this field.

Hall suggests five questions that you can use to help decide how ethical a certain decision is:

1. Is the decision legal?

2. Is the decision fair?

3. Does the decision hurt anyone?

4. Have I been honest with those affected?

5. Can I live with my decision?

These questions can provide much guidance.

THE SUPERVISOR AS MENTOR

This topic is a wonderful way to finish this chapter on supervision. As you become more experienced and proficient at being a hospitality supervisor, it is more likely that you will be a mentor to those who are less experienced and less skilled. A mentor is a leader, an excellent role model, and a teacher. A supervisor often functions as a mentor to a worker by providing guidance and knowledge on learning the operation and moving up the career ladder. The relationship often resembles that between a teacher and a student. At other times, the mentor simply provides an example of professional behavior with minimal or no interaction with the worker. Being a mentor can provide feelings of pride and satisfaction because you have contributed to someone else's career development.

Being a Winner!

The Winner—is always part of the answer.

The Loser—is always part of the problem.

The Winner—always has a program.

The Loser—always has an excuse.

The Winner—says, "Let me do that for you."

The Loser—says, "That's not my job."

The Winner—sees an answer for every problem.

The Loser—sees a problem for every answer.

The Winner—sees a green near every sand trap.

The Loser—sees two or three sand traps near every green.

The Winner—says, "It may be difficult but it's possible."

The Loser—says, "It may be possible, but it's too difficult."

BE A WINNER

KEY POINTS

1. Hotels and restaurants depend on large numbers of people to fill entry-level low-wage jobs that have little interest and no perceived future.

2. Turnover in the hospitality field is generally high. For example, your typical full-service restaurant will lose every one of its hourly employees during one year and have to fill every position.

3. There is really no valid stereotype of today's hospitality workers. The industry employs people of all ages and backgrounds. As a matter of fact, an already diverse

workplace is becoming more diverse than ever. The hospitality industry employs many young people, many women, and many members of minority groups.

4.   Being a leader means guiding or influencing the actions of your employees to reach certain goals. A leader is a person who people follow voluntarily.

5.   As a supervisor, you have been given the formal authority to oversee your employees. Your subordinates confer real authority, and you have to earn the right to lead them.

6.   As a supervisor and leader, your job is to do the right things right.

7.   Leadership style refers to your pattern of interacting with your subordinates, how you direct and control the work of others, and how you get them to produce the goods and services for which you are responsible.

8.   The old-style boss uses an autocratic method of managing employees that relies on the motivators of money or fear.

9.   According to McGregor, the autocratic style is typical of Theory X bosses. Theory Y bosses believe that workers will work of their own accord toward objectives to which they feel committed.

10.   In situational leadership, the leadership style is adapted to the uniqueness of each situation. The four primary styles of leading are directing, coaching, supporting, and delegating.

11.   Transactional leaders appeal to workers' self-interest. Transformational leaders appeal to workers' higher-order needs.

12.   Employers and employees must develop mutual respect for success.

13.   Ethics can be thought of as a set of moral principles or rules of conduct that provide guidelines for morally correct behavior. The five questions presented in the chapter provide guidance for making ethical decisions.

14.   A supervisor often functions as a mentor to a worker by providing guidance and knowledge on learning the operation and moving up the career ladder. The relationship resembles that between a teacher and a student.

KEY TERMS

autocratic method	do the right things right	Generation X
carrot-and-stick technique	empowerment	Generation Y
coaching style	ethics	goals
delegating style	formal authority	informal leader
directing style	formal leader	leader

leadership	real authority	Theory X
leadership style	reward and punishment	Theory Y
MBWA	situational leadership	transactional leader
mentor	strategies	transformational leader
mission statement	supporting style	vision
power	tactics	

REFERENCES

1. www.leadingtoday.org/onmag/jan01/leadership12001.htm

2. Larry J. Gitman and Carl McDaniel, *The Future of Business*, 5th ed. South-Western Publishing, Cincinnati, Ohio, 2005. p. 209.

3. Stephen P. Robins and David A. DeCenzo, *Supervision Today*, 4th ed. Prentice Hall, Upper Saddle River, NJ. 2004, p. 235–6.

4. www.leadingtoday.org/onmag/jan03/transaction12003.html

5. Peter F. Drucker, "Foreword," in F. Hessel-bein, M. Goldsmith, and R. Beckhard (eds.), *The Leader of the Future*. San Francisco: Jossey-Bass, 1966, pp. xii–xiv.

6. Larry J. Gitman and Carl McDaniel, *The Future of Business*, 5th ed. South-Western Publishing, Cincinnati, Ohio, 2005, p. 211.

7. Ricky W. Griffen and Ronald J. Ebert, *Business*, 7th ed. Prentice Hall, 2004. p. 445.

8. *Foodservice Leadership: Becoming an Effective Leader*. The Educational Foundation of the National Restaurant Foundation, Video.

EQUAL OPPORTUNITY IN THE WORKPLACE*

Outline

E qual opportunity, diversity, and inclusion in the workplace sounds simple enough but we all know it simply isn't so. For years women and minorities were not, and in some cases, still are not, treated equally. The Equal Employment Opportunity Commission (EEOC) was established in 1978 as a central authority,

---

* Authored by Jack E. Miller, John R. Walker, and Karen Eich Drummond.

responsible for leading and coordinating the efforts of federal departments and agencies to enforce all laws relating to equal employment opportunity without regard to race, color, religion, sex, national origin, age, or handicap. A visit to the Equal Employment Opportunity Commission's Web site at www.eeoc.gov will likely have an example of a hospitality company being sued by the EEOC for violation of the equal opportunity laws.

The fact that equal opportunity was denied to so many is the reason that in June of 1963, then President John F. Kennedy sent comprehensive civil rights legislation to Congress. Later that summer, in front of the Lincoln Memorial, Dr. Martin Luther King Jr. gave his famous "I Have a Dream" speech that came to symbolize the insistence for meaningful legislation to address the demand for racial equality and justice.[1]

As a hospitality supervisor, you will be responsible for equal opportunity in the workplace, for employing and supervising people from cultures different from your own. A "standard" approach to equal opportunity in the workplace, which does not consider each employee's cultural background, will often create communication barriers. Culturally appropriate communication strategies are needed. But what exactly is equal opportunity in the workplace? What is diversity? Why should we want equal opportunity, diversity, and inclusiviness?

What role does culture play? Our culture is defined as our values, which are manifested in the way we behave, speak, think, dress, our religious beliefs, the music we like, the way we interact, and the food we eat. Culture strongly influences behavior. Failure to understand and respect the diverse cultural backgrounds of your employees, and the differences among them, can result in misunderstandings, tension, poor performance, poor employee morale, and higher rates of absenteeism and turnover. On the other hand, when differences are respected, the working environment is richer, much more fun, and even more interesting. Employee satisfaction and performance improve because of this. The need for equal opportunity, diversity, and inclusiviness in the workplace is of critical importance in the hospitality industry.

In this chapter we help you to:

- Define equal opportunity in the workplace
- Describe the equal opportunity laws
- Explain what every supervisor needs to know
- Outline EEO and the hiring process
- Define the term *diversity*
- Describe steps that increase positive cross-cultural interaction
- Give examples of managing diversity issues positively

EQUAL OPPORTUNITY, DIVERSITY, AND INCLUSION IN THE WORKPLACE

Today, whenever a job is advertised and candidates are recruited, interviewed, tested, and selected, it is necessary to take equal opportunity into account. Progressive corporations create offices and programs responsible for planning, developing, implementing, and evaluating a comprehensive equal opportunity and diversity program with multifaceted opportunity and diversity initiatives to support the company's commitment to equal opportunity, diversity, and inclusiveness. Many large hospitality companies have an office of Equal Opportunity and Diversity (EO&D). They may also be called by similar names, such as Diversity and Equal Opportunity (DEO).

The Equal Opportunity and Diversity Office provides effective leadership to ensure that diversity and equal opportunity are a thriving part of the fabric of your company. The Equal Opportunity and Diversity Office provides an array of services, such as:

- Education and training the public about equal opportunity and diversity
- Advocacy for diversity
- Support for companies' initiatives toward equal opportunity and diversity
- Consultation on best strategies for equal opportunity and diversity recruitment
- Conflict mediation and resolution
- Monitoring employers' equity and affirmative action goals
- Reviewing compliance with state and federal regulations
- Processing and resolving complaints

Applebee's is one of the restaurant industry's progressive companies. CEO Lloyd Hill takes a stand on racial and sexual orientation issues saying, "There have been too many 'no comments' on these matters." Operations, finance, and marketing have been the "big three" of the industry for years and something crucial has been left out of the equation, and that is human resources. Applebee's, for example, has a chief people officer, Lou Kaucic, who says that it is critical for human resources to have a seat around the executive table.[2]

Sodexho, which is rated one of the top 50 employers for diversity, says that it is committed to respecting, leveraging, and celebrating the diversity of its workforce, its clientele, and the community in which they live, work, and serve.[3]

Marriott International, one of *Fortune* magazine's 100 best companies to work for, says that its commitment to diversity is absolute. It is the only way to attract, develop, and retain the best talent available.[4]

Diversity in the workplace is on the increase.

EQUAL EMPLOYMENT OPPORTUNITY LAWS

A lot of laws have been instituted to ensure that no individual or group is denied the respect deserved. Understanding the legal requirements of equal opportunity in the workplace is important for three reasons: It will help supervisors to do the right thing; realize the limitations of you company's HR and legal departments; and minimize your company's potential liability. Equal employment opportunity is a concept that means that people should be treated equally in all employment matters. Figure 13.1 lists important federal laws commonly referred to as equal employment opportunity (EEO) laws. In general, EEO laws make it unlawful for you to discriminate against applicants or employees with respect to recruiting, hiring, firing, promotions, compensation, or other employment-related activities, on the basis of race, color, religion, gender, nationality, age, or disability. Discrimination in the workplace can be thought of as making employment decisions based on factors that have nothing to do with a person's ability to do the job.

The starting point for EEO laws was probably passage of the Equal Pay Act of 1963. This law requires equal pay and benefits for men and women working in jobs

Federal Laws	Type of Employment Discrimination Prohibited	Employers Covered
Equal Pay Act of 1963	Gender differences in pay, benefits, and pension for substantially equal work	Almost all companies, private and government
Title VII, 1964 Civil Rights Act (amended in 1991)	Discrimination in all human resource activities based on race, color, gender, religion, or national origin; established Equal Employment Opportunity Commission to administer the law	Companies with 15 or more employees
Age Discrimination in Employment Act of 1967 (amended in 1986)	Age discrimination against those 40 years of age or older	Companies with 20 or more employees
Pregnancy Discrimination Act of 1978	Prohibits discrimination in hiring, promoting, or terminating because of pregnancy; pregnancy to be treated as medical disability	Same as Title VII
Immigration Reform and Control Act (1986 and 1990)	Prohibits discrimination on the basis of citizenship status and nationality	Companies with 4 or more employees
Americans with Disabilities Act (1990)	Bars discrimination of disabled persons in hiring and employment	Businesses with 15 or more employees
Family Medical Leave Act of 1993	Mandates 12 workweeks of leave for husband or wife upon birth or adoption of a child or sickness in the family	Companies with 50 or more employees
Fair Employment Practice Acts of States and Local Governments	Bars discrimination; varies	Varies

FIGURE 13.2 Equal employment opportunity laws.

requiring substantially equal skills, effort, and responsibilities under similar working conditions.

Congress passed the Civil Rights Act of 1964, Title VII (amended in 1991), to bring about equality in employment decisions. The act makes it unlawful for you to discriminate against applicants or employees with respect to recruiting, hiring, firing, promotions, or other employment-related activities, on the basis of race, color, religion, gender, or national origin. Other employment-related activities include, but are not limited to, wages, overtime pay, job assignments, training opportunities, leaves of absence, and retirement plans.

Title VII does not require you to hire, promote, or retain employees who are not qualified. The law does provide for you to hire a person of a particular gender if it is based on what is called a bona fide occupational qualification (BFOQ). For instance, it is permissible to hire a man to clean lounges and restrooms reserved for men.

The Equal Employment Opportunity Commission (EEOC) was created by the Civil Rights Act of 1964, and it is responsible for enforcing the employment-related provisions of the Civil Rights Act of 1964 as well as other EEO laws. Employees with the EEOC, which also develops and issues guidelines to enforce EEO laws, can file complaints of discrimination.

Age discrimination was addressed in the Age Discrimination in Employment Act of 1967 (ADEA), amended in 1978 and 1986, which makes it unlawful for you to discriminate in compensation, terms, or conditions of employment because of a person's age. The ADEA applies to all people 40 years of age and older. This act also bans forced retirement.

The Pregnancy Discrimination Act of 1978 makes it unlawful to discriminate against a woman on the basis of pregnancy, childbirth, or related medical conditions. You cannot refuse to hire (or promote) a woman just because she is pregnant. According to this law, pregnancy is a temporary disability and women must be permitted to work as long as they are physically able to perform their jobs. Employers cannot determine the beginning and ending dates of a pregnant employee's maternity leave.

The Immigration Reform and Control Act (IRCA; 1986 and 1990) was prompted by problems associated with the increasing numbers of immigrants living in the United States. This act makes it illegal to discriminate in recruiting, hiring, or terminating based on a person's national origin or citizenship status. In these kinds of cases, fines can be charged and judges can order employers to provide back pay, pay court charges, and reinstate an employee. Although Title VII of the Civil Rights Act of 1964 has long prohibited this type of discrimination, IRCA covers employers with four or more employees, and Title VII covers employers with 15 or more employees.

The only people you can discriminate against are those you are not legally allowed to hire (or continue to employ): illegal aliens. IRCA imposes penalties for hiring unauthorized aliens. To help ensure that you don't hire an illegal alien, IRCA requires employers to verify that the people they hire are eligible to work in the United States. This is done by completing an I-9 Employment Eligibility Verification form within three days after hire. Using this form, the employer may ask for certain documents that establish the person's identity (such as a driver's license) and employment eligibility (such as a U.S. birth certificate or valid Immigration and Naturalization Services' Employment Authorization Card). To be fair and nondiscriminatory, you cannot request certain work status documentation from some applicants but not others.

The Americans with Disabilities Act (ADA) of 1990 makes it unlawful to discriminate in employment matters against the estimated 43 million Americans who have a disability. Under the ADA, a person has a disability if he or she has a physical or mental impairment that substantially limits one or more major life activities, such as hearing, seeing, speaking, or walking. It also covers recovering alcohol and drug abusers (as long as they are in a supervised treatment program) and people infected with the HIV virus.

It is unlawful to ask an applicant whether he or she is disabled or about the disability itself. You can ask an applicant questions about his or her ability to perform job-related functions as long as the questions are not phrased in terms of a disability. You can also ask the applicant to describe or demonstrate how (with or without reasonable accommodation) he or she will perform job duties. The ADA does not interfere with your right to hire the best-qualified applicant, and a disabled applicant must satisfy your job requirements and be able to perform essential job functions.

Reasonable accommodation, which is legally required, refers to any change or adjustment to a job or the work environment that will enable someone with a disability to perform essential job functions. For example, a work table may be lowered to enable someone to work while seated, a work schedule may be modified, or a job may be restructured. Employers are not required to lower quality or quantity standards to provide an accommodation, nor are they required to make an accommodation if it would impose an undue hardship on the operation of the business. Undue hardship is defined as an "action requiring significant difficulty or expense" and is determined on a case-by-case basis.

In addition to the federal EEO laws, state and local governments have fair employment practice acts (FEPs) that often include further conditions. For example, some states forbid employment discrimination on the basis of marital status. It is important to learn about EEO laws because you need to be able to select applicants in a fair and nondiscriminatory manner.

The Family and Medical Leave Act of 1993 allows employees to take an unpaid leave of absence from work for up to 12 weeks per year for any of the following reasons:

- Birth or adoption of a child
- Serious health condition of a child
- Serious health condition of a spouse or parent
- Employee's own serious health condition

When the employee returns from leave, he or she is entitled to his or her former position or an equivalent position. To be eligible for a leave of absence, the employee must have worked for the employer for at least 12 months. If it was provided before the leave was taken, the employer is obligated to maintain group health insurance during the leave.

EEO LAWS AND THE HIRING PROCESS

Figure 13.2 lists recommended ways to ask questions of job applicants, whether on job applications or during interviews, to avoid charges of discrimination. The kinds of questions that are not allowed relate to race, gender, age (except to make sure that the applicant's age meets labor laws), family and marital status, religion, national origin, appearance, and disabilities unrelated to the job.

Job requirements or qualifications, such as those regarding education and work experience, must be relevant to the job, nondiscriminatory, and predictive of future job performance. Although requiring a high school diploma for an entry-level food-service job, such as server, seems to be acceptable, there are certainly many servers who do their jobs well without the diploma. The requirement of a high school diploma when it is not related to successful performance of the job can be viewed as discriminatory.

Any type of pre-employment test must be valid, reliable, and relevant to the job. To be valid, tests must be related to successful performance on the job. To be reliable, tests must yield consistent results. Tests should be given to all applicants, with a single standard for rating scores, and must be given under the same conditions. Even when a test is given to all concerned, it may be considered discriminatory if the test eliminates members of protected groups (the groups protected or covered by EEO laws) more frequently than members of nonprotected groups.

A good way to check yourself to ensure that you are not discriminating when evaluating job applicants is to be sure you can answer "yes" to the following five questions:

1. Are the qualifications based on the actual duties and needs of the job, not on personal preferences or a wish list?

2. Will the information requested from the applicant help me to judge his or her ability to do the job?

3. Will each part of the selection process, including job descriptions, applications, advertising, and interviews, prevent screening out those groups covered by EEO laws?

4. Can I judge an applicant's ability to do the job successfully without regard to how he or she is different from me in terms of age, gender, race, color, nationality, religion, or disability?

5. Is the selection process the same for all applicants?

Subject	Inappropriate Questions (May Not Ask or Require)	Appropriate Questions (May Ask or Require)
Gender or marital status	• Gender (on application form) • Mr., Miss, Mrs., Ms.? • Married, divorced, single, separated? • Number and ages of children • Pregnancy, actual or intended • Maiden name, former name	• In checking your work record, do we need another name for identifcation?
Race	• Race? • Color of skin, eyes, hair, etc. • Request for photograph	
National Origin	• Questions about place of birth, ancestry, mother tongue, national origin of parents or spouse. • What is your native language? • How did you learn to speak [language] fluently?	• If job-related, what foreign languages do you speak?
Citizenship, immigration status	• Of what country are you a citizen? • Are you a native-born U.S. citizen? • Questions about naturalization of applicant, spouse, or parents.	• If selected are you able to start work with us on a specific date? If not, when would you be able to start? • If hired, can you show proof that you are eligible to work in the United States?
Religion	• Religious affiliation or preference • Religious holidays observed • Membership in religious organizations	• Can you observe regularly required days and hours of work? • Are there any days or hours of the week that you are not able to work? • Are there any holidays that you are not able to work?
Age	• How old are you? • Date of birth	• Are you 21 or older? (for positions serving alcohol)
Disability	• Do you have any disabilities? • Have you ever been treated for (certain) diseases? • Are you healthy?	
Questions that may discriminate against minorities	• Have you ever been arrested? • List all clubs, societies, and lodges to which you belong. • Do you own a car? (unless required for the job) • Type of military discharge. • Questions regarding credit ratings, financial status, wage garnishment, home ownership.	• Have you ever been convicted of a crime? If yes, give details. (If crime is job-related, as embezzlement is to handling money, you may refuse to hire.) • List membership in professional organizations relevant to job performance. • Military service: dates, branch of service, education, and experience (if job-related).
Assumptions related to gender, age, race, disability, etc.	• Work is too heavy for women or handicapped. • Stereotypes: buspersons should be men and typists should be women, bartenders should be under 40, etc.	• Can you do the job?

FIGURE 13.3 Equal employment opportunity: Appropriate and inappropriate questions sometimes used in hiring a new employee.

Check Your Knowledge

1. Define equal employment opportunity.

2. List four important federal laws commonly referred to as equal employment opportunity laws.

3. What is the function of equal employment opportunity laws?

NEGLIGENT HIRING

Could your employer be sued if a guest was injured by a hostile employee who had a violent background that would have been uncovered if a reference check had been done? Yes, your employer could be sued for negligent hiring. In the past 10 years, lawsuits for negligent hiring have been on the rise. If a violent or hostile employee injures a guest or employee, the injured party may sue the employer and will probably win if he or she can prove that the employer did not take reasonable and appropriate precautions to avoid hiring or retaining the employee.

As a supervisor, you have the responsibility of taking reasonable and appropriate safeguards when hiring employees to make sure that they are not the type to harm guests or other workers. Such safeguards include conducting a reasonable investigation into an applicant's background and, especially, inquiring further about suspicious factors such as short residency periods or gaps in employment. You also have a responsibility to counsel or discipline your employees when they become abusive, violent, or show any other deviant behavior. Follow up on complaints your employees and customers may make about another employee's negative behaviors. Use your employer's policies to dismiss dangerous or unfit employees after appropriate warnings.

EQUAL OPPORTUNITY IN THE WORKPLACE: WHAT SUPERVISORS NEED TO KNOW

The following is excerpted from The U.S. Equal Employment Opportunity Commission "Training and Technical Assistance Program."[5]

Q & A: Race, Ethnicity, Color—What Practices are Discriminatory?

Title VII of the Civil Rights Act of 1964 prohibits employment discrimination based on race, color, religion, sex, or national origin.

It is illegal to discriminate in any aspect of employment including:

- Hiring and firing
- Compensation, assignment, or classification of employees
- Transfer, promotion, layoff, or recall
- Job advertisements
- Recruitment
- Use of company facilities
- Training and apprenticeship programs
- Pay, retirement plans, and disability leave; or
- Terms and conditions of employment

Interviewing

Questions you can and cannot ask at interview are discussed in more detail in the chapter on recruiting and selecting applicants. But we should mention here that there are several inappropriate questions that should be avoided. Questions such as: How many children do you have? What country do your parents come from? What is your native language? What is your height? What is your weight? How old are you? What church do you go to? What religion are you? Are you a United States citizen? Do you have any disabilities? Are you dating anyone right now? When did you graduate from high school?

A simple rule to follow is if it's not job related—don't ask. When facing charges of discrimination, the employer bears the burden of proving that answers to all questions on application forms or in oral interviews are not used in making hiring and placement decisions in a discriminatory manner prohibited by law.

The guiding principle behind any question to a job applicant is: "Can the employer demonstrate a legitimate job-related or business necessity for asking the question?" Both the intent behind the question and how the information is to be used by the employer are important for determining whether a question is an appropriate pre-employment enquiry.[6]

DIVERSITY

Understanding and embracing diversity is of critical importance in today's increasingly multicultural and diverse society. The term *diversity* is often used when discussing people of different cultures. Diversity refers to the following cultural as well as physical dimensions, which separate and distinguish us both as individuals and as groups.

- Culture
- Ethnic group
- Race
- Religion
- Language
- Age
- Gender
- Physical abilities and qualities
- Sexual orientation

Culture, ethnic group, and race are related terms. Culture is a learned behavior consisting of a unique set of beliefs, values, attitudes, habits, customs, traditions, and other forms of behavior. Culture influences the way that people behave. Cultural behavior varies from culture to culture. Culture refers to the behaviors, beliefs, and characteristics of a particular group, such as an ethnic group. Ethnic groups share a common and distinctive culture, including elements such as religion and language. Race refers to a group of people related by common descent.

The population of the United States is becoming more multicultural, and diverse, every day. Almost one in four Americans has African, Asian, Hispanic, or Native American ancestry. It is estimated that by 2020, the number will rise to almost one in three, and by 2050, the number will be almost one in two. The fastest-growing segments of the U.S. population are minority groups.

As the United States becomes more diverse, so does the workplace. The hospitality workplace employs a particularly diverse group of employees. A restaurant's staff often resembles a miniature United Nations, with employees from all around the globe. According to the U.S. Department of Labor, 12 percent of foodservice employees are foreign-born, compared to 8 percent in other occupations. Foodservice also employs many more Hispanics and African-Americans than other industries. In fact, Hispanics have been the largest minority in foodservice for almost a decade.

The National Restaurant Association's web site states that:[7]

1. Restaurants employ more minority managers than any other industry.

2. More than two-thirds of the supervisors in the foodservice industry are women; 16 percent are African American; and 13 percent are Hispanic.

3.   Since 1994 African-American spending on food away from home increased by 46 percent. For Hispanics, that increase was 78.6 percent.

Profile

GERRY FERNANDEZ

Courtesy of Gerry Fernandez

Gerry Fernandez began working as a cook at Royal's Healthside Restaurant in Rutland, Vermont. Ernest Royal, owner of the restaurant and a noted New England restaurateur, was the first African-American board member of the National Restaurant Association. Royal had experienced considerable racism, and in his honor, Gerry Fernandez conceived the Multi-Cultural Foodservice and Hospitality Alliance (MFHA) www.mfha.net. The MFHA is dedicated to promoting diversity within the foodservice industry.

Since his first position as cook at Royal's, Gerry has had a successful career beginning with a bachelor of science in food service management from Johnson and Wales University where he also earned a degree in culinary arts, followed by terms as sous chef, manager, and general manager of various New England restaurants. Gerry spent more than 10 years as a senior manager opening and operating fine dining restaurants.

In 1995, Gerry moved to General Mills as a technical service specialist in foodservice research and development. He provided support and training as well as sales marketing and product development teams. Additionally, he evaluated current new competitor products; conducted recipe development, concept testing, tolerance testing, photo shots, and product presentations. Gerry has received numerous awards including the General Mills "Champion's Award" and Nations Restaurant News "50 Power Players."

In a recent interview Fernandez spoke about the vision of the MFHA organization and its intended impact on foodservice operations worldwide.

How does diversity affect foodservice in general? "Comprehensive diversity issues exist in many large companies, and they are asking foodservice operators, 'Where do you stand?' It is coming, whether or not you like it. Diversity is not simply a social agenda issue; it is a bottom-line issue. When people talk about diversity, they think about inclusion of more women and more people of color. They tend to think only about the soft issues, the green issues. Diversity really is a green discussion more than it is any other color. MFHA is striving to make this an economic discussion rather than a social discussion."

What is the object of MFHA? "To be the solutions bridge for multiculturalism in the foodservice industry so that operators can leverage diversity as a positive influence on the bottom line. We think of multicultural diversity as a way to improve the foodservice business in all aspects: human resources, marketing, training, community relations, and so on. We are the multicultural Yellow Pages for the industry. We are solution focused: a connector of people to issues and people to information."

What does MFHA offer operators? "This is a place to start the diversity process. If operators are looking for opportunities, recipes, programs, or qualified diversity experts, they can call on us. Whether you are an on-site operator—self-op or contract managed—there is a concern regarding bids for city, state, and federal contracts. These potential clients are inquiring directly as to what percentage of your business purchases are from women and minority-owned businesses. Companies are realizing that they need a way to address this issue. We offer a context in which such issues can be explored constructively."

What kind of services does MFHA have available? "We help identify qualified women and minority-owned business operators who can do business with the big boys. Additionally, MFHA can provide in-house solutions in the form of awareness and skills training, recruiting and retention, marketing, purchasing, and referral services."

How is MFHA evolving? "The last three years have been internally focused as we have developed the infrastructure. Now we are focused externally on our members. We will be able to provide more research and, through focus groups and bench marking, help operators by training in ways to be more strategic in their diversity effort and to recruit better talent. It's not about one company or one ethnic segment, it's about our industry as a whole reaching out and recruiting from and to every segment of the population."

Source: Diane Ridge, "Diversity Runs Deep," *Food Management*, Vol. 35, No. 7, pp. 48–52, July 2000. Last update March 21, 2005.

Up until the late 1980s, white males made up the majority of the U.S. workforce. Now this group represents less than 50 percent of the workforce. Many of the new workers entering the labor force are minorities, such as Hispanics, Latinos, Asians, and many immigrants. The reasons behind these trends include a young, growing minority population and a continuing high rate of immigration.

The market-savvy businesses of today are responding to the changing demographics by targeting diverse consumers, employees, and supply partners in ways that build meaningful and reciprocal relationships. If companies' marketers and service providers do not reach out to minority communities in a holistic way, they're setting themselves up for failure in the long run. Promote inclusion in the supply chain by partnering with minority-owned firms that support our businesses as patrons.

Promote inclusion in the supply chain. By partnering with minority-owned firms demonstrating a commitment to inclusion and create jobs in the very communities that support our businesses as patrons. If companies' marketers and service providers do not reach out to minority communities in a holistic way, they're setting themselves up for failure in the long run. The market savvy businesses of today are responding to the changing demographics by targeting diverse consumers, employees and supply partners in ways that build meaningful and reciprocal relationships.[8]

In the hospitality workforce it is vital that multicultural management recognizes cultural differences among employees, and allows and encourages them. It is important to have cross-cultural awareness and to respect the cultures of others. In today's hospitality industry understanding and harmonizing with other cultures is necessary for all employees in order to avoid misunderstandings. By allowing and encouraging variation, blends of people from all different kinds of backgrounds are able to learn from one another and grow in aspects of the workplace.[9]

ARAMARK's definition of diversity is, "The mosaic of people who bring a variety of backgrounds, styles, perspectives, values, and beliefs as assets to ARAMARK and our partners." Kaleidoscope Vision states that ARAMARK is composed of unique individuals who, together, make the company what it is and can be in the future. Only when all individuals contribute fully can the strength and vision of ARAMARK be realized. The guiding principles for diversity are: "Because we are committed to being a company where the best people want to work, we champion a comprehensive diversity imitative. Because we thrive on growth, we recruit, retain, and develop a diverse workforce. Because we succeed through performance, we create an environment that allows all employees to contribute to their fullest potential."[10]

WHY DOES CULTURAL DIVERSITY MATTER?

Cultural diversity matters to every single one of us, both professionally and personally. When a group or segment is excluded or oppressed, all of us are denied. For businesses and communities to not only survive, but to thrive, each of us needs to be aware and sensitive to *all* members of the community. Our communities are rich in resources. When all segments are respected and utilized, it benefits everyone involved.

America is the most diverse nation in the world. Our ethnicity, religion, life experience, etc., makes each one of us unique.

DEVELOPING CROSS-CULTURAL INTERACTION

Diversity in itself is not a challenge but, in fact, an opportunity. It is an opportunity for us to build diverse teams; diverse knowledge perspective and experiences can solve business problems and create value for our shareholders and guests. The second prong in the initiative is moving beyond awareness training and moving toward diversity skills training, which helps to enhance the skills of managers and supervisors in communication across lines of difference. This enhances the ability to recognize and respond to the needs of our diverse customers. Every successful business needs to practice sensitivity to diversity as well as to our diverse makeup.

By developing cross-cultural interaction skills, you will be better equipped to do your job and to motivate diverse employees to accomplish company goals. But don't think you will be able to develop these skills overnight or, for that matter, even over a few months. By considering the major steps listed in Figure 13.3, you will better appreciate that this process is complex and will take time to master. The effective supervisor is aware that employees come from different cultural backgrounds, learns about how their cultures differ, and works with employees without passing judgment about their cultures.

Shifting demographics make practicing diversity more than just a politically correct idea in the hospitality industry. Diversity is anything that makes people different from each other, such as gender, race, ethnicity, income, religion, and disabilities. Foodservice has welcomed minorities for a long time, and minorities make up the largest percentage of workers in the foodservice industry. For supervisors in the hospitality

1. Increase personal awareness.
2. Learn about other cultures.
3. Recognize and practice cross-cultural interaction skills.
4. Maintain awareness, knowledge, and skills.

FIGURE 13.3 Developing cross-cultural interaction skills.

industry it is important to encourage minority talent. Promoting people based solely on their abilities, skills, and job performance into supervisory positions helps promote minority advancement in the foodservice industry.

HOW TO INCREASE PERSONAL AWARENESS

Without realizing it, it is possible to become *culture bound*, meaning that you believe that your culture and value system are the best, the one and only. You think your way of talking, perceiving, thinking, valuing, and behaving are normal and right. For example, when you hear someone talking with an accent, you are likely to think how strange it sounds, or even how wrong or abnormal it is. How many of us realize that each of us has an accent, which probably sounds strange to those of different backgrounds?

The first step in developing your cross-cultural skills is to examine how your own culture has influenced who you are. Consider, for example, how your culture has influenced your attitudes toward the following:

- Education
- Work
- Family
- Self-sufficiency
- Money
- Authority
- Expression of emotions

An activity at the end of this chapter will help you look more deeply at your own cultural attitudes and compare them to others.

Learning About Other Cultures

After becoming more aware of your own culture, the next step is to learn various facts of other cultures. As a supervisor, it is crucial to see other cultures as objectively as possible and not pass judgment. By learning about another culture, it is hoped that you will be better able to understand people from that culture, as well as to be understood better in turn. Some aspects of another culture that are interesting to learn include verbal and nonverbal language differences, values, customs, work habits, and attitudes toward work.

A danger in learning about any culture is that the information may be overgeneralized, thereby promoting stereotypes. It is important to keep in mind that regardless of cultural background, a person is still an individual and needs to be treated and respected as someone with a unique personality, wants, and needs.

You can learn about other cultures in various ways: reading about them in books and magazines, attending cultural fairs and festivals, and interacting with individuals from other cultures. By learning about other cultures and interacting with people of varying backgrounds, you can work on valuing your differences as well as uncovering and overcoming any of your own fears, stereotypes, and prejudices.

HOW TO RECOGNIZE AND PRACTICE CROSS-CULTURAL INTERACTION

A person's nationality, culture, race, and gender affect how he or she communicates. However, communication between people of different cultures can often be difficult when neither person is familiar with the other's style of communicating. Three specific problem areas that supervisors must take steps to overcome are:

1. The tendency not to listen carefully or pay attention to what others are saying,

2. Speaking or addressing others in ways that alienate them or make them feel uncomfortable, and

3. Using or falling back on inappropriate stereotypes to communicate with people from other cultures.

To be an effective supervisor in a culturally diverse workforce, you must be able to recognize the different ways that people communicate, be sensitive to your own employees' cultural values, and adapt your own supervisory style accordingly.

For example, in some cultures, people rely primarily on verbal communication. In other cultures the spoken word is only part of communication; people express themselves "in context"—language, body language, the physical setting, and past relationships are all parts of communication.

The use of personal space is another important culture difference. If you step into someone's personal space, they will often step back, in order to maintain their space. People from Latin America, Africa, the Middle East, and South America often prefer to communicate at much closer distances than would seem comfortable for people from Canada or the United States. Asians, by contrast, sometimes prefer even more personal space. As a supervisor, if an employee steps into your personal space and you step back, your action may be seen as being aloof or not wanting to talk. To adjust to situations

Creating opportunities to learn about other cultures is helpful in creating cultural harmony.
Courtesy of PhotoDisc/Gerry Images.

when talking with someone, stay put and let the other person stand where he or she is comfortable.

Eye contact and facial expressions are two other nonverbal communication techniques that vary among cultures. Whereas in North America it is common to maintain good eye contact and employ facial cues such as nodding the head when listening to someone speak, not all cultures share those practices. In many Asian and African cultures, people will make greater eye contact when speaking, but when listening, make infrequent eye contact. They also might not use facial expressions when listening to others. These nonverbal communication differences may lead to misunderstanding. A supervisor may wrongly misinterpret that an employee who does not make eye contact or nod in response is simply not listening or doesn't care, when in fact, the employee is listening in a respectful manner.

Cultural differences also affect other areas of communication, such as the rate at which people speak, the volume, speech inflections, and the use of pauses and silence when speaking. It is common in Europe and North America to speak whenever there is silence in a conversation, and to speak loudly. This is not always the case in other cultures. In Asian cultures, silence is not regarded as an interruption or indication that the conversation has ended but is often considered as much a part of conversation as speaking is. Silence is also often used as a sign of politeness and respect for elders rather than a lack of desire to keep talking. Whereas a North American's loud speech in many Asian countries is often interpreted as being aggressive or even angry, an Asian's soft-spoken voice in the United States might be seen as a sign of weakness or shyness.

Another communication difference is the tendency in Europe and the United States to be direct in conversation and get to the point. In many other cultures, this practice is considered impolite and rude. To an Asian-American, being direct might be interpreted as being insensitive to the feelings of others. Native Americans, Asian-Americans, and some Hispanic-Americans value respect and harmony and will use indirect speaking methods to achieve those ends.

It is also important to remember that not everyone from one culture will act the same. Even though it is a common perception that Asian people are soft-spoken, it is not uncommon for Asian people to speak loudly. Furthermore, not all people who look like they are of certain cultures are. For example, someone who "looks" Hispanic might have been born and raised a few blocks away from your establishment, right next door to another employee.

As a supervisor, you should be sensitive to your employees' cultural values and understand their different communication styles. Always be open for feedback when communicating. Feedback can tell you how you are perceived by others as well as how well you are getting your point across. Also, keep in mind that it is only natural that people from other cultures speak with a different tone of voice, rhythm, and pace. Finally, as a supervisor, you can also focus on core values that transcend cultural boundaries by creating a workplace where all employees feel valued, safe, and respected.

Check Your Knowledge

1.   Describe the process of developing cross-cultural interaction skills.

2.   Define *culture bound*.

THE VALUE OF CULTURAL DIVERSITY

In the 21st century supervisors and managers, in order to be effective, have to handle greater cultural diversity. Supervisors and managers who are not able to handle

More women are members of the executive committee or guidance team. Courtesy of
PhotoDisc/Getty Images.

diversity in the workforce are a liability. Poor supervision can cost companies dearly in
the following ways:

- Discrimination lawsuits
- Litigation time and money
- Legal fees/settlements
- High employee turnover rates
- Negative community image

Understanding what cultural diversity is, why it matters, and how to effectively
manage your diverse team of associates can minimize risks.

MANAGING CULTURAL DIVERSITY IN THE WORKPLACE

Managing diversity in the workplace means to recognize, respect, and capitalize
on the different backgrounds in our society in terms of race, ethnicity, gender,

and sexual orientation. Different cultural groups have different values, styles, and personalities, each of which may have a substantial effect on the way they perform in the workplace.

Rather than punishing or stifling these different management styles because they do not conform to the traditional white (male) management methods, employers should recognize these differences as benefits. Not only can diverse management styles achieve the same results as traditional methods, but a diverse workforce can also help improve the company's competitive position in the marketplace.

Diversity, or sensitivity, training is now commonplace in the corporate world. However, small businesses need to be aware of these issues just as well. As a small business owner, your awareness and respect of diversity truly matters to your employees and client base.

You must create a balance of respect and understanding in the workplace to have happy and optimally productive workers. In addition to this, it is important that you *and* your employees are aware of the importance of respecting diversity when dealing with your clients. When you work effectively with your community, both you and the community benefit.[11]

Rohini Anand, senior vice president and chief diversity officer, Sodexho USA, says that diversity has an extremely broad definition at Sodexho. It includes all those differences that make us unique, including race and gender, ethnicity, sexual orientation, religion, class, physical and mental abilities, language abilities, etc. We also have a very clear mission statement about diversity being the right thing to do and making business sense for our company. It's about creating a work environment for our employees as well as giving back to the community and providing socially responsible services to our clients.

There needs to be a real commitment for top management to "walk their talk." Plus, senior management needs to establish goals and monitor their accomplishment, otherwise they won't succeed. In some companies people only do it because the president says so, but what if the president leaves? The next president may not have the same agenda. It is better to have diversity, inclusion, and multiculturalism in the mission statement and in the departmental goals with objectives as to how the goals will be met.

Sodexho strives to be the best in class in the hospitality industry and is rapidly becoming a benchmark for corporate America. This is being achieved by six strategic imperatives, diversity being one of them. Alongside financial results they report on how they are doing on diversity and inclusion. The second is an incentive program where bonuses of 10 to 15 percent are linked to the diversity scorecard. Twenty-five percent of the executive team's bonus is linked and the CEO has guaranteed that this bonus will be paid out regardless of the financial performance of the company. Now that's putting your money where your mouth is!

A third recommendation is to have someone whose sole job is to attend to the diversity and inclusion because it's such a broad scope in terms of the kinds of things that are involved in a diversity effort. Plus, it really shows the commitment. The symbolic aspect is as important as the actual work.

According to Anand, "There are so many pieces included in a diversity effort. It ranges from recruiting and sourcing to retention ... my recommendation is that somebody be responsible for diversity and inclusion and report to senior management—preferably the president. You want to have influence at the top. A diversity effort can only be successful if you get top level buy-in along with grass roots efforts."[12]

ESTABLISHING A DIVERSITY AND INCLUSION PROGRAM

The following five steps are the how to's for establishing a diversity and inclusion program:

1. Develop a mission statement that includes diversity and inclusion.
2. Develop goals for diversity and inclusion for each key operating area.
3. Develop objectives/strategies to show how the goals will be met.
4. Develop measurements to monitor progress toward the goals.
5. Monitor progress toward goal accomplishment.

Gerry Fernandez, president of the Multicultural Foodservice and Hospitality Alliance (MFHA), says that with more than one trillion dollars in buying power, minorities of today will be the majority of tomorrow. That's not a philosophical argument; it's based purely on facts and data found in the U.S. Census. Focusing on multiculturalism isn't about doing the right thing; it is about doing the right thing for your business.[13]

Hotel corporations are also reaching out to minority groups to help them become hotel owners. For example, Hilton says it has picked all the low-hanging fruit by approaching minority athletes and entertainers, and now it's going after people who are pooling their money.[14]

Some might be concerned about the costs of promoting diversity and education about other cultures. According to Salvador Mendoza, director of diversity at Hyatt Hotels, it is possible to leverage diversity to the bottom line. Multicultural initiatives are bottom-line issues. You have to be sensitive to the needs of employees, and you have to make money. There's a way to do both while promoting a multicultural environment.[15]

Many of the larger well-known hotel and restaurant corporations have a diversity initiative to encourage minority ownership of franchised hotels and restaurants as well as becoming suppliers to those companies. Cendant's Keys to Success program aims to give minorities a leg up in the hotel business by offering an allowance of $1,000 per room for properties up to 74 rooms and $1,500 per room for larger ones. At Starwood Hotels and Resorts, which *Fortune* magazine recently named among the top 50 companies for minority employees, 80 percent of the associates are women and minorities.[16]

At the W Hotel on Union Square in New York, they celebrate the holidays of many religions and countries, theme days in the employee recreation room and coffee breaks, as well as provide opportunities for more formal communication by employee survey index, which measures how successful they were in creating a multicultural workplace of excellence. Supervisors and managers take this seriously because one third of their bonus in based upon the survey results.[17]

MANAGING DIVERSITY ISSUES POSITIVELY

The following list of tips and suggestions will to help you to remember that your staff is made up of individuals, which is important to keep in mind, no matter how diverse your staff.

General Guidelines

- Get to know your employees, what they like about their job, what they do not like, where they are from, what holidays they celebrate. Listen to their opinions. Help to meet their needs.

- Treat your employees equitably but not uniformly. Do not treat everyone the same when, after all, they are all different. Of course, there must be some consistency to what you do, but as long as you apply the same set of goals and values to each situation, you can treat each employee individually and consistently.

- Watch for any signs of harassment, such as employees telling jokes that make fun of a person's cultural background, race, sexual preference, religion, and so on. Know your company's policies on harassment.

- Foster a work climate of mutual respect.

- Encourage the contributions of diverse employees at meetings, in conversations, in training. Recognize their valuable contributions. Also, allow differences to be discussed rather than suppressed.
- Avoid touching employees.

Gender Issues

- Make sure that you are not showing favoritism to males or females, by, for instance, granting time off more readily or allowing certain employees to come in late or leave early.
- Show the same amount of respect and listen actively to both genders.
- Know your company's policy on sexual harassment and take seriously any charge of misconduct.

Cultural Issues

- Learn some of the foreign language phrases that are used by your employees. It shows respect for the employees who speak that language and improves communication.
- Find out how your employees want to be addressed in their own language and how to pronounce their names correctly. Avoid using slang names such as "Honey," "Sweetheart," "Dear," "Fella," and so on. They are disrespectful and annoying.
- Give rewards that are meaningful and appropriate to all employees.
- If an employee is having trouble with English, be careful when speaking to them. Speaking a little more slowly than usual might be helpful, but speaking too slowly might make your employees feel that you think they're stupid. Speaking very loudly will not make things easier to understand. Make sure that slang terms and idioms are understood. It's always important that employees (even those who speak English well) know and are comfortable enough to tell you when they don't understand what you're saying.
- Be cautious about the use and interpretation of gestures. Gestures such as thumbs up are by no means universal. For example, in the United States, a customer may gesture "one" to a server in a restaurant by putting up an index finger. In some European countries, this gesture means "two." If you are not sure what someone's gesture means, ask for the meaning.

Religious Issues

■   Be consistent in allowing time off for religious reasons.

Age Issues

■   Both the young and the old sometimes feel that they do not get the respect they deserve. They need to know what is going on in the department and how well they are doing their jobs, just like anyone else. Make them feel like part of the team.

■   Young workers want to do work they consider worthwhile and to have fun doing it. They want their supervisors to listen to them, to let them participate in decision making. Not surprisingly, they do not want supervisors to bark orders military-style. They like to have time and money invested into their training and development.

■   Do not have higher expectations of older adults than of their peers, and don't patronize them.

Differently Abled Issues

About 43 million Americans have a physical disability. At work, people with disabilities often feel that supervisors do not see beyond their disabilities and do not think they are capable. Coworkers may seem to patronize them and, because of embarrassment, may avoid speaking directly to them.

■   Look at the differently abled employee the same way you look at other employees, as a whole person with likes, dislikes, hobbies, and so on, and encourage the employee's coworkers to do so.

■   Speak directly to the differently abled employee.

■   Hiring of handicapped workers does have a positive effect on the economy.

■   Disabled workers are good for the community and for employers.

■   The hospitality industry has a responsibility to provide job opportunities for all.

■   Employees with disabilities are just as productive as other employees. You might have to make some adjustments for disabled employees, but this does not affect the quality of their work.

Even with great cross-cultural interaction skills, you will occasionally do something that offends an employee. When this happens, do the commonsense thing: Apologize sincerely.

KEY POINTS

1. Equal employment opportunity was denied to so many for so long that eventually in 1963 Congress passed the Equal Pay Act and, in 1964, the Civil Rights Act, Title VII, which established the Equal Employment Commission.

2. Progressive companies embrace equal opportunity, diversity, and inclusiveness. Many have EEO/Diversity officers who plan, develop, implement, and monitor EEO, diversity, and inclusion programs.

3. The equal employment opportunity laws are reviewed.

4. Hiring and negligent hiring include knowing the questions you can/cannot ask and an outline of what supervisors need to know.

5. Failure to understand and respect the differences, or the diversity, of your employees can result in misunderstandings, tension, poor performance, poor employee morale, and higher rates of employee absenteeism and turnover. On the other hand, when differences are respected, the working environment is richer, more fun, more interesting, and employee satisfaction and performance improve.

6. Steps to develop cross-cultural interaction skills are:
    - Increasing personal awareness
    - Learning about other cultures
    - Recognizing and practicing cross-cultural interaction skills
    - Maintaining awareness, knowledge, and skills

7. The chapter lists tips that can be used to manage diversity issues positively.

KEY TERMS

Age Discrimination in Employment Act of 1967	Family and Medical Leave Act of 1993	Equal Employment Opportunity Commission
Americans with Disabilities Act of 1990	inclusion	Immigration Reform and Control Act of 1986 and 1990
Civil Rights Act of 1964, Title VII	culture	negligent hiring
Equal Pay Act of 1963	diversity	Pregnanacy Discrimination Act of 1978

REFERENCES

1. www.eeoc.gov/abouteeoc/35th/pre1965/index.html

2. Charles Bernstein, "The Missing Piece," *Chain Leader*. June 2004. Vol: 9 Iss: 7, p. 10.

3. www.sodexhousa.com/diversity.asp

4. www.marriott.com/corporateinfo/culture/diversity

5. www.eeoc.gov/facts/qanda.html

6. www.isis.fastmail.usf.edu/eoa/interview_faq.asp

7. www.restaurantsusa.

8. Gerry A. Fernandez, "Multicultural Diversity: It's the Right Thing to Do for Your Business," *Nation's Restaurant News:* New York: May 19, 2003. Vol: 37, Iss: 20, p. 42, 183.

9. John R. Walker, *Introduction to Hospitality Management*. Upper Saddle River, NJ: Prentice Hall, 2002, p. 532.

10. www.aramark.com/aboutaramark.asp?topic=diversity

11. Texas Center for Women's Business Enterprise, Austin, TX. SBA Online, 8-10-2004.

12. Rohini Anand, "Make Diversity Part of the Business Plan," *Restaurants and Institutions*. Vol. 114, Iss: 10, p. 22. May 2004.

13. Gerry A. Fernandez, "Multicultural Diversity: It's the Right Thing to Do for Your Business," *Nation's Restaurant News*. May 19, 2003. Vol: 37, Iss: 20, p. 43.

14. John P. Walsh, "Putting It Together," *Hotel and Motel Management*. September 1, 2003. Vol. 218, Iss. 15, p. 4.

15. Jeff Higley, "Hospitality Leaders Promote Diversity During Conference," *Hotel and Motel Management*. September 18, 2000. Vol. 215, Iss. 16, p. 4.

16. Carlo Wolf, "Hotel Companies Diversify their Diversity Targets Even as Growth Lags," *Lodging Hospitality*. July 15, 2004. Vol. 60, Iss. 10, p. 46–48.

17. Personal Conversation with Arash Azarbarzin, July 23, 2004.

CREATING A POSITIVE WORK CLIMATE*

* Authored by Jack E. Miller, John R. Walker, and Karen Eich Drummond.

Susan just started working a month ago at the front desk of an airport hotel. So far she is not very happy with the job. To begin with, she has trouble finding a parking spot every afternoon when she comes to work, although she was promised that there were plenty. When she reports to work, she is lucky if she can find her boss, who is often away from the work area, to question him about her training program, which is going very slowly. Most of her peers manage to say hello, but that is usually all. She wonders if anyone would notice if she just took off out the front door and did not come back.

Randy, a cook in a downtown restaurant, loves where he works. Although his pay and benefits are good, there are many other reasons why he loves his job. He feels like part of a quality team at work, management always keeps him informed of what's going on, hourly employees frequently get promoted when there are open positions, the kitchen is comfortable to work in and he has just the equipment he needs, everyone is on a first-name basis, he gets bonuses based on the number of guests served, and the restaurant owners give him time off to go to college and pay his tuition.

Employees want to be treated first as individuals and as employees second. They want a lot more out of work than just a paycheck. They want, for example, respect, trust, rewards, and interesting work.

In the first section of this chapter we discuss employee expectations and needs. The concept of motivation is then discussed, followed by a section on how to build a positive work climate. This chapter will help you to:

- Explain common employee expectations of their supervisors.

- Define the term *motivation* and explain the supervisor's responsibility to motivate his or her employees.

- Discuss the essential points of current theories and practices for motivating employees on the job.

- Explain the challenge of applying common motivational theories in the hospitality work environment.

- Identify nine ways to build a positive work climate by focusing on employees as individuals.

- Describe two ways a supervisor can build a positive work climate by focusing on him or herself.

EMPLOYEE EXPECTATIONS AND NEEDS

When you become a supervisor, you will have certain expectations of your employees. You will expect them to do the work they have been hired to do—to produce the products and services to the quality standards set by the enterprise that is paying you both. You may wonder whether their performance will meet your expectations, and you may have some plans for improving productivity.

But you may not realize that what these people expect from you and how *you* meet *their* expectations may have as much to do with their performance as your expectations of them. If you handle their expectations well, if they recognize your authority willingly, you will have a positive relationship going for you, one on which you can build a successful operation. Let us look at some categories of things workers typically expect and need from the boss.

Your Experience and Technical Skills

Your people expect you to be qualified to supervise. First, they want you to have worked in the area in which you are supervising: a hotel, a hospital kitchen, a restaurant, whatever it is. Coming into a restaurant from a hospital kitchen may discount your experience and you will have to prove yourself. Coming into a big hotel from a job in a budget motel, you may also have to prove yourself. Your workers want to feel that you understand the operation well and appreciate the work they are doing. They want to feel that they and their jobs are in good hands—that you are truly capable of directing their work.

In some circumstances, being a college graduate will make you distrusted. Your workers may assume that you think you know it all and they are afraid you will look down on them. They may think that they know it all and that you have not paid your dues by coming up the hard way. In other places, if you are not a college graduate and other supervisors have college degrees—in a hospital setting, perhaps—you will have to work harder to establish yourself with your workers. If they are satisfied with what you have done on other jobs and how you are doing on this one, they will each decide at some point, okay, you are qualified to supervise here. But it may take time and tact and determination on your part.

Second, they want you to be not only experienced but technically competent. Every employee who works for you expects you to be able to do his or her particular job. They may not expect you to have their own proficiency or skill, but you must be able to do that job. This can become a sort of game. They will question you, they will check you, they will make you prove you know what you are doing—"Why doesn't the bread rise?" "Why doesn't the sauce thicken?"—and there will be instances when they will have sabotaged that recipe just to see if you know what is wrong. They may unplug the slicer and tell you it is broken, and you will start checking the machine and the fuses before you catch on. You are going to have to prove your right to supervise.

The Way You Behave as a Boss

Nearly everyone wants a boss who will take stands and make decisions, who will stay in charge no matter how difficult the situation is, who is out there handling whatever emergency comes up. Hardly anyone respects a boss who evades issues and responsibilities, shifts blame, hides behind the mistakes of others, or avoids making decisions that will be unpopular even though they are necessary.

Many people expect authority and direction from the boss. These people want you to tell them what to do; they may not know how to handle too much independence. Some of them will want you to supervise every single thing they do—"Is that okay?" "Is this the way you want it?" Others just want you to define the job, tell them what you want done, and let them go at it—"Hey, get off my back and leave me alone." Sometimes you will have a worker who is totally opposed to authority, who will reject everything you say simply because you are the boss; this one will give you a hard time. When you get to know each person's special needs and expectations, you can adjust your style of directing them accordingly—your style, but not what you require of them. You must do what is correct, not what pleases them.

Your people expect you to act like a boss toward them, not like one of the gang. They want you to be friendly, but they expect you to maintain an objective, work-oriented relationship with each person. They do not want you to be everyone's pal, and they do not like you to have special friends among the workers.

If you do socialize off the job with some of the people you supervise, you are running certain risks. Can you go out and party with them, form close friendships, and then come back and supervise them on the job without playing favorites or making other workers jealous? Maybe you can. But can your worker friends handle this closeness, this double relationship? Will they think they are special and that they can get away with things? These are friendships to approach with caution or to avoid altogether.

Your people expect you to treat them fairly and equally, without favoritism. The fairness that people expect is fairness as they see it, not necessarily as you see it. There may be someone on your staff that you don't like, and it is going to be difficult, if not impossible, for you to treat this person without bias. There may be someone else who you like a lot. And there is going to be a world of difference in the way you instruct, discipline, and deal with these two people. Is it fair in the minds of your employees? They may think that you are playing favorites or are really putting somebody down. You must always think of how these things look to the other workers, how it will affect their acceptance of you. Sometimes they may be right and you are not aware of it.

Fairness includes honesty with your workers and with the company. Your people expect you to evaluate their work honestly, to follow company rules, to put in your time, to fulfill your promises, and to carry out your threats. One of the worst mistakes you can make is to promise something you cannot deliver, whether it is a threat or a reward. People will not respect the authority of a boss who does this. If you do not come through for your workers, they will not come through for you.

Communication between Boss and Workers

Your workers expect several things from you in the way of communication. First, *they expect information*. They expect you to define their jobs and to give them directions in a way they can comprehend. Probably 90 percent of the people who work for you want to do a good job, but it is up to you to make it clear to them what the job is and how it should be done. It often takes a little extra time to make sure that each worker has grasped the full meaning of what you have said. But if you expect them to do a good job, they expect you to take the time necessary to tell them clearly exactly what a good job is.

Telling them what to do and how to do it should include the necessary skills training. In the foodservice industry it is typical to skip this training or to ask another worker to train the new person while the two of them are on the job. It is not uncommon to hire people to bus tables, put them to work without training, yell at them for doing everything wrong, and then fire them for breaking so many dishes. Unless they leave first. They may leave first because they expected to be told the right way to bus tables, and they were not told. Lack of clear direction is a major reason for the high rate of employee turnover in this industry. The boss does not meet the worker's expectations.

The second type of communication that people want from the boss is *feedback on their performance*. The most important thing a worker wants to know is, "How am I doing? Am I getting along all right?" Yet this expectation, this need, is usually met only when the worker is *not* doing all right. We tear into them when they are doing things wrong, but we seldom take the time to tell them when they are doing a good job. A few seconds to fill that basic human need for approval can make a world of difference in your workers' attitude toward you, and the work they do for you.

A third form of communication that employees expect from you is to have you *listen* when they tell you something. They can give you useful information about their jobs and your customers, and they can often make very valuable suggestions if you will take the time to listen—really listen—to what they have to say. But they do expect you to take that time and to take them seriously, because they are offering you something of their own.

Clear communication between supervisors and associates is critical in a creative and positive work climate. Courtesy of Action Systems, Inc.

Two cardinal rules on suggestions from employees are:

1. Never steal one of their suggestions and use it as your own.
2. If you cannot use a suggestion, explain why you can't, and express your appreciation.

If you violate either of these rules, suddenly your people will stop telling you anything. They are not even going to respond when you ask for their input. You have closed the door they expected to be open, and they are not going to open it again.

Unwritten Rules and Customs

In most enterprises certain work customs become established over the years, and employees expect a new supervisor to observe them. They are not written down anywhere, they have just grown up, and they are treasured by workers as inviolable rights, never to be tampered with, especially by newcomers. In many kitchens, for example, a new worker is always given the grungy jobs, such as vegetable prep or cleaning shrimp. In a hotel, a new night cleaner will have to clean the lobby and the public restrooms. If the boss brings in somebody new and he or she isn't started off with the grungy jobs, that's just not right. If a new waiter is brought in and given the best station in the dining room—the one with the best tips or the one closest to the kitchen—there's going to be a mutiny; that's just not done.

People will lay claim to the same chair day after day to eat their lunch, they will park their cars in the same place, and if you disrupt one of these things established by usage and custom, they will take it as a personal affront. You are expected to observe the established customs, and if you want to make changes, you will be wise to approach them cautiously and introduce them gradually.

Another type of rule or custom, sometimes written down but more often unwritten, is the content of a job as seen by the person performing it. When people begin a new job, they quickly settle in their own minds what constitutes a day's work in that job and the obligations and expectations that go with it. If you as a supervisor go beyond your workers' expectations, if you ask them to do something extra or out of the ordinary, you have violated their concept of what they were hired to do and they feel you are imposing on them, taking advantage. They will resent you, and they will resent the whole idea.

Suppose that you are a dishwasher and you finish early, and the boss is so pleased that she asks you to clean the walk-in. The next day you finish early again and the boss says, "This is terrific, today we are going to clean the garbage cans." "Hey, no," you say, "I was hired to wash dishes, not to clean walk-ins and garbage cans." And you are about ready to tell her off but you think better of it; you need the job. On the third day you have only 30 people for lunch instead of your usual 300, but how long does it take you to finish the dishes? All afternoon and 30 minutes of overtime at least.

In sum, people expect the boss to observe what workers believe their jobs to be, whether they have been defined on paper by management or defined only in the workers' own minds. Rightly or wrongly, they resent being given more to do than they were hired to do, and they may refuse to do the extra work, or won't do it well, or will take overtime to do it.

One way to avoid this kind of resistance is to make clear when you hire people that you may ask them to vary their duties now and then when the work is slow or you are shorthanded or there is an emergency. An all-purpose phrase included in each job description—"other duties as assigned"—will establish the principle. However, as a new supervisor you need to be aware of the way people perceive what you ask them to do. In our example, the worker who finishes early is rewarded with two unpleasant jobs totally unrelated to running the dishmachine. There is no immediate and urgent need and no warning that the worker might be expected to fill idle time with other tasks. We will have more to say about defining job content in later chapters. A clear understanding is essential to a successful relationship between worker and boss.

Person-to-Person Relationships

Today's workers expect to be treated as human beings rather than as part of the machinery of production. They want the boss to know who they are and what they do on the job and how well they are doing it. They want to be treated as individuals, and they want to feel comfortable talking to the boss, whether it is about problems on the job or about hunting and / or fishing and / or the weather and the new baby at home. They want the boss's acceptance and approval, including tolerance for an occasional mistake or a bad day. They want recognition for a job well done. Whether they are aware of it or not, they want a sense of belonging on the job.

To your people you personify the company. They don't know the owners, the stockholders, the general manager, and the top brass. To most hourly workers, you are the company—you are it. If they have an easy relationship with you, they will feel good about the company. If they feel good about the company, they can develop that sense of belonging there. And if they feel that they belong there, they are likely to stay.

Successful supervisors develop a sensitivity to each person, to the person's individual needs and desires and fears and anxieties as well as talent and skills. They handle each person as much as possible in the way that best fills the worker's personal needs. If you can establish good relationships on this one-to-one level with all your workers, you can build the positive kind of work climate that is necessary for success.

Check Your Knowledge

1. Name expectations that employees often have of their supervisors.

2. Why is communication between boss and workers important?

MOTIVATION

The term motivation refers to what makes people tick: the needs and desires and fears and aspirations within people that make them behave as they do. Motivation is the energizer that makes people take action; it is the *why* of human behavior. In the workplace, motivation goes hand in hand with productivity. Highly motivated people usually work hard and do superior work. Poorly motivated people do what is necessary to get by without any hassles from the boss, even though they may be capable of doing more and better work. Unmotivated people usually do marginal or substandard work and often take up a good deal of the boss's time. Sometimes, people are motivated by resentment and anger to make trouble for the supervisor, to beat the system, or to gain power for themselves. Such motivations are at cross-purposes with the goals of the operation and have a negative effect on productivity.

Motivation, as we have noted many times, is a major concern of the supervisor. Supervisory success is measured by the performance of the department as a whole, which is made up of the performance of individuals. Each person's performance can raise or lower overall productivity and supervisory success. The big question is how to motivate poor performers to realize their potential and raise their productivity, and how to keep good performers from going stale in their jobs or leaving for a better opportunity.

Actually, you cannot motivate people to do good work. Motivation comes from within. The one thing you as a supervisor can do is to turn it on, to activate people's own motivations. To do this you must get to know your people and find out what they respond to. It may be the work itself. It may be the way you supervise. It may be the work environment. It may be their individual goals: money, recognition, achievement, or whatever.

Are there benefits to fun work environments? The answer is an unequivocal "Yes!" Managers reported that two of the most important benefits of fun workplaces are increases in the commitment (loyalty, dedication, lower turnover) of their employees, and their organizations' ability to successfully recruit new employees.

Source: Robert Ford, John Newstrom, Frank McLaughlin, "Making Workplace Fun More Functional," *Industrial and Commercial Training*, Vol. 36, No. 3, pp. 117–120, 2004.

How do you find out what will turn people on? It isn't easy. There are many theories and few answers. What motivates one person may turn someone else off completely. Everybody is different. People do the same things for different reasons and different things for the same reasons. People's needs and desires and behaviors change from day to day and sometimes from minute to minute. You can never know directly why they behave as they do, and they may not know why either, or would not tell you if they could.

In sum, motivation is a complicated business, and motivating people to do their jobs well has no one simple answer. It takes something of an experimental approach; you try to find out what each person responds to, and if one thing doesn't work, maybe the next thing will.

But it need not be just a trial-and-error process. You can get quite a bit of insight into human behavior from people who have spent their lives studying the subject, and you will find much in their theories that will help you to figure out how to motivate individual workers to do their best for you.

But the one thing that you can seldom do is to develop a set of rules applying this or that theory to a certain person or particular situation on the job. For this reason we give you the various theories first. Then we spend the balance of the chapter investigating ways of motivating people by using your broadened understanding of human nature along with a mixture of theory, sensitivity, and ingenuity.

THEORIES OF MOTIVATION

Whether they realize it or not, everyone has a theory of how to get people to perform on the job. Several of them are familiar to you, although you may not think of them as theories.

Motivation through Fear

One of the oldest ways of motivating people to perform on the job is to use fear as the trigger for getting action. This method makes systematic use of coercion, threats, and punishment: "If you don't do your job and do it right, you won't get your raise." "I'll put you back on the night shift." "I'll fire you."

This approach to motivation is sometimes referred to as a "kick in the pants." It is still used surprisingly often, with little success. Yet people who use it believe that it is the only way to get results. They are typically autocratic, high-control, authoritarian bosses with Theory X beliefs about people, and they think other theories of motivation are baloney, that you must be tough with people.

Motivation through fear seldom works for long. People who work in order to avoid punishment usually produce mediocre results at best, and fear may actually reduce the ability to perform. At the same time it arouses hostility, resentment, and the desire to get even. Absenteeism, tardiness, poor performance, and high turnover are typical under this type of supervision.

Fear will sometimes motivate people who have always been treated this way, and it can function as a last resort when all other methods have failed. But it will work only

In the workplace, motivation goes hand in hand with productivity. Courtesy of San Antonio CVB.

if the supervisor is perceived as being powerful enough to carry out the punishment. If the boss continually threatens punishment and never punishes, the threats have no power to motivate. In fact, not even fear works in this situation.

No one recommends motivation through fear except the people who practice it. On average, workers in the United States simply will not put up with that kind of boss unless they are desperate for a job.

Carrot-and-Stick Method

A second philosophy of motivation is to combine fear with incentive reward for good performance, punishment for bad. You may recognize this as carrot-and-stick motivation: the carrot dangled in front as a promised reward, the stick hitting the worker from behind as goad and punishment. It is another high-control method, one that requires constant application. Once the reward is achieved or the punishment administered, it no longer motivates performance, and another reward must be devised or punishment threatened or applied.

In effect, the boss is pushing and pulling workers through their jobs; they themselves feel no motivation to perform well. At the same time, workers come to feel that they have a continuing right to the rewards (such as higher wages, fringe benefits), and these get built into the system without further motivating effect. Meanwhile the punishments and threats of punishment breed resentment and resistance.

Economic Person Theory

A third motivation theory maintains that money is the only thing that people work for. This classical view of job motivation was known as the **economic person theory**. Frederick Taylor was perhaps its most influential advocate. Taylor developed his scientific management theories on the cornerstone of incentive pay based on amount of work done. He firmly believed that he was offering workers what they wanted most, and that the way to motivate workers to increase their productivity was to relate wages directly to the amount of work produced. What he did not know was that the workers in his plant were far more strongly motivated by their loyalty to one another. In fact, for three years they united to block every effort he made to increase output despite the extra wages that they could have earned.

There is no doubt that money has always been and still is one of the most important reasons that people work. For some people it may be the most important reason. That paycheck feeds and clothes and houses them; it can give them security, status, a feeling of personal worth. For people who have been at the poverty level, it can be the difference between being hungry and being well fed or between welfare and self-support with self-respect. For teenagers it can mean the difference between owning a car and being without transportation. For most people on their first job, whether it is an hourly job or an entry-level management job, money is the primary motivator.

But the amount of money in the paycheck does not guarantee performance on the job. The paycheck buys people's time and enough effort to get by, but it does not buy quality, quantity, and commitment to doing one's work well. If people work for money, does it follow that they will work better for more—the more the pay, the better the performance? There are certainly instances in which it works: the expectation of wage increases, bonuses, tips, and rewards is likely to have this outcome. But money does not motivate performance once it is paid; the incentive comes from the expectation of more to come.

Furthermore, people do not work for money alone. A number of research studies have shown that, for most people, money as a motivator on the job has less importance than achievement, recognition, responsibility, and interesting work. In sum, money is only one of the resources you have for motivating people, and it does not necessarily have a direct relationship to productivity.

Human Relations Theory

After the Hawthorne experiments (Chapter 11) uncovered the human factors affecting productivity, the social person succeeded the economic person in motivation theory. The human relations enthusiasts pushed their convictions that if people are treated as people, they will be more productive on the job. Make people feel secure, they said, treat them as individuals, make them feel they belong and have worth, develop person-to-person relationships with each one, let them participate in plans and decisions that affect them, and they will respond by giving their best to the organization.

Putting this theory to work brought about higher wages, better working conditions, pension plans, paid vacations, insurance plans, and other fringe benefits, making workers happier but not necessarily more productive. The question remained: What motivates people to work?

Maslow's Hierarchy of Needs

An influential answer to this question was the motivation theory of psychologist Abraham Maslow. Human beings, he pointed out, are *wanting animals*, and they behave in ways that will satisfy their needs and wants. Their needs and desires are inexhaustible; as soon as one need is satisfied, another appears to take its place. In *Motivation and Personality* (New York: Harper & Row, 1954), Maslow proposed a hierarchy of universal human needs representing the order in which these needs become motivators of human behavior. This hierarchy of needs is represented by the pyramid in Figure 14.1.

At the bottom of the pyramid are people's most basic needs—the *physiological needs* related to *survival*, such as food and water. When these needs are not being met, every effort is directed toward meeting them. People who are truly hungry cannot think of anything but food. For many hospitality employees this equates to salary or wages.

But when survival needs are being met, they no longer motivate behavior, and the next level of needs comes into play. These relate to *safety*; they include protection, security, stability, structure, order, and freedom from fear, anxiety, and chaos. For hospitality employees this equates to benefits and pension plans.

As these needs in turn are more or less satisfied, *social needs* become the predominant motivators. These include the need to be with others, to belong, to have friends, to love, and be loved. For hospitality employees this means socializing at work—and we do plenty of that—don't we!

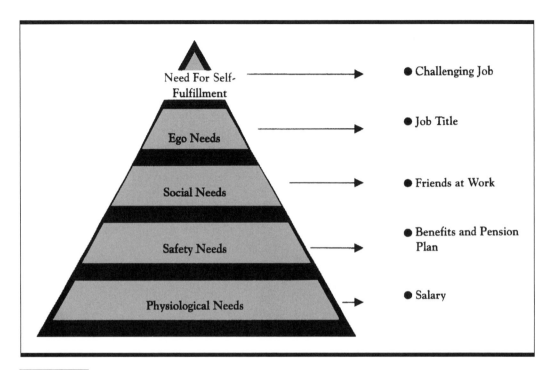

FIGURE 14.1 Maslow's hierarchy of needs.

Above these three groups of needs (sometimes called *primary needs*) is a higher level of needs centered on esteem. These are sometimes referred to as ego needs. One of them is the desire for *self-esteem* or *self-respect* and for the strength, achievement, mastery, competence, confidence, independence, and freedom that provide such self-esteem. Another is the desire for the *esteem of others*: for status, fame and glory, dominance, recognition, attention, importance, dignity, appreciation. The need for esteem gives rise in some people to the need for power as a way of commanding the esteem of others. Satisfaction of the need for self-esteem leads to feelings of self-confidence, strength, and worth. When these needs go unsatisfied, they produce feelings of inferiority, weakness, and helplessness. For hospitality employees this equated to job title and perks.

At the top of the hierarchy is the need for *self-fulfillment*, or what Maslow called self-actualization. This includes the need to be doing what one is best fitted for, the desire to fulfill one's own potential. For the hospitality employee this equates to a challenging job where people can always learn more.

One or another of all these personal needs or various combinations of needs is what motivates people to do what they do. If a lower need goes unsatisfied, people will spend all their time and energy trying to fill it, and they will not experience the next level of needs until the lower needs are met. When a need is satisfied it is no longer a motivator, and the next level of needs becomes the predominant motivation.

Thus motivation is an unending cycle of need and satisfaction, need and satisfaction. You have a need, you look for a solution, you take action to satisfy the need, and another need appears, because human beings are wanting animals whose needs and desires are never completely satisfied. This continuing cycle explains why workers' needs evolve and change as their own situation changes.

Maslow's theory of motivation does not give you a tool you can use directly; you cannot sit down and analyze each person's needs and then know how to motivate that person. What it can do is to make you aware of how people differ in their needs and why they respond to certain things and not to others. It can help you understand why some of your workers behave as they do on the job.

Theory Y and Motivation

Maslow's theories were the springboard for McGregor's Theory X and Theory Y, two opposing views of the way that supervisors and managers look at their workers (Chapter 12). Theory X and Theory Y applied Maslow's theories directly to the problem of motivating workers on the job. McGregor made two particularly significant contributions with Theory Y. One was to revise the typical view of the way that people look at work: It is "as natural as play or rest" when it is satisfying a need. This is a flat reversal of the Theory X view of the worker, and it suggests a clear reason why people work willingly.

McGregor's second contribution to motivational theory was the idea that people's needs, especially their ego and self-actualization needs, can be made to operate on the job in harmony with the needs and goals of the organization. If, for example, people are given assignments in which they see the opportunity for achievement, for responsibility, for growth, for self-fulfillment, they will become committed to carrying them out. They will be self-directed and self-controlled, and external controls and the threat of punishment will be unnecessary. In other words, if you can give people work that will fill some basic need, their own motivation will take care of its performance. People will work harder and longer and better for the company if they are satisfying their own needs in the process.

Herzberg's Motivation-Hygiene Theory

The work of another psychologist, Frederick Herzberg, explained why human relations methods failed to motivate performance and identified factors that truly motivate

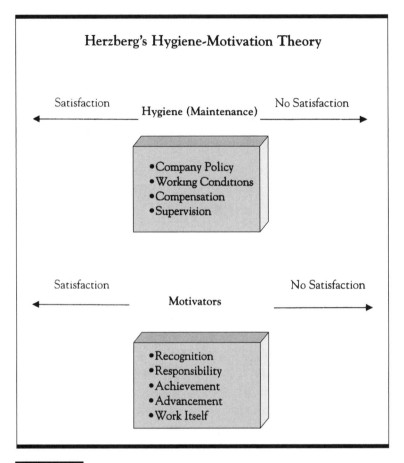

FIGURE 14.2 An adaptation of Herzberg's Hygiene-Motivation Theory, which was originally proposed by Dr. Frederick Herzberg, B. Mausner, and B. Snyderman in *The Motivation to Work* (New York: John Wiley, 1958).

(see Figure 14.2). Herzberg found that factors associated with the job environment (compensation, supervision, working conditions, company policy, and so on) create dissatisfaction and unhappiness on the job when they are inadequate; they become dissatisfiers.

But removing the causes of dissatisfaction (the human relations approach) does not create satisfaction, and it therefore does not motivate performance. Herzberg called these environmental factors hygiene factors. They are also commonly called maintenance factors. For example, if you think you are underpaid, if you don't get along with your boss, if the kitchen isn't air-conditioned—these things can reduce motivation and cause absenteeism, poor work, and less of it. They are related to motivation only in the sense that they reduce it. Such factors must be maintained at satisfying levels to avoid negative motivation. But air-conditioning the kitchen or raising wages will not make the cooks work harder once the novelty wears off.

In contrast, a second group of factors provides both motivation and job satisfaction. These, Herzberg found, consist of opportunities in the job itself for achievement and growth—such factors as recognition, responsibility, achievement, advancement, the work itself. He called these factors motivators. If you give a cook who loves to invent new dishes a chance to develop a special menu item, you will see a motivator at work.

The answer to motivating employees, then, lies in the job itself. If it can be enriched to provide opportunity for achievement and growth, it will not only motivate the worker to perform well but will also tap unused potential and use personnel more effectively. We look at job enrichment in more detail later in the chapter.

Behavior Modification

Behavior modification, a newer method for improving performance, simply bypasses inner motivation and deals instead with behavior change. It takes off from the behaviorist's theory that *all behavior is a function of its consequences*; people behave as they do because of positive or negative consequences to them. If the consequences are positive, they will tend to repeat the behavior; if they are negative, they will tend not to.

If you want to improve performance, then, you will give positive reinforcement (attention, praise) whenever people do things right. You look actively for such behavior, and when you catch people doing something right, you praise them for it.

If you were going to carry out the theory literally, you would provide some form of negative consequence for undesired behavior, but in practice negative consequences (blaming, punishment) tend to have side effects such as hostility and aggressive behavior. However, you cannot ignore the undesired behavior. You can deal with it positively without threatening the person by suggesting the correct behavior in coaching fashion. "Let me show you how." But the really important side of behavior modification is positive reinforcement. It reverses the usual story of nothing but negative feedback ("The boss never notices me except when I do something wrong"), and it satisfies the need for attention with the kind of attention that builds self-worth.

The use of behavior modification has burgeoned in recent years, and it can sometimes be very effective. There have been instances where positive reinforcement has not only corrected undesired behavior but has actually increased productivity. Whatever its theoretical base, positive reinforcement can be another resource for you to try out with your people.

Reinforcement Theory

The reinforcement theory praises and rewards employees good behavior and undesired behavior is not reinforced. Supervisors can modify behavior by giving appropriate praise and rewards. *Positive reinforcement* should be given right after the behavior occurs. Good performance is rewarded by praise, preferably in front of other associates, and other incentives like bonuses, gifts, promotions, pay increases and other perks can be given. *Negative reinforcement* is the withholding of praise and rewards for inferior performance.

Expectancy Theory

The expectancy theory explains that employees are concerned about three important questions.[1]

1. How much effort, diligence, care, etc., should I devote to my work?
2. If I perform well as a result of my effort, diligence, care etc., will I obtain desired outcomes to satisfy my needs?
3. Does my employer provide work outcomes that satisfy my needs?

With the work expectancy theory it is vital that supervisors provide the training and coaching necessary so that the associates will have the expectancy of achieving superior performance. If however, the superior performance goes unrewarded or even if the reward does not match up to the associates' expectations, then dissatisfaction will result. It is important to realize that not all employees want the same reward. The best approach is to find out what will motivate them and offer a selection of rewards.

Check Your Knowledge

1. Explain what is meant by *person-to-person* relationships.
2. Define *motivation*.
3. Briefly discuss the motivation theories.
4. Define *behavior modification* and *positive reinforcement*.

APPLYING THEORY TO REALITY: LIMITING FACTORS

Now, what can you do with all this theory? There is a great deal in it that you can put to work if you can adapt it to your particular situation and to your individual workers. There are also circumstances that limit how far you can go. One limiting factor that immediately comes to mind is the *nature of many jobs* in the hospitality industry. They are dull, unchallenging, repetitive, and boring. On the surface at least there does not seem to be much you can do to motivate the potwasher, the security guard, the cleanup crew, the makers of the beds, and the changers of the light bulbs to keep them working up to standard and to keep them from leaving for another job.

Even among the less routine jobs there is little you can change to make the work itself more interesting and challenging. The great majority of jobs are made up of things that must be done in the same way day after day. At the same time, many jobs depend to some extent on factors beyond your control: What people do each day and how much they do varies according to customer demand. Unless your workers happen to find this interesting and challenging (and some people do), it is difficult to structure such jobs to motivate people. But the situation is not hopeless. Later in the chapter we will see what creative management can do for even the dullest jobs.

A second limiting factor is *company policy, administration, and management philosophy*. Everything you do must be in harmony with company goals (customer-oriented and cost-effective) and must meet company rules and regulations. Furthermore, you do

Positive reinforcements can encourage associates to improve their performance.

not control wage rates, fringe benefits, promotion policies, controls, and other companywide systems and practices. If jobs are totally standardized by scientific management methods, you cannot tamper with job content and method at all unless you go through proper channels and procedures established by the company.

The style of management characteristic of the organization will greatly influence what you can and cannot do. If the philosophy if management is authoritarian and high-control, you will have a hard time practicing another approach. In particular, your relationship with your own boss and your boss's management style will influence the nature and scope of what you can do to motivate your people.

A third factor, closely related to the second, is the *extent of your responsibility, authority, and resources.* You cannot exceed the limits of your own job. You may be limited in your authority to spend money, to make changes in job duties, and so on. Remember, too, that your boss is responsible and accountable for your results, and this goes all the way up the chain of command. If you are going to innovate extensively, you will need the blessing of your superiors. But maybe you can get it!

Another limiting factor is the *kinds of people who work for you.* If they are only working there *until,* the job does not really motivate them; they are just putting in time. They do not put forth their energy and enthusiasm because work is not the central interest in their lives. They have something going on outside—family, studies—that takes care of most of their personal needs and interests, and they don't want to work any harder than they have to.

The large numbers of workers who are dependent personalities often pose a motivation problem—they want you to tell them what to do at every turn, until they sometimes seem like millstones around your neck. How do you shake them loose and put them on their own?

The *constant pressures* of the typical day in the life of the hospitality manager tend to fix attention on the immediate problems and the work itself. It is all too easy to become work-oriented rather than people-oriented, especially if you have been an hourly worker and are more at home managing work than managing people. This is a limitation that managers can deliberately strive to overcome once they see how motivating people can help to accomplish the work better.

Another limitation is *time.* You probably think your day is already too full, and it may well be. It takes time to get to know your people. It takes time to figure out ways of changing things that will make people more motivated. It takes a lot of time to get changes through channels if that is necessary. It takes time to get people used to changes in their jobs, and it usually takes time before you begin to see results. But the effective manager will make the time and will gain time in the end by making more effective use of people.

There are limitations in the theories themselves when it comes to applying them. The primary one is that there is no law of motivation or set of laws that you can apply as you can apply scientific or mathematical formulas. This, of course, is true of everything having to do with human beings. Everyone is different, and their needs and desires and behavior respond in a kaleidoscope of change triggered by anything and everything—other people, the environment, the task, their memories, their expectations, *your* expectations, and what they ate for breakfast.

The theories themselves change. New experiments shed new light. The enthusiasms of the past give way to the fads of the future.

Who has the answers? What works? You have to translate the findings of others in terms of your individual workers and the jobs you supervise. These are judgments you make; there are no sure-fire answers. But there is plenty of guidance along the way.

Check Your Knowledge
List factors that may limit your use of motivational techniques.

BUILDING A POSITIVE WORK CLIMATE

A positive work climate is one in which employees can and will work productively, in which they can do their best work and achieve their highest potential in their jobs. Meeting employee expectations and needs is one way to create a positive work climate. Before we take a look at others, let's discuss a similar concept: morale.

Morale is a group spirit with respect to getting the job done. It can run the gamut from enthusiasm, confidence, cheerfulness, and dedication to discouragement, pessimism, indifference, and gloom. It is made up of individual attitudes toward the work that pass quickly from one person to another until you have a group mood that everyone shares. It may change from moment to moment. You see it when it is very high and you notice it when it is very low; and if it is average, nobody says anything about it.

When people are unhappy in their jobs, they just plain don't feel good at work. They feel exhausted, they get sick easily and miss a lot of days, and eventually, they give up because the job is not worth the stress and unhappiness. In an industry where many people are working "until" and do not have a sense of belonging, these kinds of feelings and behavior are contagious and morale becomes a big problem. Absenteeism, low-quality work, and high employee turnover multiply production problems and cost money. It probably costs at least $1,000 every time you have to replace a busperson.

High morale has just the opposite effects and is the best thing that can happen in an enterprise. Napoleon claimed that 75 percent of his success on the battlefield was due to the high morale of his troops.

1. Write effective vision, mission and goals statements and ensure everyone knows them
2. Actively listen to your employees
3. Give a hand to your employees when appropriate
4. Treat employees fairly and consistently
5. Keep your employees informed
6. Involve and empower your employees
7. Use up-to-date and accurate job descriptions
8. Orient, train, and coach your employees
9. Formally evaluate employee performance at least twice yearly
10. Praise and reward your employees
11. Pay for performance
12. Institute a profit-sharing or other gain-sharing program for employees
13. Let your employees make as many of their own decisions as possible
14. Cross-train employees, rotate their positions, and have a career ladder and promote from within
15. Be able to perform the job you supervise
16. Manage your time
17. Be a good role model
18. Establish competitive and equitable pay rates
19. Offer a competitive benefit package suited to your employees
20. Provide a pleasant, safe, and clean work environment

FIGURE 14.3 Twenty ways to build a positive work climate. *Source:* Jay R. Schrock.

To build a positive work climate, you need to focus on these three areas: the individual, the job, and the supervisor. Figure 14.3 lists 20 ways to build a positive work climate. Let's look at some of the most important ways that you can make work enjoyable.

FOCUS: THE INDIVIDUAL

The starting point is your individual workers—one by one. The idea that everybody works for some one thing, like money, is no longer credible. Everybody is glad to have the paycheck, but whether they are willing to work hard for that money or for something else or for anything at all is what you want to determine. Because everybody is different, you are going to need an individual strategy of motivation for each person—not a formal program, just a special way of dealing with each one that brings out their best efforts and offers them the greatest personal satisfaction.

Getting to Know Your People

Getting to know your people takes an indirect approach. People are not going to open up to the boss if you sit down with them at the coffee break and ask them questions about what they want from their jobs. They will tell you what they think you want to hear, and they will probably feel uncomfortable about being quizzed. You may have hired them for one reason, but they probably come to work for altogether different reasons, which they may think is none of your business. They have taken the job as a vehicle for getting where or what they want, but that is a hidden agenda. For some people it is money, for some it is pride, for some it is status, for some it is something to do *until*. If you can find out what kind of satisfactions they are looking for, it will help you to motivate them.

You can learn about them best by observing them. How do they go about their work? How do they react to you, to other workers, to customers? What questions do they ask, or do they ask any? How do they move—quickly, slowly, freely, stiffly? How do they look as they speak or listen? Notice their gestures and facial expressions. What makes them light up? What makes them clam up? Pay special attention to what they

High morale helps keep employee turnover low. At this hotel the employee turnover rate is 23 percent per year.

tell you about themselves in casual conversation. This may be an entirely new approach for you, but people-watching is really quite interesting, and you can quickly become good at spotting clues.

> The key to deploying the five essential motivation steps for employers and employees are: First, clearly articulate goals and reasons. Second, involve people in finding solutions. Third, explain the rules of the game. Fourth, link people's personal goals with the organization's goals. Finally, move negative people off the team.
>
> *Source:* John Streleckly, "You Can Motivate Unmotivated People," *Restaurant Hospitality*, Vol. 88, Iss. 4, p. 66, April 2004.

Clues to what? Needs and desires, discontents and aspirations. Frustrations, drive, and achievement. Ability and performance, too, and whether performance is up to par for that job and whether this person has abilities the job does not call on. But primarily needs, desires, and responses, because these are the motivators you want to channel into high performance that will satisfy both you and them.

Observing your people has a purely practical purpose. You are not going to try to psychoanalyze them, probe for hidden motives, delve into what really makes them tick. You can't. That takes years of training you don't have, and a great deal of time you don't have either. Furthermore, you shouldn't. If you are wrong in your amateur analysis, your employees will consider you unjust, and if you are right, they will feel vulnerable—you know them too well. Either way it is going to interfere with motivation rather than improve it.

Your approach, in contrast, should be practical, pragmatic, and experimental; you could even call it superficial. You observe your people and get ideas of what you might do to motivate this or that person to perform better for you as well as get more personal satisfaction from the work. You try out an idea, and if this person does not respond, you try something else. What they respond to is what is important and what you have to work with. The personal whys—the inner needs—are simply clues that you sometimes use to reach the what-to-do.

Dealing with Security Needs

It is relatively easy to spot people with high security needs. They look and act anxious, uncertain, and tentative. They may be among those who ask you how to do everything, or they may be too scared even to ask. Fear and anxiety are demotivators; they reduce motivation. When security needs are not satisfied, people cannot function well at all; in fact, these people are among those who leave during the first few days on the job.

Here is where Maslow's theories come in handy. If you see that someone has a need for security and you can help that person satisfy that need, you ease that person along to a higher motivational level. To satisfy these needs, you do all the things that we have been recommending in earlier chapters. You tell them what to do and how to do it; you tell them exactly what you expect. You train them. All these things provide a reassuring structure to the work that protects them from the uncertainties of working. It reduces their mistakes and builds their motivation and confidence.

You let them know where they stand at all times. You support them with coaching and feedback and encouragement. You give them positive reinforcement for things they do right, and you retrain them to help them correct their mistakes. You do not solve their problems, you do not cuddle and coddle, you help *them* to do their jobs *themselves*.

You keep on making positive comments about their work even when they are fully trained and you are satisfied with their performance. It is natural for a supervisor to stop paying attention to a worker once things are going well, but even a short absence of approving comments can trigger doubt and uncertainty again in workers who are insecure. Recognition, even if it is only a big smile and a passing "Hey, keep up the good work!" is an affirmation that life on the job is, after all, not uncertain and threatening. Above all, you must avoid any use of fear as a motivator. This is the last thing that these people need.

Evaluate their work frequently, and give praise for things done right, especially for improvement of any sort. Use improvement to build confidence: Accentuate the achievement and the potential—"See how far you have come; see where you can go from here." Show them that you expect them to do well. Your confidence will give them confidence. And if you can build confidence, you may eventually activate self-motivation and aspiration. Satisfaction of primary needs allows these higher-level needs to emerge.

Dealing with Social Needs

Everybody has social needs (Maslow again). You may not think of work as being a place to satisfy them, but it often is. For many people a job fills the need to be with others, the need to be accepted, the need to belong. These are powerful needs. Often they will fall into Herzberg's category of hygiene factors: They cause dissatisfaction when they are unsatisfied, but they do not motivate when satisfied. But for some people they can be motivators, too.

For example, consider the homemaker who gets a job because she wants to talk to people who are more than three feet tall. If you hire her as a cashier or a switchboard operator, she probably won't be very good at it because this is not what she came to work for. But if you make her a desk clerk or a waitress or a sales rep where she can talk to people all day long, she could easily become a higher achiever.

Whether or not social needs can be turned into motivators, it is useful when people find such needs being satisfied on the job, both in terms of their individual development and in terms of the general work climate. People whose social needs are unmet may just not work very well, or they may even provoke trouble and conflict.

What can you do to help meet people's social needs? There are two specific needs you can work on, and it takes hardly any of your time. One is the *need for acceptance*. We have talked about this before: You build a person-to-person relationship and you treat each person as a unique individual who has dignity and worth. You respect their idiosyncrasies (unless they interfere with the work): you speak softly to Peter because that is what Peter responds to. You scream and yell at Paul because that is your unique way of relating to Paul and you both know it, and Paul will think he doesn't matter to you anymore if you treat him any other way.

You deal with each person differently, but you treat each according to the same standards, whether she is good-looking or plain, whether his mother is on welfare or owns the biggest bank in town. Each one is a person who has value, has worth, and you treat them all that way.

You also make it clear that you value each person's work and that it is important to the organization no matter how menial it is. The well-made bed, the properly washed salad greens, the sparkling-clean restroom all please customers; the crooked bedspread, the gritty salad, the empty tissue holder send customers away. This attention to detail can be as important to the success of the hotel or restaurant as the expertise of the sommelier or the masterpieces of the chef. You can make people feel that they are an essential part of the entire organization, that you need them, that they belong there. A sense of belonging may be your most powerful ally in the long run—and it helps the long run to happen.

This *need to belong* is the other social need that you can do a lot to satisfy. Things you should be doing anyway help to satisfy this need, such as making people feel comfortable in their jobs by training them, coaching them, telling them where they stand, evaluating their work frequently. Open communications also encourage belonging; people feel free to come to you with suggestions or problems. Keeping people informed about changes that affect them is a way of including them in what is going on—and if you leave anybody out you reduce that person to a nobody. You can also include people in discussions about the work, inviting their ideas, feelings, and reactions. If you can build a spirit of teamwork, that, too, will foster a sense of belonging.

One's peer group also nurtures belonging. You need to be aware of social relationships among your workers and to realize that these relationships are just as important as their relationship with you, and sometimes more so. Often, peer pressure is more influential than the boss is.

You need to have the group on your side—if it ever comes to taking sides—and that is best done through good relationships with each person. These people work under you, and they look at you as their boss. They expect you to be friendly and to sit down with them if they invite you, but they do not expect you to be one of the gang. In fact, your uninvited presence for more than a moment or two may act as a constraint to their socializing.

Groups and group socialization are a normal part of the job scene. Often, groups break into cliques, with different interests and sometimes rivalries. You should not try to prevent the formation of groups and cliques. But if competition between cliques begins to disrupt the work, you will have to intervene. You cannot let employee competition interfere with the work climate.

Rewarding Your Employees

Incentive pay, bonuses, and various kinds of nonmonetary rewards can be very effective motivators if they activate people's needs and desires or are related to their reason for working. One of the problems, of course, is that what motivates one person leaves another indifferent, yet to treat people fairly you have to have rewards of equal value for equal performance.

These methods of triggering motivation begin with the carrot principle of dangling a reward for good performance. When people need or want the reward, they will work hard in expectation of getting it. If they do not want the carrot, it has no effect.

Once the reward is achieved, the cycle must start again: The desire must be activated by the *expectation of reward*, as Herzberg points out. No expectation, no achievement, and performance slumps back to a nonreward level unless people begin to derive satisfaction from the achievement itself. However, there is no doubt that rewards are useful motivators. In many jobs the boring repetition of meaningless tasks precludes a sense of achievement that is fulfilling, and rewards may be the only resource you have for motivating.

Rewarding associates contributes to a positive work climate. Courtesy of The Cendant Corporation.

The entire system of rewards, both monetary and otherwise, must be worked out with care, not only for getting the maximum motivation but also for fairness in the eyes of the employees. The performance required to achieve the reward must be spelled out carefully, and the goal must be within reach of everyone. People must know ahead of time what the rewards are and must perceive them as fair or they will cause more dissatisfaction than motivation.

How do you make rewards into effective motivators if people's needs and desires are so different? Somebody with eight children to feed might work very hard for a money reward or the chance to work more overtime. Another person might outdo himself for an extra day of paid vacation. Still another would do almost anything for a reserved space in the parking lot right near the door with her name on it in great-big letters. Such rewards might be suitable prizes in an employee contest, with the winner being allowed to choose from among them.

You might get people involved by letting them suggest rewards (keeping the final decision to yourself). Any involvement increases the likelihood of sparking real motivation. Actually, any reward can be more than a carrot. It can be a recognition of achievement, of value, of worth to the company. It can build pride; it can generate self-esteem. It can also be a goal. Once employees earn a reward, if it gives them satisfaction, they will probably go for it again. Then you have activated motivation from within, with commitment to a person's own goal. And that, in miniature, is what successful on-the-job motivation is all about—fulfilling individual goals and company goals in the same process. The more both the employee's and the company's goals overlap, motivation is increased.

Developing Your Employees

Another way of maintaining a positive work climate is to help your people to become better at their jobs and to develop their potential. This may be one of the most critical things you do. A large percentage of the people in foodservice and hospitality enterprises are underemployed, and as managers we really do not utilize the skills and abilities of the people who work for us as fully as we could. Your goal should be to make all your people as competent as you can, because it makes your job easier, it makes you look better to your superiors, and it is good for your people.

You can develop your beginning workers through training, feedback, encouragement, and support, as well as by providing the right equipment and generally facilitating their work. By the way you deal with them, you can also give them a feeling of importance to the operation, a sense of their own worth, and a feeling of achievement and growth. Concrete recognition of improvement, whether it is an award, a reward, or merely a word of praise, can add to the pride of achievement.

If you have people with high potential, you should do all these things and more. You should try to develop their skills, utilize any talents you see, challenge them by asking for their input on the work, give them responsibilities, and open doors to advancement to the extent that you can. One thing is certain: If you have trained someone to take your place, it will be a lot easier for your company to promote you. But if none of your subordinates can fill your job, the company is less likely to move you up because it needs you where you are.

Developing your people also helps morale. It gives people that sense of moving forward that keeps them from going stale, marking time, moving on a treadmill. It is also important to your acceptance as a leader to have people feel that you are helping them to help themselves.

You develop your employees by involving them. Employees who are asked to influence what happens at work tend to develop a sense of ownership; this feeling of ownership breeds commitment. Employees can become effectively involved in many managerial activities, such as evaluating work methods, identifying problems, proposing suggestions, and deciding on a course of action. Your employees can tell you better than anyone else how their own jobs should be done.

For instance, McGuffey's Restaurants, a dinner-house chain based in North Carolina, asks for employee input on ways to improve service and also asks employees to elect representatives to an associate board at which employees concerns will be addressed. In some cases, when you involve your employees, you are actually empowering them. Empowering your employees means giving them additional responsibility and authority to do their jobs. Instead of employees feeling responsible for merely doing what they are told, they are given greater control over decisions about work. For example, in some restaurants, servers are empowered, or given the authority, to resolve customer complaints without management intervention. A server may decide, in response to a customer complaint, not to charge the customer for a menu item that was not satisfactory.

At McGuffey's Restaurants, the company gives employees their own business cards, which they can use to invite potential customers in for free food or beverages. The company even lets employees run the restaurants two days a year, during which they can change the menu and make other changes.

Following are some guidelines for empowering your employees:

- Give your employees your trust and respect, two essential ingredients for empowerment of employees.

- Determine exactly what you want employees to be empowered to do.

- Train your employees in those new areas. Be clear as to what you want them to do.

- Create an environment in which exceptions to rules, particularly when they involve customer satisfaction, are permissible.

- Allow employees to make mistakes without being criticized or punished. Instead, view these times as opportunities to educate your employees.

- Reward empowered employees who take risks, make good decisions, and take ownership.

Finally, you should also continue to develop yourself. Chances are that you won't have much time for reading and studying, but you should keep pace with what is going on in other parts of your company and in the industry as a whole—read trade publications and attend trade association meetings. You can also watch yourself as you practice your profession, evaluating your own progress and learning from your mistakes. Make a habit of thinking back on the decisions you have made. What would have happened if you had done something differently? Can you do it better next time?

FOCUS: THE JOB

Providing an Attractive Job Environment

The worker's job environment includes not only the physical environment and working conditions but the other workers, the hours, rate of pay, benefits, and company policies and administration. You may recognize these as *hygiene* or *maintenance factors*.

As Herzberg pointed out, such job factors do not motivate. But any of them can cause dissatisfaction and demotivation, which can interfere with productivity and increase turnover. So it behooves the supervisor to remove as many dissatisfiers as possible. To the extent that you have control, you can provide good physical working conditions: satisfactory equipment in good working order; adequate heating, cooling, and lighting; comfortable employee lounges; plenty of parking; and so on. You can see that working hours and schedules meet workers' needs as closely as possible. If you have anything to say about it, you can see that wages and benefits are as good as those of your competitors or better, so that your people will not be lured away by a better deal than you can give.

There is not much that you can do about company policy and administration if it is rigid and high-control, except to work within its limits, stick up for your people, and do things your own way within your sphere of authority. We will assume that the management philosophy is not based on fear and punishment or you would not be there yourself.

Providing a Safe and Secure Work Environment

It is a universal human need to want to be safe and secure. As a supervisor, one of your top priorities is making sure that the workplace is safe and secure for both workers and guests. Safety hazards abound in a hospitality operation: There are cleaning chemicals that can burn your skin, slicers that can cut more than bologna when you're not watching, heavy boxes to lift that can wrench your back, computer keyboards that can cause numbness in your hands, wet floors that you can go sliding across, and poorly lit stairs that you can fly down (with an order of hot soup in your hands).

After negotiating the numerous safety hazards, keep your eyes open because the back door has been left wide open. Before a thief sees this wonderful opportunity, slam that door shut, and lock it, then find out who left the door open in the first place.

Safety hazards in hospitality operations range from knives put in a kitchen sink full of water to hazardous chemicals housekeepers used to clean hotel rooms. Cuts, falls, fires, and electric shock are all examples of accidents that can and do happen. They occur because employees are fooling around, rushing, being careless, working under the influence, not paying attention, or overdoing it. Accidents sometimes also occur because employees are ignorant or just feel that accidents are inevitable, so they don't bother trying to prevent them.

Profile

RICK NARGI

Courtesy of Rick Nargi

An amusing story about Rick is that when he was being considered for his present position as general manager for Sodexho, his area manager went to Rick's account and asked some of the employees, "Was Rick a good manager?" "The best we've ever had," was the response. Then the area manager remembered that he had also been a manager there!

When asked what makes him such a good supervisor/manager, Rick replies: "My philosophy is simple. If it's good for the guest, we'll do it." Rick's leadership style is to lead by example. He finds that employees respect the fact that he works hand in hand with employees—training as he goes by showing and then letting employees do the task, with objective feedback. In this way, his employees know that he knows how to do all their jobs.

Rick develops employees to think for themselves, based on standards that are set for the operation. He empowers employees to make guests happy. For example, if someone asks for a tortilla, and although they are not on the line, the employee goes and gets one instead of saying, "I'll have to ask the manager." In an effort to make employees happy, Rick has open communications with his employees. He feels that if employees are happy, then guests will also be happy.

The qualities and characteristics that Rick feels make for a great supervisor/manager are:

- To be multitasked
- To have a high tolerance for stress and pressure

- To maintain a calm demeanor

- To be able to focus on detail

- To be friendly and outgoing

- To be a good listener and take an interest in employees' families during break times, but not becoming their personal friend or going out drinking with them

- To build up a diverse culture in your team

- To be caring and dedicated

In conclusion, Rick says that his biggest challenge is to recruit and retain good employees. But he is always optimistic and thinks about the "big picture" of keeping guests happy.

The foodservice sector of the hospitality industry has fortunately become a safer place to work. According to the Bureau of Labor Statistics, the number of nonfatal on-the-job injuries to employees of eating and drinking establishments has been steadily decreasing.

Besides causing pain and suffering to the injured employee and incurring the cost of lost work time, there are other direct and indirect costs to consider when an accident occurs.

- Lost time and productivity of uninjured workers who stop work to help the injured employee or simply watch and talk about the incident (Productivity normally decreases for a number of hours, but if morale is negatively affected, it could be much longer.)

- Lost business during the time that the operation is not fully functioning

- Lost business due to damaged reputation

- Overtime costs to get the operation fully functioning again

- The costs to clean, repair, and/or replace any equipment, food, or supplies damaged in the accident

- Cost to retrain the injured employee upon return to work

- Increased premiums for workers' compensation

- In the case of a lawsuit, legal fees and possible award to the injured employee

Of course, not only employees become involved in accidents; guests do also.

In 1971, the Occupational Safety and Health Administration (OSHA) was created as an agency within the U.S. Department of Labor. Its purpose is to "assure so far as possible every working man and woman in the Nation safe and healthful working conditions and to preserve our human resources." OSHA sets mandatory job safety and health standards, encourages both employers and employees to decrease hazards in the workplace, conducts compliance inspections, issues citations in cases of non-compliance, and asks for record keeping of injuries. OSHA also requires you, as the supervisor, to train your employees as to any known hazards in their work area.

Safety programs are common in hospitality operations as a way to increase safety awareness and to prevent accidents. Safety programs usually include the following components.

1. Safety policies and procedures
2. Employee training
3. Safety committee
4. Safety inspections
5. Accident reporting and investigation
6. Constant supervision

Supervisors themselves are very involved in the safety program. After all, you oversee the day-to-day monitoring and enforcement of safety rules, report and correct unsafe conditions, train and retrain employees, maintain safety records, check that the first-aid kit is well stocked, and act as a role model. If you are safety-minded, you are more likely to create an environment where safety is practiced and respected.

Safety policies and procedures state what behaviors are expected from employees in order to prevent accidents, what safety training employees receive, how often safety inspections occur, and what to do when accidents happen. Figure 14.4 is a sample safety policy and procedure regarding safety inspections.

Policies and procedures form the basis for your employee training program. Safety training should start at orientation and this information should be put into the employee handbook. The accident rate for employees is higher during their first month of employment than for any subsequent month. Safety training should be repeated and updated at least once a year for all employees. At the end of training, employees need to be evaluated on what they know, and rewarded or recognized for

Policy: In order to maintain adequate safety to meet or exceed the standards for all regulatory agencies, the General Manager will perform monthly safety audits of the restaurant.

Procedures:

1. At the beginning of each month, the General Manager asks two supervisors and two employees to set a time to do a safety inspection of the entire facility.
2. The Safety Inspection Team uses the "Restaurant Safety Survey" form to inspect the facility, noting problems as appropriate.
3. Copies of the survey are given to the supervisors, who are given two weeks to resolve any problems noted and to document this on the survey form.
4. The General Manager reviews the returned surveys and takes any additional appropriate action. The results of the survey are discussed with the Owner.
5. Reports are saved for three years.

FIGURE 14.4 Policy and procedures for safety inspections.

working safely. Figure 14.5 is a page from a training plan on kitchen safety rules.

Safety committees are often formed within hospitality operations. They meet periodically to discuss safety matters. The safety committee is often involved in reviewing data on the number and types of accidents to date, inspecting the facility, suggesting new and revised policies and procedures, and overseeing safety training.

As a supervisor, you may periodically be in charge of a safety inspection to check for and correct any unsafe conditions, such as a slicer's frayed electric cord. In addition to managers and supervisors, employees can take part in the inspection process to encourage them to take a more active role in preventing accidents.

When accidents do happen, regardless of how minor the injury appears to be at the time, it is the supervisor's responsibility to report them. Early reporting of all the facts works to the advantage of all concerned. The supervisor can move quickly to correct the unsafe condition that caused an accident, the injured person can receive prompt and effective medical care if needed, and in the case of an employee who can't return to work immediately, he or she can receive workers' compensation benefits without unnecessary delay. Also, the company can make preparations in the event of pending legal action such as a lawsuit.

The fact that all accidents should be properly reported cannot be overemphasized. In many cases, incidents that appear trivial develop into major hazards at a later time.

> **Kitchen Safety Checklist**
> **Preventing Cuts**
>
> 1. Know how to operate equipment
> 2. Pay attention when using sharp equipment
> 3. Use guards when provided on equipment
> 4. Use tampers to push food into equipment, not your hands!
> 5. Turn equipment off before adjusting
> 6. No loose sleeves, ties or dangling jewelry should be by equipment
> 7. Use knives carefully
> 8. Carry dishes and glassware carefully
> 9. Sweep up broken glass
> 10. Use a special container to dispose of broken glass, dishes, and other sharp objects
> 11. Remove nails and staples in shipping cartons and crates, and wear gloves
> 12. Remove can lids entirely from cans and put back into empty cans for disposal

FIGURE 14.5 Page from a training plan on kitchen safety rules.

If accurate and complete facts are not recorded at the time of the accident, it could be difficult to compile information should the incident develop into a claim against the company.

Implementing the Hazard Communication Standard

Most U.S. businesses must comply with the Hazard Communication Standard issued by OSHA. The purpose of this standard is to give employees the right to know what chemicals they are working with, what the risks or hazards are, and what they can do to limit the risks. You probably know of a number of hazardous materials in your workplace, such as all-purpose cleaners, detergents, oven cleaners, degreasers, and pesticides. These products often present physical hazards, such as exploding or burning, and/or health hazards, such as irritating or burning skin.

The Hazard Communication Standard requires employers to do the following:

1. Post a list of hazardous substances found in your operation.

2. Post Material Safety Data Sheets (MSDSs). For each hazardous product you have, the manufacturer has an MSDS that explains what the product is, why it is hazardous, and how you can use it safely.

1. **Do** know where the Material Safety Data Sheets are posted and read them.
2. **Do** read the labels of all products before you use them.
3. **Do** follow the directions for proper storage, handling, and use for all chemicals you use. Measure chemicals carefully.
4. **Do** ask your supervisor any questions or express any concern you may have about a certain product.
5. **Do** know how to call for medical help in case of an emergency.
6. **Do not** ever mix chemicals together.
7. **Do not** store chemicals in unmarked containers. If chemicals are transferred to different containers, each new container must be labeled with the contents and hazards.
8. **Do not** store chemicals in or close to food storage, preparation, or serving areas.
9. **Do not** leave aerosol spray containers near heat or spray close to an open flame or your eyes.
10. **Do not** dispose of any empty chemical container until you have checked the label for the proper procedure.

FIGURE 14.6 Do's and don'ts of safe chemical handling.

3. Explain to employees how to read and use the MSDS and also the labels on hazardous products.

4. Train employees how to use hazardous chemicals properly and what to do in case of an emergency.

Basic tips on safely handling hazardous chemicals are given in Figure 14.6.

Guest Safety

You may think that guests face far fewer hazards than workers do, but even though they are far away from deep-fat fryers and slicers, guests still fracture bones slipping on your stairs, get serious burns from spilled hot coffee, die from allergic reactions to certain foods, and get foodborne illnesses. Not paying attention to guest safety can cost your operation hundreds of thousands and even millions of dollars in lawsuits.

As a supervisor you don't want to see guests get hurt any more than you want employees to get hurt. So what can you do about it? You are already involved in the operation's safety program as just described, so you know your safety policies and procedures, train employees, take part in safety committee meetings and/or safety inspections, report accidents, and supervise with safety uppermost in your mind. Many guest safety concerns revolve around the following:

- *Slips, trips, and falls.* Steps are most often the culprit behind slips, trips, and falls. Stairs and steps, both inside and outside, should be well lit, covered with a nonskid surface, and have handrails. Wet floors cause their share of problems as well. Try to mop during off-hours and be sure to use "Wet Floor" signs and possibly even rope off the area. Guest parking areas should be clear of trash and free of ice in the winter.

- *Burns.* Hot beverages, such as coffee, can be a danger when not handled carefully. Your operation may have special hot beverage temperatures and rules to prevent burns. Guests should always be warned about hot plates.

- *Food allergies.* Some people experience a severe response when they eat certain foods to which they are allergic. Their throat swells up to the point where air can't get down to the lungs. This type of reaction, called anaphylactic shock, can kill. Two things can be done to prevent this problem: have a policy and procedure that tells servers how to handle a guest's question about a dish containing an allergic ingredient, and stock the first-aid kit with "Epi Pens," a medication that suppresses anaphylactic shock symptoms (managers must be trained to use it).

- *Foodborne illness.* Foodborne illnesses make millions of Americans sick each year and kill almost 10,000 people. High-quality sanitation standards and well-supervised procedures are needed to prevent outbreaks.

First aid is emergency treatment given before regular medical services can be provided. To protect both guests and employees who fall ill and are hurt, it is important to have at least one person per shift trained in first aid and in cardiopulmonary resuscitation (CPR), a procedure used in case of cardiac arrest (the heart stops beating).

Security Concerns

According to the National Restaurant Association Educational Foundation, the purpose of a security program is to protect the belongings or assets of your facility (including the building, grounds, equipment, furnishings, food, beverages, supplies, cash, employees, and guests) from incidents such as employee theft, violent crime, and burglary. Much of your work as a supervisor involves security, from doing reference checks on applicants to following cash-handling procedures, restricting access to keys, and handling a security emergency such as theft. To protect yourself, your employees and guests, and your company from damage, familiarize yourself with all security policies and procedures, and more important, enforce them without hesitation.

Check Your Knowledge

1. Safety programs are common in hospitality operations as a way to increase safety awareness and to prevent accidents. What do these safety programs include?

2. What is the purpose of the Hazard Communication Standard?

Putting the Right Person in the Right Job

If you get to know your workers, you are in a good position to figure out what jobs are right for what people. People with high security needs may do very well in routine jobs: Once they have mastered the routine they will have the satisfaction and security of doing it well. Putting them in a server's job would be a disaster. Putting people-oriented workers in routine behind-the-scenes jobs might be a disaster, too.

Many cooks enjoy preparing good things for people to eat. Even when they must follow other people's standardized recipes, there is the satisfaction of being able to tell exactly when a steak is medium rare, of making a perfect omelet, of arranging a beautiful buffet platter. Bartenders often enjoy putting on a show of their pouring prowess. These people are in the right jobs.

Pride in one's work can be a powerful motivator. Some people get a great sense of achievement from tearing into a room left in chaos by guests and putting it in order again, leaving it clean and inviting for the next guest. They, too, are in the right jobs. The professional dishwasher we have mentioned several times obviously took great pride in his work and wore his occupation as a badge of honor. He belonged in his job, and it belonged to him, and in a curious way it probably satisfied all levels of needs for him.

Making the Job Interesting and Challenging

People do their best work when something about the work involves their interest and stimulates their desire to do it well. People who like what they are doing work hard at it of their own accord. People who don't like their jobs drag their heels, watch the clock, do as little as they can get by with, and are called lazy by the boss.

Different things about the work turn different people on. Some are stimulated by working with guests: They get a kick out of making them welcome, serving them well,

Making the job interesting and challenging is a key part of a supervisor's job.

pleasing them, amusing them, turning an irate guest into a fan by helping to solve a problem. Some people are miserable dealing with guests and enjoy a nice routine job with no people hassles where they can put their accuracy and skill to work straightening out messy records and putting things in order. Some people like jobs where there is always some new problem to solve; others hate problems and like to exercise their special skills and turn out products they are proud of.

What these people all have in common is that something about the content of their job both stimulates and satisfies them. Stated in theoretical terms, it satisfies their higher needs, those related to self-esteem and self-fulfillment. Specifically, people work hard at jobs that give them opportunity for achievement, for responsibility, for growth and advancement, for doing work they enjoy doing for its own sake.

There are two ideas here that you as a supervisor can use in motivating your people. One is to put people in jobs that are right for them as just discussed. The other is to enrich people's jobs to include more of the motivating elements. Of course, there are limits to what you can do, but the more you can move in this direction, the more likely you are to create a positive work climate.

Workers who are bored are underemployed: The job does not make use of their talents, their education, and their abilities. They are only there *until*—until they find a more interesting and challenging job. Not only will you have to train their replacements sooner or later, but you are not making use of abilities right now that could contribute a great deal to your department and to the entire organization. Furthermore, as we said in Chapter 11, supervisors have an obligation to develop their people.

You cannot move people into better jobs unless jobs are available, but you can look for ways to enrich their present jobs by building some motivators into them. This does not mean asking them to take on additional, but similar, tasks—this is called *job loading*. Job enrichment means shifting the way things are done so as to provide more responsibility for one's own work and more opportunity for achievement, for recognition, for learning, for growth.

You might start by giving people more responsibility for their own work. Relax your control; stop watching every move they make. Let them try out their own methods of achieving results as long as they do not run counter to the standards and procedures that are an essential part of the job. In other words, decrease controls and increase accountability. This must all be discussed between you, and there must be a clear understanding, as in any delegation agreement.

From there you can experiment with other forms of job enrichment. You can delegate some of your own tasks. You can rearrange the work in the jobs you are enriching to add more authority and responsibility for the workers. You can give new and challenging assignments. You can assign special tasks that require imagination and develop skills.

If, for example, you find that you have creative people in routine kitchen jobs, let them try planning new plate layouts or garnishes. If someone who majored in English is working as a payroll clerk, let her try her hand at writing menu fliers or notices for the employee bulletin board or stories for the company magazine. Look for people's hidden talents and secret ambitions and use them, and keep in mind reporting them when more suitable jobs are available.

Another idea that is being tried out in a number of industries is replacing the assembly-line method of dividing the work into minute, repetitious parts by giving a worker or group of workers responsibility for an entire unit of work or complete product, including quality control. Is there a way of avoiding assembly-line sandwich-making that would give each worker or a group of workers complete responsibility for one kind of sandwich, letting them work out the most efficient method? Could you give a cleaning team responsibility for making up an entire corridor of rooms, dividing the tasks as they see fit?

There are many jobs in which the work is going to be dull no matter what you do. But even in these a shift in responsibility and point of view can work near-miracles. A concerted program of job enrichment for cleaning and janitorial services carried out at Texas Instruments is an example of what can be done with routine low-skill tasks. These services were revamped to give everyone a role in the planning and control of their work, although the work itself remained the same. Extensive training embodying Theory Y principles was given to supervisors and working foremen, while worker training included orientation in company goals and philosophy and their part in the overall operation. A team-oriented, goal-oriented, problem-solving approach encouraged worker participation in reorganizing, simplifying, and expediting the work.

Increased responsibility, participation, and pride of achievement generated high commitment as well as better ways of doing the work. In the first year's trial the cleanliness level improved from 65 percent to 85 percent, the number of people required dropped from 120 to 71, and the quarterly turnover rate dropped from 100 percent to 9.8 percent. The annual savings to the company was a six-figure total. The average educational level of these workers was fourth or fifth grade, proving that Theory Y management is applicable all up and down the scale.

A major program such as this takes a long time to develop and implement and is out of the reach of the first-time supervisor working alone. But it shows what can be done when dedicated leadership and enlightened company policies activate employee motivation.

Any job enrichment effort is likely to produce a drop in productivity at first as workers get used to changes and new responsibilities. It takes a coaching approach to begin with and a lot of support from the boss. It is also essential to initiate changes slowly and to plan them with care. Too much responsibility and freedom too soon may be more than some workers can handle, either out of inexperience or because of the insecurities involved. Again, it is a situation in which your own sensitivity to your workers is a key ingredient.

FOCUS: THE SUPERVISOR

Ultimately, it is the supervisor who holds the keys to a positive work climate. It is not only the steps he takes, the things she does to spark motivation; it is the way that supervisors themselves approach their own tasks and responsibilities—their own performance of their own jobs. If they themselves are highly motivated and enthusiastic about their work, their people are likely to be motivated, too. If they have high expectations of themselves and their people, and if they believe in themselves and their people, the people will generally come through for them. It is motivation by contagion, by expectation, by example.

In some operations the manager conveys a sense of excitement, a feeling that *anything is possible, so let's go for it!* You find it sometimes in the individual entrepreneur or the manager of a new unit in a larger company. If the manager is up, the people are up, too, and it is an exciting place to work. It is not unusual for people who have worked for such managers to end up as entrepreneurs themselves, putting their own excitement to work in an enterprise of their own.

Tony's Restaurant in St. Louis is a case in point. Owner Vincent Bommarito's enthusiasm, high standards, and involvement with employee development and performance, coupled with an anything-is-possible approach, have spawned at least 20 restaurants owned and operated by former employees. Of course, there are the added incentives of ownership in such cases, but it really begins with the excitement and enthusiasm of the original restaurant experience.

At the opposite extreme, supervisors who are not happy in their jobs, who are not themselves motivated, will have unmotivated workers who are faithful reflections of themselves—management by example again. You cannot motivate others successfully if you are not motivated yourself. And if you are not, you need a change of attitude or a change of job.

If you give 75 percent of your effort to your job, your people will give 25 to 50 percent. If you put forth a 100-percent effort, your people will give you 110 percent. If you expect the best of people, they will give you their best. If you expect poor performance, poor performance is what you will get. If you tell people they can do a certain thing and they believe in you, they can do it and they will. If you tell them it is beyond their ability, they won't even try.

This contagious kind of motivation can run back and forth between supervisor and workers; they can motivate you if you will let them. If you have good relationships with your people, they can spark your interest with new ideas about the work. They can help you solve problems. Their enthusiasm for the work will sustain your own motivation in the face of setbacks and disappointments. When a "we" attitude prevails, it builds belonging, involvement, and commitment.

Setting a Good Example

Whether you are aware of it or not, you set an example for your workers; they are going to copy what you do. The psychologist's term for this is role model. If you expect the best work from your people, you've got to give your best work to your job. If you give 100 percent of your time and effort and enthusiasm, chances are that your workers will give you 110 percent. But if they see you giving about 75 percent and hear you groaning about your problems, they will give you only 25 to 50 percent of their effort. So if you want a fair day's work from your people, give a fair day's work to them: management by example, it is sometimes called.

Giving your best means keeping your best side out all the time. Everybody has a good side and a bad side, and most of us are vulnerable to a certain few things that can turn that bad side out and cause us to lose our cool. This is disastrous when you are a role model, particularly if you are supervising people who deal with customers. If you lose your temper with a group of workers and shout at them, they are going to carry the echo of your voice and the feelings it arouses in them right into the hotel lobby or the dining room or the hospital floor. They are going to be impatient and hostile and heedless of the customers' needs. And there goes the training you have given them in customer relations.

Your good side is as influential as your bad side. If you want your people to treat customers courteously and serve them well, treat your workers courteously and well. If bad moods are contagious, so are good moods. Enthusiasm is contagious. If you would like your workers to enjoy their work, be enthusiastic yourself. Is that a big order? Sometimes. But if you can do it, it works.

Set your sights high; expect the best of your workers. If you expect their best, they will usually give you their best if you approach the subject positively. If you show them you believe in them and have confidence in their ability to do the job, if you cheer them on, so to speak, they will attach the same value to their performance that you do. They will take pride in their work and in their own achievements. On the other hand, if you suddenly tell them to improve their work, without warning and in a critical way, implying that they are slackers and don't measure up, they are likely to resent the criticism and resist the demand.

Establishing a Climate of Honesty

A positive work climate requires a climate of honesty. We have talked about honesty as one of the things that workers expect of the boss. It means that you are honest with them when you talk to them about their performance and their potential and their achievements and mistakes. It means that you keep your promises and give credit where credit is due. It means that you do not cheat, lie, or steal from the company: you do not take food home from the kitchen or booze from the bar, you do not take money from customers in return for a better room or a better table. You are a role model and you do not do these things, not only because they are unethical, but also because you want your workers to be honest; they are going to imitate you. Management by example again.

You do not say one thing and do another. Nothing confuses a worker more than a supervisor who gives good advice but sets a bad example. You are consistent and fair. You do not manipulate; you are open and aboveboard; you can be trusted.

A climate of honesty encourages the growth of loyalty. If you are loyal to the company that employs you and are honest and fair and open with your people, they will develop loyalty to both you and the company. If you put down the company, you destroy your entire work climate because your workers will begin to believe that the company is a lousy place. If you feel like running down the company now and then, keep it to yourself. If you feel like that all the time, get out. You cannot do a good job as supervisor with those feelings bottled up inside.

KEY POINTS

1. Employees want their supervisor to be qualified to supervise, be experienced, take charge, treat people fairly and equally, communicate, and treat people as human beings.

2. Motivation is the "why" of human behavior.

3. There are various theories of motivation: Use fear (McGregor's Theory X); combine fear with incentives (carrot-and-stick motivation); give money (economic person theory); give them consideration (human relations or social person theory, Maslow's hierarchy of needs); satisfy employee work needs, such as a need for growth or achievement (McGregor's Theory Y); and give positive reinforcement when a worker does something right (behavior modification).

4. Factors that may limit your use of motivational techniques include the boring nature of many jobs, company management policies, the extent of your authority and resources, the employees themselves, and the constant time pressures.

5. A positive work climate is one in which employees can and will work productively.

6. Morale is a group spirit surrounding getting a job done.

7. In order to build a positive work climate, you need to focus on the individual, the job, and yourself (the supervisor) by getting to know your people, dealing with security and social needs, rewarding and developing your people, providing an attractive job environment, providing a safe and secure work environment, making the job interesting and challenging, setting a good example, and establishing a climate of honesty.

8.   Besides causing pain and suffering to the injured employee and the cost of lost work time, there are other direct and indirect costs to consider when an accident occurs, such as lost business and possibly a lawsuit.

9.   OSHA sets mandatory job safety and health standards, encourages both employers and employees to decrease hazards in the workplace, conducts compliance inspections, issues citations in cases of noncompliance, and asks for record keeping of injuries.

10. Safety programs are common in hospitality operations as a way to increase safety awareness and to prevent accidents. They usually include the following components: safety policies and procedures, employee training, safety committee, safety inspections, accident reporting and investigation, and constant supervision. Supervisors are very involved in the safety program.

11. The purpose of the Hazard Communication Standard issued by OSHA is to give employees the right to know what chemicals they are working with, what the risk or hazards are, and what they can do to limit the risks. Supervisors must post Material Safety Data Sheets and train employees how to use MSDS and labels so that hazardous chemicals can be used safely.

12. Some of the concerns for guest safety revolve around slips and falls, burns, food allergies, and foodborne illness. Appropriate policies and procedures, employee training, and constant supervision are essential to ensure guest safety.

13. To protect both guests and employees who fall ill or become hurt, it is important to have at least one person per shift trained in first aid and in cardiopulmonary resuscitation.

14. Security programs are involved with preventing theft and other unlawful acts within a company.

KEY TERMS

anaphylactic shock	hierarchy of needs	Occupational Safety and Health Administration
behavior modification	hygiene factors	
cardiopulmonary resuscitation (CPR)	job enrichment	positive reinforcement
	maintenance factors	role model
dissatisfiers	management by example	safety committees
economic person theory	Material Safety Data Sheets	safety programs
empowering	morale	security program
first aid	motivation	self-actualization
Hazard Communication Standard	motivators	social person

REFERENCE

1. Joseph W. Weiss, *Organizational Behavior and Change: Managing Diversity, Cross Cultural Dynamics, and Ethics*. Minneapolis: West, 1996.   As cited in Charles R. Greer and Richard W. Plunket, *Supervision: Diversity and Teams in the Workplace*. Upper Saddle River, NJ: Prentice Hall, 2003, p. 234.

DEVELOPING PERFORMANCE STANDARDS⋆

Picture a scared young employee named Joe reporting to work in a big hotel kitchen on his first job. The day's work is in full swing, nobody pays any attention to him, and he has trouble even finding Chef Paul to report for duty. When he finally finds him,

---

⋆ Authored by Jack E. Miller, John R. Walker, and Karen Eich Drummond.

Joe has to follow him around to tell him he is the new cook's helper. Paul tells him to go over and help Roger.

Roger is making salads and he tells Joe to go to the cooler and get another crate of romaine. Joe doesn't know what a cooler is, or where it is, or what romaine is. He feels like heading for home. Joe doesn't know what his job is. Roger knows that Joe is supposed to be his helper, but it doesn't occur to Roger to tell Joe what that means. Even Chef Paul doesn't think to tell Joe what his duties are; he assumes that what Roger will tell him to do is all that is needed.

Many operations are as casual and disorganized as this. A supervisor can quickly go crazy trying to run such a department because things will constantly go wrong and the chief management activity will be coping with this or that crisis. Fortunately, there are ways of bringing order out of this kind of chaos by defining each job and telling people what it is and how to do it.

One of the most useful tools for sorting out this kind of confusion is a job description that incorporates performance standards. Once you start to grasp these concepts and learn how to use them, they will become some of the most useful devices in your entire supervisory repertoire.

In this chapter we explain how to develop job descriptions and performance standards and examine their use in standardizing routine jobs. It will help you to:

- Define *job analysis* and describe the process for creating one.
- Explain the importance of defining jobs clearly and telling employees the what, how, and how-wells of their jobs.
- Define *performance standard* and list several examples of performance standards that might be used in the hospitality industry.
- Write a job description using performance standards.
- Describe how performance standards can be used to develop a system of managing employees and their work.
- Explain why some performance standard systems succeed and others fail.

When we start to discuss job descriptions there are many related terms that come up, such as position, job analysis, job specification, and job evaluation. Before beginning this chapter, let's define some of these terms.

A position consists of duties and responsibilities performed by one employee. For example, in an operation there are four cook positions occupied by four employees, yet each of them has only one job or job classification, that of *cook*. A job is a group of positions with the same duties and responsibilities. It is the entirety of the work, the sum total of what a person is paid to do. Other common hospitality jobs include server, housekeeper, and front desk clerk.

Job analysis is the process that tries to present a picture of how the world of work looks for a specific job. A job analyst determines the content of a given job by breaking it down into units (work sequences) and identifying the tasks that make up each unit. For instance, for a cashier, there are a number of tasks or steps involved in ringing up sales. The primary purpose of job analysis is to form the basis of the job description.

The job description describes what the job is as a whole. It explains what the employee is supposed to do, *how* to perform job duties, and *how well* they are to be done. As such, it describes a fair day's work and sets the performance standards. The job description also explains the context of the job (or the conditions in which the work takes place), including the factors of working conditions (often hot and steamy) and the social environment (hopefully, warm and friendly).

The job specification spells out the qualifications that a person must have in order to get the job. Qualifications often fall into the following areas: knowledge, skills and abilities, work experience, education, and training.

Job evaluation is the process of examining the responsibilities and difficulties of each job in order to determine which jobs are worth more than others. Job evaluation is used primarily to determine which jobs should pay more than others. There are several ways to perform job evaluation.

Before discussing job descriptions, it is important first to talk about analyzing a job.

JOB ANALYSIS

Every job in the hospitality industry or in a managed services setting includes several distinct work segments or units of work. For example, the job of server in a restaurant includes taking orders, serving food, serving wine, and so on. Each of these is a separate unit of the work that, when combined, comprise a job. Figure 15.1 shows a typical list of units of work for a server. You will see that our list includes such units as dress and grooming, sanitation, and guest relations, which are not true work sequences but are, nevertheless, critical activities in the server's job. They require the setting of standards, training, and evaluation just as the actual work sequences do. Such units appear in other jobs as well, and the same standards will apply in each case.

Each unit consists of a number of tasks—perhaps 5, 10, 20, or 100 things that the server has to do in carrying out the work of that unit. A task is an identifiable activity that constitutes a skill or activity necessary to complete a unit of the job. For example, what are the tasks performed in taking an order? Figure 15.2 lists the tasks in order of

---

SERVER JOB UNITS

1. Stock service station.
2. Set tables.
3. Greet guests.
4. Explain menu to customers.
5. Take food and beverage orders and complete guest check.
6. Pick up order and complete plate preparation.
7. Serve food.
8. Recommend wines and serve them.
9. Total and present check.
10. Perform side work.
11. Operate equipment.
12. Meet dress and grooming standards.
13. Observe sanitation procedures and requirements.
14. Maintain good customer relations.
15. Maintain desired check average.

FIGURE 15.1 Example of job analysis: breakdown of one job classification into units (page from a procedures manual for one operating unit).

performance. You may have trouble at first deciding what is a unit and what is a task that is part of a unit. Is *explains menu* a separate unit or is it part of *takes order*? The line between unit and task is fluid at times, and you could go either way. You can even set it up both as a separate unit and as a task in another unit.

Once you have a list of tasks or procedural steps for each unit, you have the complete description for that job (Figure 15.3): the entirety of the work, the sum total of what each person in that job is paid to do, the fair day's work.

The Uses of Job Analysis

Job analysis examines the content and relative importance of the different job duties and responsibilities. This information helps companies comply with government

---

TASKS IN ONE UNIT

Job classification: Server

Unit of work: Takes food and beverage orders

Tasks performed:

1. On guest check, numbers seats at tables

2. Asks each guest in turn what he or she wants and records it following the appropriate seat number

3. Uses correct abbreviations

4. Asks for all "Choice of" selections and records on check

5. Suggests additional items such as appetizer, soup, salad, beverage, wine, specials

6. Turns in order to kitchen

7. Completes guest check with prices

FIGURE 15.2 Example of task analysis: these tasks make up one unit of the server job (page from a procedures manual for one operating unit).

regulations and defend their actions in the event of legal challenges that allege unfairness or discrimination. As we shall see in Chapter 16, the standard defense against a charge of discrimination is that the contested decision (to hire, to give a raise, to terminate) was made for job-related reasons. Job analysis provides the documentation for such a defense.[1] For instance:

The owner of a fast-food restaurant who pays an assistant manager a weekly salary (without any overtime pay) may be able to defend himself from charges of an overtime pay violation with a job analysis proving that the assistant manager job is exempt

A well-written job description clearly defines the essential functions of a job that help to determine a job's worth in an organization and form the basis of a sound (read: defensible) wage and salary structure.

Source: "Why Job Descriptions Are so Necessary for Your Payroll Staff," *IOMA's Payroll Manager's Report*, Vol. 03, No. 4, p. 5, April 2003.

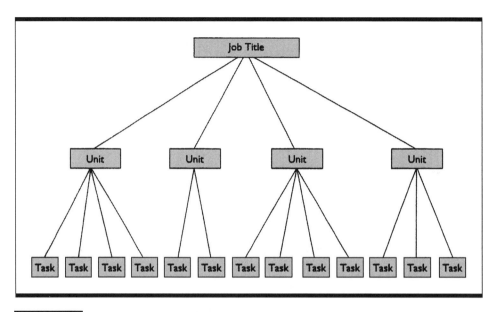

FIGURE 15.3 Anatomy of job classification. This diagram represents the content of an entire job. Numbers of units and tasks vary with the job and often from one enterprise to another. The sum of all the parts represents the total work requirements for that job.

from the overtime provisions of the Fair Labor Standards Act. The owner can prove this by showing that most of the job duties and responsibilities involve supervision and directing others rather than preparing food and providing service to guests.[2] Job analysis is also helpful in recruitment and selection, performance appraisal, compensation and training.

Now let's see how we use units of work and tasks in writing job descriptions.

JOB DESCRIPTION

There are five major reasons for low productivity and high turnover among people working at routine hospitality jobs:

1.   Workers don't know what they are supposed to be doing.

2.   They don't know how to do what they are supposed to be doing.

3.   They don't know how well they are doing what they are supposed to be doing.

4.   The supervisor has not given them any direction, help, or support.

5.   The workers have a poor relationship with the supervisor, largely for the first four reasons.

Do's when writing job descriptions

- Make sure that the requirements listed in the job description support the essential functions.

- Include a statement that allows supervisors to assign other duties as necessary.

- Avoid vague, generalized statements.

- List all the knowledge, skills, and abilities necessary to perform the job.

Source: "Why Job Descriptions Are so Necessary for Your Payroll Staff," *IOMA's Payroll Manager's Report*, Vol. 03, No. 4, p. 5, April 2003.

You could certainly lump all these reasons together as communications failures. However, far more than communication is involved. It is likely that the supervisor has never really defined the whats, how-tos, and how-wells of the jobs. (It is likely that no one has defined the supervisor's job in these terms either.) There are probably all sorts of gray areas in the supervisor's mind about who does what and how. Who, for instance, is supposed to clean the bar floor and dispose of the empty bottles: the bartender or the cleanup staff? Who is supposed to replace burned-out lights in hotel rooms and report television sets that don't work? In a hospital, who is supposed to serve the food to the patients, and who is supposed to pick up all the dirty trays from the rooms? How much work can one waiter or cleaning person or cook's helper be expected to do in one shift? In fact, what is a "fair day's work" for any job? What's more, how many people are doing a fair day's work right now? Enter the job description with performance standards. Let's start with a discussion of performance standards.

Performance Standards

Performance standards form the heart of the job description and they describe the whats, how-tos, and how-wells of a job. Each performance standard states three things about each unit of the job:

1. What the employee is to do

2. How it is to be done

3. To what extent it is to be done (how much, how well, how soon)

ANATOMY OF A PERFORMANCE STANDARD

Job classification: Server (waiter/waitress)

Unit of work: Takes food and beverage orders

Performance standard:

The server will take food and beverage orders for up to five tables with 100 percent accuracy using standard house procedures.

Breakdown:

The server will:

What: *take food and beverage orders*
How: *using standard house procedures*
To what standard: *for up to five tables with 100 percent accuracy*

FIGURE 15.4 Anatomy of a performance standard.

Traditionally, job descriptions have simply listed the duties and responsibilities (what the employee is to do) for each job. Although this approach is better than no approach, a job description using performance standards is much more useful, as will be discussed soon.

Here is an example of a performance standard for one unit of the waiter or waitress job at a certain restaurant: "The server will take food and beverage orders for up to five tables with 100 percent accuracy, using standard house procedures." Figure 15.4 breaks this standard down for you to give you the structure of a performance standard. The "what" of the standard is the work unit. The tasks become the "hows" that make up the standard procedure. When you add a performance goal for each unit, you set a performance standard: how much, how many, how good, how fast, how soon, how accurate—whatever it is that is important for establishing how well that unit of work should be done in your operation.

Supporting materials explaining or illustrating the specifics of the how (in this case, "standard house procedures") are necessary to complete each performance standard. They explain the action to be taken in order to reach the goal or standard.

Other Parts of the Job Description

Figure 15.5 is a sample job description for a server. Although there is no standard format for a job description, it usually includes the following:

JOB DESCRIPTION

JOB IDENTIFICATION

JOB TITLE   Server

DEPARTMENT   Dining Room   REPORTS TO   Dining Room Manager

HOURS   10:30 AM – 2:30 PM, 2:30 – 6:30 PM, 4:30 – 10:30 PM

EXEMPT OR NONEXEMPT   NONEXEMPT

GRADE   6

JOB SUMMARY

Serve guests in a courteous, helpful, and prompt manner.

PERFORMANCE STANDARDS

1. Stocks the service station for one serving area for one meal completely and correctly, as specified on the Service Station Procedures Sheet, in 10 minutes or less.

2. Sets or resets a table properly, as shown on the Table Setting Layout Sheet, in not more than 3 minutes.

3. Greets guests cordially within 5 minutes after they are seated and takes their order if time permits; if too busy, informs them that he or she will be back as soon as possible.

4. Explains menu to customers: (a) accurately describes the day's specials (as posted); (b) if asked, accurately describes the quality or cut, portion size, and preparation method of each menu entrée and specifies items accompanying it; (c) if asked, accurately specifies allowable substitutions for items on a complete meal menu; (d) if asked, accurately describes ingredients and taste of any menu item.

5. Takes food, wine, and beverage orders accurately for a table of up to six guests; accurately and legibly completes guest check as specified on the Guest Check Procedures Sheet; prices and totals check with 100 percent accuracy.

6. Picks up order and completes plate preparation correctly as specified on the Plate Preparation Sheet.

7. Serves a complete meal to all persons at each table in an assigned station in not more than 1 hour per table using the tray service method correctly as specified in the Tray Service Sheet.

FIGURE 15.5 Sample job description.

8. If asked, recommends wines appropriate to menu items selected, according to the What Wine Goes with What Food Sheet; opens and serves wines correctly as shown on the Wine Service Sheet.

9. Totals and presents check and carries out payment procedures with 100 percent accuracy, as specified on the Check Payment Procedures Sheet.

10. Performs side work correctly as assigned, according to the Side Work Procedures Sheet and to the level required on the Sanitation Checklist.

11. Operates all preparation and service equipment in the assigned area correctly according to the operations manuals and the safety regulations prescribed on the Operational Procedures Sheet.

12. Meets at all times all the uniform, appearance, and grooming standards specified in the Appearance and Grooming Checklist.

13. Observes at all times the sanitation procedures specified for serving personnel in the Sanitation Manual; maintains work area to score 90 percent or higher on the Sanitation Checklist.

14. Maintains good customer relations at all times according to the Customer Relations Checklist; maintains a customer complaint ratio of less than 1 per 200 customers served.

15. Maintains a check average of not less than $5.00 per person at lunch and $11.00 per person at dinner.

JOB SETTING

CONTACTS ___ Guests, dining room personnel, cooking staff ___

WORKING CONDITIONS ___ Works in temperature controlled dining ___ room and service area which become congested at busy times ___

PHYSICAL DEMANDS ___ Standing and walking most of the time, ___ frequent lifting of heavy trays ___

WORK HAZARDS ___ Hot surfaces, steam, wet floors, heavy lifting, ___ sharp knives ___

Approval Signature _____

Approval Signature _____

Date _____

FIGURE 15.5 (Continued)

- Job title, such as cook or server

- Job summary; a brief one- or two-sentence statement of the major or overall duty and purpose of the job

- Units of work, preferably in the format of performance standards

- Job setting, including physical conditions, physical demands, and work hazards

- Social environment: information on the extent of interpersonal interaction required to perform the job.

Some operators also put qualifications, such as education and experience, into the job description. Although qualifications are technically included in the job specification, many operators put them in the job description for convenience. The job-setting section describes the conditions under which the job is to be done. This should include physical conditions, such as the temperature, humidity, noise, and ventilation in a kitchen (be honest—they are usually disagreeable). Physical demands, such as frequent heavy lifting and work hazards, such as hot surfaces and slippery floors, also need to be noted. Job setting also includes the personal contacts required by the job—in other words, who the employee interacts with.

In addition to the job title, you may want to include some or all of the following descriptive information at the beginning of the job description: the department name, grade level, location of the job, whether the job is exempt or nonexempt, work hours, and reporting relationship. When discussing the reporting relationship, include the title of the person supervising this employee (and when applicable, who this employee supervises).

Always keep in mind that a job description should not refer to the person doing the job, since the job description refers to a job, not to the people doing the job. As the employee's supervisor, you need to approve and sign the job description for each of the job classifications under your control. Depending on your operation, your job descriptions may also have to be approved and signed by a representative from the human resources department and/or your superior.

Ken Blanchard, the renowned management author, gives a great example of Jim, whose work performance is only "so-so" but who is the star of the Wednesday night bowling league. The story goes ... imagine that you are Jim as he is about to bowl ... and a curtain comes down so that he can't see where to bowl the ball. Sounds familiar—there are numerous associates who are not clear as to what they are aiming at—in other words, they have no clear goals. So Jim knocks down six skittles, but he doesn't know that because no one tells him—also sounds familiar—well, thousands of associates carry on working without any feedback on how well they did. Suppose that a supervisor stood there and said "Jim, you missed four skittles"—we would know how Jim would feel. But guess how many times this actually happens to associates? Wouldn't it be better to have no certain and clear goals—to knock down all 10 skittles—but have immediate feedback and encouragement?

Source: From an address to the National Restaurant Association by Ken Blanchard, May 14, 2001.

Luckily, there are now sources of generic job descriptions available to hospitality supervisors. The National Restaurant Association has available a publication titled Model *Position Descriptions*, which contains 117 job descriptions for both lodging and restaurant occupations. The National Skills Standards Board (www.nssb.org) has available sample job descriptions and additional information on a number of food-service and lodging jobs as well.

Uses of the Job Description

Job descriptions are used often in recruiting, evaluating applicants, and training. They are also useful in assigning work, evaluating performance, and deciding on disciplinary action. In the next section we discuss the uses and benefits of performance standards in more detail.

Check Your Knowledge

1. Define the following terms:
    (a) Position
    (b) Job analysis
    (c) Job description
    (d) Job specification
    (e) Job evaluation

2. What is meant by *performance standards?*

WHAT A GOOD PERFORMANCE STANDARD SYSTEM CAN DO

If you develop a full set of performance standards for each job classification that you supervise, you have the basis for a management system for your people and the work they do. You can use them to describe the jobs, to define the day's work for each job, to train workers to meet standards, to evaluate workers' performance, and to give them feedback on how they are doing. You can use performance standards as a basis for rewarding achievement and selecting people for promotion. You can use them as diagnostic tools to pinpoint ineffective performance and as a basis for corrective action. You can also use them in disciplining workers as a means of demonstrating incompetence. They provide the framework for a complete system of people management. This system operates successfully in many areas of supervisory responsibility.

Don'ts when writing job descriptions

- Don't write a job description to be all-inclusive.

- Don't use abbreviations or terms that are not commonly understood.

- Don't include temporary duties in a job description—or note that they are temporary if they must be included.

Source: "Why Job Descriptions Are so Necessary for Your Payroll Staff," *IOMA's Payroll Manager's Report*, Vol. 03, No. 4, p. 5, April 2003.

On the Job

Intelligent and consistent use of a performance standard system reduces or eliminates those five major reasons cited earlier for low productivity and high turnover. Employees are told clearly what to do. They are taught how to do it. They know how well they are doing because there is an objective standard of measurement. The supervisor helps and supports them with additional training or coaching when standards are not being met. All this makes for much better relationships between workers and supervisor.

Performance standards improve individual performance. When people are not given explicit instructions but are left to work out their own ways of getting their work done, they usually choose the easiest methods they can find. If this meets your standards, well and good, but often it does not. People also begin to find certain parts of their job more to their liking than other parts and will slack off on the parts they like least. The procedures and standards put all these things into the right perspective.

Once workers know what to do and how to do it, they can concentrate on improving their skills. Improved skills and knowledge, coupled with goals to be met, encourage people to work more independently. If a reward system is related to achievement—as it should be—people will respond with better and better work. Better and better work means better productivity, better customer service, more sales, and higher profits. Who could complain about that?

Morale benefits greatly. People feel secure when they know what to do and how to do it, and when their work is judged on the basis of job content and job performance. If they have participated in developing the objectives, they have a sense of pride and a commitment to seeing that the objectives work. Participation also contributes to their sense of belonging and their loyalty to the company.

A performance standard system can reduce conflict and misunderstanding. Everybody knows who is responsible for what. They know what parts of the job are most important. They know the level of performance the boss expects in each job. This reduces the likelihood that one person is doing less than another who is being paid the same wage—often a cause for discontent and conflict.

Performance standards help ensure quality and consistency.

Well-defined standards can eliminate problems caused by the overlapping of functions or duties. Sometimes in a restaurant, for example, the functions of busing and serving overlap. Who resets the tables after customers leave? Both the bus person and the server may try to do it and run into each other, or each of them may think it is the other's job and it does not get done, and the table is out of service while people are waiting to be seated. At the front desk of the hotel, who will do the report for the housekeeper, the night auditor, or the early morning desk clerk, and will there be two reports or none? In the hospital, who picks up all the dirty trays, the kitchen personnel or the aides on the floor, or do they sit in the patients' rooms all day? All these gaps and overlaps will be eliminated in a performance standard system because the responsibility for performing the tasks will be spelled out.

In Recruiting and Hiring

The typical job description spells out in general terms the content of the job, the duties, and perhaps the kind of experience or skill desired. Performance standards, on the other hand, clearly define the jobs and the duties, the methods of performing the duties, and the competencies required. This will help you as a supervisor to find the right people and to explain the jobs to prospective employees. It will also help in planning and forecasting personnel needs, because you will know exactly what you can expect from each trained employee. If you are looking for experienced people, performance standards are helpful for testing skills.

When you select a new employee, you have a ready-made definition of the day's work for the job. You and your new worker can start off on the right foot with a clear understanding of what is to be done in return for the paycheck. It is a results-oriented approach to defining the job.

We discuss recruiting and selection more fully in Chapter 16.

In Training

A complete set of performance standards gives you the blueprint for a training program. Each standard sets the competency goals for on-the-job performance toward which the training is guided. The training that forms the heart of a successful performance standard system begins with a written procedure. Developing a training program is discussed at length in Chapter 18.

In Evaluating Performance

A complete performance standard system should include periodic evaluations of each worker's performance, with feedback to the workers on how they are doing. Realistic and well-developed standards of performance form a solid basis for objective evaluation. After evaluation, the supervisor is responsible for helping those who are working below standard to improve their performance.

An evaluation system based on performance standards can pinpoint specific deficiencies needing corrective training. It is a positive approach; the focus is on the work, not the person; it does not put the person down. The problem is addressed and corrected, and everyone benefits. A performance standard evaluation system can also help you to identify superior workers by the way they meet or exceed the standards set. Such people merit your attention as candidates for development and promotion. Evaluation is discussed at length in Chapter 19.

Profile

RYAN ADAMS

Courtesy of Ryan Adams

There are many examples of good supervision that I could cite. However, there is a distinctive difference between what is taught and what is realistic. The first three words that I think of in terms of good supervision are legal, ethical, and moral. Books tend to give black-and-white examples with black-and-white results. This is not reality in the hospitality industry.

A good supervisor must be respectful of everyone on every level. You are in the middle of the line-level employees, the middle managers, and the top management. You have to be able to juggle the concerns of your direct manager, with the challenges of your staff and still try to impress the top-level managers when they are around. This can be a difficult balancing act.

You have to draw a line—often the most difficult decision for a supervisor. Most supervisors have climbed their way up the ladder and are often viewed as one of the crew. You must distinguish yourself as a manager or else your staff will try to take advantage of you. Everything you do is being watched on every level. Now more than ever it is essential to put your foot down and establish your mark. It is often said that "being a manager is not a popularity contest"—this could not be more true. Being a supervisor can often be a lonely position.

When an employee comes to you, stop what you are doing and give the person your undivided attention. Look the employee in the eye and really hear what he or she is saying. When the person has finished talking, paraphrase what has been said so that you understand and can empathize with the feelings expressed so that he or she is validated, and then offer counseling to help resolve the concern. This is easier said than done. As a supervisor, you always have to be on top of your game. This means knowing policy and procedures, knowing the union contract if your business is unionized. You have to be an expert in the human resources field. If you do not know, you always have your manager to fall back on or the human resources department. If you are not sure, ask; it is better to find out than to make an error that can cost big money. If you do not know the answer to a particular question, tell the employee that you will get back to him or her with the answer. Make sure that you follow up or the person will feel that you are incompetent and untrustworthy. If this occurs, you will have to make huge strides to improve that relationship.

Trust and empower your people. If you really want to shine and make your staff feel good about their jobs, trust them. Delegate side duties and additional responsibilities. Make sure that you give them the proper praise for their work; they will not forget that you did not praise them for their help and may be reluctant to offer in the future. Let your staff make decisions. Give them the guidelines to make decisions and train them. Role-playing is a great way to prepare them for the chaos they will experience. This will enable you to take on more responsibility from your managers, and your staff will be confident to respond to smaller problems that would otherwise tie up your day.

In discipline situations, never have the paperwork already filled out. Make notes, but do not just present the write-up without talking to your employee first. They will feel like you did not even give them a chance to explain. You assumed they were guilty right off the bat and they will feel like they never had a chance.

Always check on your staff and make sure that you take time out of your day at some point to make small talk. Often, when an employee makes the transition to supervisor, he or she forgets how he or she wanted to be treated when an employee. It is easy to adopt negative or undesirable traits of managers of the past. Always be objective and never lose the person you are—that is what got you there in the first place. Always be on time to meetings or at least call in advance to notify someone that you cannot attend. Make your manager's concerns your priority, your staff's needs mandatory, and the vision and values of your company your guiding principles. If you do not believe in what the company stands for, it is difficult to share that vision with others. Remember, you are not just a manager you are a leader. This means taking your staff to a place they would not have gone otherwise. As a manager, what gets done gets measured. Not that this is right—it is a fact and thus a big part of your evaluation.

In Your Job and Your Career

A performance standard system will simplify your job as supervisor. Once it is in place and running, you will spend less of your time supervising because your people will be working more independently and things will run more smoothly of their own accord. You will have fewer misunderstandings, fewer mistakes in orders, fewer broken dishes, and fewer irate customers. You will have more time to spend in planning, training, thinking, observing, and improving product and method instead of managing on a crash-and-crisis basis.

After experiencing the standard-setting process, you will have a much better conceptual grasp of your own department, your own area of command, and everything that goes on there. You will be able to coordinate better the various aspects of the work you are responsible for, be able to see how things can better be organized, and be able to run a tight ship. It will be a growth experience for you, and it will make you a better manager. The experience will stand you in good stead as you pursue your career, and so will the improved results in your department.

Check Your Knowledge

1.   What can a good performance standard system do?
2.   The performance standard system operates successfully in many areas of supervisory responsibilities. What are these areas?

SETTING UP A PERFORMANCE STANDARD SYSTEM

Developing a complete performance standard system is not something you can do overnight. There are a number of steps to the process, and there are certain essentials for success that must be included in the planning and operation.

Three essentials for successful operation must be built into the system from the beginning. The first is *worker participation*. The people who are currently working in a given job category should work with you as you analyze that job, set the standards for performance, develop the standard procedures, and determine a fair day's work. One worker's input is very important to you. Often, they know the job better than you do, particularly the procedural steps involved.

The give-and-take of discussion will often produce better results than one person working alone. In many cases your workers will set higher standards of performance than they would have accepted if you alone had set them. In the end, there must be mutual agreement between supervisor and workers on the procedures and the standards and the fair day's work, although the supervisor always has the final say.

Helping to hammer out the *whats, hows*, and *how-wells* will inevitably commit workers to the goals. They will work much harder for something they have helped to develop than for something handed down by the boss. The experience will make them feel recognized, needed, and important, as well as helping to build that sense of belonging that is so necessary to morale.

The second essential for a successful system is *active supervisory leadership and assistance throughout*. As supervisor, you will make the final decisions on the work units to be included and their relative importance. You will determine how much leeway to give your people in working out the procedures and standards of performance. As leader, you will be in charge at all times. But you will all work together as much as possible in identifying the units, specifying the methods and procedures, and setting the performance standards. Under your leadership, performance standards will represent a joint acceptance of the work to be done and responsibility for achieving it.

In training and on the job, the supervisor's leadership continues. Now your role is the supportive one of facilitating the learning of skills, giving feedback, and providing additional training as necessary. Frequent evaluations, whether formal appraisals or a "Hey, you're doing fine," must be an integral part of the system. If the supervisor neglects this aspect of the system, the entire system will soon deteriorate.

The third essential is a *built-in reward system* of some sort, with the rewards linked to how well each worker meets the performance standards. People who do not want to work hard must understand that the better shifts, the promotions, and the other rewards will go to those whose work meets or exceeds the standards set. In some instances you may not have a great deal of leeway in handing out rewards, but you can always give the extra word of praise or written note of thanks for a job well done. Often, this means as much as a material reward. People feel that you are recognizing them as individuals and are appreciating their contributions.

For some people in some jobs, the sense of achievement measured against a defined standard of excellence is a reward in itself, as long as it is recognized and *not taken for granted*. This probably does not operate so effectively in dull and repetitive jobs such as washing dishes and vacuuming carpets. But in such jobs as desk clerk or server, dealing with customers offers many challenges, and the worker can take pride in improving skills and handling difficult situations well. There is nothing in this system that limits excellence to the standards set, and workers should be encouraged to excel.

There is a definite order of steps to be taken in developing a performance standard system. Figure 15.6 is a flowchart depicting the entire process. The next several pages will follow in detail each progression on the chart. As you read, you will find it helpful to refer back to the flowchart to see the relationship of each step to the whole process.

Defining the Purpose

The first step is to define the purpose for which the standards are to be used. Our purpose here is to develop a system for one job classification that can be used to define a day's work, set standards, develop training plans, and evaluate on-the-job performance. A performance standard is to be developed for each unit of the work.

Analyzing the Job

Once you have defined your purpose, your next step is to analyze the job and break it down into units. First, your employees can help to identify all the different work units they perform. When your list of units is complete, you and your crew should list in order of performance all the tasks or steps to be taken in completing that unit of work.

Once you have agreed on a list of tasks or procedural steps for each unit, you have the data for the first two parts of each performance standard that you are going to write. The unit is the *what* of the objective. The tasks become the *hows* that make up the standard procedures. When you add a standard for each unit, you have a complete performance standard.

The supervisor and the people working at the job should set the standards of performance together, as already discussed. Although the supervisor has the final say in the matter, it is critical to have the workers' input on the standard and their agreement that it is fair. If they don't think that it is fair, they will stop cooperating and your entire system will fail. They will let you succeed only to the degree that they want you to succeed.

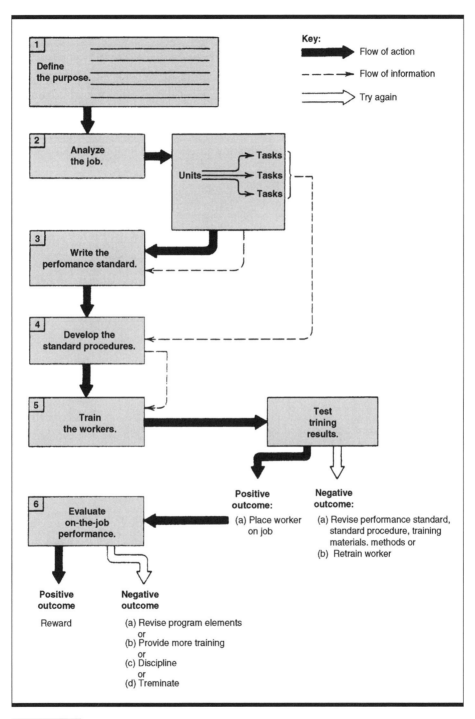

FIGURE 15.6 Flowchart for developing a performance standard system.

Sometimes it is appropriate to define three levels of performance: an optimistic level, a realistic level, and a minimum level. An optimistic level is your secret dream of how a fantastic crew would do the work. A realistic level is your estimate of what constitutes a competent job and the way that good steady workers are doing it now. A minimum level is rock bottom—if people did any less, you would fire them.

It is best to write your performance standards for a realistic level. A minimum level simply sets the standard at what a worker can get away with—and some of them will. This level is appropriate only for trainees or new employees during their first days on the job.

An optimistic level is appropriate for the high achiever who is not challenged by a goal that is too easy. Achievement on this high level must be rewarded if you want that kind of effort to continue.

When you have determined all the elements of each performance standard in a given job—the *what*, the *how*, and the actual standard itself for each unit—you should rate each unit in terms of the importance that you, as a supervisor, attach to it in on-the-job performance, as is done in Figure 15.7 for the job of server. This value scale should be made very clear to your servers and should carry considerable weight in a formal evaluation and in any reward system you set up. You may want to ask your servers for their ideas about relative importance, but the final decisions are your responsibility alone. You are the one with the management point of view and the company goals in mind. It will help your people if you explain clearly just why you rate the units as you do. In Figure 15.7, their relative importance is shown by assigning a point value to each unit. The rewards go to those people with the highest total points on their evaluation score.

Writing the Performance Standards

Now we are ready for step 3 on the flowchart (Figure 15.6), writing the performance standards for each unit of the job. First, let us review the essential features of a performance standard. It is a concise statement made up of three elements that together describe the way a unit of work is to be carried out in a given operation:

1.   What is to be done?

2.   How is it to be done?

3.   To what extent (quality, quantity, accuracy, speed) is it to be done?

Writing performance standards is crucial to setting up a performance standard system.

You can use the form in Figure 15.8 and simply fill in the blanks as we go. Let us take the first unit on the server list (Figure 15.1) and go through the process step by step. The first unit is *stock service station*. You make this abbreviated description more precise by limiting the scope of the work sequence: "The server will stock the service station for one serving area for one meal. . . ." Notice two things here:

1. You must use an action verb: the server will do something, will perform—not "be able to" or "know how to" or "understand," but actually do something. (The other phrases are used in objectives written for training purposes. Here we are writing objectives for day-in, day-out, on-the-job performance.) Use Figure 15.9 for help choosing a verb.

2. You limit the action as clearly and precisely as possible—which service station, what for. Limiting the action in this way makes it easier to measure performance.

SERVER UNIT RATINGS

1.	Stocks service station	4 points
2.	Sets tables	4
3.	Greets guests	8
4.	Explains menu to customers	8
5.	Takes food and beverage orders and completes guest check	8
6.	Picks up order and completes plate preparation	4
7.	Serves food	6
8.	Recommends wines and serves them	8
9.	Totals and presents check	8
10.	Performs side work	4
11.	Operates equipment	4
12.	Meets dress and grooming standards	8
13.	Observes sanitation procedures and requirements	8
14.	Maintains good customer relations	10
15.	Maintains desired check average	8
		100

FIGURE 15.7 Server unit ratings. Point values represent the importance of good performance in each unit of work (page from a procedures manual).

Next you define the *how*: "... as described in the Service Station Procedures Sheet..." or "... following standard house procedures. ..." The standard simply states how or where this information is spelled out.

Finally, you state the standard of performance: "... completely and correctly in ten minutes or less. ..." That is, everything must be put in its assigned place within ten minutes and nothing must be missing.

Now you can put together the whole performance standard: "The server will stock the service station for one serving area for one meal as described in the Service Station Procedures Sheet. The server will stock the station completely and correctly in 10 minutes or less."

Here are the requirements for the finished product: a good, useful, workable performance standard.

WRITING A PERFORMANCE STANDARD

Job classification:

Unit of work:

What must be done?   (state the performance)

The worker will:

How is it to be done?   (the standard procedures are
                           where they are spelled out)

. . . according to . . . using . . . as shown in . . .

To what standard?   (how you measure it or what
                       you must be able to observe):

FIGURE 15.8 Sample form to use in writing a performance standard.

Calculate
Classify
Construct
Define
Demonstrate
Describe
Diagram
Discuss
Display
Distinguish
Estimate
Evaluate
Explain
Give examples
Identify
Interpret
Label
Lead
List
Locate
Make
Measure
Name
Operate
Organize
Pace
Predict
Recognize
See
Show
Smell
Solve
Use
Work

FIGURE 15.9 Action verbs for performance standards.

1. *The statement must be specific, clear, complete, and accurate.* It must tell the worker exactly what you want. Instructions cannot be vague so that it is not misinterpreted or misread. If it is not specific, clear, complete, and accurate, it can be more confusing than anything else.

2. *The standard of performance must be measurable or observable.* "Good" and "well" are not measurable or observable; they are subjective judgments. "Correct" and

"accurate" are measurable *if there is something to measure by*—a set of instructions, a diagram, mathematical accuracy. The waiter delivers the order correctly if he serves the customer what the customer ordered. The bartender measures accurately if she pours ten 2-ounce martinis and 20 ounces are gone from the gin bottle. There are ways to measure these performances. There *must* be a measurable or observable way for the supervisor to tell whether a person is meeting the performance standard.

3. *The standard must be attainable.* It must be within the physical and mental capabilities of the workers and the conditions of the job. For example, servers cannot take orders at a specified speed because they have no control over the time it takes customers to make up their minds. Sometimes a standard is set too high the first time around. If nobody can meet it, expectations are unrealistic and you should reexamine the objective.

4. *The standard must conform to company policies, company goals, and applicable legal and moral constraints.* It must not require or imply any action that is legally or morally wrong (such as selling liquor to minors or misrepresenting ingredients or portion sizes).

5. *Certain kinds of standards must have a time limit set for achievement.* This applies to training objectives and performance improvement objectives, to be discussed shortly.

Figure 15.5 includes a set of performance standards for the job of server in a specific restaurant, developed for the units of work identified in Figure 15.1.

Performance standards are a specialized and demanding form of communication, and writing them may be the most difficult part of developing a performance standard system. But it is precisely this process that requires you to make things clear in your own mind. If you have problems with writing performance standards, don't worry—even experts do. But try it anyway. If it forces you to figure out just what you as a supervisor expect of your workers, you will have learned a tremendous lesson.

Check Your Knowledge

1. Name the three essentials to setting up a successful performance standard system.

2. What is meant by *optimistic level, realistic level*, and *minimum level?*

Developing Standard Procedures

The fourth step on the flowchart (Figure 15.6) is to develop standard procedures. Standard procedures complete each package and in many ways are the heart of the matter.

The procedures state what a person must do to achieve the results—they give the instructions for the action. They tell the worker exactly how things are supposed to be done in your establishment. Spelling out, step by step, each task of each unit in a given job develops them. There may be many tasks involved—5, 10, 20, 100—whatever is necessary to describe precisely how to carry out that unit of the job. Turn back to Figure 15.2 to refresh your memory.

The standard procedures have two functions. The first is to standardize the procedures you want your people to follow; the second is to provide a basis for training. You can use various means of presenting the how-to materials that make up each standard procedure: individual procedure sheets, pages in a procedural manual, diagrams, filmstrips, videotapes, slides, and photographs. It depends on what will be easiest to understand and what will best meet the requirements of the individual standard. For stocking the service station you might use a list of items and quantities along with a diagram showing how they are placed. For opening a wine bottle you might have a videotape or a series of slides or pictures showing each step. For dress and grooming you would have a list of rules (Figure 15.10). The important thing is to have them in some form of accessible record so that they can be referred to in cases of doubt or disagreement and so that the trainers can train workers correctly. Show-and-tell is not enough in a performance standard system.

Career ladders create common language for defining jobs

It is easier to undertake a major journey when one has a map of the potential stops along the way. The sign posts make for a smoother, more productive passage. The same can be said of career management.

Source: Claudine Kapel and Catherine Shepherd, *Canadian HR Reporter*. Vol. 17, No. 12, p. 15, June 2004.

Two areas of caution: Don't get carried away with unnecessary detail (you don't need to specify that the menu must be presented right side up), and don't make rigid rules when there is a choice of how things can be done (there are many acceptable ways to greet a customer). You do not want your people to feel that they have tied themselves into a straitjacket in helping you to develop these procedure sheets. In fact, this entire process should free them to work more creatively. You simply specify what must be done in a certain way and include everything that is likely to be done wrong when there

---

APPEARANCE AND GROOMING CHECKLIST

Immaculate cleanliness is required.
1. Clean body: take a daily shower or bath, and use deodorant.
2. Clean teeth and breath: brush your teeth often, use mouthwash after meals if brushing is impossible.
3. Clean hair: shampoo at least once a week.
4. Clean hands and nails at all times: wash frequently.
5. Clean clothing, hose, and underwear daily.
6. Clean shoes: polish well, in good repair.

Grooming must be neat and in good taste.
7. Hair neatly styled.
8. Nails clean, clipped short, no polish.
9. Minimal makeup.
10. No strong scents from perfume, cologne, after-shave, soap, or hair spray.
11. No jewelry except wedding ring and/or service award pins.

Uniforms will be issued by hotel. You must care for them.
12. Clean, wrinkle free, in good repair at start of shift.
13. Hose required.
14. Closed-toe shoes, low heels.

Health and Posture
15. Report any sickness, cuts, burns, boils, and abrasions to your supervisor immediately.
16. Stand straight, walk tall, and look confident!

FIGURE 15.10 Standard procedures for the unit on appearance and grooming: 16 tasks must be completed to meet the objective (page from a procedures manual).

are no established procedures. The rest should be left up to the person on the job as long as the work is done and the standards are met.

Training Workers to Meet the Performance Standards

Training is the fifth step in developing a performance standard system (see Figure 15.6). A training program should have its own training objective for each standard. Each training objective will have a time limit added within which the worker must reach a required performance standard. For example: "After 1 hour of training and practice, the trainee will be able to stock the service station for one serving area for one meal completely and correctly in 15 minutes or less following standard house procedures." You will notice that the performance time limit is changed from the previous example because this is a training goal and not an on-the-job goal. In training, the procedures form the basis of the training plans and the training itself. We talk about this in Chapter 18.

At the end of the training period, the results of the training will be tested. In a new performance standard program this is a test of both the worker and the various elements of the program. If the results are positive, you can put the worker right into the job (or that part of the job for which training is complete). If the results are negative, you have to consider where the problem lies. Is it the worker? The standard? The procedures? The training itself? Something calls for corrective action.

Evaluating On-the-Job Performance

The final step in developing a performance standard system (see Figure 15.6) is to evaluate worker performance on the job using the performance standards that apply to that job. This first evaluation is a test of both the workers and the system so far. If a worker meets all the standards, the outcome is positive and a reward is in order. A positive outcome is also an indication that your standards and procedures are suitable and workable.

If a worker rates below standard in one or more areas, you again have to diagnose the trouble. Is the standard too high? Are the procedures confusing, misleading, or impossible to carry out? Or is it the worker? If it is the worker, what corrective training does he or she need? If the worker is far below standard in everything, is there hope for improvement, or should the worker be terminated?

IMPLEMENTING A PERFORMANCE STANDARD SYSTEM

Once you have fine-tuned your system, you have a permanent set of instruments for describing jobs, defining a fair day's work for each job, training workers to your standards, evaluating performance, and rewarding achievement. How well can you expect it to work?

How to Make a Performance Standard System Pay Off

The first key to making your system work is the *workers' cooperation* in the developmental stage and their agreement to the standards of performance. If they have participated fully in developing them, they will participate fully in carrying them out. If, on the other hand, the development sessions were full of wrangling, bargaining, and manipulation, and in the end you more or less forced your people to agree to your decisions, they will find ways to sabotage the system. They will also be resentful and uncooperative if they are required to put in time and work in addition to their regular duties and hours without extra compensation or reward.

The second key to success is to *put the system to work slowly* over a period of time, one job at a time. It cannot be done in a day or a week or a month. A performance standard system is a total management system, and it takes a great deal of time to develop it and put it in place. It takes a long time to develop good standards, to standardize the procedures, to translate the standards and procedures into training programs, and to train your people to meet the performance standards. It takes total commitment to the system, and if you do not have that commitment it will never work for you.

The third key to success is *an award or incentive system*. This is something you work out alone, since you are the only one who knows what you have to offer. It could be money: a bonus, a prize, a pay raise, a promotion. But it does not have to be money; it could be a better shift, an extra day off, a better serving area, a bottle of champagne, or a certificate of merit displayed for all to see. Whatever it is, it is important that all your people understand what the rewards are for and how they are allotted, that they feel the system is fair, and that you practice it consistently.

The fourth key to success is to *recognize your workers' potential* and use it as fully as you can within the limits of your authority. Performance standards tend to uncover talent that has been hidden under day-after-day drudgery. Numerous surveys have shown that many people in the hospitality industry are truly underemployed. If they are encouraged to become more productive, to take more responsibility, to learn new skills, you will get a higher return. Human assets are the most underutilized assets in the hospitality industry today. A performance standard system gives you new ways to capitalize on them. Better products, better service, more customers—who knows how far you can go?

The fifth key to continued success is to *review your system periodically*, evaluating and updating and modifying if your ways of doing things have changed. For example, you may have changed your menu or your wine list. Have you also changed the list of what wine goes with what food? You may have put in some new pieces of equipment. Have you adapted your procedures to include training the workers to use them properly?

If you do not keep your materials up to date, if you begin to let them slide, you may begin to let other things slide, too—the training, the evaluations, the reward system. It will run by itself for a time, but not indefinitely. It works best when everyone is actively involved in maintaining it.

How a Performance Standard System Can Fail

Performance standards do not work everywhere. Good, clear, accurate, understandable standards are often hard to write unless you or one of your workers is good at putting words together. (This may be one of those hidden talents that the process uncovers.) *If the standards are not clearly stated and clearly communicated to everyone, they can cause confusion instead of getting rid of it.* The objectives are communications tools, and if they do not communicate well—if the people do not understand them—the program will never get off the ground.

The supervisor can cause the system to fail in several ways. The worst thing that you can do is to change standards without telling your people. You just do not change the rules of the game while you are playing it, especially without telling anyone. You can make changes—often you have to—but you have to keep your people informed, especially when such critical matters as evaluations and rewards are at stake.

Another way in which the supervisor can bring about the failure of the system is to neglect its various follow-up elements. It is especially important to help your people attain and maintain the performance standards you and they have set—to correct underperformance through additional instruction and training, and to do this in a positive, supportive way rather than criticizing or scolding. You must help, and you must maintain a helping attitude.

If you neglect the follow-up elements—if you do not help underperformers, if you fail to carry out a consistent reward system, if you do not recognize superior achievement and creativity, if you do not analyze individual failures and learn from them—all these things can make a system die of neglect. *Similarly, it will die if your people find no challenge or reward in the system—if the goals are too low to stimulate effort, if the supervisor is hovering around all the time "evaluating," or if for some reason the system has not succeeded in putting people on their own.*

What it often comes down to is that if the supervisor believes in the system and wants to make it work, it will, bringing all its benefits with it. If the supervisor is half-hearted, you will have a half-baked system that will fail of its own deadweight.

Sometimes a supervisor can become so preoccupied with maintaining the system that the system will take over and become a straightjacket that prevents healthy change in response to new ideas and changing circumstances. This happens at times in large organizations where the deadweight of routine and paperwork stifles vitality and creativity. It can also happen with a rigid, high-control supervisor whose management style leans heavily on enforcing rules and regulations. A performance standard system should not lock people in; it should change and improve in response to changes in the work and the needs of the workers.

Sometimes the system is administered in a negative way: "You didn't meet your objectives." "You won't get a raise." "You're gonna be fired if you don't meet these standards." People can experience it as a whip or a club rather than as a challenge, and that is the end of its usefulness. This is not the fault of the system, however, but of the way in which it is administered. Truly, the supervisor is the key to success.

Check Your Knowledge

1. Explain the two functions of standard procedures.
2. What are the keys to making a performance system work?

Some Alternatives

One obvious drawback of a performance standard system is the time and effort necessary for developing it. Most first-line supervisors would have trouble finding the time, and in fact they might not have the authority to develop such a system on their own initiative. It is more suited to the job of manager of a large unit or an individual restaurant. Sometimes it is made part of a companywide system in which individual supervisors are directed to develop such a system for their own units within a prescribed framework and with company training.

Another way of developing a company is to hire an outside expert to do the job analysis and write the objectives. However, a homegrown system developed by a supervisor together with the workers who actually carry out the duties and tasks is more likely to succeed than is a system grafted onto an operation from outside. A system developed by outsiders is not likely to provide the same motivation to make it succeed. It is better to have imperfectly phrased objectives embodying the spirit of the homegrown product than technically correct standards imposed from the outside that no one has any interest in meeting.

Many large companies approach the problems of defining jobs and standardizing procedures without using performance standards. Job analysis and procedures manuals are used widely and successfully, especially in organizing, recruiting, and training. They avoid the time and effort of developing a performance standard system. But they also lose its advantages. They go halfway, without taking the final step of developing performance standards. Without the goals and standards this approach does not have the challenge or the controls of a performance standard system. It does not tie together all aspects of managing people—daily performance, selection, training, evaluation, recognition, and rewards—as a proper system does. It does not ensure that workers will be told what to do and how to do it and to what standard. It does not go far enough.

As a supervisor, you can derive great benefit from understanding and applying these concepts even if you never have the chance or the desire to develop a written system. You can use the *what, how-to,* and *how-well* principles to analyze and organize your jobs, train your workers, and let them know how they are doing. You can formulate clearly in your own mind what you want them to do, how you want them to do it, and what standard of performance you expect without formalizing anything in writing. Then, if you can communicate it all to your people and establish it as a way of life on the job and a system of management for yourself, you have the best part of a formal written system. But it may take just as much thought and effort and just as long a time.

KEY POINTS

1. Every job in the hospitality industry includes several distinct work segments or units of work. Each unit of work is made up of a number of tasks.

2. Job descriptions often include job title, job summary, units of work (preferably in the format of performance standards), job setting, and the social environment.

3. Performance standards form the heart of the job description and describe the whats, how-tos, and how-wells of a job.

4. If you develop a full set of performance standards for each job that you supervise, you have the basis for a management system for your people and the work they do. You can use them in recruiting, training, and evaluation. You can use them with employees to reduce conflict and misunderstanding. Everyone knows who is responsible for what.

5. Three essentials to setting up a successful performance standard system are worker participation, active supervisory leadership and assistance throughout, and a built-in reward system.

6. Figure 15.6 depicts how to develop a performance standard system: define the purpose, analyze the job, write the performance standard, train the workers, and evaluate on-the-job performance.

7. Figure 15.8 shows a sample form to be used when writing performance standards.

8. Performance standards must be specific, clear, complete, accurate, measurable or observable, attainable, and in conformance with company policies and legal and moral constraints.

9. The first key to making your system work is the workers' cooperation and agreement in the developmental stage. The second key to success is to put the system to work slowly over a period of time, one job at a time. Other keys to success

include having an award or incentive system, recognizing your workers' potential, and reviewing the system periodically.

10. A performance standard system can fail if the standards are not clearly stated and communicated to everyone, if the supervisor does not follow up properly, if the supervisor does not provide enough challenge or reward, or if the system is administered in a confining or negative manner.

KEY TERMS

job	job specification	performance standards
job analysis	job title	position
job description	levels of performance: optimistic level, realistic level, minimum level	tasks
job evaluation		training objective
job setting		units of work

REFERENCES

1. Luis R. Gomez-Mejia, David B. Balkin, and Robert L. Cardy. *Managing Human Resources*, 3rd ed. Upper Saddle River, NJ: Prentice Hall, 2001, p. 66.

2. Ibid, p. 66.

RECRUITING AND SELECTING APPLICANTS*

You've run an ad in the Sunday paper for a weekend housekeeper, but the only person to put in an application is a high school student looking for her first job. You interview her, and you look at the housekeeper's work schedule and realize that if you don't hire her today, you'll have to spend the weekend doing housekeeper duties yourself. So you hire her, and the next day, when she starts, you ask an experienced (but not very friendly) housekeeper to get the new hire started. By next Saturday, she has quit, so you put another ad in the Sunday paper and you think, "There's got to be a better way."

---

* Authored by Jack E. Miller, John R. Walker, and Karen Eich Drummond.

How do you find the people you need? How can you choose people who will stay beyond the first week, do a good job, and be worth the money you pay them? Does it always have to be the way it is today?

No, it doesn't. There is no foolproof system: Human beings are unpredictable and so is the day-to-day situation in the typical hospitality operation. But the knowledge and experience of people who have faced and studied these problems can be helpful to you, even though you must adapt it to your own situation.

In this chapter we examine the processes and problems of recruiting and selecting hourly employees for hospitality operations. It will help you to:

- Describe the typical characteristics of entry-level jobs in the hospitality industry.

- Identify common sources of workers for the hospitality industry.

- Define a job's qualifications.

- List factors that affect forecasts of personal needs.

- Identify and avoid discriminatory language and practices in recruiting, interviewing, and selecting.

- Describe the most used methods of recruiting and evaluate their usefulness.

- Discuss and evaluate the standard tools and practices for screening people and selecting the best person for the job.

THE LABOR MARKET

The term labor market refers to (1) the supply of workers looking for jobs as well as (2) the jobs available in a given area. When you need people to fill certain jobs, you are looking for people with certain characteristics—knowledge, abilities, skills, personal qualities—and you have a certain price you are willing or able to pay for the work you expect them to do. The people who are in the market for a job are looking for jobs with certain characteristics—work they are qualified to do or are able to learn, a place they can get to easily, certain days and hours off, a pleasant work environment, people they are comfortable working with and for, and a certain rate of pay (usually, the most they can get). The trick is to get a good match between people and jobs.

When jobs are plentiful and few people are unemployed, employers have a harder time finding the people they want, and workers are more particular about the jobs they will accept. When many people are looking for jobs and jobs are scarce, employers have a better choice and workers will settle for less. The number of employers looking for the same kinds of people also affects the labor market. You are always in competition with hospitality operations like your own, as well as retail stores, which also offer many part-time, entry-level jobs.

Hospitality companies identify where they are in the marketplace for employees, meaning the Ritz-Carlton will likely attract a different person than a Motel 6. Companies assess the need for additional employees for a brief period of a "full house" versus some overtime being worked by existing staff.

Jobs to be Filled

Many of the jobs in food and lodging operations demand hard physical labor. People are often on their feet all day doing work that is physically exhausting. About the only people who sit down are telephone operators, typists, cashiers, reservationists, and many clerical workers. Kitchens are hot and filled with safety hazards. At busy times, pressure is intense and tension is high. Many jobs are uninteresting and monotonous—eight hours of pushing a vacuum cleaner, making up guest rooms, polishing silver, setting up function rooms, washing vegetables, spreading mayonnaise on bread, placing food on plates, washing dishes.

In many of these jobs the pay is low, but there is the possibility of promotion. It is not surprising that the duller and more demanding a job is, the harder it is to fill it with a good worker and the more often you have to fill it. The main attraction of such jobs is that they are available, and you are willing to take people with no experience and no skills. For example, operators may offer starting positions to employees whose English communication skills need improving. These individuals can, once they are more proficient in English, advance to other positions within the operation. Examples of this in a hotel would be in housekeeping and stewarding.

For certain jobs you must look for specific skills and abilities. Front desk clerks, servers, and bartenders must have several kinds of skills: verbal and manual skills and skill in dealing with customers. Cooks must have technical skills, varying in complexity with the station and the menu. All these jobs require people who can function well under pressure. The rate of pay goes up for skilled workers, except for waiters and waitresses, who are usually paid minimum wage or less and make most of their money in tips.

Days and Hours of Work

In the hospitality industry, people needs have a pattern of daily peaks and valleys, with the peaks forming around mealtimes and the valleys falling between. This makes for some difficulty in offering the regular eight-hour day that many people are looking for. You also have some very early hours if you serve breakfast, evening hours if you serve dinner, and late-night hours if you operate a bar or feature entertainment or serve an after-theater clientele. This irregular kind of need encourages split shifts, part-time jobs, and unusual hours, which can work both for you and against you in finding workers.

Sometimes you cannot guarantee a certain number of hours of work per week: Workers are put on a call-in schedule and must simply take their chances of getting as many hours as they want. But if they cannot count on you, you may not be able to count on them.

You also have varying needs according to days of the week. These form a fairly predictable pattern, predictable enough for you to plan your hiring and scheduling. In restaurants, staff needs are lighter during the week and heavy on weekends, which closes your doors to people looking for a Monday-to-Friday week. In business hotels the pattern is the reverse, heavy during the week and light on weekends, however resorts are busier on weekends. Restaurant employees typically work when other people are playing—evenings, weekends, and holidays—which complicates finding people to fill your jobs. Restaurants may also have urgent temporary needs for parties and promotions and emergencies when regular employees are out sick or leave without warning. This requires a banquet server call-in system or overtime for regular employees.

In some facets of the foodservice industry, the timing of people needs is regular and predictable. In hospitals and nursing homes the population is generally steady seven days a week, and the only variation in need comes with the daily peaks and valleys of mealtimes. Schools have steady Monday-to-Friday patterns with short days built around lunch, and they follow the school calendar, closing down for vacations, when they lose many people. Business and industry feeding follows the workweek of the business or plant.

In hotels the pattern of need is likely to be irregular but fairly predictable. Reservations are typically made ahead except in the restaurants, and need is generally geared to coming events in the community or in the hotel itself, or to predictable vacation and travel trends. Often, a hotel will require large numbers of temporary workers for single events such as conventions and conferences. Temporary extra help is often supplemented by having regulars work overtime. Where needs vary widely and frequently, supervisors can spend a great deal of time on staffing and scheduling alone. Hospitality operators normally have a number of "on-call employees" who are called upon to work banquets and catering functions as required.

The types of jobs, unusual working hours and days, minimum wages, and the up-and-down character of the need for workers limits the appeal of hotel and foodservice jobs to people who can fit this pattern or can slip in and out of it easily. Accordingly, it attracts people who are looking for short-term jobs, part-time work, or jobs requiring no skills or previous experience. Some people deliberately seek the unusual hours to fit their own personal schedule: people going to school, moonlighters, parents who must be at home to take care of the kids. Many people are looking for temporary work and have no interest in long-term employment or a career in the industry. "I am only working here until I can find a *real* job" is a common attitude.

Sources of Workers

The source of workers continues to change as the composition of the U.S. labor forces changes. The majority of new workers entering the workforce are women, minorities, and immigrants. Why is this? It is due to the combination of a shrinking, older, white U.S. population; a younger, growing minority population; recent easing of immigration restrictions; and increasing numbers of women entering or returning to work.

If the job you need to fill is anything above the lowest level in terms of pay, interesting work, and decent hours, *the first place to look for someone to fill it is inside your own operation.* Upgrading someone whose attitudes and performance you already know is far less risky than hiring someone new and will probably assure you of a good, loyal worker. You will spend less time in training, and the adjustment will be smoother all around.

Consider also how people would feel if you brought someone in from outside to fill a job or a shift they would like to have. It is important for morale to give your workers first chance, even when you might find it easier to fill the vacant job from outside than to fill the job your current employee will vacate. It is part of being a good leader to consider your own people first and to move them along and develop their capabilities for better jobs.

In the labor market at large, a major source of workers for foodservice and lodging jobs consists of *people looking for their first job.* Of these, most are teenagers. The percentage of teenagers in the total population is not as large as it used to be. This valuable source of labor has shrunk while our need for workers has grown. Overall, the hospitality industry employs many younger workers, and operators need to become familiar with the Child Labor laws in their state.

As an industry, we are always looking for people, and we are among the few employers who will hire people without experience. Usually, first-timers want the jobs for the money, the experience of working, and the advantage it gives them in getting their next job. A few, but not many, apply because they think the work will be interesting. Often, they choose a particular place because a friend is working there or because it is close to home. Many are looking for part-time work because they are students. Many are working *until*—until school starts or until they get enough money to buy a car. Some hospitality companies are now helping new employees with English classes so they can become more valuable employees. One hotel even offered a quick course overview of the hotel to recently graduated but unemployed former high school students and ended up hiring several of them to work at the resort.

Another group of potential hospitality employees is *women* who want to go to work to supplement the family income or simply to get out of the house. A woman with children may be very happy with part-time work, three or four hours spanning the lunch period while the kids are at school, or an evening shift when her husband can take care of the children.

Another group of part-time workers is interested in evening work: *the moonlighters*, people looking for a second job. This is not ideal for either you or them, since they may be tired from working their first job. However, students and homemakers also carry a double load, so perhaps moonlighting is no more difficult.

Another source of workers is the *unemployed*. If they have worked in an operation like yours, they may have skills and experience useful to you. If they were in another line of work, you may be competing with unemployment compensation, which is often more than the wages you pay. Workers from the automobile industry, for example, may have been making $25 an hour, and although their unemployment compensation is not as high as that, it is still above hospitality wages. If compensation runs out and they go to work in a hotel or restaurant, workers from higher-paying industries rarely find satisfaction in their jobs. They are likely to see both the pay and the work as a step down from the jobs they lost. They are truly *until-type* employees.

Top Recruiting Methods

1. Newspaper/magazine

2. Online

3. Company Web site

4. In-house job referral

5. Professional/industry association

6. Job fairs

7. Schools

8. Employment agencies

9. Online resumes

Source: Anonymous, "HR Proceeds with Cautious Optimism on Hiring" *HR Focus*, Vol. 81, No. 4, p. S1, April 2004.

Some people seek work in hotels or restaurants just to get away from what they have been doing. Sometimes, recent college graduates find that they are not happy with the jobs they have taken or the field they prepared for, and they just want to get out. Sometimes these people just want a breather, some time to think things over and make new plans. Sometimes they are thinking of switching to the hotel or restaurant field and want to experience it from the inside before they make up their minds. A number of people today are interested in learning professional cooking because the pay at the top is high and a certain glamour goes with it.

Hiring *retired people* is becoming more commonplace, although the number of retired people who do return to work is still quite small. The over-65 group is growing and will increase to 20 percent of the population in 2030. Retirees often want to work to fill some empty time or perhaps to supplement their income. Although some of our jobs may not be suitable because of physical demands and odd hours, this is not a

First-time job hunters apply for lodging and foodservice jobs because the jobs are available. Courtesy of Photo-Disc/Getty Images.

labor source you should dismiss routinely. Not only is it against the law to discriminate based on age, but also, older workers often have stability and an inner motivation that younger people have not yet developed. One national fast-food chain has made a special effort to develop jobs and hours that fit the availability and skills and talents of the retired. They have found this group to be an excellent source of employees: they are dependable, work-oriented people who are happy to have the jobs. In general, retirees have proven to be loyal, willing, and service-oriented workers. They come to work on time, have much prior work experience on which to draw, and do their jobs well.

Another group of people that might be interested in working in the hospitality industry is the *disabled*. A disabled person has a physical, mental, or developmental impairment that limits one or more of life's major activities. For example, a disabled person may have a visual or hearing impairment or may be mentally retarded. Although you may spend more time training some disabled employees, they tend to be loyal, enthusiastic, hardworking, and dependable. There are disabled employees doing many different hospitality jobs. For instance, a cashier or payroll clerk can work from a wheelchair, a hearing-impaired person can do some food preparation tasks, or a mentally retarded person may be able to wash dishes and pots. It is illegal not to hire a disabled worker unless the disability would interfere with the person's ability to perform the work.

As supervisor, you need to be aware of the fact that your employees may be reluctant to work with a disabled person. This is usually due to a fear of the unknown; most of your employees probably don't know what it is like to interact and work with someone who is disabled. It is your job to build a supportive environment in which the disabled employee, and your other employees, will work well together. Discussing with your employees ahead of time what the new employee will be doing and what to expect can do this. Encourage your employees to talk honestly about how they feel and about their concerns. Be positive about the placement of disabled people in the workplace and what they can accomplish.

> Although you may be shifting your attention to external recruiting, the loyal employees who have stuck by your organization through the past few difficult years may be your best candidates for job openings.
>
> *Source:* Anonymous, "Recruit from Within—or Else," *HR Focus.* Vol. 81, No. 4, p. S3, April 2004.

Often, we set up qualifications for jobs we want to fill that are totally unrealistic (and quite possibly illegal), and if we get what we say we are looking for we will have overqualified and unhappy people. We do not need high school graduates to make beds, bus tables, cook hamburgers, wash vegetables, push vacuum cleaners, or wash pots or floors.

Setting such requirements, in fact, can be interpreted as discriminatory. For some jobs, people do not even need to be able to read and write. All they need is the ability to perform the required tasks. Requirements we set up for a job must be based on the requirements of the work.

Check Your Knowledge

1. To what does *labor market* refer?
2. Compare and contrast the need for staff in a restaurant and in a hotel.

Characteristics of Your Labor Area

You will find it helpful to know something about the labor market in your own area: such things as prevailing wages for various kinds of jobs, unemployment rates for various types of workers, the makeup of the labor force, and the kinds of enterprises that are competing with you for workers, both in and out of your own industry. You should know something of the demographics of your area: ethnic groups, income levels, education levels, and where in your area different groups live. Where do low-income workers, young marrieds, immigrants, and the employable retired typically live? Employers sometimes note the zip code of the area in which the majority of their employees live to know where to do community advertising.

There are other useful things to know about your community. Where are the high schools and colleges that can provide you with student workers? What agencies will work with you to find suitable disabled workers? What are the transportation patterns in your area? Are there buses from where your potential workers live that run at hours to fit your needs? Can workers drive from their homes in a reasonable length of time? Operations such as airports or in-plant cafeterias in outlying areas often find transportation the greatest single problem in finding employees.

In a large organization your human resource department may have such information. In fact, they may take care of much of the routine of recruiting. But the more you participate and the better you know the labor resources of the area, the more likely you are to know how to attract and hold the kind of people you want.

DETERMINING LABOR NEEDS

If you are a busy supervisor and you see a heading like this, your first reaction may be to laugh. What the heck, you need people all the time. You've got no time to make out lists, you need whoever walks in the door, and you are just afraid nobody will walk in. But what if you could turn things around and avoid panic and crisis by hiring workers who are right for the job and will not walk off and leave you in the lurch? And do you realize the hidden costs when you hire unqualified people or people who are wrong for the jobs you ask them to do?

Hiring such workers is worse than useless. Either you will keep those workers and suffer their shortcomings, or you will have to fire them and start all over—and perhaps make the same mistakes. If you train those workers and the ones you replace them with, your training costs will skyrocket and the work will suffer until you get them trained. If you do not train them, they will not do their jobs right and they will waste things and break things and turn out inferior products and give inferior service.

If they are unhappy or incompetent, they will be absent or late a lot, and their morale will be poor and so will everyone else's. They will not get the work done on time, and you will have to pay overtime. They will give poor service and drive customers away, and your sales will dwindle. When you finally do fire them, your unemployment compensation costs will go up and you will have to hire people to take their places: and the next people you hire may be even worse. It is a very, very costly way to choose people, and in time it could cost you your reputation as a good employer, your job, or your business. There are better ways to go about hiring people based on the thinking and experience of experts, and the place to start is to figure out exactly what to look for.

Defining Job Qualifications

To define a job's qualifications, you need to list the knowledge, skills and abilities, work experience, and education and training required. This is known as a job specification. Figure 16.1 shows a sample job specification. Note that there is a heading "Preferred Qualifications"—the reason for this is to avoid any problems with affirmative action. If some applicants do not have the preferred qualifications then they are not as qualified for the position as those who do have the preferred qualifications. Training and certifications may also be added to the specification.

Knowledge consists of the information needed to perform job duties. For example, a cook must know that one cup holds eight ounces, and other measurements, just as the dietary manager in a hospital kitchen must know which foods are not allowed on

---

Job Specification: <u>Server</u>

Department: Dining Room

Grade   6

Job Qualifications:

KNOWLEDGE <u>Basic knowledge of food and cooking.</u>

SKILLS AND ABILITIES <u>Present a good appearance—neat and</u>
<u>well-groomed, interact with guests in a courteous and helpful</u>
<u>manner, work well with other personnel, write neatly,</u>
<u>perform basic mathematical functions (addition, subtraction,</u>
<u>multiplication, and division), set tables, serve and clear.</u>

WORK EXPERIENCE <u>Six months satisfactory experience as a</u>
<u>server required. One year preferred.</u>

EDUCATION AND TRAINING <u>High school graduate and/or</u>
<u>service training preferred.</u>

PREFERRED QUALIFICATIONS <u>a) 1 year in a fine dining</u>
<u>restaurant environment. b) must be able to work on weekends.</u>

FIGURE 16.1 Job specifications.

modified diets. You can use verbs such as *knows, defines, lists*, or *explains* to begin a knowledge statement.

Skills and abilities refer to competence in performing a task or behaving in a certain manner. Must a person be able to lift 100-pound bags and boxes? Add and subtract and multiply? Convert recipes? Mix *x* number of drinks per hour? Cook eggs to order at a certain rate? Have a responsive, outgoing approach to people? Be as specific as possible.

Performance standards, if you have them, will tell you the specific skills you are looking for. You must decide whether to buy these skills or do your own skills training. If you plan to train, you need to define the qualities that will make people trainable for a given job. A bartender, for example, needs manual dexterity. Desk clerks and serving personnel need verbal skills.

The qualifications that you list in your job specification must not discriminate in any way on the basis of race, national origin, gender, age, marital or family status, religion, or disability. The place to begin in avoiding discrimination is with your job specifications. It is important that you phrase them in concrete terms of what each job requires and that you think in these terms as well.

According to Office Team (Menlo Park, California; www.officeteam.com), interviews and reference checks are the most effective tools for identifying top performers. Interviewers look for motivation, versatility, and a proactive approach. Other qualities to consider:

1. Passion

2. Favorites

3. Optimism

4. Expectations

5. Tone

Source: Anonymous, "Keeping Current: Recruitment and Hiring," *Partner's Report*, Vol. 04, No. 3, p. 5, March 2004.

Forecasting Personnel Needs

Anticipating your needs for workers will give you time to look for the right people. If you need extra people for holiday and vacation periods, hire them ahead of time or your competitors will beat you to the best people. Records of past sales or occupancy or special events may indicate trends in people needs. Look ahead to changes in your business: Is your employer planning to expand? And how will it affect your department's need for people?

Scheduling is a key factor. Your work schedules form a day-to-day forecast of the people you need at each hour of the day. Plan them in advance. Make sure that your workers are aware of any changes you make, and make sure that they tell you well in advance of any changes that they have in mind.

Employees need an environment that motivates them and offers benefits. Let employees know that you value their opinion. If at all possible, allow schedules to be flexible. This gives employees a feeling of control and the comfort of knowing that if something comes up, they will not be criticized. Today, more people are demanding that their personal lives be taken as seriously as their work lives. People want to be taken seriously; they are concerned about pursuing their own personal goals. Your employees need to feel respected by you.[1]

As an employer it is important that you try to meet the needs of both your employees and the company. Examine your scheduling as a whole. First, does it provide efficiently for your needs? Second, are there ways of organizing the shifts that would be more attractive to the type of person you would like to hire? Do you ask people to work short shifts at unattractive hours, such as early in the morning or late at night? A country club advertised a split shift of 11 to 3 and 5 to 11, three days a week—is that likely to appeal to anyone? That's a 10-hour day with hardly enough time between shifts to go home, yet it is not a full 40-hour week.

Consider revamping your schedules with people's needs and desires in mind. Look at the hours from their point of view. How far do they have to travel? How much useful personal time does your schedule leave them? How much money do they make for the time involved in working for you, including travel times? Ask your present workers how they feel about their days and hours, and try to devise schedules that will not only fill your needs but will be attractive to new people as well. Your people will appreciate it if you give them a chance to move to a shift they like better before you hire someone new to fill a vacancy. Often, before making decisions it is important to implement new plans or policies with the staff. Include staff in decision-making process and find out how they feel on certain policies; you may be surprised at what they have to say.

Another key factor in forecasting personnel needs is *downtime*, the length of time that a position is vacant until a new employee who can fully perform the job fills it. Let's consider how long downtime might normally be: An employee resigns and gives you only two days' notice. It's not unusual, particularly if you don't make a point of requiring proper notice (usually two weeks) and withhold something of value to the employee, such as accrued vacation time, if proper notice is not given. Once the employee resigns, depending on your employer's procedures, you may have to fill out an employment requisition form. A requisition is something like a purchase order that must be signed by the appropriate person before you can begin the recruiting process.

Let's say that this takes one week. If you want to advertise the job, you will probably have to wait another week before the ad appears and you get responses. Now you can probably plan on one to two weeks to screen applicants, interview and test applicants, check references, and make a final selection. Often, the person you hire must give his or her current employer two weeks' notice, so you wait a little more.

Scheduling is an important task, which, when done well, helps ensure a smooth-running operation. Courtesy Sarasota Memorial Hospital.

Now if you believe in magic, when the new employee shows up for the first day of work, you will think your problems are over and put the new employee right to work. Wrong! Now it will take at least one week, probably more, before your new employee gets up to speed in the new position. It has now been about six to seven weeks since your employee resigned. One way to help reduce downtime is to forecast your personnel needs periodically. Figure 16.2 shows a staffing guide form that can be used every two months to help determine when to hire new employees so that downtime is minimized. Staffing guides are based on the budget and expected volume of business.

Training versus Buying Skills

In determining your personnel needs, you must decide whether to buy skills or to train new people yourself. Most managers will tell you they simply don't have time to

STAFFING GUIDE

Department: _____   Date: _____

Positions	Number Full Staff	Staff on Hand	Current Openings	Anticipated Openings	Total to Be Hired	Time Required to Recruit and Train

FIGURE 16.2 Staffing Guides help supervisors determine when to hire new employees.

train people—they are too busy with the work itself. They look for people who have experience in the jobs they are hiring for, even when they have to pay a higher wage.

There is no security in hiring experience, however. You may pay more to break someone of five years of forming bad habits than it would cost you to train an inexperienced person from scratch. For exactly this reason, a number of corporations hire only people with no experience for certain jobs. If you do hire experience, it is important to verify it by checking references and to evaluate it by testing performance.

Training takes the time of both trainer and trainee, and that is expensive. But putting people in jobs without enough training is likely to be more costly in the end. The worker does not perform well and is not happy, the customer suffers and is not happy, and you will suffer, too, and you will not be happy. You really don't have time not to train people. There is more on this subject in Chapter 18.

Check Your Knowledge

1.   Discuss why it is important to know the characteristics of your labor needs.

2.   Explain what is known as *job qualification*.

RECRUITING

General Recruiting Principles

Since the legal aspects of recruiting and selection were covered in Chapter 3 we will move on to recruiting. Recruiting—looking actively for people to fill jobs—is a form of marketing. You are in the labor market to sell jobs to people who might want them. Because your need is constant and urgent, because you have many competitors, and because many of your jobs are not the most exciting ways of making a living, you really need to work at making your recruiting effective.

The first word to keep in mind is *appropriate*. You must put out your message in appropriate places and aim it toward people you would like to hire. Use techniques appropriate to your image and to the kinds of people you want to attract. A "Help Wanted" sign in a dirty and fly-specked window is going to reach only people who pass by and attract only people who reflect that image themselves—if it attracts anyone at all. "Now Hiring" hanging in a clean window is only one step up.

Take a look at some of the classified ads found in Figure 16.3. Which one might you respond to? Can you decipher what all the abbreviations mean? Which advertisement tells you the most about the restaurant and the nature of the jobs available? If you project an image of being a desirable employer through your advertisements, you are probably going to attract desirable applicants.

Your message must be appropriate: Tell them what they want to know. They want to know (1) what the job is, (2) where you are, (3) what the hours are, (4) what qualifications are needed, and (5) how to apply. "Bartender Wanted" and a phone number is not going to pull them in until after they have tried everyone else. They are also interested in (6) attractive features of the job, such as good wages and benefits.

Recruiting excellent candidates is requisite to ensuring excellent morale and guest satisfaction.

It is also essential to use channels of communication appropriate to the people you want to reach, the same channels that they are using to look for jobs. You must get the message to the areas where they live and use media of communication they see and hear.

The second word to keep in mind is *competitive*. You are competing with every other hotel and foodservice operation in your area for the same types of people. For unskilled labor you may also be competing with other types of operations as well: retail stores, light industry, and so on. You must sell your jobs and your company at least as well as your competitors sell theirs, if not better.

The third word to remember is *constant*. It is a good practice to be on the lookout for potential employees all the time, even when you have no vacancies. Even the best and luckiest of employers in your field will probably replace at least six out of every 10 employees in a year's time, and many operations run far higher than that. Keep a file of the records of promising people who apply each time you fill a job, and look through them the next time you need to hire.

FIGURE 16.3 Classified advertisements.

You will also have drop-in applicants from time to time. Pay attention to them; they have taken the initiative to seek you out. Ask for a resume and let them know that you will add it to the talent bank. Give them a tentative date to call back, and be cordial. They should leave with a feeling of wanting to work for you; remember that you are marketing yourself as a good employer, and you may need them tomorrow.

The final words of wisdom are: *use a multiple approach.* Do not depend on a single resource or channel; try a variety of methods to attract people. There are many channels: schools and colleges giving hotel and foodservice and bartending courses, well-chosen word-of-mouth channels such as current employees, notices on the right bulletin boards (the student union, the school financial aid office, even the Laundromat if you are after a part-time homemaker), newspaper and radio ads, online job resources, trade unions, employment agencies, community organizations, summer job fairs, and organizations working to place certain groups of people such as refugees or minorities or disabled persons. You can also go out into the field and recruit workers directly wherever they are.

Let us look at some of these resources and channels in more detail.

Profile

PATRICK ACCORD

Courtesy of
Patrick Accord

Regardless of industry, supervision is a key constant: key because the quality of supervision affects the bottom line as well as most of the operations required to reach that point; constant because you can be assured that there will always be someone looking over your shoulder. Regardless of industry, there are certain qualities and characteristics that define a good supervisor. My personal experience, based on work as a kitchen/chef supervisor, coupled with other experiences as an employee under supervision, has taught me that certain traits common to the most effective supervisors cross industry boundaries.

While supervising a kitchen, I learned quickly that personal communication is one of the main ingredients needed by an effective supervisor. Actually, I think I learned this while working under supervisors who weren't able to communicate effectively. There is nothing more disheartening for an employee than when he or she is blamed for something that was altered or lost in the channels of communication. To minimize the chance that information is lost in the chain of command, shorten the chain. The most effective supervisors and managers that I've witnessed are the ones who are in the field with employees, talking with them and keeping lines of communication intact. There is no need to ask Cook 1 what Cook 2 has been doing when you can just ask Cook 1 himself.

Through hard work and communication, a supervisor can then begin to foster a team atmosphere. A supervisor shapes a group's atmosphere or company culture through his work ethic, attitude, and set regulations. The supervisor must set the standard for hard work, do it in an affable manner, and set rules for the benefit of the entire unit. These rules might include a certain dress code or even a dress-down day. Functioning as a group in the workplace, so that the work can be accomplished efficiently, is the key to profitability.

Hopefully, a supervisor who begins to foster a good atmosphere will be able to retain employees. Quality in almost any industry is synonymous with consistency. Two out of the four employees left during my first week of supervising the kitchen. Even though they had served notice and we started training in preparation, their loss set our consistency off for almost a month. Customers were complaining that their favorite recipes over the last several years tasted different and they weren't going to give us another chance. I stress the importance of consistency in everything that a supervisor does.

Obviously, good supervision is multidimensional and much more involved than the limited discussion above indicates. But I believe that the basic tenet of open lines of communication leads to good relationships, a good working environment, and retention of employees. Quality is consistency, and as we keep employee turnover at a minimum and build a valued and trusted staff, our jobs as supervisors become that much easier and more profitable.

Internal Recruiting

Internal recruiting is the process of letting your own employees know about job openings so that they may apply for them. Often, the most successful placements occur through people who already work for you. Internal recruiting often results in promoting from within, a practice in which current employees are given preference for promotions over outside applicants with similar backgrounds. Promoting from within has several advantages: It rewards employees for doing a good job, it motivates employees and gives them something to work toward, and it maintains consistency within the enterprise.

Now how can you be sure of letting all employees know about open positions? Using a practice called job posting, a representative (usually from the human resources or personnel department) posts lists of open positions (Figure 16.4) in specific locations where employees are most likely to see them. Usually, employees are given a certain period of time, such as five days, in which to apply before applicants from the outside will be evaluated. In most cases, employees must meet certain conditions before responding to a job posting. For instance, the employee may be required to have a satisfactory rating on his or her last evaluation and have been in his or her current position for at least six months. These conditions prevent employees from jumping around too often to different jobs, a practice that benefits neither you nor your employee.

When you can't find a current employee to fill an open position, your employees may refer their friends and acquaintances to you. Some employers give a cash or merchandise reward to employees who bring in somebody who works for at least a certain time, such as 90 days. Many employers trying to draw in new employees have used these types of programs, called employee referral programs, very successfully. Employees who refer applicants are usually asked to fill out a referral form or card that may be handed in with the applicant's application form.

Date: Monday, September 25

Department: Food and Nutrition Services

Job Title: Food Service Worker

Job Code: 600026

Reports to: Operations Supervisor

Job Qualifications:

1. Six months experience in a health care facility.
2. High school graduate.
3. Courtesy and diplomacy in dealing with patients, hospital staff, fellow workers, and the department's management team.
4. Ability to consistently demonstrate the values of Sarasota Memorial Health Care System.
5. Communication skills, verbal and reading: required to read and understand written instructions, recipes, and labels.

Mental/Physical Demands:

1. Adaptability to routine work involving short-cycle repetitive duties under specific instructions.
2. Demonstration of good judgment consistently showing insight into problems.
3. Continuous physical activity involves standing, walking, bending and stooping. Amount of weight lifted is routinely 25–30 pounds, and up to 50 pounds. Must be able to push carts weighing to 400 pounds.
4. Talking, hearing and visual acuity essential.
5. Versatility required to adapt to frequently changing conditions in job duties covering a broad range of food service and production activities.
6. Finger and manual dexterity and motor coordination as required to manipulate kitchen utensils and food service supplies skillfully.

FIGURE 16.4 Job posting.

The idea behind this type of program is that if your present employees are good workers and are happy working for you, they are not likely to bring in someone who won't suit you or who won't fit into the work group. Bringing a total stranger into a group of workers can be very disruptive. Sometimes employees bring in relatives. Among employers there are two schools of thought about this: Some say that it is an absolute disaster, whereas others find that it works out well. It probably depends on the particular set of relatives. If a family fights all the time, you do not want them working for you. Some people point out that if one family member leaves or is terminated, the other will probably quit, too, and then you will have two jobs to fill. You have a similar problem if there is a family emergency; you will be short both employees.

> When screening, it is important to strike a balance. Extensive screening of potential and existing staff risks falling foul of the law, failing to respect individuals' rights and treating people in a discriminatory manner. Conversely, organizations could miss out on people who could be a highly valuable asset. Tread carefully.
> *Source:* Liz Hall, "Looks Good on Paper?" *Personnel Today*, p. 17, March 2004.

Other internal recruiting methods include speaking with applicants who walk in, call in, or write in. These applicants should be asked to fill out an application form and should be interviewed when possible.

External Recruiting

The remaining recruiting methods are all considered external recruiting, that is, seeking applicants from outside the operation. An advantage of bringing in outsiders is that they tend to bring in new ideas and a fresh perspective.

Advertising   The classified ad section of the Sunday paper is probably the most common meeting place for job seekers and employers. It is also the best source for reaching large numbers of applicants, although it does not necessarily bring in the best candidates. Probably 90 percent of employers looking for non-college-educated employees advertise in newspapers, which makes it a competitive job market as well as a popular one for job seekers. You can run an ad at a better rate for seven days or for three days than for one, but Sunday is your best day.

There are two types of ads: *classified* and *display*. Because they take up less space, classified ads are less costly than display ads. However, display ads using the company's logo attract more attention and set your ad apart from others (Figure 16.5). Regardless of the type of ad, be sure to include information on (1) what the job is, (2) where you are, (3) what the hours are, (4) what qualifications are needed, and (5) how to apply. Regarding how to apply, there are two types of ads: open, which give your company name and address, and *blind*, which do not reveal company identity, but instead, give a box number for responses. Blind ads pull in fewer responses than open ads because

JW Restaurants has a career for you

RESTAURANT MANAGERS
&
ASSISTANT RESTAURANT MANAGERS

We are a high-quality tablecloth restaurant company based in Chicago and Atlanta with 24 restaurants, expanding to 28 this year. We are looking for outstanding individuals to join our team.

We offer:

> ➤ Moving and relocating expenses

> ➤ A $3000 signing bonus

> ➤ An exciting work environment

> ➤ Paid medical, dental, and optical insurance

> ➤ Paid vacation

> ➤ A 401(k) plan

> ➤ Career development, training, and seminars

> ➤ Exceptional salary and bonus package

• VIEW OUR WEB SITE AT **JWRESTAURANTS.COM** •

Email or send your résumé to: Jwrestaurants.com
                                           1000 Restaurant Way
                                           CHIGAGO, IL 12345

FIGURE 16.5 Display ads attract more attention and can give more information than classified ads.

readers don't know who the company is (it could even be their current employer). The open ad brings in larger numbers of applicants, or it can screen applicants by listing job requirements in detail.

Another way to screen is to include a specific instruction such as "Call Joe 9–11 A.M." The people who call Joe at 2 P.M. obviously do not follow written instructions, so if the job requires following written instructions, you can eliminate these callers then and there (unless nobody calls between 9 and 11 and you are in a panic). Your company name and address will screen out people who do not want to work there for whatever reason.

When you are writing job advertisements, avoid terms that may be perceived as discriminatory, such as *busboy* or *hostess*. These terms indicate that the applicants should be male in the case of the busboy, or female in the case of the hostess. This is discriminatory, and therefore illegal, but you see it frequently in the newspapers. Also, avoid references to age, such as "young" or "recent high school graduate."

The number of applicants an ad pulls will vary greatly with the state of the economy. In good times even an enticing ad may pull fewer responses than you would like. But when unemployment is high, even your most careful attempts to screen will not keep the numbers down. People who need that job are going to apply for it no matter what your ad says. You may have 250 applicants for one potwashing job.

If you are going to advertise in the paper, it is well worth studying the ad pages to see what your competition is doing. Read all the ads with the mind-set of a job seeker, and then write one that will top them all. Display ads such as those in Figure 16.5 attract attention and project a good image. Many ads mention incentives such as benefits, equal opportunity, job training, career growth, and other attractions. Usually, such ads are for large numbers of jobs (hotel openings, new units of chains, and so on) or for skilled labor or management jobs. If you are only looking for one potwasher, you may not want to go all out in your ad, but if you want a competitive potwasher, run a good-looking, competitive ad.

Some companies advertise all the time. There are two types: the third-rate place whose third-rate ad isn't pulling anyone in ("Needed: intelligent, well-groomed person for nightclub work; call Pete") and the large corporation that runs a two-line ad to keep its name in the job seeker's consciousness ("TGI Friday's, have a nice day!" or "Plaza of the Americas Hotel is the finest").

In addition to advertising in the major area paper, consider running ads in special places where your potential workers will see them. Many cities have special area newspaper and shopping guides. Place your ads in those areas where your target workers live—people within commuting distance who may be candidates for your types of jobs. For instance, if many of the potential employees in your area speak Spanish, consider running an ad in Spanish-language newspapers. Other special places are the school, college, and local newspapers in your area. There are also Web sites that list job opening in the same ways as newspapers.

In addition to newspaper advertising, some employers use Web sites, radio, and television. These media can reach many more people and do so, of course, at a much higher price. The higher price is due in part to the cost of using an advertising agency to develop the ad for you. Radio and television can be used very effectively to reach certain groups, such as teenagers.

A low-cost place to advertise is right in your operation. You can use any of the following to bring in applicants: placemats, indoor or outdoor signs (if done professionally), receipts, or table tents, to name just a few. Finally, you can advertise open jobs by posting notices in supermarkets, libraries, churches, synagogues, community centers, and health clubs.

Employment Agencies Employment agencies are a resource you should look into under certain circumstances. We will look at three common types of agencies: private, temporary, and government. Private employment agencies normally charge a fee, which is not collected until they successfully place an applicant with you. In most cases, if this person does not stay with the company for a specified period of time, the agency must find a suitable replacement or return the fee. The fee is often 10 percent of the employee's first-year salary. These types of agencies most often handle management or high-skills jobs and should be used only if they specialize in your field.

Temporary agencies have recently grown in size and importance, and now a small number specialize in filling positions, including entry-level positions, for hotels, restaurants, and caterers. Temporary agencies charge by the hour for personnel who work anywhere from one day to as long as needed. Using temporary employees is advantageous during peak business periods or other times when emergency fill-in personnel are needed. However, you can't expect a temporary employee to walk into your operation and go straight to work. You must be willing and able to spend time and money to orient and train these employees.

Another source of employees, at no cost, is the U.S. Employment Service, a federal and state system of employment offices called Job Service Centers. Your local Job Service Center will screen and provide applicants for entry-level jobs. The centers have many unemployed people on their books who are looking for jobs. It is a question of whether they are well enough staffed to be able to sift through the people and send you suitable applicants who will not waste your time.

Direct Recruiting Direct recruiting, going where the job seekers are, is practiced primarily by large organizations seeking management talent or top-level culinary skills. Such organizations send recruiters to colleges that teach hospitality management or culinary skills to interview interested candidates. There are also certain situations in which direct recruiting is appropriate for entry-level and semiskilled personnel. For example, when a hotel or restaurant closes, you might arrange to interview its employees. A large layoff at a local factory might be another such situation. It may be worthwhile to interview foodservice students in secondary or vocational schools.

Some large cities hold job fairs in early summer to help high school students find summer work. This would be an appropriate place for direct recruiting. Summer employees, if they like the way they are treated, can also become part-time or occasional employees during the school year that follows.

One of the advantages of direct recruiting is that you may get better employees than you would by waiting for them to drop around or to answer your ad in the Sunday paper. Another advantage is the image-building possibilities of direct recruiting. You are not only hiring for the present; you are creating a good image of your company as a place of future employment. Some companies also have internal job fairs where managers are available to talk with employees about their jobs so they have a better idea of what it takes to be a manager. It shows the companies willingness to promote from within.

Additional External Recruiting Sources Organizations that are involved with minorities, women, disabled workers, immigrants, or other special groups will usually be very cooperative and eager to place their candidates. Examples of such organizations include the National Association for the Advancement of Colored People, the National Organization of Women, and the American Association for Retired Persons. Since these organizations do not work only in hospitality, they may not be familiar with the demands of your jobs, and it is absolutely necessary that you be very clear and open and honest about what each job entails. Here again your detailed job descriptions and performance standards are available. In addition, community organizations such as church groups, Girl Scouts, and Boy Scouts can be sources of employees.

It is a good idea to tell people with whom you do business when you are trying to fill a job. Many of the salespersons you deal with, for example, have wide contacts in the field, and they have good reason to help you out if you are a customer.

Sometimes friends and acquaintances in other fields know of someone who needs a job. Clergy, whose parishioners have confided in them about their financial problems may be able to send people looking for work to you. Sometimes parents are looking for jobs for their children. Through individual contacts you often reach people who are not yet actively looking for jobs but intend to start soon.

Many people say that one person's telling another that yours is a good place to work is the best advertising there is and that it will provide you with a steady stream of applicants. Whether the stream of applicants appears or not, there is no guarantee that it will send you the people you want. You are more likely to get the type of people you are looking for through a systematic marketing plan to reach your target groups. But one thing is true: If yours is a good place to work, you will not need as many applicants because they will stay with you longer.

Evaluating Your Recruiting

To determine which sources give you the best workers, you need to evaluate the results over a period of time. What is your successful rate of hire from each source? What is the cost, not only the cash paid out for ads but the hire ratio to numbers interviewed from each source? Interviewing is time consuming, and if interviewing people from a certain source is just an exercise in frustration, that is not a good source.

What is the tenure of people from each source: How long on average have they stayed? How many have stayed more than 30 days or three months? How good is their performance? If you find that you are getting poor workers from a particular source, you should drop that source. If you are getting good people from a certain source, stick with it.

You should also evaluate your own recruiting efforts. Are you staying competitive? Do you explain the job clearly and completely and honestly, or do you oversell the job? Do you project a good image for your enterprise, or do you oversell the company? If you oversell, your mistakes will come back to haunt you.

Check Your Knowledge

1.   What is *negligent hiring?* As a supervisor, what responsibilities should you have to take into consideration?

2.   Discuss briefly the principles for recruiting.

3.   What are *internal recruiting* and *external recruiting?*

SELECTING THE RIGHT PERSON

Let us suppose that you now have a number of applicants for a job you want to fill. Ten applicants for one job is considered by experts to be a good ratio, but that number will vary. Up to a point, the more you have to choose from, the better your chances are of finding someone who is right for the job. But even if you have only one applicant, you should go through the entire selection procedure. It may save you from a terrible mistake.

It is critical to select the right person for the open position. Companies like Ritz-Carlton arrange for final applicants to complete a "Talent" interview to determine if the candidate will fit with the Ritz-Carlton culture and be able to provide genuine caring service to guests. The most successful person may not be the most experienced person—natural talent plus a really positive attitude and desire to be a team player and to learn more every day, will frequently be a better person for hospitality companies.

Other positive signs of a good candidate are things like—do they smile in the first few seconds, and what feeling do I get from them, and do they exhibit a passion for the hospitality business?[2] Some companies use current employees on a selection committee because they will be working with the new hire.

We all know that the hospitality industry has a high turnover rate and much of this high turnover is due to poor selection. The cost of replacing employees is about $8,000 in a high-end hospitality business. This sounds like a lot, but by the time you add up all the costs involved with every stage of the process—position announcements, advertising, recruiting, selection, interviewing, testing, drug screening, talent interview, background checks, and job offers, you can see that this is no overstatement.[3] For line employees in mid-market hospitality organizations the typical cost of turnover is about $5,000 per position. However, the payoff is more than offset in reduced turnover that can occur with effective and efficient selection.

So, if you want friendly, courteous service, you must hire friendly, courteous people. Hiring employees is like casting stars for a movie—if we do the job well people will believe that the actor is actually the person they are portraying. Walt Disney World allows its best employees, known as star "cast members," to select future cast members. Disney gives these star cast members three weeks of training in the selection process before they join the selection team.

Assuming that you have already established job specifications and have done some preliminary screening through your ads or on the phone, the selection procedure from here on has five elements:

1. The application form
2. The interview and evaluation
3. Testing
4. The reference check
5. Making the choice

Application Form

An application form is a fact-finding sheet for each applicant. It is a standard form (Figure 16.6) that asks relevant and job-related questions such as name, address, and phone number, type of job wanted, work history, education, references, and how the applicant heard about the job. As explained in Chapter 13, questions that can be viewed as discriminatory are not allowed (refer to Figure 13.2). You should instruct applicants to complete

APPLICATION FOR EMPLOYMENT
PLEASE PRINT ALL INFORMATION

Date

Month	Day	Year

Equal Opportunity Employer

The Company will not discriminate against an applicant or employee because of race, sex, age, religious creed, political affiliation, national origin, sexual preference, disability, or any veteran status.

Last Name	First	Middle Initial	Social Security Number

Present Address (Street & Number)	City	State	Zip Code	Home Phone Number ( )

Address where you may be contacted if different from present address	Alternate Phone Number ( )

Are you 16 years of age or older?   U.S. Citizen or Resident Alien?   If no, indicate type of Visa
☐ YES ☐ NO   ☐ YES ☐ NO

JOB INTEREST

Position you are applying for:	Type of position you eventually desire:

Available for:
☐ Full-Time   ☐ Day Shift   ☐ Weekends
☐ Part-Time   ☐ Evening Shift   ☐ Other _____
☐ Per Diem   ☐ Night Shift

When would you be available to begin work?

Have you previously been employed by us? ☐ Yes ☐ No If yes, when	Previous Position(s)

Have you previously submitted an application to us?
☐ Yes   ☐ No   If yes, when

How were you referred to the Company?   ☐ Employment Agency   ☐ Your Own Initiative
☐ Advertisement - Publication _____   ☐ Employee Referral - Name _____

EDUCATION

School	Name and Address	Circle Highest Year Completed	Type of Degree	Major Subject
High School Last Attended		1 2 3 4		
College, University, or Technical School		1 2 3 4		
College, University, or Technical School		1 2 3 4		
Other (Specify)				

FIGURE 16.6 Application for employment.

PREVIOUS EMPLOYMENT — BEGIN WITH PRESENT OR MOST RECENT POSITION

1. Employer

Employed _____ to _____

Address (include Street, City, and Zip Code)

May we contact?   ☐ Yes   ☐ No

Telephone Number   ( )

Starting Position

Salary

Last Position

Salary

Name and Title of Last Supervisor

Telephone Number   ( )

Brief description of duties:

Reason for Leaving:

Disadvantages of Last Position:

2. Employer

Employed _____ to _____

Address (include Street, City, and Zip Code)

May we contact?   ☐ Yes   ☐ No

Telephone Number   ( )

Starting Position

Salary

Last Position

Salary

Name and Title of Last Supervisor

Telephone Number   ( )

Brief description of duties:

Reason for Leaving:

Disadvantages of Last Position:

3. Employer

Employed _____ to _____

Address (include Street, City, and Zip Code)

May we contact?   ☐ Yes   ☐ No

Telephone Number   ( )

Starting Position

Salary

Last Position

Salary

Name and Title of Last Supervisor

Telephone Number   ( )

Brief description of duties:

Reason for Leaving:

Disadvantages of Last Position:

FIGURE 16.6 (Continued)

IF MORE THAN THREE PREVIOUS EMPLOYERS, PLEASE LIST OTHERS HERE

Employment Dates		Company and Address	Position or Type of Work	Salary or Wage	Reason for Leaving
From	To				

Please indicate if you were employed under a different name than the one shown on the first page of this application in any of your previous positions.

Employer	Name Used

U.S. MILITARY RECORD (If related to the job you are applying for)

Branch of Service _____

Active Duty _____ From _____ To _____

Nature of Duties _____

_____

CONVICTIONS/COURT RECORD

Have you been convicted of a crime within the last 7 years?

_____ Yes   _____ No   The existence of a record of convictions for criminal offenses is not considered an automatic bar to employment.

Date of Conviction _____   Describe circumstances: _____

_____

ACKNOWLEDGMENT

I understand that this employment application and any other Company documents are not contracts of employment and that any individual who is hired may voluntarily leave employment upon proper notice and may be terminated by the Company at any time and for any reason. I understand that no employee of the Company has the authority to make any agreement to the contrary and I acknowledge that any oral or written statements to the contrary are hereby expressly disavowed and should not be relied upon by any prospective employee.

I hereby grant permission for the authorities of the Company, or its agents, to investigate my references, and I release the Company and all previous employers, educational institutions, persons, and law enforcement agencies from any and all liability resulting from such an investigation. Upon my termination, I authorize the release of information in connection with my employment.

I certify that the statements made on this application are true and correct, and thereby grant the Company permission to verify the information contained herein.

I understand that giving false information or the failure to give complete information requested herein shall constitute grounds, among others, for rejection of my application or my dismissal in the event of my employment by the Company.

DATE: _____   SIGNATURE OF APPLICANT: _____

FIGURE 16.6 (Continued)

everything, especially the work history, including places and dates of employment, and names of supervisors.

Before you interview an applicant, you should familiarize yourself with the material on the application and jot down questions. What about gaps in employment? Unanswered questions? The way applicants fill out applications can also be very revealing. Do they follow instructions? Can they read and write? Do they understand the questions? Are they neat or messy? Is their handwriting legible? Did they complete everything? Such things may relate to the job requirements. Did they sign the application form—because if they didn't, and you later find out that they had been convicted of a crime, they can always say, "I didn't sign the application form."

The Interview

The first essential for a good interview is a quiet place free of distractions and interruptions, and the first task is to put the candidate at ease. You can tell how they feel by looking for nonverbal clues: a worried look on the face, tensed posture. It is important to remember that people get nervous about interviews. If you can make them feel comfortable and nonthreatened, they are more likely to open up and be themselves, and this is what you are after. Listen attentively; this calls for your best listening skills. And remember that you want to impress them favorably on behalf of your organization. A careless mistake in the beginning can ruin the entire interview.

Prepare a list of questions based on the job description—this underlines the importance of a good job description. With lower-level jobs it is best to follow a preplanned pattern for the interview, so that you cover the same territory with every applicant. You can start off with general information about the job and the company. The interview involves a two-way exchange of information: you want to know about the applicant, and the applicant wants to know about the job. Some employers use a highly structured type of interview known as a patterned interview, in which the interviewer asks each applicant a predetermined list of questions. It is important to ask the same questions to all candidates. There may also be additional questions on the interviewer's form that are not asked of the applicant but are provided to help the interviewer interpret the applicant's responses. The training required for a patterned interview is minimal compared to other methods, and the standardized questions help to avoid possible charges of discrimination.

You are after two kinds of information about the applicant: hard data on skills and experience and personal qualities important to the job. As you go over the application in the interview, fill in all details that the applicant left unanswered and ask questions about gaps of thirty days or more on the employment record. Often, people will not

Getting applicants to talk takes practice. Courtesy of Flat Earth.

list jobs on which they had problems. If they have something to hide, they will hide it, and these are exactly the things you need to find out. Don't hesitate to probe if you are not satisfied with either the applicant or his or her answers to your questions. Take care to avoid questions that could be considered discriminatory.

As to personal qualities, you may never really know what they are like until you put them to work. If you can get them talking, you can judge such traits as verbal skills or ease with people. But you will not be able to tell anything about motivation, temperament, absenteeism, honesty, reliability, and all the other things you are looking for.

Getting people to talk may be agonizing the first time you interview. The best method is to avoid questions that have yes or no answers. Ask: "What did you do at. . .?" "What did you like best about . . .?" "Tell me why . . . ."One owner always asked server applicants about the funniest thing that ever happened to them on the job. He would not hire people who said that nothing funny had ever happened to them because he believed that they could not deal with people effectively if they couldn't see the funny side of things. You should talk only about 20 percent of the time, with the candidate filling in the remaining 80 percent.

Other good work-related questions to ask are: Tell me about the strengths you bring to this job. This position requries good organizational skills; tell me about how organized you are. How did you handle these situations: When a guest was unhappy with the room? When a guest has eaten most of an entree and then says, "I don't like it?" When a guest says, "Why do I have to stand in line for two hours, just to go on one ride at your theme park?" or "You forgot my dinner" to the hospitality server in a hospital room?

Avoid asking about what the applicant likes to do for fun—what if the answer is "on Wednesday night I have Bible study," and he or she doesn't get the job? The applicant could claim that you discriminated on religious grounds. If it doesn't pertain to the job, don't ask it.[4]

Ask if you may make notes (but not on the application form because it goes in the applicant's file and can later be used as evidence in a legal case and your comments may come back to haunt you). You can do this during the interview if it does not inhibit the applicant; otherwise, do it immediately after, lest you forget. Avoid writing down subjective opinions or impressions; instead, write down specific job-related facts and direct observations. Be objective, factual, and clear.

Evaluate the applicant immediately on your list of specifications for the job, using a rating system that is meaningful to you, such as a point system or a descriptive ranking: (1) exceptional, hire immediately; (2) well qualified; (3) qualified with reservations; (4) not qualified. Some large companies have evaluation forms or systems they may require you to use. Look at the applicants from the perspective of what they can do and what they will do. Can-do factors include the applicant's job knowledge, past experience, and education—in other words, whether the applicant can perform the job. Will-do factors examine an applicant's willingness, desire, and attitude toward performing the job. You want the person who you hire to be both technically capable to do the job (or be trainable) and willing to do the job. Without one or the other, you are creating a problem situation and possibly a problem employee.

Evaluation is a subjective business; it is based primarily on feelings and emotions. People turn you off or they turn you on; you like them or you don't; and you will make your decision to hire or not to hire primarily on this interview, whether your judgment is valid or not. Studies have shown that there is very little correlation between interview evaluation and success on the job. They also show that interviewers make up their minds in the first four minutes.

Yet you would not dare skip the interview. So how can you get the most value out of it? If you are aware of what is going on in your head and in the other person's behavior, it will help you to evaluate applicants more objectively.

One thing that is happening is that applicants are giving you the answers they think you want to hear and projecting the image they think you are looking for, and they may not be like that at all in real life. Yet often they let their guard down when the interview is just about over and reveal their true selves in the last few minutes. If you are aware of this, perhaps you can exchange the first four minutes with the last few in making your evaluations.

It is very easy, in that first four minutes, to be influenced by one or two characteristics and extend them into an overall impression of a person. This is known as the halo effect or overgeneralization. You may be so impressed with someone who is articulate and well dressed that you jump to the conclusion that this applicant will make a great bartender. The first day on the job, this impressive person has drunk half a bottle of bourbon two hours into the shift.

A negative impression may be just as misleading. One restaurant manager interviewed a man for a dishwasher job and was so shaken by what he perceived as a wild look in the man's eyes that he was literally afraid to have the man in the place at all. So in the usual panic and crisis, he hired a young kid. He told a friend in the business about the wild-looking man, and the friend said, "You have just turned down the only absolutely professional dishwasher in this entire city." So after the young kid quit two days later, the manager got in touch with the wild-looking man, who accepted the position, stayed 15 years, never was absent, never was late, never broke anything, kept the dishroom spotless, polished the dishmachine every day, and retired on a company pension.

Another form of overgeneralization is to assume that all applicants from a certain school or all people your potwasher knows personally and says are okay are going to be good workers. This is not necessarily so; it is a generalization about personality rather than knowledge or skill.

Another thing that happens easily is to let *expectations* blind you to reality. If someone has sent you an applicant with a glowing recommendation, you will tend to see that applicant in those terms, whether or not they are accurate.

Still another thing that is easy to do is to see some facet of yourself in someone else and to assume that this person is exactly like you. You discover that this person grew up in your old neighborhood, went to the same school that you did, had some of the same teachers, and knows people you know. A spark is kindled and you think, "Hallelujah, this person has got to be great!" This reaction is known as projection—you project your own qualities onto that person. Furthermore, you are so excited about finding someone exactly like you (you think) that you may even forget what that has to do with the job for which you are interviewing this person.

What it all comes down to is that in interviewing and evaluating, you need to stick closely to the personal qualities needed *on the job* and to be on guard against your subjective reactions and judgments. Do not make snap judgments and do not set standards that are higher than necessary. Not all positions require people who are enthusiastic, articulate, or well educated, so don't be turned off by a quiet school dropout who can't put six words together to make a sentence.

When it comes to telling applicants about a job, you should be open and honest and completely frank. If they will have to work Sundays and holidays, tell them so. One supervisor told an applicant she would work a five-day week. The applicant assumed that it was Monday through Friday, and that was fine. But when she reported for work and they told her it was Wednesday through Sunday, she quit then and there. She felt that the supervisor had cheated, and from that point on the trust was gone.

Be frank about days and hours, overtime, pay and tips, uniforms, meals, and all the rest, so the new employee will start the job with no unpleasant surprises. You might call this truth in hiring. Sure, you want to sell your jobs, but overselling will catch up with you.

Explain your pay scale and your promotion policy: "This is what you start at, this is what you can make with overtime, this is what you can realistically expect in tips, this is what you will take home, this is as high as you can go in this job, these are the jobs you can eventually work up to, these are your chances of that happening." Give them a chance to ask questions, and then end the interview. Tell them when you will make your decision and ask them to call you the day after that if they have not heard from you. All together it should take you 20 to 30 minutes to interview an applicant for an entry-level job and up to 60 minutes for a supervisory position. Tips for interviewing are summarized in Figure 16.7.

During the interview, clarify the important aspects of the job. For instance: "This job requires that you work Tuesday to Saturday, are you able to do that?" or "This position requires you to work evenings and weekends, are you able to do that?" Or, "This position requires you to lift up to 50 pounds. Can you do that?"

Testing

Some companies use tests as an additional method of evaluating applicants. Sometimes tests are given before the interview to screen out candidates. Sometimes they are given after interviews to the small group of candidates still in the running, to add objective data to subjective evaluations. Various kinds of tests are used:

1. Skills tests measure specific skills.

2. Aptitude tests are intended to measure ability to learn a particular job or skill. Manual dexterity tests are a form of aptitude test and measure manipulative ability.

3. Psychological tests are designed to measure personality traits; large companies often use them in hiring management personnel.

4. Medical examinations measure physical fitness.

1. Be nonjudgmental during the entire interview process. Do not jump to conclusions. A poor interviewer reaches a decision in the first 5 minutes.
2. Recognize your personal biases and try not to let them influence you. Be objective. Do not look for clones of yourself. Do not let an applicant's age, gender, attractiveness, or verbal fluency influence your opinions.
3. Spend most of your time listening attentively. Allow the candidate to do at least 70 to 80 percent of the talking. Listen to each answer before deciding on the next question. Do not interrupt.
4. Make notes so that vital information is not forgotten.
5. Repeat or paraphrase the applicant's statements to make sure that you understand the applicant and perhaps get more information, or you may repeat the last few words the applicant just said with a questioning inflection. Also, summarize the applicant's statements periodically to clarify points and to bring information together. A summary statement may begin with, "Let's state the major points up to now. . . ." In this manner, the applicant can confirm or clarify what has been discussed.
6. Another technique to get a quiet applicant to talk and show interest is to ask open-ended questions (questions without a yes or no answer) and use pauses. Pauses allow the applicant to sense that more information is desired and hopefully, the interviewee will feel compelled to fill the silence.
7. Use body language to show interest and elicit information. Use direct eye contact, nod, smile, and lean forward slightly.
8. Do not be bashful about probing for more information when it is needed.
9. Instead of asking about an applicant's "weaknesses," refer to areas of improvement.
10. Paint a realistic picture of the job. Be honest.
11. Always be sincere, respectful, courteous, friendly, and treat all applicants in the same way.
12. Allow the applicant to ask questions of you.

FIGURE 16.7 Tips for interviewing.

Except for medical examinations and skills tests, most hospitality enterprises do not use tests for nonmanagement jobs. There are several reasons for this. One is the time it takes to give tests and score them. Another is that many of the tests available have little relevance to the requirements of nonmanagement jobs. A third is that many tests, having been constructed for populations of a certain background and education, discriminate against applicants who do not have that background and education. It is illegal to use such tests either in hiring or in promotion.

To be usable, a test must be valid, reliable, and relevant to the job. To be valid, it must actually measure what it is designed to measure. To be reliable, it must be consistent in its measurement, that is, give the same result each time a given person takes it. To be relevant, it must relate to the specific job for which it is given. The user of any test must determine that it meets these criteria and must use it properly as its publisher designed it to be used. All in all, the complications of testing, the risks of discrimination, and the possibilities for error at the hands of an untrained user make most tests more trouble than they are worth.

Skills tests and specific aptitude tests such as manual dexterity tests are the exceptions. Your best bet, and the one most closely geared to your job needs, is a set of skills tests derived from your performance standards. They must be adapted somewhat since the applicant will not know all the ins and outs of your special house procedures, but this can be done. It will give you an objective measure of an applicant's ability to perform on the job and an indication of how much additional training is needed.

Psychological tests are used to test for honesty and even broader qualities such as integrity. These tests are based on the assumption that honest and dishonest people have different values and see the world differently. Some employers use honesty tests in the hopes of providing a secure workplace for their employees.

Using honesty tests properly requires some work. First, some states and localities do not allow such testing, so check the regulations. Next, you need to examine independent reviews and validity tests (provided that the instrument actually tests what it is supposed to test) of the instrument you want to use. Even if you find a good instrument, and it is legal in your location, don't forget that testing also requires money and time and that the results are not a substitute for any of the other selection steps you take, such as interviewing or making reference checks.

A medical examination can be required only after a job offer has been made to the applicant. When a job offer is made prior to the medical exam, it is considered a conditional job offer because if the applicant does not pass the medical exam, the job offer is normally revoked.

The Employee Polygraph Protection Act of 1988 prohibits the use of lie detectors in the screening of job applicants. Although lie detectors have been used in the past in some states, they are now illegal to use in the employment process.

Check Your Knowledge

1.   What are the elements that the selection process includes?

2.   Give a tip that is useful when interviewing.

3.   What does the Employee Polygraph Protection Act of 1988 prohibit?

Reference Check

You have now narrowed your choice to two or three people. The reference check is the final step before hiring. It is a way to weed out applicants who have falsified or stretched their credentials or who in other jobs have been unsatisfactory. Reference information can be thought of in two ways: substance and style. *Substance* concerns the factual information given to you by the applicant. *Style* concerns how the person did in previous jobs, how he or she got along with others, how well he or she worked under pressure.

First, verify the substance issues, such as dates of employment, job title, salary, and so on. You may wonder why applicants would falsify information on an application, but they do. One applicant writes that he graduated from a culinary school that he only attended briefly, another says that she was the front desk manager when in reality she filled in twice for the regular manager. If your job requires a particular educational degree or certification, ask applicants to supply a copy of the appropriate document. Otherwise, get the applicant's written permission to obtain a transcript.

Once you have confirmed that the person is who they say they are on paper, you can start checking previous work references. Often, former employers will only reveal neutral information such as job title, dates of employment, and salary, because of fear of being charged with libel, slander, or defamation of character by the former employee. Although there is nothing wrong with providing objective documented information, such as an attendance problem, past employers are often reluctant to discuss this sort of concern or even answer the one question you really need an answer to: "Would you rehire?" To reduce any possible liability, you should ask applicants to sign a release on the application form (Figure 16.7) that gives you permission to contact references and holds all references blameless for anything they say.

Because it is fast, checking references by phone is very common. Be sure to document your calls on a form. Ask to speak to the employee's former supervisor. Always identify yourself and your company, and explain that you are doing a reference check. Start by asking for neutral information such as salary and job title and work your way up to more telling information.

Despite the importance of checking references, few people in the hospitality industry bother with a reference check. It may be habit or tradition, or it may be fear and desperation: fear of finding out there is a reason not to hire and desperation to fill the job. It may just be too time consuming or you may think that your gut feeling or intuition says it all. But it is really a serious mistake to neglect the reference check and thus run the risk of hiring a problem worker.

When calling for a reference check talk to human resources, not the department supervisor—who may be a friend of the applicant or who may want to be rid of the applicant and therefore give him or her a good reference regardless. Do get background checks: these will include a credit check—you don't want someone with credit problems working in a cash-handling situation. Do also get a criminal background check—you don't want a sex offender working for you.

Making the Choice

Choosing a new employee is your decision and your responsibility. Making the choice may mean choosing between two or three possibilities or looking further for the right person for the job. When making the hiring choice, avoid making any of these common mistakes:

1. Don't jump to hire someone who simply reminds you of yourself. Also try not to fall prey to the halo effect. Look at the big picture!

2. Many problems in hiring come about when you hire too quickly. Use the time involved in the selection process to go through each step thoughtfully. Aim to hire the best candidate, not simply the first reasonably qualified applicant who comes forth.

3. Don't rush to hire the applicant who interviewed the best. Although the interview process can certainly tell you a lot about an applicant, the applicant with the best interviewing skills (which can be learned and practiced by anyone) is not necessarily the best person for the job. Also keep in mind that during an interview, some applicants will use their charismatic personalities and ability to tell you what you want to hear to get top consideration for the job in question.

4. Don't hire someone just because your "gut feeling," or intuition, says that this applicant is the best. Intuition is fine to use, but always combine it with the other tools of the trade, such as reference checking and testing.

5. Don't hire someone just because they come highly recommended. Perhaps an applicant comes highly recommended as a breakfast cook, but you are looking for an experienced pizza maker. It's fine to listen to a recommendation for an applicant, but as usual, that's only part of the story.

Every time you hire someone, even when you feel confident about your choice, there is the chance that you have made a mistake. You will not know this, however, until your new people have been with you awhile and you can see how they do the work, whether they follow instructions and learn your ways easily and willingly, how they relate to the customers and the other workers, whether they come in on time, and all the other things that make good workers. To give yourself the chance to make this evaluation, it is wise to set a probationary period, making it clear that employment is not permanent until the end of the period.

If you see that some of your new people are not going to work out, let them go and start over. Do not let them continue beyond the end of the probation period. It is hard to face the hiring process all over again, but it is better than struggling with an incompetent employee. It may be as hard to fire as it is to hire, but that's another story.

Making the Offer

Offers for all jobs should be made in writing. The offer letter typically is sent, or given, to the new hire after an offer has been made and accepted over the phone. When you are making an offer, be sure to include all the conditions that were discussed with the applicant. The following points should appear in the offer letter, as appropriate:

- Department
- Position title
- Supervisor
- Location
- Rate of pay
- Schedule of shift, days off
- When jobs start, where to report, whom to report to
- Clothing and equipment needed
- Meal arrangements
- Parking
- Arrangements for orientation / training
- Brief description of benefits
- Probationary period
- Appointment time or whom to call for an appointment concerning filling out additional personnel forms (such as the I-9 form)

KEY POINTS

1. *Labor market* refers to the supply of workers looking for jobs and the jobs available in a given area.

2. Many hospitality jobs require hard physical labor, and the pay is often low. The days and hours of work vary, but many employees work part-time hours, including weekends and evenings.

3. Most new workers entering the labor force are women, minorities, and immigrants.

4. Possible sources of workers include those already working in your operation, people looking for their first job, women, immigrants, retired people, moonlighters, the unemployed, the disabled, and people who just want to get away from what they have been doing.

5. You will find it helpful to know something about the labor market in your own area, such things as prevailing wages for various jobs, unemployment rates for various types of workers, demographics, and the kinds of companies you are competing with for workers.

6. To determine labor needs, you must define the qualifications for each job in a document called a job specification. Job qualifications include knowledge, skills and abilities, work experience, and education and training.

7. When forecasting personnel needs, look at your schedules and consider the amount of time it takes to replace an employee and get the new employee trained. Anticipate openings using a personnel forecast form, shown in Figure 16.2.

8. Figure 13.2 states recommended ways to ask questions of job applicants to avoid charges of discrimination.

9. Recruiting should be appropriate, competitive, constant, and use a multifaceted approach.

10. Recruiting is either internal or external. Examples include employee referral programs, direct recruiting, advertising, employment agencies, community organizations, personal contacts, and word of mouth.

11. The selection process includes the application form, the interview and evaluation, testing, the reference check, and making the choice.

12. Tips for interviewing are given in Figure 16.7.

13. To be usable, a test must be valid, reliable, and relevant to the job.

14. Checking references by phone using a form such as that shown is common.

KEY TERMS

can-do factors	employee referral programs	internal recruiting
demographics	employment requisition	job posting
direct recruiting	external recruiting	Job Service Centers
Employee Polygraph Protection Act of 1988	halo effect (overgeneralization)	job specification
		labor market

REFERENCES

1. Phillip Perry, "A carrot a day," *Restaurants USA*, January–February 2001.

2. Personal conversation with Charlotte Jordan, October 25, 2004.

3. Personal correspondence with Chris Chapman, September 14, 2004.

4. Katerina Ameral, presentation to USF HR class, November 4, 2004.

TEAMWORK AND TEAMBUILDING*

One vital factor is necessary in order to be successful in the hospitality industry, having an effective team. But, what is an effective team and how do we turn groups into teams and make them winning teams? Many hospitality corporations realize that their main competitive advantage is their employees. One hospitality product is much the same as another until we add personal service. We have all likely experienced a hospitality service that was less than what was expected and, hopefully, many more of the opposite. Why is it that in one place the employees are standing around talking amongst themselves and not attending to their guests' needs? Yet, in another, there is a group synergy, with employees helping and encouraging each other to excel. Figure 17.6 illustrates the synergy created by a team.

In this chapter we will examine teams and teamwork and how to establish winning teams, a vital part to achieving success in the hospitality industry. Successful concepts

---

* Authored by Jack E. Miller, John R. Walker, and Karen Eich Drummond.

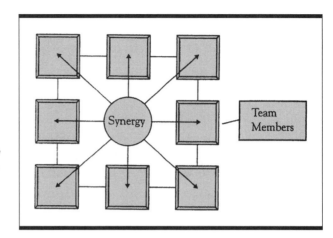

FIGURE 17.1 Team members can create a synergy (when the output is greater than the sum of the individual input). This is accomplished by group members encouraging each other to accomplish goals.

like *Total Quality Management (TQM)* and *empowerment* are presented with industry examples to reinforce the learning. It will help you to:

■   Explain the difference between *groups* and *teams*

■   Describe *team norms, cohesive teams,* and three ways to influence a team

■   Discuss the building of teams, turning groups into teams, creating successful teams, and the characteristics of successful teams

■   List and describe the steps in installing a TQM process

■   Discuss empowerment and coaching

WHAT IS A TEAM?

Teams are very different than groups. A group is defined as a number of people working together, or considered together because of similarities. If working together they interact to achieve a certain objective. The group usually shares information but remains neutral. A team is a special kind of group. Teams are task-oriented work groups; they can evolve or be appointed, either formally or informally (which will be discussed further in the following section). The team attempts to achieve a positive collaboration among its members. A successful team will work well with each other, achieve set goals, and each member will have a feeling of self worth. The successful team will also be adaptive, flexible, and able to deal with conflicts as they arise.

A formally appointed team has an appointed team leader. The team leader possesses the power to influence others and may have more decision-making authority than others. The power to influence others is not the only difference between team members and leaders. A head server is a good example of a formally appointed team within a restaurant. Power may be delegated to this server from management. Delegation is when one gives a portion of their responsibility and authority to a subordinate. The manager may delegate the head server to do nightly checkouts or voids throughout the evening.

An informally appointed team will evolve on its own. It has a rotation of leadership. The group leader does not have formal power over the group. The informally appointed team has some advantages over the formally appointed. For instance, one person probably does not possess every quality needed to be the perfect leader. With the rotation of leadership everyone has a chance to show the qualities that they possess. Formally appointed team leaders may also lose popularity among the group because of their connection with management. With an informally appointed team, this is not likely to happen due to the fact that when their turn comes, everyone is linked with management.

People join teams for many different reasons. One main reason for joining in a team in the hospitality industry is to accomplish tasks as efficiently and swiftly as possible. It would be a lot harder to survive a night as a server if you try to do everything on your own. In actuality, it would be virtually impossible to expedite, deliver, and serve food, while clearing, resetting tables, and waiting on people! Being part of the team assures you that you have others to fall back on if the going gets rough. People may also simply join a team to feel like they are a part of a whole. They may want to feel like they contribute something to the overall success of the team. This may help to develop, enhance, and/or confirm some underlying identity needs.

A team that will be highly successful consists of members who care for and trust each other. They know how to listen to each other as well as express their own ideas. This will form interdependence within the team. The interdependence leads to a team collaboration. They find that working together will be more effective then working apart. Efficiency will increase, as well as team morale. Team morale is another factor in having a successful team. A team with high morale has harmony among its members. They work well together, know how to communicate openly, and trust each other. In order to have high team morale within the team you must have teamwork, as well as team players.

Teamwork is the actual action that a team performs. It is defined as the cooperative effort by a group of persons acting together as a team. In order to have teamwork in the hospitality industry you must have team players. Team players are individuals that participate in a collective effort and cooperation to get the job done efficiently. This may range from clearing a table for a coworker on a busy night to taking an order for them because they seem overburdened. One common form of teamwork in the restaurant industry is the rule of having "full hands" going in and out of the kitchen whenever possible.

It is interesting to note that with self-managed teams the dynamics change if a member leaves or transfers to another "store" (as in restaurant) or hotel. Is this true only for self-managed teams? The new member takes time to adjust to the dynamics and culture of the group. Because we frequently work in groups in the hospitality industry, it is essential that teamwork is a major requirement for selection of the associate. Being a team player is more important than being an independent-minded superstar. Ask any team coach.

WORKING TOGETHER

Now that we have learned the differences between a team and a group, let's consider how team norms affect work behavior. In the hospitality industry teams as well as team norms are constantly evolving. Team norms are defined as implicit, in addition to explicit rules of behavior. Norms occur inevitably within every type of group or should we say, *team* interaction. They are how each member of the team communicates and conducts himself or herself in the workplace. Norms work best when the team is allowed to create them amongst themselves. Teams may resent it if preexisting norms are imposed upon them or are appointed to them.

Norms can be lead in a positive direction. This makes it sound like norms should be stopped because they are inherently negative. Positive team norms are behaviors that are agreed upon and accepted within the group. They range from communication to performance. The team should have a positive norm among them for open communication, as well as wanting to strive for peak performance. For example, a team might agree that if a team member is running late, the other team members will cover for him or her. This can help service overall by ensuring that one person's delayed bus won't delay service for customers. However, a supervisor must keep an eye out for the employee who decides to come in late frequently. Negative norms can develop by abusing team norms.

One way a manager may increase positive team norms in the hospitality industry is by giving rewards for high sales. This could be a nightly, weekly, or monthly contest where the server with the highest sales gets a reward. The rewards could range from a dinner on the house or a gift certificate. This creates a positive norm among the team members and allows them to have fun, while all of them all striving for the same goal.

Negative team norms are behaviors that are against the interest and are not accepted by the overall group. An example of a negative team norm is an employee who feels that he does not need a pre-shift meeting; therefore he always comes to work late. This employee should not just be made an example of in this book; he should also be made an example of at work. As a supervisor it is your duty to evaluate anything or anyone that may have a negative impact on your team. You will never be able to stop negative norms from arising, but you can assess them so that the team may move forward.

In hospitality companies, there are work-area teams such as a dining room team in a hotel restaurant. There may also be project teams where a member of the dining room team joins a project team for a period of usually about two months to work on a special project. The project could be creating a new menu, or making suggestions for re-conception of the theme of the outlet.

Cohesive Teams

Why are some teams more efficient than others? Think of it as putting pieces of a puzzle together. Each member of the team is interconnected and represents a piece of this puzzle. In order for the puzzle to be put together correctly you must have cohesion. Building a cohesive team is a major factor in the success of any hospitality company. A cohesive team communicates well with each other and has well-defined norms, unity, respect, and trust among its members. As in all teams the members of cohesive team have strengths and weaknesses; hopefully what one member lacks another will make up for. This cohesion will result in a team that works well and fits together well. When members of the team fit well together, there is more of a chance that the team will reach its peak performance. If a team lacks cohesion, performance will be hindered because the group will not have any sense of unity.

To build a cohesive team goals and objectives need to be set. How would a team be able to strive for cohesion if they do not know what their goals are? Through close interaction with one another, the team will learn each other's strengths and weaknesses (as mentioned above) and how each member works. Interaction and communication among the members of the team will eventually lead to group norms, respect, trust, and unity. In the restaurant industry everyone has the same objective and goals in mind: let's make this shift as smooth and efficient as possible, and have fun while we are doing it. It is also easier to give negative feedback when there are agreed-upon goals.

Three Ways to Influence an Informal Team

There are some ways that you are able to influence an informal team. One question that you may ask yourself is, have you been giving the team enough and appropriate feedback? What type of feedback are you giving them? You should not give only negative feedback (or only positive feedback). The amount of feedback given to employees generally should meet somewhere in the middle. Unfortunately, it is more common in the restaurant industry to hear when something is done wrong than when something is done right. Positive reinforcement is often neglected, but employees need it just as much as criticism. It takes only two words from you to change an employee's whole perspective—those two words are, "Great job!" Therefore, employees need to be told when their actions are unacceptable as well as when they've done a job well.

In addition to feedback, you should be able to *identify the key players within the group*. Although it is stated above that there are no formally appointed leaders in the informal team, there are always some members who have more of a control over the team. The

Getting team members' input is crucial to obtaining their full commitment to achieving goals.
Courtesy The Ritz Carlton, Sarasota.

manager should identify the "unappointed" leaders and assess whether they are positive or negative impacts. If they are negatively impacting the group, then appropriate steps should be taken to address the issue. (The manager talks with the individual to find out why they are doing negative things, and to formulate a plan to get them to change their ways.)

Finally, another way to influence the informal team is *communication*. Management will not have any direction to go in unless they communicate with the team. Open communication not only builds a trusting, open relationship with the staff, but it helps to confirm that you are addressing the right issues. If you are consistent at openly communicating with staff, they are more likely to come to you with problems that are occurring within the establishment. If you had a manager that never or rarely spoke to you, the chances of your going to him or her with an issue are slim to none.

BUILDING TEAMS

One of the biggest challenges a manager will face is building a successful team. Before actually implementing the plan of building a team, managers should consider what they want out of the team they are about to build. What needs to be the focus of the team? What is the major goal that you want the team to accomplish? In the restaurant/hotel industry the goal may be increased sales or simply more customer appreciation and/or feedback. After you have a clear answer to these questions, you may then start on building the team.

The first step to take is clarifying these goals to preexisting members (if there are any). Next, you should be very selective with who you hire, and always conduct a reference check! It happens often in this industry, but you should never hire employees simply to fill a position. You should always hire based on the idea that the applicant may provide something for the team (skills, personality, good attitude, etc.). There is rarely a shortage of applicants in this industry; more often managers make rash decisions on hires due to a lack of time. In the long run these rash decisions will take more time to fix than the time it would have taken to screen out possibilities, before the rash hire. Management should also seriously take recommendations about who to hire from team members. It is not likely that a team would intentionally recommend a "bad apple" as a new team member.

Keep in mind that one team member's problem affects the whole group. Essentially, if a team member has a problem that is not addressed it will create a downward spiral. One team member's problem will end up being the entire staff's problem. Although you are working on a team, you should consider each person as an individual, and even work with him or her on issues that do not concern the group. Once team members see that you are concerned with them individually, in addition to the team as a whole, you start to build a sense of trust and confidence.

Build a positive work environment. If you are delegating tasks to team members, or simply asking the team to kick performance up a notch, provide incentives. Incentives may range from actual rewards to extra positive feedback to the chance promotion. You want the team to know that you are actively looking for rising stars. Once the team knows that you have appreciation for those who work hard and that you recognize those who are slackers, chances are you will find more team members rising in performance.

Turning Groups into Teams

Many supervisors may mistakenly assume that they have a team when, in actuality, what they have is a group. A group is two or more interacting and interdependent individuals who come together to achieve particular objectives. Groups may be

Team power. Courtesy of PhotoDisc/Getty Images.

formal or informal. Formal groups are work groups established by the company. Formal groups include committees, group meetings, work teams, and task forces. Formal groups are either permanent or temporary. For instance, the executive committee of a resort hotel is permanent and meets regularly to run the resort. A temporary committee is established to work on a particular project like a staff appreciation banquet. After the banquet, the temporary committee, having achieved its goals, is disbanded.

By contrast, informal groups are more social by nature. These groups form naturally in the workplace due to friendships and common interests. Examples are, people sharing lunchtime together or forming a club. Remember, a group is based on independence: a team is based on interdependence. In order to have a team you must have trust, communication, and collaboration. There are many ways that a supervisor may attempt to change a group into a team. Here we will discuss a few of the most critical.

First, as a supervisor you want to get the team's input toward establishing team goals. Working with the group to define goals involves the individual as a part of the whole, and a group with common goals is more likely to work as a team to achieve them.

Second, allow some team decision making. When a decision needs to be made about something concerning the team, consult them and hear them out. This does not necessarily mean that the outcome decision has to be that of the team, but give them a say. They will appreciate having a voice in the workplace, but understand that the final decision comes from management. If you have a cohesive team then they should all want to participate in the decision-making process. If you have a group, conformity tends to appear and not everyone has an interest in the decision-making process or the outcome. Some ways to involve the team in decision making are to have a regular meeting at which changes in policy are discussed. Make it clear that the supervisors take employees' suggestions seriously. Figure 17.2 shows the steps involved in turning groups into teams.

Third, stress communication. In a team, members know each other's motives and what makes each other tick. In the typical group the members do not really know each other and may even distrust other members of the group because communication is not key, unlike a team. In a team supervisors must stress the importance of communication. When team members feel comfortable enough to communicate their point of view to each other, they in turn are more apt to give other members of the team support and trust. If it seems that there are problems, address them. Make sure the team feels comfortable enough with each other and with management to point out problems. Letting employees know about changes, even those that

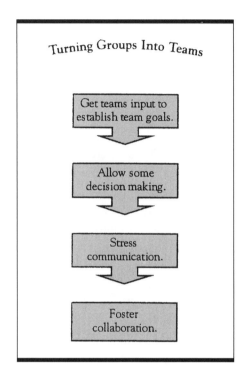

FIGURE 17.2 The steps involved in turning groups into teams.

don't affect them directly can make them feel like they ate working as a part of a whole.

Finally, you must have collaboration among team members. In a group the members may all have an individual goals, but a successful team strives together to reach the same goal. Team members must be committed to reaching the goal. If members are not striving for the same goal then you have a group, and you may want to do some reassessing of the group members to establish a team. As we stated above in the Working Together section, keep in mind that even if the team is striving for the same goal, team members have strengths and weaknesses; hopefully what one member lacks another will make up for. If the team collaborates and works through each other's strengths and weaknesses, they will have a sense of unity. When members of the team have unity, there is more of a chance that the team will reach its peak performance.

Creating Successful Teams

Creating successful teams depends on creating the climate for success. We know that teams must have a passion for the company's vision, mission, and goals, but supervisors need to give clear guidelines as to exactly *what* is to be done *by whom, when, where,* and *what resources* are required. The supervisor also ensures that the resources are available when needed.

The word TEAM stands for Together Everyone Achieves More. Team members should be selected for their attitudes and skills and trained by a "coach" not a boss. Training for group decision making and interpersonal communications as well as cross-training makes for success. Select people who like teamwork—not everyone does—and reinforce behaviors that make for good teamwork by having formal recognition awards for those who "walk the talk." Some companies make a DVD and give them along with framed photos taken with senior management to team members. Other companies profile members in newsletters. Give teams an opportunity to show their work to senior management.

Team selection, especially team leader selection is important. It's best not to select the most senior member, who may be a member of the executive committee or guidance team (to use the Ritz-Carlton term) because other team members will simply agree with whatever the senior manager says. It's better to select another team member.

A good example of creating a successful team was at a major resort hotel where the servers at the Beach Club reported to two different departments. Guest comments alerted management to a *challenge* (which sounds better than *problem*) of poor timeliness in the delivery of food and beverage orders, yet the service received an outstanding score. The pool and beach attendants reported to one department and the bartenders and cooks to another. When both groups were united to form one team, there was some initial resentment, but as the teamwork improved so did the tips. Figure 17.3 illustrates the elements of a successful team.

Characteristics of Successful Teams

Having described the creation of successful teams we can now take a look at how a successful team looks and behaves. There are ten main characteristics of successful teams:

1. The team understands and is committed to the vision, mission, and goals of the company and the department.
2. The team is mature—not necessarily in age—but in realizing that members sometimes need to place the team before their personal interests.
3. The team works to continually improve how it operates.

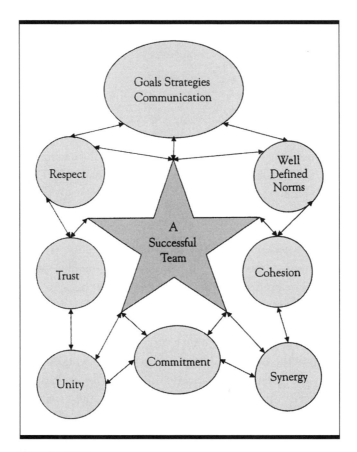

FIGURE 17.3 Elements of a successful team.

4. Team members treat each other with respect: they listen and feel free to express their thoughts.

5. Differences are handled in a professional manner.

6. Members have respect for their supervisor.

7. Members are consulted and their input is requested in decision making.

8. Members encourage and assist other team members to succeed.

9. The team meets or exceeds its goals.

10. There is a synergy where the output of the team is greater than the input of each team member.

In order to become successful, teams need to have the skills required for the job. They also need to be empowered to do the job and to be held accountable for their performance. Teams should be rewarded for meeting or exceeding goals. In the fast-paced hospitality industry people with insufficient skills are quickly discovered—they need to be trained or replaced for the benefit of team the other members—otherwise the team morale will suffer.

TOTAL QUALITY MANAGEMENT

Given an increasingly competitive market and fluctuations in guest service levels in many hospitality organizations, it is no wonder that so many companies have adopted a Total Quality Management (TQM) continuous improvement process. TQM is a concept that works well in the hospitality industry, because its goal is to ensure continuous quality improvement of services and products for guests.

With TQM the word *guest* is preferred over *customer*, the inference being that, if we treat customers like guests, we will exceed their expectations. Successful and progressive companies realize that quality and service go hand in hand. A good meal poorly served results in guest dissatisfaction and a consequent loss of revenue.

TQM works best when top management, middle management, supervisors, and hourly employees all believe in the philosophy and concept of TQM. It is a never-ending journey of continuous improvement, not a destination.

How to Install a TQM Process

TQM is applied in all areas of the business at every level. It works like this: A detailed introduction of the TQM concept and philosophy is given by a senior member of management to underline the importance of the TQM process. The best example of a TQM philosophy is the Ritz-Carlton Hotel Company, which has built a reputation for exceptional guest service. Horst Schulze, former president and CEO, nurtured the tradition of excellence established by the celebrated hotelier, Cesar Ritz. Beginning with the motto, "We are ladies and gentlemen serving ladies and gentlemen. We practice teamwork and lateral service to create a positive environment." The mission, "To provide the finest personal service and facilities, instill well-being, and even fulfill the unexpressed wishes of our guests," expresses the need for uncompromising service.

Profile

TOBIE CANCINO

Courtesy of Tobie Cancino

My typical Saturday night involves heart-pounding bass and synchronized lights, cocktails of all colors of the rainbow, and about 1,000 of my closest friends … just like yours does. I am on the other side of it, however. I pour drinks in the VIP Room of the Zanzabar, the most posh nightclub in Waikiki. Glamorous? Maybe. Does it involve supervision? Yes and no. Officially, my job description does not entail this. But achieving a moneymaking, happy medium between cocktail servers, customers, management, owners, bar backs, and security certainly requires super vision. At least in my world, super vision is the ability to see and prevent possible disasters before they happen. In this atmosphere of alcoholic uncertainty, bionic power is definitely an advantageous trait.

Saturdays have become a concert, and I am the maestro. When I walk in at eight o'clock, my bar is already set up. The ice well is full, mixers are topped off, garnishes are cut, and the water and solutions in the three-compartment sink are at the right temperatures. My bar back, Jack, asks for my liquor pull list, and returns promptly with a stacked hand truck in tow. I tell him simply, "You are the best," and he smiles.

The "early" cocktail server arrives one half hour before me, and the room is immaculate. We share a little "girl talk," then I ask her to please push the Chilean Bordeaux blend. She sells three bottles. Our largest shareholder strolls in, and I immediately pour his regular drink, a glass of iced water and two cherries. The cocktail server and I tempt him to tie the cherry stems into knots with his tongue, and then joke with him about his oral abilities. He laughs and buys us dinner. As the night begins to pick up, the general manager storms in mumbling something about "mutts and morons wearing baggy pants in line downstairs." I hand him his black coffee and tell him that three bottles of the Chilean Bordeaux were sold. His frown disappears and he greets a few guests. As one of the bouncers comes in from the fire exit, I can tell that he just had to kick out a belligerent drunkard. All he needs is a "Hey there, Big Boy," a sexy smile, and a fruit punch. Life at Zanzabar did not always harmonize so well. Understanding people and coordinating their responsibilities to make music took a bit of rehearsal. The second movement of the concerto begins.

Customers march to different tunes, however. For the most part, 90 percent of our customers are regulars in the VIP Room. The staff and I have come to know most members by name, their drinks, their supplementary habits, and how far they can go without disrupting the music. There have been cases, though, when the bionic powers weakened and disaster was imminent.

- A table of six ordered a bottle of Cristal champagne ($300). They were in a festive mood, and decided to have another. The cocktail server was obviously elated, and I proceeded to serve it thinking that two glasses of champagne per person is acceptable. Suddenly, they started dropping like flies. One by one, they slouched in their chairs and fell asleep. Since overserving customers is a serious violation of liquor laws, I began to worry about unpleasant consequences. It is later discovered that these party animals had decided to wash down a few ecstasy tablets with their champagne.

- An appreciative boss buys a shot of MacCallan 18 ($15.00) for his strawberry daiquiri-drinking employee. It is a nice gesture, and I served it. In no time, I noticed chunks of red on the ivory tablecloth before her. I helped her to the restroom, washed my own hands, and then ran them under a sanitizer with full faith in quaternary ammonium.

Supervising is only for a certain type of person. You must be a public relations professional in dealing with customers, especially irate ones. You have to be a mentor by setting good, if not perfect, examples, and thereby commanding respect. You have to be a cheerleader even in times of distress, by continuing to lead with positive energy and empowering words. You have to be a mother and sometimes remind your employees to tidy up after themselves and keep their mouths clean (in more ways than one). It is being a secretary since paperwork is unavoidable, in terms of forecasting, scheduling, controlling labor reports, and so on; the list can go on and on. You have to be a boss who strictly enforces rules and regulations. And above all, you should be a friend. It is said if an employee feels that he or she can turn to a manager with problems, even ones of a personal nature, a stronger work relationship will be built. After all, no employee will want to work hard for a boss who is not liked.

I am confident in saying that this is the career for me. Supervision is the first step to executive management and ownership. Forecasting and planning are extended to longer terms as one rises to higher levels. For now, though, short-term planning, both in my life and in the workplace, is gratifying.

Once upon a time, though, I was a bar manager at a restaurant that seated 600. A young owner noticed my drive, organization, and affinity for knowledge. Sure, I had the integrity, ability to communicate well, hard-working ethic, and positive personality that all supervisors should have. I quickly found out, though, that supervision necessitates management of people, whether your internal or external customer, above all else; and needless to say, the maturity to understand varied and complex human beings was not there.

It is the classic: "If I knew then what I know now...." Great supervisors are all of the above. However, exceptional ones have the super vision to see what motivates employees and pleases guests.

It is no wonder that the Ritz-Carlton was the first hospitality company to win the coveted Malcolm Baldrige National Quality Award. The main reason for The Ritz-Carlton Company winning this award, not once but twice, is due to TQM. Ritz-Carlton associates are empowered to "move heaven and earth" to fulfill a guest's request. All associates are "schooled" in the Company's Gold Standards, which include a credo, motto, three steps of service, and twenty Ritz-Carlton basics. Each employee is expected to understand and adhere to these standards, which describe the process for solving guest problems.

Figure 17.4 shows the steps for a successful TQM continuous improvement process. Top and line management is responsible for the process. Once they commit to ownership of the process, the team participants will be energized to focus their energy on the process. Notice how step one calls for leadership (existing, or in need of leadership training). It is critical to have good leader-managers in place to maximize the effectiveness of TQM.

- *Step one* in the process: Have excellent leaders as supervisors and managers. The more successful companies develop leader-managers who can inspire the TQM teams to exceed guest expectations.

- *Step two:* Build and train teams of volunteer associates within each department and later cross departmentally in problem solving.

- *Step three:* Have the teams decide on and write down the appropriate levels of guest service and relative weighting for "their guests" because front-line associates best know the service expectations of "their" guests. Of course, management has input, but the whole point of TQM is that management has to give up some

TQM being introduced to a team. Courtesy of Sodexho.

of its power and allow associates to share in the decision-making process for determining the criteria and performance levels for guest service. For example how many rings should the telephone give before it is answered? Or, how long should guests have to wait for a hostess to seat them at a restaurant? The answers are, answer the phone within three rings if possible, and, in the absence of the hostess, someone to acknowledge the guests and let them know that the hostess will be there momentarily. The list of performance criteria for each department will vary according to the type of hospitality business and the guest expectations. In a restaurant situation, guests can be asked in a survey how much they liked their food. A Likert type scale of 1–10 or 1–7 can be used to score each criterion. Food quality is further broken down into taste, smell, appearance, and temperature. Other restaurant meal quality criteria include service = courtesy, friendly, efficient, prompt, professional, etc. The total dining experience includes ease of access to the restaurant, parking, curbside appeal, cleanliness, condition of bathrooms, decor, noise levels, lighting, ambiance, music, and so on.

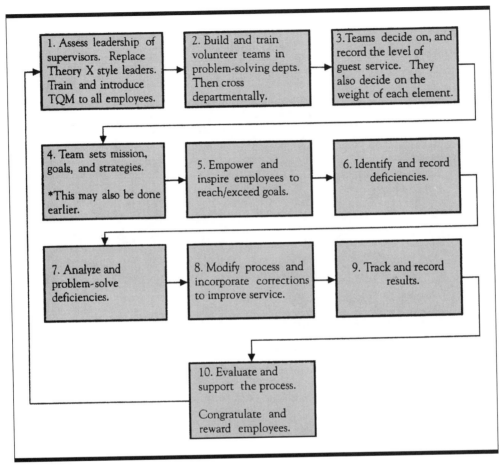

FIGURE 17.4 Ten steps to a Total Quality Management continuous improvement process.

Once a score has been determined for each element of the guest experience, a base has been arrived at for future comparison. The team of associates comes up with ideas and "how-tos" of improving the guest experience for each of the elements that is below the level of quality expected by guests.

■ *Step four:* Set mission, goals, and strategies based on guest expectations. Write the company, property/unit, or department mission and goals, and create strategies to meet or exceed those goals.

■ *Step five:* Empower and inspire associates to reach goals.

■ *Step six:* Identify deficiencies, which are areas where service falls below expectations.

- *Step seven:* Analyze and resolve identified deficiencies.

- *Step eight:* Modify processes to incorporate corrections and to improve service to expected levels.

- *Step nine:* Track results—improvements in service, guest satisfaction, employee satisfaction, cost reduction, and profit.

- *Step ten:* Evaluate and support the process. If the goals are not being met, begin again with step one. If the goals are met, congratulate team members for their success and reward them.

Installing TQM is exciting because, once everyone becomes involved; the teams find creative ways of solving guest-related problems and improving service. Other benefits include increased guest and employee satisfaction, cost reductions, and, yes, increased profit. TQM is a top-down, bottom-up process that needs active commitment and involvement of all employees, from top managers to hourly paid employees. With TQM, if you are not serving the guest, you had better be serving someone who is serving the guest. To the guest, services are experiential; they are felt, lived through, and sensed.

EMPOWERMENT

More hospitality companies are empowering teams and employees to deliver outstanding guest service. Empowerment means ensuring that employees have the skills, knowledge, and authority to make decisions that would otherwise be made by management. The goal of empowerment is to have enthusiastic, committed employees who do an outstanding job because they believe in it and enjoy doing it. Empowerment encourages employees to be creative and to take risks, both of which can give a company a competitive edge.

There are two types of empowerment: *structured* and *flexible.* Structured empowerment allows employees to make decisions within specified limits, an example being "comping" an entree, not the whole meal. Flexible empowerment gives employees more scope in making decisions to give outstanding guest service.

As described in the TQM section, employees are empowered to problem-solve and do whatever it takes to delight the guest (so long as it's legal). With Ritz-Carlton, associates are empowered by *"owning"* the guest's request. Associates can spend up to $2,000 without consulting management to solve a guest's problem. An example was when the laundry was pressing a bridesmaid's dress and accidentally burned a hole in it. The concierge took the guest to the nearby Versace store and bought a new dress on her own credit card. Empowerment enables companies to get quick decisions to satisfy guests. An associate no longer has to find a manager to approve a request; the associate is *empowered* to handle the situation.

Empowerment also means fewer levels of management are required. For example, a hotel had several floor housekeepers whose job it was to inspect all rooms serviced by housekeepers. Finally, management wised up and asked themselves the question, why aren't we doing it right to start with? Now, certified housekeepers no longer need their rooms checked; the first person in the room after it's cleaned is the guest. This has saved thousands of dollars in salaries and benefits. Empowered employees can schedule, solve TQM problems, budget, do performance evaluations, and participate in employment selection. Today, the supervisor's role is to formulate a vision, show trust, provide resources, coach, train, offer encouragement, and help when needed.

The steps in establishing an empowerment program are similar to those for TQM—a meeting of all employees to announce (with the use of specific guest survey data) the need to increase guest satisfaction. This is followed by an introduction and explanation of empowerment. A training session goes over problem resolution, decision making, and guest service. The program is monitored and recorded so guest and employee satisfaction—both of which hopefully increase—can be celebrated. The number of times a manager is called to deal with a request is also recorded along with any costs involved with empowering employees to give away or comp a service. Hospitality companies find that the cost of reducing or comping a few charges is more than made up by the increased business they receive as a result of any "guarantee" program.

Another story that illustrates how empowerment can encourage an associate to go the extra mile is: Picture a fabulous resort hotel on a cool day in February. Two guests arrive and decide that they want to have their lunch out on the terrace, rather than in the restaurant. A table is duly set for them, and, because it was cold, the server went to the laundry and had them put two blankets in the dryer to warm them up. When the guests were presented with the blankets, they were really impressed. It so happened that the guests were travel writers for a major newspaper, and they wrote up the story as an example of exemplary service.

Empowered employees tend to feel more in control of and have a greater commitment to their work and are also more productive than nonempowered employees. So it's no wonder that many hospitality companies like Marriott and TGI Friday's gain their associates' feedback and ideas on a regular basis. They empower their employees and they, in turn, score highly in guest and employee satisfaction surveys. It's a win–win situation.

Guest feedback is an important part of TQM. Some hospitality businesses have outside companies conduct guest surveys, asking such questions as: Did you have a sense of well-being? Did you feel cared for as an individual? Did you feel wanted as a guest? These questions are measuring the emotional attachment that the guest has with the company and brand.

TEAM CHALLENGES

Every team must overcome some challenges to be successful. Regardless of how much supervisors strive to overcome them, some of these challenges must work out on their own. For instance, you can implement ways that the team may gain personal development, cohesion, positive norms, etc., but the supervisor cannot simply make them happen. The people in the team must want to gain these qualities and must want a positive workplace.

One major team challenge that management must help to overcome is negativity. No matter how selective supervisors are at hiring employees, they will always come across an unexpected negative hire. You must remember that when you are interviewing someone, they always have their best face on. The first impression is not necessarily what is behind the real person. If someone is applying for a position in the company, they are probably not going to come in being negative (if they do, then you should not hire them in the first place). Therefore, it is important (once again) for the supervisor to be an active part of the team. If one person is bringing everyone down, either the active supervisor will see it for themselves, or a team member will be comfortable enough with the supervisor to bring it to their attention. This issue should be immediately addressed; otherwise it may create a domino effect.

Another major challenge that management must overcome is learning how to delegate responsibilities. Supervisors must learn how to let go of certain responsibilities, and which responsibilities are to be let go of. Even if you think that it will be much quicker and easier to just do it yourself, this is another way to gain the respect of the team. Some examples of things that may be delegated to the team in a restaurant are reservations, server cash-outs, nightly station checks, and time for evening "cuts" (when you cut the server staff down from a full staff to a smaller staff at the end of the night). When a job is delegated, make sure you explain what to do clearly and precisely. Also make sure that the person you are delegating the job to possesses a full understanding of what is to be done and that he or she is confident in doing it.

High turnover is one of the major obstacles in the hospitality industry. You cannot have a cohesive, successful team if the team members are always changing. Although there is no clear-cut way of how to overcome high turnover, there are some strategies that may reduce it. One way is to be in tune with your staff. If it seems that members of the team are distraught, take the time to talk with them. Ask what the problem is and try to reach a compromise. Maybe the only problem is that they are having scheduling conflicts, and it can be resolved simply by giving them more or less hours.

Finally, supervisors must overcome the challenge of gaining the respect of the team. This is a tricky one because you must learn how to be their friend to gain trust as well as their leader to gain respect. A supervisor who is too friendly may get walked all over. A supervisor who is not friendly enough will not gain trust. Where do you draw the line? The answer to this is not so simple. You should always be professional when talking with the staff. Never use inappropriate language; you never really know who it may offend. Also, limit activities that you attend together outside of the company. Take part in organized activities, but do not make a regular appearance at the local hangout after shifts.

Coaching

There is a big difference between a supervisor and a coach. A coach does not use fear or status as a form of motivation to get the job done. The coach uses energy and positively (guess what, it works)! The coach of a team must remember that they are also part of that team. They are essentially the team's backbone. Successful coaches must organize, give moral support, delegate, challenge, and inspire their team members. The following are a few ways that a manager may learn how to turn into a team coach:

- One way to coach your team is to have a pre-shift meeting. At this time you may want to go over what the night's forecast looks like, delegate some tasks, give general feedback on the teams overall performance, go over the evening specials, etc. Pre-shift meetings may show the team that you are concerned for their well-being, as well as the organization's. This is also a good time for the staff to voice their concerns and opinions. They should be given the opportunity to have an active role in group decision making. Remember that communication is one of the key factors in having a successful team.

- Take advantage of moments that you may be able to use to teach a team member something. Instead of automatically reacting to something a team member is doing wrong, take a step back and think about how you can best handle the situation and how can you teach them a better way to do it. The staff will respect this way a lot more than your scolding or reprimanding them.

- Organize team activities. Take an active role in arranging outside activities that the staff will be able to do together. Go beyond the yearly Christmas party. You

Coaching a team member on the closing procedures. Courtesy Sarasota Memorial Hospital.

may want to organize some type of field trip to an amusement park for your staff. Oh, and but be sure to post a sign-up sheet so that you know how many of your staff will attend (this way you don't end up shorthanded for that day).

KEY POINTS

1. A group is defined as a number of persons working together, or considered together because of similarities. They share information but remain neutral. A team is a special kind of group that attempts to achieve a positive collaboration among its members.

2. A formally appointed team has an appointed team leader. The team leader possesses the power to influence others; power may be delegated to this server from management. An informally appointed team will evolve on its own, it has a rotation of leadership, and the group leader does not have formal power over the group.

3. One main reason for joining in a team in the hospitality industry is to accomplish tasks as efficiently and swiftly as possible. People may also simply join a team to feel like they are small part of a whole (this may help to develop, enhance, and/or confirm some underlying identity needs).

4. Teamwork is the actual action that a team performs. It is defined as the cooperative effort by a group of persons acting together as a team. In order to have teamwork in the hospitality industry you must have team players.

5. In the hospitality industry teams as well as team norms are constantly evolving. Team norms are defined as implicit, in addition to explicit rules of behavior. Positive team norms are behaviors that are agreed-upon and accepted within the group. Negative team norms are behaviors that are against the interest and are not accepted by the overall group.

6. A cohesive team communicates well with each other, has well-defined norms, unity, respect, and trust among its members. To build a cohesive team goals and objectives need to be set.

7. Three ways to influence an informal team: feedback, identify the key players, and communication.

8. Before actually implementing the plan of building a team, managers should consider what they want out of the team they are about to build. They should be very selective with whom they hire, and conduct reference checks. A supervisor should also keep in mind that one team member's problem affects the whole group.

9. Groups may be formal or informal. Formal groups are work groups established by the company; informal groups are more social by nature.

10. There are four steps to take at turning a group into a team:
    - Get the team's input into establishing team goals.
    - Allow some team decision making.
    - Stress communication.
    - Have collaboration among team members.

11. A team that will be highly successful understands and is committed to the vision, mission, and goals of the company and the department, is mature, works to continually improve how it operates, treat each other with respect, handle differences in a professional manner, have respect for their supervisor, are consulted for their input in decision-making, encourage and assist other team members to succeed, meets or exceeds its goals, and has synergy.

12. Total Quality Management's goal is to ensure continuous quality improvement of services and products for guests. TQM is applied in all areas of the business at every level. There are ten steps to a Total Quality Management:
    - Have excellent leaders as supervisors and managers.
    - Build and train teams of volunteer associates within each department and later cross departmentally in problem solving.
    - Have the teams to decide on and write down the appropriate levels of guest service and relative weighting for "their guests."
    - Set mission, goals, and strategies based on guests' expectations.
    - Empower and inspire associates to reach goals.
    - Identify deficiencies.
    - Analyze and problem solve identified deficiencies.
    - Modify process to incorporate corrections to improve service to expected levels.
    - Track results—improvements in service, guest satisfaction, employee satisfaction, cost reduction, and profit.
    - Evaluate and support the process.

13. There are two types of empowerment: *structured* and *flexible*. Structured empowerment allows employees to make decisions within specified limits; flexible empowerment gives employees more scope in making decisions to give outstanding guest service.

14. Major team challenges are negativity, learning how to delegate responsibilities, high turnover, and gaining the respect of the team.

15. The coach uses energy and positively, not fear or status, as a form of motivation to get the job done.

KEY TERMS

coach	formally appointed team	team
cohesive team	group	synergy
delegated	informal groups	team morale
empowerment	informally appointed team	team players
feedback	norms	teamwork
formal groups	project teams	Total Quality Management (TQM)

18

EMPLOYEE TRAINING
AND DEVELOPMENT*

An agitated coffee shop manager was overheard shrieking into the telephone: "But Shirley, you can't leave me like this . . . but Shirley, I've got a new server coming in tomorrow morning . . . but Shirley, you've got to come in tomorrow morning at six and train her for me . . . *but Shirleeee . . .!*"

Chances are good that Shirley did not come in at 6 A.M.—she has left for good. Chances are even better that if Shirley did come in, she would give her replacement a sketchy run-through of the job little better than a magic apron, plus a full-scale account of the difficulties of working with Ms. Manager. Yet this method of training is not at all uncommon in the hospitality industry.

---

* Authored by Jack E. Miller, John R. Walker, and Karen Eich Drummond.

We give many excuses for not training: We don't have the time, we don't have the money, people don't stay long enough to make training worthwhile, they don't pay attention to what you tell them anyway, they'll pick it up on the job, and so on. There is an edge of truth to all of this, but the edge distorts the truth as a whole. When you look at the whole picture, you find that the money saved by not training is likely to be spent on the problems that lack of training causes. And those problems involve more than money; they involve customer satisfaction and the well-being of the enterprise.

In this chapter we explore the subject of training in detail and offer a system for developing a training program tailored to a particular enterprise. It will help you to:

- Discuss the importance of training in the hospitality industry.
- Cite both the benefits of training and the problems encountered providing it.
- Outline factors that help employees learn.
- Explain steps for developing a job training program.
- List the major steps in job instruction training and describe how to apply them.
- List the six skills necessary for effective classroom training.
- Identify when retraining is needed and how to retrain.
- Explain the importance of orientation and enumerate the kinds of information that should be covered.
- Identify the essential elements in a successful training program and the major steps in developing such a program.

IMPORTANCE OF TRAINING

In a hospitality setting, training simply means teaching people how to do their jobs. You may instruct and guide a trainee toward learning knowledge (such as certain facts and procedures), skills necessary to do the job to the standard required (such as loading the dishmachine), or attitudes (such as a guest-oriented attitude). Three kinds of training are needed in food and lodging operations:

1. Job instruction is just that, instruction in what to do and how to do it in every detail of a given job in a given enterprise. It begins on the first day and may be spread in small doses over several days, depending on how much needs to be taught and the complexity of the job.

2. Retraining applies to current employees. It is necessary when workers are not measuring up to standards, when a new method or menu or piece of equipment is introduced, or when a worker asks for it. It takes place whenever it is needed.

3.   Orientation is the initial introduction to the job and the company. It sets the tone of what it is like to work for the company and explains the facility and the nitty-gritty of days and hours and rules and policies. It takes place before beginning work or in the first few days at work.

Need for Training

In our industry as a whole, we do very little of all three kinds of training. There is always that time pressure and that desperate need for someone to do the work right now, so we put untrained people to work and we hassle along with semicompetent or incompetent workers. Yet somehow we expect—or hope—that they will know how to do the work or can pick it up on the job, because we are not quite sure ourselves exactly what we want them to do.

Orientation acquaints new associates with the organization and its policies and procedures relating to the job. Courtesy of The Cendant Corporation.

As an industry, we are spoiled by our history in this respect. Our early inns and taverns were family affairs. The innkeeper was the host, the wife did the cooking, and the family did the chores with perhaps a servant or two, and there was no need for special training because the work was just extended housekeeping. In the nineteenth century, as hotels and restaurants and taverns followed the railroads across the country, we had floods of immigrants from Europe who had grown up as servants or had served long apprenticeships in hotel or restaurant kitchens. In the 1920s new immigration laws dried up this source of trained labor, but during the Depression we had willing workers from other industries who worked hard at learning their jobs because they needed them to survive.

It was during World War II with its shortage of workers that our labor problems really began and our need for training became acute. The capable people who were not off fighting the war worked in well-paying jobs in war plants, while hotels and restaurants had to get along with untrained, unskilled workers who couldn't find any other work but left as soon as they found jobs they liked better.

We have been struggling with such problems ever since. We are nearly always shorthanded; we don't take time to train; we need a warm body on the job and that is what we hire and put to work. How do people manage people if they do not train them? We have mentioned the magic apron training method—if you put them to work, they can learn the job. Anyone can make a bed. Anyone can carry bags and turn on the lights and the television set. Anyone can take orders and serve food. Anyone can push a vacuum cleaner, wash dishes, and bus tables. That is the prevalent wishful thinking.

Many employers assume that experience in a previous job takes the place of training—a busboy is a busboy; a salad person can make any salad. They depend on these people to know how to do the job to their standard and according to their methods.

The coffee shop manager who tried to persuade Shirley to come in at 6:00 A.M. and train her replacement was practicing another common method of training—having the person who is leaving a job train the person who will take it over. This method is known as *trailing* if the new worker follows the old one around. Another method is to have a big sister or big brother or buddy system; an old hand shows a new worker the ropes, often in addition to working his or her own job.

None of these training methods provides any control over work methods, procedures, products, services, attitudes toward the customers, and performance standards. You do not control the quality of the training, and you do not control the results.

You may serve a 1-ounce martini on Thursday and a 3-ounce martini on Friday because your two bartenders got their experience at different bars. The blankets may pull out at the foot of the beds because no one showed the new housekeeper how much to tuck in. The cups may be stacked three deep in the dishmachine because no one trained the new dishwasher—anyone can run a dishmachine. The draft beer gets a funny taste because they did not have draft beer where the new bartender worked before and no one has told him how to take care of the lines. The fat in the fryer takes on a nauseating smell, but the new fry cook does not know it should be changed or filtered because on his last job someone else took care of that. (In fact, he was not even a fry cook, but you didn't check his references.)

Food costs may be high because kitchen personnel have not been trained in waste and portion control. Breakage may be high because servers, bartenders, bus personnel, and dishwashers have not been trained in how to handle glassware and dishes. Equipment breaks down frequently because no one has been trained in how to use it. Health department ratings are likely to be low because sanitation always suffers when training is poor, and pretty soon the local television station may send around an investigative reporting crew to expose your shortcomings to the entire community.

When good training is lacking, there is likely to be an atmosphere of tension and crisis and conflict all the time because nobody is quite sure how the various jobs are supposed to be done and who has responsibility for what. Such operations are nearly always shorthanded because someone did not show up and somebody else just quit, and people are playing catch-up all the time instead of being on top of their work. Service suffers. Customers complain or they just do not come back, and managers begin to spend money on extra advertising that they could have spent on training and avoided all these problems. Yes it is true that "proper food safety training and more sophisticated equipment are more costly. But in the long run customers gain confidence in restaurants that are well run."[1] The benefits of training indeed outweigh the cost in the long run.

A small mistake or oversight made by a poorly trained employee can have enormous impact. This lesson was brought home a few years ago when a night clerk whose training was obviously incomplete turned off a fire alarm "because it was bothering me" and several people died in the fire.

Benefits of Training

Perhaps you are already beginning to think that what is needed is some sort of system like performance standards that would define the last detail of every job so that each person could be trained to do the job correctly. You are absolutely right. Each new person would learn the same information and procedures as everyone else. Everybody would learn the same ways of doing things. Job content, information, methods, and procedures would be standardized, and performance goals would be the same for everyone. The new employee would end up producing the same product or service to the same standards as everyone else doing that job.

Suppose that you had such a system in place and used it to train your people. *How would it help you on the job?*

- *It would give you more time to manage.* You would not have to spend so much time looking over people's shoulders, checking up, filling in, putting out fires, and improving solutions to unexpected problems.

- *You would have less absenteeism and less turnover,* because your people would know what to do and how to do it, they would feel comfortable in their jobs, and you would spend less of your time finding and breaking in new people.

- It *would reduce tensions between you and your people.* You would not be correcting them constantly, and you would have more reason to praise them, which would improve morale. It would also reduce tension between you and your boss. When your people are performing smoothly, the boss is not on your back. You worry less, sleep better, and work with less tension.

- It *would be much easier to maintain consistency of product and service.* When you have set standards and have taught your people how to meet these standards, the products and the service are standard, too. Guests can depend on the same comfort, the same service, the same excellence of food, the same pleasant experience they had the last time.

- *You would have lower costs*—less breakage, less waste, fewer accidents, less spoilage, better cost control. New workers would be productive sooner. You might be able to get the work done with fewer people because everyone would work more efficiently.

- *Trained personnel would give you happier guests and more of them.* The way that employees treat customers is the single most important factor in repeat business. One worker untrained in customer relations can make several guests per day swear that they will never set foot in your place again.

- *Training your workers can help your own career.* Your performance depends on their performance. And if you have not trained anyone in your job, you may never be promoted because you will always be needed where you are.

By keeping workers interested and motivated, cross-training cuts turnover. It creates loyal, multi-skilled employees that chains need to open new locations. Cross-training increases productivity and pares labor costs, and it lays a foundation for careers rather than dead-end jobs.

Source: Lisa Bertagnoli, "Ten-Minute Managers Guide to Cross Training Staff," *Restaurants & Institutions,* Vol. 114, No. 18, p. 26, August 2004.

Good training will benefit your associates, too. Here are some things that it can do for them:

- It *can eliminate the five reasons why people do poor work:* not knowing what to do, or how to do it, or how well they are doing; not getting any help from the supervisor; not getting along with the supervisor at all. Good training can get them through those first painful days and make them comfortable sooner.

- *Trained employees do not always have to be asking how to do things.* They have confidence; they can say to themselves, "Hey, I know my job; I can do my job." This gives them satisfaction, security, and a sense of belonging, and it can earn praise from the boss.

- *Training can reduce employee tension.* The boss is not on their backs all the time with constant negative evaluations, and they are not worried about how they are doing.

- *Training can boost employee morale and job satisfaction.* When employees know exactly what the boss expects from them, they tend to be more satisfied and relaxed with their jobs. Wouldn't you be?

- It *can also reduce accidents and injuries.* If you have been trained how to lift heavy luggage or cases of food, you are not going to hurt your back. If you have been trained how to handle a hot stockpot, you are not going to scald yourself.

- *Training can give people a chance to advance.* The initial training, even at the lowest levels, can reveal capabilities and open doors to further training, promotion, and better pay.

Good training will benefit the entire enterprise. Training that reduces tensions, turnover, and costs and improves product, service, and guest count is certainly going to improve the company image and the bottom line. Many corporations recognize this and have developed systematic training programs.

However, not everyone in the industry sees training as an investment that pays its way. Many managers of small operations consider training an exercise in futility because, they say, it takes more time than it is worth, because people do not stay, because people are not interested in being trained, because it does not work, because it should not be necessary. The myth persists that people in entry-level service jobs should be able to do these jobs without training. When times are bad, with lack of volume and low guest counts, training is the first thing that a manager gives up, as though it were a frill.

It is hard to convince these people that training is worth the investment. It is difficult to measure and prove the difference that training makes because there are always many variables in every situation. Perhaps the best way to be convinced that training pays off is to compare individual operations where the training is good with those that do little or no training. The differences will be obvious in atmosphere, in smoothness of operation, in customer enjoyment, and in profit.

Among larger establishments, there are some that have gained a reputation for their training, that train people so well they are hired away by other firms. It is a nice reputation to have—a nice image for bringing in customers as well as attracting good workers. How do you measure an image? Usually, you do not have to.

On the downside there have been instances where cutting down on training to cut expenses has proved to be false economy and has resulted in deterioration of service, decline in customer count, and eventually the demise of the enterprise.

Think back to the theory that ROI means *return on individuals*. Training is an investment in people. In an industry whose every product and service depends almost entirely on individual people at work—people who deal directly with guests—investing in training those people is a major key to ROI of any sort.

Check Your Knowledge

1.   What is *training?*

2.   List the three kinds of training needed in hospitality operations.

3.   What are the benefits of training your new personnel? Briefly explain each benefit.

Problems in Training

Managers who do not train their people are not all stubborn fools or cynics; the problems are real. Perhaps the biggest problem is *urgent need*; you need this person so badly right now that you don't have time to train, you can't get along without this pair of hands. You put the person right into the job and correct mistakes as they happen and keep your fingers crossed.

A second critical problem is *training time:* your time and the worker's time. While you are training, neither of you is doing anything else, and you do not have that kind of time. Your time and the worker's cost the company money. A training program requires an immediate outlay of money, time, and effort for results that are down the road. This is especially a problem for the small operation with cash-flow problems and a day-to-day existence. Training is an investment in the future they cannot afford; their problems are here today.

A third problem is *turnover*—people leave just as you get them trained, and you have spent all that time and money and effort for nothing. Training may reduce turnover, but it does not eliminate it, given the easy-come, easy-go workers in the hospitality industry.

The *short-term worker* is a training problem in many ways. People who do not expect to stay long on a job are not highly motivated. They are not interested in the job and they are not interested in getting ahead; they just want the paycheck at the end of the week. They do not like training programs. They do not like to read training materials. They do not get anything out of lectures. Most of them have poor listening, reading, and studying skills. They do poorly with the general, the abstract, and the complex. They are impatient; they are looking for a *now* skill—something they can do this afternoon.

The *diversity of workers* can be a training problem. Some are pursuing college degrees; others are poorly educated. Many have never had a job before; others have been in the industry for years. (Some of these are floaters who move from one operation to another; they like to work openings, stay about a month, and move on.) Some are know-it-alls; others are timid and dependent. Some are bright; others are below average in intelligence and aptitudes. Some do not speak English. Overall, they are not a promising classroom crowd. How can you train such different people for the same jobs and expect the same performance standards?

We also have problems with the *kinds of jobs* we train for. One type is the dull, routine job that takes no high degree of intelligence or skill: vacuuming carpets, mopping floors, prepping vegetables, and running a dishmachine. The problem here is the very simplicity of these jobs: We tend to overlook the training. Yet these jobs are very important to the operation, and it is essential that they be done correctly.

Most housekeeping jobs, for example, involve sanitation. Yet because sanitation can be technical and at times boring, and much of it is not visible to the untrained eye, it is easy to skip over it lightly. Techniques may not be properly taught or their importance emphasized—the sanitizer in the bucket of water, the indicator on the temperature gauge in the right place, the dishmachine loaded so that the spray reaches every dish and utensil.

Also overlooked are techniques of doing routine tasks quickly, efficiently, and safely. The optimum stroke of the vacuum cleaner, the order of tasks in cleaning a room, how to handle your body in making a bed or scrubbing a tub so that you don't strain your back—these little things can make a critical difference to efficiency, absenteeism, and employee well-being.

At the other extreme is the *complexity* of jobs containing up to 200 or 300 different tasks, plus the subtle skills of customer relations. Such jobs—server, bartender, and desk clerk—are so familiar to people who supervise them that they do not stop to think how much there is for a new person to learn. Training time for these multiple tasks can be a real problem. Therefore, you skimp on the training, you rush it, or you hire experienced people and skip the training. You forgo the control, the consistency of product and service, and the high-grade performance of people you have trained to your own standards.

The final typical training problem is *not knowing exactly what you want your people to do and how.* If you do not know this, how can you train them?

What you need is a system of training that defines what your people are to do and how, trains everyone to the same standards, adapts to individual needs and skills, and lends itself to one-on-one training. We talked in Chapter 15 about using performance standards in such a system, and we are going to discuss in detail how to develop a training program for this kind of system. Although not many people are going to take the trouble to develop a full-blown system, you can still see how its principles and techniques apply in training, and you can go as far as you find practical in applying them.

Before we look at the three different types of training, let us first consider who will do the training and how employees learn best.

WHO WILL DO THE TRAINING?

We have mentioned various ways of assigning the training responsibility: the magic apron, having an employee who is leaving train her replacement, the buddy or big brother/sister system. They do not work because such training is haphazard and incomplete, but most of all because the wrong person is doing the training.

With the magic apron, people train themselves. They are the wrong persons to do the training. They make a mistake and are yelled at, and what they train themselves to do is what will keep them from being yelled at. They will also train themselves to do things the easiest way and, in general, to do what is to their own best interest, and often, these things are opposed to the interests of the house.

Shirley is leaving or has already left. She will do only enough to placate Ms. Manager and get her paycheck. She will tell her replacement only what she knows, which may be very little, and only what she can cram into the shortest possible time, and she will not care whether the new person learns anything. She will also teach shortcuts and ways of getting away with breaking rules.

Big brother, big sister, and buddy will also teach only what they know, and only as much of that as they happen to think of, and they too will not care how well the new person understands. Unless they are paid extra for training, they may resent the assignment. They may also resent the new person as a competitor. In addition, they will hand on to the new worker all their own bad habits and all their accumulated gripes, and they will condition the trainee to their view of the job, the boss, the customers, and the pay.

The logical person to train your people is you, the supervisor. It is your responsibility, whether you delegate it or do it yourself. Training is one of those obligations to your people that goes with your job—giving them the tools and knowledge to do theirs. However, you have a thousand other responsibilities and your day is interrupted every 20 to 48 seconds.

If you can possibly make the time, you owe it to yourself to do the training. It is the beginning of leadership. A good teacher forms a lasting impression in the learner's mind, a special regard that will color the relationship from that point on. It gives you a chance to get to know your new people, to establish that one-to-one relationship necessary to being an effective leader.

On the other hand, you may have someone on your staff with the right potential who might be able to train new people even better than you can, considering all the demands on your time and attention. If you have established a good training program, you can delegate the training to someone like this.

Such people must be trained. They must know how to do everything they have to teach. They must learn the skills needed to train others: how to treat people as individuals, how to put themselves in the learner's place, how to gear the lesson to the learner, how to increase motivation, how to lead—all the good things you have been learning yourself.

Profile

MARIA SOMMERHAUZER HORTA

Courtesy of Maria Horta

Throughout my experience in the hospitality industry, I have always played on what I call my *Brazilian jeitinho*, which embraces some qualities I have gained from growing up in Brazil. *Jeitinho* is the Brazilian optimistic attitude of being especially creative in a variety of ways suitable to work out certain situations, such as making extra efforts to satisfy guests and employees when resolving certain issues. Indeed, most things can be accomplished somehow, in order to please guests and employees, as long as you keep your goals in mind.

First of all, let me tell you a little about myself. Upon my graduation from high school I promised myself I would continue my education. In fact, I decided to study hospitality management in San Diego, California, because San Diego is a beautiful city, with a high volume of tourism. Shortly after I moved to San Diego and started going to school, I wanted to experience the hospitality industry. I started at the front desk of a major hotel and I did not see working my way through college as a hardship, but rather as an opportunity, requiring that I manage my time and priorities and exert every effort to be productive. Although I started at a front desk position, my curiosity and initiative took me all over many departments of the hotel industry, such as reservations, sales and marketing, and the food and beverage division. Moreover, my greatest accomplishment was to supervise one of the food and beverage departments of another major hotel in San Diego. My new target customers were East Coast companies that sent groups of employees to our hotel in San Diego, mostly for work and conferences. We provided these preferred guests with a friendly, welcoming "happy hour," featuring a complimentary buffet and a full bar, from Monday through Friday. We usually had baseball, basketball, or football games playing on a big-screen TV during happy hour, which made an even more relaxed and fun atmosphere in which to "hang out." I found it very much fun to develop a relationship with some of these guests, especially because they always came back to our hotel. Some of them stayed for weeks, sometimes months; and some of them came back for a week every month of the year. I believe that most of these guests always came back because they got to meet a lot of people in our happy hour, and they felt very comfortable.

Next, as a supervisor, I found it effective to have a vision, or to set goals you want to accomplish during a given period of time. Then, communicate these goals to the team. Goals should be achievable given sufficient effort, and it must be possible to tell when they have been achieved. Recognizing and prizing employees who are accomplishing goals and devoting themselves to their work is crucial for employee motivation and satisfaction, leading to a higher quality of work.

Furthermore, I found it wonderful to build strong relationships with employees; you can understand them, and get sincere feedback from them on many aspects of work; and they can understand you, including what you expect from them. Supervisors make a great impact on an employee's performance; it is important to be aware of this fact. Whenever you have to correct a certain behavior or employee attitude, always mention the good things about that employee, building his or her self-esteem before criticizing the person's work.

In conclusion, I believe that effective supervising is, essentially, using common sense when making decisions in every situation. Also treating people fairly and with respect; recognizing and prizing their good work; and knowing how to criticize someone's conduct, if needed, without hurting their feelings, is very important. Finally, supervisors should listen to employees and guests and have a good sense of humor and a little *jeitinho* to please guests and employees while complying with the set goals for the company.

It is essential for these people to receive appropriate compensation: extra pay for extra work, a promotion, whatever fits the situation. They must also want to do the training. You remain responsible for the training, and if it is not done well, it will come back to haunt you.

By the way you train, you are teaching more than rules, procedures, skills, and job standards. You are teaching basic attitudes toward work, personal standards of performance, the importance of the person, getting along with other people (both guests and colleagues), your own work values, and many subtle but lasting lessons in human relations and values. People on their first jobs are particularly susceptible to this type of learning. Their first job will probably affect their attitude toward work performance, work relationships, and work values for the rest of their lives. It is important to be aware of this. You do not have to save their souls, but you do owe it to them to set high standards and a good example and to teach a work ethic of being on time, meeting standards, and giving their best efforts to the job. You owe it to yourself, too, and to the organization.

> When screening, it is important to strike a balance. Extensive screening of potential and existing staff risks falling foul of the law, failing to respect individuals' rights and treating people in a discriminatory manner. Conversely, organizations could miss out on people who could be a highly valuable asset. Tread carefully.
>
> *Source:* Liz Hall, "Looks Good on Paper?" *Personnel Today*, p. 17, March 2004.

HOW EMPLOYEES LEARN BEST

Training is a form of communication, and as in all communication, the sender (trainer) controls only the first half of the interaction. The second half, the receiving of the message—the learning—depends on the trainee. Learning is the acquisition of knowledge, skills, or attitudes. How do adults learn best? Many of the following tips for helping employees learn are derived from a field of study called adult learning theory.[2]

1. *Employees learn best when they are actively involved in the learning process.* When employees participate in their own training, they retain more of the concepts being taught. To get employees involved, you need to choose appropriate teaching

Good potential trainers need to be identified and receive additional compensation for training.

methods. Teaching methods are the ways we convey information to learners. You are no doubt familiar with the lecture method because it has dominated U.S. education for many years. Using the lecture method, content is delivered primarily in a one-way fashion from a trainer to the participants. Little or no interaction occurs between the trainer and the participants. Although the lecture method may be an efficient method to get across needed information to employees, it is most inefficient at getting employees to use the information. Figure 18.1 lists teaching methods that more actively involve employees.

2. *Employees also learn best when the training is relevant and practical.* Adult learners are picky about what they will spend their time learning. They often pursue learning experiences in order to cope with life-changing events such as a job change. Learning must be especially pertinent and rewarding for them.

3. Besides *being relevant, training material needs to be well organized and presented in small, easy-to-grasp chunks.* Adults need to be able to learn new skills at a speed that permits mastery. Unlike children, adults come to the classroom with prior experience, so they need to integrate new ideas with what they already know. Using

Discussion	Role-play
Demonstration	Simulation
Practice/skill	Dramatization
rehearsal	Instructional games
Case study	Brainstorming
Guest speaker	Field trip

FIGURE 18.1 Teaching methods to promote employee involvement in training.

visual aids, such as posters, during training helps to focus employees' attention, reinforce main ideas, save time, and increase understanding and retention.

4. *The optimal learning environment for employees is an informal, quiet, comfortable setting.* The effort you put into selecting and maintaining an appropriate environment for training shows your employees how important you think the training is. You give a message that training isn't that important when employees are stuffed into your office, made to stand in a noisy part of the kitchen, or when you allow yourself to be interrupted by phone calls. Employees like to feel special, so find a private room, and consider having beverages, and perhaps some food, available.

5. In addition to training in an appropriate setting, *employees learn best with a good trainer.* Figure 18.2 lists characteristics of successful trainers, some of which we have already discussed. As you go through the table, you will see that the characteristics listed also apply to successful supervisors. A good supervisor is usually a good trainer.

6. Toward the end of training, employees are generally evaluated on how well they are doing. *Employees learn best when they receive feedback on their performance and when they are rewarded* (perhaps with a certificate or pin) for doing well.

Formalized employee-education programs improve customer experiences and profits

Initiatives range from coaching and mentoring to watching videos, learning online, and role-playing. They include group tasting and discussion sessions and converting customer evaluations to actions and improvements. Regardless of the form it takes, training can grow business and nurture employees.

Source: Margaret Sheridan, *Restaurants & Institutions*, Vol. 114, No. 35, p. 127, July 2004.

1. Displays enthusiasm and has a sense of humor
2. Communicates clearly in a way that participants understand
3. Is knowledgeable
4. Is sincere, patient and listens to participants
5. Encourages and positively reinforces all participants
6. Is organized
7. Plans the training session
8. Involves all participants
9. Presents the material in an interesting and appropriate way for participants to learn
10. Checks the outcome to see that all participants have learned and has them sign that they have learned the training topics

FIGURE 18.2   Characteristics of a good trainer.

Check Your Knowledge

1.   What are some of problems you may come across when you do not train your employees?

2.   Who will train your employees?

3.   When do employees learn best?

DEVELOPING A JOB-TRAINING PROGRAM

A good job-training program should be organized as a series of written training plans, each representing a learnable, teachable segment of the job. Once you have prepared such plans, you can use them for every new person you hire for the job: They are all ready to go. You can use as much or as little of each plan as you need, depending on what the new employee already knows.

Performance standards provide a ready-made structure for a training program for a given job: Each unit of the job with its performance standards provides the framework for one training plan. In this section we describe how to develop a training program using performance standards. Although you may not complete the system in every detail, you can apply the principles and content to any training program.

Establishing Plan Content

Even if you do not have performance standards, you still have to go through pretty much the same procedures to develop a good training program. You must analyze the job as a whole, identifying all the units that make up that job classification and then the tasks that make up each unit. Then you must decide how you want each unit and task done and to what standard. You then develop a procedure manual or some other way of showing how the tasks are to be carried out. These steps are described in detail in Chapter 15. When you have done all this, you are ready to prepare training plans, one plan for each unit of the job.

Figure 18.3 traces the progress of one training plan from its beginning to its implementation on the job. Let us follow it through, using an example from the bartender's job. The job of bartender contains a dozen or so units, such as setting up the bar, mixing and serving drinks, recording drink sales, operating the cash register, and so on. You will write a training plan for each unit. Your first training plan will be for *setting up the bar*.

1.   Write your performance standard: "The bartender will set up the bar correctly according to standard house procedures in half an hour or less."

2.   Write a training objective derived from your performance standard: "After 3 hours of instruction and practice, the trainee will be able to set up the bar correctly according to standard house procedures in 45 minutes." This training objective expresses what you expect the person to do after training, the training goal. It differs from the on-the-job performance objective in three ways:
     ■   A time limit is set for the training.
     ■   The verb expresses trainee achievement rather than on-the-job performance.
     ■   The performance standard is lower for this learning level (45 minutes) than for the day-in, day-out performance level.

3.   Incorporate your standard procedures that you may already have developed. If not, here is what you do. You list all the tasks of the unit in the order in which they are performed, and you spell out each task in the form of a procedures sheet or visual presentation stating or showing exactly how you want that task carried out in your operation. Figure 18.4 is a procedures sheet for the first task of setting up the bar. Figure 18.5 goes with it to illustrate some of the procedures. All the procedural materials taken together define the content of the instruction for the unit, and they become both guides and standards for the training. You are now ready to plan the training itself.

Developing a Unit Training Plan

A training plan (Figure 18.3 step 4) sets forth not only what you will train someone to do, but how, and when, and where, what supplies and materials you need, and how

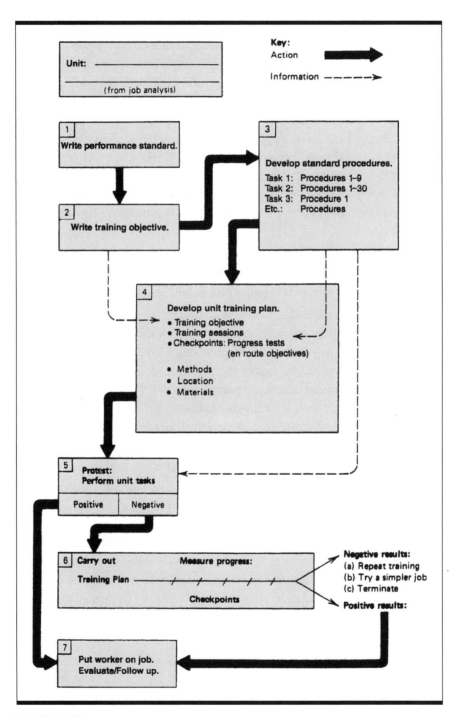

FIGURE 18.3 Flowchart for developing and carrying out a training plan for one unit of a job.

Standard Procedures

Job: Bartender.   **Unit 1**: Setting up the bar

Task no. 1: Replenishing liquor supplies, standard house procedures

1. Count the number of full or partly full bottles of each brand and compare with the Par Stock Sheet posted at the bar. This will give you the numbers to be replaced.
2. On requisition sheet, enter name, unit size, and number needed for each brand.
3. Count empty bottles (box under bar) brand by brand and compare numbers with requisition. If they do not agree, report differences to supervisor. Supervisor will OK discrepancies or tell you what to do.
4. Sign and date completed requisition form on line 1 and have supervisor sign.
5. Lock the bar gate. Take requisition and empties to storeroom (use dolly or cart). Storeroom will count empties, issue fulls, and sign requisition.
6. Count full bottles to make sure you have received the numbers storeroom has shown on requisition. Sign and date on bottom line. Storeroom keeps requisition.
7. Take full bottles to bar. Wipe them and arrange all bottles as shown on well and backbar diagram below.
8. Set up two reserve bottles with pourers for each bottle in well.
9. Check all pourers and replace corks as necessary.

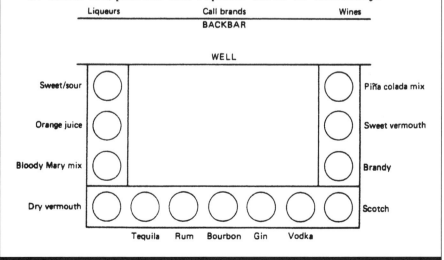

FIGURE 18.4 Portion of a procedure for setting up the bar: procedures for one task (page from a procedures manual for the job of bartender).

REQUISITION

DEPT _Bar_   DATE _June 12_

Item (Brand)	Unit	Quantity Requested	Quantity Issued	Unit Cost	Total Cost
J & B	L	2			
Chivas	L	1			
Jim Bean	L	1			
C.C.	L	1			
Beefeater	L	2			
Smirnoff	L	3			
Teq - Cuervo	L	2			
Bacardi	L	2			
Brandy - C.B.	L	1			
Amaretto	750	1			
Baileys I.C.		1			
Cr. Cacao - W		1			
Burgundy - Gal	1.75	1			
Chablis - Alm	1.75	4			
Cinzano dry	750	1			
Mary mix	case	1			

REQUISITIONED BY _Mike Smith_   DATE   6/12

SUPERVISOR   DATE

ISSUED BY   DATE

RECEIVED BY   DATE

FIGURE 18.5 Example of a requisition filled out by a bartender (page from a procedures manual for the job of bartender).

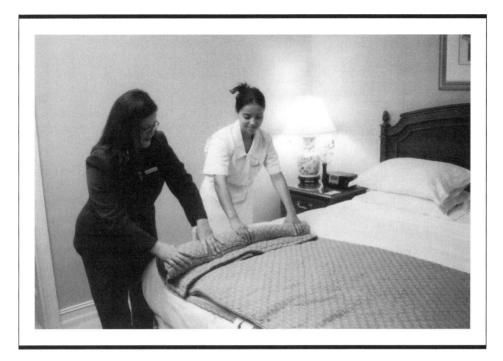

Training objectives are based on performance standards.

much training you will do at one time. Figure 18.6 is an example of a training plan for the first unit of the bartender job. Let us go through that plan item by item.

Notice first that the training objective is stated, so that you can keep the goal in mind and shape the training to reach it. The unit is taught in several *training sessions*. The primary reason for this is to avoid giving the trainee too much to learn at once. Another reason is to avoid tying up the person doing the training for too long a time. In this particular case it is also to avoid tying up the bar itself.

The tasks are taught in the order in which they are performed on the job. (Some tasks do not have an order; in Dress and Grooming, for example, all "tasks" are carried on simultaneously.) One training session may include several tasks, some taking as little as 5 or 10 minutes. Length of time for each session will vary according to the trainee's previous experience. An experienced bartender, for example, will learn your par-stock-empty-bottle-requisition routine far more quickly than someone who has never tended bar before. (Most operations look for experienced bartenders because training from scratch takes too long, but even an experienced bartender must be trained in *your* bar and *your* procedures.)

```
                          TRAINING PLAN


Job classification:  Bartender

Unit 1:  Setting up the bar

Learning objective: After 3 hours of instruction and
practice, trainee will be able to set up the
bar correctly according to standard house procedures in
45 minutes.

Training sessions:   1. Replenish liquor (Task 1, training
                        time 30 minutes)
                     2. Replenish other supplies (Tasks
                        2-6, training time 30 minutes)
                     3. Set up draft beer, check soda
                        system (Tasks 7-8, training
                        time 20 minutes)
                     4. Prepare garnishes (Tasks 9-13,
                        training time 30 minutes)
                     5. Set up register (Tasks 14-15,
                        training time 20 minutes)
                     6. Set up ice bins, glasses, sinks,
                        mixing equipment, bar top,
                        coffee (Tasks 16-21, training
                        time 25 minutes)

Method:  Demonstrate and do (JIT), one on one. Video-
         tape on beer setup.

Location:  Bar, 1 hour before opening (bar must be as
           left after closing)

Materials:  Liquor and all other  Cocktail napkins
              supplies as of       Ice
              closing              Bar knife and cutting
            Liquor empties from      board
              previous day         Bar spoon, jiggers
            Par Stock Sheet        Mixing glasses
            Requisition forms      Guest checks
            Well and backbar       Credit card slips
              diagram              Cash register
            Pourers, replacement   Opening bank
              collars              Dolly or cart
            Ashtrays               Coffee machine and
            Matches                  coffee
            Picks                  Procedure sheets, Tasks
            Snacks                   1-21

Checkpoints:  After each task
```

FIGURE 18.6 Training plan for one unit (page from a training manual).

The training plan should provide *checkpoints* along the way, as shown in step 6 of Figure 18.3. These allow you to measure a worker's progress toward achieving the objective. They may follow groups of tasks within the unit of work, or they may follow the whole unit with a series of less demanding performance standards (a more lenient time limit, a greater margin for error). You can write special intermediate objectives for the checkpoints or set several successive levels of performance for the entire unit of work.

The *method of training* must include two elements: (1) showing and telling the trainee what to do and how to do it, and (2) having the trainee actually do it and do it right. These elements are combined in a widely used formula known as *job instruction training*, which we examine in detail shortly. There are various ways to show and tell: demonstration, movies, videotapes, CD-ROMs and DVDs.

The closer the training method and setup are to the on-the-job situation, the better the training. You can teach table setting by actually setting up tables for service, teach bed making while you are actually making a room ready for the next guest. But there are many things you cannot teach while doing them on the job. In such cases you simulate on-the-job conditions as closely as you can: You use the real equipment and real supplies and you set up the equipment and the task as realistically as possible.

One-on-one training generally works best. In a classroom, a person does not learn as well. Everybody absorbs the material at different rates or has different problems with it. The slow learners are lost and the fast learners are bored. The classroom also causes anxiety and inhibits everyone except the know-it-all.

However, group presentations have certain advantages. They are useful for giving general information and background that may be overlooked by the individual trainer. Because group presentations can be more closely controlled, it is a good way to convey company policy so that it is always stated accurately and everyone gets the same message. Groups are also used for material presented in movies and videos.

A number of chains use audiovisual presentations such as videotapes or slidetapes that are developed at headquarters and are sent out for use by individual stores or several stores in an area. Training in customer relations, for example, can be given in this fashion. It is effective and ensures not only a consistent message but also consistent training quality.

The *location* of the training should be a quiet place free of interruptions. Ideally, training is done in the actual job setting during off hours. Some corporations have special training facilities completely equipped to simulate the actual job environment.

Your *training materials* should include the same equipment and supplies that will be used on the job, and they should all be on hand and ready before the training starts. You must prepare your entire session in advance if training is to be effective.

Developing a written training plan helps you to think out all the aspects of the training and to orient everything to the new employee and the details of the job. Each completed plan gives you a checklist for readiness and a blueprint for action.

Like many good things prepared for a well-run operation, training plans take a long time to develop, and the manager or supervisor will have to do one plan at a time one piece at a time, probably over a long period. It may be helpful to schedule development along the lines of an improvement objective (Chapter 15), setting overall goals and interim goals. Then each completed piece of the plan will provide a feeling of achievement and the momentum to continue. Of course, if you already have job analyses, performance objectives, and procedures manuals, your work is half done at the outset.

Moving from Plan to Action

Now you are ready to train the worker. But before you train new employees you must find out how much training they really need. If they have knowledge and skills from previous experience, it wastes both their time and yours to teach them things they

Training plans need checkpoints to measure the trainees' progress.

already know. For this reason the training of people who have some experience begins with a pretest (Figure 18.3, step 5): You have them actually do the unit of work. If the unit consists of operating the dishmachine, you have them operate the dishmachine; if it is serving wine, you have them serve wine; if it is setting up the bar, you have them set up the bar.

You observe the new worker's performance and confine your training to what the person does not know, what does not measure up to your standard, what varies from your special ways of doing things, and what the person must unlearn in the way of habits and procedures from other jobs. Experienced workers should end up meeting the same standards as people whom you train from scratch.

Not all units and tasks are suitable for pretesting. Some are too complex, and some are different every day. In this case you can ask experienced new workers to describe how they would carry out the tasks in question and then adjust the training accordingly.

Now suppose that you are training Gloria and David, who have never had a job before. You carry out your first unit training plan (Figure 18.6), teaching each of them every task in the unit's action plan. You test them at every checkpoint to make sure that they are following you and are putting it all together and meeting your time requirements. Finally, when you have taught all the tasks in the unit, you evaluate Gloria and David by having them perform the entire unit in sequence.

Does Gloria meet the performance standard of your learning objective? If so, you move on to the second unit of the job and the second objective. Suppose that David fails to meet the standard for the first unit. You retrain him in those procedures that he is not doing correctly. If he did not meet the time requirement, you have him practice some more.

If he just can't get it all together, you might try him on the second unit anyway. If he can't do that either, he may not be able to handle the job, and you may have to place him in a less demanding job. It is also possible that your training was at fault, and you have to take a hard look at that. If you do not have a simpler job, or if he cannot team that simpler job either, you may have to let him go. The training has not been wasted if it has identified an untrainable employee in time to save your paying unemployment compensation. (It sure was frustrating, though!) Don't frustrate yourself with someone who cannot or will not learn.

Ideally, you will put a new employee on the job (Figure 18.3, step 7) after training for all units of the job has been completed. But you may need Gloria and David so badly that you will have them work a unit of the job as soon as they have been trained for that unit. In complex jobs it may even be easier for them to work certain units of the job for awhile before going on to learn the entire job.

Once the formal training process is completed, there is still one very important step: evaluation. Making an evaluation is the crucial process of determining whether training objectives were met. It can occur both during and after training. Formative evaluation uses observation, interviews, and surveys to monitor training while it is going on. Summative evaluation measures the results of the training after the program is completed, looking at it in five ways.

1. *Reaction:* Did the employees like the training?
2. *Knowledge:* Did the employees learn the information taught?
3. *Behavior:* Are the employees using the new skills or behavior on the job?
4. *Attitudes:* Do the employees demonstrate any new attitudes?
5. *Productivity:* Did the training increase productivity, and was it cost-effective?

Various techniques can be used to answer these questions. Participants can report on what they liked and did not like about the training by filling out evaluation forms. Tests are frequently given at the end of training sessions to determine whether the employees know the information and/or skills covered. For instance, a dishwasher may be asked the correct temperature for the final rinse and then asked to demonstrate how to pick up dishes without contaminating them. Results can also be measured through observation of employee behavior and monitoring of critical indicators such as the number of guest complaints, level of repeat business, and so on. After collecting information from various sources, the person doing the evaluation needs to compare the results to the learning objectives to determine whether the training indeed succeeded in bringing about the desired changes.

> Customer service and guest satisfaction are the primary measuring sticks for a successful training program. A training program not only benefits a hotel, but it could have a long-term impact on the overall industry.
>
> *Source:* Jeff Higley, "Companies Refocus on Training," *Hotel and Motel Management*, Vol. 219, No. 13, p. 1, July 2004.

Job Instruction Training

Successful training observes the flow of the learning process. During World War II, when war plants had to train millions of workers quickly, a training method was developed that took maximum advantage of the learning flow. It was so successful that it has been used in various forms ever since in all kinds of training programs in all types of industries. This is job instruction training (JIT), sometimes also called on-the-job training.

The method consists of four steps:

1. Prepare the worker for training.

2. Demonstrate what the worker is to do (show and tell).

3. Have the worker do the task, as shown, repeating until the performance is satisfactory.

4. Follow through: Put the worker on the job, checking and correcting as needed.

These four steps are applied to one task at a time. Figure 18.7 shows the steps and the relationship to learning flow.

Step 1, preparing the worker (call him Bob), consists of several things you do to let him know what is coming, make him feel at ease, and motivate him to learn. One thing is telling Bob where his job fits into the overall operation and why it is important

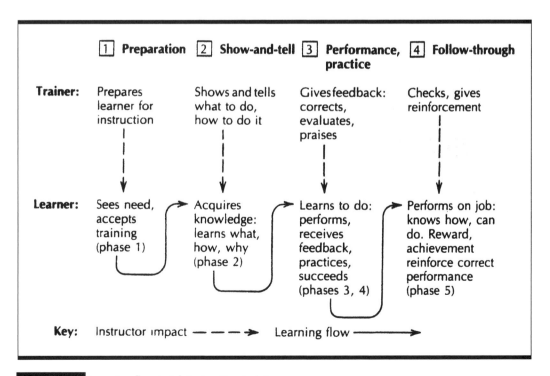

FIGURE 18.7 Learning flow in job instruction training.

to the operation. Another is giving Bob a reason to learn ("It will benefit you." "It will help you to do your job." "You will be rewarded in such and such a way.") A third is telling him what to expect in the training and expressing confidence that he can do the job.

Step 2, demonstrating the task, is show-and-tell: "This is what I want you to do and this is how I want you to do it." You explain what you are doing and how you are doing it and why you are doing it the way you are. You use simple language and stress the key points. You tell Bob exactly what he needs to know but no more (unless he asks). If you tell him too much, you will confuse him. You do not go into the theory of the dishmachine: the temperature it has to reach, the bacteria that have to be killed, and why bacteria are such an issue. You tell him, "The dish must get very hot. The needle must be at this number." The core of the action stands out clearly—no theory, all application. You take care to demonstrate well, because what you do is going to set the standard of performance, along with teaching the how-to. You cannot give a second-class demonstration and expect the worker to do a first-class job.

Step 3, having Bob do the task as you showed him, is really the heart of the training. The first time is a tryout. If he can do it correctly right off, he is stimulated. If he cannot, you correct the errors and omissions in a positive way and have him do it again, showing him again if necessary. As he does it, have him tell you the key points and why they are done the way they are; this will reinforce the learning. Have him do the task several times, correcting himself if he can, telling you why he made the correction, letting him experience the stimulation of his increasing understanding. Encourage his questions, taking them seriously no matter how simpleminded they sound to you. Praise him for his progress and encourage him when he falters or fails. Have him repeat the task until you are satisfied that he can do it exactly as you did, to the standard you have set for him. Let him see your satisfaction and approval.

Step 4, following through, means putting Bob on his own in the actual job. You do this not for individual tasks but for units or groups of units or when the worker has learned the entire job. You stay in the background and watch him at work. You touch base frequently, correct his performance as necessary, and let him know how he is doing. Now, briefly, you are a partner in his success. You praise and reward as promised. When he continues to do things just the way you have trained him to do, you can leave him on his own.

Check Your Knowledge

1. Why is evaluating important?

2. Briefly explain the four steps of job instruction training.

RETRAINING

Training people for jobs does not always take care of their training needs. Further training is necessary in several instances.

One such situation arises when changes are made that affect the job. You might make some changes in the menu. You might put in a different type of cash register. Your boss might decide to use paper and plastic on the hospital trays instead of china and glasses. Your food and beverage director might decide to install an automatic dispensing system for all the bars.

When such changes affect the work of your people, it is your responsibility to tell them about the changes and see that they are trained to deal with them. If the changes are large, you might develop new performance standards, procedural sheets, and training plans and run your people through additional training sessions. If the changes are small, such as a new kind of coffeemaker or a new linen supplier with different routines and delivery times, they still affect people's work, but in the usual daily rush it is easy to overlook letting people know or to assume they will find out and know what to do. Even posting a notice or a set of instructions is not enough; a person-to-person message is in order, with show-and-tell as called for.

It is as important to keep your people's knowledge and skills up to date as it is to train them right in the first place. They cannot do the job well if the job has changed, and it makes them feel bad to know that no one has thought to tell them of the change and show them what to do.

A second kind of training need arises when an employee's performance drops below par, when he or she is simply not meeting minimal performance standards. It may be caused by various things—difficulties involving the job itself or other people, personal problems outside the job, or simply job burnout—disenchantment with doing the same old thing day after day and lack of motivation to do it well any more.

Suppose that Sally's performance as a cocktail waitress has deteriorated noticeably in the last few weeks and there have been guest complaints of poor service, ill temper, and rudeness. The old-style manager, of course, would be on Sally's back yelling at her and ordering her to shape up, but threats and coercion are not going to do the trick. Nor will it help to ignore the problem. A person whose previous work has been up to standard is usually well aware of what is happening. If you tolerate Sally's poor performance, it will reduce her respect for you, for the job, and for herself.

This situation calls for a positive one-on-one approach, generally referred to as coaching. Coaching is a two-part process involving observation of employee performance and conversation focusing on job performance between the manager and the employee. It is discussed in detail in Chapter 19.

Job instruction training prepares the associate for training and demonstrating what the associate is supposed to do—show and tell. Courtesy of Sodexho.

A few other situations also call for retraining. For example, you may notice that a worker has never really mastered a particular technique (such as cleaning in the corners of rooms) *or has gone back to an old bad habit* (such as picking up clean glasses with the fingers inside the rims). In such cases, you simply retrain the person in the techniques involved.

In other instances, people themselves may ask for further training. If you have good relationships with your people, they will feel free to do this, and of course, you should comply. It is testimony to your good leadership that they feel free to ask and that they want to improve their performance.

ORIENTATION

Orientation is the prejob phase of training. It introduces each new employee to the job and workplace as soon as he or she reports for work. It is not uncommon in the hospitality industry for people to be put to work without any orientation at all: "Here is your workstation; do what Virginia tells you." You don't even know what door to come in and out of and where the restrooms are, and on payday everyone else gets paid and you don't, and you wonder if you have been fired and didn't even know it.

The primary purpose of orientation is to tell new staff members (1) what they want to know, and (2) what the company wants them to know. As with any training, it takes time—the new person's time and the supervisor's time—anywhere from thirty minutes to most of the day.

Nevertheless, it is worth the time needed to do it and to do it well. It can reduce employee anxiety and confusion, ease the adjustment, and tip the balance between leaving and staying during the first critical days. In addition, it provides an excellent opportunity to create positive employee attitudes toward the company and the job.

Therefore, you have two goals for an orientation:

1. Communicating information: getting the messages through
2. Creating a positive response to company and job

Let us look at the second one first because it makes the first one easier and because it is more likely to be overlooked.

Creating a Positive Response

If you do not have an orientation for each new employee, somebody else will—your other workers. Their orientation will be quite different from yours, and it may have a negative impact. They want to give a new person the inside story, the lowdown, and it will include everybody's pet gripes and negative feelings about the company and warnings to watch out for this and that, and your new worker will begin to have an uneasy feeling that this is not such a good place to work. People are always more ready to believe their coworkers, their peer group, than their boss, so it is important for you to make your impact first. Then, in the days that follow, you must live up to what you have told them in your orientation or their co-workers may undermine the impression you have made.

You want to create an image of the company as a good place to work. You also want to foster certain feelings in your new people: that they are needed and wanted, that they and their jobs are important to the company. You want to create the beginnings of a sense of belonging, of fitting in. You want to reduce their anxieties and promote a feeling of confidence and security about the company and the job and their ability to do it. This is the beginning of establishing that positive work environment discussed in Chapter 14.

You do all this not only through what you say but how you say it and even more through your own attitude. You speak as one human being to another; you do not talk down from a power position. You avoid Theory X assumptions; you assume that each is a person worthy of your concern and attention who can and will work well for you. You do not lay down the law; you inform. You treat orientation as a way of filling their need to know rather than *your* need to have them follow the rules (although it is that, too). You accentuate the positive.

If you can make a favorable impact, reduce anxieties, and create positive attitudes and feelings, new employees will probably stay through the critical first seven days. It will be much easier for you to train them, and they will become productive much more quickly.

Communicating the Necessary Information

Employees want to know about their pay rate, overtime, days and hours of work, where the restrooms are, where to park, where to go in and out, where the phone is and whether they can make or receive calls, where their workstation is, to whom they report, break times, meals, and whether their brother can come to the Christmas party. The company wants them to know all this plus all the rules and regulations they must follow; company policy on holidays, sick days, benefits, and so on; uniform and grooming codes; how to use the time clock; emergency procedures; key control; withholding of taxes; and other boring and bewildering things. They must also fill out the necessary forms and get their name tags, and they should have a tour of the facility and be introduced to the people they will work with.

It is a lot to give all at once. It is best to give it one-on-one rather than waiting until you have several new people and giving a group lecture. A lecture is too formal, and waiting several days may be too late.

You can have it all printed in a booklet, commonly called an employee handbook. But you cannot hand people a book of rules and expect them to read and absorb it. It will really turn them off if you ask them first thing to read a little booklet about things they cannot do. *Tell them.* Give them the booklet to take home.

An orientation checklist, shown in Figure 18.8, is an excellent tool for telling your employees what they need to know. It lists sample topics covered during an orientation program, such as how to request a day off. These topics are grouped into three categories: "Introduction to the Company," "Policies and Procedures," and "The New Job." One benefit of using such a checklist is that it ensures consistency among managers and supervisors who are conducting orientation and makes it unlikely that any topic will be forgotten.

INTRODUCTION TO THE COMPANY

_____   Welcome.

_____   Describe company briefly, including history, operation (type of menu, service, hours of operation, etc.) and goals (be sure to mention the importance of quality service).

_____   Show how company is structured or organized.

POLICIES AND PROCEDURES

_____   Explain dress code and who furnishes uniforms.

_____   Describe where to park.

_____   How to sign in and out and when.

_____   Assign locker and explain its use.

_____   Review amount of sick time, holiday time, personal time, and vacation time as applicable.

_____   Review benefits.

_____   Explain how to call in if unable to come to work.

_____   Explain procedure to request time off.

_____   Review salary and when and where to pick up check, as well as who can pick up the employee's paycheck. If applicable, explain policy on overtime and reporting of tips.

_____   Discuss rules on personal telephone use.

_____   Explain smoking policy.

_____   Explain meal policy, including when and where food can be eaten.

_____   Review disciplinary guidelines.

_____   Explain guest relations policy.

_____   Review teamwork policy.

_____   Explain property removal policy.

_____   Explain responsible service of alcohol, if applicable.

_____   Explain Equal Employment Opportunity policy.

_____   Discuss promotional and transfer opportunities.

_____   Explain professional conduct policy.

_____   Explain guidelines for safe food handling, safety in the kitchen, and what to do in case of a fire.

_____   Explain notice requirement if leaving your job.

THE NEW JOB

_____   Review job description and standards of performance.

_____   Review daily work schedule including break times.

_____   Review hours of work and days off. Show where schedule is posted.

_____   Explain how and when employee will be evaluated.

_____   Explain probationary period.

_____   Explain training program, including its length.

_____   Describe growth opportunities.

_____   Give tour of operation and introduce to other managers and co-workers.

FIGURE 18.8 Sample orientation checklist.

Similarly, you cannot expect new employees to soak up everything you say. As you are aware, communication is a two-way process, and you can send message after message but you cannot control the receiving end. They will listen selectively, picking out what interests them. Try to give each item an importance for them. (For example: "You can get any entree under $5 free." "The employee parking lot is the only place that isn't crowded." "The cook will poison your lunch if you come in through the kitchen.") Give reasons. ("The money withheld goes to the government.") Phrase things positively. ("You may smoke on breaks in designated areas outside the building" rather than "Smoking is forbidden on the job.")

Watch your workers carefully to make sure that you are understood, and repeat as necessary. Encourage questions. ("Can I clarify anything?") Be sure you cover everything (use a checklist). Even so, you will need to repeat some things during the next few days.

Taking the trouble to start new employees off on the right foot will make things easier as you begin their training for the job. They will feel more positive, less anxious, and more receptive to the training to come.

OVERCOMING OBSTACLES TO LEARNING

When you think of the many barriers to communication, it should not be surprising that training should have its share of obstacles. Some of them are learning problems, and some have to do with teaching, the trainer, or the training program. (You can see the two halves of the communication process again: sending and receiving the message.)

One problem for the learner may be fear. Some people are afraid of training, especially if they did not finish school and never really learned how to learn. This kind of anxiety clouds the mind and makes learning difficult. Some people have fear as their basic motivation. Contrary to prevalent belief in this industry, fear is usually a barrier to learning, not a motivator. It interferes with concentration and inhibits performance. People who are afraid of the boss or the instructor will not ask questions. They will say that they understand when they do not.

You can reduce fear and anxiety with a positive approach. Begin by putting the new employee at ease, conveying your confidence that he or she can learn the job without any trouble. Everyone will learn faster and better if you can reduce their anxieties and increase their confidence. Work with the trainee informally, as one human being to another, and try to establish a relationship of trust. Praise progress and achievement.

Some people have little natural motivation to learn, such as ambition, need for money, desire to excel, desire to please, and self-satisfaction. If they don't see anything in the training for them, they will learn slowly, they will not get things straight, and they will forget quickly.

There are several ways of increasing motivation:

1. *Emphasize whatever is of value to the learner:* how it will help in the job, increase tips, or make things easier. As you teach each procedure, point out why you do it as you do, why it is important, and how it will help.

2. *Make the program form a series of small successes for the learner.* Each success increases confidence and stimulates the desire for more success.

3. *Perhaps the most important motivator is to build in incentives and rewards for achievement as successive steps are mastered.* These can range from praise, a progress chart, and public recognition (a different-colored apron, an achievement pin) to a bonus for completing the training.

Some people are not as bright as others. They may have trouble with the pace and level of the instruction: too fast, too much at once, too abstract, too many big words. They may be capable of learning if the teaching is adjusted to their learning ability. *One-to-one instruction, patience,* and *sensitivity* are the keys here. Often, things learned slowly are better retained.

Some people are lazy and indifferent. And if they are lazy about learning the job, they will probably be lazy about doing it. Others will resist training because they think they know it all. They expect to be bored and they pay little attention to the instruction. These are potential problem types and they will be either a challenge or a real headache.

Sometimes we do not deal with people as they are. We assume that they know something they do not know, or we assume that they don't know something they do know. Either way, we lose their attention and their desire or ability to learn what we want them to learn. To overcome this obstacle, we need to *approach training from the learner's point of view.* Instead of teaching tasks, teach people. Put yourself in their place, find out what they know, teach what they do not know, and interest them in learning it.

Keep it simple, concrete, practical, and real. Use words they can understand: familiar words, key words they can hang an idea on. Involve all their senses: seeing, hearing, feeling, experiencing. It is said that people remember 10 percent of what they read, 20 percent of what they hear, 30 percent of what they see, 50 percent of what they hear and see, and they remember more of what they do than what they are told. Teach by show, tell, and do—hands-on.

Sometimes the training program is the problem. If it is abstract, academic, impersonal, or unrealistic, it will not get across. If you have not carefully defined what you want the trainee to learn and you have no way of measuring when learning has taken place, the trainee may never learn the job well. If the training sessions are poorly organized, or if the training materials are inadequate or inappropriate, or if the setting is wrong (noisy, subject to constant interruptions, lacking in equipment or other on-the-job realism), the sessions will be ineffective. If the program does not provide incentives to succeed, the program itself will not succeed.

Sometimes the instructor causes the learning problems. Trainers need to know the job well enough to teach it. They need to be good communicators, able to use words other people will understand, sensitive enough to see when they are not getting through. They need to be able to look at the task from the learner's point of view, a very difficult thing when you know it so well that it is second nature to you. They need patience. They need leadership qualities: If people do not respond to the trainer as a leader, they do not learn willingly from that person.

Above all, trainers must not have a negative attitude toward those they are training. Never look down on either the person or the job, and take care to avoid Theory X assumptions (people are lazy, dislike work, must be coerced, controlled, and threatened). Assume the best of everyone.

When a mistake is made, correct the action rather than the person, and correct by helping, not by criticizing. A useful technique is to compliment before correcting. Say, for example, "You are holding the bottle exactly right and you have poured exactly the right amount of wine. What you need to do to avoid spilling is to raise the mouth and turn the bottle slightly before you draw it away from the glass" (instead of "Look what you did, you dribbled wine all over the table; don't *do* that, I *told* you to raise the mouth!"). Emphasize what is right, not what is wrong.

Be patient. Hang on to your temper. Praise progress and achievement. Think success. Cheer your people on as they learn their jobs, and stick with them until they have reached your goals.

KEY POINTS

1. Training means teaching people how to do their jobs. You may instruct and guide a trainee toward learning knowledge, skills, or attitudes.

2. Three kinds of training are needed in hospitality operations: job instruction, retraining, and orientation.

3. Training has the following benefits: more time to manage, less absenteeism and less turnover, less tension, higher consistency of product and service, lower costs, happier customers and more of them, and enhancement of your career. By making sure that your employees know what to do, tension is reduced, morale and job satisfaction are boosted, the number of accidents and injuries are reduced, and your workers have a better chance of advancing.

4. The problems involved in training are real: urgent need for trained workers, lack of time, lack of money, short-term workers, diversity of workers, kinds of jobs and skills, complexity of some jobs, and not knowing exactly what you want your people to do and how.

5. The logical person to train your people is you, the supervisor. It is your responsibility, whether you delegate it or do it yourself. Training is one of those obligations to your people that goes with your job—giving them the tools and knowledge to do theirs.

6. Employees learn best when they are actively involved in the learning process, when the training is relevant and practical, when the training materials are organized and presented in small chunks, when the setting is informal and quiet, when the trainer is good, and when employees receive feedback on their performance and reward for achievement.

7. Figure 18.3 portrays the steps involved in developing and carrying out a training plan.

8. Once the formal training process is completed, there is still one very important step: evaluation. Formative evaluation uses observation, interviews, and surveys to monitor training while it is going on. Summative evaluation measures the results of the training after the program is completed, looking at it in five ways: reaction, knowledge, behavior, attitudes, and productivity.

9. The procedure for job instruction training is illustrated in Figure 18.7.

10. Classroom training may be used at times for job instruction or retraining. Teaching in a classroom requires certain skills: Be aware of and use appropriate body language and speech, convey respect and appreciation, use informal and familiar language, correct in a positive and friendly manner, handle problem behaviors effectively, avoid time-wasters, facilitate employee participation and discussions, and use visual aids properly.

11. Retraining is needed when changes are made that affect the job, when an employee's performance drops below par, or when a worker simply has never really mastered a particular technique.

12. Orientation is the prejob phase of training that introduces each new employee to the job and workplace. Your goals for orientation are to communicate necessary information, such as where to park and when to pick up a paycheck, and also to create a positive response to the company and job.

13. Some keys to training include the following: Use a positive approach to reduce fear and anxiety, look at ways to increase employee motivation, such as building in incentives and rewards as steps are mastered; adjust the teaching to the employee's learning ability; don't assume anything; approach training from the learner's point of view; keep it simple and practical; and make sure that the trainer is doing a good job.

KEY TERMS

adult learning theory	job instruction	summative evaluation
big sister/big brother or buddy system	job instruction training	teaching methods
coaching	learning	training
employee handbook	orientation	training objective
formative evaluation	pretest	training plan
	retraining	

REFERENCES

1. Pamela Parseghian "For Raw Recruits, Training Is the Best Defense Against Food Poisoning," *Nation's Restaurant News*, Vol. 34, No. 33.

2. Adapted from "Inservice Training: How Do Employees Learn Best?" *Hospital Food & Nutrition Focus*, Vol. 6, No. 4, pp. 1–4, © 1989, Aspen Publishers, Inc. Reprinted with permission.

EVALUATING PERFORMANCE*

Among the five reasons why people do poor work or leave their jobs entirely is that they don't know how well they are doing. This chapter is about finding out how well they are doing and telling them about it.

Good supervisors are out among their people every day, observing, coaching, evaluating: "Hey, that's a great job!" "Here, let me show you how to do that." "Look, there's a quicker way." Informal evaluation or coaching is an everyday part of their involvement with their people. It goes with getting the work done, achieving the results they are responsible for. They may not think of it as evaluation, but they are on the

---

* Authored by Jack E. Miller, John R. Walker, and Karen Eich Drummond.

lookout all the time to see if people are doing what they are supposed to do in the way they are supposed to do it. And if they have good human relations skills, they let their people know in a positive, upbeat fashion.

Unfortunately, the hospitality industry also has its share of supervisors who are not long on human relations skills. They may be out there every day, too, watching, checking up, looking for mistakes, and getting after people when they are doing something wrong. They take a totally negative approach, and their people receive continuous negative evaluations or none at all. If they are doing all right, the boss sees no need to comment. However, the absence of negatives does not add up to a positive. This makes people uneasy.

We need a systematic approach to evaluation that will let people know how well they are doing and help them to improve. We cannot get along without the day-by-day approach, but we need to stop and assess performance over a period of time. This provides a chance to recognize achievement, point out paths to improvement, and formalize it all for the record.

This chapter deals with day-to-day coaching and periodic performance evaluations and how they can contribute to increased production, employee satisfaction, and supervisory success. It will help you to:

- Describe the concept of coaching, and outline the guidelines of effective coaching.

- Explain the complementary relationship between ongoing day-by-day evaluation and periodic performance reviews.

- Enumerate the purposes and benefits of performance reviews.

- Outline the steps of the performance review process.

- Explain common hurdles to evaluating employee performance fairly and objectively.

- Describe how to handle an appraisal interview, and list mistakes that commonly occur during appraisal interviews.

- Explain how follow-up can extend the benefits of performance review.

Success in foodservice and lodging operations depends on the individual performance of many people. We have said this often. To get the results you are responsible for, all your associates must be performing up to standard—to the standard you have set and trained them for. Are they? That is what evaluation is all about. First, we look at coaching, then performance evaluation.

COACHING

Coaching is a two-part process involving observation of employee performance and conversation focusing on job performance between the manager and the employee. Coaching can take place informally at the employee's workstation or formally by having coaching sessions in an office. It is different from counseling, a process used to help employees who are performing poorly because of personal problems such as substance abuse.

The overall purpose of coaching is to evaluate work performance and then to encourage optimum work performance either by reinforcing good performance or confronting and redirecting poor performance. Coaching therefore provides your employees with regular feedback and support about their job performance and helps you to understand exactly what your employees need to know. It also prevents small problems from turning into big ones that may require much more attention later.

> What every good manager needs is continuous feedback about performance. Anyone who has sat in the manager's chair knows how little feedback you get during the course of a day. In fact, being promoted often means the end of virtually all feedback.
> *Source:* Bob Gunn, *Strategic Finance*, Vol. 86, No. 1, p. 9, July 2004.

If coaching employees is so beneficial, why do supervisors often avoid it? Possible reasons are:

- Lack of time (In most cases, coaching requires only a few minutes.)
- Fear of confronting an employee with a concern about his or her performance (A mistake—the problem not faced may only get worse, not better.)
- Assuming that the employee already knows that he or she is doing a good job, so why bother saying anything? (Your employee would love to hear it anyway.)
- Little experience coaching (You can start practicing now.)
- Assuming that the employee will ask questions when appropriate and does not need feedback (Many employees are too proud or shy to ask questions.)

The first step in coaching is to observe employees doing their jobs. Be sure you are completely familiar with pertinent performance standards and job duties. If an employee is doing the job well, do not hesitate to say so. Everyone likes to be told that

The first step in coaching is to observe employees doing their job. Courtesy of VISIT FLORIDA.

they are doing a good job, so praise employees as often as you can. Work on catching your employees doing things right, and then use these steps.

1. Describe the specific action you are praising.

2. Explain the results or effects of the actions.

3. State your appreciation.

In some cases you may want to write a letter of thanks and make sure that a copy goes into the employee's personnel file. You could instead use a standard form, which is quicker to complete.

When observing employees, sometimes you'll see what appears to be a problem with performance. If Ted left a pallet of canned goods outside the storeroom, ask him: "Is there a reason why these canned goods aren't put away yet?" If Sally isn't using the new procedure for cleaning flatware, ask her, "Are you aware of the new procedure for washing flatware?" before you assume that she is trying to get away with something. It could be that Ted stopped putting the canned goods away when a delivery of milk (which has to be put in the refrigerator immediately) came in, or perhaps Sally was on vacation when the cleaning procedure was changed. Consider the following questions *before* correcting an employee.

- Does the employee know what is supposed to be done, and why?
- Are there any reasons for poor performance that the employee can't control, such as inadequate equipment?
- How serious are the consequences of this problem?
- Has the employee been spoken to about this concern before?

By asking questions before you point a finger at someone, you help maintain the self-respect of the employee. After asking questions, if it is obvious to you that a correction is needed, be careful not to correct one employee in front of another. No one likes being corrected in front of his or her peers. Arrange to talk privately with the employee to define the performance problem, agree on why it is happening, make your standards clear, and work with the employee to set goals for improvement.

Let's say that Kim's performance as a cocktail server has deteriorated noticeably in the last few weeks and there have been guest complaints of poor service, ill temper, and rudeness. If you tolerate her poor performance, it will reduce her respect for you, for the job, and for herself. So you arrange to talk to her privately and try to get her to do most of the talking. You get Kim to tell you what is wrong and let her know how you perceive the problem as well. The goal is to resolve the problem, and you encourage her to make her own suggestions for doing this. This leads to her commitment to improve. You make sure that she understands the performance you expect, and you get her to set her own improvement goals: measurable performance goals such as a specific reduction in customer complaints within a certain period of time.

If the problem is related to the job, you do what you can to solve it. For instance, one fast-food employee's poor performance turned out to be caused by a large puddle of water in which she had to stand while working. The supervisor had the plumbing fixed and that solved the performance problem. Kim's problem may have an equally simple solution.

If the problem involves other people on the job, the solution may be more complex, but you do everything you can to resolve it. In the meantime you have a management obligation to help Kim meet performance standards.

If the problem is personal, it may help Kim to talk about it, but you cannot solve it for her. You can only listen in order to help her overcome its interfering with her work.

If the problem is burnout, you may be able to motivate her with some change of duties and responsibilities that would add variety and interest to her job. In any case, she will probably respond to your supportive approach, and when she has set her own goals, she will feel a commitment to achieving them.

When goals have been set that you both agree to, establish checkpoints at which you meet to discuss progress (get Kim to set the times—perhaps once a week or every two weeks). You express your confidence in her ability to meet her goals, make it clear that you are available when needed, and put her on her own.

During the improvement period, you observe discreetly from the sidelines, but you do not intervene. Kim is in charge of her own improvement; you are simply staying available. You compliment her when you see her handle a difficult customer; you give her all the positive feedback you can; you keep her aware of your support.

You wait for the checkpoints to discuss the negatives, and you let Kim bring them up. You use the checkpoints as informal problem-solving sessions in which you again encourage Kim to do most of the talking and generate most of the ideas.

To summarize, make sure that a counseling session includes the following:

1. Speak in private with the employee. Be relaxed and friendly.

2. Express in a calm manner your concern about the specific aspect of job performance you feel needs to be improved. Describe the concern in behavioral terms and explain the effect it has. Do so in a positive manner.

3. Ask the employee for his or her thoughts and opinions, including possible solutions. Discuss together these solutions and agree mutually on a course of action and a time frame.

4. Ask the employee to restate what has been agreed upon to check on understanding. State your confidence in the employee's ability to turn the situation around.

At a later time, you should follow up and make sure that the performance concern has been addressed. Figure 19.1 lists general coaching guidelines.

In many operations, you will be asked to document (meaning you will need to write on paper) coaching sessions. Some supervisors document coaching sessions in a supervisor's logbook, which is much like a diary of day-to-day events in the operation. Depending on the policy, coaching sessions may be recorded on forms intended for that purpose. Any documentation of coaching sessions should include the date and place of the coaching and a summary of the coaching session. Although you may feel this is time-consuming, documentation is essential if you ever need to terminate an employee or simply to do yearly performance evaluations, the next topic.

1. Be specific about the employee's job performance.
2. Focus on the employee's behavior, not the employee. Always maintain the self-respect of the employee. To reduce employee defensiveness, use "I" statements rather than "you" statements.
3. Reinforce or confront job performance issues as soon as possible after observation. However, if you are at all angry or upset, do not confront the employee until you have cooled down.
4. Praise in public, correct in private. We are all very sensitive about being told in front of our peers that we are doing something wrong. Unless the error could have serious consequences, wait until you can at least take the employee aside long enough to discuss it.
5. Explain the impact of the employee's job performance on the work group and the entire operation.
6. Be a coach, not a drill sergeant.
7. Allow some time each day to walk around and coach employees.
8. Document coaching sessions.

FIGURE 19.1 General coaching guidelines.

Check Your Knowledge

1. What is *coaching?* What is the overall purpose of coaching?

2. Why do supervisors often avoid coaching?

ESSENTIALS OF PERFORMANCE EVALUATION

In management terms, the phrase performance evaluation refers to a periodic review and assessment of each employee's performance during a given period: three months, six months, a year, or a certain number of hours worked. The assessment is recorded, usually on a company rating form, and is then discussed with the employee in an interview that answers the perennial question, "How am I doing?" and explores the possibilities for improvement.

Other terms used for this process are performance appraisal and performance review. We will use these terms to distinguish the system of periodic evaluation from the informal performance evaluation that is a daily part of the supervisor's job.

Performance reviews are not always used for hourly workers in the hospitality industry. This is partly because supervisors are so busy, partly because so many workers do not stay long enough to be evaluated, and partly because so many operations are under the immediate direction of the owner. But the practice is increasing, especially in chain operations. It is part of their general thrust toward maintaining consistency of product and service, improving quality and productivity, and developing the human resources of the organization.

A performance review does not substitute in any way for the informal evaluations you make in checking on work in progress. Where things happen so fast, where so many people are involved and so much is at stake in customer satisfaction, you cannot just train your people, turn them loose, and evaluate their performance six months later. You must be on the scene every day to see how they are doing, who is not doing well, and how you can help those who are not measuring up. This is an informal blend of evaluation and on-the-job coaching and support to maintain or improve performance right now and to let people know when they are doing a good job. Performance reviews every six months or so cannot substitute for it. Feedback must be immediate to be effective.

In fact, if you had to choose between periodic reviews and daily evaluations, the daily evaluations would win hands down. But it isn't a choice; one complements the other.

Purpose and Benefits

If you are evaluating people every day, why do you need a performance review? There are several good reasons or purposes.

1. *In your day-to-day evaluations you tend to concentrate on the people who need to improve,* the people you have trouble with, the squeaky wheels who drive you crazy. You may also watch the outstanding performers, because they make you look good and because you are interested in keeping them happy and in developing them. But you seldom pay attention to the middle-of-the-road people. They come in every day, they are never late, they do their work, they don't cause any problems, but they never get any recognition because they do not stand out in any way. Yet they really are the backbone of the entire operation and they ought to be recognized. Everybody who is performing satisfactorily should be recognized. In a performance review you evaluate everybody, so you will notice these people and give them the recognition they deserve.

2. *Looking back over a period of time gives you a different perspective.* You can see how people have improved. You will also look at how they do the entire job and not just the parts they do poorly or very well. You evaluate their total performance.

3. A *performance review is for the record.* It is made in writing, and other people—the personnel department, your own supervisor, someone in another department looking for a person to fill another job—may use it. It may be used as data in a disciplinary action or in defending a discrimination case. It may be and should be used as a basis for recognition and reward.

4. A performance review requires you to get together with each worker to discuss the results. It *lets people know how well they are doing.* You may forget to tell them day by day, but you cannot escape it in a scheduled review. And if you know you will have to do ratings and interviews at evaluation time, you may pay more attention to people's performances day by day.

5. A *performance review not only looks backward, it looks ahead.* It is an opportunity to plan how the coming period can be used to improve performance and solve work problems. It is a chance for setting improvement goals, and if you involve the worker in the goal setting, it increases that person's commitment to improve. The improvement goals then become a subject for review at the next appraisal, giving the entire procedure meaningful continuity.

> A good manager tells employees what could be improved as the workers are doing the job. Or tells the employees what they are doing right and should continue to do. It sounds like such common sense. Let people know along the way, and the whole system runs much more smoothly.
>
> *Source:* Amy Joyce, "Making Reviews Meaningful; Clear and Frequent Communication Between Manager and Worker Is Key," *The Washington Post*, p. F.05, June 2004.

Performance reviews have many uses beyond their primary concern with evaluating and improving performance. *One is to act as the basis for an employee's salary increase.* This type of salary increase is called a merit raise and is based on the employee's level of performance. For example, an employee who gets an outstanding evaluation may receive a 6-percent increase, the employee who gets a satisfactory evaluation may receive a 4-percent increase, and the employee with an unsatisfactory evaluation may not receive any increase. In one survey of U.S. businesses, 75 percent of respondents reported using appraisals to determine an employee's raise.

Another use is to identify workers with potential for advancement: people you can develop to take over some of your responsibilities, people you might groom to take your place someday or recommend for a better-paying job in another department. As you know, managers have an obligation to develop their people, and a performance review is one tool for identifying people capable of doing more than they are doing now.

Other managers may use your performance reviews. Since they are a matter of record, others may use them to look for people to fill vacancies in their departments.

If they are going to be used this way, it is important that you make your evaluations as accurate and objective as you can. (It is important anyway—more on this subject later.) If someone has been promoted on the basis of your inaccurate evaluation and the promotion does not work out, you may be in hot water.

Your boss, to rate your own performance as a supervisor, may use your performance reviews. If the records show that most of your workers are poor performers, this may indicate that you are not a very good supervisor.

Performance reviews can *provide feedback on your hiring and training procedures.* When workers turn out to lack skills they should have been trained in, it may indicate that your training procedures were inadequate. Workers you hired who rate poorly in every respect reflect on your hiring practices. Both indicate areas for improvement on your part. (Good selection and training programs were discussed in Chapters 16 and 18.)

Workers who rate poorly across the board are of special concern and may be candidates for termination. Performance evaluations can help to identify such workers. If they do not respond to attempts to coach and retrain, their performance evaluations may document inadequacies to support termination and help protect your employer from discrimination charges.

Finally, *performance reviews may provide the occasion for supervisors to get feedback from employees about how they feel about their job, the company, and the way they are treated.* Supervisors who are skilled interviewers and have good relationships and open communication with their people may be able to elicit this kind of response. It takes a genuine interest plus specific questions such as "How can I help you to be more effective at your job?" "Are there problems about the work that I can help you solve?"

Many people will hesitate to express anything negative for fear it will influence the boss to give them a lower rating, but questions with a positive, helpful thrust can open up some problem areas.

When carried out conscientiously and when there is constant communication between reviews, performance reviews have many benefits. They help to maintain performance standards. By telling workers how they are doing, they can remove uncertainty and improve morale. By spotlighting areas for improvement, they can focus the efforts of both worker and supervisor to bring improvement about. They can increase motivation to perform well. They provide the opportunity for improving communication and relationships between supervisor and worker. They can identify workers with unused potential and workers who ought to be terminated. They can give feedback on supervisory performance and uncover problems that are getting in the way of the work.

All these things have great potential for improving productivity, the work climate, and person-to-person relations. And all this benefits the customer, the company image as an employer, and the bottom line.

Steps in the Process

A performance review is a two-part process: making the evaluation and sharing it with the worker. There should also be a preparation phase in which both supervisors and workers become familiar with the process, and there should be follow-up to put the findings to work on the job. In all there are four steps:

1. Preparing for evaluation
2. Making the evaluation
3. Sharing it with the worker
4. Providing follow-up

Companies that use performance review systems usually give supervisors some initial training. They are told why the evaluation is important and what it will be used for: promotions, raises, further employee training, whatever objectives the company has. They are given instruction in how to use the form, how to evaluate performance fairly and objectively, and how to conduct an appraisal interview. This initiation may take the form of a briefing by the supervisor's boss, or it may be part of a companywide training program. It depends on the company.

The people being   evaluated should also be prepared. They should know from the beginning that performance reviews are part of the job. Good times to mention it are in the employment interview, in orientation, and especially during training, when you can point out that they will be evaluated at review time on what they are being trained to do now. Showing people the evaluation form at this point can reinforce interest in training and spark the desire to perform well.

People must also know in advance when performance reviews will take place, and they must understand the basis for evaluation. They should be assured that they will see the completed evaluation, that they and the supervisor will discuss it together, and that they will have a chance to challenge ratings they consider unfair.

When carried out conscientiously and when there is constant communication between reviews, performance reviews have many benefits.

MAKING THE EVALUATION

The performance evaluation is typically formalized in an evaluation form that the supervisor fills out. There are probably as many different forms as there are companies that do performance reviews, but all have certain elements in common. Figures 19.2 and 19.3 are sample evaluation forms.

Performance Dimensions

An evaluation form typically lists the performance dimensions or categories on which each worker is to be rated. Examples include the quality and quantity of the work itself, attendance, appearance, work habits such as neatness or safety, and customer relations. The dimensions of job performance chosen for an evaluation form should be:

■   Related to the job being evaluated

■   Clearly defined in objective and observable terms, as in a performance standard

APPRAISAL FORM: COUNTER PERSON

Name: _____   Job Title: _____

Employee Number: _____   Unit: _____

Supervisor: _____   Appraisal Period: _____

Reason for Appraisal: Probationary_____   Yearly_____

Major Job Duties: _____   Standards: _____

1. **Guest Service**   Smiling, cheerful, makes guests feel welcome and want to return. Concentrates on fast, friendly service.

Low		Satisfactory		Excellent
1	2	3	4	5

2. **Productivity**   Efficient, works at a fast pace, always trying to improve and increase amount of work done.

Low		Satisfactory		Excellent
1	2	3	4	5

3. **Work Habits**   Maintains a neat, clean work area. Always leaves it that way for the next shift.

Low		Satisfactory		Excellent
1	2	3	4	5

4. **Attendance**   Always on time. Regular attendance and works late when needed.

Low		Satisfactory		Excellent
1	2	3	4	5

5. **Appearance**   Well groomed, neat appearing, meets uniform, hair and jewelry policies.

Low		Satisfactory		Excellent
1	2	3	4	5

FIGURE 19.2 Performance review form. Adapted from a form used by Carl's Jr.

6. Team Oriented   Works well with others and is concerned about the
                               entire team.

Low   Satisfactory   Excellent
├─────────────┼─────────────┼─────────────┼─────────────┤
1   2   3   4   5

7. Station Proficiency   Meets the standards of quality, proper portioning,
                               waste control, and speed of service of each station
                               worked.

Low   Satisfactory   Excellent
├─────────────┼─────────────┼─────────────┼─────────────┤
1   2   3   4   5

8. Safety   Works safely. Follows all safety procedures and
                               precautions. Identifies unsafe conditions
                               immediately.

Low   Satisfactory   Excellent
├─────────────┼─────────────┼─────────────┼─────────────┤
1   2   3   4   5

Overall Assessment: _____Total Score: _____

_____

_____

_____

_____

<u>Goals for Improvement for the Next Review Period.</u> Based on the evaluation on the
front of this form, develop specific improvement goals for the employee to
accomplish by the next review period.

1. _____

_____

_____

2. _____

_____

_____

FIGURE 19.2 (Continued)

3. _____

_____

_____

<u>Employee's Reaction to the Performance Review.</u> Please be specific in describing your agreement or disagreement on the evaluation as well as identifying areas in need of further clarification or discussion.

_____

_____

_____

_____

_____

_____

Management Signature _____ Date _____

Employee's Signature _____ Date _____

Restaurant Manager's Signature _____ Date _____

FIGURE 19.2 (Continued)

Many evaluation forms go beyond specific performance to include such personal qualities as attitude, dependability, initiative, adaptability, loyalty, and cooperation. Such terms immediately invite personal opinion; in fact, it is hard to evaluate personal qualities in any other way. The words mean different things to different people, the qualities are not in themselves measurable, and they do not lend themselves to objective standards. Yet some of these qualities may be important in job performance. Some evaluation forms solve the problem by defining the qualities in observable, job-related terms. For instance, dependability can be defined as "comes to work on time."

Some qualities that are pleasant to have in people who work for you are not really relevant to doing a certain job. A dishmachine operator does not have to be "adaptable" to run the dishmachine. A "cooperative" bartender may cooperate with customers by serving them free drinks. "Initiative" may lead people to mix in areas where they have

SERVER PERFORMANCE EVALUATION

Name: _____

Position: _____

Date of Hire: _____ Yearly or 60-Day Evaluation: _____

Department: _____

Please use COMMENT section whenever "Exceeds" or "Does Not Meet" is checked. POINTS: Exceeds—5, Meets—3, Does not meet—0.

Performance Standards	Exceeds	Meets	Does Not Meet
1. Stocks the service station for one serving area for one meal completely and correctly, as specified on the Service Station Procedures Sheet, in 10 minutes or less.	Comments: _____	_____	_____
2. Sets or resets a table properly, as shown on the Table Setting Layout Sheet, in not more than 3 minutes.	Comments: _____	_____	_____
3. Greets guests cordially within 5 minutes after they are seated and takes their order if time permits; if too busy, informs them that he or she will be back as soon as possible.	Comments: _____	_____	_____
4. Explains menu to customers: accurately describes the day's specials and, if asked, accurately answers any questions on portion size, ingredients, taste, and preparation method.	Comments: _____	_____	_____

Performance Standards	Exceeds	Meets	Does Not Meet
5. Takes food, wine, and beverage orders accurately and legibly for a table of up to six guests according to Guest Check Procedures; prices and totals check with 100 percent accuracy.	Comments: _____	_____	_____
6. Picks up order and completes plate preparation according to Plate Preparation Procedure.	Comments: _____	_____	_____
7. Serves a complete meal to all persons at each table in an assigned station in not more than 1 hour per table using the Tray Service Procedures.	Comments: _____	_____	_____
8. If asked, recommends wines appropriate to menu items selected, according to the What Wine Goes with What Food Sheet; opens and serves wines correctly as shown on the Wine Service Sheet.	Comments: _____	_____	_____
9. Accepts and processes payment with 100 percent accuracy as specified on the Check Payment Procedures Sheet.	Comments: _____	_____	_____
10. Performs side work correctly according to the Side Work Assignments Sheet and as requested.	Comments: _____	_____	_____
11. Operates all equipment in assigned area according to the Safety Manual.	Comments: _____	_____	_____

FIGURE 19.3 Performance appraisal form based on performance standards.

Performance Standards	Exceeds	Meets	Does Not Meet
12. Meets at all times the Dress Code requirements.			
	Comments:		
13. Uses at all times the sanitation procedures specified for serving personnel in the Sanitation Manual; maintains work area to score 90 percent or higher on the Sanitation Checklist			
	Comments:		
14. Maintains a "Good" or higher rating on the Customer Relations Checklist; maintains a customer complaint ratio of less than 1 per 200 customers served			
	Comments		
15. Maintains a check average of not less than $7 per person at lunch and $15 per person at dinner			
	Comments:		
16. Is absent from work less than 12 days in a year.			
	Comments:		
17. Is late to work less than 12 times in a year.			
	Comments:		
18. Can always be found in work area during work hours or supervisor knows where he or she is.			
	Comments:		
19. Attends or makes up all required meetings and training.			
	Comments:		
20. Supervisor receives positive feedback from peers with minimal complaints.			
	Comments:		

OVERALL RATING:
Outstanding Performance: 75–100 points (must meet or exceed all standards)
Good Performance: 50–74 points
Marginal Performance, Reevaluate in 60 Days. Below 50 points

EVALUATOR'S COMMENTS

_____
_____

EMPLOYEE'S COMMENTS. Please comment freely on this evaluation.

_____
_____
_____

EMPLOYEE'S OBJECTIVES: What would you like to accomplish in the next 12 months?

_____
_____
_____

EMPLOYEE'S OBJECTIVES FOR THE NEXT 12 MONTHS:
(Plan should be specific, realistic, measurable, and include target dates.)

_____
_____
_____

SIGNATURES:

_____   _____   _____
Employee   Evaluator   Reviewer
Date:_____

FIGURE 19.3 (Continued)

no authority or competence or to depart from standard procedures (change recipes or portion size).

Sometimes the personal qualities found on company evaluation forms are included because they are important in assessing potential for advancement. But where you are concerned only with evaluation of the performance of routine duties, it is not appropriate to include such qualities in an overall evaluation on which rewards may be based. People who polish silver or wash lettuce should not be penalized for lacking initiative. In such cases the question can be answered "NA," not applicable. Concern with promotions should not be allowed to distort an evaluation system intended primarily for other purposes.

Performance Standards

A quality evaluation form defines each performance dimension in measurable or observable terms by using performance standards (Figure 19.4). There should be standards, measurable or observable standards, wherever possible to make evaluation more objective. Unfortunately, subjective evaluations are not legally defensible if an employee for matters such as employment discrimination ever takes you to court. To be legally defensible, your evaluation of job performance should be based on measurable and objective performance standards that are communicated to employees in advance.

On the face of it, an evaluation based on performance standards may look intricate and difficult to carry out. But supervisors who have used performance standards in training and in informal day-by-day evaluations find them to be a very simple way to rate performance. Usually, they don't have to test people; they recognize performance levels from experience.

Probably not many organizations have such a system, and not all jobs lend themselves to this kind of evaluation. It is best suited to jobs where the work is repetitive and many people are doing the same job, a situation very common in hospitality operations.

Performance Ratings

Many evaluation forms use a rating scale ranging from outstanding to unsatisfactory performance. A common scale includes ratings of outstanding, above average, average, needs improvement, and poor. In the case of performance standards, you can simply check off that the employee either meets or does not meet the standard. In some systems, there is also a category for "exceeds standard" (Figure 19.3).

The major problem with ratings such as outstanding or excellent is figuring out what they mean in performance terms. What constitutes excellent? What is the

Performance (abbreviated here)	Point Value		Performance Level*		Overall Evaluation**
1. Stocks service station	4	×	2	=	8
2. Sets/resets a table properly	4	×	2	=	8
3. Greets guests	8	×	3	=	24
4. Explains menu	8	×	3	=	24
5. Takes orders	8	×	3	=	24
6. Picks up and completes order	4	×	2	=	8
7. Serves meal	6	×	3	=	18
8. Recommends and serves wines	8	×	1	=	8
9. Totals and presents check	8	×	3	=	24
10. Performs side work	4	×	0	=	0
11. Operates equipment	4	×	2	=	8
12. Meets dress and grooming standards	8	×	3	=	24
13. Observes sanitation procedures	8	×	2	=	16
14. Maintains good customer relations	10	×	3	=	30
15. Maintains check average	8	×	3	=	24
	100				248

*Superior = 3   **Overall rating of 300 = outstanding: highest reward
Competent = 2   250–300 = superior: middle reward
Minimal = 1   200–250 = competent: minimum reward
Below minimum = 0   100–200 = improvement needed
100 = marginal
below 100 = hopelessly inadequate

FIGURE 19.4 Performance dimensions rated using point values.

difference between fair and poor? If there is no definition, the ratings will be entirely subjective and may vary greatly from one supervisor to another. Where raises and promotions are involved, the results are not always fair to everyone. And nothing bugs employees more than seeing an employee who puts in half the amount of work they do receive the same raise as everyone else.

Some forms take pains to describe what is excellent performance, what is average, and so on. The more precise these descriptions are, the fairer and more objective the ratings will be. In some cases, point values are assigned to each performance dimension (Figure 19.4), indicating its relative importance to the job as a whole. These point values add up to 100 percent, the total job. A different set of point values is used to weight each level of performance (3 points for superior, 2 for competent, 1 for minimum, 0 for below minimum). After evaluating each item you multiply the point value by the performance level. Then you add up the products to give you an overall performance rating. This will provide a score for each person based entirely on performance; raises can then be based on point scores. This system allows you to rate performance quality in different jobs by the same standard—a great advantage. Perhaps the most valuable feature of this rating method is that it pinpoints that part of the job the employee is not doing well and indicates how important that part is to the whole. It gives you a focus for your discussions with the worker in the appraisal interview, and it shows clearly where improvement must take place.

The evaluation forms in Figures 19.2 and 19.3 achieve a good balance in what they ask of the supervisor. They are simple, yet they require a fair amount of thought. The required ratings provide both a means of assessing excellence for reward purposes and a way of determining where improvement is needed. Both evaluation forms feature another element often used in the overall review process—improvement objectives. Each evaluation considers how well past objectives have been met and sets new objectives for the upcoming period. This tends to emphasize the ongoing character of the performance review process rather than a report-card image.

No evaluation form solves all the problems of fairness and objectivity. Probably those that come closest are designed exclusively for hourly workers, for specific jobs, and for evaluating performance rather than promotability. Some experts suggest that a single form cannot fulfill all the different purposes for which performance reviews are used, and that questions needed for making decisions on promotion and pay be eliminated where reviews are used primarily for feedback, improvement, and problem solving.

The form you encounter as a supervisor will probably be one developed by your company. Whatever its format and its questions, its usefulness will depend on how carefully you fill it out. You can make any form into a useful instrument if you complete it thoughtfully and honestly for each person you supervise.

If your company doesn't have an evaluation system, you can develop your own forms, tailored to the jobs you supervise. If they evaluate performance rather than people and are as objective as you can make them, they will serve all the basic purposes of performance review on the supervisory level: feedback, improvement, incentive, reward, and open communication between you and your people.

Pitfalls in Rating Employee Performance

Whatever form or system you use, evaluating performance consists of putting on paper your ratings of each person's work over the period since hiring or since the last performance review. It is based on your day-to-day observations plus relevant records such as attendance records. No matter how well you think you know an employee's work, the process demands thought and reflection and a concentrated effort to be fair and objective.

There can be many pitfalls on the way to objectivity. We *have noted how the form itself* may in some cases encourage subjective judgments. Another pitfall is the *halo effect*, which you encountered in Chapter 6 in the selection interview. Something outstanding, either positive or negative, may color your judgment of the rest of a person's performance. Kevin may sell more wine than anyone else, so you may not observe that he comes in late every day. Sharon broke a whole tray of glasses her first day on the job, so you don't even notice that she has not broken anything since and that her check average has risen steadily.

Profile

DEMIAN RODILES

Courtesy of Demian Rodiles

I used to work in a restaurant in Dallas, Texas. I started out there as a waiter and quickly moved my way up the ladder. I went from a waiter to a headwaiter, who was responsible for taking the money from all the staff at the end of a shift. Then I made my way into the bar and in no time at all I was the head bartender. I stayed in the bar for a while and then found that I was not doing what I really wanted to do—and that was working in the kitchen. After I worked in the kitchen and learned all the positions, management felt that I was not being used to my full potential. So they asked me if I would like to become a manager. This was great, but I guess that at the time I really did not want all that responsibility, so we came to an agreement; I became a head cook, which is something like an assistant sous chef.

While being a head cook I learned a lot about supervising, both good and bad things about supervising. As supervisor I had to choose how I acted with the other employees a little differently than when I was just a cook like them. You have to treat everyone as an equal and try not to show any favoritism. I had to respect what my superiors wanted and work toward achieving their goals. I do not mean that I treated anyone badly; it just meant that I had to keep a professional relationship with employees while we were at work. Since I was friends with some of the employees outside work, they knew that at work we interacted as professionals and did not let anything at work affect our relationships as friends. This sounds like it is easy to do, but there were difficult times determining where the lines were drawn. One thing I feel that gave me so much success was that I had earned respect from the kitchen staff because I had worked as one of them and performed at an equal or higher level than some of the staff. It was very noticeable how they would act when I would ask for something to be done as opposed to another supervisor, who were actually managers, but could not perform on the line and would sometimes ask for things that were unreasonable. I also began to notice that the kitchen staff would not perform to their maximum output when this particular manager was working. Or just the opposite, they would work fast and try to show him up and make him look bad in front of the wait staff. It was clear that they did not respect him and it became a problem later on down the line. It was interesting that I did not notice this until I started to look at it from a supervisor's position. So I believe that to be a good supervisor, this is a very important part of being successful. Whatever job it is you are asking your employees to do, make sure that you can do the job as well as, if not even better than, they can.

Letting your feelings about a person bias your judgment is another easy mistake. If you don't like someone, you see their mistakes and forget about their achievements. If you like someone, you reverse the process.

Comparing one person with another is another trap: If John were as good as Paul . . . if he were even half as good as Paul . . . But Paul really has absolutely nothing to do with John. You have to compare John's performance with the job standards, not John with Paul.

Sometimes supervisors' feelings about the entire evaluation process will affect their ratings. They may be impatient with the time that evaluations take and the cost of taking people away from work for interviews. Even supervisors who believe in evaluation and practice it informally all the time may resent putting pencil to paper (and the interviews too) as an intrusion into their busy days. Some supervisors do not take evaluations seriously and simply go through the motions. Some are really not familiar with the details of their employees' work. Some simply hate paperwork and feel that daily informal evaluation and feedback are enough.

Some supervisors let concern about the consequences influence their ratings. They may fear losing good workers through promotions if they rate them high. They may fear worker anger and reprisals if they rate them low. They may not want to be held responsible or take the consequences of being honest, so they rate everybody average. That way they do not have to make decisions or face the anger of people they have rated negatively, and nobody is going to argue.

Procrastination is another pitfall. Some people postpone ratings until the last minute on grounds of the press of "more important" work. Then the day before evaluations are due they work overtime and rush through the evaluation forms of 45 people in 45 minutes. Obviously this is not going to be a thoughtful, objective job.

Another pitfall is the *temptation to give ratings for the effect they will have.* If you want to encourage a worker, you might give her higher ratings than her performance warrants. If you want to get rid of somebody, you might rate him low—or recommend him for promotion. If you want to impress your boss, you might rate everybody high to show what a good supervisor you are.

If you are a *perfectionist*, and few employees measure up to your standards, you might rate everyone poorly. Another pitfall occurs when you *rate employees on their most recent performance* because you kept insufficient documentation of their past performance. This often results in vague, general statements based only on recent observations. This can upset the employee, especially if earlier incidents of outstanding performance are forgotten.

Sooner or later, false ratings will catch up with you. Unfair or wishy-washy evaluations are likely to backfire. You are not going to make a good impression with your superiors, and you will lose the respect of your workers. Such evaluations tend to sabotage the entire evaluation system, the value of which lies in accuracy and fairness.

The defense against such pitfalls and copouts lies in the supervisor's own attitude. You can never eliminate subjectivity entirely, even by measuring everything. But you can be aware of your own blind spots and prejudices, and you can go over your ratings a second time to make sure that they represent your best efforts. You can make the effort needed to do a good job. You can also do the following:

- Evaluate the performance, not the employee. Be objective. Avoid subjective statements.

- Give specific examples of performance to back up ratings. Use your supervisor's log or other documentation to keep a continual record of past performance so that doing evaluations is easier and more accurate.

- Where there is substandard performance, ask "Why?" Use the rule of finger, which means looking closely at yourself before blaming the employee. Perhaps the employee was not given enough training or the appropriate tools to do the job.

- Think fairness and consistency when evaluating performance. Ask yourself, "If this were my review, how would I react?"

- Get input from others who have some working relationship with the employee. Write down some ideas to discuss with the employee on how to improve performance.

- If you set out to be honest and fair, you probably will be. If you keep in mind what evaluations are for and how they can help your workers and improve the work, you will tend to drop out personal feelings and ulterior motives and to see things as they are.

Employee Self-Appraisal

As part of some performance appraisal systems, some employees are asked to fill out the performance appraisal and evaluate themselves. Employee self-appraisal is surprisingly accurate. Many employees tend to underrate themselves, particularly the better employees, whereas less effective employees may overrate themselves. If the employee is given the chance to participate, and the manager really reads and takes the self-appraisal seriously, the employee gets the message that his or her opinion matters. This may result in less employee defensiveness and a more constructive performance appraisal interview. It may also improve motivation and job performance. Self-appraisal also helps put employees at ease because now they know what will be discussed during their appraisal. Employees may also tell you about skills they have or tasks they have accomplished that you may have forgotten. Self-appraisal is particularly justified when an employee works largely without supervision.

Check Your Knowledge

1. Why do you as a supervisor need to conduct a performance review?

2. What are the four steps in the performance review process?

3. What is the purpose of a rating scale?

THE APPRAISAL INTERVIEW

The appraisal interview (evaluation interview, appraisal review) is a private face-to-face session between you and an employee. In it you tell the worker how you have evaluated his or her performance and why, and discuss how future performance can be improved. The way you do this with each person can determine the success or failure of the entire performance review.

Planning the Interview

Each interview should take place in a quiet area *free of interruption*. Schedule your interviews in advance, and allow enough time to cover the ground at a comfortable pace. A sense of rush or hurry will inhibit the person being appraised. If you encourage people to feel that this is a time with you that belongs to them alone, they are likely to be receptive and cooperative.

It is important to review your written evaluation shortly before the interview and to plan how you will communicate it to the employee for best effect. Indeed, in some companies you may give a copy of the evaluation to the employee ahead of time. Your major goal for the interview is to establish and maintain a calm and positive climate of communication and problem solving rather than a negative climate of criticism or reprimand. Although you may have negative things to report, you can address them positively as things that can be improved in the future rather than dwelling on things that were wrong in the past. If you plan carefully how you will approach each point, you can maintain your positive climate, or at the very least stay calm if you are dealing with a hostile employee.

You will remember that in communications the message gets through when the receiver wants to receive it. Successful communication is as much a matter of feeling as of logic, so if you can keep good feeling between you and the worker, you have pretty much got it made. Your own frame of mind as you approach the interview should be that any performance problems the worker has are your problems, too, and that together you can solve them.

Conducting the Interview

Usually, a bit of small talk is a good way to start off an interview—a cordial greeting by name and some informal remarks. You want to establish rapport; you want to avoid the impression of sitting in judgment, talking down, or laying down the law. You want to be person-to-person in the way you come across. You want your workers to know you are there to help them do their jobs well, not to criticize them. Criticism diminishes self-esteem, and people who have a good self-image are likely to perform better than people who don't.

Workers who are facing their first appraisal interview may be worried about it. Even though they have been told all about it before, it may seem to them like a day of judgment or like getting a school report card. It *is important to make sure that they understand the evaluation process*: the basis for evaluation, its purpose, how it will be used, and how it affects them. Stress the interview as useful feedback on performance and an opportunity for mutual problem solving. Conveying your willingness to help goes a long way toward solving problems: "How can I help you to do a good job?"

After explaining the purpose of the interview, *it is often useful to ask people to rate their own performance on the categories listed on the form.* If you have established clear standards, they usually know pretty well how they measure up. Often, they are harder on themselves than you have been on them. The two of you together can then compare the two evaluations and discuss the points on which you disagree. Stress the positive things about their work, and approach negative evaluations as opportunities to improve their skills with your support.

Encourage them to comment on your judgments. Let them disagree freely with you if they feel you are unfair. You could be wrong: You may not know the whole story or you may have made a subjective judgment that was inaccurate. Do not be afraid to change your evaluation if you discover that you were wrong.

Get them to do as much of the talking as possible. Ask questions that make them think, discuss, and explain. Encourage their questions. Take the time to let them air discontent and vent feelings. Let them tell you about problems they have and get them to suggest solutions. (The problem of the worker standing in the puddle of water mentioned in Chapter 16 surfaced in the open communication of a good appraisal interview.)

Be a good listener. Don't interrupt; hear them out. Maintain eye contact. If the people being reviewed feel that you are not seeing their side, if they begin to feel defensive, you have lost their cooperation. An evaluation that is perceived as unfair will probably turn a complacent or cooperative employee into a hostile one.

Although you encourage them to do most of the talking, you do not relinquish control of the interview. Bring the subject around to improvement goals and *work with them on seeing objectives for improvement.* Many evaluation systems make goal setting a requirement of the appraisal interview. The worker, with the supervisor's help and guidance, sets goals and objectives with specific performance standards to be achieved between now and the next appraisal. These goals are recorded (as in Figure 19.2) and become an important part of the next evaluation. It is best to concentrate on two or three goals at most rather than on the whole range of possibilities. Goals should be measurable and attainable.

If you can get people to set their own improvement goals, they will usually be highly motivated to achieve them because they themselves have made the commitment.

You should make it clear that you will support them with further training and coaching as needed to meet their goals.

It is a good idea to *summarize the interview* or ask the worker to summarize it and to make sure that you both have the same understanding of what the employee is to do now. Have the employee read the entire evaluation and sign it, explaining that signing it does not indicate agreement and that he or she has the right to add comments. Discuss your reward system openly and fully and explain what is or is not forthcoming for the person being interviewed. Make sure that the employee receives a copy of the completed evaluation form.

End the interview on a positive note—congratulations if they are in order, an expression of hope and support for the future if they are not. Your people should leave their interviews feeling that you care how they are doing and will support their efforts to improve, and that the future is worth working for.

Common Mistakes in Appraisal Interviews

A poorly handled appraisal interview can undermine the entire evaluation process, engender ill feeling and antagonisms, cause good people to leave, and turn competent workers into marginal performers and cynics. Interviewing is a human relations skill that requires training and practice.

If you have established good relations with your people, the appraisal review should not present any problems. It is simply another form of communication about their work—a chance to focus on their problems, reinforce acceptable behavior, and help them improve—no big deal for either of you. If you are new to supervision or if you are a hard-driving, high-control type of person, you may have difficulty at first in carrying out the human relations approach recommended for a productive appraisal review. But you will find it worth the effort. Here are some major mistakes to avoid.

If you take an *authoritarian approach* (this is what you have done well, this is how I want you to improve, this is what you will get if you do, this is what will happen if you don't), it will often antagonize employees rather than produce the improvements you want. It may work with the employee who thinks you are right or with dependent types of people who are too insecure to disagree. But people who think your evaluations are unfair in any way and do not have a chance to present their point of view may not even listen to your message, and they probably won't cooperate if the message does come through. *You* cannot improve their work; only they can improve their work, and few will improve for a carrot-and-stick approach unless they desperately need the carrot or truly fear the stick. They will leave, or they will remain and become hostile and discontented.

Be a good listener. Do not interrupt; hear them out. Maintain eye contact.

Discontented people complain about you to each other, morale declines, and problems multiply. Improvement does not take place.

The tell-and-sell approach is a mild version of the authoritarian approach: The supervisor tells the worker the results of the evaluation and tries to persuade the employee to improve. It is a presentation based on logic alone, rather like a lecture. It seems to be a natural approach for someone who has not developed sensitivity in handling people.

The assumption is that the worker will follow the logic, see the light, and respond to persuasion with the appropriate promise to improve. No account is taken of the feelings of the people being evaluated, and the supervisor has no awareness of how the message is being read as the interview proceeds. There is also the assumption that the supervisor's evaluation is valid in every respect, so there is no need for the worker to take part in discussing it.

The result for the people being evaluated is at best like getting a report card; it is a one-sided verdict handed down from the top, and it leaves them out of the process. Usually, they sit silent and say nothing because the format does not invite them to speak. If they do challenge some part of the evaluation, the supervisor brushes aside the challenge and doubles the persuasion (being sure that there are no mistakes or perhaps being afraid to admit them). The supervisor wins the encounter but loses the worker's willingness to improve. The results are likely to be the same as in the hard-line authoritarian approach.

Certain mistakes in interviewing technique can destroy the value of the interview.

- *Criticizing and dwelling on past mistakes* usually make people feel bad and may also make them defensive, especially if they feel you are referring to them rather than to their work. Once they become defensive, communication ceases. The best way to avoid such mistakes is to talk in terms of the work, not the person, and in terms of the future rather than the past, emphasizing the help and support available for improvement.

- *Failing to listen, interrupting, and arguing* make the other person defensive, frustrated, and sometimes angry. Avoiding these mistakes requires you to be aware of yourself as well as of the other person and to realize continuously what you are doing and the effect it is having. It takes a conscious effort on your part to maintain a cooperative, problem-solving, worker-focused interview.

- *Losing control of the interview* is a serious mistake. There are several ways this can happen. One is to let a discussion turn into an emotional argument. This puts you on the same level as the worker: You have lost control of yourself and have abdicated your position as the boss. Another way of giving up control is to let the worker sidetrack the interview on a single issue so that you do not have time for everything you need to cover. You can recoup by suggesting a separate meeting on that issue and move on according to plan. Still another way of losing control is to allow yourself to be manipulated into reducing the standards for one person (such as overlooking poor performance because you feel sorry for someone or in exchange for some benefit to yourself). Although you may think you have bought future improvement or loyalty in this way, you have actually given away power and lost respect.

Your first appraisal interviews may not be easy. Many supervisors have trouble telling people negative things about their work in a positive, constructive way. As with so many other management skills, nobody can teach you how; it is something you just have to learn by experience, and if you are lucky you will learn it under the skillful coaching of a good supervisor. A good interview comes from preparing yourself, from practicing interviewing for other purposes (hiring, problem solving), from knowing how to listen, from knowing the worker and the job, from staying positive, and from keeping tuned in to the interviewee, whose feelings about what you are saying can make or break the interview. It is probably one of the best learning experiences you will have in your entire career in the industry.

FOLLOW-UP

The evaluation and the appraisal review have let employees know how they are doing and have pointed the way toward improved performance. If you have done the reviews well, they have fostered momentum for improvement in responsive employees. You have become aware of where people need your help and support and probably also of where your efforts will be wasted on people who will not change or are unable to meet the demands of their job. So the appraisal review has marked the end of one phase and the beginning of a new one. How do you follow up?

The first thing you do is to see that people receive the rewards they have coming to them. You must make good on rewards promised, such as raises in pay, better shifts, better stations, and so on. If there is some problem about arranging these things, devise several alternative rewards and discuss them promptly with the people concerned. Never let people think you have forgotten them.

Employment Review Tips:

Some things to do:

- Give the employee advance notice of the review.
- Start the review with small talk and a greeting.
- Bring all relevant documents.
- Be specific in discussing goals and deadlines.

Source: Monique Balas, "Make Your Performance Review Work for You," *Knight Ridder Tribune Business News*, p. 1, February 2004.

For people you have discovered need more training, arrange to provide it for them. For people you feel will improve themselves, follow their progress discreetly without hovering or breathing down their necks. Coaching is in order here, day-to-day counseling as needed. Remember that in the appraisal review you emphasized your help and support. It doesn't take much time: just touching base frequently to let people know you will come through for them, frequent words of praise for achievement, readiness to discuss problems. Put them on their own as much as possible, but do not neglect them.

There will be some people who you are sure will make no attempt to improve, who will continue to get by with minimum performance. Reassess them in your mind: Was your appraisal fair? Did you handle the interview well? Is there some mistake that you are making in handling them? Are you hostile or merely indifferent? Are *they* able to do better, or is minimal performance really their best work? Would they do better in a different job? Is their performance so poor on key aspects of the job (customer relations, absenteeism, sanitation, quality standards) that discipline is in order? Should they be retrained? Should they be terminated (hopelessly unwilling or unable to do the job)?

If employees are complacent or indifferent, you might as well give up trying to make them improve unless you can find a way to motivate them. If employees are hostile, you should try to figure out how to turn them around or at least arrive at an armed truce so that they will do the work and get their pay without disrupting the entire department. We have more to say on motivation and discipline in later chapters.

There are two important facets of follow-up. One is actually carrying it out. If, after you have done your reviews, you let the process drop until the next appraisal date, you will let all its potential benefits slip through your fingers. The other important facet is using all you have discovered about your people and yourself to improve your working relationship with each person you supervise. It can be a constantly expanding and self-feeding process, and it will pay off in the morale of your people and in your development as a leader.

Check Your Knowledge

1. List four common mistakes in appraisal interviews.

2. List the steps to follow when conducting an interview.

LEGAL ASPECTS OF PERFORMANCE EVALUATION

Four major equal employment opportunity laws affect the process of performance evaluation: Title VII of the Civil Rights Act of 1964, the Equal Pay Act, the Age Discrimination in Employment Act, and the Americans with Disabilities Act (see Chapter 13). Knowing how to avoid violations of these laws in the evaluation process can save time and money as well as create goodwill with your employees and a positive public image. Following are ways to ensure fair and legal evaluations:

1. Evaluation of performance should be based on standards or factors obtained from a job analysis of the skills, tasks, and knowledge required to perform the job.

2. Performance standards should be observable, objective, and measurable.

3. Keep a positive rapport during your discussions with the employee. This helps tremendously to avoid complaints of being unfair and, possibly, charges of discrimination.

4. Do not enter into discussions that focus on qualities of employees based on their membership in a group protected by EEO laws. If employees refer to their membership, it is best not to respond. For example, suppose that Jack, who is sixty, says: "At my age it gets harder to see the small details. I guess that explains my trouble with this." It would be appropriate for you to focus on how to ensure that Jack is able to see well enough to perform his job. It would be an error for you to make any mention of his age, both to him or anyone else, and certainly not on the written part of his appraisal, even though he brought up the subject.[1]

5. Employee performance should be documented more frequently than once a year at appraisal time. An employee should not be surprised at performance appraisal time.

6. If an employee disagrees with his or her evaluation, he or she should be able to appeal.

KEY POINTS

1. The overall purpose of coaching is to evaluate work performance and then to encourage optimum work performance by either reinforcing good performance or confronting and redirecting poor performance. Figure 9.1 lists coaching guidelines.

2. Performance evaluation refers to the periodic review and assessment of each employee's performance during a given period, such as a year. This is in addition to the informal performance evaluation that is a daily part of a supervisor's job.

3. When carried out conscientiously and when there is constant communication between reviews, performance reviews have many benefits. They help to maintain performance standards. By telling workers how they are doing, they can remove uncertainty and improve morale. By spotlighting areas for improvement, they

can focus the efforts of both worker and supervisor to bring about improvement. They can increase motivation to perform well and provide the opportunity for improving communication and relationships. They can identify workers with unused potential and workers who ought to be terminated. They can give feedback on supervisory performance and uncover problems that are getting in the way of the work.

4. The performance review process includes these four steps: preparing for evaluation, making the evaluation, sharing it with the worker, and providing follow-up.

5. An evaluation form typically lists the performance dimensions or categories on which each worker is to be rated. The performance dimensions should be related to the job being evaluated and defined clearly in objective and observable terms, as in a performance standard.

6. A rating scale is used for each performance dimension, such as outstanding to unsatisfactory. The more precise the descriptions for each rating, the more objective the ratings will be.

7. No evaluation form solves all the problems of fairness and objectivity. Probably those that come closest are designed exclusively for hourly workers, for specific jobs, and for evaluating performance rather than promotability.

8. Some pitfalls when rating employee performance include the halo effect, letting your feelings about a person bias your judgment, comparing one person with another, letting your feelings about the evaluation process affect rating, procrastination, giving ratings for the effect they'll have, and being too lax or too much of a perfectionist.

9. Evaluate the performance, not the employee.

10. Employee self-appraisals are especially justified when an employee works largely without supervision.

11. Plan a quiet location for appraisal interviews, review your written evaluation shortly beforehand, and plan how you will communicate it to the employee for best effect.

12. When conducting the appraisal interview, start with a bit of small talk. Make sure that the employee understands the evaluation process, ask the employee to rate his or her own performance first, encourage employees to comment on your judgments, get the employee to do most of the talking. Work with them on setting improvement objectives, summarize the interview, and end on a positive note.

13. Common mistakes in appraisal interviews include taking an authoritarian or tell-and-sell approach, criticizing, dwelling on past mistakes, failing to listen, and losing control of the interview.

14. Follow-up after performance appraisals is crucial. If you let the process drop until the next appraisal date, you will let all its potential benefits slip through your fingers.

15. Equal employment opportunity laws apply to performance evaluation, so the evaluation process needs to be nondiscriminatory.

KEY TERMS

appraisal interview (evaluation interview, appraisal review)

coaching

counseling

employee self-appraisa

evaluation form

merit raise

performance appraisal (performance evaluation, performance review)

performance dimensions or categories

rating scale

REFERENCE

1. Adapted from William S. Swan, *How to Do a Superior Performance Appraisal*. New York: Wiley, 1991.

DISCIPLINE AND EMPLOYEE ASSISTANCE PROGRAMS*

Overview

---

* Authored by Jack E. Miller, John R. Walker, and Karen Eich Drummond.

H ere are five true–false statements about the serious subject of discipline; one of them is true. Do you know which it is?

- Discipline = punishment.

- Whether or not you are plagued with discipline problems is a matter of how lucky you are in the people you supervise.

- A supervisor who is fairly relaxed about enforcing rules is likely to have fewer discipline problems than one who makes people toe the line.

- "You do that once more and you're fired!" is a good way to make a worker shape up.

- Most employees really want to obey the rules and do their jobs well.

The last one is true: Most of your employees will come to work each day, do their jobs satisfactorily, and leave without causing any problems. The first four statements are in most cases false; each is discussed in this chapter.

There is more to discipline than meets the eye. Discipline is not a black-and-white issue; there are many shades of gray. It is a fluctuating product of the continual interplay between the supervisor and the people supervised within the framework of the rules and requirements of the company and the job.

As a whole, the hospitality industry is not famous for disciplinary success. Often, discipline is administered across a crowded room at the top of the lungs, and disciplinary measures make a direct contribution to the high rate of employee turnover in the industry.

In this chapter we explore the subject of discipline from several points of view. It will help you to:

- Define the four essential elements of successful discipline and explain the importance of each.

- Compare and contrast the negative and positive approaches to discipline.

- State basic guidelines for administering discipline, and explain how to avoid common mistakes and pitfalls.

- Weigh and discuss the problems of terminating a worker who has underperformed.

- Discuss the legal implications of termination and learn how to avoid unwarranted charges of discrimination.

- List guidelines for conducting a termination interview.

- Explain the basics of dealing with sexual harassment and substance-abuse problems.

ESSENTIALS OF DISCIPLINE

I f you were to walk around your work area one day and ask your employees what discipline is, it is very likely that the most frequent response would be that discipline means punishment. Does discipline really mean punishment? Let's take a closer look.

The word discipline has two somewhat different but related meanings. One refers to a *condition* or *state* of orderly conduct and compliance with rules, regulations, and procedures. If everyone follows the rules and procedures and the work moves along in an orderly fashion, we say that discipline is good in this department or operation. But if people are not following the rules and procedures, and maybe do not even know what the rules and procedures are, and the work is not getting done and people are fighting and the place is in chaos and nobody is listening to what the supervisor is trying to say, we say that the discipline is terrible.

The second meaning of the word *discipline* refers to *action* to ensure orderly conduct and compliance with rules and procedures. When people break rules, you discipline them; you take disciplinary action. Disciplinary action, depending on your

Ensure that associates know what the rules and procedures are by telling and showing them what to do. Courtesy of Sarasota Memorial Hospital.

policy, may or may not include punishment such as a written warning or suspension. If your employees are relatively self-disciplined, it is not necessary to discipline often.

In this chapter we are concerned with both kinds of discipline. We are concerned with maintaining a condition of discipline, and we are concerned with the most effective kinds of disciplinary action to ensure compliance to rules. *Both sides of discipline are the responsibility of the supervisor, and discipline, in both senses of the word is essential to supervisory success.*

The discipline process contains three steps:

1.   Establishing and communicating ground rules for performance and conduct

2.   Evaluating employee performance and conduct through coaching, performance appraisals, and disciplinary investigations (Coaching and performance appraisals are discussed in Chapter 19.)

3.   Reinforcing employees for appropriate performance and conduct and working with employees to improve their performance and conduct when necessary

As a supervisor, you are involved in each step of this process, as discussed throughout this chapter. Let's start by looking at the *four essentials of successful discipline*:

1.   A complete set of rules that everyone knows and understands

2.   A clear statement of the consequences of failing to observe the rules

3.   Prompt, consistent, and impersonal action to enforce the rules

4.   Appropriate recognition and reinforcement of employees' positive actions

The first essential—a complete set of rules—consists of all the policies, regulations, rules, requirements, standards, and procedures that you and your workers must observe in your job and theirs. These should include:

■   Company policies, regulations, and directives that apply to your department and your people. Of particular importance to you are company policies and procedures relating to disciplinary action (Figure 20.1).

■   Work rules relating to hours, absences, tardiness, sick days, meals, use of facilities and equipment, uniforms and grooming, conduct on the job (smoking, drinking, dealing with customers, patients, or guests).

■   Legal requirements and restrictions, such as health code provisions, fire and safety regulations, liquor laws.

- Job requirements, performance standards, and job procedures for each job you supervise.

- Quality and quantity standards required (such as standardized recipes, portion sizes, drink sizes, guestroom amenities).

All this material will form a basic operations and procedures manual for your department. From it you can prepare a manual for new employees and plan their first-day orientation (Chapter 16). Then you can use it in developing your training programs (also Chapter 18), incorporating all the rules, procedures, and penalties that the workers

---

Discipline Policy and Procedure

Policy: It is necessary to establish rules of conduct to promote efficient and congenial working conditions and employee safety. Further, it is our intention to provide equality in the administration of discipline when these rules of conduct are violated. Discipline is to be administered fairly without prejudice and only for just cause.

Procedure: In order that all disciplinary actions by supervisors are consistent, one of the following actions will be used according to the seriousness of the offense.

1. Oral warning with documentation
2. Written warning
3. Suspension
4. Termination

An employee will be subject to disciplinary action ranging from oral warning to discharge for committing or participating in any of the acts listed below. The normal level of discipline is also listed. All suspensions, terminations, or exceptions must have the approval of the Director of Human Resources.

1. False statements or misrepresentation of facts on the employment application—termination
2. Absence for one day without notifying the department manager prior to the start of the shift—written warning
3. Absence for two consecutive work days without notifying the department manager prior to the start of the shift—suspension
4. Absence for three consecutive work days without notifying the supervisor prior to the start of the shift—termination
5. Excessive absenteeism with or without medical documentation—within a calendar year—
   - 6 absent incidents—oral warning with documentation
   - 8 absent incidents—written warning
   - 9 absent incidents—suspension
   - 10 absent incidents—totaling 13 days or more—termination
6. Excessive lateness—within a calendar year—
   - 8 latenesses—oral warning with documentation
   - 12 latenesses—written warning
   - 16 latenesses—three-day suspension
   - 20 latenesses—termination

FIGURE 20.1 A discipline policy and procedure.

7. Falsification of time sheets, recording another employee's time or allowing others to do so—termination
8. Failure to record own time when required—oral warning with documentation
9. Leaving work area without permission—written warning
10. Leaving the facility without permission during normal working hours—written warning
11. Stopping work early or otherwise preparing to leave before authorized time, including meal periods—oral warning with documentation
12. Sleeping on the job—suspension
13. Failure to carry out job-related instructions by the supervisor where the failure is intentional—suspension
14. Threats or intimidation to managers, guests, or other employees—termination
15. Use of abusive language to managers, guests, or other employees—suspension
16. Stealing or destruction of company or guest's property—termination
17. Not performing up to performance standards—oral warning with documentation
18. Disorderly conduct during working time or on company property—suspension
19. Violations of sanitation and safety regulations—level 2, 3, or 4 depending on situation
20. Reporting to work unfit for duty—written warning
21. Possession or use of alcohol or nonprescribed drugs during working time or on company property—termination
22. Possession of explosives, firearms, or other weapons during working time or on company property—termination

Multiple or Cumulative Violations

1. Subsequent violations of a related nature should move to the next higher step in the discipline pattern (e.g., a related violation following a written warning will call for a 3-day suspension, etc.).
2. Violations of an unrelated nature will move to the next higher level after two disciplinary actions at the same level (e.g., after two written warnings for unrelated violations, the next unrelated violation would call for a suspension rather than another written warning).
3. Cumulative violations that occur more than 12 months before the violation in question will not be used to step up the discipline for an unrelated violation.
4. The above listed violations are the basic ones and are not intended to be all-inclusive and cover every situation that may arise.

FIGURE 20.1 (Continued)

must know, so that they start out well-informed. You can use your manual as a reference for verifying the proper ways of doing things and for settling any disputes that arise. Keep it in loose-leaf form so that you can update it easily when policies, regulations, and procedures change.

It is your responsibility to see that all your people know the rules and procedures that apply to them and to their jobs. These rules and procedures form a set of boundaries or limits for employee behavior, a framework within which they must live their occupational life. You might compare it to a box or a fence that encloses them while they are on the job (Figure 20.2). Most employees really want to do a good job, and if they know what they are supposed to do and not do, most of them will willingly stay

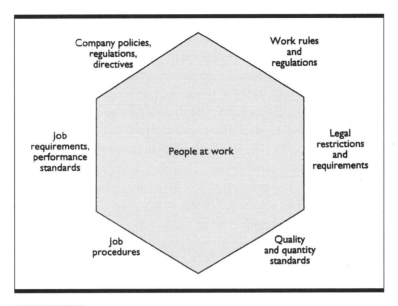

FIGURE 20.2 A framework of policies, rules, restrictions, standards, procedures, and requirements within which employees carry out their work.

in the box and abide by the rules. Knowing the rules and the limits makes most people more comfortable in their jobs.

The second essential is to make very clear the consequences of going beyond the limits, of not following the rules and procedures. If there are penalties for breaking the rules, people must know from the outset what the penalties are. This information should be stated in matter-of-fact terms: "This is what we expect you to do; this is what happens when you don't." It *should not take the form of warnings and threats.* There should be no hint of threat in either your words or your tone of voice.

The penalties for breaking rules are usually written into your disciplinary policy and procedures (Figure 20.1). The policy and procedures may prescribe the specific disciplinary action for each rule violation each time a given employee breaks that rule, or the penalties may be more loosely defined.

Knowing the consequences has its own security: People know where the boss stands, and they know what will happen if they go beyond the limits. Even when the penalties seem severe, and even when people do not like their supervisor personally, you often hear them say, "At least with the boss, you know where you stand."

The third essential is to enforce the rules promptly, consistently, and impersonally and to comply with the rules yourself. It is very common for supervisors to threaten punishment—"If you are late once more, I'm gonna fire you"—and never carry out the threat. After a while, other people see that the threat is never carried out and they begin to think, "Why should I be here on time?" And pretty soon, the supervisor has lost control and the workers are setting the rules and standards. Once you have made a threat, you have no choice but to carry it out or back down.

The principle applies not only to threats but also to rule breaking in general. If you pay no attention when people break rules, if you walk on by and do nothing, everyone will begin to break the rules and discipline will crumble. And if you break rules yourself, people will have no respect for you because you are applying a double standard. They will think, "What is good enough for you is good enough for me, too," and you will have problems with compliance. There won't be any ground rules left.

Many people suggest the hot stove as the perfect model of administering discipline:[1]

- It gives *warning*. You can feel the hot air around it.

- Its response is *immediate*. The instant you touch it, it burns your finger.

- It is *consistent*. It burns your finger every time you touch it.

- It is *impersonal*. It reacts to the touch, not the person who touches.

These are all sound guidelines to follow with any approach to discipline. You give *warning* by making sure that people know the rules and the consequences—what to do and how to do it and what happens if they don't. Your response is *immediate;* by tomorrow the mistake or transgression is past history and the worker has gotten away with something and three others have seen it happen and will try it today. You are *consistent:* You hold everybody to the same rules all the time; and you are *impersonal:* You are matter-of-fact, you don't get angry, you don't scold, you don't preach, you simply act as an adult. You deal with the specific incident, not with the person's bad attitude or thick skull. You eliminate your personal feelings about individual people: you do not prejudge someone you don't like, and you do not let favoritism creep in.

But there is more. Although impersonal, discipline ought to be carried out as part of a positive human relations approach to the people who work for you. In disciplining, you must focus on things that people do wrong, but your people can handle this negative feedback better if you use a lot of that positive reinforcement we talked about in the last chapter. Don't be like the manager who said, "Every time you do something wrong I'll be there to catch you. But when you do something right—well, that's what I pay you for."

The fourth essential is to recognize and reinforce your employee's positive actions. Discipline is not just making sure that employees follow rules, but includes recognizing those who are following rules and performing up to standards. Recognizing your employees need not be a laborious process; it can be as simple as saying, "Thanks for taking care of our guests in such a prompt and courteous manner," or filling out a positive action memo (Figure 20.3). Other ways to recognize your employees are discussed in Chapter 14.

APPROACHES TO DISCIPLINE

There are two different approaches to disciplinary action. One is the negative approach of discipline by punishment. The other is the positive approach of discipline by information and corrective training. Philosophically, they divide along Theory X and Theory Y views of people and management styles.

Negative Approach

Most people associate discipline with punishment. The theory is that if you enforce the rules by punishing people who break them, those people will learn not to break the rules and the punishment will be a warning to others that will keep them in line. It is the old theory of motivation through fear. The punishment may be anything from a

---

You've Done A Great Job!

For: _Denise Smith, Cook_

From: _Joe Brown, Chef_

Date: _8/22/06_

Thank you for giving two of our long-term guests Mr. and Mrs. Jones, the extra-special treatment last night. They were most unhappy about their meal until you came out of the kitchen to help them make another selection. You did a great job of reassuring them and keeping their visit enjoyable. Thanks for going the extra mile.

FIGURE 20.3 Positive action memo.

public dressing-down or threat of dismissal or private reprimand to penalties tailored to fit the violation, culminating in termination.

Negative discipline has been used a great deal in the foodservice and lodging industries. It is commonly used by the rigid, high-control, autocratic, Theory X-style manager who believes that people are lazy and irresponsible and that you have to be on them all the time. Never mind the reason it happened: If they break rules, they've got to be punished; it's the only way to get it through their heads. It is also used by managers who are civilized and friendly but simply believe that punishment is the way to enforce rules.

The fear-and-punishment approach has never worked very well. Punishing one person may deter others from breaking rules, but it does not correct the behavior of the person punished. Punishment simply does not motivate employees to shape up and do their work in an orderly and obedient manner. It may motivate them to avoid the punishment a second time—"Hey, you got me once, but you will never get me again"—but from then on, they will do just enough work to get by.

Fear and punishment are in fact *demotivators*. People who are punished feel embarrassed, defensive, angry, and hostile. It often arouses a desire to get back at the boss and to get the other workers on their side. They look for ways to cause trouble for the boss without getting caught, and the boss is probably going to have to punish them again and again. Punishment almost never turns a first offender into a good worker. It is, however, likely to turn that worker into an adversary.

Managers who are rigid rule followers are usually very conscious of their right to punish and their duty to control, so they go by the book: If a rule is broken, punishment follows. Rigidity is the strongest feature of this kind of discipline: It is consistent. It does deter rule breaking, and it maintains a certain kind of controlled order.

On the other hand, punitive managers tend to have chronic discipline problems, which they are likely to blame on their "no-good workers." They do not recognize how their own shortcomings as managers and leaders have contributed to the problem: They probably haven't explained the rules, communications are poor, people don't like the constant negative feedback, don't like working for them, and so on. Some Theory X managers are really very insecure people, and their inability to control their workers' behavior makes them even more insecure. They vent their anger and frustration on their workers, reassuring themselves that the workers, not they, are to blame.

In a fear-and-punishment approach to discipline there is a traditional four-stage formula for disciplinary action:

- An *oral warning*, stating the violation and warning the employee that it must not happen again

- A *written warning*, stating that the offense has been repeated and that further repetition will be punished

- *Punishment*—usually suspension without pay for a specific period, typically one to three days

- *Termination* if the employee continues to repeat the offense after returning to work

This four-stage formula is called progressive discipline because of the progressive severity of each stage. (The term does not in any way imply a forward-looking or humanitarian approach.) The stages are similar to those specified in most union contracts and written into most company policy manuals. The formula is not confined to hard-line Theory X managers: It is widely used with hourly employees in all types of industries.

Over all the years that negative discipline has been used, it has never been successful at turning chronic rule breakers into obedient and cooperative employees. There is nothing in it that will motivate change that will help anyone to become a better employee. It generally creates adversarial relationships and a sort of underground power struggle between worker and boss that is harmful to the work climate and the general morale. This is a power struggle that the supervisor must win if relationships with other workers are to be successful.

Positive Approach

If you stop thinking discipline = punishment and start thinking discipline = rule compliance, you can begin to see that other ways of enforcing the rules are possible. For example, what is the most frequent cause for breaking rules or going against company policies or failing to follow procedures? Up to 90 percent of the time, people do not know that they are doing something that they are not supposed to be doing. They didn't know that you must not leave the hollandaise sitting all day on the back of the range. They didn't know they shouldn't let the patient in Room 302 have the sugar packets left on other patients' trays. They didn't know that champagne had to be chilled. They didn't know that they had parked in the general manager's parking space. They didn't know that guests weren't allowed in the wine cellar and you taught them that the customer is always right.

So when rules are broken, the action you take is to inform and correct. Even though you have handed out employee manuals and have told people the rules and trained them in their jobs, there are still things they don't know, or don't understand, or don't recognize in a new situation, or forgot, or they saw somebody else doing something and thought it was all right. So the positive approach to discipline is continuous education and corrective training whenever the rules and procedures are not being observed.

The philosophy behind the corrective approach is a Theory Y view of people: By and large people are good, they will work willingly, they want to learn, they welcome responsibility, they are capable of self-direction and self-discipline. They will do their job right if you tell them what you want them to do. The approach to discipline is educative and developmental: You inform people why the rule or procedure is important and how to carry it out correctly. The goal is to turn workers into productive employees who are self-motivated to follow the rules and procedures.

This approach to discipline is really an extension of the coaching process—observation, evaluation, and continued training as needed. It approaches rule breaking as a problem to be solved, not as wrongdoing to be punished. It does not threaten people's self-respect, as punishment does; rather, it enlists their efforts in solving the problem.

There will still be some people who go on breaking rules, people who are irresponsible or lazy or hostile or who just don't care. So there must still be some last-resort disciplinary action if rule breaking persists. But persistent rule breaking doesn't happen nearly as often as it does with the punishment approach.

For chronic rule breakers, there is a three-stage formula for disciplinary action that parallels the stages of negative discipline. However, it is not punitive: Rather, it places the problem of correction squarely in the hands of the offender. The employee now has the responsibility for discipline.

- *Stage 1: oral reminder*. In a friendly way, you point out the rule violation as you see it happen. You talk to this person—let us say that it is Jim—formally about the seriousness of the offense, the reason for the rules, and the need to obey them. You listen to what Jim has to say in explanation and express confidence that he will find a way to avoid repeating the action.

- *Stage 2: written reminder*. This follows further rule breaking. You discuss privately, in a very serious manner, the repeated or continual violation of the rules, and you secure Jim's agreement that he will conform in the future to company requirements. Your attitude is that of counselor rather than judge or law enforcement officer: You avoid threatening him. Following this meeting you write a memorandum summarizing the discussion and agreement, which both you and Jim sign. It is wise to have a third party present at this discussion to act as a witness if needed later. This memo goes into Jim's permanent file.

- *Stage 3: termination*. Since Jim has broken not only the rules but also the agreement, there is a clear reason for the termination.

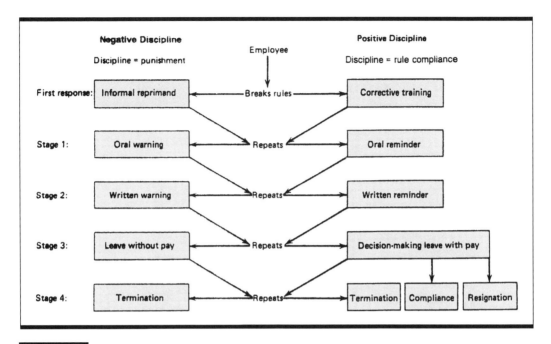

FIGURE 20.4 Negative and positive disciplinary action compared.

This punishment-free formula for disciplinary action is known as positive discipline. Figure 20.4 compares it stage by stage with the negative discipline method. Positive discipline works. Many people who use it report that about 75 percent of the time employees decide to come back and follow the rules. They may not maintain their turnaround indefinitely, but three months or even three weeks of productive behavior is preferable to finding someone new—and it is infinitely better than the hostile employee you are likely to end up with after an unpaid layoff.

Check Your Knowledge

1. What is *discipline?* Whose responsibility is it?
2. List the three essential steps of successful discipline.
3. What is *negative discipline?*
4. What is the positive approach to discipline?

Advantages of the Positive Approach

Using a positive approach from the outset has distinct advantages over the negative system. Honest mistakes, infringements of rules, and violations of policies and

It is better to avoid confrontational situations by adapting a positive proactive approach to policy and procedure violations.

procedures are educated out of people's work habits early, before they have time to become issues demanding confrontation. Many discipline problems simply do not happen. The negative consequences of punishment do not fester their way through the work climate. The worker feels no need to get even. The boss and the worker do not become adversaries.

Under a negative system the worker is likely to see the supervisor as someone to avoid and fear. With a positive approach the boss becomes the good guy in the white hat, the coach and counselor who facilitates the employee's work. There is an opportunity for a good relationship to develop. Even if a problem reaches the point of taking leave, the worker is not likely to come back hostile because the employee has no need to save face.

With a positive discipline system the supervisor is more likely to deal with problems early and to be consistent in discipline. A reminder is quick and easy. A reprimand takes time and is unpleasant; you are busy so you look the other way, and pretty soon everybody is taking advantage of you.

Positive discipline lowers costs by reducing the number of disciplinary incidents, reducing turnover, reducing mistakes and poor workmanship, and providing an orderly work environment and a positive work climate favorable to productivity and good morale. Such savings are hard to measure. Punitive discipline raises costs by increasing turnover, reducing motivation, and causing hostility and disruptive behavior. Such costs are also hard to measure.

The cost of the paid leave is one that many managers boggle at: Why should you pay a rule-breaker to stay home and think about it, on top of paying someone to replace the rule-breaker at work? However, that is all you pay for the opportunity to end the rule breaking once and for all. Overall, considering the savings of the positive system and the hidden costs of the punitive system, you come out way ahead.

One of the most important contributions of a positive discipline system is that the decision-making leave with pay does turn some people around permanently. It brings them face-to-face with themselves and puts their future in their own hands. This can become a new starting point for them. The supervisor can then play a key role by supporting all attempts to improve and by giving encouragement, positive reinforcement, and recognition for success. This is one of the few ways of transforming a hostile employee into a responsible and productive worker. It is a very rewarding kind of supervisory success.

Shifting from Negative to Positive Discipline

The biggest problem of using the positive approach is in shifting from one approach to the other. As a person starting out in your first supervisory position, you might not have this problem. But supervisors who are used to administering penalties and punishments often have trouble shifting gears. To begin with, they may have difficulty accepting the idea of paying an employee to stay home and think things over. It seems like a reward for bad behavior, and it seems unfair to the people who follow the rules and are working hard for their day's pay.

The second problem is shaking loose the habit of thinking in terms of punishment and substituting the attitude of educating and helping people to avoid breaking rules. Supervisors may *believe* in punishment. They may have been brought up with this type of discipline both at home and at school. It is hard to begin to teach, to help, to develop a rule-breaker when you have always reprimanded, warned, threatened, and punished. It requires an entirely new set of attitudes as well as a new tone of voice.

ADMINISTERING DISCIPLINE

We talked in Chapter 11 about management in the hospitality industry being reactive rather than planned—that is, reacting to events as they happen, dealing with problems as they come up. Certainly, enforcing the rules is one of the most reactive aspects of the supervisor's job. Even when the general outlines and the essentials are clear in your mind, each instance of enforcing the rules and procedures makes its own special demands, and positive and negative approaches seem less clear-cut and obvious.

Adapting Discipline to the Situation

Many companies have a uniform discipline system that prescribes the specific disciplinary action for each rule violation each time a given employee breaks that rule. Figure 20.1 gives you an example. A system such as this provides a companywide set of directives that tells the supervisor exactly what to do. It takes the subjectivity out of disciplinary action and gives support to the supervisor, especially when drastic action is needed.

Yet even with a company system there is a good deal of room for your own method of administering it. Seldom are discipline situations black and white. You have to investigate the facts and exercise your own judgment in the light of all the relevant factors. Human skills and conceptual skills are involved.

Usually, disciplinary action should be adjusted to circumstances. One of the things that you should consider is the intent of the rule-breaker. Was it an accident? Was the person aware of the rule or requirement? Was it a case of misinformation or misunderstanding? Could it have been your fault? Another consideration is extenuating circumstances such as severe personal problems or a crisis on the job. Still another consideration is the number of times that a person has done this type of thing before. Another is the seriousness of the offense. What are its consequences for the product, the customer, your department, the company? What will be the impact of your response as a deterrent to others?

You may handle different people differently for the same violation: You may take a hard-line approach with a hostile troublemaker but treat an anxiety-ridden first-time offender gently. This does not mean that you are being inconsistent; you are enforcing the rules in each case; you are not permitting either of them to go against regulations. As with everything else in this profession, you must be able to adapt your discipline to your own leadership style, to your workers and their needs and actions, and to the situation at any given time and all the time.

Some Mistakes to Avoid

One of the biggest mistakes that new supervisors make is to start off being too easy about enforcing the rules. They want people to like them, and they let people get away with small things that are against the rules, and perhaps even a few big things, just because they think people will like them for it. For example, you see one of your people lighting up a cigarette five minutes before closing and you just look the other way. If you were promoted from an hourly position, you may still have the worker's view of the rules and you can empathize with that person's feeling about that cigarette and that rule against smoking on the job. You may even disapprove of some of the rules you are supposed to enforce. It is very easy to let many things slip by.

This is just about the most difficult way you can start off your supervisory career. By saying nothing when a violation occurs, you are actually saying, "It's okay to do that." Right off, some people will begin to test you, to see how far they can go before you take any action, and pretty soon you will have a real problem on your hands getting people to follow rules and meet standards.

It is always easier to start out by strictly enforcing every rule and regulation than it is to try to tighten up later. People feel betrayed when you switch from leniency to enforcement, and they suddenly decide that you are bad, mean, and tough to work for. Besides, it is your obligation as a manager to enforce the rules. Even when you think rules are unfair, you do not take it upon yourself to change them by not enforcing them. Rules can be changed, but the way to do it is to go through channels and get the changes approved. Often, supervisors look the other way because they are simply too busy to cope with discipline. You just don't have time for this today, you don't want the hassle, and you've got to get the work out, so you let things slide.

Sometimes, correcting people's behavior just doesn't seem to do any good. You go over and over and over a procedure with a certain worker but nothing seems to change, and you reach a point where you start taking those little white pills your doctor gave you for indigestion, and finally, you stop wrestling with the problem and do nothing. Still another reason for doing nothing is that if you fire this person, you might get a new employee who is even worse. Another reason is that you don't think your supervisor will back up your action, so you just don't take any.

All these reasons for letting people get by with rule-breaking or substandard performance add up to the same problem: It gets harder and harder to maintain discipline. And it gets harder and harder to manage your people in other ways as well, because you lose their respect. In effect, *they* gradually take charge of the way they do things. The work suffers, quality of product and service suffers, customers complain, costs go up, and you are failing at your job as a manager.

Another mistake in disciplining is to act in anger. Anger will make the worker defensive and hostile, and you will seldom use good judgment in what you say and do. You won't stop to get the facts straight, you may be harsh and vindictive, you may make a threat you can't carry out, or do some other thing you will regret later. If you overreact, if you are wrong, you lose face and you lose some of your control over your people.

Threatening to take any action that you do not carry out is very common, and it is always a mistake. It is like looking the other way: It invites testing and rule-breaking. You have to stick to whatever you say you will do: You have no alternative.

Putting somebody down in front of other people is another way to ask for an uncooperative employee. It is one thing to correct someone quietly in the presence of others: "I just want to remind you that we always use the guard on the slicer." This approach informs and teaches on the spot, and although it is a form of public discipline it does not belittle, embarrass, or humiliate. But yelling, threatening, or making a fool of someone in front of others will certainly have the familiar consequences of resentment and hostility.

A *different kind of mistake is to exceed your authority in taking disciplinary action.* You must know exactly what your job empowers you to do as well as everything there is to know about company policy and practice. If there is a company system of procedures and penalties, you must follow it. If you are thinking of terminating someone, make certain that you have the authority to do so and find out the termination procedures your company requires. It could be quite embarrassing if you threatened to fire someone and then found out you couldn't. And it would be a disaster all the way around if you fired somebody and then had to take that person back.

Another critical error is to try to evade the responsibility for taking disciplinary action by shifting it to your boss or the personnel department or by delegating it to someone under you. If you do this, you simply become a straw boss and your people will have no respect for you. Discipline is an obligation of supervision, and your success as a manager depends on it.

Unexpected discipline will always meet with resistance and protest. This often happens when a rule has not been enforced for some time and the supervisor suddenly decides to tighten up. It is important to give warning about either a new rule or a new policy of enforcing an old rule, with a clear statement of the consequences of breaking it.

Some other things to avoid are:

- *Criticizing the person rather than the behavior.* Keep personalities out of discipline.

- *Waiting too long to take action.* The longer the gap between incident and action, the more likely the action is to be interpreted as a personal attack.

- *Touching someone when you are disciplining.* It can be interpreted as intent to do physical harm or as sexual harassment.

- Being *inconsistent.* You must avoid partiality, and your actions must be fair in your workers' eyes.

Taking the Essential Steps

The set of procedures that follows is one you should use when you are confronted with a serious infringement of regulations or a less serious but chronic failure to observe the rules of the operation or the requirements of a job. There are six formal steps to enforce compliance. These steps apply no matter what approaches to disciplinary action—negative or positive—you intend to follow. They apply to each stage of the disciplinary sequence (Figure 20.4) and they amplify what should take place at each stage.

1. *Collect all the facts.* Interview any employees involved and any witnesses, especially other supervisors or managers. Write it all down. Make every effort to sort out fact from opinion, both in what others say and in your own mind. Avoid drawing conclusions until you have the full picture. Use these questions as a guide:
   (a) Was the employee's action intentional? Was it an accident? Was it the result of misinformation or misunderstanding? Could it have been your fault?
   (b) Was the employee aware of the rule or requirement?
   (c) Were there extenuating circumstances, such as severe personal problems or a crisis on the job?
   (d) How serious is the offense? What are its consequences for the product, the guest, your department, the company?
   (e) What is the employee's past record? Is this the first time something like this happened, or has it happened before? How long has the employee worked here?
   (f) Did you witness the violation? If not, what kind of evidence do you have? Are your sources other management personnel? Do you have enough evidence to justify action?

2. *Discuss the incident with the employee.* Do this as soon as possible after the incident; after all, justice delayed is justice denied. Plan to sit down with the employee in a quiet setting where you will not be interrupted. Also, line up a witness to sit in on the interview. Here are the steps to follow:
   (a) Tell the employee that you are concerned about the incident that took place and that you would like to hear his or her side after you describe the facts as you see them.

(b)   Stay calm and without assigning blame, go over what you know. Also explain the consequences of the action. For example, if a server failed to clean up her station at the end of the shift, explain how this affects the other servers and the guests.

(c)   Now ask the employee to tell you his or her side. Listen actively, encourage, stay calm, and do not get into an argument. Ask questions as needed. This step is crucial because it gives the employee due process. Due process is the opportunity to defend yourself against charges.

3.   *Decide on the appropriate action if any is to be taken.* To do this, you must consider what both yourself and others have done in similar cases. Your action should be consistent with that of others throughout the company or you may inadvertently set a precedent. You want to make sure that any action you take is not discriminatory. Before deciding on any action, be sure to consult your boss, and you may also be required to discuss this with a representative from the human resources department.

4.   *Take the appropriate actions, such as a written warning, and develop an improvement plan with the employee using these steps:*

(a)   Explain to the employee the action you are taking, in a serious but matter-of-fact tone of voice, avoiding any trace of vengefulness or anger. Also state clearly the consequences that will follow if the behavior recurs.

(b)   Ask the employee to identify some actions that he or she can take so that this does not happen again. Develop mutually an improvement plan and a date by which it is expected that the improvement will be made. Make it clear that you are willing to work with the employee but that it remains the employee's responsibility to make the changes.

(c)   If your policy requires it, ask the employee to sign a disciplinary report. This is normally done so that you have written proof that the employee was informed of the contents of the report. From time to time you will have an employee who refuses to sign the report because he thinks that his signature will signify that he agrees with the contents of the report, or in other words, he is guilty as charged. When this happens, explain that the signature signifies understanding of, not agreement with, what is stated. If the employee continues to refuse to sign, you should write "Refused to Sign" on the report.

(d)   Close on a positive note by stating your confidence in the employee to improve and resolve the issue. Also express your genuine desire to see improvement.

5. *Make sure that you have everything written down.* Why is it important to have everything written? There are several reasons. First, in the event that the employee ever takes you to court or an unemployment compensation hearing, you will need written documentation to help build your case. Second, the process of writing down helps you see the situation more objectively and focus on job-related issues. Third, because your documentation includes the employee's improvement plan, it helps the employee to improve.

    When documenting, be specific about what the employee did and the circumstances surrounding the situation. Focus on observable, verifiable facts; be non-judgmental. Document facts, not opinions or hearsay—they have no place in documentation. Include who, what, where, when, and how. Document accurately and thoroughly, including information obtained during your investigation and during the disciplinary meeting. Always document as quickly as possible; otherwise, you will forget many of the details. Also include objectives for future performance and the consequences for not meeting the objectives.

6. *Follow up.* You do everything you can do to help the worker meet your expectations while staying on the lookout for further troublemaking of any kind. If the behavior does not meet your stated expectations, you must take the next step as promised.

Check Your Knowledge

1. Positive discipline can result in a reduction in what three areas?

2. What is the *uniform discipline system?*

Profile

ALEXIA GREENBERG

Courtesy of Alexia Greenberg

There are many key qualities that a supervisor must have not only to get the job done but also to satisfy clients and the staff that serves them. Great supervisors must have technical expertise in the department they supervise. It is essential that a supervisor demonstrate a depth of knowledge in his or her technical or specialized areas in order for the department to run smoothly and have mistakes corrected before they occur. For example, when one is supervising in the convention floor department, focusing on the customer is crucial. By being knowledgeable about the department, focusing exactly on what the meeting planner wants in regards to meeting room setups is simplified. My knowledge enables me to prepare the staff and myself mentally to deliver what is asked for, with even some time to spare for last-minute changes. If a supervisor is able to develop and maintain effective relationships with both internal and external customers and at the same time promote a customer-service orientation within an organization, customers will continue to return based on the specialized one-on-one service they are given when patronizing the organization.

When supervising my staff I think of myself not only as a leader but also as an "organizational leader." When working with staff I show the example I want others to follow and make clear what is expected of them on a daily basis. By pursuing self-development and learning new information pertaining to my area of expertise, I am able to improve my personal, professional, and most important of all, unit growth. These actions pay off by allowing me to enhance the shared learning that occurs in my department. I am also very big on developing others. A supervisor who provides a staff member with the opportunity to grow and develop his or her skills in turn benefits from a more knowledgeable worker who is able to handle a more difficult task level than expected. Such trained workers will become more confident when performing tasks and have a better chance of meeting any challenges with which they are faced. This will improve overall customer satisfaction and distinguish the department from others.

Fostering teamwork and relationships is essential in the hospitality environment. By fostering relationships and a positive climate to build effective teams that are committed to organizational goals and initiatives, I am able to supervise a staff that consists of team players that are willing to rally and work together to accomplish any task with which they are faced. Even though my staff and I are faced with difficult times, we are able to work successfully under pressure as a team because we constantly motivate each other to get the job done and in turn are rewarded with positive comments on our guest satisfaction scores.

As a supervisor, I concentrate on managing work execution in order to ensure that all work is completed effectively in the convention floor department. Monitoring the progress of work completed against schedules and budgets can easily help a supervisor accomplish this goal. To be effective when overseeing staff functions, a supervisor must obtain leadership. By providing steps forward to access difficulty issues and guiding others toward the accomplishment of identified meaningful goals, I feel I am able to exemplify the leadership skills I have acquired while working in the industry. Also, communication is an important asset of being a successful supervisor. Communicating openly with others creates an atmosphere in which timely and high-quality information flows smoothly both upward and downward through the organization. This open form of communication allows all associates to be on the same page and facilitates the decision-making process.

A supervisor who demonstrates such top qualities along with dedication, detail orientation, and patience will be able to provide exceptional service when performing on the job. However, a supervisor can never say that he or she has mastered the art of overseeing a staff because in the hospitality industry one learns something new every day. This ongoing learning process is what allows supervisors continually to incorporate new practices into everyday tasks and improve their ability to manage responsibilities.

TERMINATION

Salvage or Terminate?[2]

If you had performance standards, you trained people carefully, and have evaluated and coached and corrected them on a more-or-less daily basis, you would pretty quickly spot people who are never going to make it in their jobs. They aren't exactly rule-breakers, they just don't perform well, are absent a lot, or do some dumb thing over and over and over and you just can't get them straightened out.

If you hired them, your best bet is to terminate them before their probationary period runs out, as suggested in Chapter 16. But you may think that you can turn them around, and you work and work and work with them, and finally, you have to admit that they are hopeless and you are stuck with them. You may also have inherited some of these people.

What are you going to do? Should you fire Jerry for going right on overpouring drinks although you have showed him every blessed day the right amount to pour? How can you get rid of Kimberly when you can't even figure out what to pin her trouble on, because it's something different every day? Can you terminate Alfred for being an alcoholic when he has been here five times as long as you have and is twice your age? Should you terminate any of them, no matter how bad their work is?

Sometimes managers will try to dehire people by making them want to leave the job or look for something else. In this approach, a manager gives other people all the work and leaves this person with nothing to do or in other ways hints that it would be wise to look for another job. It is a destructive way of handling a person, and it does not work very well for the manager either. Legally, it is a practice that is open to all kinds of discrimination lawsuits and should be avoided. You have no control and you have to wait for this person to take the step of leaving while you go on paying wages for little or no work done. It is both kinder and better either to terminate outright or to keep on trying to salvage this worker.

From the productivity point of view and your own frustration level, it would probably be far better if you simply terminated all these very poor performers. But there are other considerations. Length of service is one. The longer people have been working for a company, the harder it is to fire them. Company policy and if there is a union, union rules, come into play here; you may not have a choice. Seniority is one of the most sacred traditions in U.S. industry.

A person's past record is another consideration. You may have people who are chronically late to work, and if they always have been, they probably always will be. On the other hand, if a person has had a good performance record and there is a sudden change, whether it is coming in late or some other drop in performance, that person is probably salvageable. Another consideration is how badly you need a person's skill or experience. In a tight labor market, even somebody who does not meet standards is better than nobody.

It is very difficult to fire someone who desperately needs the job even if the person is terrible at it. You might bring yourself to do it if you had to look forward to 30 years of coping with this substandard worker. If the person in question is a senior, you cannot terminate him or her on the basis of age, but you can terminate the person for inability to do the job to the standard required, once you have given the employee ample chance to improve and have been through the steps of verbal warning, written warning, and so on.

It is also difficult to fire someone who you are pretty sure will make trouble about it. In this case it is wise to consult with your boss or the human resources department or both. (Some companies have a policy that only the director of human resources and the general manager or department head may terminate an employee. In any event, there should always be a warning of the termination, in case of later legal action.)

Perhaps the most difficult question to figure out is the effect on your other workers of terminating someone. They may have resented that person's poor work and be glad to see you hire someone who they do not have to fill in for all the time. On the other hand, they may have been imitating this person and slowing down the whole operation—a bad example is always easier to follow than a good one. Or they may be fond of this character and will be angry if he or she is terminated. Some of them will be worried and upset about whether the same thing will happen to them. A termination is always something of an upheaval, and you may have to cope with some repercussions.

You have to consider the cost and trauma of hiring a replacement against the cost and trauma of retaining this person. You also have to consider whether your authority entitles you to terminate. In fact, you should consider this first.

If you decide to salvage, you have a few options open. You can try people in different jobs. You can look for special talents and interests and try to motivate them with some form of job enrichment. You can counsel the alcoholic to go to a clinic for rehabilitation. You can investigate the case of the sudden performance drop and try coaching this person back to the old level. Or you can grin and bear it.

Given the risk of legal complications—which can cost an employer from $15,000 to defend whether they are right or wrong—the job of terminating someone has become more difficult and important than ever. Every year thousands of employers are hauled into court by former employees claiming they were fired illegally. Attorney James P. McElligott offers these suggestions to help avoid the nightmare of a wrongful termination lawsuit:[3] Establish clear performance expectation; maintain clear communications; document everything; ensure you allow the employee a chance to respond; do not discriminate—almost everyone belongs to a "protected group"; conduct regular employee evaluations; and deal promptly with performance problems.

Just-Cause Terminations

If you think that it may be an appropriate time to terminate an employee, first make sure that it isn't something for which you can't fire the employee, such as discrimination (Figure 20.5). You can fire employees for *just cause*, meaning that the offense must affect the specific work the employee does or the operation as a whole in a detrimental way. Before terminating anyone, ask yourself the following questions:

1. Did the employee know the rule, and was he or she warned about the consequences of violating the rule? Are these understandings confirmed and acknowledged in writing?

2. Were management's expectations of the employee reasonable? Was the rule reasonable?

3. Did management make a reasonable effort to help the employee resolve the problem before termination, and is there written proof of this?

4. Was a final written warning given to the employee explaining that discharge would result from another conduct violation or unsatisfactory performance?

5. In the case of misconduct, did the employee act in willful and deliberate disregard of reasonable employer expectations? Was the situation within his or her control?

1. Race, color, gender, or national origin (Title VII of the Civil Rights Act of 1964).
2. In retaliation for filing discrimination charges (Title VII of the Civil Rights Act of 1964).
3. For helping other employees who have been discriminated against by a company for exercising their civil rights (Title VII of the Civil Rights Act of 1964).
4. For testifying against a company at an Equal Employment Opportunity Commission hearing (Title VII of the Civil Rights Act of 1964).
5. Because the employee is over 40 years old (Age Discrimination in Employment Act of 1967, as amended).
6. Forcing retirement or permanent layoff of an older employee (Age Discrimination in Employment Act of 1967, as amended).
7. Because she is pregnant (Pregnancy Discrimination Act of 1978).
8. In retaliation for reporting to a state or federal agency unsafe working conditions (Occupational Safety and Health Act of 1970).
9. For filing an OSHA complaint (Occupational Safety and Health Act of 1970).
10. For testifying against the company in an OSHA related hearing or court related action (Occupational Safety and Health Act of 1970).
11. A handicapped employee because of the handicap (Americans with Disabilities Act of 1990).
12. To avoid a pension or benefit plan, such as group health insurance (Employee Retirement Income Security Act of 1974).
13. For performing National Guard duties.
14. For "whistle-blowing" illegal acts by the employer or other employees.

FIGURE 20.5 Inappropriate reasons for terminating an employee.

If the situation was out of the employee's personal control, he or she cannot be charged with misconduct.

6. Was management's investigation of the final offense done in a fair and objective manner, and did it involve someone other than the employee's direct supervisor? It is best that the employee's supervisor not function alone and fill the roles of accuser, judge, and jury. Is there substantial proof that the employee was guilty?

7. Is dismissal of the employee in line with the employee's prior work record and length of service? When an employee has many years of service that are documented as satisfactory or better, he or she is generally entitled to more time to improve before being dismissed.

8. Did the employee have an opportunity to hear the facts and respond to them in a nonthreatening environment? Was the employee able to bring someone into the disciplinary interview if requested?

9. Has this employee been treated as others in similar circumstances? Has this rule been enforced consistently in the past? If the rule has not been enforced consistently, you may have to forgo terminating the employee and instead, go back a step, such as to suspension. In the case where a rule that hasn't been enforced starts to be enforced again, you have to inform employees beforehand of the change.

10. Is the action nondiscriminatory? Has equal treatment been given to members of protected groups (minorities, women, employees over 40 years of age) and nonprotected groups?

These questions are only guidelines for determining just-cause termination. Even if you can answer yes to every question presented here, there is still no guarantee that you won't wind up in court. If you decide to terminate, all the basic procedural steps spelled out for disciplinary action apply to this final decision. You state the problem in writing, collect the facts, make your decision, and take the action.

The Termination Interview[4]

Few people like telling an employee that he or she is terminated, fired, dismissed. The best way to reduce your nervousness and make it less stressful for the employee is to prepare for the termination interview by using something like a termination interview checklist. The checklist can help you to:

1. Select a good time and place to conduct the interview.

2. Determine who will be present at the meeting (you should have at least one person as a witness), as well as whether the employee needs to be escorted out of the building.

3. Develop your opening statement and practice it.

4. Determine how best to respond to possible employee reactions.

5. Determine the final pay, severance pay, and benefits to which the employee is entitled.

6. Develop a list of clearance procedures to be performed at the end of the interview. The timing and place for the interview are important. Although conventional wisdom says to fire an employee at the end of a workweek, that is not necessarily

the best line. By firing the employee at the beginning of the workweek, you give him or her a chance to start immediately looking for a new job, instead of complaining and becoming upset at home. Nor is it wise to terminate employees near major events such as holidays, birthdays, or dates of their anniversary of beginning work with the company. Try to arrange a time when the employee can clean out his or her locker without other employees present.

The meeting should take place in a private room so that should the employee become unruly, guests and coworkers will not be disturbed. A room in the human resources department is ideal. Having prepared for the interview, it is time to speak with the employee. Although you may be nervous, it is probable that the employee is nervous as well. The employee probably knows what's going on and is anxious to get it over with, too. Employees who are fired are often relieved and go on to find new jobs that are much more satisfying. In some cases you might even feel that you did the employee a favor. Following are steps for a termination interview.

1. Do not beat around the bush. Avoid small talk and tell the employee that he or she is being dismissed, and why. Do so in a firm, calm manner. Avoid a discussion of all the details leading up to this decision. This is not the time for that; there have surely been plenty of previous counselings. Instead, state the category under which the discipline problem falls, such as excessive absenteeism, and mention the last step taken and how it was made clear that the employee faced termination for one more offense. Clearly communicate that the decision has been made and there is no possibility for negotiation. Explain that the decision is a joint decision in which others, such as the general manager and human resources director, have been involved. Reinforced in this manner, your authority will not be questioned as readily.

2. At this point, listen to and accept the responses of the employee. Be prepared for any type of response, such as anger, tears, amazement, or hostility. Figure 20.6 describes how to react to four different types of responses.

3. Now is the time to say something positive to the employee to maintain his or her self-esteem, which at this point is probably sagging. Make a statement about something that you, and others, really like about the employee. Perhaps the employee has a good sense of humor or was thoughtful of coworkers.

4. Move on to a discussion of final pay, severance pay, and benefits to which the employee is entitled.

Type of Emotional Response	What You Can Do
1. Crying	• Let the employee cry it out. • Do not apologize for your actions. • Show concern by offering a tissue, something to drink, or a moment of privacy if appropriate. • Staying calm and businesslike, think about the next step in the interview.
2. Shouting and cursing	• Keep your own emotions under control and maintain a calm and cool demeanor. • Make it perfectly clear to the employee that you will continue the conversation only when the shouting stops. Use your normal tone of voice; do not show irritation. • Tell the employee that you would like him or her to know the arrangement for termination pay and benefits.
3. Unresponsive	• Be empathic, but also continue the interview. • Do not ask the employee questions such as "How could you be shocked at this news?" Do not play counselor when the employee withdraws. • Confirm all details in a letter.
4. Employee leaves after your opening statement	• Tell the employee that you really do not want him or her to miss hearing the arrangements made for termination pay and benefits.

FIGURE 20.6 How to react to employees' emotional responses.

5. Finally, explain your clearance procedures and give the employee clear instructions about what to do after your discussion. Do you want the employee to go straight to his or her locker, clean it out, and leave quietly? Is there someone who will escort the employee out of the building?

6. End the interview by standing up and moving toward the door. Avoid making any physical gesture, such as shaking hands or putting your hand on the employee's shoulder, which could be taken the wrong way by someone who is upset and angry. Try to close on a positive, friendly note.

Keep the pace moving during the termination interview. The entire interview should be over in about 10 to 20 minutes.

After the interview, be sure to document important details, including the employee's reaction, any threats that may have been made, and any comments made about the fairness of the decision. Routine terminations lacking clear resolutions can come back to haunt a business. Be sure to keep everything confidential; inform only those employees who must know. If you tell the employee's former coworkers about the dismissal, you are leaving yourself open to be sued for slander.

SPECIAL DISCIPLINARY CONCERNS

Sexual Harassment[5]

As a supervisor you need to be able to recognize and confront sexual harassment. The Equal Employment Opportunity Commission (EEOC) issued guidelines on sexual harassment in 1980, indicating that it is a form of gender discrimination under Title VII of the 1964 Civil Rights Act. The EEOC states that sexual harassment consists of "unwelcome advances, requests for sexual favors, and other verbal or physical conduct of a sexual nature when: (1) submission to such conduct is made, either explicitly or implicitly, a term or condition of an individual's employment, or (2) submission to or rejection of such conduct by an individual is used as the basis for employment decisions affecting the person." This definition of sexual harassment is known as the quid pro quo definition. *Quid pro quo* means that something is given in exchange for something else. In this type of sexual harassment, submission to or rejection of a sexual favor is used as the basis for employment decisions regarding that employee. The employment decision may be an increase in pay, a promotion, or keeping your job. Only supervisors or other members of management can engage in quid pro quo harassment.

Another type of sexual harassment is environmental sexual harassment. In this case, comments or innuendoes of a sexual nature or physical contact are considered a violation when they interfere with an employee's work performance or create an "intimidating, hostile, or offensive working environment." In this situation, the harassment must be persistent and so severe that it affects the employee's well-being.

A final type of sexual harassment is third-party sexual harassment. Third-party sexual harassment involves a customer or client and an employee. The customer or client may harass an employee, or the other way around. For example, a male customer may harass a female bartender.

The following examples of sexual harassment include an example of quid pro quo, environmental, and third-party sexual harassment. See if you can determine which is which.

1. Beth is a new employee who works as a cook's assistant in a crowded kitchen. The men in the kitchen are constantly making crude, sexually oriented comments and jokes, and leave their X-rated magazines in full view of anyone walking by. Beth feels very intimidated and ill at ease. Unfortunately, the situation doesn't improve over the first two months, and Beth feels too stressed to continue working.

2. For the past few nights, after the dining room has closed, Susan's boss has asked her to go to his place for a drink. Although Susan has gone out with him and some friends once before, she is not interested in pursuing a relationship with him. When she tells him she is not interested, he tells her that a dining room supervisor job will be opening soon and that he could make sure she gets it if she takes him up on his invitation.

3. Barbara is a regular customer at a popular after-work bar where Bob works as a bartender. Barbara finds Bob to be a very good-looking fellow, so much so that she can't keep her eyes, or hands, off him. Bob doesn't like the attention Barbara gives him, but he feels he can't do much about it since she is the customer.

Such instances of sexual harassment can cost a company lost productive time, low morale, harm to its reputation, court costs, and punitive damages to harassment victims. In each of the situations above, there is an element of sexual harassment. While the second situation represents the typical exchange of sexual favors for employment opportunities, the first situation is an example of environmental sexual harassment in which the working environment was intimidating, hostile, or offensive due to physical, verbal, or visual (such as pornographic pictures) sexual harassment. The third situation represents third-party sexual harassment.

As a supervisor you are responsible for *recognizing, confronting, and preventing the sexual harassment of both female and male employees by other employees or by nonemployees* such as guests or people making deliveries. "An employer can be liable for customers who harass employees when the employer knew or should have known of the harassment and failed to prevent it."[6] Both you and your employer will be considered guilty of sexual harassment if you knew about, or should have known about, such misconduct and failed to correct it. If you genuinely did not know that sexual harassment took place, liability can be averted if there is an adequate sexual harassment policy *and* the situation is corrected immediately.

Following are some specific actions that you can take to deal effectively with the issue of sexual harassment:

- Be familiar with your company's sexual harassment policy. Figure 20.7 is a sample policy. This policy should include disciplinary guidelines for people who are guilty of sexual harassment and guidelines for harassers who retaliate against those who turn them in. This policy may also include a formal complaint procedure for employees to use if they think they have been victims of sexual harassment, with provisions for immediate investigations and prompt disciplinary actions when appropriate.

- Educate your employees on how to recognize sexual harassment, how to report it when it occurs, and the steps that will be taken if an employee is guilty of sexual harassment.

- When an employee informs you of a possible case of sexual harassment, investigate the situation promptly according to your company policy. Your investigation is much the same as that done for any possible case of misconduct as just described. Don't assume that anyone is guilty or innocent.

- When you witness an example of sexual harassment, follow your policy and take appropriate and timely disciplinary action.

- Provide follow-up after instances of sexual harassment. Check with victims and witnesses that harassment has indeed stopped and that no retaliation is taking place.

- Prevent sexual harassment by being visible in your work areas, being a good role model, and taking all reported incidents seriously.

Check Your Knowledge

1. What is meant by *dehire?*

2. What is a *third-party sexual harassment?*

Other Forms of Harassment

Harassment in the workplace is not limited to sexual harassment. All forms of harassment based on national origin, race, color, religion, gender, disability, or age are illegal. *Harassment* is defined as intimidating, hostile, or offensive behavior toward someone, or the creation of an intimidating, hostile, or offensive environment for someone, based on that person's national origin, race, color, religion, gender, disability, or age.

I. Policy

The policy of XYZ Hotels is that all of our employees should be able to enjoy a work environment free from all forms of discrimination, including sexual harassment. Sexual harassment is a form of misconduct that undermines the integrity of the employment relationship, debilitates morale, and therefore interferes with the work effectiveness of its victims and their co-workers. Sexual harassment is a violation of the law and will not be tolerated or condoned.

II. Definition of Sexual Harassment

Sexual harassment consists of unwelcome advances, requests for sexual favors, and other verbal or physical conduct of a sexual nature when:

1. submission to such conduct is made either explicitly or implicitly a term or condition of an employee's employment, or
2. submission to or rejection of such conduct by an employee is used as the basis for employment decisions, or
3. the conduct interferes substantially with an employee's work performance or creates an intimidating, hostile, or offensive work environment.

Sexual harassment is not limited to actions of hotel employees. Customers and clients may also be victims, or perpetrators, of sexual harassment.

Following are examples of sexual harassment.

- Unwelcome intentional touching or other unwelcome physical contact (such as pinching or patting).
- Unwelcome staring or whistling.
- Unwelcome sexually suggestive or flirtatious notes, gifts, electronic or voice mail.
- Offering an employment-related reward in exchange for sexual favors.
- Verbal abuse of a sexual nature.
- Unwelcome display of sexually suggestive objects or pictures such as pinups.
- Conduct or remarks that demean or are hostile to a person's gender.

III. Coverage: XYZ Hotels

XYZ Hotels prohibits sexual harassment during work hours or while on company property by all employees and by all nonemployees, such as customers and suppliers.

IV. Responsibilities

XYZ Hotels managers are responsible for preventing sexual harassment and educating employees about this subject. They are also responsible for setting a good example, taking every complaint seriously, investigating complaints fairly, and maintaining confidentiality.

XYZ Hotels requests that any employee with a complaint regarding sexual harassment make every effort to promptly present the complaint to their immediate supervisor or the human resources director. If the complaint involves the employee's immediate supervisor, or if the employee feels uncomfortable discussing the complaint with the immediate supervisor, the employee may speak to another supervisor.

V. Investigation Procedures and Disciplinary Action

Once a supervisor has received a complaint, he or she is to immediately contact the Human Resources Department. After notification of the employee's complaint, a fair and confidential investigation will be initiated. The results of the investigation will be reviewed by the Human Resources Director for possible disciplinary action.

If warranted, disciplinary action up to and including termination will be imposed. Retaliation against employees who file complaints or assist in investigating complaints may also result in discipline up to and including termination.

FIGURE 20.7 Sample sexual harassment policy.

Intimidating behavior may involve threatening someone with harm of some type. Hostile behavior could include asking an employee to do something that is completely unrealistic, such as asking a potwasher to be in charge of washing all dishes as well. Offensive behavior is generally ridiculing or taunting someone because of his or her color, for example. As a supervisor, you should be constantly on the lookout for intimidating, hostile, or offensive behavior, because it has no place in the workplace.

Substance Abuse

The problem of substance abuse in the workplace is pervasive. Although it is not always apparent, its effects can be devastating. Job performance or safety of employees and/or guests is adversely affected. Substance abuse is usually defined as working under the influence of, using, or being impaired by alcohol or any drug. Drugs include illegal and some legal drugs, prescription or over-the-counter medications, such as painkillers that can alter conciousness. Although drug abuse probably gets more publicity, the extent of alcohol abuse in the workplace is actually greater than that of all the illegal drugs combined.

The U.S. Department of Labor reports that an estimated 6.5 percent of full-time and 8.6 percent of part-time workers in the United States are current illicit drug users. In the hospitality industry, this number is higher.[7] Aside from the immediate risk to the employee, substance abuse problems present certain concerns to you as the supervisor. Drug abuse may lead to robbery or violence. Although there is no sure way to spot a restaurant employee who is having a substance abuse problem, there are signals to look out for.

Some of these behaviors will be visible in the workplace. These employees tend to be late for work more often, take more days off for sickness, be involved in accidents more often, and be more likely to file for workers' compensation claims. The U.S. Department of Labor estimates that, in one year, employee alcohol and drug abuse has cost American businesses roughly $81 billion in lost productivity, lost time, accidents, breakage, healthcare, and workers' compensation. Frequently, these employees have difficulties meeting performance standards and getting along with their peers. Employee involvement with alcohol and drugs also affects employee morale and can affect your company's image adversely.

Based on the fact that substance abuse in the workplace has become a tremendous concern and that it can be dealt with effectively, there have been numerous government initiatives to deal with it. Of particular interest is the Drug Free Workplace Act of 1988, which requires that most federal contractors and anyone who receives federal grants provide a drug-free workplace by doing the following:

■ Informing employees that they are prohibited from doing any of the following in the workplace: unlawful manufacture, distribution, dispensation, possession, or use of a controlled substance. Inform employees what actions they can expect if they do (this policy must be in writing).

■ Give employees a copy of the policy and ask them to abide by it as a condition of continued employment.

■ Inform employees of the dangers of drug abuse at work and available counseling, rehabilitation, and employee assistance programs.

■ Make a good-faith effort to maintain a drug-free workplace.

These represent some of the major requirements. As a supervisor, you have several responsibilities for dealing with substance abuse in your workplace.

1. *Any disciplinary action that you take should be based on observable, job-related factors, such as substandard job performance or inappropriate workplace behavior rather than on the existence or suspicion of a substance abuse problem.* Substance abuse is generally regarded as a health problem, a disease, and as such disciplinary action based only on an employee's substance abuse problem is illegal. Discipline is legal only if the focus is on the employee's inability to meet job and conduct requirements.

2. *You need to be familiar with your company's policy on substance abuse.* More and more companies are developing substance abuse policies, such as the one shown in Figure 20.8 In a substance abuse policy, the following topics are usually addressed:
   ■ Rules regarding alcohol and drug possession and use
   ■ Penalties for rule violations
   ■ When employees may be subject to drug testing
   ■ Programs available for counseling, education, and rehabilitation, such as employee assistance programs

   Drug testing is one way to reduce drug abuse in the workplace. More and more employers are doing drug testing of applicants, with applicants being denied employment if the results come back positive. Of companies that do drug testing, *for-cause testing* of employees is common. With for-cause testing, an employee is asked to take a drug test if the person's supervisor has a reasonable suspicion that the employee may be impaired due to substance abuse. Random testing is also used by some companies to monitor their employees for drug use.

3. *You need to be able to identify and confront constructively employees who are substance abusers to urge them to accept professional help.* Figure 20.9 lists indicators of an

SUBJECT: SUBSTANCE ABUSE POLICY   EFFECTIVE DATE: 3/1/XX

I. *GENERAL POLICY*

We are committed to programs that promote safety in the workplace, employee health and well-being, and which promote a positive image of the institution in the community. Consistent with the spirit and intent of this commitment, we developed this policy statement regarding the sale, use, possession or distribution of drugs and alcohol by all employees.

Employee involvement with drugs and alcohol can adversely affect job performance and employee morale, jeopardize employee and patient safety and undermine the public's confidence. Such involvement is particularly unacceptable in an industry like ours in light of the nature of our role in society and the potentially disastrous consequences to patients which may result from an employee's impaired condition. Our goal, and the purpose of this policy, therefore, is to establish and maintain a safe workplace and a healthy and efficient workforce free from the effects of drug and alcohol abuse, and to extend to employees having an addictive disease an opportunity for effective treatment and rehabilitation.

II. *EMPLOYEE ASSISTANCE PROGRAM*

We encourage any employee with a drug or alcohol problem to contact the EAP, the Occupational Health Department, or any recognized external evaluation, referral, or treatment agency for assistance. We subscribe to the premise that addictive diseases are entitled to the same consideration and offer of treatment which is extended to any other disease. All communications and records will be maintained on a confidential basis. Employees will not be subject to discipline for voluntarily acknowledging their drug/alcohol problems; nor will job security or promotional opportunities be jeopardized as a consequence only of having an addictive disease except to the extent that the manifestations of the disease interfere with the employee's performance of his or her job. However, this will *not* excuse violations of the Substance Abuse Policy for which the employee is subject to discipline. Employees who utilized the Employee Assistance Program or any other treatment resource will be expected to meet existing job performance standards and established work rules within the framework of established administrative practices. A request for assistance does not exempt the employee from routine performance expectations, nor does it confer any immunity, legal or disciplinary, from the consequences of misconduct.

1. There may be limited exceptions to this guarantee in (1) instances where there may be a clear and present danger presented to the welfare of the employee or another person; (2) where records or testimony might be subject to subpoena or other legal process; or (3) where the employee consents to disclosure.

III. *RULES REGARDING DRUGS AND ALCOHOL*

Whenever the capacity of an employee to function on the job has been diminished to the point where he is unable to perform his job duties and/or is acting in an unsafe manner, supervisory personnel will have the responsibility for taking immediate action to: (a) remove the impaired employee from the work area; (b) initiate procedures; and (c) refer the individual to the Employee Assistance Program. The justification for taking such actions shall be observable unsatisfactory job performance or behavior.

A. *Use, Possession, Transportation, Sale, Distribution*

The use, possession, sale, or distribution of drugs or alcohol while on Medical Center property or Medical Center business shall be cause for immediate discharge. Illegal substances will be confiscated and the appropriate law enforcement agencies may be notified.

B. *Drugs/Alcohol in System*

1. *Alcohol*

An employee found to have a blood-alcohol concentration of .05% or more (or its equivalent as determined by a different diagnostic test such as a Breathalyzer) while on company property shall receive a 5-day suspension on the first offense and shall be required to participate in the Employee Assistance Program. In addition, the employee shall be subject to random drug and alcohol testing. If the employee refuses to participate in the EAP and the terms of a chemical dependency treatment agreement and/or violates any rules set forth in this policy at any time thereafter, he/she shall be subject to immediate discharge.

FIGURE 20.8 Substance abuse policy and procedure.

2. Marijuana/Hashish

An employee found to have detectable concentrations of marijuana (or its metabolites) in his or her system shall receive a 5-day suspension on the first offense and shall be required to participate in the Employee Assistance Program. In addition, the employee shall be subject to random drug and alcohol testing. If the employee refuses to participate in the EAP and the terms of a chemical dependency treatment agreement and/or violates any rules set forth in this policy at any time thereafter, he/she shall be subject to immediate discharge.

3. Drugs Other Than Marijuana or Alcohol

An employee found to have detectable concentrations of any drug other than marijuana or alcohol in his or her system, including, but not limited to, heroin, cocaine, morphine, phencyclidine (PCP), amphetamines, barbiturates, or hallucinogens (or metabolites of any such drugs), shall receive a 5-day suspension on the first offense and shall be required to participate in the Employee Assistance Program. In addition, the employee shall be subject to random drug and alcohol testing. If the employee refuses to participate in the EAP and the terms of a chemical dependency treatment agreement and/or violates any rules set forth in this policy at any time thereafter, he/she shall be subject to immediate discharge.

4. Testing for Drug/Alcohol in System

An employee may be required to submit to blood, urine, or other diagnostic tests to detect alcohol and/or drugs (or drug metabolites) in his or her system whenever the employee is involved in an on-the-job accident or the employee's observed behavior raises a reasonable suspicion of drug or alcohol use. See Fitness for Duty guidelines for criteria for what constitutes reasonable suspicion. (A bargaining unit employee is entitled to have a union representative present, if immediately available, during the initial collecting of a specimen.) If an initial screening test indicates positive findings, a confirmatory test will be conducted.

Employees with a prior violation of the Drug and Alcohol Policy will be subject to random testing.
Any employee who refuses to submit to testing shall be subject to disciplinary action up to and including discharge.

C. Other Rules and Provisions

1. Searches

The company reserves the right to carry out reasonable searches of employees and their property, including, but not limited to, lockers, lunch boxes and private vehicles, if parked on company property. (A bargaining unit employee whose person or property is to be searched is entitled to have a union representative present, if immediately available, while the search is being conducted.) An employee who refuses to submit immediately to such a search shall be subject to disciplinary action up to and including discharge.

2. Drug Paraphernalia

Employees are prohibited from bringing drug paraphernalia onto company property at any time. An employee who possesses or distributes such paraphernalia while on company property shall be subject to disciplinary action, up to and including discharge.

3. Off-Duty Arrests/Convictions

An employee who is arrested for, or convicted of, a drug offense which involves the off-duty sale, distribution, or possession of illegal drugs must promptly inform his supervisor of the arrest, the nature of the charges, and the ultimate disposition of the charges. Failure to do so is grounds for discipline, up to and including discharge. Such arrest/conviction may subject the employee to discipline, up to and including discharge, depending upon the circumstances involved.

4. Over-the-Counter or Prescribed Medications

Over-the-counter or prescription medications may have pharmacological effects which can impair job functioning and performance. Additionally, many such medications may be abused even if obtained through legal means by exceeding the customary dosage. Employees taking such medications are responsible for using such drugs in an appropriate manner, becoming aware of the potential side effects of any such drug, and informing their supervisor of their use of medications which might potentially impair their

FIGURE 20.8 (Continued)

job performance. Employees who intentionally abuse medications such as (but not limited to) tranquilizers, sedative-hypnotics, analgesics, anti-depressants, or diet pills shall be subjected to the same disciplinary sanctions prescribed for illicit drugs in this policy (i.e., a 5-day suspension, random testing and referral to the EAP). Employees whose impairment can be demonstrated to be the result of an inadvertent unpredictable, or a typical reaction to an over-the-counter or prescription medication shall be absolved of any responsibility for such an incident.

5. *Reporting Violations of the Drug and Alcohol Policy*

It is each employee's responsibility to immediately report unsafe working conditions or hazardous activities that may jeopardize his or her safety or the safety of fellow employees or guests. This responsibility includes the responsibility to immediately report any violation of the Substance Abuse Policy. An employee who fails to report such a violation may be subject to disciplinary action, up to and including discharge.

6. *Job Applicants*

Applicants for employment may be given blood, urine or other diagnostic tests to detect alcohol and/or drugs (or drug metabolites) in their system. Successful completion of the test is a condition of employment.

7. *Re-employment*

Any individual who leaves the company through layoff, resignation or termination for a period exceeding 90 days will be required to submit to blood, urine or other diagnostic tests to detect alcohol and/or drugs (or drug metabolites) in their system prior to re-entry into the workforce. Positive test results for alcohol or drugs will be considered in deciding whether the employee shall be permitted to return to work.

8. *Progressive Discipline Not Applicable*

The disciplinary steps set forth in the Employee Handbook providing for progressive discipline (e.g., 1st written warning, 2nd written warning, probation, discharge) or the 3 step process for Level II Infractions *do not apply* to violations of the Substance Abuse Policy. The discipline to be imposed for violations of the Substance Abuse Policy shall be governed solely by the provisions set forth herein.

FIGURE 20.8 (Continued)

impaired employee. Obviously, a supervisor cannot intervene unless you identify a problem needing your intervention. Early intervention is important, as the longer a problem exists, the more difficult it will be to resolve it. In addition, confronting the problem is most effective in producing a positive outcome when it occurs before the situation has deteriorated to the point where you have to take disciplinary action.

No one relishes confronting an employee with his job deficiencies, or informing him that his continued employment is in jeopardy. However, for an employee with a substance abuse problem that is causing impaired job performance, this intervention can be not only job-saving, but, in some cases, literally life-saving as well.

When confronting constructively an employee whom you suspect to be a substance abuser, you are basically saying two things to the employee about his or her poor performance. On the one hand, you are asking for accountability and change relative to the issue of job performance, while on the other hand, you are

The following list of indicators ranges from those which are very clear and compelling to others which may be ambiguous. The supervisor is in the position of having to make a judgment based upon the facts at hand (i.e., the employee's immediately observable behavior as it relates to job performance). Supervisors should be particularly alert to behaviors which are abnormal, uncharacteristic, or inappropriate to the context of the work emvironment.

Physical Appearance:

Impaired coordination, unsteady gait, staggering, poor balance
Tremors, shakiness, dizziness, seizures
Impaired muscular control, poor performance of gross or complex motor tasks
Bloodshot eyes, dilated or constricted pupils, watery eyes
Excessive sweating, chills, nausea
Abnormal drowsiness, "nodding off," excessive fatigue, stupor
Blank expression, unresponsive
Inappropriate or bizarre dress, neglect of personal hygiene or appearance

Unusual/Abnormal Behavior:

Markedly poor judgment, impulsivity
Carelessness, risk-taking behavior, neglect of safety procedures
Marked irresponsibility, indifference, or rigidity
Marked anxiety, agitation, panic
Mood swings, erratic behavior
Apathy, lethargy, depression, despondency, suicidal thinking
Euphoria, elation, "high," excessively talkative, overactive (restless)
Over-reactiveness (verbal or physical)—boisterousness, irritability, argumentativeness, quarrelsomeness, belligerency, explosiveness, threats, assaultiveness, combativeness
Slurred speech

Cognitive (Mental) Factors:

Inability to concentrate or comprehend, distractibility
Memory deficits, lapses, forgetfulenss
Preoccupation, brooding, excessive daydreaming
Confusion, disorientation, incoherence, irrelevancy
Diminished level of consciousness, "out of touch"
Impairment of communication—expressive or receptive
Hallucinations (perceptions which are false/unreal)
Marked suspiciousness, feelings of persecution, homicidal thoughts

FIGURE 20.9 Behavioral indicators of possible impairment/unfitness for duty.

expressing sincere interest and concern coupled with an offer of help in the form of a referral to an EAP or other program. You need to strike a balance between these complementary facets of the process: being firm and being empathic. The employee has to experience both of these facets so that the probability of acceptance of the need for help is maximized. The use of confrontive messages is most effective in breaking through denial, which is often characteristic of substance abuse, while the constructive messages have the intent of motivating the troubled employee to comply with a referral.

4. *Don't try to diagnose or give employees advice on their substance abuse problems.* To do so complicates the entire situation, often leaves you open to manipulation, and may anger the employee, who may feel that the intrusion into his or her personal life is not warranted. Instead, focus on observable workplace behavior and leave the issue of possible substance abuse to professionals who are properly trained in this area.

Things are not always as they seem, and for the manager, a consistent focus on job-related behaviors is the most secure footing.

EMPLOYEE ASSISTANCE PROGRAMS

Counseling programs called employee assistance programs (EAPs) are an expansion of traditional occupational alcoholism programs, which began appearing years ago. Larger companies are more likely than smaller companies to have EAPs. Companies such as Marriott, KFC, and Lettuce Entertain You offer counseling and referral services to some or all of their employees.

An EAP is an employer-paid benefit program designed to assist employees with personal problems. EAPs offer outsourced counseling and referral to a range of professional services. The rationale behind the programs is that getting a valuable employee "back on track" is worth doing for them, their families, and the company.

Signs of employees in need of help are increased tardiness, fatigue, missed goals, inappropriate behavior, medical problems, psychological problems, stress, and increased sick days. If there is a performance-related work problem, then supervisors and human resources can investigate the situation and require all concerned to submit a report. EAPs work with employee discipline and counseling to retain employees who need temporary assistance. The approach to take is called intervention rather than confrontation. Most larger companies have an EAP program that employees can use free of charge for counseling and for various types of assistance such as legal, financial, and family needs.

Another reason for companies to offer EAPs is because legally alcohol abuse is classified as a sickness and should be treated as such to allow an employee a chance to get help and hopefully recover.

The general purpose of an EAP is to provide a confidential, professional counseling and referral service to employees with problems such as addictions and dependencies, family problems, stress, and financial problems. An EAP can provide a comprehensive range of services:

- *Assessment*: identification of the nature of the problem
- *Intervention*: in the form of focused counseling by a counselor or referral to an appropriate community resource
- *Follow-up*: including monitoring of employee progress and assisting with reentry of the employee into the workplace when the employee has left rehabilitation
- *Managerial assistance*: providing technical assistance and emotional support to supervisors handling troubled employees

There are four steps to an EAP program: first: *identifying a troubled employee*, and advising them of available confidential counseling. Employees have the right to decline participation in an EAP but, refusing to do so may mean termination if the problem has a negative impact on the employee's work. Second: *visit with a counselor*, who talks with the employee and may arrange for specialized treatment of the problem. Third: *solve the problem*—naturally this could take just a couple of sessions, such as with a financial problem, or much longer for other problems. In either case, the employee is directed to someone who does not work for the company. Fourth: *depending on the outcome of the treatment*, which, if successful, the employee returns to work. If however the treatment is not successful and the employee's performance is below expectations, then he or she is usually terminated. (Remember, termination is based solely on unaccceptable work—nothing else. And also remember to give some grace, meaning, give them something positive like a week's pay so they are hopefully not so bitter that they commit an act of violence. Make sure you have someone with you all the time when terminating someone and an escort to your car after work.)

How to Make EAPs Work

There are five steps that make EAPs work, and like most other HR programs they are quite logical:

1. Write a statement of policy and purpose with the goals and objectives of the EAP program and let all supervisors and all employees know that the program is freely available.

2. Train supervisors and managers what to do, how to recognize a troubled employee, and how to let the employee know of available help.

3. Set procedures for the referral of employees who need help.

4. Establish communications to let employees know about the EAP and for what to do when referrals are necessary.

5. Evaluate the program.

Remember, it's up to the supervisor to recognize the "troubled" employee and to discretely talk to them in private (troubled employees will often be grateful to have someone to talk to, but remember you are *not* a trained counselor). Most employees will accept professional help and be appreciative of it. As a supervisor, you must document all the occurrences of underperforming employees specifically where their performance is below expectations. Then the supervisor must talk with the employee about the poor work performance. The conversation should be in private and focus only on the work performance.

Check Your Knowledge

1. Employees with substance abuse problems present certain concerns to you as supervisor. What are these concerns?

2. As a supervisor you have several responsibilities for dealing with substance abuse in your workplace. What are your responsibilities?

3. Describe an EAP program.

THE SUPERVISOR'S KEY ROLE

The orderly and obedient carrying out of the work of an enterprise depends almost entirely on the effectiveness of the first-line supervisor in establishing and maintaining discipline. It is the supervisor who transmits the rules and policies laid down by management. It is the supervisor who orients, trains, and provides continuous information to workers so that they know what to do, how to do it, to what standards, and what will happen if they don't. And if it comes to that, it is the supervisor who sees to it that what is supposed to happen does happen.

But the effective supervisor does not let it come to that. With prompt action, a teaching-helping approach to discipline, and sensitivity to people's motivations and feelings, supervisors can usually keep incidents from developing into disciplinary problems. Supervisors who are consistent and fair, who follow the rules themselves, who create and maintain a positive work climate with good communications and good person-to-person relations are usually able to maintain good discipline with a minimum of hassles, threats, and disciplinary actions.

On the other hand, the supervisor who attempts to maintain discipline through threat and punishment is usually plagued with ongoing disciplinary problems because of the resentment and anger that such methods provoke. Such supervisors often cop out by blaming workers for problems they have created themselves: "You just can't get good workers today." In this case, too, it is the supervisor who creates the prevailing condition of discipline.

Nobody ever claims that discipline is easy, and nobody has a foolproof prescription for success. It is supervisory leadership and example that set the climate and the direction, and it is the supervisor, acting one on one, who makes it all happen.

SAFETY AND SECURITY MANAGEMENT

It is a universal human need to want to be safe and secure. As a supervisor, one of your top priorities is making sure that the workplace is safe and secure for both workers and guests. Safety hazards abound in a hospitality operation: There are cleaning chemicals that can burn your skin, slicers that can cut more than bologna when you're not watching, heavy boxes to lift that can wrench your back, computer keyboards that can cause numbness in your hands, wet floors that you can go sliding across, and poorly lit stairs that you can fly down (with an order of hot soup in your hands).

After negotiating the numerous safety hazards, keep your eyes open because the back door has been left wide open. Before a thief sees this wonderful opportunity, slam that door shut, and lock it, then find out who left the door open in the first place.

A Safe Workplace

Besides causing pain and suffering to the injured employee and incurring the cost of lost work time, there are other direct and indirect costs to consider when an accident occurs:

- Lost time and productivity of uninjured workers who stop work to help the injured employee or simply watch and talk about the incident (Productivity normally decreases for a number of hours, but if morale is negatively affected, it could be much longer.)

- Lost business during the time that the operation is not fully functioning
- Lost business due to damaged reputation
- Overtime costs to get the operation fully functioning again
- The costs to clean, repair, and/or replace any equipment, food, or supplies damaged in the accident
- Cost to retrain the injured employee upon return to work
- Increased premiums for workers' compensation
- In the case of a lawsuit, legal fees and possible award to the injured employee

Of course, not only employees become involved in accidents; guests do also.

In 1971, the Occupational Safety and Health Administration (OSHA) was created as an agency within the U.S. Department of Labor. Its purpose is to "assure so far as possible every working man and woman in the Nation safe and healthful working conditions and to preserve our human resources." OSHA sets mandatory job safety and health standards, encourages both employers and employees to decrease hazards in the workplace, conducts compliance inspections, issues citations in cases of noncompliance, and asks for record-keeping of injuries. OSHA also requires you, as the supervisor, to train your employees as to any known hazards in their work area.

Safety programs are common in hospitality operations as a way to increase safety awareness and to prevent accidents. Safety programs usually include the following components:

- Safety policies and procedures
- Employee training
- Safety committee
- Safety inspections
- Accident reporting and investigation
- Constant supervision

Supervisors themselves are very involved in the safety program. After all, you oversee the day-to-day monitoring and enforcement of safety rules, report and correct unsafe conditions, train and retrain employees, maintain safety records, check that the

Policy: In order to maintain adequate safety to meet or exceed the standards for all regulatory agencies, the General Manager will perform monthly safety audits of the restaurant.

Procedures:

1. At the beginning of each month, the General Manager asks two supervisors and two employees to set a time to do a safety inspection of the entire facility.

2. The Safety Inspection Team uses the "Restaurant Safety Survey" form to inspect the facility, noting problems as appropriate.

3. Copies of the survey are given to the supervisors, who are given two weeks to resolve any problems noted and to document this on the survey form.

4. The General Manager reviews the returned surveys and takes any additional appropriate action. The results of the survey are discussed with the Owner.

5. Reports are saved for three years.

FIGURE 20.10 Policy and procedures for safety inspections.

first-aid kit is well stocked, and act as a role model. If you are safety-minded, you are more likely to create an environment where safety is practiced and respected.

Safety policies and procedures state what behaviors are expected from employees in order to prevent accidents, what safety training employees receive, how often safety inspections occur, and what to do when accidents happen. Figure 20.10 is a sample for policy and procedure regarding safety inspections.

Policies and procedures form the basis for your employee training program. Safety training should start at orientation and this information should be put into the employee handbook. The accident rate for employees is higher during their first month of employment than for any subsequent month. Safety training should be repeated and updated at least once a year for all employees. At the end of training, employees need to be evaluated on what they know, and rewarded or recognized for working safely. Figure 20.11 is a page from a training plan on kitchen safety rules.

Safety committees are often formed within hospitality operations. They meet periodically to discuss safety matters. The safety committee is often involved in reviewing data on the number and types of accidents to date, inspecting the facility, suggesting new and revised policies and procedures, and overseeing safety training.

Kitchen Safety Checklist
Preventing Cuts

1. Know how to operate equipment.

2. Pay attention when using sharp equipment.

3. Use guards, when provided, on equipment.

4. Use tampers to push food into equipment, not your hands!

5. Turn equipment off before adjusting.

6. No loose sleeves, ties, or dangling jewelry should be near equipment.

7. Use knives carefully.

8. Carry dishes and glassware carefully.

9. Sweep up broken glass.

10. Use a special container to dispose of broken glass, dishes, and other sharp objects.

11. Remove nails and staples in shipping cartons and crates, and wear gloves.

12. Remove can lids entirely from cans, and put back into empty cans for disposal.

FIGURE 20.11 Page from a training plan on kitchen safety rules.

As a supervisor, you may periodically be in charge of a safety inspection to check for and correct any unsafe conditions, such as a slicer's frayed electric cord. In addition to managers and supervisors, employees can take part in the inspection process in order to encourage them to take a more active role in preventing accidents.

When accidents do happen, regardless of how minor the injuries appear to be at the time, it is the supervisor's responsibility to report them. Early reporting of all the facts works to the advantage of all concerned. The supervisor can move quickly to correct the unsafe condition that caused an accident, the injured person can receive prompt and effective medical care if needed, and in the case of an employee who can't return to work immediately, he or she can receive workers' compensation benefits without unnecessary delay. Also, the company can make preparations in the event of pending legal action such as a lawsuit.

The fact that all accidents should be properly reported cannot be overemphasized. In many cases, incidents that appear trivial develop into major hazards at a later time. If accurate and complete facts are not recorded at the time of the accident, it could be difficult to compile information should the incident develop into a claim against the company.

Implementing the Hazard Communication Standard

Most U.S. businesses must comply with the Hazard Communication Standard issued by OSHA. The purpose of this standard is to give employees the right to know what chemicals they are working with, what the risks or hazards are, and what they can do to limit the risks. You probably know of a number of hazardous materials in your workplace, such as all-purpose cleaners, detergents, oven cleaners, degreasers, and pesticides. These products often present physical hazards, such as exploding or burning, and/or health hazards, such as irritating or burning skin.

The Hazard Communication Standard requires employers to do the following:

1. Post a list of hazardous substances found in your operation.
2. Post Material Safety Data Sheets (MSDSs). For each hazardous product you have, the manufacturer has an MSDS that explains what the product is, why it is hazardous, and how you can use it safely.
3. Explain to employees how to read and use the MSDS and also the labels on hazardous products.
4. Train employees how to use hazardous chemicals properly and what to do in case of an emergency.

Basic tips on safely handling hazardous chemicals are given in Figure 20.12.

Guest Safety

You may think that guests face far fewer hazards than workers do, but even though they are far away from deep-fat fryers and slicers, guests still fracture bones slipping on your stairs, get serious burns from spilled hot coffee, die from allergic reactions to certain foods, and get foodborne illnesses. Not paying attention to guest safety can cost your operation hundreds of thousands and even millions of dollars in lawsuits.

As a supervisor you don't want to see guests get hurt any more than you want employees to get hurt. So what can you do about it? You are already involved in the operation's safety program as just described, so you know your safety policies and procedures, train employees, take part in safety committee meetings and/or safety

---

1. *Do* know where the Material Safety Data Sheets are posted and read them.
2. *Do* read the labels of all products before you use them.
3. *Do* follow the directions for proper storage, handling, and use for all chemicals you use. Measure chemicals carefully.
4. *Do* ask your supervisor any question or express any concern you may have about a certain product.
5. *Do* know how to call for medical help in case of an emergency.
6. *Do not* ever mix chemicals together.
7. *Do not* store chemicals in unmarked containers. If chemicals are transferred to different containers, each new container must be labeled with the contents and hazards.
8. *Do not* store chemicals in or close to food storage, preparation, or serving areas.
9. *Do not* leave aerosol spray containers near heat or spray close to an open flame or your eyes.
10. *Do not* dispose of any empty chemical container until you have checked the label for the proper procedure.

FIGURE 20.12 Do's and don'ts of safe chemical handling.

inspections, report accidents, and supervise with safety uppermost in your mind. Many guest safety concerns revolve around the following:

- *Slips, trips, and falls.* Steps are most often the culprit behind slips, trips, and falls. Stairs and steps, both inside and outside, should be well lit, covered with a nonskid surface, and have handrails. Wet floors cause their share of problems as well. Try to mop during off-hours and be sure to use "Wet Floor" signs and possibly even rope off the area. Guest parking areas should be clear of trash and free of ice in the winter.

- *Burns.* Hot beverages, such as coffee, can be a danger when not handled carefully. Your operation may have special hot beverage temperatures and rules to prevent burns. Guests should always be warned about hot plates.

- *Food allergies.* Some people experience a severe response when they eat certain foods to which they are allergic. Their throat swells up to the point where air can't get down to the lungs. This type of reaction, called anaphylactic shock, can kill. Two things can be done to prevent this problem: have a policy and procedure that tells servers how to handle a guest's question about a dish containing an allergic ingredient, and stock the first-aid kit with "Epi Pens," a medication that suppresses anaphylactic shock symptoms (managers must be trained to use it).

- *Foodborne illness.* Foodborne illnesses make millions of Americans sick each year and kill almost 10,000 people. High-quality sanitation standards and well-supervised procedures are needed to prevent outbreaks.

First aid is emergency treatment given before regular medical services can be provided. To protect both guests and employees who fall ill and are hurt, it is important to have at least one person per shift trained in first aid and in cardiopulmonary resuscitation (CPR), a procedure used in case of cardiac arrest (when the heart stops beating).

Security Concerns

According to the Educational Foundation of the National Restaurant Association, the purpose of a security program is to protect the belongings or assets of your facility (including the building, grounds, equipment, furnishings, food, beverages, supplies, cash, employees, and guests) from incidents such as employee theft, violent crime, and burglary. Much of your work as a supervisor involves security, from doing reference checks on applicants to following cash-handling procedures, restricting access to keys, and handling a security emergency such as theft. To protect yourself, your employees and guests, and your company from damage, familiarize yourself with all security policies and procedures, and more important, enforce them without hesitation.

Check Your Knowledge

1. Safety programs are common in hospitality operations as a way to increase safety awareness and to prevent accidents. What do these safety programs include?

2. What is the purpose of the Hazard Communication Standard?

AIDS and the Hospitality Worker

AIDS, or acquired immunodeficiency syndrome, is a serious illness that harms the body's ability to fight infection. A virus called HIV (human immunodeficiency virus) causes AIDS. The HIV virus is spread by sharing body fluids, which can occur via tainted plood transfusions, unprotected sex or sharing needles with someone who is HIV positive, body piercing, and tattoos. There is no evidence that the HIV virus can be spread through food handling or casual contact. Persons with HIV initially show no signs or symptoms. As time goes on, and it may be years, they display symptoms of HIV infection, such as fatigue, diarrhea, weight loss, and wounds that don't heal. An infected person is diagnosed with AIDS when he or she develops serious infections or cancers.

Employees with HIV/AIDS are now protected by the Americans with Disabilities Act, so it is illegal to fire an HIV-positive employee or otherwise discriminate in employment matters. They can continue to work as long as they are able to perform the essential functions of their position. Reasonable accommodations, such as flexible work assignments and hours, may be necessary.

Now that you know you can't get AIDS from working with an HIV-infected employee, and you can't discriminate against these employees, what do you do when one of your employees tells you that he is HIV-positive? As usual, there is plenty you can do as a supervisor, but first see if your employer has a written AIDS policy that you should follow.

- Show support. Many HIV-infected employees fear for their jobs and their benefits. Explain that he or she will continue to be treated according to existing policies and will continue to receive the same medical benefits. Review the employee's sick time, vacation time, and insurance coverage. Offer other support that may be available in the workplace, such as employee counseling services or employee-financed emergency funds.

- If the employee is starting to show symptoms, discuss any reasonable accommodations that you can make, such as more frequent breaks or fewer work hours.

- Review the basics of the Family and Medical Leave Act (to be discussed in a moment).

- Keep the employee's medical information confidential.

- If you haven't done so already, train your employees about AIDS to reduce any fears. This could involve a guest speaker from the local American Red Cross, a videotape about AIDS, and printed materials.

Of course, if you have one or more employees who are HIV-positive, you want to make sure that your employee sanitation and safety training is up to par to make sure that the employee's condition does not present any health concerns.

KEY POINTS

1. *Discipline* refers to a condition or state of orderly conduct and compliance with rules, and also refers to action to ensure orderly conduct and compliance with

rules. Both aspects of discipline are the responsibility of the supervisor, and both are essential to supervisory success.

2. The four essentials of successful discipline are a complete set of rules that everyone knows and understands; a clear statement of the consequences of failing to observe the rules; prompt, consistent, and impersonal action to enforce the rules; and appropriate recognition and reinforcement of employees' positive actions.

3. Negative discipline uses a fear-and-punishment approach and a four-stage progressive formula for disciplinary action: oral warning, written warning, punishment (such as suspension), and termination.

4. The positive approach to discipline is continuous education and corrective training whenever the rules and procedures are not being observed. The four-stage formula for disciplinary action includes oral reminder, written reminder, decision-making leave with pay, and termination (see Figure 20.4).

5. With positive discipline, the negative consequences of punishment do not fester their way through the work climate, and the boss and worker do not become adversaries. Positive discipline can result in reduced turnover, absenteeism, and disciplinary problems.

6. Some mistakes to avoid include starting off too easy about enforcing the rules, acting in anger, threatening to take any action that you do not carry out, putting somebody down in front of others, exceeding your authority, evading responsibility for taking action by shifting it to someone else, or disciplining unexpectedly.

7. The set of procedures to use when confronted with a serious infringement of rules include collecting all the facts, discussing the incident with the employee, deciding on the appropriate action (if any is to be taken), documenting the process, and following up.

8. You can fire employees for just cause, meaning that the offense must affect the specific work the employee does or the operation as a whole in a detrimental way. In this chapter we outlined 10 questions that need to be asked, such as, "Has the employee been treated as others have been in similar circumstances?" before deciding whether or not to terminate.

9. During a termination interview, you need to get right to the point, listen to the employee's response, state something positive about the employee, and then move on to severance arrangements and clearance procedures.

10. As a supervisor you need to be able to prevent, recognize, and confront the forms of sexual harassment (quid pro quo, environmental, and third-party) in the workplace.

11. Harassment in the workplace is not limited to sexual harassment. All forms of harassment based on national origin, race, color, religion, gender, disability, or age are illegal.

12. Employees with substance abuse problems present certain concerns to you as supervisor. These employees tend to be late for work more often, to take more days off for sickness, to be involved in accidents more often, and to be more likely to file for workers' compensation claims.

13. As a supervisor, you have several responsibilities for dealing with substance abuse in your workplace. First, any disciplinary action that you take should be based on observable, job-related factors, such as substandard job performance or inappropriate workplace behavior rather than upon the existence or suspicion of a substance abuse problem. Second, you need to be familiar with your company's policy on substance abuse. Third, you need to be able to identify and confront constructively employees who are substance abusers to urge them to accept professional help.

14. An employee assistance program provides confidential and professional counseling and referral service to employees with problems such as addiction and dependencies, family problems, stress, and financial problems.

REFERENCES

1. The original hot-stove model is generally attributed to Douglas McGregor of Theory X and Theory Y fame. It gave warning by being red hot.

2. This section is adapted from Lawrence Steinmmetz, "The Unsatisfactory Performer: Salvage or Discharge?" *Personnel*, Vol. 45, No. 3, 1968; and from Richard Martin, "Costly Liability Can Result from Botched Dismissals, Faulty Paperwork," Nation's Restaurant News, September 15, 2000.

3. James J. Lynott, "How to Discharge an Employee and Stay out of Court," *Restaurant Hospitality*, July 2004. Vol. 88, Iss. 7, p. 62.

4. This section is adapted from Richard Martin, "Costly Liability Can Result from Botched Dismissals, Faulty Paperwork," *Nation's Restaurant News*, September 15, 2000.

5. Amy Zuber, "EEOC Suits Put Harassment on Operators Front Burner," *Nation's Restaurant News*, Vol. 33, No. 5, February 1, 1999.

6. Susan E. Long, "When Customers Harass, Employees Can Be Liable," *HR Focus*, Vol. 76, No. 3, March 1999.

7. http:www.dol.gov/asp/programs/drugs/workingpartners/stats/stats.asp

PLANNING AND ORGANIZING*

Overview

Planning Your Own Time   **Reference**
Key Point

As we mentioned briefly in Chapter 11, there are various management functions, such as planning, organizing, communicating, coordinating, staffing, motivating, controlling, and evaluating. These management functions can be seen as a sequence of steps that you take to get your job done:

1. Plan
2. Organize
3. Lead
4. Decision Making
5. Control

During the final step, you evaluate whether the objectives of your original plan have been met, and you may end up revising your plan or leaving it intact. In this manner, you have gone full circle through the management process.

---

* Authored by Jack E. Miller, John R. Walker, and Karen Eich Drummond.

In this chapter we present planning, organizing, and controlling as a means of solving some problems, avoiding others, maintaining better control over events, and giving the supervisor more time to manage. It will help you to:

■   Describe how hospitality supervisors can best plan their time on the job.

PLANNING YOUR OWN TIME

The most relentless reality about working as a supervisor in the hospitality industry is the lack of time. There is never enough private time for planning and reflective thinking. There are never enough long blocks of time in which to plan your time. Furthermore, how can you plan your time when most of your managing consists of reacting to things as they happen? How can you plan for that?

Planning your time is not going to give you any more of it; there are just so many hours in your working day. What it will do is enable you to make more effective use of those hours you work.

Your job requires that you spend the time in your day in several different ways:

■   Planning, organizing, and communicating the day's work

■   Responding to the immediate needs, demands, and inquiries of others (customers, workers, bosses, salespersons, suppliers, health inspectors, and so on)

■   Managing your people: hiring, training, directing, coaching, evaluating, disciplining

■   Dealing with crises, solving problems

■   Making reports, keeping records, enforcing rules (maintenance activities)

■   Doing some of the work yourself if you are a working supervisor

There are certain parts of the day when the job controls your time, when customer needs and demands are high: check-in and checkout times at the front desk, early mornings in housekeeping, food preparation for mealtimes in the kitchen, serving periods in the restaurant, and so on, depending on the function you supervise. At these times you must be at the disposal of anyone and everyone who needs you to answer questions, settle disputes, deal with crises, make decisions, and observe your people in action. It is important for you to be visible at such times, especially if your people serve customers directly. It is important to greet guests and to let them see that you take a personal interest in them and the way they are being treated. And it is important to your people to have you out there with them: They feel your support and they see your example. It is management visibility.

Profile

K. BRUCE FOLKINS

Courtesy of Marina Jock Restaurant

I have learned through my experience in the hospitality industry that in order to be a successful supervisor, one must master and build upon certain key fundamentals. I have been a supervisor in the field for 20 years. Currently I am the assistant director of operations at Marina Jacks in Sarasota, Florida. In my opinion, the keys to being successful are rapport, responsibility, and respect.

The first, *rapport*, must be built with both employees and clientele. It is a necessity in the hospitality industry to have good rapport with employees. This will build a relationship with each person as an individual, and provide them with a sense of security. A good rapport will not only make the shifts go by smoother, but also helps to lead everyone in the same direction. Supervisors are also obliged to build a good rapport with clientele. If the customers are treated as individuals, they will sense a connection with the restaurant, which will make them want to keep coming back.

The second key is *responsibility*. A manager must be responsible for their own actions as well as those whom they are supervising. Responsibility means being reliable, dependable, and capable of making moral decisions. Every position in the hospitality industry relies on the fundamental of responsibility, from the bottom to the top of the ladder. As a supervisor your superior, employees, and clientele are all counting on you.

Finally, after establishing rapport and demonstrated responsibility a supervisor will gain the *respect* needed to be successful. If everyone in your surroundings respects you, they know the decisions you make are for the good of the team as a whole. This will make it easier for them to follow your lead when faced with a challenging situation and do what is right both for the customer and the business.

These are segments of your time that you cannot plan for other than to set them aside and let nothing else intervene. Certain other responsibilities may also be pegged to fixed points in the day: the housekeeper's report, end-of-shift sales figures, cash deposits, and so on. The rest of the time is yours to fill with all the other duties you are required to do.

What *do* you do? If you analyze the ways in which you spend your time now, you can probably find ways to spend it better. The first step is to keep a running log for at least one typical day, several days if possible. Put down everything, including interruptions, with a beginning and an end time for each activity. Figure 21.1 is a suggested format. To save making extensive notes, you can devise symbols such as those on the chart. But make your notes complete enough to make sense to you later when you analyze them. (If you can, get someone to help you with this activity; otherwise, making the notes may interfere with doing your job.)

The next step is to see what the record shows. Total the time you spent in each activity, and divide by the number of days to figure your daily average for each. Then ask yourself several questions:

- Is the amount of time spent per day appropriate to the activity? How can you reduce the time: Do it faster? Less often? Organize it better? Delegate it?

- How does the time spent on unimportant activities compare with time spent on highly important activities? Can you distinguish important from unimportant? How can you improve the ratio?

- Are you doing things that are not really necessary? Why are you doing unproductive work?

- Are you doing things that you could delegate to someone else?

- Can you group activities better as to time and place (for example, make all your phone calls for purchases at one time during the day)?

- Was time wasted that could have been avoided by better planning? Standing plans? Better training? Better communications? Less supervision, more trust? Better records and better housekeeping? Saying no to unnecessary requests? Better decision making? An ounce of prevention?

- Does the log reveal that you do not spend any time at all on certain important but time-consuming activities you should be doing, such as making a list of sales prospects, developing holiday promotions, revising recipes, developing a procedures manual? Was it because you did not want to get started on a long project? When will you get started?

No doubt your log will raise other questions, and no doubt you will be able to work out some good answers to all the questions.

First, get rid of activities that waste time or are not worth the time they take. Major wastes of time for supervisors include the following.

- Too much socializing
- Accepting drop-in visitors

Begin	End	Total (min.)	Activity	With Whom	Importance (Rate 1–5)
7:45	7:52	7	Plan for day	self	1
7:52	7:52½	½	Q – sched change	Sam	3
7:52½	7:53	½	Plan	S	1
7:53	7:53½	½	Tel	Alice	1
7:53½	7:56	3½	Tel – replace Alice	4 people	1
7:56	8:00	4	Plan	S	1
8:00	8:13	13	Howdy rounds	O	1–2

C-E	Coaching-evaluating	Pl	Planning	1 = Most important
CR	Crisis	Pro	Production	5 = Least important
Cus	Customer	Q	Answering	
Dec	Decision		questions	
Dir	Giving directions	R	Report	
Dis	Discipline	S	Self	
Int	Interviewing	Sol	Solving problems	
O	Other(s)	Tel	Telephone	
		Tr	Training	

FIGURE 21.1 Format for keeping track of how you spend your time.

- Allowing interruptions and distractions
- Inability to say "no"
- Poor organization of papers
- Procrastination and indecision
- Reading junk mail

Stephen Covey, author of *The Seven Habits of Highly Effective People*,[1] writes about how crucial it is to spend your time on important matters and to control the amount of time spent on urgent matters, such as when the cook announces that the kitchen is running out of a popular entrée. Just because a matter is urgent doesn't mean that it is automatically important, although you will certainly have to deal with the cook's problem in a timely but not time-consuming manner.

1. To keep socializing to a minimum, ask friends and family to call at work only if there is an emergency. Also make sure that you don't spend too much time socializing with your peers and employees. To cut down on outside visitors dropping in, make it a policy that visitors must have an appointment. When you find that certain employees are forever running to you with every problem and question, help them to find their own answers, and if this doesn't help, ask them to save up several questions to go over at one time.

2. To organize your papers well, consider setting up your desk with these boxes or trays: in, out, action, pending, read, and file. All incoming papers go in the "in" box, and similarly, all outgoing papers such as memos you've written go in the "out" box. The "action" box contains papers and projects you are currently working on. The "pending" box has papers that need to be taken care of in the future. Some supervisors set up 31 file folders numbered from 1 to 31 to represent the days of the month. Pending papers are then put into the proper date. This type of file system should be checked daily. The "read" box contains magazines and other material that can be read at your leisure. The "file" box contains papers that can simply be filed away. Each of these boxes is important, but the most important file in your office sits under your desk: the wastebasket. Don't think you have to hold on to everything!

3. Now that you have eliminated some of the time-wasters, *set priorities*. List all the things you want to get done today and divide them into *musts* and *shoulds* or number them 1 and 2. Do the must things (the 1's) first. It is said that 80 percent of your results can come from 20 percent of your efforts. Use a desk calendar (Figure 21.2) to plan and schedule the must items into the top 20 percent of your time.

DECEMBER

S	M	T	W	T	F	S
						1
2	3	4	5	6	7	8
9	10	11	12	13	14	15
16	17	18	19	20	21	22
23	24	25	26	27	28	29
30	31					

TUESDAY, DECEMBER 11

7:00	●		12:00
15	·		15
30	·	*service*	30
45	·		45
8:00	●		1:00
15	·		15
30	·	*Production meeting*	30
45	·		45
9:00 *Evaluations – Jane*	●		2:00
15 *John*	·		15
30 *Jim*	·	*Make catering calls*	30
45	·		45
10:00 *New employee*	●	*Planning time*	3:00
15 *orientation*	·		15
30	·		30
45	·		45
11:00 *Taste lunch production*	●	*Order produce*	4:00
15 *service*	·	*Order beverage*	15
30	·		30
45	·		45

Evening

5:00 *Meet Art re menu design*	●	*Meet w/ banquet servers*	6:30
15	·		45
30	·		7:00
45	·	*service*	15
6:00	●		30
15	·		45

FIGURE 21.2A Planning your day with a desk calendar.

Thursday XX/XX/XX	**DAY**	Week	Month

8 am	
9 am 9.30	Meeting with Sysco management " "
10 am 10.30	Interviewing servers Interviewing servers
11 am 11.30	AM staff pre-shift meeting Monitor lunch
12 pm 12.30	Monitor lunch Monitor lunch
1 pm 1.30	Monitor lunch Lunch
2 pm 2.30	Wedding planning with the Smith's " "
3 pm 3.30	Budget meeting " "
4 pm 4.30	Order supplies PM staff pre-shift meeting
5 pm 5.30	Check dinner Monitor dinner
6 pm 6.30	Monitor dinner Monitor dinner
7 pm	Monitor dinner
8 pm	Hand over to closing manager (if all is going well on a quiet night)

Add Event	Add Alternate Time

FIGURE 21.2B Planning your day with an electronic calendar.

A weekly planning sheet is a useful supplement to your daily calendar. At the end of the day, transfer what you didn't get done to tomorrow's list, add today's accumulation of new musts and shoulds, reassess your priorities, and discard anything that no longer seems important. You will soon become adept at sorting out the time-wasters.

4. Set *aside regular periods of time without interruption* for interviews, problem solving, training, important decisions, and long-range projects. Every manager needs a quiet time each day for creativity and problem solving. Begin those time-consuming projects; divide them into manageable segments and get started on them. Getting them under way, and getting one or two of them accomplished, will renew your energy and confidence. Sometimes a small success is a big boost for self-motivation.

5. *Initiate long-range solutions to your time problems*—standing plans, better training, more delegation, reduced turnover, better communications—things that will eliminate the need for you to be in the thick of everything all the time (although still remaining visible). You will have fewer crises, fewer fires, because everyone will know what to do and how to do it. You will have more people taking more responsibility. You will have time to develop your people, to motivate, to build trust, to exercise true leadership.

There will be many days when your plans are wiped out by unexpected events. When this happens, reschedule priority items for another day and go home and get a good night's sleep. Hanging on to feelings of frustration will eat you up. But don't give up planning just because your plans don't work out some of the time. Adjusting your plans continuously is part of the planning process in your kind of job. And you can't adjust your plans if you haven't made any.

Check Your Knowledge

1. How do workers respond to change?

KEY POINT

1. To make good use of your time, eliminate time-wasters, set priorities, use a planning calendar, set aside regular periods of time without interruption for interviews, and initiate long-range solutions to your time problems.

REFERENCE

1. Steven R. Covey, *The Seven Habits of Highly Efficient People*, New York: Simon and Schuster, 1989, pp. 146–182.

DELEGATING*

Delegation is always recommended by management experts, yet the harassed management people in our industry seldom delegate. It is the least used of all management tools. Supervisors and managers will drive themselves to the point of exhaustion, ulcers, and those little white pills the doctor prescribes rather than entrust their employees with any of their own responsibilities. Why won't they share them? And why won't the people who work for them take on such responsibilities if, indeed, they will not?

In this chapter we examine how to delegate successfully in a hospitality enterprise. It will help you to:

- List the essential steps in successful delegation and discuss the importance of each.

- List common delegation mistakes and explain techniques for avoiding them.

HOW TO DELEGATE SUCCESSFULLY

Certain conditions are essential to successful delegation. You have met them in earlier chapters.

---

* Authored by Jack E. Miller, John R. Walker, and Karen Eich Drummond.

Conditions for Success

One condition is *advance planning*. This should include an overall review of who is responsible for what in your department at this time, what further responsibilities could be delegated, who is qualified to assume greater responsibilities, what training would be necessary, how various shifts in responsibilities would affect others, and when these shifts would appropriately take place. Delegation involves rearranging things, and it brings your conceptual skills into play. You have to look beyond the daily operational detail to the larger picture and get it all into focus. In addition to general overall planning, delegation requires a specific plan for each instance of delegation so that everything is clear to everyone concerned and the groundwork is prepared properly. We will say more about this in the next section.

A second condition for successful delegation is a *positive attitude toward your people*. You cannot have Theory X beliefs about your people and expect delegation to work. You don't have to be an all-out Theory Y manager, but you must have good relationships with your people, know their interests and their capabilities, and be sensitive to their needs and their potential. You must respect them as individuals and be interested in developing them, for both your sake and theirs. You need to develop the kind of leadership skill that gives people belief in themselves and makes them want to come through for you.

A third condition is *trust*. There has to be trust between you and the people to whom you delegate: You trust them enough to share your responsibility with them, and they trust you not to put something over on them or get them in over their heads. Only if you both have this trust can you get the commitment necessary to make delegation work.

A fourth condition of successful delegation is the *ability to let go and take risks*, to let your workers make some mistakes and to give yourself the same privilege. Each time you delegate a responsibility it is going to be new for you and new for the other person, and some mistakes are bound to be made; it is not going to be perfect from day one. But when a mistake happens, you don't panic and you don't jump on the other person. You take a coaching approach. The worker learns under your leadership, and you improve your leadership skills, and that is what true on-the-job training is all about. You can both learn something from every mistake, and that is how you both grow.

A fifth condition of successful delegation is *good communications*. You must keep the channels open and use them freely, send clear messages, and keep everyone informed who is affected by the delegation: the person to whom you delegate, the workers in that area, and your boss. Make sure that the people to whom you delegate know the terms of their authority and the extent of their responsibility. The more you delegate—the more people there are who share your responsibility—the more important good communications become.

The sixth condition is *commitment*. If you can involve your people in the planning and goal setting for their new tasks, they will become committed to achieving the results. You, in turn, must be committed to train, coach, and support as needed. You don't just dump the job on somebody else and abdicate.

Steps in Delegation

The first step in delegation is to *plan*. You need to identify tasks that can be assigned to someone else, and you need to figure out which of your people are able and willing to take them on. You begin by listing all the things you do. You might find it useful to keep a chart for several days on which you note absolutely everything you do in each quarter-hour. Then you sort out your activities and responsibilities into groups, as shown in Figure 22.1. After you have done this, you can arrange things that should and

Successful delegation. One of the conditions of successful delegation is to have a positive attitude toward your associates. Courtesy of The Cendant Corporation.

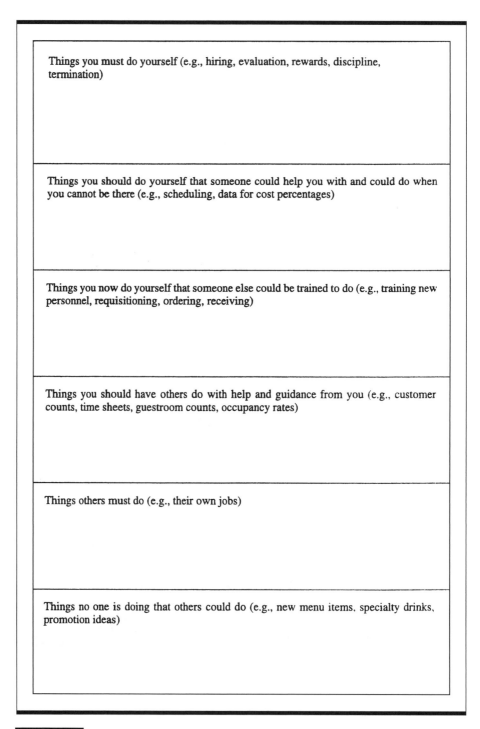

FIGURE 22.1 A way of organizing tasks that can be delegated.

Able and willing (great candidate)	Unable but willing (needs training)
Able but unwilling (needs motivation)	Unable and unwilling (poor candidate)

FIGURE 22.2 A way of planning the assignment of tasks to be delegated.

could be delegated in some kind of order: order of importance, or ease of delegating, or time saved, and choose which one or two you will tackle first.

Next you must look at your people. Choosing the right person for the responsibility is a key ingredient in successful delegation. Figure 22.2 can be useful to you here. Motivation and ability are both essential to success. Who among your people is both able and willing? If there is no one with both qualities, is there someone you can train, or someone who would be willing if you could overcome their fears or make the content of the task more attractive or offer appropriate recognition and reward?

Once you have identified the task and the person you want to have perform it, the second step is to *develop the task in detail* as a responsibility to be delegated. You define the area of responsibility, the activities that must be carried out, the results you expect, and the authority necessary to fulfill the responsibility. This is all very similar to the procedure you use in developing performance standards. In fact, a system of performance standards is an excellent tool for use in delegating responsibility. You can turn people loose in their jobs because you have told them exactly what you want, have set the achievement goals, and have trained them in the skills needed. They can take the responsibility from there and leave you free to manage.

In any delegation you do the same thing. You spell out the essential content and detailed requirements of the task, you define the limitations, and you specify the results expected. Within these limits people will be free to do the job in their own fashion. You will also spell out the specific authority that goes with the responsibility delegated: what kinds of decisions can be made without checking with the boss, what money can be spent, what actions they are authorized to take on behalf of the boss or the enterprise, and so on. You figure all this out ahead of time, and then you take the third step—you delegate.

The third step has three parts: you *delegate responsibility* for the task and the results expected, you *delegate the authority* necessary to carry it out, and you establish accountability. As we have seen, these are the three interlocking parts of delegation, and they must be spelled out clearly.

When you delegate, you meet with the chosen employee—John and Susan or whoever—in a private interview in which you describe the task, the results you expect, and the responsibility and authority it entails. It should be an informal person-to-person discussion. You should present the new assignment in a way that will stimulate interest and involvement: ask for ideas, make it a challenge, mention its present and future benefits, offer rewards if appropriate, and express confidence. Take a "we" approach, indicating your availability for support and your continuing interest in John's or Susan's success. Promise training if it is needed. However, do not put pressure on by ordering, threatening, or making it impossible to refuse. *There must be agreement on the employee's part to accept the delegation.*

Delegation is a contract. You cannot just give responsibility to people; they must accept the responsibility. They must also accept the accountability that goes with the responsibility. Unless you have fully given responsibility and authority and the other person has fully accepted responsibility and accountability, true delegation has not taken place.

It is important for your employees to know that you are sharing your responsibility with them; you are not dumping it on them and abandoning them. You, too, are accountable for the results. Give them plenty of chance for questions and plenty of reassurance for lingering doubts.

If you have matched the right person with the right assignment and have communicated it in the right way, John and Susan will be interested, pleased, motivated, challenged, and glad to have more responsibility. If you include them in setting goals for the project, you will gain their commitment to achieving them.

Set checkpoints along the way for following progress. They give you the means of keeping the employee and the assignment on target. You can modify or adjust the assignment, correct mistakes, and give advice at critical points without taking back the entire job. Checkpoints are your controls. If you can't set up controls, either don't delegate the job or redesign it so that you have some other means of tracking performance.

The fourth step in delegation is to *follow up*. Train your people as needed. This is something they have never done before, so you go through the whole story: what you want done, how you want it done, to what standard. If you don't, they will take the easiest way to do it. When they are ready to go, communicate the new status to everyone concerned, following channels, and make good on immediate rewards promised, such as relieving them from other duties to make time for the new ones. Then slip into the coaching role. Stay off their backs: Don't oversupervise and overcontrol; let them work out their own problems if they can. If they have trouble making decisions and keep asking you what to do, turn the questions back to them—ask them what *they* think. Encourage them to go it on their own. Don't let the responsibility you have given them dribble back to you.

When employees try to dump their assignment back to you, it is called reverse delegation. It may occur because the employee lacks confidence, doesn't really know enough to do the job, is afraid of making a mistake, or simply does not want the added responsibility. You need to listen to the employee and discuss the impasse, but make it perfectly clear that the task is still the employee's responsibility to complete. If you take back incomplete work, you will support the employee's dependence on you. The best way to handle reverse delegation can be stated as follows: "Don't bring me problems, bring me solutions."

Observe the checkpoints, assess progress, give feedback, and help Susan and John reach independence in their new assignments. Then congratulate yourself on two things: You are learning how to delegate successfully, and you are developing your promising employees. This is genuine on-the-job training (not the magic apron type), and you are developing genuine management skills.

Check Your Knowledge

1. Certain conditions are essential to successful delegation. What are these conditions?

2. Why do some supervisors have trouble delegating?

Common Mistakes in Delegation

When you have had no experience in delegating, it is easy to make mistakes. Perhaps one of the most common is *not communicating clearly*. Susan and John must understand what you want done, how you want it done, what results they are accountable for, and what the goals and standards are. They must understand the area, extent, and limits of their responsibility. They must know what authority they have and its limitations—what they are empowered to do, what decisions they can make on their own, and what decisions they must refer to you.

If you have done your homework carefully before you meet with them, you can communicate to John and Susan clearly. You can make sure they have understood by asking them to summarize for you the essentials of the agreement. In many cases it may be wise to put things in writing.

But often in this time-pressure industry it is easy to skip the planning stage, and it is easy to crowd the delegation of a responsibility into one of those 48-second interchanges of which your day is made. This is taking a big risk. You cannot communicate the details of the assignment itself and the implications of responsibility, authority, and accountability in that length of time. After you have delegated for a while to people who have become experienced in sharing your responsibilities, 48 seconds may be enough. But the first time you delegate to first-time delegates, make it a big deal. Communicate everything clearly, and check to see that everything is understood between you.

Another mistake it is easy for a first-timer to make is to *oversupervise*, simply because you are nervous about the whole thing. In this case you soon revert to being the boss and taking back the responsibility you have delegated. You have to remember that it won't all go perfectly, that you have picked someone you trust, that you do have checkpoints and controls, and that the only way to learn to delegate is to stop being bossy. If you jump in and correct small mistakes all the time, John and Susan are not going to come to you for help when they have a real problem.

It is also easy to make the opposite mistake—*not taking time enough to train* John and Susan in their new responsibilities and *not giving them enough support*. In this case they may become discouraged and lose their enthusiasm. The may do a poor or mediocre job, or they may leave because things are not going well for them and they are discouraged about themselves. You must take time to give them the training they need, and they must always have the feeling that you are supporting them and that they can come to you to discuss problems. Furthermore, they must experience success and build confidence if the delegation is to prove fruitful.

Delegating without setting up controls—built-in ways to monitor performance—is another common mistake. If you have not had much experience with delegation, you may overlook this essential. You need checkpoints—periodic reports, reviews, conferences—so that you can keep track of things without being involved in the work but can intervene if necessary to keep things from getting out of hand.

Still another common mistake is *job loading*, mentioned earlier—increasing the workload without adding any new responsibility, interest, or challenge. Suppose that you raise the number of rooms that must be cleaned in a given time period. This is not delegation. It is bound to cause resentment and will complicate rather than simplify your life. It demotivates the worker. In contrast, a task that includes new responsibilities can be a motivator even when extra work is involved, as long as the worker welcomes the responsibility and as long as the work can be done in the time there is to do it.

A similar mistake is to *assign dead-end, meaningless, boring, unchallenging tasks without offering any kind of incentive or reward*. In this case an increase in responsibility is not enough—it is just an extra burden, and there is nothing in it for them. You have to make it worth their while: extra money, more status, shorter hours, a promise of something better at a specific time, whatever will cause a worker to accept the responsibility willingly.

Delegating to the wrong person is another common mistake. If you know your people well and plan the delegation carefully, this will not happen to you.

A few supervisors make the mistake of *delegating unpleasant parts of their job that involve the boss-subordinate relationship, such as discipline or termination*. This simply amounts to abdicating the role of boss. The employee cannot handle it and everyone loses respect for the boss who passes the buck. As President Truman said, "The buck stops here."

Setting up overlapping responsibilities is another mistake that people sometimes make. You may carelessly give the same task to two different people, or give someone an assignment that involves someone else's department without clearing it with that department head. If your own boss is a disorganized person and the lines of authority and responsibility are not too clear, you may even find yourself delegating a responsibility that does not belong to you. Be sure that you know where you stand in the organization and what you are doing, and be careful to keep everyone informed.

You can avoid these mistakes if you plan carefully, know your people and your own responsibilities, keep in touch with what is going on, and keep your overall goals in sight—to manage your people to produce a smooth-running operation with everyone contributing the best of which each is capable.

KEY POINTS

1. Conditions for delegating successfully include advance planning, a positive attitude toward your people, trust, the ability to let go and take risks, good communications, and commitment.

2. The steps in delegation include planning, developing the task in detail, delegating responsibility for the task and results expected, delegating the authority and establishing accountability, setting checkpoints along the way for following progress, and follow-up.

3. Reverse delegation is when employees try to dump their assignment back to you.

4. Common mistakes in delegating include not communicating clearly, oversupervising, not taking time enough to train and give support, not setting up controls, job loading, assigning dead-end work without any reward, delegating to the wrong person, delegating unpleasant parts of the job that involve the boss–subordinate relationship, and setting up overlapping responsibilities.

WRITE YOUR RESUME ⋆

INTRODUCTION

The resume is one of the most critical steps in securing a job. Remember that your resume precedes the interview and is the only impression you make on your potential employer before you are (hopefully) asked to make a personal impression in an interview. Most resumes are glanced at for less than a minute—less time than

---

⋆ Authored by Lisa M. Brefere, Karen Eich Drummond, and Brad Barnes.

you might wait for a red light to turn green. Resumes that are wordy or hard to read end up in the trash, and many resumes wind up being filed away forever. Only a small percentage of resumes ever make it to the interview step.

But employers still ask for resumes, and a good resume provides a competitive edge. Your resume tells potential employers what you have accomplished already and what you can do for them now. Look at the resume as an advertising tool; it sells your talents and skills to an employer, much as a 60-second commercial sells to a consumer. Good resumes can awaken an employer's interest in you and get you what you want—an interview.

TYPES OF RESUMES

Resumes fall into one of three categories: chronological, functional, or combination (combines characteristics of both the chronological and functional). The type you choose should emphasize your strengths and deemphasize your weaknesses. most resumes these days are combination resumes, as you will see shortly.

The *chronological resume* (Figure 23.1) lists the jobs you've had by date of employment, starting with your most recent job and working backward. The education section lists your education in reverse chronological order as well. Use the chronological resume if:

- You have recent and continuous work history in the field you are looking for a job in.

- You have progressed up a clearly defined career ladder and are looking for advancement.

Employers especially like to see a clearly defined career ladder in your listing of jobs; it lets them know what you can do right now. Do not use this type of resume if you are just starting out, trying to switch fields, or have large gaps in employment—then it would be better to use the functional resume.

The *functional resume* (Figure 23.2) also includes a listing of your work experience and education, but in a brief form toward the end of the resume. Most of the functional resume is a summary of your skills and accomplishments, such as specific culinary skills you've used or menus you've developed and served. Use the functional resume if:

- You are applying for a job that is quite different from your current or past job.

- You have little to no work experience in this field.

- You are reentering the job market after a break.

Cheryl Richardson

Permanent Address:
92 Longwood Road
Aurora, NY 11593
315-555-1212

cherylrich@yahoo.com

Current Address until June:
233 University Avenue
Ithaca, NY 12830
315-555-1213

Summary

Dean's List college student in culinary arts, recently promoted to Line Cook at nationally known Moosehead Restaurant.

Work Experience

7/04–Present   **Line Cook** at Moosehead Restaurant, Ithaca, NY
Work at sauté or grill station for lunch or dinner meals in a well-known restaurant featuring healthful natural foods cuisine. Perform mise en place and food preparation. Follow safe and sanitary food procedures.
o   Test and evaluate new recipes.
o   Won Employee of the Month (June 2005).

10/02–6/04   **Preparation Cook** at Moosewood Restaurant, Ithaca, NY
Performed all preparation tasks in kitchen emphasizing scratch cooking and vegetarian dishes. Completed all duties in timely fashion while maintaining sanitation standards.
o   Received "Excellent" performance evaluations.

Summers 2001 and 2002   **Assistant Cook** at Lenape Summer Camp, Seneca Falls, NY
Under Head Cook's direction, did basic food preparation tasks, cooking, and baking. Assisted in purchasing, receiving, and inventory management.

Education and Certification

May 2006   Bachelor of Professional Studies in Culinary Arts, Olympia University, Ithaca, NY

Dean's List every semester (Anticipated)

Treasurer, Culinary Club (sophomore year)

ServSafe® Food Protection Manager, #2364656 (National Restaurant Association Educational Foundation)

FIGURE 23.1 Chronological Resume.

The functional resume emphasizes what you can do and deemphasizes where you have worked. Many skills, such as management skills, are transferable between industries, and this type of resume especially helps people who are switching to the culinary field or just starting out after college.

Tim Fitzpatrick

3626 Chestnut Drive, Salina, CA 84529   408-392-8942   tfitz@aol.com

Seeking an entry-level Cook position in a restaurant.

College student in culinary arts with diverse cooking and foodservice experience, including food preparation and supervising.

Culinary Arts:
- Experienced with kitchen food preparation and cooking equipment.
- Competent in basic food preparation techniques, including cutting.
- Use standardized recipes.
- Follow portion control guidelines.
- Plate and garnish foods.

Sanitation
- ServSafe® certified.
- Follow appropriate cleaning and sanitation procedures.

Supervision
- Supervised five employees.
- Scheduled, trained, motivated, and coached employees.
- Solved problems.

Employment

Cold Food Preparation, Bay Community College.   September 2004 to present. Part-time.

Head Waiter, The Tides Retirement Community.   June 2003 to August 2004. Part-time.

Waiter, The Tides Retirement Community.   June 2002 to June 2003. Part-time.

Education

Associate in Occupational Studies in Culinary Arts anticipated May 2005. Bay Community College.

FIGURE 23.2 Functional Resume.

Many employers look on functional resumes with some level of distrust. While they can see what sorts of skills and abilities you have, they don't know where you learned them. This is a good reason to consider the next type of resume.

The *combination resume* (Figure 23.3) combines features from both the chronological and functional resumes into a type of resume that is increasingly popular. Basically, you showcase your skills and achievements at the beginning of the resume, typically in a section entitled *Profile* or *Summary*. Then you go on to describe your jobs and education in reverse chronological order. It's a format that almost any jobseeker can customize to meet his or her needs.

THE INGREDIENTS OF A GREAT RESUME

A great resume sells a potential employer the idea that you are the person to do the job. Your resume will do this most effectively if you remember that it is not just a job description of your current and past jobs. For a resume to be great, you need to:

- Choose and highlight the parts of your background that position you for the type of job you are currently seeking.
- Discuss what you did in other jobs, but especially how well you did it.
- Include measurable achievements and accomplishments.

Following are guidelines for what to include and what not to include on your resume.

What You Must Include

Most professional resume writers agree that you must include these sections in your resume.

- Contact information (including a businesslike email address)
- Profile (short summary of qualifications)
- Professional experience
- Education
- Professional licenses/certifications (such as ServSaf®)
- Professional affiliations (such as membership in the American Culinary Federation)

Richard Plumb, C.E.C., A.A.C.

211 West Greenwich Avenue
Greenwich, CT 07041
203-437-9365 (h) 203-530-8821 (c)
brewchef@yahoo.com

Profile

- Experienced Executive Chef and Director of Operations. Have operated multiple restaurants accommodating over 500 guests.
- Developed kitchen and menus for new brewery restaurants.
- Excel in developing successful menus and recipes.
- Proven team-building and motivational skills have kept staff turnover below 40%.

Experience

Director of Operations/Corporate Executive Chef
Boston Hops, Inc., New York, NY   May 2000–present
Responsible for menu development, kitchen/bar design, opening plan and execution, training, and staff hiring for three new brewery restaurants.

- Redesigned kitchen.
- Upgraded menus.
- Developed corporate buying policies, recipes, restaurant standards, and training manuals.

Executive Chef/Back of House Director of Operations
Greenwich Regency, Greenwich, CT   May 1996–May 2000
Responsible for 32 Cooks and 6 Sous Chefs in a $9.5 million food and beverage operation. Also supervised stewarding, purchasing, and receiving.

- Five-year average of 29% food cost and 30% labor cost.
- Employee retention improved 75%.
- Operation featured in numerous publications.

Chef de Cuisine
Pebble Creek Café, Purchase, NY   June 1993–March 1996
Instrumental in kitchen and restaurant design of American regional restaurant. Responsible for all costs for front and back of the house. Developed menus, monthly marketing tools, and advertising strategies.

- Increased quarterly sales 25%.
- Demonstrated project planning and design skills.

FIGURE 23.3 Combination Resume.

Education	A.O.S. in Culinary Arts, April 1991 New Jersey Culinary Institute Nutritional Cuisine, January 2000, New Jersey Culinary Institute, 20-hour course
Certification	Certified Executive Chef, January 2000 American Culinary Federation
Associations	Active Member, American Culinary Federation, since 1991 The Chefs Association of Westchester and Lower Connecticut since 1991, President from 1994 to 1995
Awards	1998 Chef of the Year, The Chef's Association of Westchester and Lower Connecticut Delaware Valley Chefs Association Culinary Competition, ACF Silver Medal, 1997 U.S. Team Member, International Ice Carving Competition, Gold Medal, 1996 Southern New Jersey Chefs Association Culinary Competition, First Prize, Poultry Platter, 1995

FIGURE 23.3 (Continued)

Additional sections that present information such as computer skills and awards are also appropriate.

What You Might Include

You might include a job objective, a short statement of the type of job you are looking for. It is important that the job objective be concise and not too broad—for example, "Job Objective: Sous Chef in Club Setting." Some applicants like to use an objective; others don't. The information stated in your objective will be stated in your cover letter, so it is not absolutely essential that it be on your resume. However, if you are not sending your resume in for a specific job opening, it's a good idea to include a job objective because the employer is not immediately associating your resume with a specific opening.

Place your job objective below the contact information on the resume and check that it is appropriate each time you send your resume out. You want your stated job objective to closely match the job you are applying for.

What to Omit

Don't put any of these on your resume:

- Reference information (just state that a list of references is available)
- Availability
- Salary history
- Diversity issues
- Photographs

It is customary to give out your reference list only at an interview or after you have been interviewed for a job. Availability is also a subject that can be addressed in an interview. You don't want to advertise that you are available immediately—it makes you look desperate! Salary is yet another issue that should be discussed later. As described in the chapter on interviewing, it is best not to discuss salary with the employer until you are offered the job. Once you receive an offer, you are in a much better position to negotiate a good salary.

WRITE YOUR RESUME

The type of resume discussed in detail here is a combination resume, which begins with a profile in which you highlight your qualifications and accomplishments. Then it moves on to a chronological review of your professional (work) experience, education and certifications, professional affiliations, and other information you want to include. See the Resume Worksheet on the student website to help organize the information for your resume.

Contact Information

At the top of every resume is your contact information, including your mailing address, telephone numbers, and email address. It is acceptable to use the postal abbreviation for your state instead of writing out the name of your state. For example, use CT for Connecticut. Don't use any abbreviations for your street address (such as Ave. for Avenue) or city (such as NYC for New York City).

When typing out your phone number(s), be sure to include your area code and designate which number is which, as shown in the following example.

(H) 272-356-7890
(C) 272-367-5237

You may put parentheses around the area code, but don't put 1 before the area code. Make sure you have a reliable answering service for every phone number you put on your resume, including cell phones. Of course, once you send your resume to potential employers, you must frequently check for voicemail messages.

If you are a student still in college, it is best to give both your college and home addresses and telephone numbers and to note when to use each address. For example, you might state next to your college address something like "Contact through May."

Email represents yet another way to communicate with employers. You should definitely list an email address, one that sounds professional. Don't type partyguy aol.com on your resume and then wonder why you aren't getting any phone calls. Job hunting requires a suitably professional email address. Your Internet provider may allow you to pick several email addresses, so choose one with a neutral feel. It's quite common for job hunters to reserve one email address for the resume. If you want a new email address, check out the free email accounts available from companies such as hotmail.com.

Profile

Your profile section appears right below your contact information so the employer can quickly get an idea of who you are, what you can do, and how you can contribute. This section can be titled Profile, any of the following names, or any appropriate name you can think of.

- Career Profile
- Professional Profile
- Summary
- Qualifications
- Summary of Qualifications

- Areas of Expertise (or Proficiency)
- Key Strengths
- Core Competencies
- Professional Highlights
- Achievements or Accomplishments
- Highlights of Skills and Experience
- Highlights of Qualifications

This section can take the form of a bulleted list, a paragraph, or both. Whichever format you choose, make this section brief and focused. Highlight your experience, accomplishments, and skills. As you write a rough draft of this section, make sure it answers this question: "If I had only 30 seconds to get someone to hire me, what would I say?"

When you mention your skills, be sure they are directly related to the type of position you want. Also, stating "hardworking employee" is not nearly as strong as evidence such as "Promoted from preparation cook to line cook within three months because of excellent knife skills and work ethic."

Here is a bulleted profile for a highly experienced Certified Master Chef.

Profile

- Successfully completed Certified Master Chef test.
- Over 20 years' experience in quality food preparation.
- Thorough understanding of all facets and styles of foodservice.
- Well versed in many ethnic and international cuisines.
- Able to produce quality results while adhering to well-planned budgets.
- Over 8 years' experience in multi-unit management.
- Excellent human resource management skills, maintaining a departmental employee retention average of 3.5 years.
- Self-motivated quality- and cost-oriented manager.
- Highly trained in nutritionally conscious cuisine.

Of course, this profile is pretty long because of the chef's extensive and noteworthy culinary career. Yours will most likely have fewer bullets. Note that the most significant achievements are noted first. The format of this profile could be changed by combining the first three bullets into a short paragraph and then bulleting the remaining points.

A profile for someone coming out of college with some work experience in the industry might look like this.

Profile Hardworking and reliable culinary student distinguished by:

- Over two years' experience as a preparation cook promoted to line cook at La Brasserie.

- Silver Medal earned in ACF-sanctioned hot food competition, category K.

- President's Honor Roll every semester.

- Strong interpersonal and organizational skills.

Make sure that some of the points you make are measurable achievements, like earning a silver medal at a culinary competition, saving the department $25,000 a year in labor, and cutting staff turnover by 25%.

You may want to write up your profile after you have completed the work experience and education sections. Once you have those sections ready, it will be easier for you to see which skills, achievements, and experience you want to highlight in the profile.

Professional Experience

After the profile, your next section will probably be professional experience, although in some cases it may be education. A good rule of thumb is to put the stronger section first. For example, if you are seeking a job as a culinary educator, the amount of formal education you have is important, so you may want to highlight your degrees at the top of the resume. For most culinary positions, put your work experience first unless you have almost no experience.

You don't have to call this section Professional Experience. Other possible names include the following.

- Professional Background
- Employment History
- Work History
- Work Experience
- Experience

- Career Track

- Employment Chronicle

- Career History

- Career Path

To start writing up your work experience, use the Resume Worksheet to write down information about your jobs. Start with your current or most recent job, and then work backward. The worksheet will help you decide what to include on the resume.

When writing up your job duties, think in terms of the broad responsibilities you had and the specific tasks or duties you performed for each responsibility. For example, on your resume you could state the broad responsibility first, and then present a bullet list of important duties and notable accomplishments. Don't just discuss what you did; also include *how well* you did it. Employers want to see measurable achievements. It helps them see how you can contribute to their organization's bottom line. Here's an example.

Executive Chef   June 2000–July 2004

Big Oak Café, Troy, New York

Supervised and coordinated the food purchasing and production for kitchen producing 1,000 meals/day.

- Purchased over $1 million of food and supplies yearly.

- Saved $25,000 in the first year after improving bid system and updating purchase specifications.

- Developed and instituted regular seasonal menu changes.

- Reduced kitchen labor cost by 5%.

- Quality of food consistently rated "good" or higher.

- Conducted formal monthly training sessions and daily coaching of employees.

Note three points in this example. First, there are no complete sentences; each statement is a phrase. Second, each phrase begins with a specific, descriptive verb. For example, instead of a general verb such as *manage*, use precise verbs such as *organize* or *direct*. Table 23.1 lists action verbs you can use when preparing your resume. Try to avoid phrases that begin with "Responsible for"; instead, find an appropriate verb. Third, once you have climbed the career ladder, it is assumed you can cook. So talk about how many people you supervised, the volume of the business, and how you

TABLE 23.1 Verbs for Resumes

COMMUNICATION SKILLS

arranged	composed	edited	motivated	publicized
addressed	conferred	explained	negotiated	published
authored	corresponded	formulated	persuaded	wrote
clarified	drafted	informed	presented	

CREATIVE SKILLS

conceptualized	designed	fashioned	illustrated	originated
created	established	focused	invented	performed

CULINARY SKILLS

arranged	cooled	garnished	planned	simmered
assembled	cut	griddled	poached	specified
baked	deep-fried	grilled	prepared	steamed
boiled	designed	identified	produced	stored
braised	determined	judged	purchased	thickened
broiled	dressed	measured	roasted	used
calculated	filleted	microwaved	sautéd	
chose	finished	pan-broiled	scaled	
converted	flavored	pan-fried	seasoned	
cooked	formulated	performed	set up	

FINANCIAL SKILLS

administered	computed	formulated	purchased	sold
analyzed	contracted	increased	recommended	trimmed
audited	cut	marketed	reconciled	
balanced	decreased	planned	recorded	
budgeted	eliminated	projected	reduced	
calculated	forecast	provided	saved	

HUMAN RESOURCE SKILLS

coached	encouraged	instructed	oriented	specified
counseled	evaluated	interviewed	placed	staffed
delegated	facilitated	mediated	promoted	streamlined
developed	guided	moderated	recruited	taught
empowered	helped	motivated	represented	trained
enabled	hired	negotiated	screened	

`TABLE 23.1` (Continued).

MANAGEMEMT SKILLS

accepted	created	finished	optimized	restored
accomplished	defined	focused	organized	restructured
achieved	delivered	founded	originated	revamped
adapted	demonstrated	formulated	overhauled	revitalized
administered	designed	generated	oversaw	saved
advanced	developed	guided	performed	scheduled
advised	devised	headed	persuaded	solved
allocated	diagnosed	identified	planned	spearheaded
analyzed	directed	implemented	prepared	streamlined
appraised	diversified	improved	presented	structured
approved	eliminated	increased	presided	summarized
assigned	engineered	innovated	prioritized	supervised
assisted	enlisted	inspected	processed	surveyed
chaired	established	installed	produced	traveled
clarified	evaluated	instituted	provided	trimmed
conducted	examined	introduced	regulated	upgraded
consolidated	executed	launched	remodeled	
contributed	expanded	led	repaired	
controlled	expedited	maintained	represented	
coordinated	facilitated	monitored	resolved	

MARKETING AND SALES SKILLS

compiled	distributed	generated	maintained	obtained
consolidated	expedited	increased	marketed	stimulated

managed costs. If your experience is mostly cooking, be careful of repetitive wording when describing your jobs. For example, don't keep listing "sautéed fish and chicken" for each job.

Another way to format your work experience is to start with a short paragraph listing your responsibilities and duties, and then have a bulleted list of your accomplishments. Here is how that approach looks:

Executive Chef   June 2000–July 2004
Big Oak Café, Troy, New York

Supervised and coordinated the food purchasing and production for kitchen producing 1,000 meals/day. Purchased over $1 million of food and supplies yearly. Developed and instituted regular seasonal menu changes. Conducted formal monthly training sessions and daily coaching of employees.

Performance Highlights

- Saved $25,000/year after improving bid system and updating purchase specifications.
- Reduced kitchen labor cost by 5%.
- Quality of food consistently rated "good" or higher.

When thinking of your accomplishments and achievements, ask yourself if you ever did the following.

1. Save your employer money—If so, how much?
2. Increase sales—If so, how much?
3. Increase profitability—If so, how much?
4. Bring in new business—If so, how much?
5. Increase employee retention—If so, how much?
6. Decrease payroll costs, including overtime—If so, how much?
7. Increase guest satisfaction—If so, how much?
8. Increase profitability—If so, how much?
9. Decrease or keep food cost constant—If so, how much?
10. Increase check average—If so, how much?
11. Reduce purchasing costs—If so, how much?
12. Update and improve policies and procedures?
13. Initiate and implement new menus or programs?
14. Implement new hardware, software, or other systems?
15. Improve productivity?
16. Improve communications?
17. Design new training programs?
18. Introduce new standards?
19. Streamline operations, functions, or support activities?

20. Realign staffing to meet business demand and/or decrease costs?

21. Receive a prize/honor/award from an employer, school, or professional organization?

22. Manage special projects, such as kitchen renovation or purchasing new equipment?

23. Develop unique skills or qualifications?

24. Have public speaking experience?

25. Have culinary industry certifications?

Quantify your achievement whenever possible, as in "Increased check average 5%."

Education and Certifications

Next, discuss your education and certifications. Conceptually divide this section into three parts:

1. College

2. Continuing education (or lifelong learning)

3. Certifications

If this section is long, you can certainly separate it into two or three sections.

As long as you are in college or have graduated from college, you probably do not need to include high school information. If you went to a particularly prestigious high school or one with a well-known culinary program you were in, you might include the name of the school and program and the year you graduated.

With regard to your college education, the following items are the bare minimum you must put on your resume.

■ Type of degree received, your major, and date of graduation—always list the degree before the name of the college or university at which you earned it. If you have graduated, you could use this format:

Bachelor of Professional Studies in Culinary Arts, 2003
Culinary University, Denver, Colorado

If you are still in school, give the month and year when you anticipate completing your degree. For example:

Associate in Occupational Studies in Culinary Arts anticipated May 2006
Culinary University, Denver, Colorado

If you are not that close to finishing your degree, you could say this:

Currently pursuing an associate degree in Occupational Studies in Culinary
Arts
Culinary University, Denver, Colorado

If you minored at college in an area related to culinary, mention that as well. If your college major was unrelated to the culinary field (such as German or history), mention your degree but don't specify your major.

- Names of colleges and universities you've attended—if you transferred from a community college, for example, to a four-year college and earned your degree, it is not absolutely essential to mention the community college. However, if it might work to your benefit to mention the community college, as when the community college's culinary program is well known, include it on your resume. You can also include your cumulative average if it is good—meaning at least over 3.0 if your school uses a standard 4.0 scale. List your cumulative average like this: 3.0/4.0.

Of course, you can include many other aspects of your college education on your resume.

- **Academic honors** — Note academic honors such as Dean's List, awards, honor societies, and scholarships.

- **Internships** — Mention where you completed your internships; note the time frame and what you did.

- **Activities** — Many college students don't have much work experience, so listing involvement in school or extracurricular activities is important. Employers look for this because such involvement shows initiative. If you were involved in a culinary club or association, especially if you held an office, include this information on your resume. Holding an office shows leadership. Include volunteer activities.

- **International study** — Include where you studied, when, and a brief statement of what you did.

- **Special projects/Team projects** — If you don't have much work experience, you may want to briefly describe a special college project, perhaps a team project, if it is related to the position you are applying for. For example, you may have worked on a project involved in catering events or culinary competitions.

- **Courses taken** — Listing four to eight relevant courses may benefit you if you are a recent graduate and don't have much work experience.

After your college section, mention relevant continuing education courses you have taken. These could include classes provided by an employer, workshops or seminars attended at industry-related conferences, continuing education courses taken to maintain American Culinary Federation certification, and formal education courses such as computer classes taken online or in the classroom. Specify the year in which you took the training. If the training was particularly lengthy, you can also add the number of hours or days it required. Don't forget to include computer courses you have taken.

You can also include certifications, such as Certified Culinarian, in this section, or you may want to list them in a separate section. Specify the certification you have, the certifying organization, and when you received the certification.

Professional Affiliations

Your memberships in appropriate professional associations show your enthusiasm and dedication to your career. Membership is also important for keeping up in the field and networking with colleagues.

Additional Sections

- **Computer skills** — Every job requires computer skills. List the software programs you can use with at least basic proficiency.

- **Foreign language skills** — If you are fluent in a language other than English, especially Spanish, do mention it on your resume. If you are not fluent but can read, write, or speak well, include this information too. Just make sure you write down, for example, "Speak Spanish" or "Read French."

- **Volunteer work** — Chefs frequently do volunteer work with food banks and other organizations. Mention relevant volunteer work you have performed, along with the name of the organization and the year.

- **Awards/Honors** — List awards and honors you received, from employer awards to medals won at culinary competitions. Give the name and year and describe the award/honor, if necessary.

■ **Military service** — Mention the branch of service in which you served, your highest rank, your dates of service, decorations or awards, and special skills or training you received that could further your career.

■ **Publications** — If you have published an article in an industry magazine, a book, or any other relevant material, list the title and publication date.

■ **Presentations** — List presentations you made at professional meetings and in other professional settings.

References

Resumes usually do not list names of references. Most resumes close with the statement "References available on request."

Rough Draft

Now that you have completed the Resume Worksheet, you are ready to make a rough draft of your resume. For your rough draft, just concern yourself with the information you want to include and how you want to say it. Don't worry about laying it out on your fancy resume paper yet. At this stage, you just want to decide what to say and what to leave out. See the Resume Draft, which is on the student web site, to start working on your rough draft.

Don't plan to tackle this project in one night. You will need a number of work sessions to get a rough draft that you can type up. Take time to edit your resume at every step. Ask friends, teachers, and family for ideas and feedback.

MORE RESUME GUIDELINES

Once you have prepared a rough draft, it's time to take a look at these points to consider as you type it.

Length

The length of your resume usually depends on the amount of work experience you have. Although you may have been told that your resume shouldn't exceed one page, if you have carefully chosen relevant material that requires two pages, that's fine. Resumes are frequently two and sometimes three pages long. If you have over ten years of experience, a two-page resume is common. Make each page a full page. If your last page has just a few lines on it, compress your information to remove the excess page.

Fonts and Formatting

Use the following guidelines to format your resume.

- As for any business document, allow 1-inch margins on the sides, top, and bottom of each page.
- Double-space between sections and entries. Single-space paragraphs and bulleted lists. Be consistent with your spacing.
- Paragraphs should be short—five or six sentences at most. Break longer paragraphs into two or more.
- Pick out a font that is up-to-date and crisp.
  - Arial
  - Bookman
  - Century Schoolbook
  - Franklin Gothic
  - Palatino
  - Tahoma

  Times New Roman is also an acceptable font, but because it is used frequently, it is less distinctive than those noted here. The serif fonts—those where the letters have small lines extending from them, usually at the top and bottom—are often easier to read than sans-serif fonts. Examples of serif fonts include Bookman, Century Schoolbook, Garamond, and Palatino. Arial, Franklin Gothic, and Tahoma are sans serif fonts. Avoid fonts such as Courier that give the same amount of space for each letter, even though some letters are wider than others.

- In most cases, your best font size will be 10, 11, or 12, although headings and your name should be taller. For example, if you use 12-point Arial for the body text, try 14-point Arial for section headings and 16- to 18-point Arial for your name at the top of the resume.
- Don't clutter your resume with too much text. Lots of white space makes your resume easier to read. White space is the space on a page not occupied by text or pictures.

- Use underlining sparingly, if at all. Instead of underlining, try boldface, which is often better at getting attention. Further, it's easier to read boldface type than underlined text. Boldface works well for section titles and job titles. Don't use boldface to attract attention to a word or phrase in a sentence.

- Don't type words with all capital letters; this is very difficult to read. Instead, capitalize the first letter (if appropriate) and then switch to lower case.

- When you make a list, use a bullet (round, square, or diamond-shaped) or a tiny box instead of a hyphen. Use the same bullet style for each section or for the entire resume.

- Use a horizontal line to separate your contact information from the rest of the resume. The line helps organize the contents of the resume. You might set off each section with horizontal lines, as in Figure 23.1.

- To give your resume a consistent flow, maintain the same style from beginning to end. Every section should have the same design elements. For example, if your education heading is bold and centered, every section heading should be bold and centered.

Formats

Most resumes are set in either one or two columns. The resumes in Figures 23.2, 23.4, and 23.5 use one column, while the resumes in Figures 23.1 and 23.3 use two columns. The one-column format allow you to fit a little more information on a page because more space is available (but you still must leave plenty of white space). You can certainly type up your resume in both formats and then decide which looks best. You can even combine both formats by using one column for your contact, objective, and profile sections and then switching to a two-column format for the rest of the resume.

Let's take a look at the five resumes in this chapter to develop a better idea of ways to format a resume.

- Figure 23.1. The body of this resume is set in 12-point Arial, the section heads in 14-point bold, and the person's name in 16-point bold. In this use of the two-column format, the dates of employment and college are in the left column, and the job and education information are in the right column. The horizontal line under each section heading, along with the appropriate use of white space, make the headings stand out and result in an easy-to-read resume.

Cheryl Richardson

Permanent Address:
92 Longwood Road
Aurora, NY 11593
315-593-8270

cherylrich@yahoo.com

Current Address until June:
233 University Avenue
Ithaca, NY 12830
315-229-5987

Summary

Dean's List college student in culinary arts, recently promoted to Line Cook at nationally known Moosehead Restaurant.

Work Experience

Line Cook at Moosehead Restaurant, Ithaca, NY   July 2004–Present
Work at sauté or grill station for lunch or dinner meals in a well-known restaurant featuring healthful natural foods cuisine. Perform mise en place and food preparation. Follow safe and sanitary food procedures.
• Test and evaluate new recipes.
• Employee of the Month (June 2005).

Preparation Cook at Moosewood Restaurant, Ithaca, NY   October 2002–June 2004
Performed all preparation tasks in kitchen emphasizing scratch cooking and vegetarian dishes. Completed all duties in timely fashion while maintaining sanitation standards.
• Received "Excellent" performance evaluations.

Assistant Cook at Lenape Summer Camp, Seneca Falls, NY   Summers 2001 and 2002
Under Head Cook's direction, did basic food preparation tasks, cooking, and baking. Assisted in purchasing, receiving, and inventory management.

Education and Certification

Bachelor of Professional Studies in Culinary Arts   Anticipated May 2006
Olympia University, Ithaca, NY

Dean's List every semester

Treasurer, Culinary Club (sophomore year)

ServSafe® Food Protection Manager, #2364656 (National Restaurant Association)

FIGURE 23.4 One-Column Resume Sample.

Brad Barnes, C.M.C., C.C.A., A.A.C.

213 Davis Avenue, Christianson, NY 10735
203.555.0150
BandBsolutions@aol.com

Qualifications

Culinary Skills

- Very strong experience in quality food preparation.
- Thorough understanding of all facets and styles of service.
- Well versed in many ethnic and international cuisines.
- Able to produce quality results while adhering to budget.
- Committed to upholding the highest standards of operation in the professional kitchen.
- Highly trained in nutritionally conscious cuisine.

Management Skills

- Self-motivated, quality- and cost-directed manager.
- Solid experience in multi-unit management.
- Excellent human resource management skills, maintaining a departmental employee retention average of 3.5 years.
- Skilled in sanitary management of food preparation facilities.
- Experienced in public speaking, presentations, and seminars.
- Developed, wrote, and presented educational videos.

Professional Experience

Chef/Owner, B & B Solutions   2001–present

Partner in Food and Beverage Management firm currently operating food and beverages operations in two Manhattan properties: the Embassy Suites Hotel in Battery Park City and the Hilton Times Square. Food and Beverages is a freestanding entity and is required to be totally self-sustaining while providing 24-hour room service, an employee cafeteria, and many other hotel services.

- Report on profitability, quality, and operations to our client.
- Reversed the operations from substantial losses to break even.

Corporate Executive Chef, ITB Restaurant Group   1992–2001

Oversaw profitability, training, menu development, and staffing of kitchens in three restaurants while acting as executive chef for the flagship operation, 64 Greenwich Avenue.

FIGURE 23.5 Resume of Very Experienced Chef.

64 Greenwich Avenue Restaurant, 125 seats/$2.4 million annual sales
Responsible for design of the kitchen as well as the purchase of all
equipment. Developed all menus. Developed profit and loss prospectus for
opening food sales.

- Increased profitability of food sales by 10% since the opening
  through a customer-driven sales-oriented approach to menu
  development as well as a concentrated effort to retain employees
  and increase productivity.
- Practiced an aggressive approach to purchasing by constantly
  researching new resources while maintaining a good business
  relationship with purveyors.
- Initiated our banquet/catering division in order to expand sales as
  well as make better use of available staff and facility.
- Banquet/catering has grown to 35% of annual sales at a higher
  profitability than à la carte service.
- Maintained a constant learning atmosphere in the kitchen through
  promotion from within and the rotation of culinary school externs
  in the facility.

The Black Bass Grille, 65 seats/$1.4 million annual sales
The Black Goose Grille, 120 seats/$2 million annual sales
Set tone and style of menus and worked with the Chef to produce profitable,
customer-driven menus that stayed within our philosophy and food standards.
Wrote and implemented all front-of-the-house training procedures.

- Assured profitability of each kitchen through guidance in food cost
  control, staffing, and time management.
- Produced all graphics for seasonal menus.

Executive Chef, The Black Bass Grille   1989–1992
Hired to change the style of food and service from a tavern-style pub to a white-
tablecloth casual dining restaurant.

- Raised check average from $20 to $37.
- Increased yearly sales from $780,000 to $1.4 million.
- Analyzed lunch business, which showed a history of poor customer
  counts, then recommended closing for that meal period, saving the
  company about $16,000 annually.
- Purchased new equipment per budget to facilitate new style of
  service.

Executive Chef, Greenwich Island Catering, $1.8 million annual sales 1987–1989
Supervised all food production and event logistics, including staffing and
equipment setup. Maintained three daily corporate accounts.

FIGURE 23.5 (Continued)

Executive Chef, The Brass Register at Four Squares, 225 seats, 240 banquet seats, $1.6 million annual sales   1980–1985

Worked as Sous Chef and then Executive Chef. Started catering and banquet service.

Education and Certifications

A.O.S. in Culinary Arts, Culinary Institute of America, 1987

Nutritional Cuisine course, Culinary Institute of America, 1995

Certified Master Chef, American Culinary Federation

Certified Culinary Administrator, American Culinary Federation

Certified ACF International Judge

Certified ServSafe® Food Protection Manager

Certified TIPS Alcohol Service Trainer

Professional Organizations

Member, American Culinary Federation

Member, American Academy of Chefs

Member, World Association of Master Chefs

Honors and Awards

President's Medal from the American Culinary Federation

Coach and Design Director for American Culinary Federation Team USA, 2004 and 2000

Hermann Rusch Humanitarian Award for Contributions to 9/11 Relief Effort

Two Gold Medals, IKA/HOGA Culinary Olympics, Frankfurt, Germany

"Chef of the Year," The Chefs Association of Westchester and Lower Connecticut

FIGURE 23.5 (Continued)

Cheryl Richardson

92 Longwood Road
Aurora, NY 11593
315-593-8270
cherylrich@yahoo.com

Summary

Dean's List college student in culinary arts, recently promoted
to Line Cook at nationally known Moosehead Restaurant.

Work Experience

7/04-Present   Line Cook at Moosehead Restaurant, Ithaca, NY
Work at sauté or grill station for lunch or dinner meals
in a well-known restaurant featuring healthful natural foods
cuisine. Perform mise en place and food preparation. Follow safe
and sanitary food procedures. Test and evaluate new recipes. Won
Employee of the Month (June 2005).

10/02-6/04 Preparation Cook at Moosewood Restaurant, Ithaca, NY
Performed all preparation tasks in kitchen emphasizing scratch
cooking and vegetarian dishes. Completed all duties in timely
fashion while maintaininq sanitation standards. Received
"Excellent" performance evaluations.

Summers, 2001 and 2002.   Assistant Cook at Lenape Summer Camp,
Seneca Falls, NY. Under Head Cook's direction, did basic food
preparation tasks, cooking, and baking. Assisted in purchasing,
receiving, and inventory management.

Education and Certification

Bachelor of Professional Studies in Culinary Arts Anticipated
May 2006, Olympia University, Ithaca, NY

Dean's List every semester

Treasurer, Culinary Club (sophomore year)

ServSafe® Food Protection Manager, #2364656 (National Restaurant
Association)

FIGURE 23.6 Scannable Resume.

- Figure 23.2. This one-column resume uses 12-point New Century Schoolbook as the body font. The section names and contact information are set in 14-point type and the person's name in 16-point. The name, job titles, and section names are bolded. Because this is a functional resume, the middle has horizontal lines that emphasize the person's skills. Italics are used in this section for the top line.

- Figure 23.3. This two-column resume uses a *T* set of lines to make it look appealing. The font is Palatino, with 12-point type for the body, 16-point for the section heads, and 18-point for the person's name. The name, section heads, and job titles are bolded. The first column contains the section names and the second column the dates and information. If you like how this format looks but have more than one address to list, you can start your vertical line just below the contact section.

- Figure 23.4. This one-column resume shows the section heads in italic bold and centered with horizontal lines above and below for emphasis. The body font is 12-point Garamond, and the name font is 18-point. Section heads, job titles, and the person's name are bold. The years of employment are kept to the right.

- Figure 23.5. This resume is typical of someone with a lot of experience, expertise, and involvement in the culinary profession. The font is Franklin Gothic (12-point body text, 14-point section heads, and 16-point name). Section names, job titles, and employer names are bolded. The section headings appear to the left and have a horizontal line coming out to add emphasis and clarity. The body text is tabbed in to make the section headings more prominent.

The formats of these resumes can also be found on the student website.

Keywords

Keywords are nouns or noun phrases that state job titles, skills, duties, and accomplishments (see Table 23.2). Some employers scan resumes into a database. Keywords help the employer identify applicants who may be able to fill a specific position. This is described in length in a moment. For now, you want to use appropriate keywords when possible in your resume. Another source of keywords is job advertisements.

Voice and Tense

Even though you never say *I* on a resume, the subject of each phrase is indeed *I*. Be sure your verbs agree with the first person. Use the past tense of verbs when talking

TABLE 23.2 Culinary and Management Keywords

CULINARY KEYWORDS

Back-of-the-house operation	Food service management	Mise en place
Banquet operations	Front-of-the-house operations	Multi-unit operations
Banquet sales	Garnish	Profit and loss responsibility
Budget administration	Guest relations	Portion control
Catering operations	Guest satisfaction	Presentation
Club management	Information technology	Product positioning
Corporate dining room	Inventory control	Project design
Customer retention	Labor cost controls	Project management
Customer service	Leadership	Purchasing
Employee training	Marketing	Sales
Food and beverage operations	Menu planning	Service management
Food cost controls	Menu pricing	

MANAGEMEMT KEYWORDS

Benchmarking	Leadership	Problem solving
Communication	Leadership development	Profit and loss management
Consensus building	Long-range planning	Quality improvement
Corporate culture	Multi-unit operations management	Sales management
Corporate mission	New business development	Team-building
Decision making	Organizational development	

about past jobs and events. Use the present tense when describing what you do in your current job.

Spelling, Punctuation, and Grammar

When in doubt, use a good dictionary and a style guide. Use the dictionary to determine when certain words are hyphenated or capitalized. Also:

- Capitalize job titles, department name, company name, and towns/cities. Capitalize the first word of each bulleted item.

- Do not use abbreviations. Spell out abbreviations and acronyms, unless they are certifications that follow your name. For example, in Ron Smith, CPC, Certified Pastry Culinarian does not need to be spelled out.

- It is common practice to spell out numbers one through nine and then write the numbers 10 and above as numerals.

- Use colons and semicolons correctly, as well as apostrophes. Remember that *it's* means "it is," and the form *its'* does not exist in English.

- Put one space between a period and the first letter of the next sentence.

- Put a comma between a job title, the company name, and the location.

- Always put a comma between the name of a town or city and the state.

Honesty

This guideline is simple: Be honest. Don't even try to be dishonest. The culinary world is really quite small, and you don't want to get a reputation for twisting facts. Even if you get something past an employer who hires you, many contracts include a clause that says dishonesty in the hiring process can result in job termination later.

Paper

As you can guess, white or conservative colors such as ivory and light gray are best for resumes.

If you use watermarked paper, be sure to print your resume on the correct side of the paper. Hold up a piece of watermarked paper to the light; the correct side is facing you if you can read the watermark. Be sure the paper you use is at least 20# weight and is suitable for your printer.

EDIT AND PROOFREAD

Once you have typed up a resume, it's time again to edit and proofread. The most common mistakes are simple typographical and spelling errors. Computer spellcheckers do not catch correctly spelled words used incorrectly—*of* for *on*, for example, or *their* for *there*. You want your resume to stand out, but not for the wrong reasons. Avoid mistakes: Have several people proofread your resume before you send it anywhere.

Use Table 23.3, Resume Checklist, to make sure you have a polished product.

SCANNABLE RESUMES

Many large companies, and a growing number of small ones, use computers to sort the hundreds of resumes they receive. These companies scan paper resumes

TABLE 23.3 Resume checklist

_____ 1. Is your resume easy to read?

_____ 2. Is your resume attractive?

_____ 3. Is there enough white space? Is each section distinct?

_____ 4. Have you kept every paragraph under five lines?

_____ 5. Is your contact information all correct?

_____ 6. Are your qualifications at the top of the resume easy to scan? Do they make you an attractive candidate? Does the list include at least one substantial accomplishment?

_____ 7. Does your resume highlight relevant education and work experience?

_____ 8. Does your work experience include measurable accomplishments?

_____ 9. Did you use action verbs when describing past work experiences?

_____ 10. Have you omitted references to salary and reasons for leaving jobs?

_____ 11. Is your highest educational attainment shown first?

_____ 12. Have you included relevant continuing education?

_____ 13. Have you included certifications you have, such as sanitation?

_____ 14. Did you mention special work-related skills?

_____ 15. If you are still in college, did you mention college activities and clubs you were involved in and offices you held?

_____ 16. Have you proofread your resume and allowed at least one other person to edit and proofread as well?

_____ 17. Can someone quickly glance at your resume and see the most important points?

into a computer database. When managers need to fill a position, they program the computer with keywords that describe the qualifications they want in a candidate. The computer then searches its database for resumes that include those keywords. The resumes with the most matches are forwarded to the managers.

Before you submit your resume to a company, call them to find out if it scans. If it does, be sure your resume's design is computer-friendly. Resumes that will be scanned should contain no graphics or formatting that a computer might misinterpret. Follow these steps to increase a scanner's ability to read your resume:

- Use nontextured white or very light paper with black letters.

- Choose a plain, well-known font such as Helvetica, Arial, or Times New Roman.

- Use a 12-point font for all body text and 14-point for all headings.

- Do not use underlines or italics, and do not use asterisks or parentheses. Modern systems can understand bold, but older systems might not. You can still distinguish headings by using capital letters.

- Use a one-column format.

- Avoid boxes, graphics, columns, and horizontal or vertical lines.

- Put your name on its own line at the top of each page. Also, give each piece of your contact information (address, phone number, email address) its own line.

- Use round, solid bullets.

- Do not staple or fold your resume.

Figure 23.6 contains an example of a scannable resume.

EVERYTHING YOU NEED TO KNOW ABOUT REFERENCES

Before making a hiring decision, most employers want to speak with people who know you well. You should find three to five people who agree to recommend you to potential employers.

Choosing references can be difficult, especially for people with little work experience. But you may have more options than you think. The people you ask to be references should be familiar with your abilities. Supervisors from paid or unpaid jobs, teachers, advisors, coaches, and coworkers are all good choices. Select the most willing, articulate people you can. Always ask permission of the people you want to speak for you before including their name on your reference list.

After choosing and contacting references, type a list with the name, address, telephone number, and email address of each one, and briefly describe his or her relationship to you. Bring copies of this list, along with your resume, to interviews.

When people agree to be references, help them help you. Send them a copy of your resume or application to remind them of your important accomplishments. Tell them what kinds of jobs you are applying for so they know what types of questions to expect.

EXERCISES

1. Learn more about resumes at the monster.com website:
   http://resume.monster.com/resume_samples/

2. Use the Resume Worksheet on the student website to write up the information for your resume. You will probably not include everything you write on this worksheet on the resume itself, so just be complete.

3. After you have gathered the information for your Resume Worksheet, write your first draft using the form on the website. Be sure to use action verbs from Table 23.1 and keywords from Table 23.2.

4.   Type your rough draft in at least two different formats. The website contains five formats. Which looks best?

5.   To evaluate your resume, use Table 23.3 or go to monster.com and click on "Quizzes." Then click on "Resume Readiness Quiz."

BEYOND THE WANT ADS: HOW TO LOCATE AND CONTACT PROSPECTIVE EMPLOYERS*

Overview

INTRODUCTION

Although the job advertisements in the Sunday newspaper seem to offer lots of positions, trying to find one only by wading through the want ads does not often work—especially as your salary requirements rise. This is because most jobs are never advertised. Research indicates that one of the most effective ways of finding out about jobs is by getting leads from people you know, a technique called *networking*. Many more positions are filled every day through word of mouth than through printed advertisements. Another effective way to find a job is to identify potential employers yourself and call them or knock on their door. This chapter discusses a variety of ways to find

---

* Authored by Lisa M. Brefere, Karen Eich Drummond, and Brad Barnes.

jobs. As you read, keep in mind that the more methods you use to find a job, the higher your odds of getting a job offer.

GENERAL GUIDELINES

You may find it frightening to look for a job because it means calling strangers, being interviewed, taking risks. While the experience may pull you out of your comfort zone, it is clearly an opportunity to meet new people, grow, and become more confident. The worst that can happen is that someone may not want to help you in your job search, may not want to interview you, or may give the job to someone else. The best that can happen is that you will find a job you love.

Responding to Job Postings

Now that you have a plain text resume to use on the Internet, here are tips for responding to job postings online.

- Put the job code, job title, or number in the subject line of your email.
- Address your cover letter directly to the recruiter.
- Unless you are asked to attach your resume, put your ASCII-formatted resume in the body of the email message. This will get your information in front of the recruiter's eyes. When you attach a resume, it takes more time for the recruiter to get to; also, the file may be rejected by email systems due to virus concerns. However, you can also attach your resume, giving the recruiter a choice.

Some job sites sort resumes by date of submission, with the most recent resumes up front. Renew your resume every two to three weeks to keep it fresh.

FOLLOWING UP ON CONTACTS

Job candidates stand out when they make the extra effort to contact and establish a relationship with the hiring manager. Although you may think you are being a nuisance, you're not. This is how you can make an impression *and* stand out from the other candidates.

FILLING OUT APPLICATIONS

Many jobs require applicants to complete an application instead of, or sometimes in addition to, submitting a resume. Application forms make it easier for employers to evaluate and compare a group of applicants because the forms ask the same questions. In many cases, it is harder to compare resumes. If an employer asks you to fill out an application, do so graciously. Don't bother offering your resume in place of the application. If an employer uses application forms, you must fill one out to be considered.

When given an application form, read it over completely before you begin. Use your resume to help you fill in the necessary information. Write neatly in black or blue ink. Answer every question on the application. Write "none" or "not applicable" if a question does not apply to you.

Although applications do not offer the same flexibility as a resume, you can still find ways to highlight your best qualifications. For example, you can use strong action verbs to describe your job duties and accomplishments. If you do not have paid experience, you can list volunteer job titles.

Applications often ask for your salary history, and your application may be considered incomplete without it. If you are unsure of the exact numbers, write in an approximation, Usually, approximations are acceptable.

If possible, make a copy of your completed application. If you go back for an interview, take the copy with you.

WRITING COVER LETTERS

Every resume you send, fax, or email must have its own cover letter. Sending a resume without a cover letter is like starting an interview without shaking hands. The purpose of the cover letter is not simply to say what job you want and repeat what is in your resume. The best cover letter:

- Conveys your enthusiasm and energy.
- Sparks the employer's interest.
- Creates an impression of competence.
- Positions you above the competition.

Ultimately, you want your cover letter and resume to generate enough excitement to get you called in for an interview.

So how do you write a great cover letter? It's not hard. Just check out these tips:

- Every cover letter should have a professional appearance. Use a block or modified block format that fits on one page, looks neat, and contains no errors. In the block format (see Figure 24.1), all text starts at the left-hand margin, except if you want to put your name and contact information centered at the top, as on your resume. In the modified block format (see Figure 24.2), indent the first line of each paragraph five spaces and place the date, "Sincerely," and your name in the middle of the page. Use the same stationery your resume is printed on for your cover letters.

  Whenever possible, send your letter to a specific person rather than to an office. Consider how differently you respond to a letter addressed to "Occupant" than one addressed to you. If you do not know whom to address, call the employer and ask who is hiring for the position. Check that the name you use is spelled correctly and the title is accurate. Pay close attention to the correct use of Mr. or Ms. Use a colon after the name in the salutation, not a comma, as follows.

  Dear Mr. Smith:

- If you are responding to a want ad, you can skip the salutation line and go right to the opening paragraph. If you absolutely can't get a name, use "Dear Sir / Madam:" as your salutation.

- The first paragraph, called the opening paragraph, should tell the employer which job you are applying for and the connection you have to the company. If someone the employer knows suggested you apply, mention that recommendation. If you are responding to an advertisement, refer to it and the source that published it. You can also put a position reference line between the address and the salutation, as in Figure 24.2.

  Your knowledge of the company might give you another opportunity to connect yourself to the job. You could briefly cite a recent success or refer to its excellent reputation for catered events, for example. You might also want to state why you would like to work for the employer. Don't go overboard; save the specifics for the interview.

- In the next paragraph, the main paragraph, you highlight your knowledge, skills, abilities, accomplishments, and successes that relate directly to the position for which you are applying. The idea is that the cover letter should *complement* your resume, not just repeat it. One way to do this is to summarize your most relevant credentials using a bulleted format. Leave no doubt in the reader's mind that you can contribute to the success of the operation.

Heather Plumb, C.W.P.C.

211 West Greenwich Avenue
Greenwich, CT 07041
203-437-9365 (h) 203-530-8821 (c)
brewchef@yahoo.com

May 6, 2005

Mr. Ted Carlisle, CEC
Executive Chef
Wamtuxet Inn
10 Shore Drive
Madison, CT 08483

Dear Mr. Carlisle:

As a Certified Working Pastry Chef, I am looking for a position in a larger operation. Marybeth Gilmore gave me your name because she said you plan to expand your bakery operation soon. I have read many fine reviews of the food at the Wamtuxet Inn and feel I could contribute to its fine reputation.

My ten years of employment in the pastry field show increasing responsibility, dedication, and solid accomplishments, such as the following.

- Developed and executed a new menu for 100-seat bakery operation.
- Increased sales 30% by selling bakery items to area restaurants.
- Reduced employee turnover from 75% to less than 25%.
- Developed new quality-control standards.

Thank you for your time reviewing my enclosed resume, which can only briefly highlight my qualifications. i look forward to an opportunity to meet with you to discuss how my interests and qualifications can best meet your needs. I will call next week to schedule a convenient time for an interview. In the meantime, please feel free to call me at 201-437-9365.

Sincerely,

Heather Plumb, CWPC
Enclosure

FIGURE 24.1 Cover letter using block format with centered name and address.

211 West Greenwich Avenue
Greenwich, CT07041
203-437-9365 (h) 203-530-8821 (c)
brewchef@yahoo.com

May 6, 2005

Mr. Ted Carlisle, CEC
Executive Chef
Wamtuxet Inn
10 Shore Drive
Madison, CT 08483

Re: Pastry Chef Position

Dear Mr. Carlisle:

As a Certified Working Pastry Chef, I am looking for a position in a larger operation. Marybeth Gilmore gave me your name because she said you are looking for a new Pastry Chef for your expanded operation. I have read many fine reviews of the food at the Wamtuxet Inn and feel I could contribute to its fine reputation.

My ten years of employment in the pastry field show increasing responsibility, dedication, and solid accomplishments, such as the following.

- Developed and executed a new menu for 100-seat bakery operation.
- Increased sales 30% by selling bakery items to area restaurants.
- Reduced employee turnover from 75% to less than 25%.
- Developed new quality-control standards.

Thank you for your time reviewing my enclosed resume, which can only briefly highlight my qualifications. I look forward to an opportunity to meet with you to discuss how my interests and qualifications can best meet your needs. I will call next week to schedule a convenient time for an interview. In the meantime, please feel free to call me at 201-437-9365.

Sincerely,

Heather Plumb, CWPC

Enclosure

FIGURE 24.2 Cover letter using modified block format.

Subject: Pastry Chef Position

Dear Mr. Carlisle:

My strong qualifications for the available pastry chef position and a referral from Marybeth Gilmore have prompted me to contact you. In addition to being a Certified Working Pastry Chef, I have over ten years of experience in the pastry field and have:
- Developed and executed a new menu for 100-seat bakery operation
- Increased sales 30% by selling bakery items to area restaurants.
- Reduced employee turnover from 75% to less than 25%.
- Developed new quality-control standards.

I would like to meet with you to discuss how I could contribute to the fine reputation of the Wamtuxet Inn. Thank you.

Heather Plumb, CWPC
****

My resume is pasted below in text format, and I have attached a Word copy if you prefer to download it.

FIGURE 24.3 Email cover letter.

- In your final or closing paragraph, thank the reader for his or her time, request an interview, and repeat your home phone number. The closing is your chance to show commitment to the job.

    Figures 24.1 and 24.2 show sample cover letters.

E-mail cover letters are much briefer than typed letters to ensure ease of readability. Addresses are not needed, but be sure to use a salutation. The position you are applying for should be typed into the subject line. As in Figure 24.3, include a bulleted list of reasons you should be considered for the job, along with a request for an interview and any other required information. Unless you have specific instructions on how to email your resume, paste it below the cover letter in text format and also attach it as a Word document. Microsoft Word is the industry's standard word-processing program.

EXERCISES

1. Write up at least 12 cards on networking contacts. Rate how well you know each contact as well as how much each can help in your job search.

2. Write a short script to use when calling someone about a job. Be sure to mention the contact who referred you.

3. Find out what services your college placement office provides.

4. Find out if there are any job fairs in your local area over the next eight weeks. Use the Internet, classified advertisements, and other sources.

5. Attend a job fair and speak to at least two recruiters. What is different about talking to a recruiter compared to having a formal interview?

6. Attend a meeting or conference of a professional organization such as the local chapter of the American Culinary Federation and make at least two networking contacts.

7. Generate a plain text (ASCII) resume and bring it to class to compare with another student's.

8. Find an advertisement for a job that interests you. Write a cover letter to the employer. Bring it to class and discuss it with another student.

9. Write a cover letter to be emailed to respond to the job advertisement in exercise 8.

THREE-STEP INTERVIEWING ⋆

Overview

INTRODUCTION

Landing an interview is important. It's like getting your foot in the door. This chapter will help you ace the interview process, get a job offer, and negotiate the details of the job offer. Interviewing is more than going in and answering somebody's questions in an intelligent manner. In an interview, you are selling yourself—your skills, abilities, accomplishments, personality, and more. The length of this chapter alone shows that

⋆ Authored by Lisa M. Brefere, Karen Eich Drummond, and Brad Barnes.

there's a *lot* more to interviewing, so start reading! You don't want the interview door to slam shut and leave you without a job offer.

So what is that interviewer thinking about? He or she is looking to see if:

- You are qualified to do the job (experience, knowledge, skills, and abilities).
- You would fit in with the company and the people with whom you would be working.
- You are hardworking, persistent, and passionate about your career.

An interviewer is always looking for a candidate who is a good fit with the job, the supervisor, and the company. Much like every restaurant has its own ambiance, each company has its own atmosphere, and you may very well prefer working for one company over another simply because it matches your style better. An interviewer is also always looking for candidates who talk about what they can do for the employer, not what the employer can do for them.

Most interviews are either with a gatekeeper or the person with the authority to hire you (often the person who will be your boss if you get the job). Gatekeepers are people in human resources departments, employment agencies, or executive search firms who interview you to determine if you should go on to the next interviewing step. They do not determine if you get the job but rather if you should stay in the running. Gatekeeper interviews are also called screening interviews. If you interview satisfactorily with the human resources representative of a managed services company, for example, you will be invited to meet directly with the supervisor of the operation where you would be working. Similarly, if an employment agency or executive search firm interviewer thinks you are a good candidate, he or she will send you to interview directly with the client—your potential employer. In many cases, especially with smaller employers, you interview with the hiring manager from the start. This type of interview is called a selection interview.

Screening interviews may be done by phone. These interviews are becoming more popular because they avoid the time and money expenses associated with face-to-face interviews. If you get through the phone interview, you will be invited for a face-to-face selection interview.

Even without a screening interview, you may be interviewed several times before a hiring decision is made. With each successive interview, you can expect more technical questions and a closer consideration of how you will fit in. For instance, in your first interview you meet the person who will be your supervisor if you are hired. The interview reveals that you are qualified to do the job. Next, you are invited back to be interviewed by other people on the team. The emphasis in the second interview is not so much on screening you out as on how you will fit in. In addition, the interview covers how you will contribute to the company and be a valuable employee.

Beyond the screening and selection interviews is the confirmation interview. In this third type of interview, the person who will be your supervisor introduces you to his or her boss, usually as a matter of courtesy for approval. In most cases, the superior approves the selection and the supervisor makes the offer. During the confirmation interview, it is important to establish a good rapport with the superior. The issue is not whether or not you are qualified for the job; the superior wants firsthand assurance that you are a great choice. This is not the time to sell yourself too hard. Just be likable and emphasize how you are productive and can meet goals.

Interviews involve three steps. The first step includes everything you need to do *before* the interview, such as learning about the employer and deciding what to wear. The second step is the interview itself. The final step is what you do after the interview, including sending a thank-you note, evaluating your presentation, and following up.

BEFORE THE INTERVIEW

Learn About the Prospective Employer

Knowing about the employer before you go in for an interview has many positive benefits.

- It increases your confidence.

- The interviewer looks more favorably on candidates who took the time to research the employer than on candidates who didn't. You appear more knowledgeable, serious, and committed.

- It will be easier for you to initiate and follow a conversation about the employer.

- It will be easier for you to determine how your knowledge, skills, and abilities can benefit the employer.

The Internet is the best place to begin researching prospective employers. Many employers have websites that are full of information—although they usually just share the good stuff! Look for sections on websites entitled About Us, Pressroom, or News Releases. These sections offer background information and the company's most recent news. Try to find the information noted in Figure 25.1, Interview Form (on pages 689–690). Here are additional resources:

- Publicly held companies publish annual reports that tell you just about everything you need to know about a company before an interview. To get a copy of the most recent one, check the employer's website, call the shareholder relations department, or ask a stockbroker. The president's message in the annual report may say a lot about the mission and future of a company.

- Other resources for business and financial information on employers include the following.
  - www.ceoexpress.com. This site has links to lots of newspapers and business periodicals. It also has several search engines.
  - www.hoovers.com. This site has business information on most American companies.
  - www.sec.com. This is the site of the Securities and Exchange Commission and has financial information on all public companies.

- Your college placement office may have information about the employer. This resource normally maintains files on employers who visit the campus to conduct interviews.

- People who work for the employer, or used to, may be good resources. Some of your college teachers may be able to give you the name of such a person. If the person says negative things about the employer, keep in mind that you might have a totally different experience.

- Current and past issues of industry periodicals such as *Nation's Restaurant News* may be helpful. You can search the contents of the following industry periodicals at www.findarticles.com: *Food Management, Hotels, Hotel and Motel Management, Nation's Restaurant News*, and *Restaurant Hospitality*.

- The employee who schedules your interview may be able to mail you descriptive literature such as company brochures, an annual report, and employee newsletters.

Prepare Your Questions

At some point during the interview, usually toward the end, you will have an opportunity to ask your own questions. This is your chance to find out more about the employer, the job, and who you would be working with. After all, you may have to decide if you want to work there.

It is important to ask questions during your interview. By asking good questions, you show the interviewer you are interested, smart, and confident. Your questions enable the interviewer to see a little more of who you are as well as establish a rapport. Even if the interviewer answers all of your questions in the course of the interview, you should ask at least one when he or she turns the interview over to you. Table 25.1 lists many questions you might ask during your interview.

TABLE 25.1 Great Questions to Ask the Interviewer.

What do you think is the most important contribution the company wants from its employees?	Which committees would I take part in
	How would I be evaluated in this position, and how often?
What is the company's mission? (If you found the mission statement on their website, ask the interviewer to discuss it.)	How will my management and leadership performances be measured? By whom?
What are the goals of the company for the next five years?	Can this job, if done well, lead to other positions in the company? Which ones?
How would you characterize the company's culture? What are its values?	Can you describe the work environment?
	What type of employee works here?
Do you have a job description for this position I can look at?	What kind of employee is successful here?
	How empowered are employees?
Why is the position being filled?	What criteria determine who gets this job?
What would be my day-to-day responsibilities?	What do you like most about working for this company?
Do you have an organizational chart I can look at? How is the kitchen organized?	How would you describe your style of management?
What specific skills and abilities are you looking for?	How does the company support personal and professional growth?
How does this position contribute to company goals?	What training opportunities are available?
If I am hired, what will be my first assignment?	Do you have any concerns about my skills, abilities, education, or experience?
What are this job's biggest challenges?	Do you need anything else from me to have a complete picture of my qualifications and suitability for this job?
What do you want the person who gets this job to achieve?	
What is the budget for this area?	What is the next step in the interview process?
What is my spending authority?	

An interview is not the time or place to inquire about salary or benefits. You don't want to seem more interested in financial rewards than in contributing to the company. If asked about salary requirements, try to convey flexibility. The best time to discuss salary and benefits is after you are offered the job. At that point, you are no longer the seller; you are the buyer, and you have more leverage.

Prepare and Rehearse Your Responses

Another important step in preparing for an interview is to anticipate the questions you will be asked and how you will respond. Pages 681 to 685 show typical questions and responses.

Choose What to Wear

Dress is not just about receiving respect but also about conveying it. Your appearance at an interview reflects your personal presence in the context of a work culture, and it says a great deal about your work. Remember that the very first contact you have with people is visual.

Make that first impression a good one by taking the right steps to be dressed appropriately. For a cook's position, it is appropriate to wear casual business attire, as described here. For a Sous Chef or higher position, wear professional business dress, as also described below. Do not go to an interview in the Chef's clothes you wore to work that morning. If you are going to take a cooking test as part of the interview and therefore plan to wear your Chef's outfit, make sure everything is perfectly clean and pressed and that your shoes are polished. Here are guidelines for professional and casual business attire:

PROFESSIONAL BUSINESS DRESS: MEN	PROFESSIONAL BUSINESS DRESS: WOMEN	CASUAL BUSINESS DRESS: MEN	CASUAL BUSINESS DRESS: WOMEN
Suit (navy blue, gray, black)	Suite (navy blue, gray, black)	Dress pants	Dark dress pants
Dress shirt	OR conservative dress	Dress shirt	OR dark skirt with blouse or sweater
Conservative tie	OR dark skirt with blouse or sweater	(jacket and tie not required but highly recommended)	Dress shoes
Dress shoes	Stockings	Dress shoes	Stockings (with skirt)
Dark socks to match shoes	Dress shoes	Dark socks to match shoes	
Matching belt and shoes		Matching belt and shoes	
NO	NO	NO	NO
Loud ties	Miniskirts	Jeans	Jeans
White socks	Very high heels	Shorts	Shorts
Boots	Sandals	Boots	Miniskirts
	Low-cut clothing	T-shirts or polo shirts	Sandals
		Loud ties	Low-cut clothing
		White socks	

The objective is to look reliable, not trendy. Don't wear clothes or accessories that draw attention *away* from you.

Avoid wearing lots of makeup, jewelry, perfume, or cologne, which can be distracting to the interviewer. Make sure your shoes are clean and polished, and check your personal hygiene—hair, fingernails, and so on.

Lastly, avoid last-minute clothing disasters by trying on your interviewing outfit a few days before the interview. Make sure it fits well, looks neat, and is clean and pressed. Also, plan for the unexpected. If you will be wearing stockings, make sure you have at least two pairs. If your shoes have shoelaces, get a spare pair in case they break.

Choose What to Bring

You must take *some* things with you to the interview, but be sure to pack light. You don't need to lug a huge briefcase stuffed with lots of papers that have nothing to do with your interview. In many cases, a simple writing pad portfolio with a pocket for copies of your resume, references, and Interview Form, plus your calendar (paper or electronic) is enough. If you have a job portfolio in a loose-leaf binder, that's fine too. You must be able to immediately locate papers you want to share with the interviewer and refer to your list of questions. Have your calendar available in case you are asked to schedule another interview. If your cooking skills are going to be tested, bring your own set of knives to be most comfortable. If you carry these things in a slim, professional-looking briefcase, that's fine. Just make sure you have everything ready at least one to two days before the interview, and bring extra copies of your resume and references to hand out.

Calm Down Already!

Most people are nervous when interviewing—but remember, you were asked to interview for the job because the employer believes you could be right for it. The interview is your chance to confirm that belief and establish rapport.

Also keep in mind that the interviewer is a little nervous too—nervous about selecting the wrong person! Employers often can't obtain a lot of feedback from your past employers, so they rely a lot on the interviewing process, which we all know doesn't always identify the best-qualified person.

To reduce nervousness, get a good night's sleep and maintain your usual routine. You might also call to mind some of your happiest memories or proudest moments before arriving for the interview. These relaxation techniques can also help.

- Take a deep, slow breath. Let the air come in through your nose and move deep into your lower stomach. Then breathe out through your mouth. Repeat this for several minutes. Imagine that the air coming in carries peace and calm and that the air going out contains your tension.

■   Slowly clench your fists. While keeping them clenched, pull your forearms tightly up against your upper arms. While keeping those muscles tense, tense all of the muscles in your legs. While keeping all those tense, clench your jaws and shut your eyes fairly tight. Now, while holding all your muscles tense, take a deep breath and hold it for five seconds. Then, let everything go all at once. Feel yourself letting go of your tensions.

A little bit of nervousness is okay. It will help you think clearly and concentrate.

DURING THE INTERVIEW

Now it is finally showtime! Because the interview is the first meeting between you and your prospective employer—and a relatively brief meeting, at that—your interviewer will have to base most decisions about you on first impressions. The manner in which you introduce yourself, your personal appearance, whether you maintain eye-to-eye contact with the interviewer throughout the conversation, the completeness and honesty of your answers to questions, whether you are on time—these factors will combine to form the interviewer's appraisal of you, both as a person and as a prospective employee.

Getting to the Interview

On the day of the interview, give yourself plenty of time to get ready and travel to the location. Plan to arrive 10 to 15 minutes early, even after allowing yourself extra driving time for traffic jams, roadwork, and other hazards. Consider taking a test drive or testing your public transportation route beforehand. You will be a lot more confident on the day of your interview if you know exactly where you are going.

Once you get there, find a restroom to check your appearance. Make sure to remove sunglasses, portable stereo, and chewing gum. Use a breath mint if needed. Then check in about five minutes early with the appropriate person. It's important to make a good impression from the moment you enter the reception area. Greet the receptionist cordially and try to appear confident. You never know what influence the receptionist has with your interviewer. If you are asked to fill out an application while you're waiting, be sure to do so completely. If you are instructed to sit down for a few minutes, look over your notes, read through company literature, and go over the major points you want to make in the interview. Keep smiling and be friendly!

General guidelines of what to do and what not to do during interviews are listed in Tables 25.2 and 25.3. Read them over now, before the interview starts!

TABLE 25.2 General Interviewing Guidelines.

- Turn off your cell phone or pager (or put it in silent mode) before you go into the interview.
- Don't chew gum or candy.
- Maintain good eye contact with the interviewer, especially when he or she is talking. This shows interest and self-confidence. Good eye contact does not mean staring; look away periodically.
- Use good body posture. Stand straight and sit correctly. Do not slouch.
- Show you are open and receptive by keeping your legs uncrossed. Don't cross your arms while you sit; it comes across as being defensive.
- Smile naturally at appropriate times.
- Check that you are not tapping your foot, running your hands through your hair, pulling on your jewelry, or using any other distracting mannerisms that show nervousness.
- Speak clearly and firmly. Don't talk too softly or too fast.
- Answer each question completely and directly. Be concise—most questions can be answered in 30 seconds to two or three minutes.
- Be specific when you answer questions. A good interviewer won't let you get away with being vague. Use specific examples to illustrate your points.
- It's okay to shed some modesty and brag a little about your accomplishments. Just don't overdo it, and don't even think about being arrogant!
- Talk about what you can do for the employer, not what the employer can do for you.
- Be honest.
- Never speak negatively about a former or current employer. It serves none of your purposes and will lower the interviewer's estimation of you. Put yourself in the place of the interviewer. If you speak poorly about one employer, what is to prevent you from speaking poorly about this employer if you get this job?
- Project enthusiasm about the prospect of working in this position.
- Be a good listener. Do not interrupt the interviewer. Instead of anticipating the interviewer's next question, concentrate on each question as it is being asked. Being a good listener is an excellent way to build a rapport with the interviewer.
- Pauses are a normal part of the interview process. It's okay to take a moment to put your thoughts together before answering tough questions.
- If you don't know the answer to a question, it's okay to say so. If you have never run a profit-and-loss account, don't fake it.
- Maintain your self-confidence throughout the interview.
- Let your personality come through.

Introductory Phase

Make a favorable impression at once by smiling and greeting the interviewer by title (Mr. or Ms.) and name, then introducing yourself in a professional, self-confident manner. Never use the interviewer's first name unless you are invited to do so. Make eye contact

TABLE 25.3 What Not to Do During an Interview.

- Be late.
- Dress informally.
- Have poor personal hygiene.
- Have bad breath.
- Tap your feet or fingers or click your pen.
- Let the interviewer pose all the questions.
- Be sarcastic.
- Be overbearing.
- Make negative statements about past supervisors or employers.
- Know it all.
- Be overassertive.
- Interrupt the interview constantly.
- Express yourself in an unclear manner.
- Overuse phrases or words such as "I guess," "yeah," and "like."
- Ask too many questions about salary and benefits.
- Ask any of the following questions.
    - Why do I have to fill out this job application when the information is on my resume?
    - Do I get compensation time for hours worked beyond 40 hours a week?
    - Can you tell me about the retirement plan?
    - Can I tape this interview?
    - I missed my lunch. Do you mind if I eat my sandwich while we talk?
    - Will this take long? My girlfriend is waiting for me outside.
    - When will I be eligible for my first vacation?
    - Is it possible to telecommute at all with this job?
    - Would I get an office or a cubicle?
    - Are you single?

and stand up straight. Be ready to shake hands if the interviewer extends a hand. Be sure your handshake is firm, but not firm enough to bruise. Sit down in the seat the interviewer indicates. Sit deep and comfortably in your seat. Take a deep breath. Try not to sit on the edge of the chair and look nervous.

The person conducting the interview will begin to form an opinion of you based on such things as the firmness of your handshake, the clearness of your voice, and whether you walk with purpose or shuffle along, so pay attention to what you are doing. This is not the time to try out the latest slang expressions or to move in low gear.

The Heart of the Interview

After introductions, the interviewer will probably discuss the company and describe the job. He or she will then ask questions meant to gauge how well you would fill the position. Many employers use resumes as guides, asking for additional details during the interview. In addition to finding out more information, they are observing how well you communicate and interact.

Some jobseekers are so focused on specific answers that they forget to relax and connect with the interviewer. An interview should be conversational, with the normal exchanges and pauses. It's okay to pause—for example, to stop and consider an answer to a difficult or unexpected question.

Certain questions will show up in many of your interviews, so it's a good idea to think about them ahead of time and plan how you will respond. Most of your responses will take from 30 seconds to two to three minutes. Your answers should be concise, but don't be afraid to adequately describe your skills, abilities, and accomplishments. Interviewers want to hear examples of how you use your knowledge, skills, and abilities. Their attitude can be summed up in two words: Show me. This is where your portfolio comes in. Use it to your advantage.

Interviewers recommend rehearsing your answers in front of a mirror or with a friend to gain confidence and poise. You may even want to videotape a mock interview to see how you really look and act. The goal is to become comfortable speaking with an interviewer about your education, experience, skills, abilities, achievement, and goals. Whatever you do, do not memorize your responses. The worst thing is to come across as if you are reading from a script.

"Tell me about yourself." This is a huge question. Don't make the mistake of giving a huge answer. What you want to do here is sum up your education and experience, then end with a statement about "how my background leads me to your company today to interview for this position." You might even start out with a mention of when you knew you were interested in the culinary field. Here's an example.

> I have been interested in working as a Chef since I worked summers on the New Jersey shore in my uncle's seafood restaurant. I worked in every position in that restaurant but loved being a line cook the most. Once I graduated from high school, I went straight to Middlesex County College to get my culinary degree. While completing my degree, I worked as a line cook at the Auberge, a fine dining restaurant. I learned a lot about à la carte dining, station setup, and mise en place. About five years ago, I got my degree and took a job with the Marriot Hotel in Princeton, where I am today. I've worked all the stations in the kitchen there, including working with banquets and catering, and was promoted to Sous Chef two years ago. I am also an ACF-certified Sous Chef. This is the background that leads me to this interview today.

"What are your strongest points?" This question is a gift, so use it wisely. Think about your knowledge, skills, abilities, experience, personality, motivation, and so on.

Mention four or five strengths, and give a specific, brief example to illustrate each. For example:

> I work well under pressure. For instance, last week the water main outside our building broke, and we had no water. Using our emergency plans, we were still able to feed all our guests satisfactorily until the water was turned back on that night.

"What are your major weaknesses?" You can take two approaches to this classic question. First, you can mention something that is actually a strength, such as:

- *I'm something of a perfectionist.*
- *I'm a stickler for punctuality.*
- *I'm tenacious.*

Second, you can mention a weakness you can easily overcome, such as:

- *I need more computer training.*
- *I need to learn more about nutritious cooking methods. I've signed up for an online course about it.*
- *I need more experience doing public speaking.*

"What do you hope to be doing five years from now?" The interviewer is not only looking for information about your ambitions but is also seeing if your expectations for advancement match what the employer can offer. It's okay to want to continue climbing the career ladder; just be reasonable about how long it takes to do so. Here is one possible answer:

> I hope I will still be working here and have increased my level of responsibility based on my performance and abilities.

Avoid citing specific time frames. Talk about what you enjoy doing and about realistic opportunities.

"What do you know about our company? Why do you want to work here?" This is where your research on the company will come in handy. Describe any encounters you have had with the company and offer positive feedback you have heard from customers or employees.

> Your company is a leader in your field and taking on new accounts every day. You run many of the college foodservices in this area, and I know, just from some friends, that

you're doing wonderfully in your accounts. I would like to work for, and learn from, an industry leader.

You might try to get the interviewer to give you additional information about the company by saying you are interested in learning more about the company objectives. This will help you focus your response on relevant areas.

"What was your greatest accomplishment in your current or last job?" Give a specific illustration from your previous or current job where the accomplishment was totally your doing and had a positive impact. If you have just graduated from college, try to find some accomplishment from your schoolwork, part-time jobs, or extracurricular activities. Don't exaggerate your achievements, and be sure to mention if others helped.

> When I started my current job, there was no catering menu, so we reinvented the wheel every time we did a catering affair. So I developed a standard catering menu, which our customers have enjoyed using. I have also gotten positive feedback from the cooks on it. It makes their jobs a little bit easier and more predictable.

Use the technique shown in this example when you are asked to describe accomplishments: describe the problem, then the action you took, and the results of your action.

"Why should we hire you?" Cast your background in light of the company's current needs. Give compelling examples. If you don't have much experience, talk about how your education and training prepared you for the job.

> From our discussion, I think you would agree with me that I have the qualifications and experience to contribute to your company. I am also excited about this position and feel I would fit in well. I am sure I can expand your clientele as I did at my last job.

"Why do you want to leave your current job?" This is not the time to mention that you can't stand your boss—although that may be true. It is generally expected that if you are looking for a new job you are looking for more money, a bigger challenge, a better shot at advancement, or simply a new environment. Make sure you point out why this job will provide you those things. Never complain, gossip, or whine about a current or past boss as this is not professional behavior.

> I want to develop my potential. I have never worked in a hotel foodservice and would like to get some experience doing catering and banquets. Also, this operation is a lot bigger than the one I left.

"Tell me about a problem you had in your last job and how you resolved it." The employer wants to assess your analytical skills and see if you are a team player. Focus on the solution. Select a problem from your last job and explain how you solved it.

"Describe a time you failed." This may not sound like a question you want to hear, but you can use it to your advantage. We have all had times when our ideas didn't work. Think of a situation when you goofed, but the mistake didn't cause major problems and you learned a valuable lesson.

> One day I forgot to tell Maintenance about problems the baker was having with the floor mixer. The baker was furious at me the next morning because the mixer was still not working right. I ran to Maintenance and luckily got someone who fixed the problem temporarily until a regular repair person came in. Now I know the value of preventive maintenance and have put all the baker's equipment on a preventive maintenance schedule with our Maintenance department. I also learned to keep a pad and pen in my pocket at all times to write things down.

"How would you approach this job?" This would be much easier to answer once you are in the job for a few weeks, but you're not that lucky! The interviewer wants to get an idea of what types of actions you will take and if those actions are appropriate. Mention that you will need time to observe and survey the operation before you take action. Name a couple of ideas you might implement after learning enough to do so.

> First, I would like to get to know the people in the kitchen and observe them. From what you have said, it seems that the room service area needs immediate attention. After seeing the menu and how the food is prepared and delivered, and after talking with the employees, I am sure to come up with solutions to the timeliness problem.

"Describe your management style." This question probes how you work with people. Are you a participative manager? Do you like to empower or delegate to employees? Which do you value more: people or production? In the best situation, you have an idea of how this company treats their employees and whether or not your style matches it.

> My employees would say that I am a very participative manager. I try hard to listen because they are on the front line every day taking care of our guests. You've got to take good care of your employees to keep your turnover low and guest satisfaction high.

"What is your philosophy of cooking?" Here you need to describe the guiding principles that drive you and your cooking, including your philosophy of foods and cooking, your work ethic, management philosophy, and so on. Your cooking philosophy may be, in brief, to emphasize local, organic foods in simple meals, or to blend traditional with contemporary cooking. In a healthcare setting, your cooking philosophy may be to provide home-style, attractive meals that patients enjoy.

You may find the interviewer asking questions that are not job-related. It is inappropriate for an interviewer to ask about your age, race, religion, or marital status. What can you do if you are asked such a question? Take a moment to evaluate the situation and respond in a way that is comfortable for you. For example, if you are asked about your age, be succinct and try to move the conversation back to an examination of your skills and abilities. Or you might say, "I'm in my forties, and I have a wealth of experience that would be an asset to your company." If you are not sure you want to answer the question, ask for a clarification of how it relates to your qualifications for the job. You may decide to answer if the explanation is reasonable. If you feel there is no justification for the question, you might say that you do not see the relationship between the question and your qualifications for the job and you prefer not to answer it.

Don't Forget to Ask Your Questions

Make sure to ask your list of questions. Just as the interviewer is evaluating you, you need to evaluate the job and the employer.

As the interviewer answers your questions, you may want to write down key points. Be sure to ask the interviewer ahead of time for permission to take notes. Asking permission shows that you are polite and respectful. You can phrase the question this way: "Do you mind if I jot down some notes about our discussion? Taking notes helps me organize all the wonderful information I am learning about your company and this job."

Ask for a Tour of the Operation

Most interviewers will want you to see the foodservice operation. We have prepared a list of points for you to investigate when you take your tour. Not all the items in Table 25.4 are set in stone, but we feel that a "yes" answer to most or all of these points indicates a quality place of employment. Keep in mind that, contingent on the type of operation, there are many ways to deal with most of these items. We have listed them to make you think about your potential workplace and how it is managed. After all, you may be spending more waking time there than anywhere else, so the place should live up to your expectations.

TABLE 25.4 What to Look at During Your Tour of the Operation.

- Uniforms clean and in good condition.
- Adequate and safe locker and changing facilities.
- Kitchen clean and orderly. No standing water, burned-out lights, or accumulated grease.
- Food production areas neat and orderly.
- Garbage area in good order.
- Staff has hats.
- Plastic gloves present.
- Break area in good shape. (This may be part of the restaurant in stand-alone facilities; that is acceptable as long as the management recognizes that breaks and nourishment are part of your workday.)
- Corners, walls, and ceilings clean.
- Refrigeration temperatures correct and temperature logs present.
- Employees happy and well directed.
- Facility maintained and in good repair.
- The kitchen stocked with needed equipment and smallwares.
- Food products wrapped, dated, labeled, and stored in proper containers.
- Temperature of the kitchen reasonable and the air fresh.
- General sanitation apparently correct.
- Hoods clean.
- China stored in an organized fashion.
- Chef certified at Chef de Cuisine or higher.
- Chef recently certified in sanitation.
- Chef's shoes clean and polished.
- Cooks taste what they are preparing.

When and How to Discuss Money and Benefits

The right time to discuss money depends on whether you are applying for an hourly job or a salaried job. For an hourly job, it is appropriate to bring up the topic during your initial interview. Often you will know the hourly rate before the interview.

For salaried positions such as managerial jobs, it is risky to bring up salary issues during the interviewing process unless the interviewer does. It is best not to discuss your specific compensation package, especially salary, with the employer until you are offered the job, at which point you are in a much better position to discuss and negotiate salary. Remember: *He who mentions money first loses.*

If an interviewer asks what your salary requirements are, say you have a range that depends on the whole compensation package of salary, bonus, and benefits. If

TABLE 25.5 Sources of Salary Information.

Internet

jobstar.org/   Jobstar.org has lots of salary review information. Click on Salary Info.

www.salary.com   Try the Salary Wizard for salary information.

www.salaryexpert.com   This website can give you local salary information for many culinary jobs.

www.bls.gov/   The Bureau of Labor Statistics has tons of salary information; just be sure to check the date. On the homepage for the Bureau of Labor Statistics, look under Occupations and click on *Occupational Outlook Handbook*. Next, click on A–Z Index. This book can tell you about earnings as well as the nature of the work, working conditions, employment, advancement, and job outlook for many occupations. Look under any of these three categories in the Index.

B—Bakers

C—Chefs, cooks, and food preparation workers

F—Food and beverage serving and related workers; foodservice managers

Make sure you are looking at the most current edition of the *Occupational Outlook Handbook*.

stats.bls.gov/oco/cg/cgindex.htm   This site is the index to the Bureau of Labor Statistics' *Career Guide to Industries*. It contains salary information about jobs in eating and drinking places, hotels and other lodgings, and health services. Some of the jobs covered are Chefs and Head Cooks, Restaurant Cooks, and Foodservice Managers.

www.bls.gov/   The Bureau of Labor Statistics posts salary information by state and metropolitan areas. On the home page, look under Wages, Earnings, and Benefits and click on Wages by Area and Occupation. Next, under State Wage Data, click on By State. You will now see a U.S. map. Click on the state you want, then click on the occupation you want, such as Food Preparation and Serving Related Occupations. Then you can click on 35-0000, Food Preparation and Serving Related Occupations, to get state salary data. At the bottom of this page are links to salary information for metropolitan areas in that state.

TRADE ASSOCIATIONS

TRADE PUBLICATIONS

COLLEGE/UNIVERSITY CAREER SERVICES OFFICE

YOUR NETWORK

YOUR PAST EXPERIENCE

pushed, have a range in mind from your minimum salary requirement to 15 to 20% above that figure. Keep in mind that employers know you are looking to make more money than your current or last job, so put your minimum salary requirement above, but not outrageously beyond, your current or most recent salary. You also need to have a handle on the going rate in your locale for the type of position you want. Sources of salary information appear in Table 25.5.

Conclude the Interview

Be sensitive enough to tell when the interview is over and it is time to leave. The interviewer may make one of the following statements to hint that the interview is coming to a close.

- I think that pretty much covers it.
- We've covered a lot of ground today.
- I really need to wrap this up.

Instead of saying something, the interviewer might look at the clock or an appointment book, or simply start shuffling papers.

Before the interview is over, be sure to find out what the next step will be. Are you to contact the interviewer, or is the interviewer to contact you? How long will it take for the interviewer to reach a decision? Should you contact the interviewer by phone or by email? If another interview is to be scheduled, get the necessary information. It is important to find out how you are supposed to follow up and then to follow the instructions.

Be sure to make your closing statement to the interviewer a positive one. You went into the interview expecting to land this job; it is hoped that you have reason to maintain this attitude throughout the interview. Now you want to leave the interviewer with the same positive feelings about you that you have presented throughout your meeting. In your closing statement, tell the interviewer that:

- You are very interested in the position.
- You are sure you would do the job well.
- You would enjoy working for the employer.

Also, don't forget to thank the interviewer for his or her time as you say good-bye.

AFTER THE INTERVIEW

Evaluate the Interview

As soon as possible after the interview, use your Interview Form (Figure 25.1) to help you go over it. Make sure to write down the names of people you met, along with their titles and any thoughts you have about them. Perhaps the Director of Human Resources was

CONTACT INFORMATION

Employer Name _____

Address/Phone/Website_____

Contacts (People you know, the interviewer, people you meet during the interview)

Name/Phone #/Title _____

Name/Phone#/Title _____

Name/Phone#/Title _____

FAST FACTS

Headquarters: _____ Public or Private: _____

Number of Units: _____ Location of Units: _____

Number of Employees: _____ Annual Revenue/Sales:_____

Services/Products/Areas of Expertise_____

Interesting Statistics _____

Competitors _____

Company Strengths _____

Company Challenges _____

MY INTERVIEW QUESTIONS

1. _____
2. _____
3. _____
4. _____
5. _____
6. _____
7. _____
8. _____

FIGURE 25.1 Interview form.

INTERVIEW IMPRESSIONS

FOLLOW-UP

1. _____
2. _____
3. _____

GOALS FOR NEXT INTERVIEW

1. _____
   _____
2 _____
   _____

FIGURE 25.1 (Continued).

bossy and curt while the person who would be your supervisor was easy to get along with. Write down additional impressions from your interview such as which questions you answered well or not so well, what was appealing and not appealing about the job, the people, the employer, or the work environment, and so on.

Next, fill in the Follow-up box with your instructions about the next step(s) in the process. Make sure to write down the appropriate names and dates; note the dates in your calendar as well.

Last, fill in the Goals for Next Interview box. Every interview is a little different, and each offers you opportunities to improve your interviewing skills. After you review the interview, set one or two goals for the next. Perhaps you have photographs of plated desserts you missed the chance to show the hiring manager. Maybe you need to work on talking at a slower pace.

Send a Thank-You Note

Even after the interview is over, your task is not complete. Secure a good impression by sending a thank-you letter to the interviewer. It is best to send the letter on the same day.

Thank-you letters should be brief—shorter than one page—and may be handwritten or word processed. Their purpose is to express your appreciation for the interviewer's time and to state again your interest in the job. Most thank-you letters have three main paragraphs (see Figure 25.2).

1. The first paragraph is your chance to thank the interviewer again for meeting with you and to show enthusiasm for the job. Refresh the interviewer's memory by mentioning the date of the interview and the position for which you applied.

2. The second paragraph is for you to briefly repeat the skills that make you well suited for the job. You might also note a topic from the interview that was especially interesting to you. Include any important information you forgot to mention during the interview.

3. The third paragraph is where you thank the interviewer again, give your phone number, and state that you look forward to hearing from him or her.

Write or type the letter on solid white, off-white, or gray stationery. Use a standard business format. Put a colon after the interviewer's name and a space after each paragraph. And don't forget to sign your first and last name.

Many employers say an emailed thank-you letter is acceptable if email correspondence was exchanged between the interviewer and the candidate. Otherwise, an email message does not substitute for standard mail in most situations.

Be sure to proofread the letter and make sure you spell the interviewer's name correctly. If a group interviewed you, write to each person on the panel or to the person who led and coordinated the interview, mentioning the other people you met. Interviewers tell tales of misspelled, misused words written in thank-you letters that

15 Spring Road
Hamlet, LS 41112
561-848-9487

April 15, 2005

Mr. Thomas Atkins
Executive Chef
Hilton Hotels
455 East Greenbush Avenue
Pittsburgh, PA 18944

Dear Mr. Atkins:

Thank you for the opportunity to interview with you yesterday afternoon. I am very
interested in the Sous Chef position you described.

My culinary education and work experience as a Sous Chef in another local hotel have
prepared me well for the open position. I am especially interested in expanding the banquet
business, as we discussed. I would welcome the opportunity to contribute to that effort.

I enjoyed meeting you and your staff and look forward to hearing from you soon. If I can
provide any additional information, please call me at 561-848-9487. Thank you again for
your time and consideration.

Sincerely,

Peter Gates

FIGURE 25.2 Sample thank-you letter.

wreck the image of an otherwise impressive candidate. As you write your thank-you
note, remind yourself that you might be writing to your next supervisor.

FOLLOW-UP

Follow-up is *crucial* to your success. Job candidates stand out when they make the
extra effort to reiterate their strong interest in a position and the company. Although
you may think you are being a nuisance, you're not. You are being graded on initiative
and persistence. This is how you can make an impression and stand out from other

candidates. Contact the employer in the manner you were instructed to—phone, email, or in person. Repeat your interest in the job and ask if you were successful in obtaining a job offer.

EMPLOYMENT TESTING

Some employers use tests or other assessment tools as part of their screening process. This section discusses tests you may encounter.

26

ADVANCING YOUR CAREER*

Overview

Introduction

Mentors

Professional Organizations

INTRODUCTION

Advancement opportunities for cooks and chefs depend on their training, work experience, ability to perform increasingly more responsible and sophisticated tasks, leadership and management skills, and level and type of education. Large establishments and managed service companies usually offer excellent advancement opportunities. Chefs and cooks who demonstrate an eagerness to learn new cooking skills and to accept greater responsibility can move up within the kitchen and take on responsibility for food purchasing, menu development, and supervision. Others may advance by moving from one kitchen or restaurant to another.

During the early part of your career, it's a good idea to stay in each job at least one year, or as long as it takes to learn everything you can there. If you are no longer challenged, perhaps it's time to look for another job to get experience with a different type of cuisine, work with a new chef, or simply work in another foodservice segment.

As Chefs improve their culinary skills, their opportunities for professional recognition and higher earnings increase. Chefs may advance to Executive Chef positions

---

* Authored by Lisa M. Brefere, Karen Eich Drummond, and Brad Barnes.

and oversee several kitchens within a foodservice operation, open their own restaurants as Chef-proprietors, or move into training positions as teachers or educators. Your career path is your own unique creation. This chapter discusses ways for you to advance.

MENTORS

Chef apprentice programs use the mentor model to train new Chefs. A mentor is a person who helps someone, usually a subordinate, grow professionally. Mentors serve as role models and teach, guide, coach, and counsel their mentees (the individuals they mentor).

Although the mentee clearly benefits from the mentor relationship, the mentor gains advantages too, including the personal satisfaction of passing on his or her successes and the recognition for being a positive role model. Being a mentor also means being able to continually practice culinary, management, and interpersonal skills. Mentors are true professionals in the sense that they directly help others. Besides giving invaluable training, mentors boost the confidence of mentees and provide guidance about career moves.

Mentoring may be formal or relatively informal. Informal mentoring occurs all the time in the workplace. It happens when one person simply helps someone, usually a subordinate, and a career-helping relationship develops. Formal mentoring is found in structured programs in which a company or organization matches mentors with mentees. A good match is one in which the mentor gets along well with the mentee, has the expertise the mentee desires, and is a good teacher.

Regardless of whether mentoring is formal or informal, the following guidelines will help both parties get the most out of the relationship.

1. Have an initial meeting to discuss the expectations of both the mentor and the mentee.

2. Plan to commit to a partnership for six months to one year and discuss a no-fault termination in which either party can back out for any reason.

3. Identify mentee goals and make an action plan. Accept that these goals may change.

4. Set up how often the mentor and mentee will meet to discuss progress.

5. The mentee must be willing to accept constructive feedback, try new things, and take risks.

6.   The mentor will use listening, coaching, guidance, career advising, and other techniques to help the mentee reach his or her goals.

7.   Many mentoring relationships continue long past the initial time commitment, especially as the partners often become friends. When the mentor and mentee decide their work together is completed, they should go over the original action plan and discuss the progress and results. They should give each other constructive feedback that may help in future mentoring relationships.

In many cases, culinary professionals have to find their own mentors, often by networking, and be willing to work hard once they find a good mentoring relationship.

PROFESSIONAL ORGANIZATIONS

Being active in professional organizations is key to job advancement and your career. Professional organizations give you lots of opportunities to network with other culinary professionals as well as these additional benefits (which vary by organization):

- Industry magazines and newsletters that keep you up to date on the culinary industry.

- Annual meetings/conferences to upgrade and update your knowledge and skills.

- Educational seminars to upgrade and update your knowledge and skills.

- Leadership opportunities.

- Industry contacts—for example, with representatives of foodservice equipment manufacturers.

- Job announcements.

- Recognition awards.

The Appendix gives detailed information about each organization.

The American Culinary Federation (ACF) is the largest and most prestigious organization dedicated to professional Chefs in the United States today. Their mission is as follows.

It is our goal to make a positive difference for culinarians through education, apprenticeship, and certification, while creating a fraternal bond of respect and integrity among culinarians everywhere.

ACF offers its members many opportunities to keep their knowledge and skills current through its monthly publications (*National Culinary Review* and *Center of the Plate*) and through seminars, workshops, national conventions, and regional conferences. ACF sanctions U.S. culinary competitions and oversees international competitions that take place in the United States. ACF accredits culinary programs at the secondary and postsecondary levels. Local chapters of ACF offer members opportunities to network with nearby culinary professionals. Also, ACF members are simultaneously enrolled in the World Association of Cooks Societies (WACS), which represents 54 countries.

Following is a list of culinary professional organizations:

American Culinary Federation (ACF)

American Dietetic Association (ADA)

American Hotel and Lodging Association (AHLA) and Educational Institute of AHLA

American Institute of Baking (AIB)

American Institute of Wine and Food (AIWF)

American Personal Chef Association (APCA)

American Society for Healthcare Food Service Administrators (ASHFSA)

Association for Career and Technical Education

Black Culinarian Alliance (BCA)

Bread Baker's Guild of America

Club Managers Association of America (CMAA)

Confrérie de la Chaîne des Rôtisseurs

Dietary Managers Association (DMA)

Foodservice Consultants Society International (FCSI)

Foodservice Educators Network International (FENI)

Institute of Food Technologists (IFT)

International Association of Culinary Professionals (IACP)

International Caterers Association

International Council of Cruise Lines

International Council on Hotel and Restaurant Institutional Education (I-CHRIE)

International Food Service Executives Association (IFSEA)

International Foodservice Manufacturers Association (IFMA)

International Inflight Food Service Association (IFSA)

Les Dames d'Escoffier

Military Hospitality Alliance (MHA)

National Association for the Specialty Food Trade (NASFT)

National Association of College and University Foodservice (NACUFS)

National Association of Foodservice Equipment Manufacturers (NAFEM)

National Food Processors Association

National Ice Carving Association (NICA)

National Restaurant Association and the Educational Foundation of the National Restaurant Association

National Society for Healthcare Foodservice Management (HFM)

Research Chefs Association

Retailer's Bakery Association (RBA)

School Nutrition Association (SNA)

Société Culinaire Philanthropique

Society for Foodservice Management (SFM)

United States Personal Chef Association

Women Chefs and Restaurateurs

Women's Foodservice Forum (WFF)

INDEX